Franz Schulze
1969

The Avant-Garde in Painting

The Avant-Garde in Painting

Germain Bazin
Conservateur en chef au Musée du Louvre

Translated from the French
by Simon Watson Taylor

With 265 illustrations, 52 in color

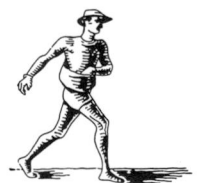

Simon and Schuster · New York

Histoire de l'avant-garde en peinture
du XIIIe au XXe siècle
Copyright Librairie Hachette 1969

First published in Great Britain under the title
The Avant-Garde in the history of painting,
Copyright © 1969 by Thames and Hudson

Published in the United States by Simon and Schuster
Rockefeller Center, New York, N.Y. 10020

SBN 671-20422-X
Library of Congress Catalog Card Number: 73-92199
Printed in Great Britain by Jarrold and Sons Ltd

Contents

Introduction

In French military terminology, the term 'avant-garde' designates an advance detachment whose task it is to prepare the way for the main fighting force, which retains the decisive role. Applied strictly to other fields of human activity, this expression should, therefore, designate precursors rather than creators, all those who are ahead of their time and who, having glimpsed some new form prematurely, leave others to exploit it when the time is ripe. So, in painting, Savoldo and Pordenone foreshadow Caravaggio, Herrera the Elder prefaces Goya, Hercules Seghers and Elsheimer anticipate Rembrandt's visionary style.

Our own epoch has given a different sense to the expression 'avant-garde', at least in the field of art, attributing to this position decisive powers of invention capable of replacing established forms with fresh ones, the anticipatory character of which is due less to their inherent qualities of innovation than to their determination to break with the society from within which they are formulated. The retrospective application of this revolutionary notion of the nature of innovation to particular painters in previous eras runs the risk of distorting the meaning of the expression completely, especially now that we are saddled with the romantic concept of the *peintre maudit*, the artist damned by fate, the value of whose creative work tends to be assessed in terms of the ostracism it engenders. Such an attitude has exalted Caravaggio, with his reputation as a stormy petrel, over Rubens who lived like a prince; it has become fashionable to ignore the fact that, far from being a social outcast, the painter of *The Calling of St Matthew* astonished his contemporaries with the revelation of his genius and immediately inspired a school of followers. It is not possible to understand the art of other times on the basis of a determination to visualize the artist as a man at odds with society. It should be realized that, on the contrary, the civilizations which preceded the modern world granted the artist the greatest possible freedom in the invention of the forms best suited to serve their ideals. Although the medieval Church inspired programmes, it refrained from coercing the image-makers. Becoming belatedly apprehensive about the spirit of the Reformation, the Church occasionally took it upon itself to be stern, but even then avoided unnecessary harshness: the Inquisition did not oblige Veronese to destroy the *Feast in the house of Levi*, merely to modify certain aspects. Similarly, those parishes or confraternities which were so horrified by Caravaggio's plebeian naturalism that they turned down certain works they had commissioned simply allowed him to keep them, and did not take offence even when some picture they had rejected, such as the *Death of the Virgin*, later became the occasion of a personal triumph for the artist.

During the Renaissance period, the artist, even when working for the Church, enjoyed considerable creative freedom. It was common knowledge at the time that Fra Filippo Lippi had bestowed upon the Madonna the features of his mistress, a nun whom he had seduced in her convent. Fouquet endowed the Virgin of his *Madonna and Child* with the face of King Charles VII's mistress. Grünewald found a patron and a monastery to harbour his terrible visions. The artist was sometimes considered to be above the law; a pope pardoned Benvenuto Cellini for a murder, while Caravaggio, who had also killed a man, had already been pardoned by Paul V when, as a fugitive, he died of fever on the barren coast of Porto Ercole.

From the time of the Renaissance onwards, the artist was particularly highly regarded for his inventive qualities. The literate princes of the sixteenth, seventeenth and eighteenth centuries were constantly on the alert for novelties and competed vigorously for their creators. Many bold ventures were due as much to the environment as to the artist. We marvel today at the inventive genius of Arcimboldi, preceding surrealism as it does by several centuries; yet in the atmosphere of a Milan steeped in academicism he made little impression as an artist, and it needed the mannerist court of Prague to reveal him to himself.

The quarrel between those with an aversion to novelty and those addicted to it is a contemporary phenomenon. Certain present-day art critics and biographers who prefer their artists to be cripples, drunkards, social outcasts, suicides, anarchists, swashbucklers or scoundrels might be well advised to consider the great innovators of the past as other than asocial beings; they would then have to admit that Goya, revered today as the quintessential rebel, was a man astute enough to scheme for his own ends with the various regimes which were squabbling over Spain, and to survive with equal resilience in the camp of 'collaboration' and that of 'resistance'.

This is not to imply that today's fundamental discord between artist and society never existed previously. Precedents are to be found in seventeenth-century Holland, where the greatest painters, Frans Hals, Ruisdael, Rembrandt and Vermeer, all had to resign themselves sooner or later to breaking with their social environment and retreating into the solitude of genius, with all the consequences that such a break implied. The condition of pariah imposed upon the 'avant-garde' artist appears, in fact, to be a specific aspect of the kind of bourgeois civilization which seems to need to compensate for the boldness of its measures in the field of action by an aesthetic and ethical conservatism designed to provide the feeling of stability necessary to its activity.

In aristocratic civilizations, on the contrary, the artist is a magician; a society eager for displays of sophisticated wit expects from him a constant and inventive flow of unexpected diversions. Without fearing the disapproval of his court, Philip IV not only recognized Velázquez's genius but indulged him in his ambition to become a grandee, treating the painter as his friend and confidant. Velázquez was the first artist to be liberated from the tyranny of commissioned work; the rank of nobility the king bestowed upon him prevented him from ever again involving his art in commercial transactions. The paintings of Velázquez's Seville period would seem to rule out the possibility that he would have developed exactly as he did without the protection of Philip IV. There were other painters at the court of Madrid, and ones with a greater aptitude for flattery, but it was the quality of genius that the king discerned in Velázquez, and that alone, that attracted him.

It must be admitted that the Bourbons showed less respect for the independence of genius than the Hapsburgs – Charles V, Philip II and Philip IV. When Louis XIII of France tore Poussin away from Rome, it was to serve his own glory rather than that of the unfortunate artist, who found himself so overwhelmed with work that he made his escape as quickly as was decently possible. Louis XIV, the inspired despot who bent all the arts of his time to his will, went even further. During the eighteenth century, the French court favoured academicism,

and the original artistic invention that went on was conducted quite outside its sphere; meanwhile in Spain the coming to power of the Bourbons brought in its train an academic despotism that was completely to undermine indigenous art.

In this book I have set out to identify as the members of the 'avant-garde' of painting all those who were pioneers, all those who have enabled it to proceed from conquest to conquest, until its reversion, in our own time, to nothingness. These pioneers may equally well be those who were in advance of their time, or on the contrary those who revealed their time to itself; in any case, no surprise should be felt at the inclusion among 'avant-garde' painters of artists such as Raphael or Correggio who launched veritable revolutions in art. One might even go so far as to say that these are both *peintres maudits*, at least posthumously! 'If he were to return today,' said Picasso speaking of Raphael, 'with exactly the same canvases, nobody would buy a single one from him. Nobody would even look at them.'

On the other hand, those artists will be excluded – without reference to the author's own preferences – whose genius fulfilled itself harmoniously within the pattern set by the achievements of their predecessors: such artists as Titian, Poussin, Gauguin, for example. This does not involve a rejection of classicism as an innovating position, since Raphael and Giotto are ranked among the great 'inventors'. Any reproaches relative to the long-lasting academicism that classicism engendered should be addressed to the succeeding generations rather than to classicism itself. It has been my aim here to consider Raphael from the viewpoint of a man of 1511 privileged to contemplate the brand-new frescoes of the Stanza della Segnatura in the Vatican, and not in the spirit of a modern exasperated by four centuries of Raphaelism.

This fresh perception of the things of the past demands a tremendous effort of will to free oneself from the whole accumulation of ideas deposited by 'tradition'. But what would become of tradition if it could not count on the revolutionaries to defend it against the traditionalists? It is the revolutionaries' perennial youthful rebellion against the past which eventually ensures the continuation of a *living* tradition, and tradition, having the continuity of human civilization in its care, is indebted to them for preserving its vitality.

As perspective recedes, the sharp detail of the original blurs and fades, to merge into the general line of evolution. Tradition and evolution are interdependent; anything that passes from hand to hand is bound to lose some substance through constant usage, and this gradual erosion needs to be compensated for by a constant deposit of new sediment. Life itself offers us the prime example of this process: its continued existence depends entirely on its being transmitted from one individual to another, and yet since the world began no individual has ever reproduced the exact characteristics of his immediate predecessor.

Even if not necessarily in conflict with the social environment, artistic creation remains very much a battle. Both bourgeois civilization and the marxism it has spawned as a reaction against it have demeaned the conflict to one between man and man, whereas its real site is deep within the soul, a conflict between man and himself, between man and God. The Greeks expressed this spiritual laceration in the myth of Prometheus. Creation involves violence, but it is essentially a violence to oneself. The artist's destiny is to assume the burden of human contradictions so as to elucidate or resolve them. The nineteenth century made the artist a scapegoat, a role which he is well qualified to play. But from time immemorial, and even in the present age, he has also been honoured as an inspired being, able by means of the visible to deliver to humanity some tidings of the invisible.

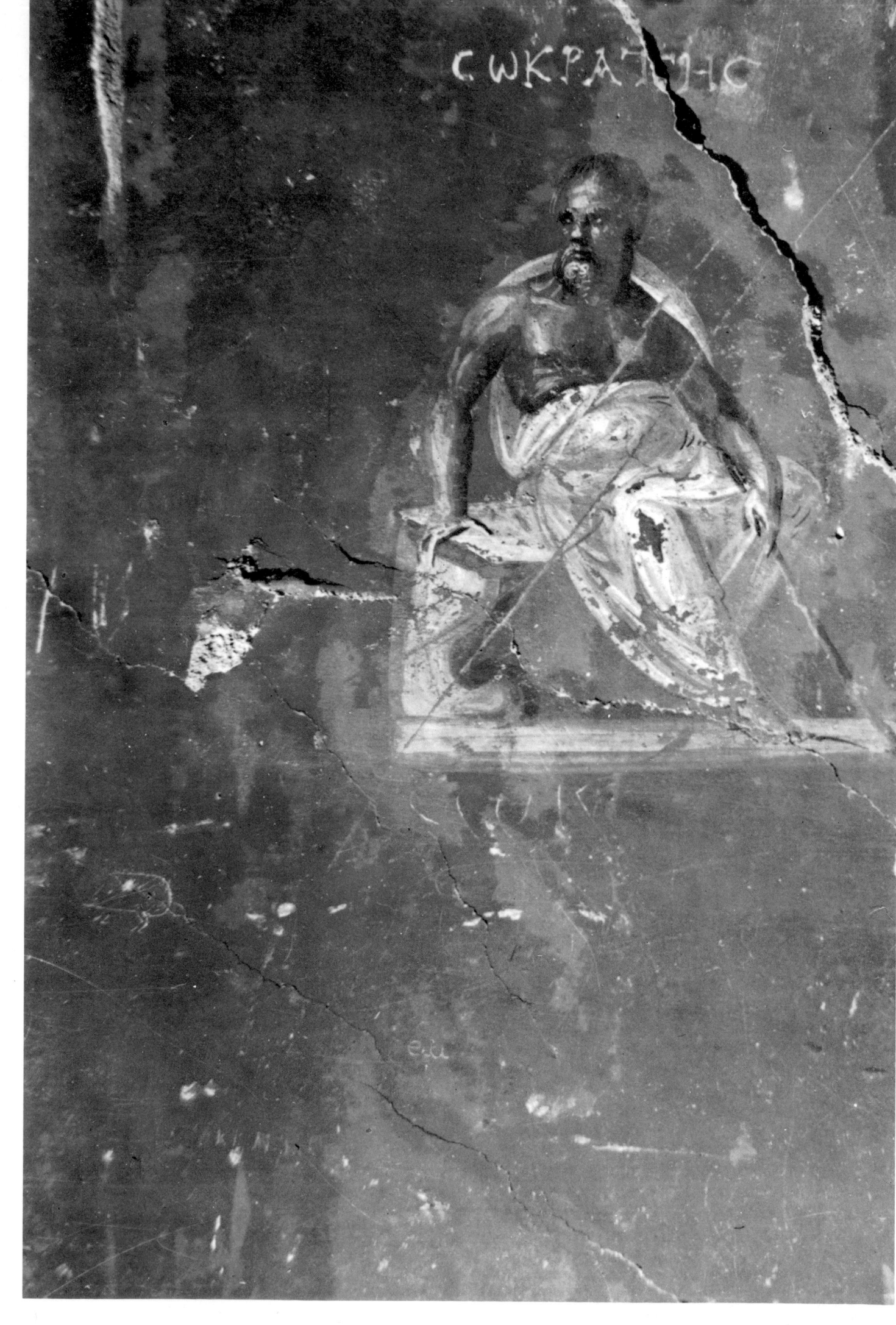

CWKPATHC

1 *Socrates*. Painting found in a house at Ephesus in 1963. 1st century BC.

1 The lost heritage

Plato, whose thought, as developed by neoplatonism, was to leave so profound a mark upon the Renaissance, professed complete contempt for art. He believed that the transition from essence to appearance always involved a fall from grace; the artist, instead of emulating the philosopher by climbing back up the slope which leads down from the One to the Infinite, allows himself to slide down it to the very bottom. The painters who were Plato's contemporaries, in the full throes of discovering nature, inevitably appeared to him to be corrupters. Even Zeuxis, who had needed five models, all young women chosen from among the greatest beauties of Corinth, in order to portray Helen's loveliness, found no favour in his eyes; Zeuxis could never attain more than a composite beauty, for absolute beauty is that which assumes no corporeal appearance and which is the sole destiny of the dialectic of love.

Plato finally admitted art into his ideal society, on the grounds that it might to some extent help the gross-minded to restore in themselves those impulses which had become distorted by the flux of events; but he remained hostile to the idea of judging a work of art by subjective criteria (that is to say, by the pleasure it afforded) and dedicated the artist to 'imitation'. However, this assigned role was by no means intended to induce the artist to reproduce appearances in process of growth; it constituted, rather, a form of approach to the reality which is essence, to be achieved by respecting just proportions, such as those defined during the previous century by Polycletus in his *Canon*. In this way, art was to be fixed permanently in an academic mould, and Plato offered the artists of his time the example of Egyptian hieratic art, which had not evolved for thousands of years.

But the philosopher's admonitions were in vain. The artists of the fourth century preferred to follow the precepts of Gorgias, who advocated the practice of illusionism. Furthermore, they were influenced by the doctrines of Aristotle, for whom art should be lively and play a healthy role in society through the process of *catharsis*, the purgation of the passions; in complete opposition to Plato, then, Aristotle favoured those two sources of creation, boldness and innovation, which typify the 'avant-garde'. So the two conflicting principles which were to nourish the whole evolution of European painting had already been laid down in the fourth century BC, the great century of Greek painting.

It is not difficult to understand why painting, in view of the determination with which it strove for likeness at that time, should have seemed to Plato to be the most dangerous of the arts. The man of genius who had forced destiny during the previous century was Polygnotus of Thasos. The paintings he had executed with Micon in Athens and those he had made alone for the *leskhe* (meeting-place) of the Cnidians in Delphi represented a *Battle between the Greeks and the Amazons*, the *Capture of Troy*, and the *Battle of Marathon*. There is no more splendid subject than a battle – Paolo Uccello was to make full use of its resources in a later epoch – for the painter seeking to capture expression, action and position in space, and this is precisely what Polygnotus had succeeded in portraying in his work, thus liberating his art from the constraints of the surface: he had transformed an art of drawing into one of painting. And yet, as a true classicist, this contemporary of Phidias upheld that truth which was subject to the rules of measurement and beauty. The theatre was at the height of its glory then, and the requirements of stage design spurred artists on to increasingly audacious feats of *trompe-l'œil* and artifice. The first stage-setting, according to Vitruvius Pollio, 'was created in Athens in the time of Aeschylus by Agatharchos; he wrote a treatise on this art, followed by Democritus and Anaxagoras who dealt with the same subject'. These recipes were perfected at the end of the fifth century by Apollodorus the skiagrapher (skiagraphy is the art of depicting shadows), who succeeded in conjuring from plane surfaces the illusion of the exterior world, with its relief and colouring. This constituted the avant-garde of painting of that time, and was already the target of criticism from the traditionalist supporters of Polygnotus's classicism. Zeuxis and Parrhasius went even further in the same direction. Pliny recounts that a bunch of grapes depicted by Zeuxis in a stage-setting was so lifelike that birds used to swoop down and peck at them; and

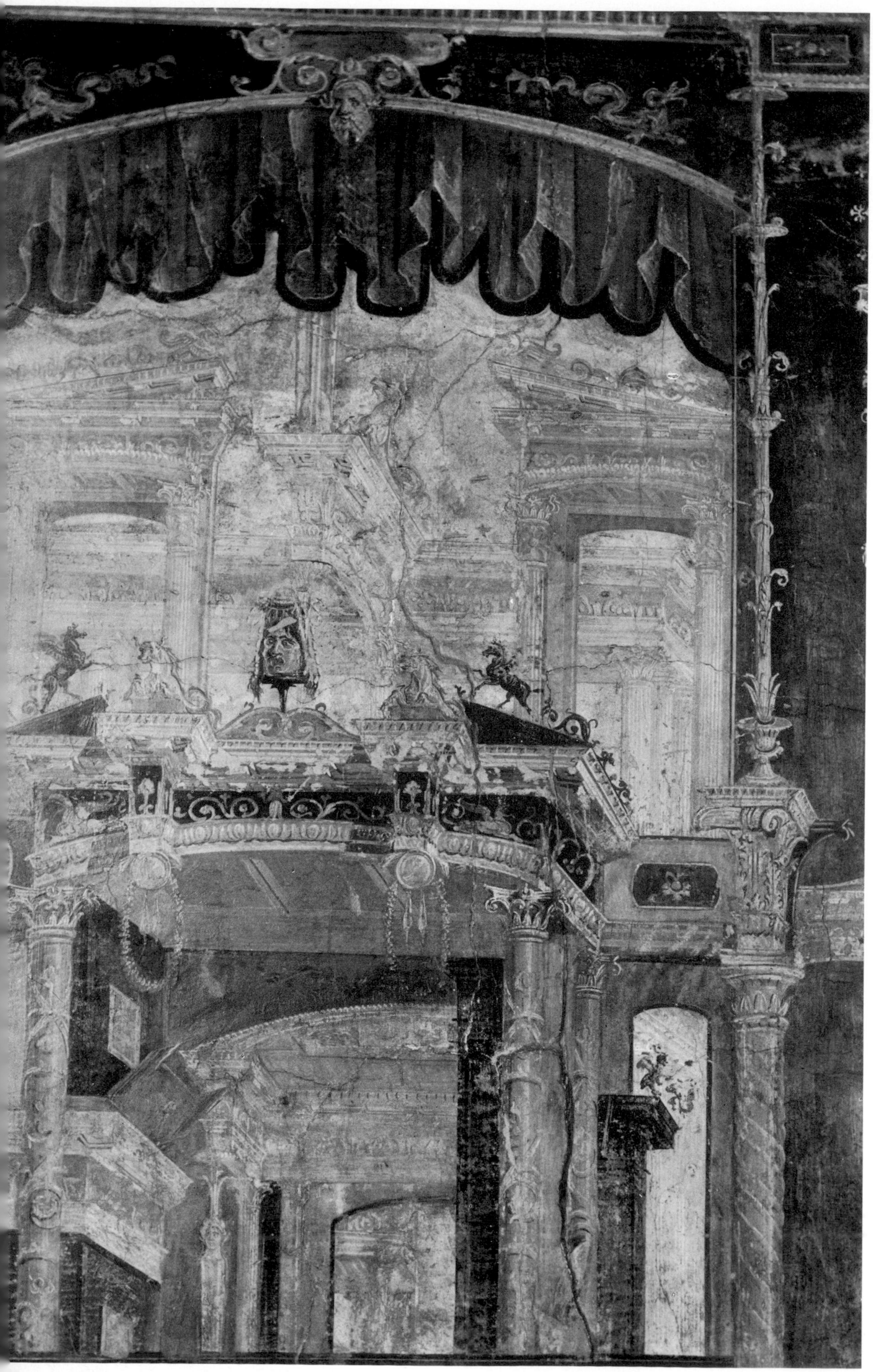

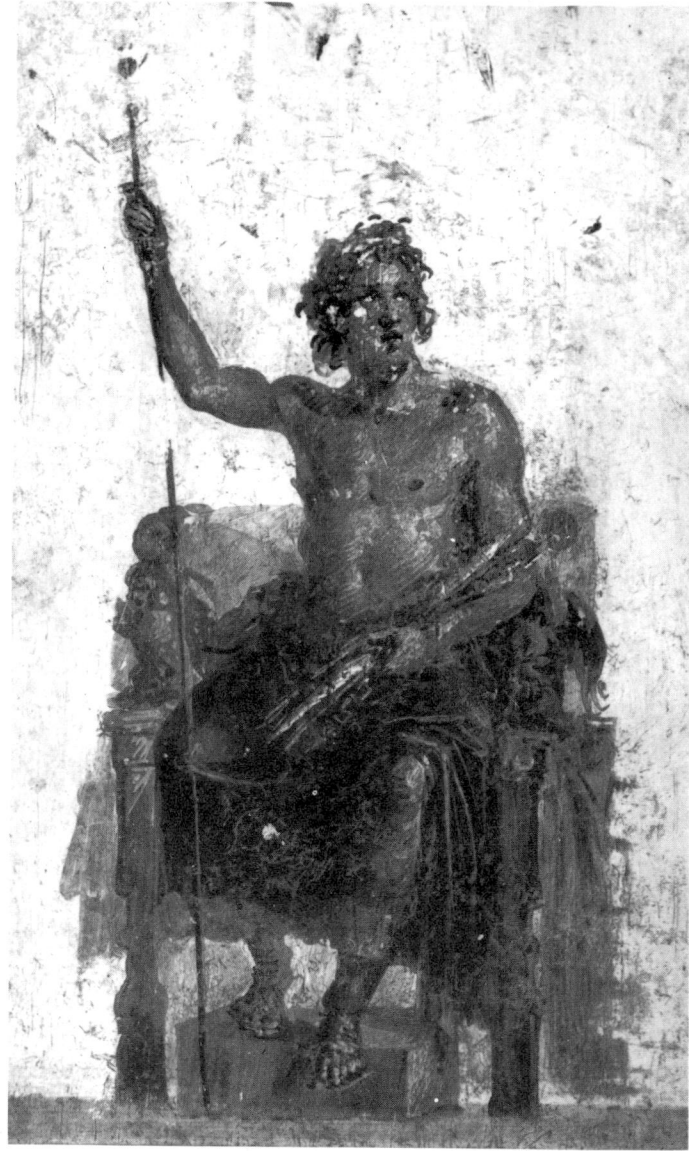

◀ 2 Decoration from a house at Herculaneum. Naples, Museo Nazionale.

3 *Zeus*. Painting in the House of the Vettii at Pompeii, probably derived from a work by Apelles.

While certain paintings at Herculaneum and Pompeii are evocative of Greek classicism, others are more concerned with the illusionistic impression sought by artists such as Zeuxis and Parrhasios.

Parrhasius once painted a draped curtain with such cunning that a fellow artist, seeing it for the first time, tried to draw it aside, thinking that it was real and concealed the picture. These exemplary anecdotes, which were doubtless invented by sophists, allow us to guess at the nature of the aesthetic conflicts involved. According to Pliny, Zeuxis remarked that if the child he had painted beside the grapes had been equally lifelike the birds would never have dared peck at them; but to the general astonishment, the artist destroyed the fruit, retaining only the child because he considered it more 'perfect'. From this period onwards, schools and sects proliferated. While Parrhasius aimed to express life through eloquence of contour, Zeuxis perfected relief by the use of light and shadow, and so invention continued its gradual progress. Shading added its effect to virile bodies that had become more muscular, and later appeared on the smooth surface of female nudes. Then 'points of light' began to make breastplates sparkle, as in works by Titian and Rubens. The foreshortening that enhanced the relief became bolder, and Apelles went so far as to make the hand of his Alexander jut out from the image, an audacity that was not to be repeated in the West until the seventeenth century. In Apelles's time, painting began to emerge from the wall surface, becoming a mobile object, hanging against a living-room wall or resting on a moulding. Everything became a suitable theme for painting: historical subjects, portraits, landscapes and still-lifes. This last genre grew particularly popular, and towards the end of the fourth century or the beginning of the third Piraikos made a speciality of it, painting barbers' and cobblers' signs. He also

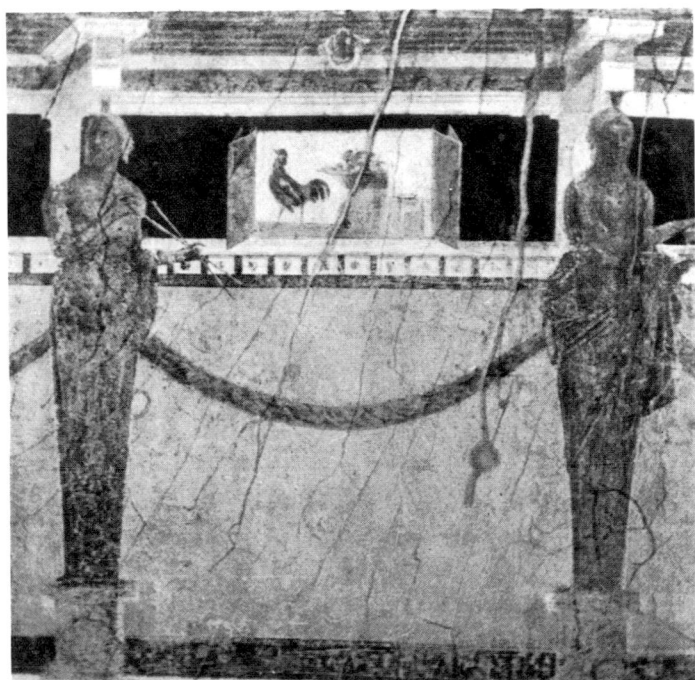

5 Detail of wall-painting from the House of the Cryptoporticus at Pompeii.

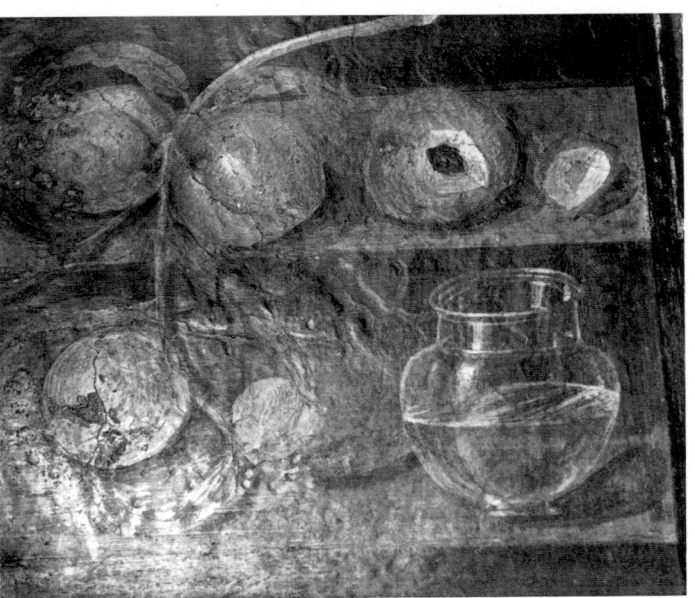

6 *Peaches, nuts and glass*. Detail of a wall-painting from Herculaneum. Naples, Museo Nazionale.

Many Romano-Campanian paintings were inspired by the *xenion*, a type of domestic still-life invented by the Greeks of the Hellenistic period; some of these paintings show how such easel pictures, with their protective shutters, were arranged in the room.

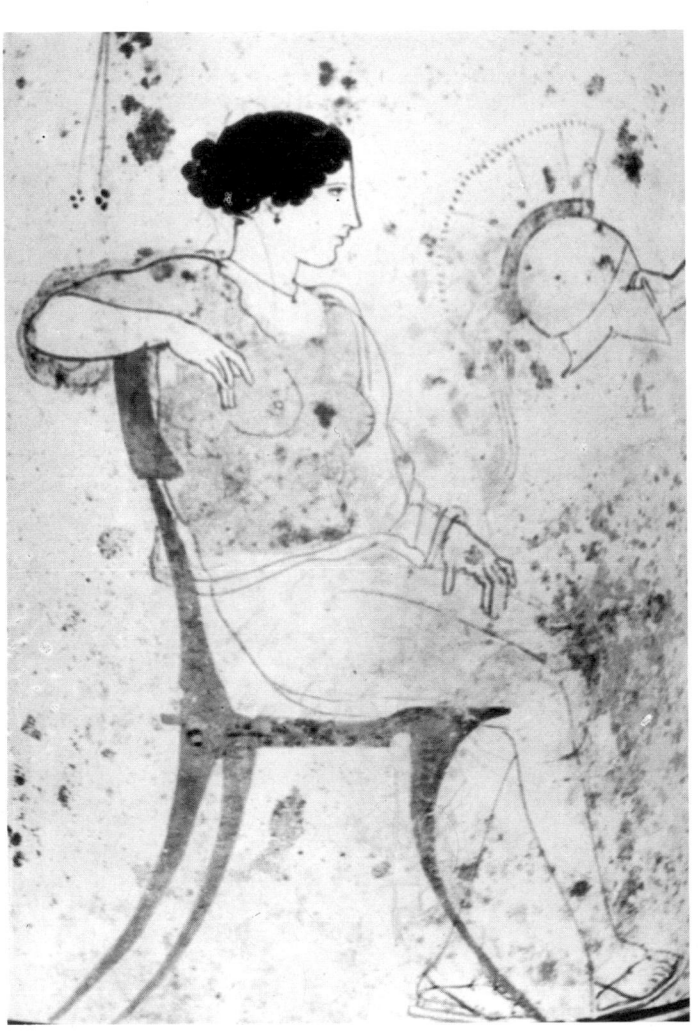

4 Detail of a *lekythos* from Eretria. Third quarter of 5th century BC. Athens, National Museum.
Unlike those vases whose red and black figures represent a decorative conception, the funerary *lekythoi* carry painted designs which give some idea of the expressive graphic skill of the great Greek masters.

depicted various foodstuffs, doubtless in the form of small pictures protected by shutters, like those to be seen represented in *trompe-l'œil* in the first-century mural designs at Pompeii and Rome. The mosaicist Sosos of Pergamum (third or second century BC) had the strange idea of representing the floor of a dining-room before it had been swept clean of the scraps from the meal; the ancients designated this particular type of painting *rhyparographia*, that is to say 'garbage painting', a word-play on *rhopographia* which meant 'painting of minute objects' and was in its turn opposed to *megalographia*, the word for mural painting. The imitation of everyday objects had a great success until the end of the ancient world. The Romans bought the Greek originals for high prices, had copies painted on their walls, or reproduced the motifs on their tessellated floors. These genre pictures were the forerunners of the Spanish *bodegones*. Others among these small pictures of still-lifes were called *xenia* (or presents) and perpetuated the old tradition of making gifts of fruit, game, glassware or silverware to one's hosts (*pl. 6*).

It is useless to attempt, as some have done, to pierce the mystery of these vanished works by examining the paintings on vases. One could as well try to visualize Raphael by studying the pottery of Urbino. In addition, the birth of classical painting coincided with the decadence of vase decoration, which had, in any case, adhered strictly to the silhouette form; the single exception is the Attic funerary *lekythoi* of the fifth and fourth centuries (*pl. 4*), oil-jars with a white ground, whose decorative technique is closer to that of painting. As for the following century, the vases of Centuripae (Sicily) and the Lipari Islands permit us to appreciate their fresh colours and blended contours in the context of Hellenistic painting. It was at this moment in time that the philosopher Philostratus wrote: 'Everything possesses its own colour, clothes, weapons, houses and living-rooms, woods, mountains, springs and the *air which envelops all things*.' Might not this remark, inspired no doubt by the paintings of his contemporaries, apply equally well to impressionist pictures? But the paintings which have survived are either partly effaced or of coarse quality and yield us little useful information. The third-century tomb at Kazanlik in Bulgaria, on the very frontier between the Greek and barbarian worlds, presents a painted scene that is doubtless somewhat archaistic: the quadriga (*pl. 7*) shows the artist's happy attempt to suggest the horses' impatience by distributing their contrasting postures across the surface with considerable animation; however, a certain 'barbarism' shows itself in the weakness of the drawing, something in which the Greeks were always unsurpassed.

It will prove more useful to examine the abundant, if belated, evidence provided by the Roman paintings rediscovered in Pompeii, Herculaneum, Stabiae and Rome. It is true that these paintings have been called into question, as much by their supporters as by their opponents, and Italian criticism is at present divided by a controversy on the subject of their real merit. The critic Carlo Ragghianti (*Pittori*

di Pompeii, Milan 1963) defends the originality of these paintings in relation to Hellenic art, whereas the archaeologists consider them to be the provincial result of an academic or unrefined imitation of the masterpieces of Hellenic painting. Ranuccio Bianchi-Bandinelli, in articles published in 1940 and 1941 (collected in *Storicità dell'arte classica*, Florence 1950), has supported this latter thesis: using precise examples, taken mostly from the celebrated Villa of the Mysteries, he has no difficulty in showing that the Campanian painters produced flagrant imitations containing blunders typical of unintelligent copyists. Taking an opposite point of view, Ragghianti has been the first to approach these paintings as works of art executed by individuals, whether copyists or not; by distinguishing 'mannerisms', that is to say elements of individual style in these works, he has been able to arrange them in an order of ascription to particular 'masters', rather than limiting them to the anonymous classification of styles in use before him. No agreement can ever be possible, probably, between the archaeological criticism of Bianchi-Bandinelli and the formal criticism of Ragghianti, since they derive from basically incompatible principles. The archaeologists base their judgments on the criterion of the absolute perfection attained by Greek classicism, a criterion that Bernard Berenson defended throughout his life, adding to it its prolongation in Italian classicism. The more modernist criticism of Ragghianti proceeds from the principles of Alois Riegl, according to which every artistic gesture is significant and expresses a formal will that may well find itself never more apparent than in imitation. Ragghianti puts forward as one example of originality within the context of imitation Arnolfo di Cambio copying the early Christian sarcophagi. As for the question of 'clumsiness', in the light of the re-evaluation of primitive civilizations which followed upon Riegl's initiative, this has ceased to represent a negative value. By virtue of these more or less conscious principles, the 'provincialism' of Roman art has been restored to honour during the last decades, so there seems no reason why similar esteem should not be extended to the particular provincial form constituted by Campanian painting.

In default of the irretrievable beauty of Greek painting, Roman Campania has at least preserved for us its genres and subjects. The platonic theory of the transmission of classic form allows us to perceive in various mythological scenes a reflection of the masterpieces of the great fifth- and fourth-century masters, although it is not possible for us to trace these interpretations back to a specific master – interpretations which are freer than the copies of

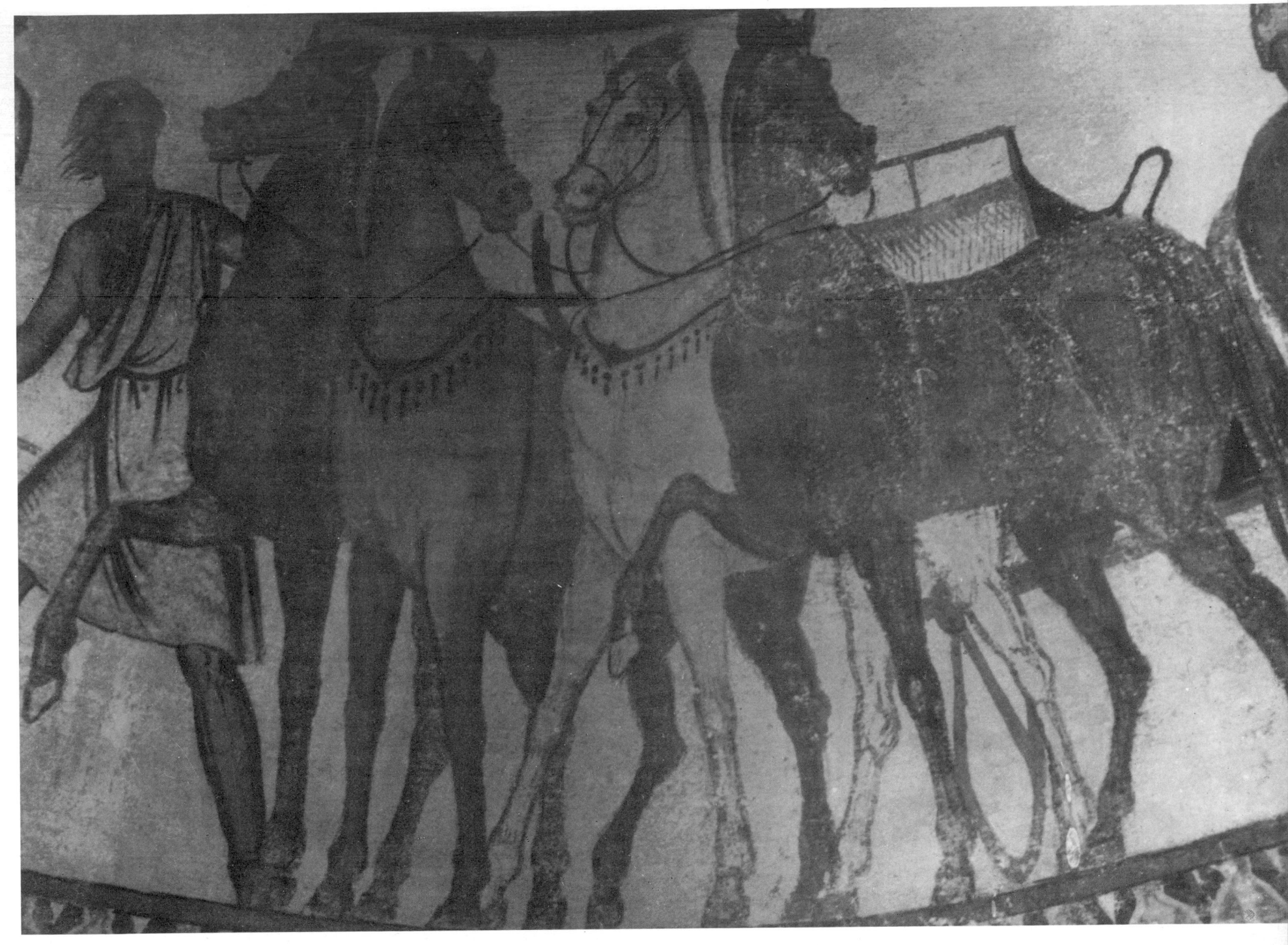

statuary made during the same epoch. Most of these scenes possess a classical grandeur, and it is a mosaic which probably expresses best the extraordinary boldness of painting during the Hellenistic period: the *Battle of Issus* (*pl. 9*) is certainly a copy of a celebrated work executed for one of Alexander's successors by some court painter (Philoxenes of Eretria, Helenus of Alexandria, Protogenes, Aetion?). Despite the loss of refinement resulting from the translation into mosaic, we can appreciate the play of hues, lights, reflections and cast shadows, the forcefulness of the expressions, the dynamism of the action and, most of all, the art of suggesting

depth. The form of the horse in the foreground, viewed from the rump, is entirely gathered back on itself; not until Rubens will an equally bold use of foreshortening be found.

The three towns buried by Vesuvius display a comprehensive panorama of antique painting, and include all the varieties of landscape which the West was later to reinvent. Here is the classical landscape, serving as framework for an epic action, reminiscent of Poussin or Claude (the Odyssey landscapes in the Vatican's Museo Profano); here is the 'sacred landscape' of Hellenistic derivation, depicting animals and temples dispersed in nature in a dream-

7 *Quadriga*. Detail of a wall-painting from a tomb at Kazanlik, Bulgaria. 3rd century B C.

Contemporary with the great masterpieces of Greek painting, these magnificent horses reflect, with an admixture of provincial crudity, the intense realism of the great masters of the classical period.

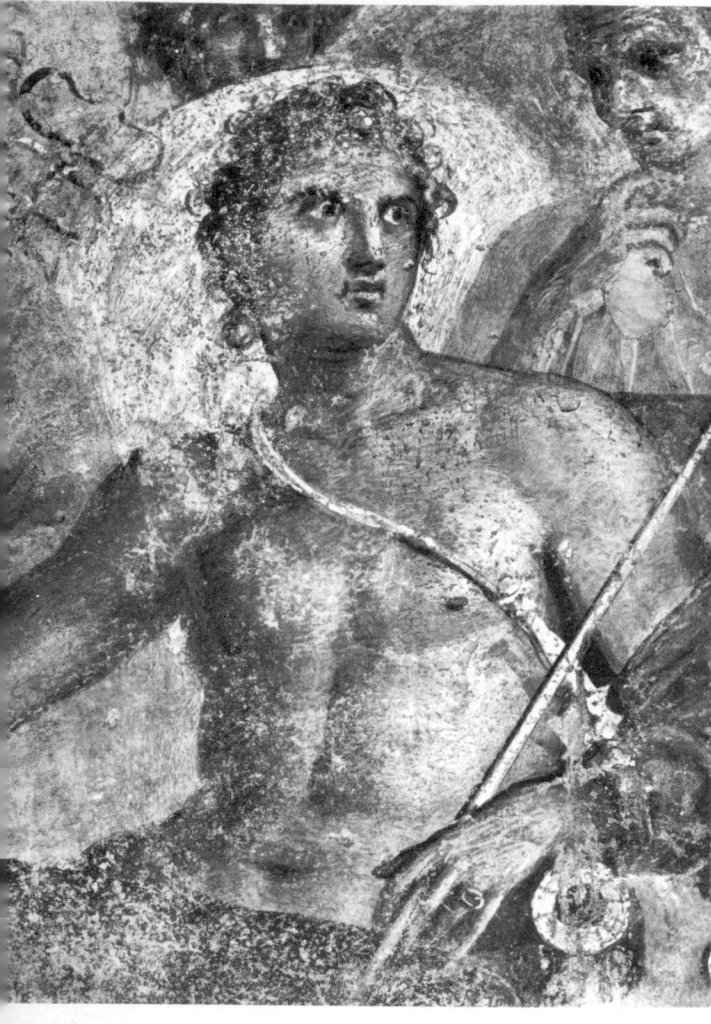

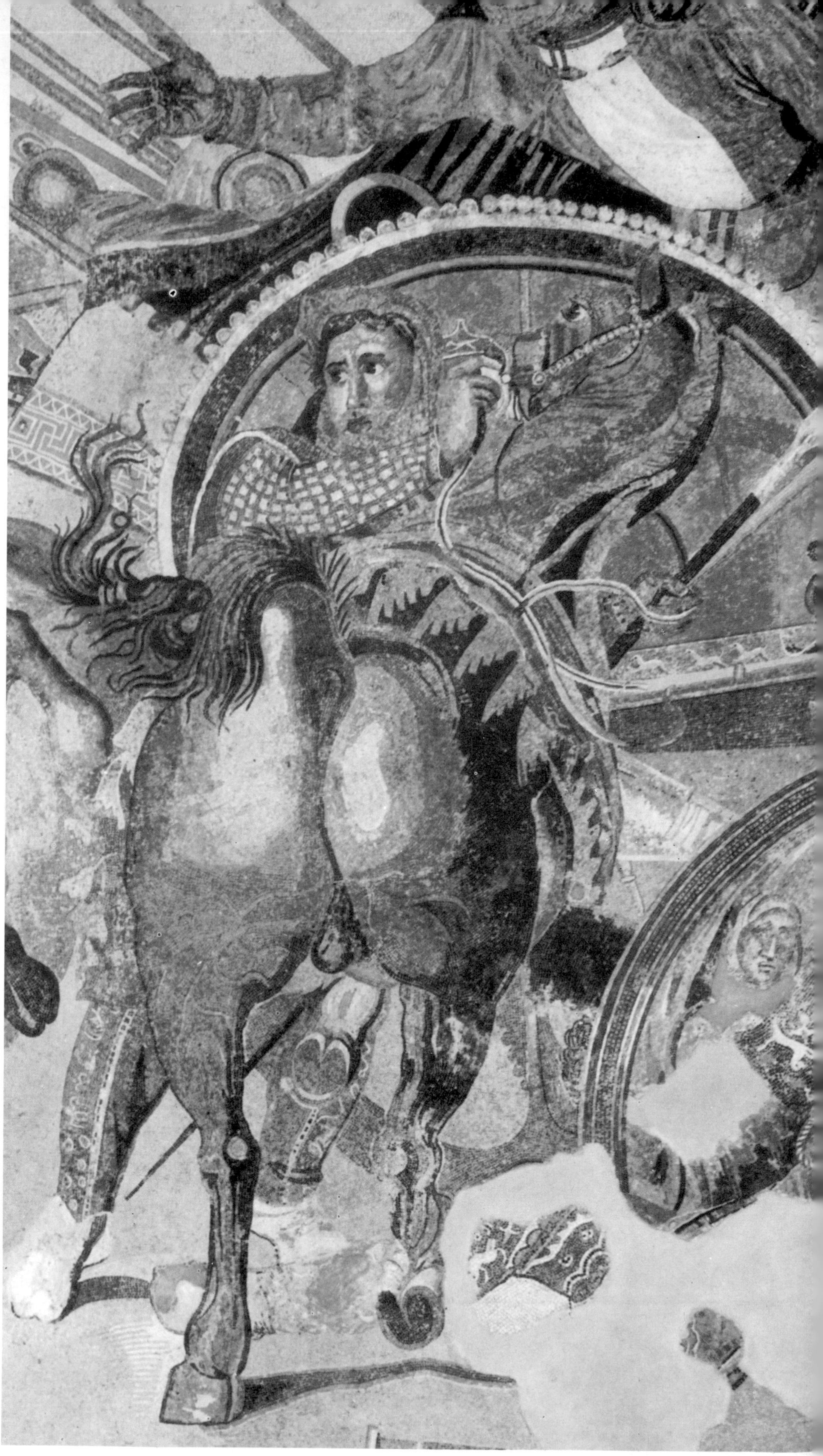

8 *Achilles and Briseis*. Detail of a painting from the House of the Tragic Poet at Pompeii. Naples, Museo Nazionale.

9 *The Battle of Issus*. Detail of a mosaic from the House of the Faun at Pompeii. Naples, Museo Nazionale.

In certain works at Pompeii and Herculaneum the expressive liveliness, powerful foreshortening and intensity of movement evoke the dynamism of seventeenth-century baroque art.

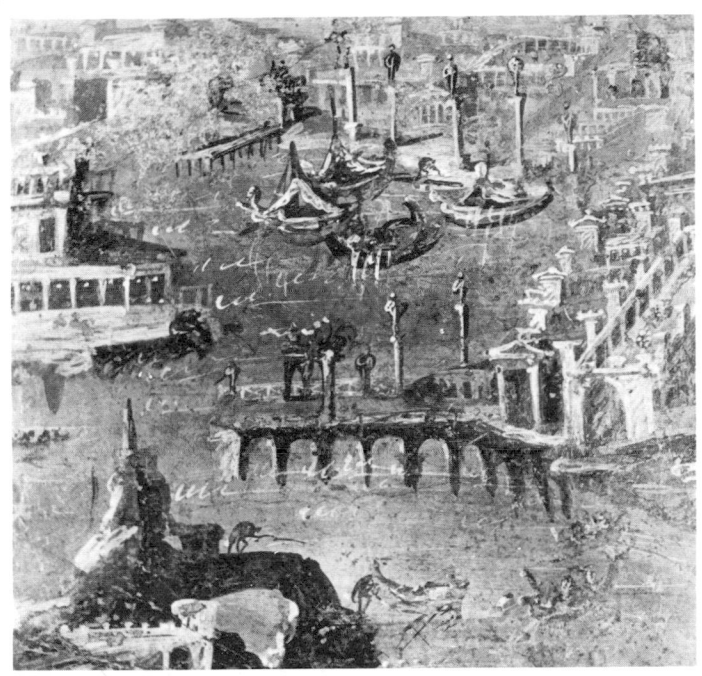

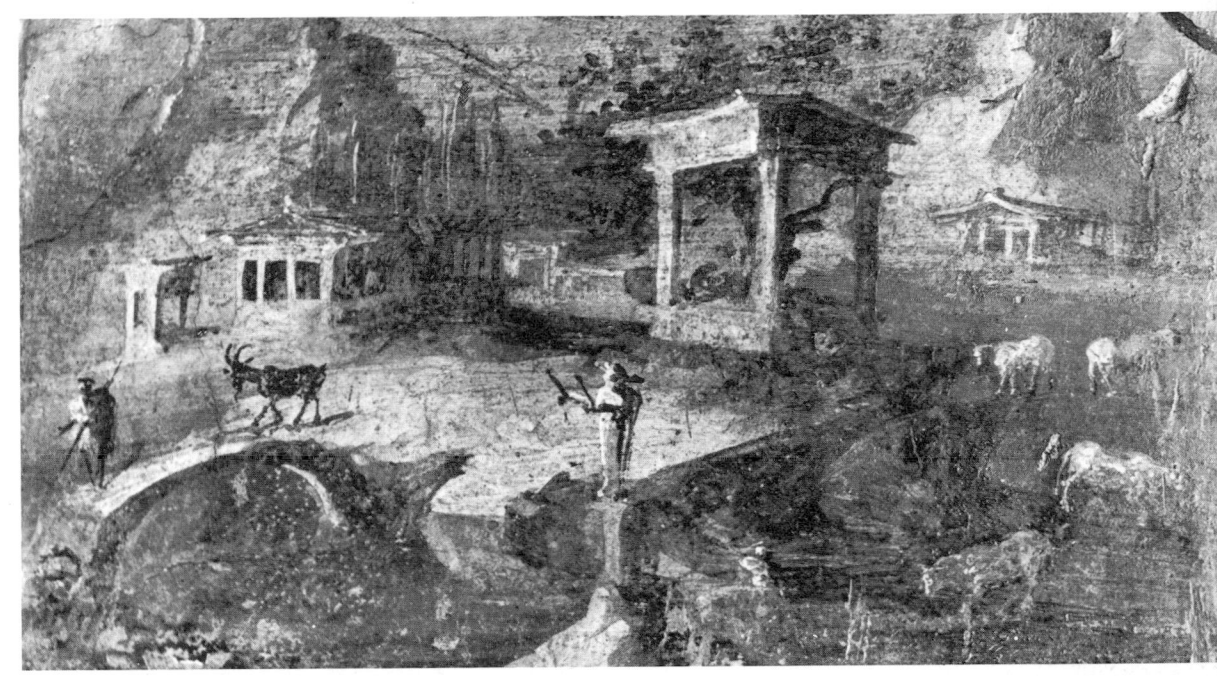

like atmosphere, whose poetic inspiration evokes eighteenth-century idyllic landscapes; the exotic landscape, introducing African animals, is of Alexandrian origin; and here, too, are seascapes, port scenes (*pl. 10*) and townscapes. The wall-paintings of the Villa of Livia at Primaporta (Rome, Museo delle Terme), and certain murals recently excavated at Pompeii, have revealed to the astonished excavators that the 'verdure' genre of painting of our Middle Ages was already practised by the ancients. This whole broad vista of the spectacle offered by nature lacked one single feature: it was left to the painters of Western art to invent the portrait-landscape *reproducing* a motif or limited aspect of nature, for the ancients conceived landscapes only as composed wholes.

Although historical painting was held in highest esteem, the Romans of Campania took special delight in genre scenes, and it is thanks to such paintings that we are fully acquainted with the details of their family and social existence, through scenes of home life, the street, the tavern and even the public brothel. Picaresque story-pictures are sometimes painted in a satirical spirit akin to that of Jacques Callot. The *xenia* inform us what food they ate and the kind of tableware they used. We know their predilection for animals, as well as for birds, flowers, butterflies and especially for the joyous forms of naked children, those *amorini* who perform every possible human task while at play. And all the stages of development of the art of skiagraphy have been revealed to us by the houses of Pompeii.

The Italians inherited from the Romans this

10 *View of a port*. Detail of a wall-painting from a house at Stabiae. Naples, Museo Nazionale.

11 Detail of a landscape. Naples, Museo Nazionale. The landscape is one of the great inventions of Greek painting, and Pompeii and Herculaneum have preserved for us several examples, although these were never realistic views painted from nature.

12 Detail of a decoration in the House of the Masks, discovered in 1961 on the Palatine at Rome. A marvellously preserved example of those imaginary architectures, condemned by Vitruvius for their audacity, which were doubtless intended to suggest theatre scenes.

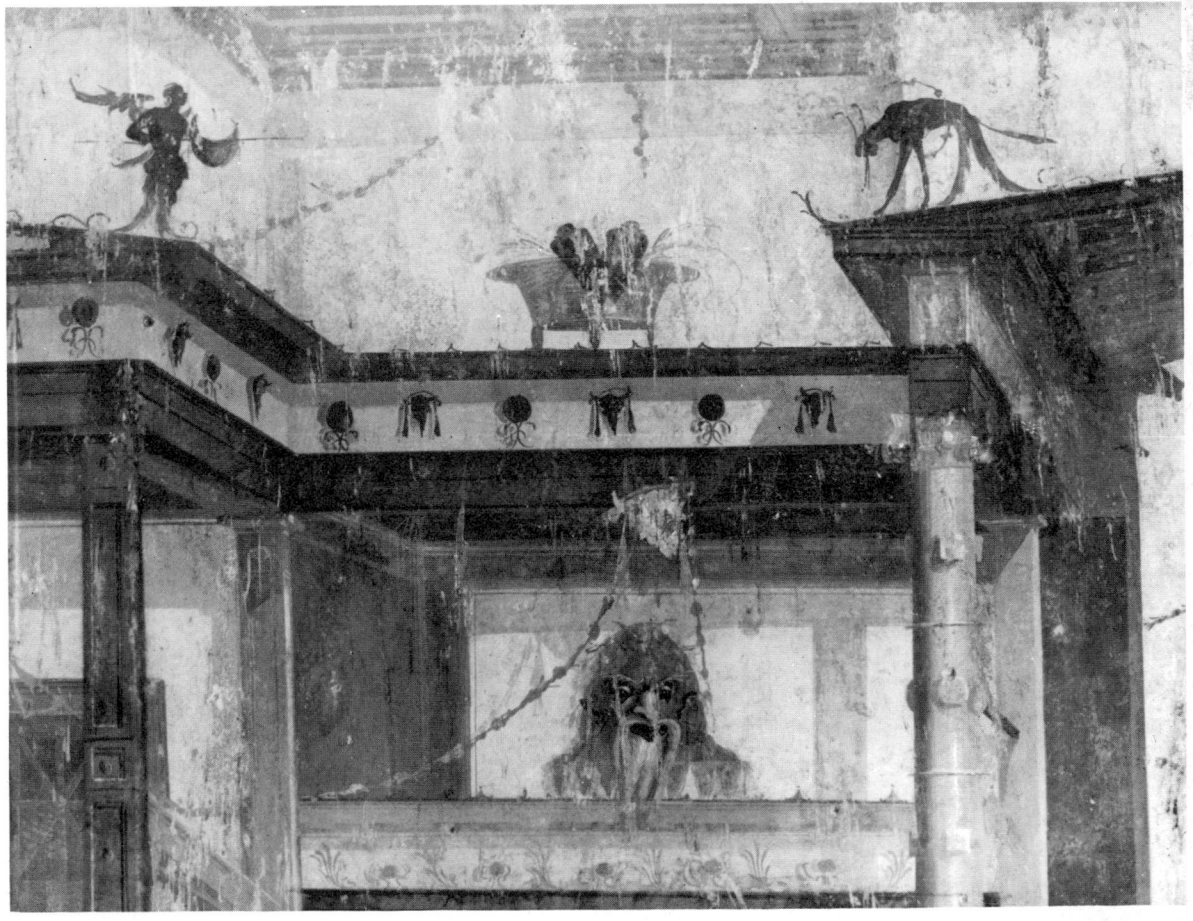

preference for domestic privacy in which it is the walls of the rooms which open on to dream-forests and fantastic architectures. There is no general agreement on the question of whether the Romans practised the art of *perspectiva artificialis* with a single vanishing-point. Judging by the Pompeiian mural decorations of the 'Second Style', it may be considered that they came very near to this through the convergence of lines upon a vanishing axis, but with several directions of lighting, as for example in a wall painting from a villa at Boscoreale (Naples). The paintings of the Third and, more especially, the Fourth Style, incorporating several vanishing points and exuberant pictorial detail, bear witness to the fact that towards the close of the Hellenistic world scenography was as rich in resources as it ever was in the baroque opera of the seventeenth and eighteenth centuries. This wall painting from Herculaneum (*pl. 2*), with its marvellously realistic curtain that makes one think of the celebrated curtain painted by Parrhasios, surely evokes also the most poetic fantasies created by Giuseppe Galli Bibiena in his eighteenth-century stage designs. It is clear, then, that in spatial invention the ancients anticipated the great baroque artists of the West, at least in terms of mural painting, although they appear to have remained ignorant of an allied art, that of ceiling painting.

We are immensely the gainers from the natural disaster which struck down the unfortunate inhabitants of Pompeii, Herculaneum and Stabiae in AD 79, and preserved for posterity, under the ashes, this astonishing treasury of antique painting. In surveying these ruins, we are able to study all the stages of antique treatment of artistic themes, from the classical style, respectful of form, to the freest possible execution, involving dabs of light and shadow, evocative of Magnasco or of Goya in the period of his deafness. This latter manner (*pl. 13*) has erroneously been termed 'impressionist'; the ancients named this cursive style *compendiaria* (abbreviated). The term 'impressionist' should be limited to work executed in pure colour, which the ancients also practised, but apparently towards the end of their artistic evolution, at the moment when painting was about to yield its supremacy to mosaic. In the first Christian mosaics, dating from the fourth and fifth centuries, in Santa Maria Maggiore at Rome, and in Hagios Giorgios and the Acheropita at Salonika, the whole effect is obtained by colour alone, an intense colour which was to lose its richness, if not its brilliance, in Byzantine art. In these mosaics, drawing and shading are entirely absent, while an absolute clarity makes the light vibrate, breaking it up into its chromatic variations. No doubt the technique of mosaic lent itself particularly to this 'divisionism'. At Hagios Giorgios, Salonika, the way in which the gradations of volume are achieved solely by variations of colour evokes Cézanne, while at Santa Maria Maggiore one thinks rather of Renoir, the Renoir of Cagnes, conjuring infinite shades of tone from his palette.

From Polygnotus to the Master of Salonika, in ten centuries, antique painting travelled along the same path that in Western art was later to lead from Giotto to impressionism. In less than two centuries, all this was to be swept away by barbarian invasions and the spiritual revolution of Christianity. The break was a brutal one, and only one art, that of the portrait, experienced all the intermediary stages involved in the transition from the real to the unreal. It is perhaps in this domain that the Romans, with their predilection for naturalism and individualism, demonstrated the greatest inventiveness. The truthful meaning of the human effigy had been vitiated by the idealized beauty or gesture imposed upon it by the Greeks. A man shown in terms of unadulterated physical truth, such as the famous baker of Pompeii, is a purely Roman work, and no comparable verism in portrait painting is to be found until the advent of Jan van Eyck. The woman accompanying the baker is depicted in a more conventional manner, as is the case throughout history with female effigies, although the Romans occasionally probed deeper than the gallantry demanded by custom; a bust from Pompeii, in the Museo Nazionale in Naples, portrays the archetypal Mediterranean matron such as may still be seen any day on the screen in Italian popular films.

The art of the portrait, realized in encaustic on panel, flourished in Lower Egypt from the first to the fourth centuries AD. These effigies, representing figures still in the bloom of youth, were hung in the atrium of the family's house, and on the death of their model they were wrapped in the mummy's bandages. A marvellous field for the study of races at the end of the ancient world is provided by this gallery portraying all the ethnic groups which intermingled in Egypt: Greeks, Jews, Syrians, Persians, Negroids, Indians, Copts and Romans. The change which overtook humanity during the closing years of the ancient world can nowhere be more effectively studied than in the Middle East, the scene of a decisive encounter with the tormenting problems of spiritual life. The earliest of these portraits look out at this world, while those from the latest period look out at the world beyond: the gaze of these enormously enlarged ocular globes begins to waver, grows anxious, then becomes fixed

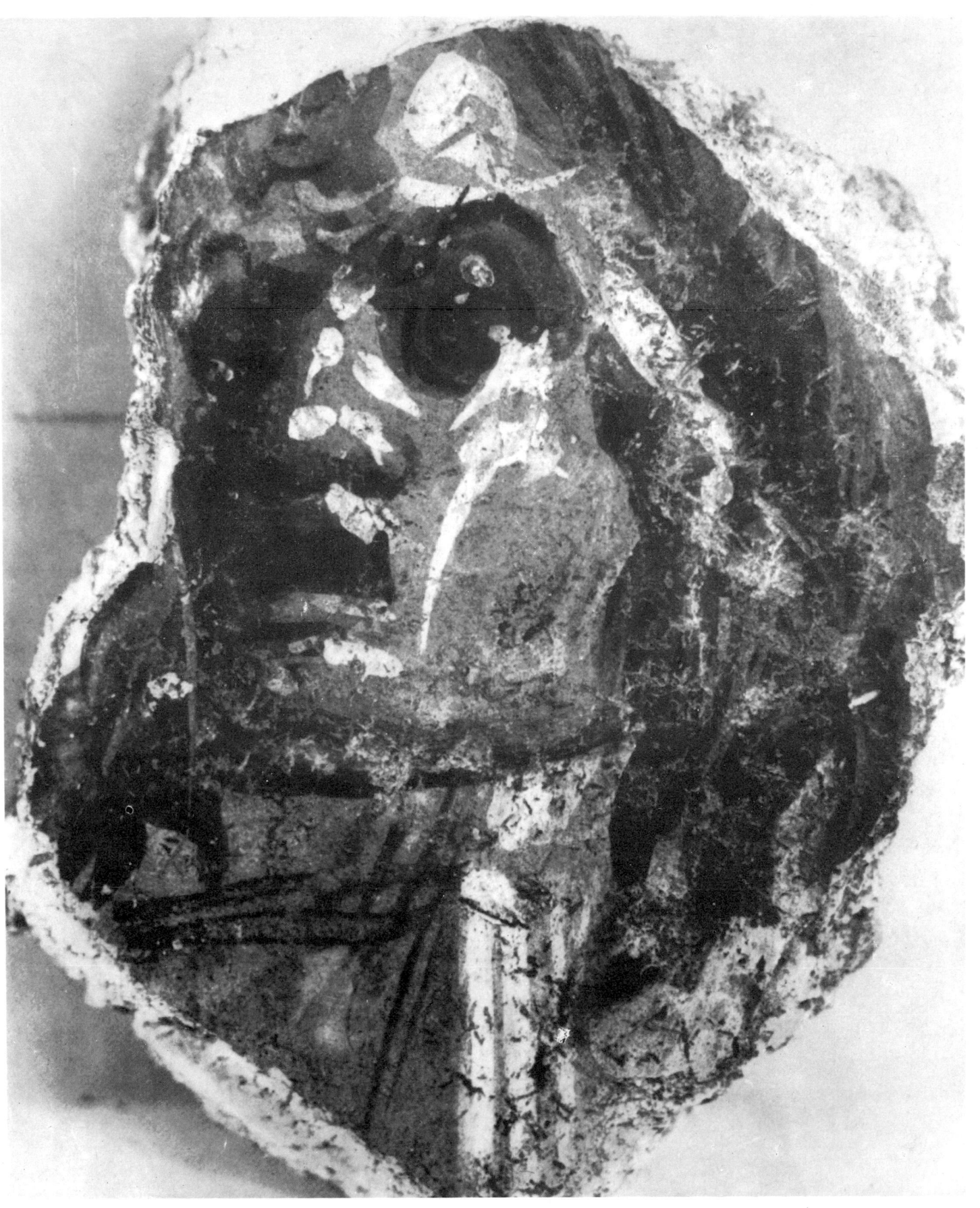

13 *Head of a woman*. Wall painting discovered at Stabiae.

The free use by Romano-Campanian painters of an abbreviated treatment called *compendiaria* is sometimes prophetically evocative of Goya's expressive vigour.

in contemplation of the invisible (*pl. 14*). After these ecstatic glances had been extinguished in Faiyum, the Coptic monks, before being overwhelmed by the tide of Islam, continued to reproduce them clumsily in the new Christian imagery, the popular reflection of the great Byzantine art. But by one of the most extraordinary paradoxes of history, antique painting was continued beyond its time by other monks, those of the monastery of St Catherine at Sinai. Preserved by the desert from the theological controversies of the sixth century and the iconoclastic quarrels of the eighth, spared by the Arabs themselves from any encroachment, these monks pursued until the seventh century the living art of antique painting, and this in the form of icons at a moment when, for theological reasons, these images were eliminating all intimate relationship with the world of appearances, retaining only the minimum of visible support necessary for the manifestation of the idea. Looking at this sixth-century face (*pl. 15*), with its heavy sensual eyes and rosy complexion, who would guess, if it were not for the Syrian *maphorion* (a head-dress worn by priests and women), that it belonged to a representation of the Virgin Mary painted at the very moment when, in Byzantine art, she was becoming pure Idea in the solemn guise of the *theotokos* (Mother of God) or the compassionate one of the *hodegitria* (divine guide)? It is strange to think that it took the 1956 Suez campaign to reveal to the world this treasure-trove of icons, preserved inviolate in Sinai and glimpsed hitherto only by a few scholars.

The West was never able to inherit the riches of antique painting. The original examples vanished with the civilization which had given birth to them, and the tradition was broken by Christianity. Being a means of exploration of the real, such painting remained unadaptable to the new Christian civilization which guided the image in the direction of an entirely different vocation that was both spiritualistic and unrealistic. This process culminated in the virtual disappearance of the art of painting, and the arts of coloration were given expression during the Middle Ages through other mediums: mosaic, stained glass, miniature, enamel. The awakening of Western art was accomplished through sculpture. The relatively uninventive style of the Romanesque fresco, and of Italian painting before 1250, bears witness to the backwardness of strictly pictorial form in comparison to the world of sculpture which, from the Master of the Miègeville Tympanum in the church of Saint-Sernin at Toulouse to Nicola Pisano, constitutes the true artistic avant-garde between 1100 and 1250.

Painting, properly so called, was, however, preserved in Byzantium in the form of icons, although these have vanished almost as completely as have the paintings of the ancient world. The sad smile on the face of the twelfth-century *Our Lady of Vladimir* (*pl. 16*), a surviving witness of an engulfed world, testifies that a flicker of life was at that moment animating Byzantine art. The frescoes of Serbia, those of Mileševa (*c.* 1235) and especially those of Sopoćani (*c.* 1260), as well as certain icons of the same school, show the development of a tendency resulting from the deep urge towards classicism which Byzantine civilization had been experiencing since the ninth century, and which constituted an important factor in the gradual relaxation of hieratic convention, the consequent increased suppleness of style, and the appearance of an impulse towards nature. This impulse found outlets in the schools deriving from Byzantium, the Greek school (the fourteenth-century wall paintings at Mistra), the Serbian and the Russian schools.

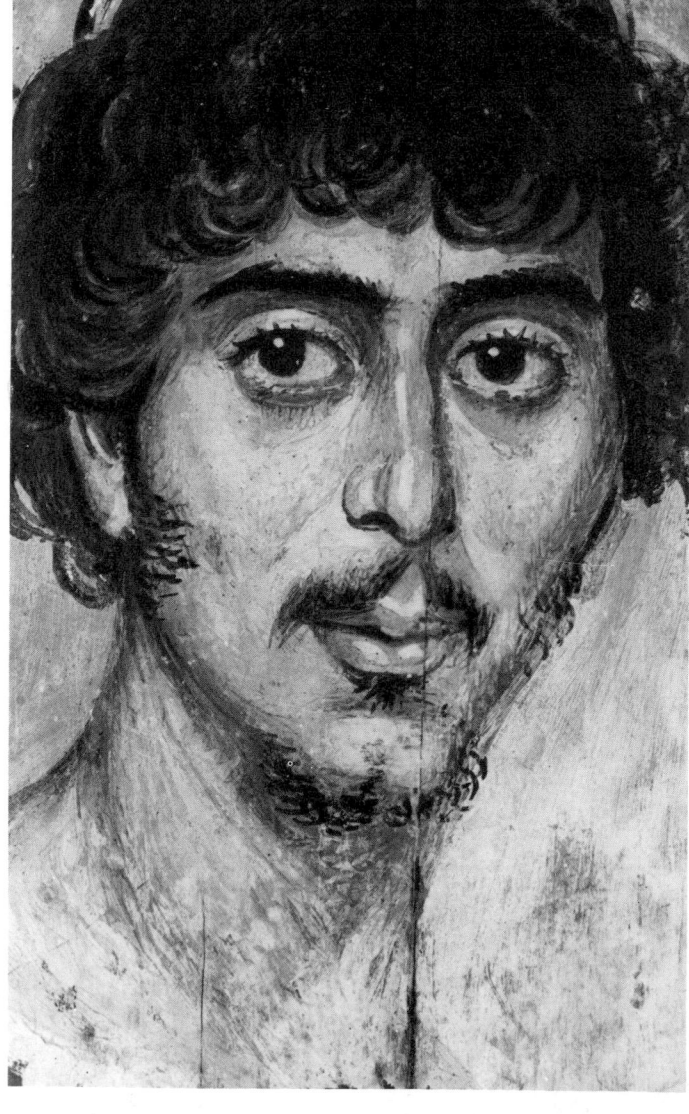

14 *Portrait of a man*. 2nd century A D. Graeco-Egyptian. Berlin-Dahlem, Staatliche Museen.

The psychological portrait, succeeding the idealized portrait of the Greeks and the realistic portrait of the Romans, expressed the spiritual anguish prevalent during the closing phases of the ancient world.

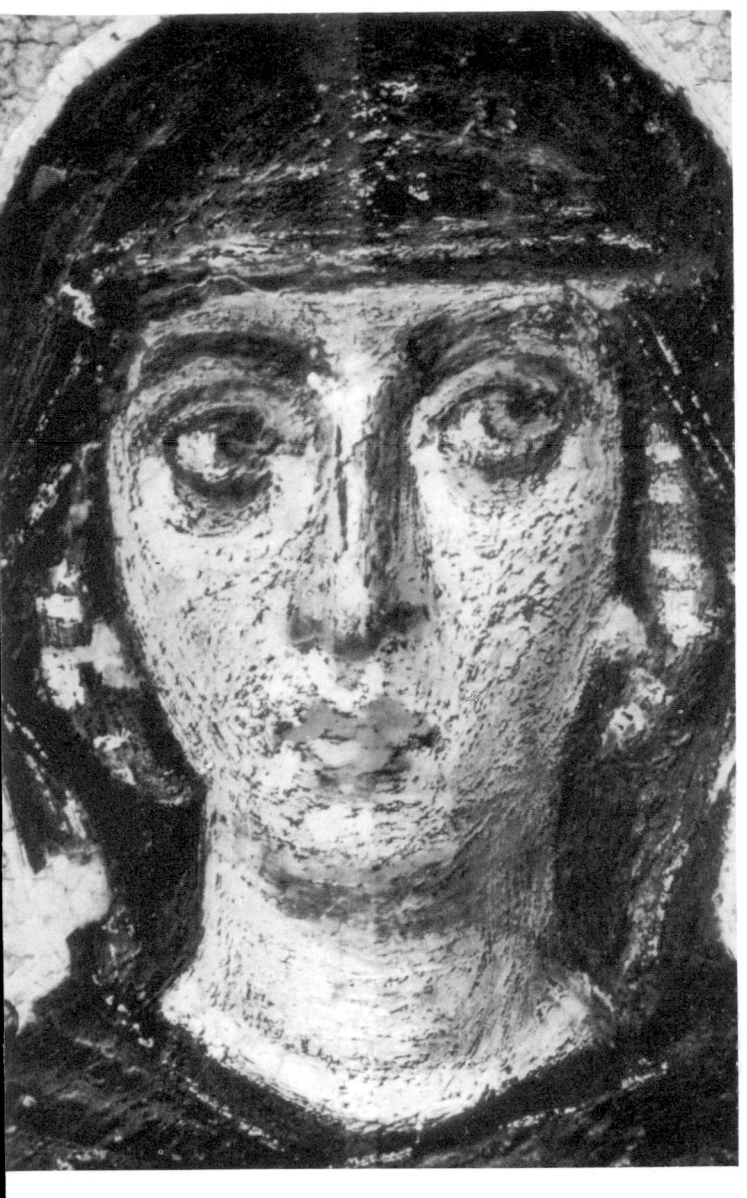

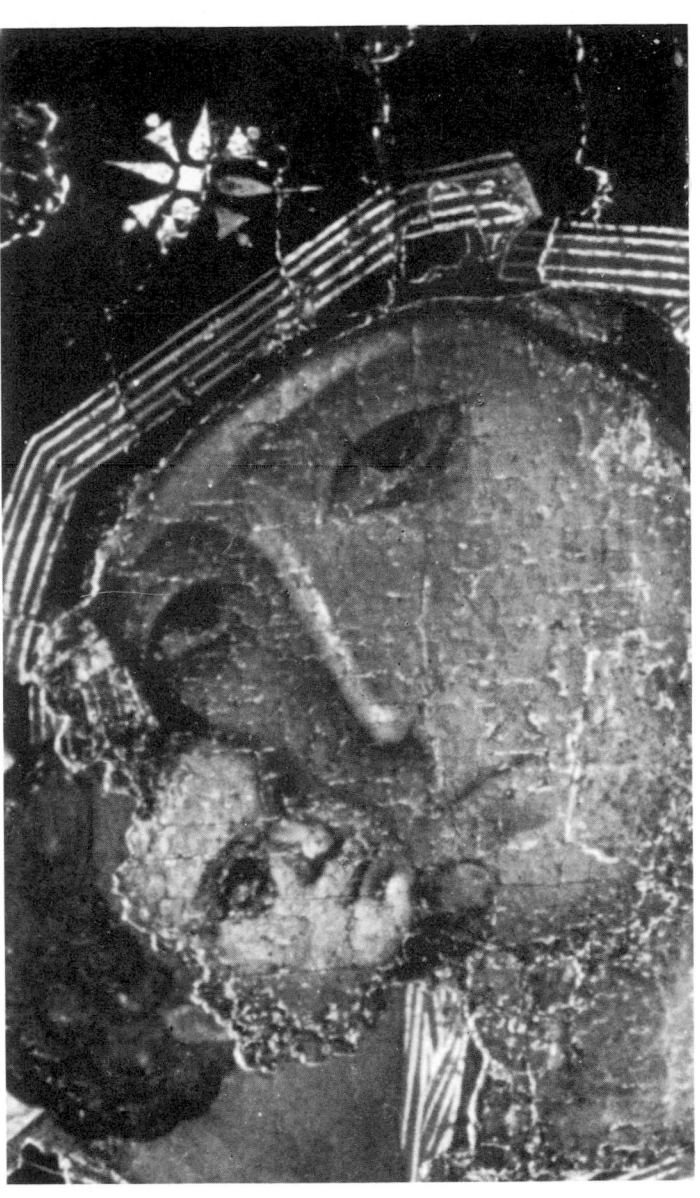

15 Detail of *Madonna and Child*. 6th century A D. Icon from the monastery of St Catherine at Sinai.

The sensual expression and crimson lips of the Madonna of Sinai allow an element of antique humanism to show through the Eastern hieratic convention which was to triumph in Byzantine art.

16 *Our Lady of Vladimir*. 12th century A D. Moscow, Tretyakov Museum.

After several centuries of theological art, a thrill of life suddenly permeated the icons of Byzantium once more, during the eleventh and twelfth centuries. This awakening of human feeling, when it occurred in the West a little later, was more profound.

The surprising points of similarity between the paintings of Mistra and those of Tuscany have led to some theorizing about the latter's influence, but these affinities prove rather that Byzantine art was in the process of rejoining the West in the course of its own evolution. The same applies to Russia. At the beginning of the fifteenth century, at the opposite pole of the Christian world, the Moscow-centred art of the icon shared with the fourteenth-century school of Siena a traditionalist attitude which, eschewing all drastic innovation, moved forward through a constant refinement of fundamental plastic and spiritual concepts; these concepts were themselves derived from the sum of Byzantine artistic production over the centuries, which still retained alive, buried deep within it, some of the ferment deposited there by antiquity. Despite everything, life insinuated itself into this formalism, as it did at Siena, so transforming this supremely anti-humanist attitude. Andrei Rublev's Christ, for example, is already on a par with the Christs of the Quattrocento; the graceful linear style of this artist evokes Duccio and his theological spirituality, and, to a lesser degree, that of Fra Angelico. Rublev, like Duccio – although in the latter's case the Gothic impulse helped stimulate his development – shows how the art of painting tended to free itself from Byzantine constraints, but without any deliberate attempt to break away.

Thus Byzantium achieved its own self-renewal within the context of a harmonious evolution. But this evolution had already been overtaken, a century previously, by the revolution accomplished in Tuscany by Giotto, who had established the new foundations of the art of painting. Byzantium's renovation no longer represented anything but the ultimate refinement of a decadent and doomed civilization.

17 Giotto (*c.* 1266–1337). Detail of
St Francis giving his cloak to a poor man.
Assisi, Upper Basilica.

2 The initiator

Certain historians, still respecting Vasari's predilections, see Cimabue as the pioneer of modern Italian art. But Cimabue should, on the contrary, be given his rightful position as the last great exponent of the Byzantine aesthetic which prospered in Tuscany throughout the first half of the thirteenth century in two forms: popular and expressive in the emotional works of the Pisa and Lucca schools, more preoccupied with abstract form in the works of the Florentine school. Cimabue's style has affinities with that of the contemporaneous frescoes at Sopoćani in Serbia, though it is even more formal and less sensitive. The tenth-century mosaics of the narthex of Hagia Sophia show that, by way of Venice, no doubt, the great Cenno di Peppe drew the inspiration for his monumental art from the very source of official tradition, solidly entrenched on the banks of the Bosphorus and carefully preserved from any foreign contact. The ossified modelling, the partitioning which transforms the figures into a game of patience, the rejection of true space, the deliberate aim to transmute every element of reality into an abstract pattern and thus to elevate every singular form to the dignity of a concept, all these, together with the virtuosity with which linear arabesque is handled, are expressed in identical fashion at Hagia Sophia, at Sopoćani and in Cimabue's Madonnas.

The strength of Byzantine tradition in thirteenth-century Italy explains why the renovation of plastic values in the West reached this country almost a whole century later than the rest of Europe. It might have been thought that the example of French Gothic art, then at the peak of its achievement, would have helped to loosen these bonds, but such was not the case. The art of Nicola Pisano derived from a separate, native tradition, and it is significant that from its very beginnings Italian art, in the person of this great sculptor, turned towards antiquity for its models. A slightly older contemporary of Giotto, Pietro Cavallini, followed the same path. Inspired by the atmosphere of the eternal city, he liberated himself from Byzantinism, not through the observation of nature but by plunging back in time to ancient Rome. He was the first to exhume this formalistic Roman-style grandeur which was destined in its turn to become a tradition, and very often a restrictive one, until the nineteenth century.

Cimabue marks the end, not the beginning, of an era. The true pioneer of Western painting, the pillar on which the whole edifice rests, is Giotto. Whether purposely (Masaccio, Raphael) or unconsciously (Caravaggio, David), painters throughout the succeeding centuries were to return to the principles that he originally posed. Giotto's contemporaries, Boccaccio, Petrarch, Dante, were keenly aware of this creative force among them, and extolled him as the founder of Western figurative painting. Protected by popes, summoned to practise his art in Assisi, Rome, Naples, Padua, Rimini, he became the first painter to rise above the status of artisan and to be elevated to the same heroic dignity of genius that the humanists had hitherto reserved for poets.

Although only part of Giotto's prolific output has survived, it is still sufficiently extensive to allow us to reconstruct the artist's career in its entirety. The three cycles which serve to define him constitute a powerful unity and present almost perfect examples of the three phases of a master's evolution. The series of frescoes he devoted to the Legend of St Francis, at Assisi (*pls 17–18*), show us the artist at grips with a new subject, in full flow of creativity, inventing attitudes, gestures, expressions and compositions, impulsively and sometimes awkwardly, and tackling the problem of spatial values well before the masters of the Quattrocento, that is to say from the very beginning of modern painting. The frescoes in the Scrovegni Chapel (*pls 20–1, 23–5, 28–9*) in the Arena at Padua (1304–6) represent the flowering of genius in full maturity, with realism perfectly balancing formal grandeur in an intensity of dramatic action that has never been surpassed. The Peruzzi and Bardi Chapels of Santa Croce in Florence, which he decorated some time after 1317, demonstrate a certain formalism, and show the artist ageing serenely and more preoccupied with composition than with expression. In truth, if the Assisi link were to be suppressed, as recent English and American criticism has sought to do, in order to reassign the merit for having founded Italian

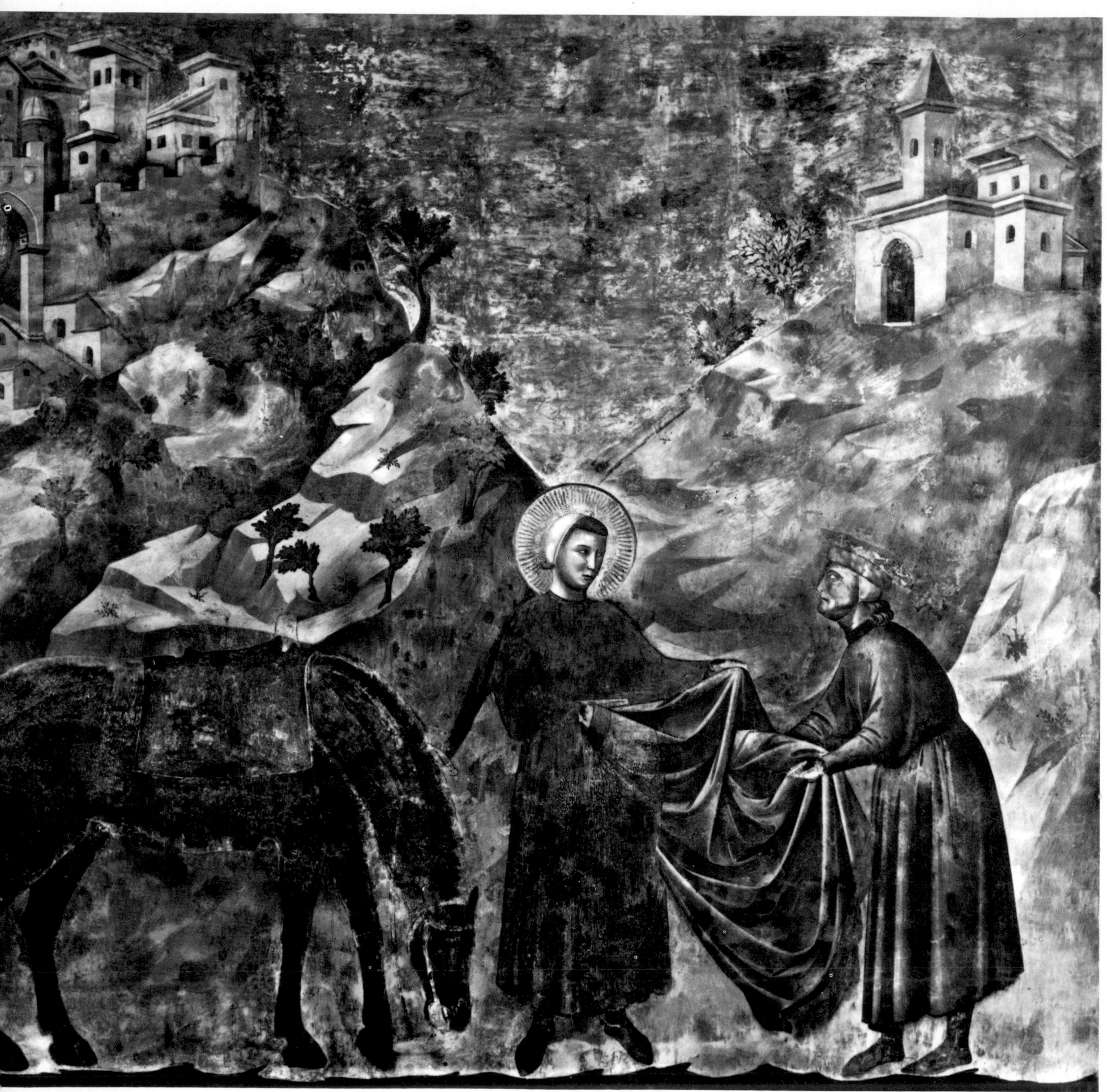

painting to a hypothetical 'Master of the Life of St Francis', Giotto's marvellous and majestic career would be shorn of its essential continuity. More than that: the stylistic evolution of the Italian school during this critical era would become entirely confused if any weight were given to the idea that the Paduan frescoes might have been painted before those of the Assisi cycle, which would then be relegated to the work of an imitator. Italian criticism, with its added advantage of innate percipience, seems to me to be better inspired in respecting a tradition which is, in any case, buttressed by very strong arguments.

At Assisi, Giotto became the creator of a new style of images that actualized religious art by situating it in an historical and heroic perspective and by inserting its representations into an inhabited space. Although the artist's encounter with the newly established legend of St Francis may have been providential in suggesting to him a hitherto unexplored theme, Giotto had no time for the Franciscan myth. His *St Francis receiving the stigmata* at Assisi, a calm and powerful hero with a robust and well-nourished body, is in a world apart from the emaciated ascetic of Monte La Verna, his body mortified, his soul engulfed in divine hypostasis, as he was depicted so often by the neo-Byzantines of the Dugento and the Sienese of the Trecento.

After the death of St Francis, his followers were split by a dispute between the 'spiritual' faction, which advocated the retention in its full purity of the spirit of poverty with all that that entailed, and the 'conventual' faction, which argued that the missionary future of the Order and the Church demanded stable foundations and, consequently, the possession of property. Supported by the popes, the triumphant conventuals celebrated their victory by the construction of a magnificent basilica and a great monastery. Working for them as he did, Giotto inevitably shared their viewpoint, but in any case his own temperament alienated him from mysticism and led him to conceive of the human body as a force which he sometimes endowed with an almost athletic intensity. In the twenty-eight frescoes of the Lower Basilica of Assisi, Giotto breaks with the Franciscan mystical tradition to present us with the emotionally charged panorama of a hero at grips with the world, imposing his will upon the forces of nature, bringing to the papacy the bulwark of a new order.

At Padua, in the frescoes of the life of Christ in the Arena Chapel, pathos is raised to the level of the essential drama, the struggle between Good and Evil, and is resolved by the triumph of the supreme hero, Christ. Giotto brings religious art down from the ideal regions to which Byzantium had elevated it, and fits it into the dimensions of the human drama. I once wrote that in this respect Giotto paved the way for the Renaissance superman, capable of fulfilling his destiny without the aid of divine grace; but this rash statement would better have been applied to his heir, Masaccio. Giotto, on the contrary, *realizes* Christianity; he realizes it in its essential truth, that of being the religion of the Man-God. Certainly his Christ is a man, but one who assumes the totality of humanness with a perfection that could derive only from the Man-God. From this perfection flows beauty. Whether God or man, the human figure ceases to be the more or less grimacing ghost that had filled the mosaics with an air of gloom, and rediscovers the harmonious proportions once given him by the Greeks. Giotto straightened the Byzantines' aquiline noses and restored the Greek profile to honour: the old Simeon of the *Presentation at the Temple* (*pl. 21*), renouncing his status as prophet, assumes the beauty of the divine Plato.

All the personages who, in the Arena Chapel, Padua, participate in the sacred drama around Christ, share in this superior humanity. Of all the themes dear to Christian artists, that of the Annunciation is certainly the favourite, for it shows a human being confronting destiny. The Virgin in Simone Martini's *Annunciation*, a frail being shrinking back in sudden terror at the apparition of the celestial messenger, is the very image of human weakness, while Fra Angelico's Virgin (*pl. 62*), a humble, gentle dove, bends her head in submission to the divine will: they both belong to the order of grace, the grace from which humanity has fallen. But Giotto's Virgin in the Arena Chapel (*pl. 20*), her head held high, her sturdy body set solidly upon the ground, is ready to come to grips with the supernatural; she draws the strength to accomplish her destiny from her Adamic nature, as the only child of man preserved by divine decree from human sin. The forces of Evil can gain no foothold upon this immovable rock, for the Mother of God is also the mother of mankind and the protectress of all sinners who seek refuge under her ample cloak.

After Giotto, one must await the Spanish sculptors of the seventeenth century to find once more such lofty Christological images, or figures of Virgins so profoundly imbued with a sense of their mission to bring to the mystery of the Incarnation all the latent power of an unblemished human being. However, in expressing the drama of the Redemption in all its impassioned and living reality, Giotto inevitably opens the way to everything human, the worst as well as the best: in embodying

18 Giotto. *St Francis giving his cloak to a poor man*. Assisi, Upper Basilica.

Giotto brought about a veritable reincarnation of painting, transposing the story into an inhabited space and creating expressive values which recall the greatness of Greek tragic poetry.

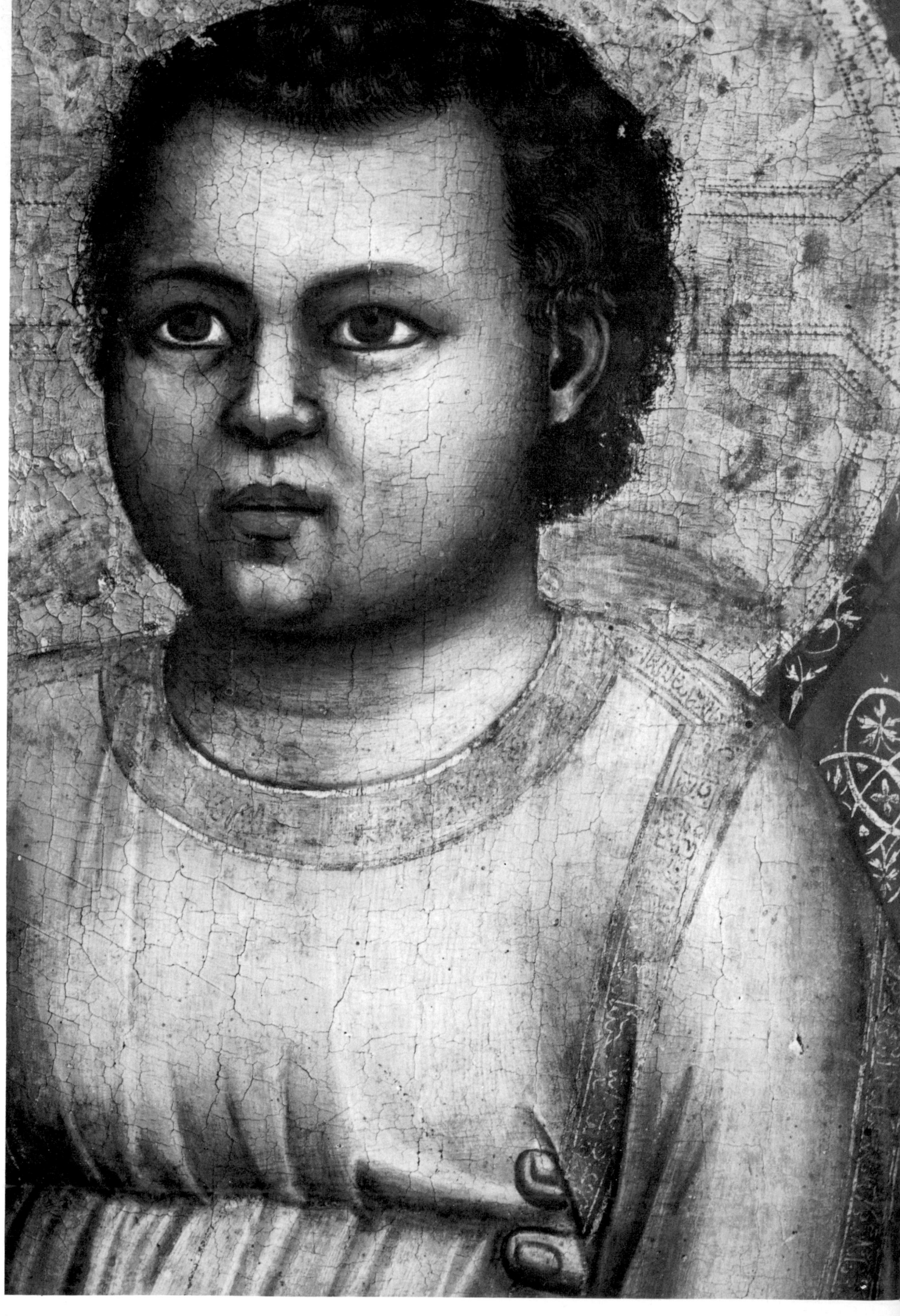

19 Giotto. The Child, detail of *Virgin and Child*. Florence, Uffizi.

No Infant Jesus painted by any other artist expresses with as much force as that of Giotto the power of a humanity assumed in its totality by Christ.

28

Good, he re-embodies Evil. The faith of preceding ages had envisaged Evil as an absence of being rather than as a specific being; Giotto, however, gives it human semblance in the face of this Judas, which incarnates Evil just as Christ himself incarnates Good *(pl. 28)*. The tragic element in Giotto's work derives from a confrontation between the rival forces of uncontrolled energies unleashed upon the world by the Evil One. And yet the artist treats the theme of the evildoer only cursorily; his executioners are unimpressive, his *Hell* is the weakest part of the Arena frescoes, and the power of the *Massacre of the Innocents* lies in the suffering of the victims rather than the cruelty of the executioners. But before Giotto, the brilliant unknown artist who drew the cartoons for the mosaic cycle of the Last Judgment in the Baptistry at Florence *(pl. 22)* had anticipated the Dantesque vision of Hell, providing a link with the satanism of the thirteenth-century French sculptors which had hitherto been unknown to the Italians.

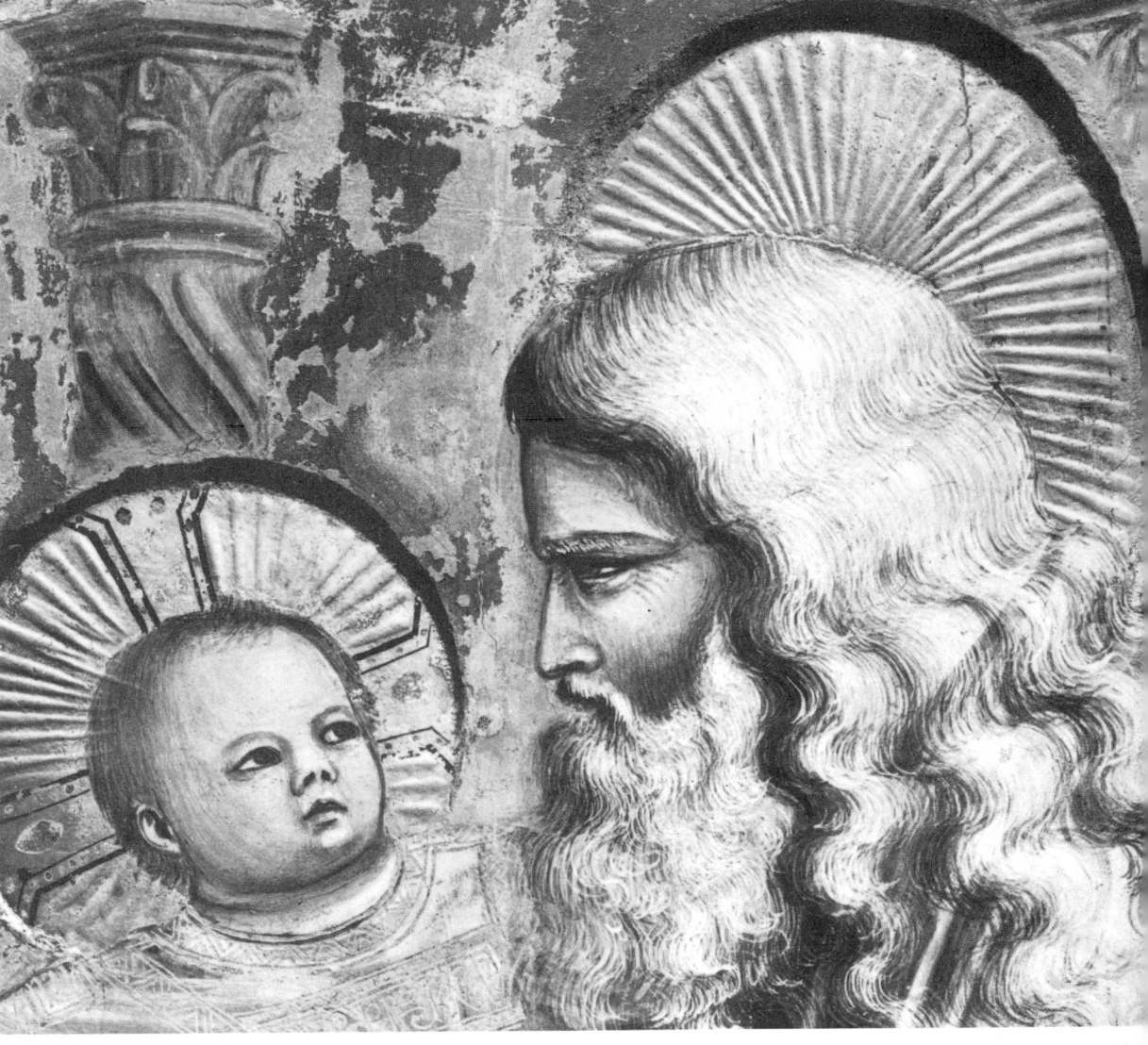

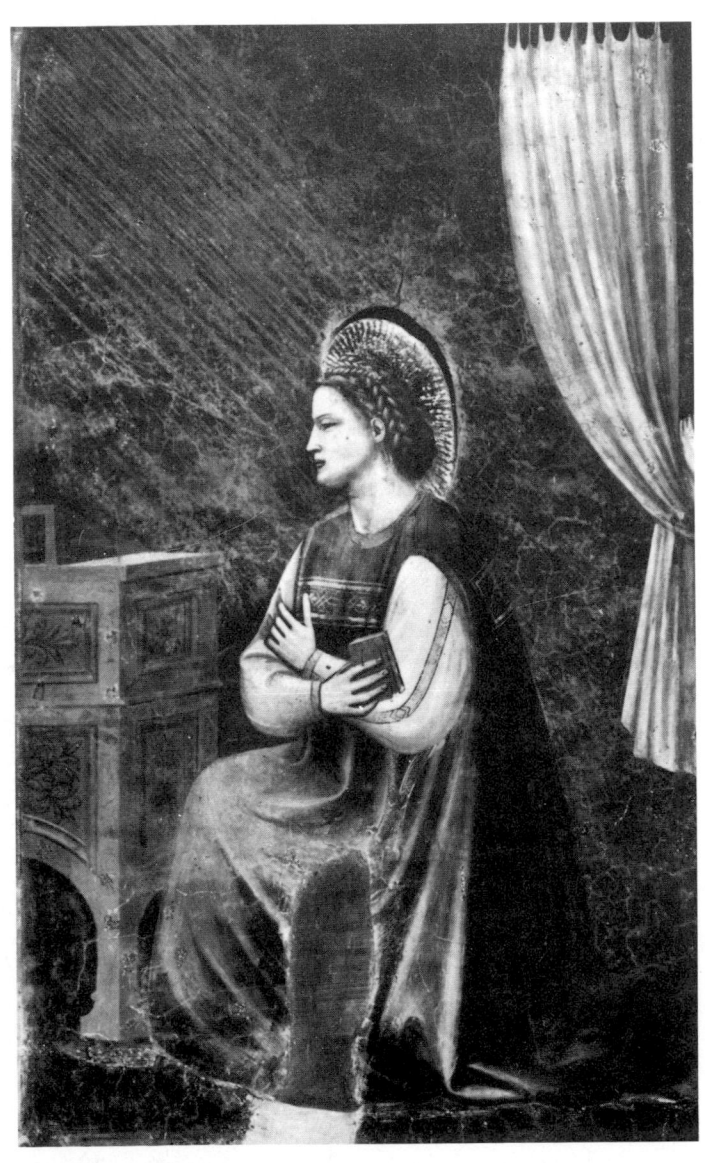

Giotto was the first to demonstrate the possibilities of painting, by showing that, because it disposed of greater powers of imaginative invention than sculpture, it was far better suited to the task of embracing the whole of mankind and the universe. From then on, painting was to become an inexhaustible source of fresh imagery. Giotto laid down the original principles of this form of art, and the subsequent history of painting lies essentially in the extent to which it conformed to or transgressed these principles. From a given surface, Giotto deduced the spatial definition which would provide the field of action. He did not seek space for its own sake, as the Renaissance painters were later to do, but was content that it should be a scenic space, adequate to contain the unfolding of the drama. The first to experiment with perspective, he assigned it several vanishing-points, not so much through archaism, as through instinct, to prevent the eye from being swallowed up by a depth which, as in Quattrocento painting, would attract it at the expense of the essential factor: the action. Giotto was

◀ 20 Giotto. *Virgin Annunciate*. Padua, Arena Chapel.

21 Giotto. *Simeon*. Padua, Arena Chapel.

Giotto drew from his knowledge of antiquity the inspiration which allowed him to restore, in all its authority, the human presence excluded from painting for centuries.

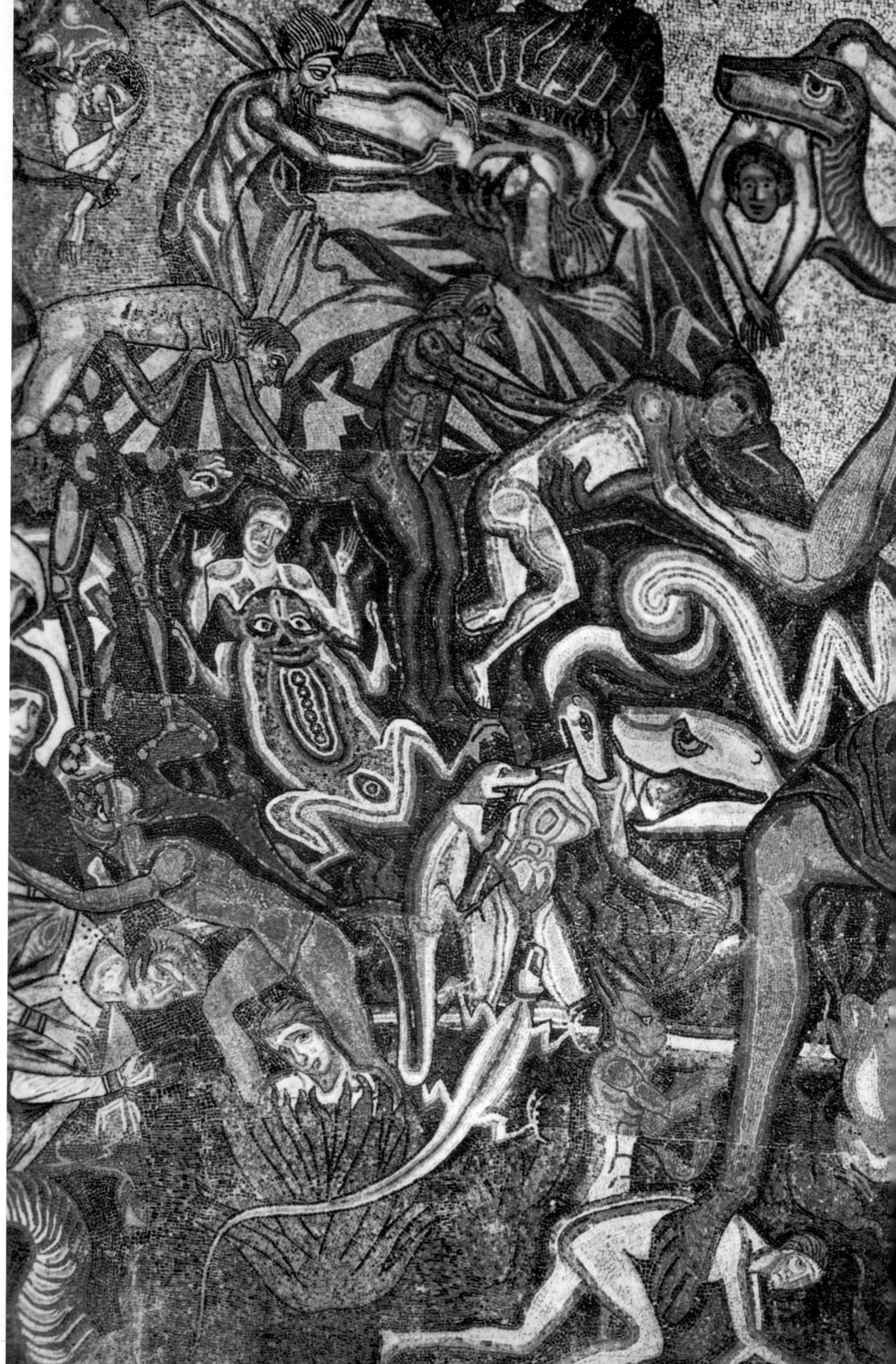

22 *The Last Judgment*. Mosaic in the cupola of the Baptistery, Florence.

The anonymous contemporary of Giotto who composed the cartoons for the mosaic cycle in the Baptistery was inspired by an expressionist violence which heralds Hieronymus Bosch.

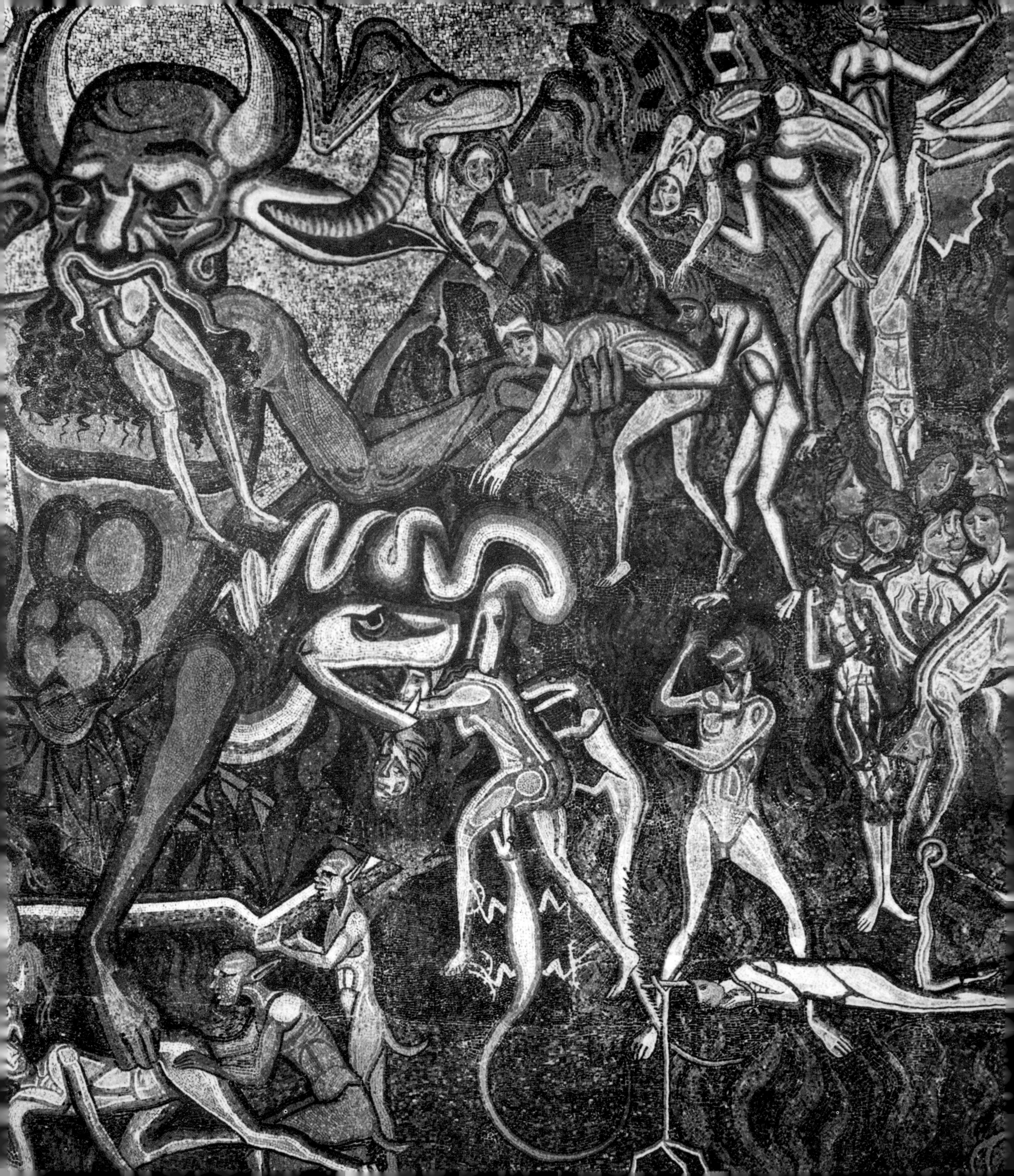

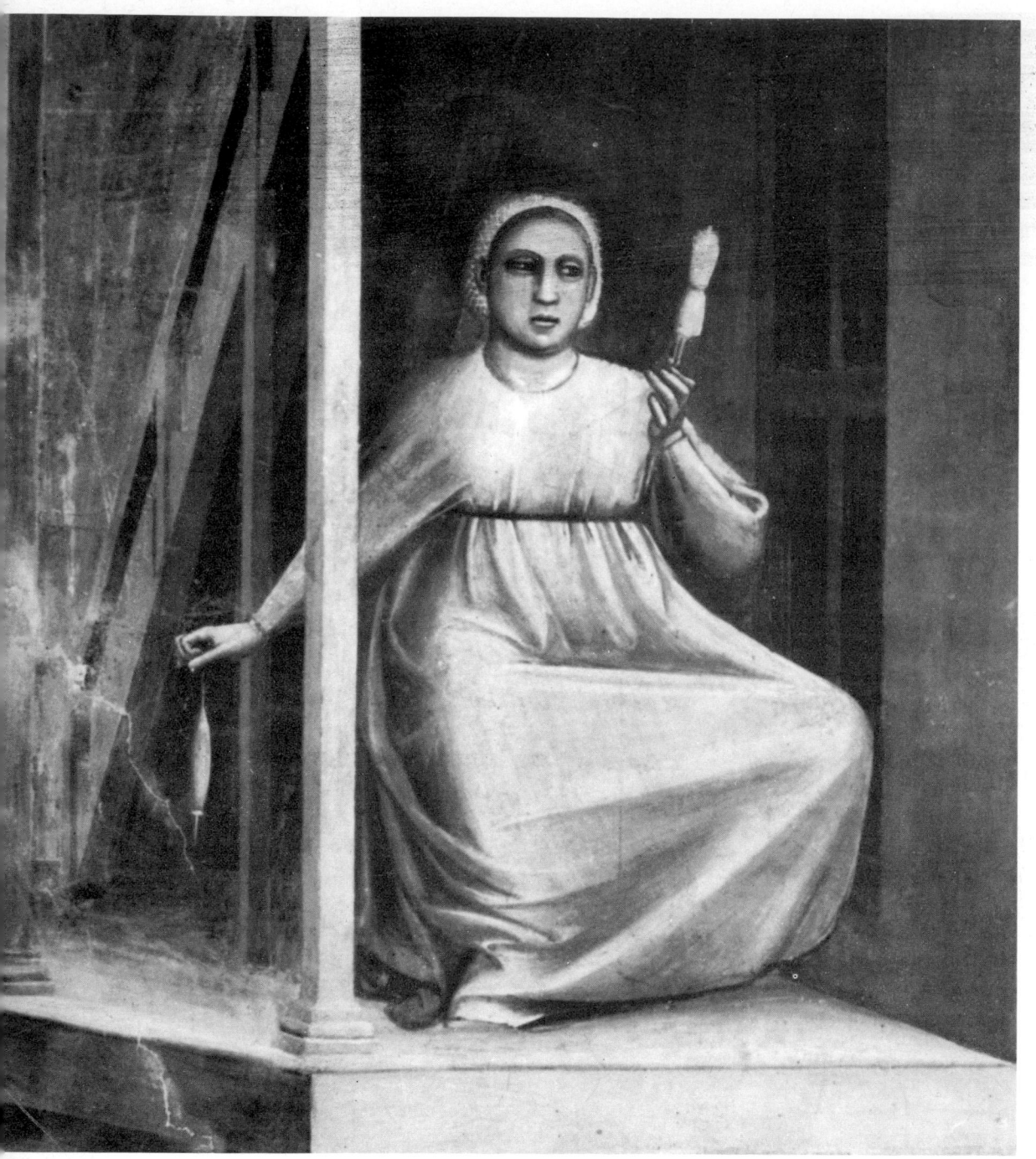

23 Giotto. Servant-girl, detail of *The Apparition of the Angel to St Anne*. Padua, Arena Chapel.

antagonistic forces create the rhythm which merges them in one destiny, making them interdependent in the unity of action. For the first time since antiquity, the human being is re-created in terms of his physical existence; the body rediscovers its volume and opacity in three-dimensional space. The human being becomes an independent reality, an active force spreading within the drama.

However, Giotto's figures never act simply for the sake of acting; their bodies, held back in a defensive attitude, lend themselves only to the minimum motion required by the drama. Yet a tremendous variety of gestures and attitudes entered into painting with the advent of Giotto: his mind fashioned the lively characteristics he observed into an abbreviated form which translated each gesture into the essential gesture, rich in all the potentialities of the action it implied. This virtue of concision, that had once typified Greek monumental sculpture, was, after Giotto, attained by only a few great classicists with the gift of discerning the essential in the multiplicity of appearances.

In the antique manner, Giotto used draping to convey action. Drapery, which for centuries had remained folded flat against the wall surfaces of cupolas or altars, suddenly regained the suppleness of life when brought out into the open. As Giotto's skill developed, so his draperies became wedded more intimately to the bodies they clothed, gaining in expressive effectiveness. At Florence, in the Peruzzi and Bardi Chapels, the drapery attains a musical cadence: the truth of a gesture is limited by its elegance, but Giotto, in the full splendour of his genius, is able to seek for a beauty which lies beyond drama.

In this swift journey through the realm of painting we may safely ignore the whole Florentine school of the Trecento, with the exception of Giotto. There was one painter, however, contemporary with Giotto and living in Florence, who provided plenty of material for the Florentine chroniclers with his reputation as a lazy, facetious dauber. This was Bonamico di Martino, called Buffalmacco, who played practical jokes on monks, nuns and even bishops; Boccaccio and Sacchetti both took pleasure in accumulating a fund of salacious stories concerning his escapades. What we are told of his revolutionary approach to painting is most intriguing: the indolent Buffalmacco improvised directly on to the wall, wielding his brush boldly in search of form. This nonchalant approach must have scandalized his fellow painters at a time when Giotto was expending so much thought and care in producing works in which the contours of the design were incised with a sharp needle or sometimes even

an innovator in that it was from nature that he borrowed the elements of the framework within which human life was to unfold. But although he thoroughly refurbished the repertoire of signs used by painters hitherto, he continued to observe the conventional hierarchy of forms by which a man was bigger than his home and as tall as the mountain he was climbing; in other words, he distinguished the secondary from the principal according to a moral order rather than a natural order.

The interplay of the active figures produces the picture's grouping, and thus its composition; the

Everyday gestures, excluded from art for centuries, were reintroduced into painting by Giotto.

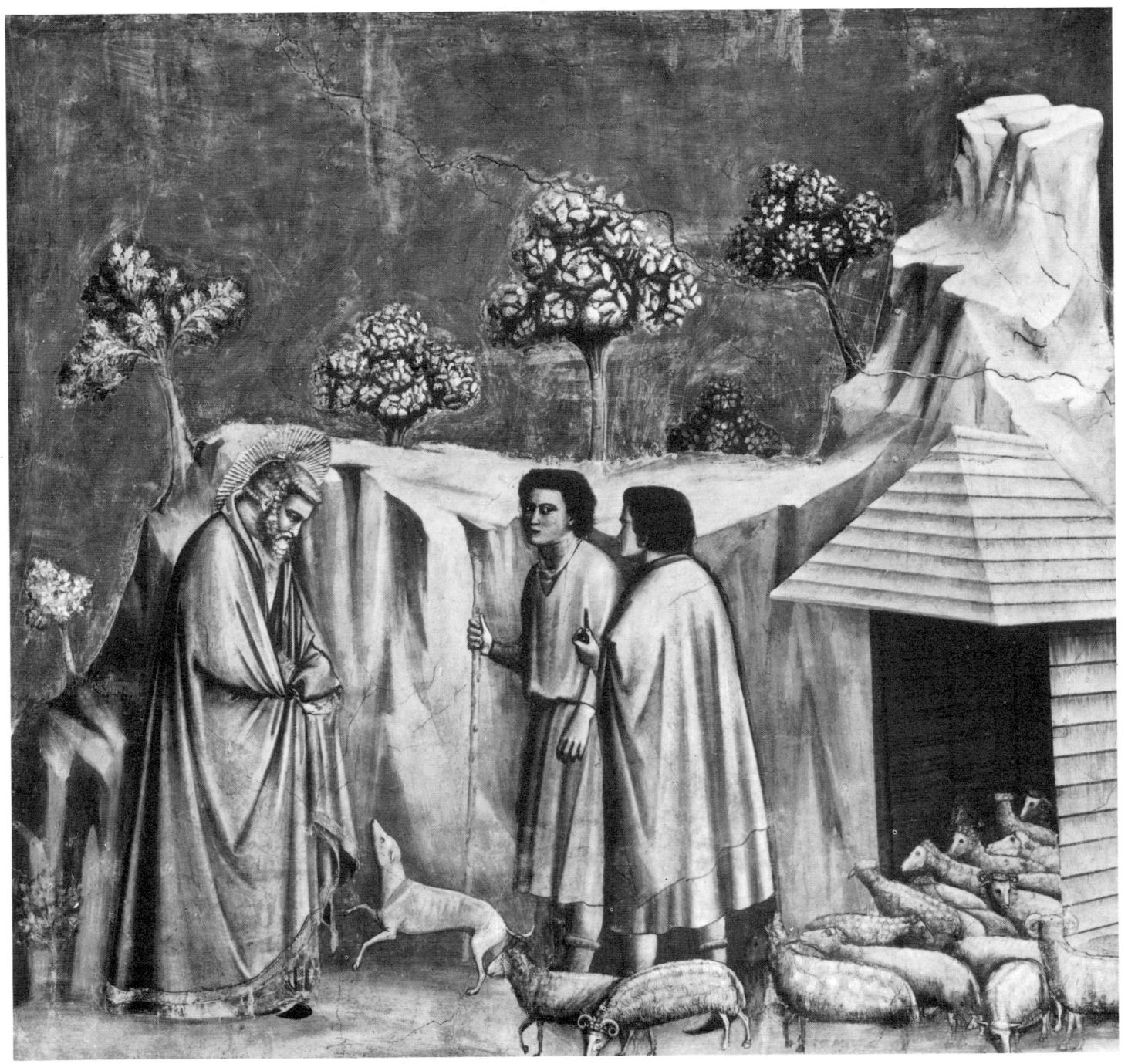

24 Giotto. *St Joachim welcomed by the shepherds*. Padua, Arena Chapel.

intaglio-engraved, following the strict principles of *buon fresco* which had transformed wall painting into an art as studied as that of architecture. The 'dauber' Buffalmacco anticipated modern painting by centuries. The fragmentary remains of his frescoes at the Badia a Settimo Church in Florence do not, unfortunately, allow us to come to any decision regarding the truth of the old legends about this painter.

Andrea Orcagna, architect, sculptor and painter, crystallized the Giottesque principles, around the middle of the century, in his Florentine workshop, and made them the basis of a prosperous enterprise. His brother Nardo di Cione was more open to innovation than he was: the saints depicted by Nardo in his *Paradise* in Santa Maria Novella show that, unlike Giotto, he was responsive to feminine grace. In his frescoes of the *Passion* in the Badia he emphasizes the pathos of the drama: the Christ of *The Meeting of Christ and the Virgin* (*pl. 26*) casts a long, sad glance over the holy women held back by a ruffianly soldier's brutal gesture; this Jesus is perhaps more human than Giotto's, but for that very reason less Christological. As for the soldier

The dog recognizing his master, and the sheep with their individual movements, like the attitude of the mule in the *St Francis giving his cloak to a poor man* (*pl. 18*), represent the humble life of domestic animals, brought back into art by Giotto in the shadow of man's own life.

33

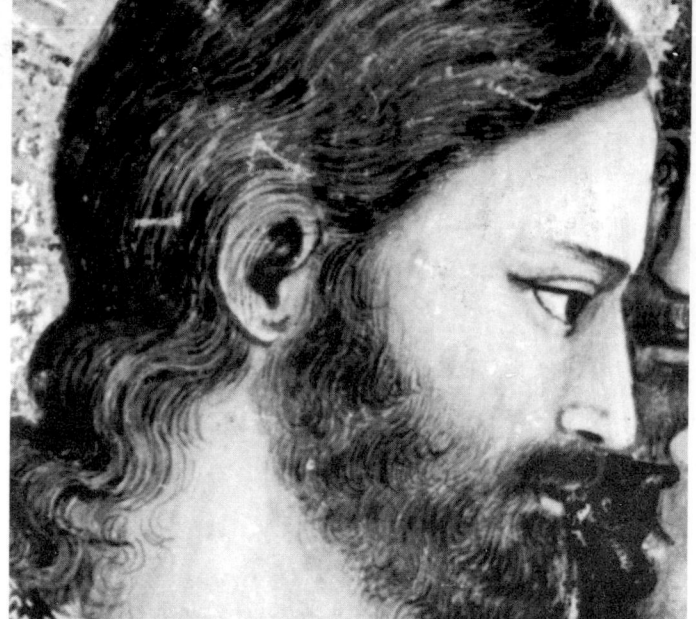

25 Giotto. Head of Christ, detail of *The Arrest of Christ in the Garden of Olives (pl. 28)*. Padua, Arena Chapel.

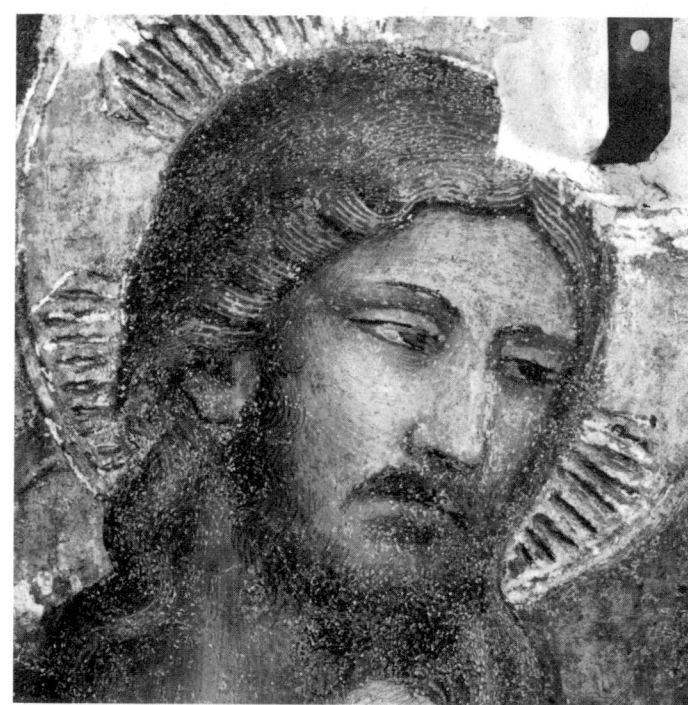

26 Nardo di Cione (active *c.* 1343–65). Head of Christ, detail of *The Meeting of Christ and the Virgin*. Fresco. Florence, Badia Church.

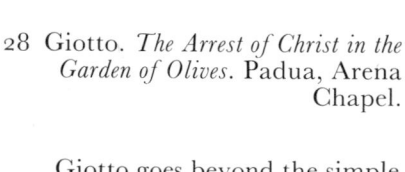

27 Nardo di Cione. Head of a soldier, detail of *The Meeting of Christ and the Virgin*. Fresco. Florence, Badia Church.

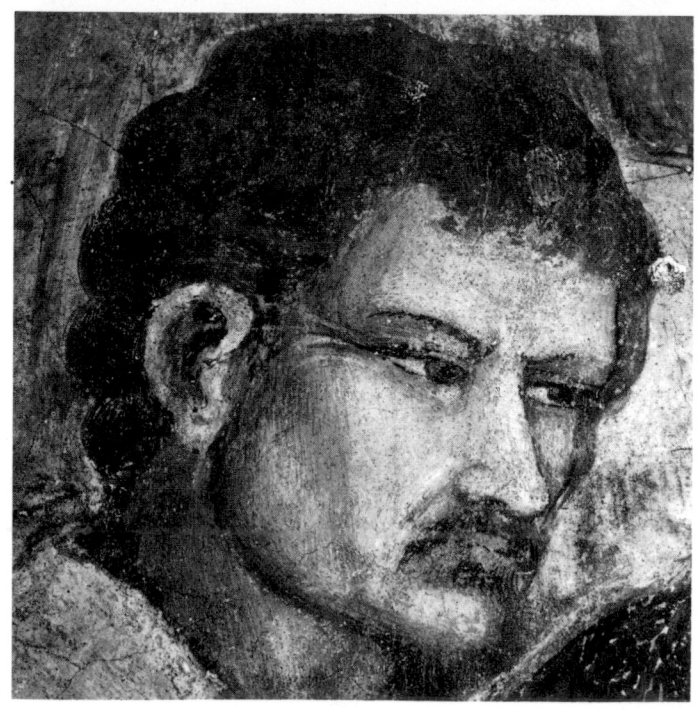

28 Giotto. *The Arrest of Christ in the Garden of Olives*. Padua, Arena Chapel.

Giotto goes beyond the simple illustration of his subject in *The Arrest of Christ* and paints the confrontation between Good and Evil. Nardo's interpretation of the Passion casts light on that of Giotto, being more realistic and lacking the same theological significance; Nardo's Judas is less of a caricature and closer to life, while the mournful look of his Christ is that of a suffering man rather than the divine judge.

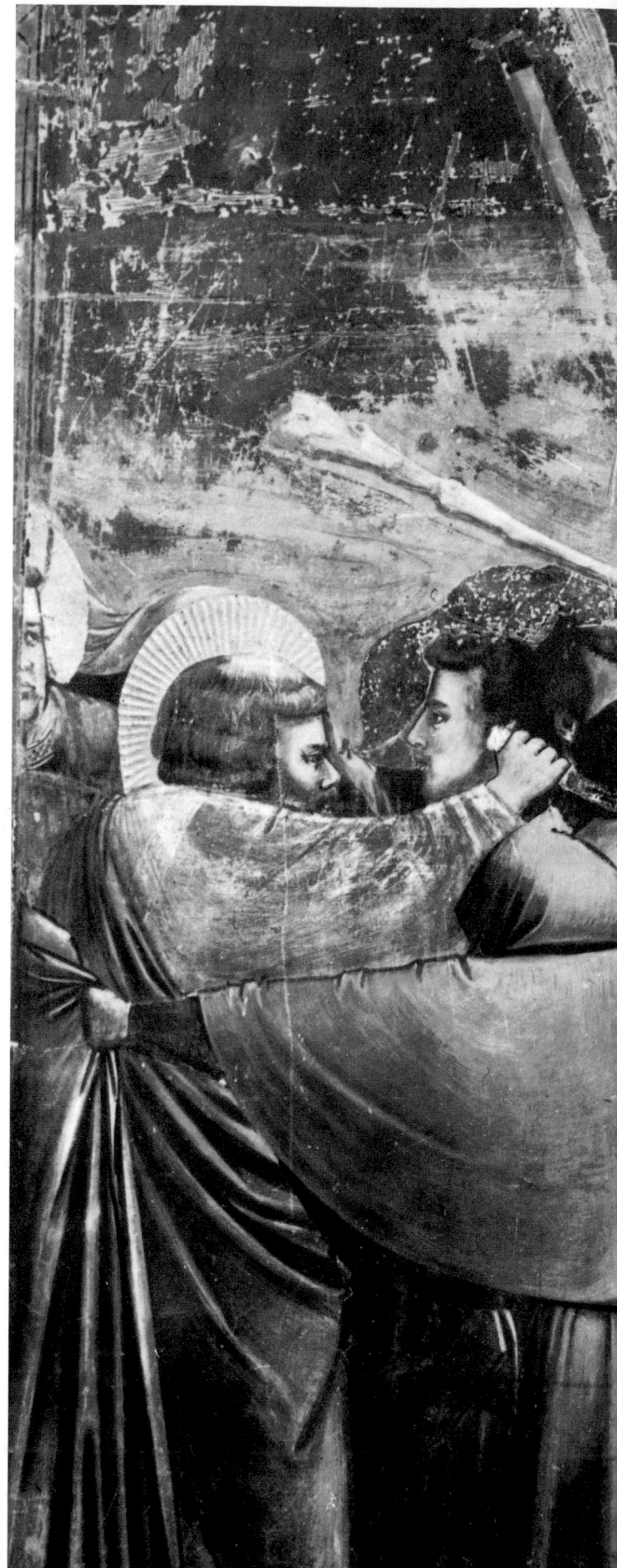

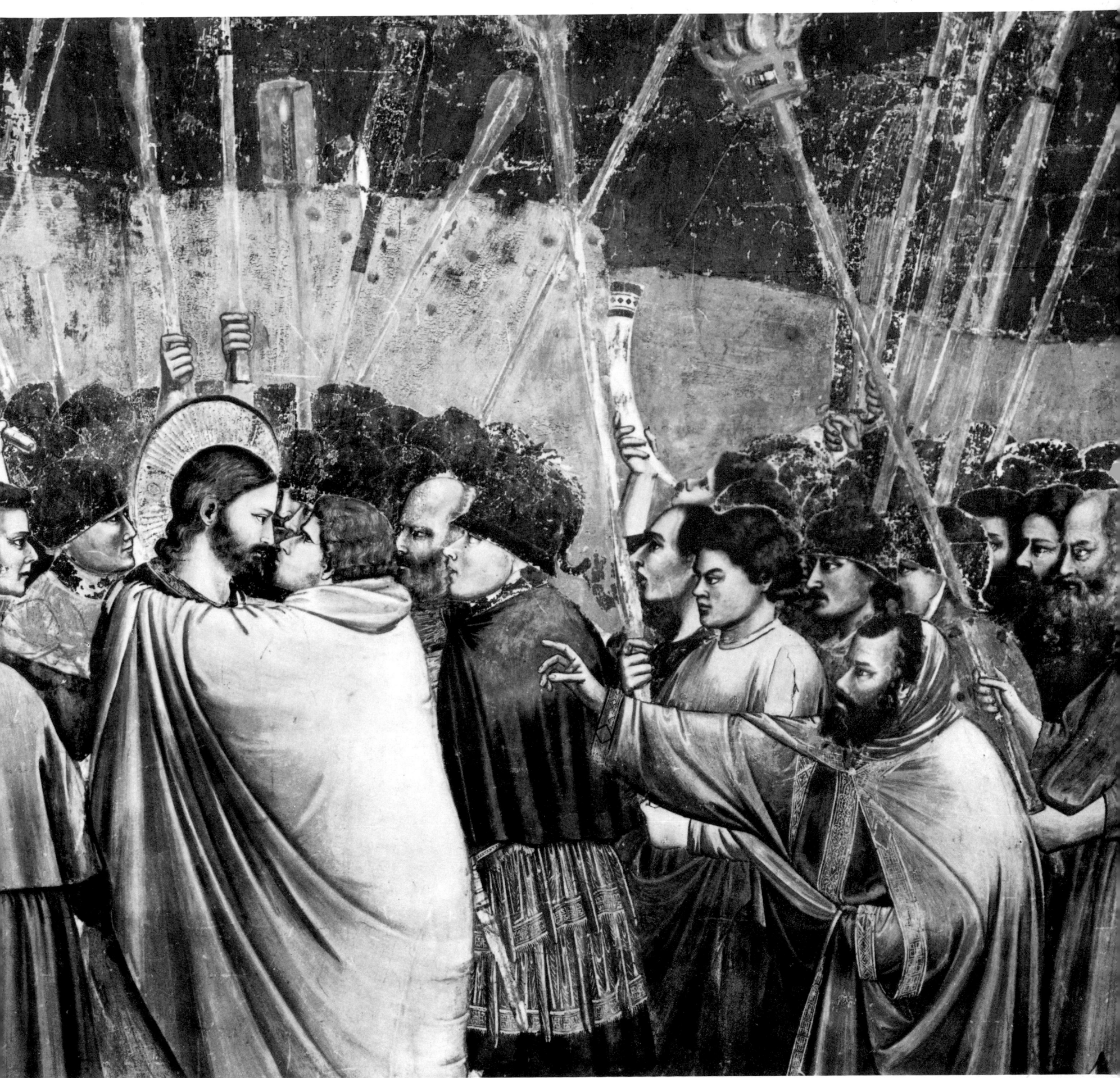

29 Giotto. Detail of the *Adoration of the shepherds*. Padua, Arena Chapel.

30 Barna da Siena (active *c.* 1350). *Adoration of the shepherds*. San Gimignano, Collegiata.

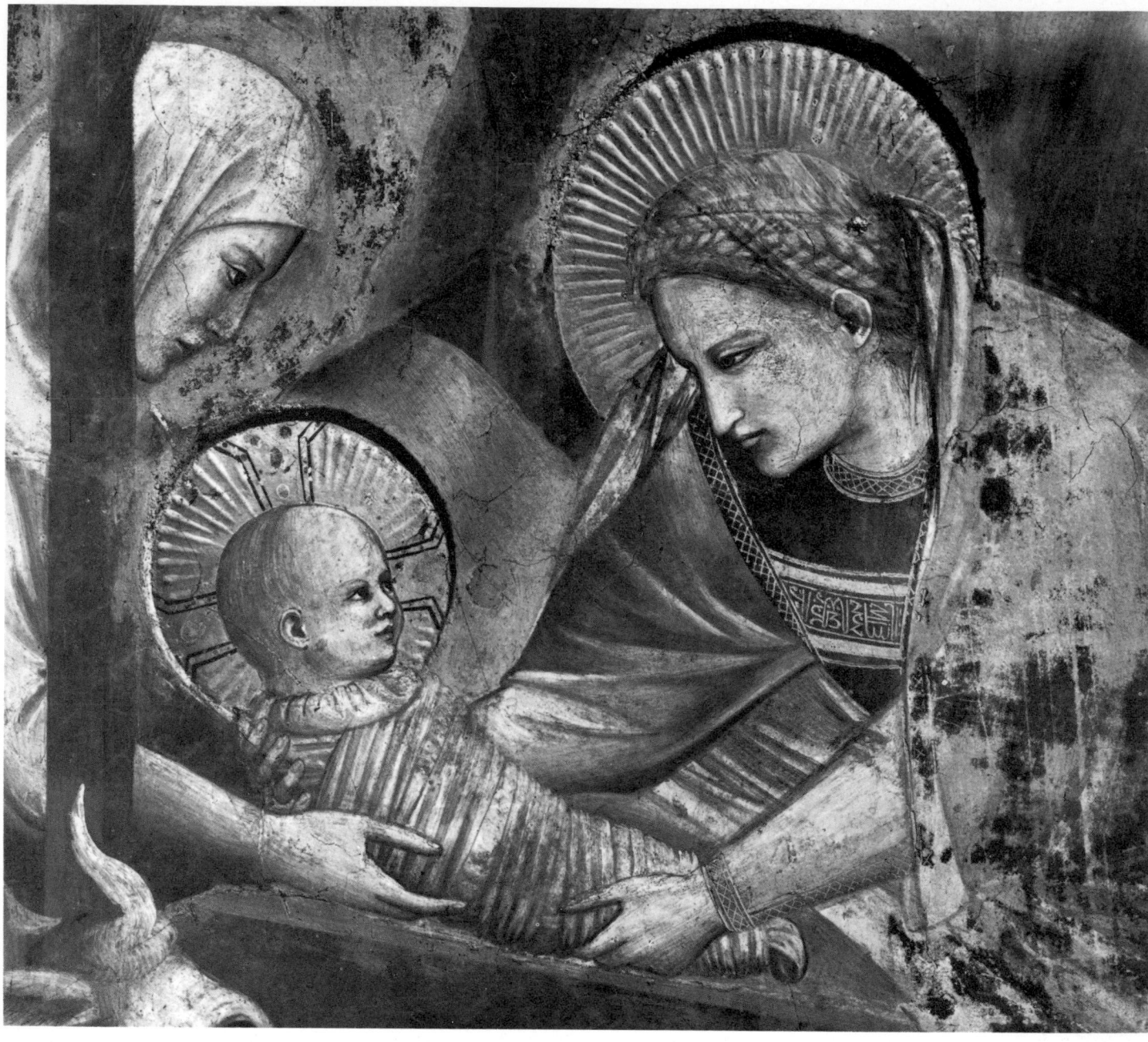

In Giotto's painting, the gesture with which Mary offers her Son to the shepherds represents a considered action. The Sienese Barna introduces a more instinctive emotion into his interpretation of the event: the Virgin literally tears the Child from her breast to offer him to the men who will one day become his executioners.

brandishing a scimitar (*pl. 27*), his gallows-bird look is more lifelike than anything else to be found in painting before Caravaggio; here is an individual face, taken from life and transposed, unembellished, in all its singular truth. This realism denotes an impulsive temperament entirely alien to that of Giotto, for whom there was no truth outside general truth.

Siena, too, was a law unto itself, a city caught up by some strange complex that forced it to live in a kind of spiritual isolation, depriving it of the stimulus that foreigners and even enemies bring with them. For Siena the enemy was Florence, and, although the Sienese hurled the Florentines back at Monta-perti in 1260, they never relaxed their guard. Siena remained a town under siege, and it was destined to see its grandeur culminate some three centuries

later in one of the most celebrated sieges in history, when a French captain, Blaise de Montluc, galvanized its expiring forces to a point of absurd heroism. The inhabitants of this fiery city were easily drawn to excesses, and while the sons of a few families achieved dubious fame by squandering their inheritance on feasting and carousing, others were scorched by the flame of mysticism. Poetry offered its resources to these young men who, in one way or another, had turned their backs on reality, and it became the only form of escape open to the beleaguered, inspiring them to celebrate the world of Heaven, lending its supple rhymes to pride and humility alike.

This strange town gave birth to a school of painting which remains a paradox in terms of Western artistic development. As against the

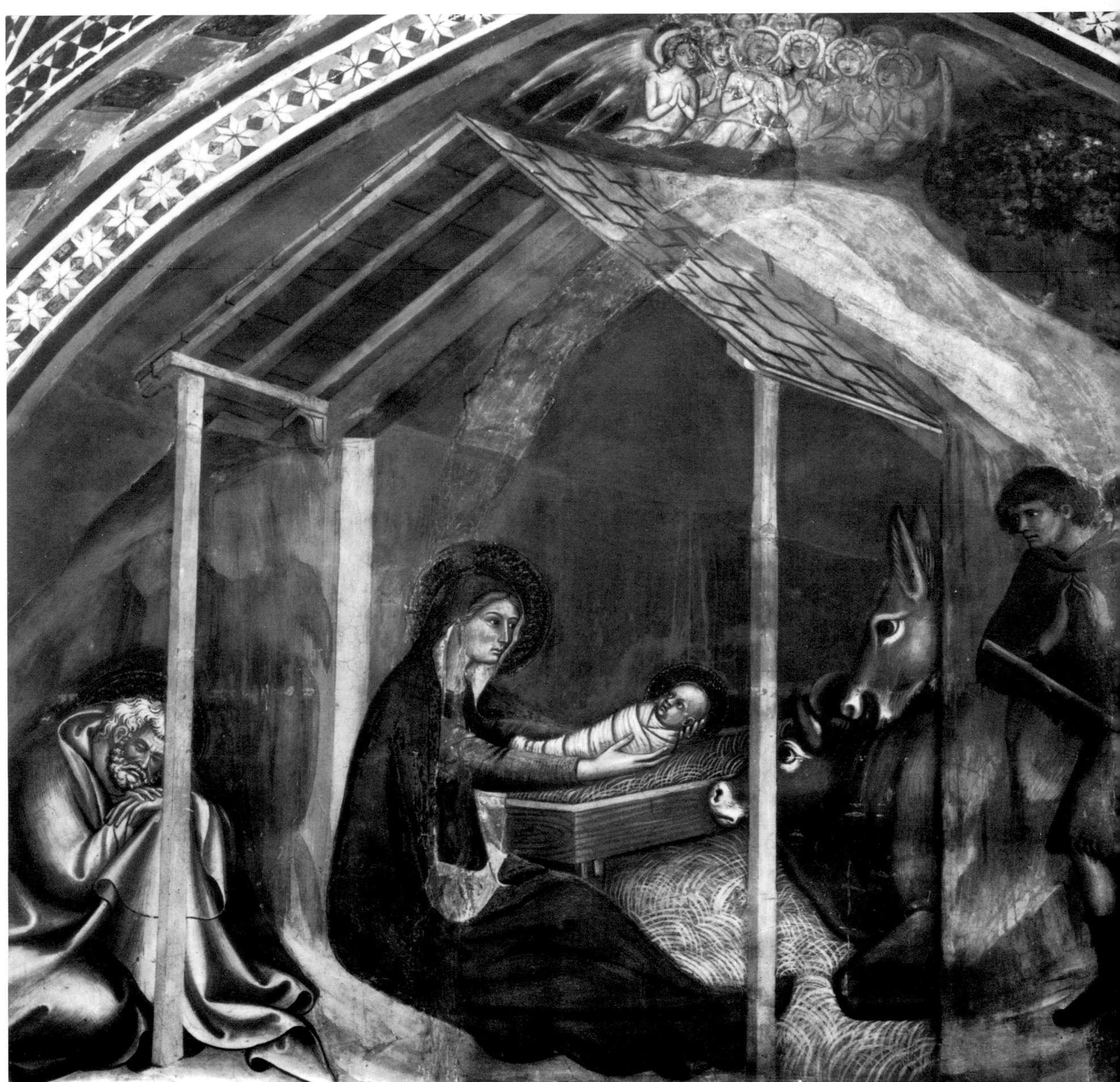

essentially progressive aesthetic to which Florence, its rival, brought the impetus of its faith in the future, Siena pursued a policy of ultra-conservatism worthy of Chinese civilization. Indeed, the work of the early Sienese masters presents many analogies with the art of China, a fact noted by Berenson some sixty years ago when, discovering Sassetta and thus adding a last essential figure to the panorama of great masters of the Quattrocentro, he opened a new chapter in art criticism. The curve of Sienese painting, which eventually reaches full circle, embraces two centuries, starting from Duccio and Simone and ending at Sassetta and Naroccio. During these two hundred years, these artists exploited the self-same style whose essence Duccio had originally rescued alive from a dying artistic civilization, the Byzantine civilization, perceiving instinctively in that essence the distant effluvia of Alexandrine art. From this desiccated plant, the Sienese coaxed forth parasitic shoots that blossomed on the very fringe of life.

The privileged field of action of Florentine painting was the fresco. Duccio took a first timid step towards releasing the easel painting from the hidden world of the miniature and the mysteries of the icon; on the limited surface thus revealed, the painting became narrative and analytical, dedicated to tenderness, suffering and death. Throughout the fourteenth century, the Sienese lament continued unabated, and Sienese painting delivered a message of anguish which can be read in all the glances, in all the unsmiling faces burning with fever, in these convulsive gestures ruled by despair rather than action. Suffering appears here in the form of disconsolate grief rather than the physical struggle with adversity that, in Giotto's art, makes a hero out of the most miserable man. Anxious mothers hug their children to their breasts, as though trying to hide them from a threatening world. Barna da Siena's Virgin (*pl. 30*) tears the Child from her heart in a despairing gesture as she holds him up for the adoration of men who will soon become his murderers; with this painter, Christ is no longer a redeemer but a man overwhelmed by his destiny, a wind of panic blows through the Gospel, and the Passion degenerates into an apocalypse. The most expressive symbol of this tormented city is the Virgin of Simone Martini's *Annunciation*, twisting her whole body round as she shrinks at the approach of the life which is rushing into her. Gothic art brought these painters a style that lent itself to their spiritual malaise, rather than an injection of vigour.

The influence of Florence might have saved them from themselves, for Ambrogio Lorenzetti, strongly influenced by Giotto, moulded his figures and objects in realistic outline. A brief pause in the struggle between the different Sienese class groups allowed Ambrogio to conceive the hedonistic dream of his allegory of *Good Government* (*pl. 31*) in which peasants garner their corn, young girls dance in the streets and Giottesque individuals with relaxed features are wrapped up in their affairs. In this great panorama, Ambrogio depicts rosy cheeks, well-nourished bodies, eyes heavy with desire; his wondering gaze is filled with the beauty of towns and the charms of country scenes. For the first time in Western painting, nature is represented for its own sake, and the man who lives in it must be content with the modest status to which he is entitled when measured against the scale of the universe: along the walls of the Palazzo Pubblico in Siena, these ants swarming over the earth's crust already evoke Bruegel's manikins toiling away at their humble daily tasks. Ambrogio, who was interested in geography and cartography, seems to have heard some indefinable cosmic summons, a summons that the happy chance of a civic commission allowed him to heed momentarily, but that others were doomed never to hear. In Siena, all was tragedy, and the pleasure-loving Ambrogio was carried off, as was his remarkably dissimilar brother Pietro, by the Black Death in 1348. One might almost say that great Sienese painting died of the plague.

The situation in the provinces occasionally allowed a greater freedom and favoured individual inspiration. In Rimini, Giotto's influence was merely frozen into a grimace by Baronzio's Byzantinism; but, in Bologna, Vitale absorbed the same influence while modifying its austerity and embellishing it with the fresh colours of life. Bologna, being a university city, within easy distance of Florence, linked by the great Emilian plain with northern Italy and, beyond that, with the Gothic world, was open to influences of all kinds. From Gothic art, Bologna was able to derive a sense of freedom to supplement the influence of Giotto, an achievement that was beyond the Sienese, whose closed minds drew from Gothic only the constraint of a new style to add to the archaism of Byzantine style. Vitale's manner, a distant echo of the refinement of the French miniaturists, is that of an elegant and profane art, using a rich, creamy relief and joyous colouring that anticipates the researches of the Lombard school. His *Madonna dei denti*, with her eyelids veiling a languorous gaze and her suggestion of a sensual smile, allows a hint of the equivocal charms of the eternal feminine to pierce through the formally correct iconographic theme.

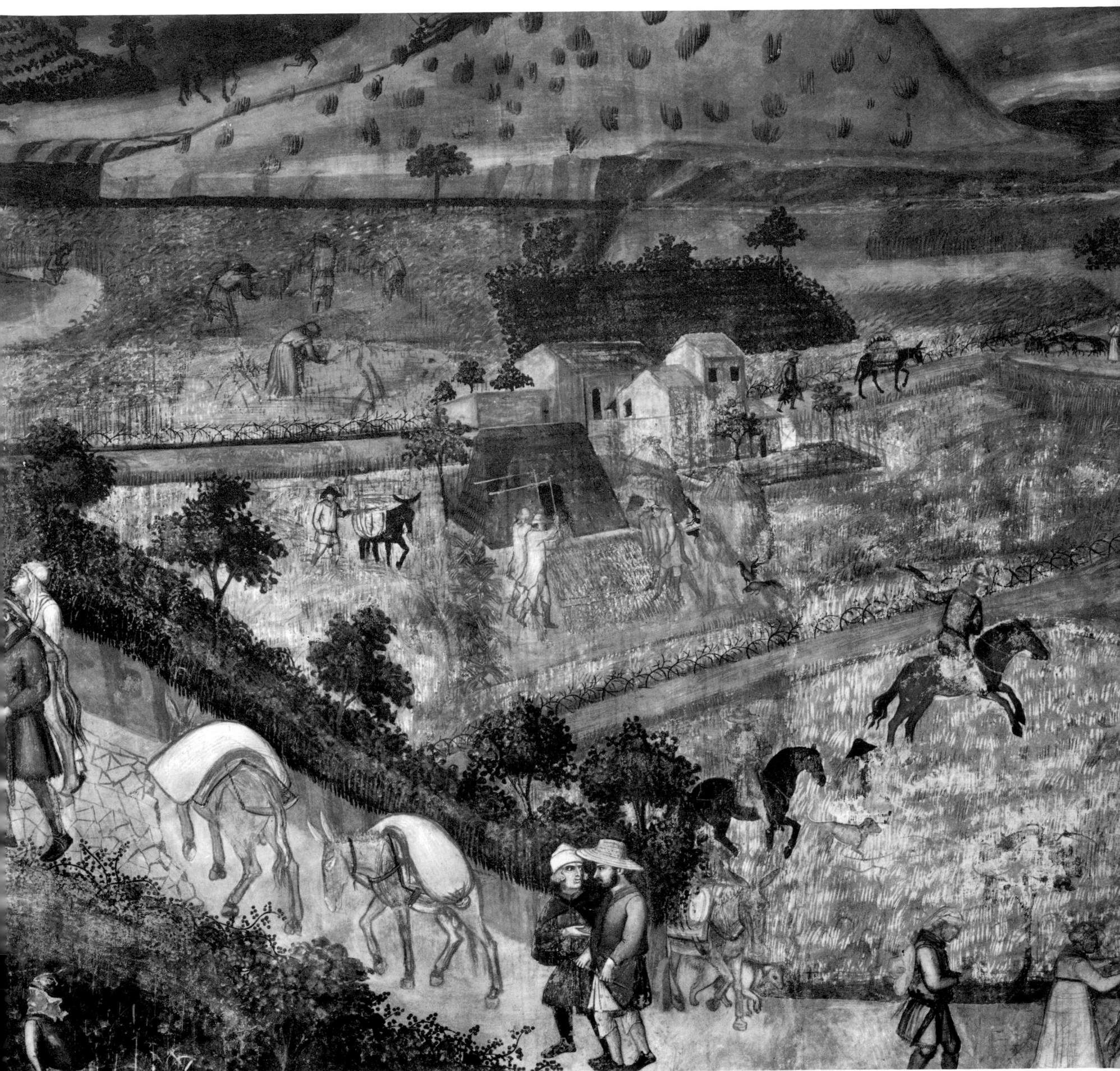

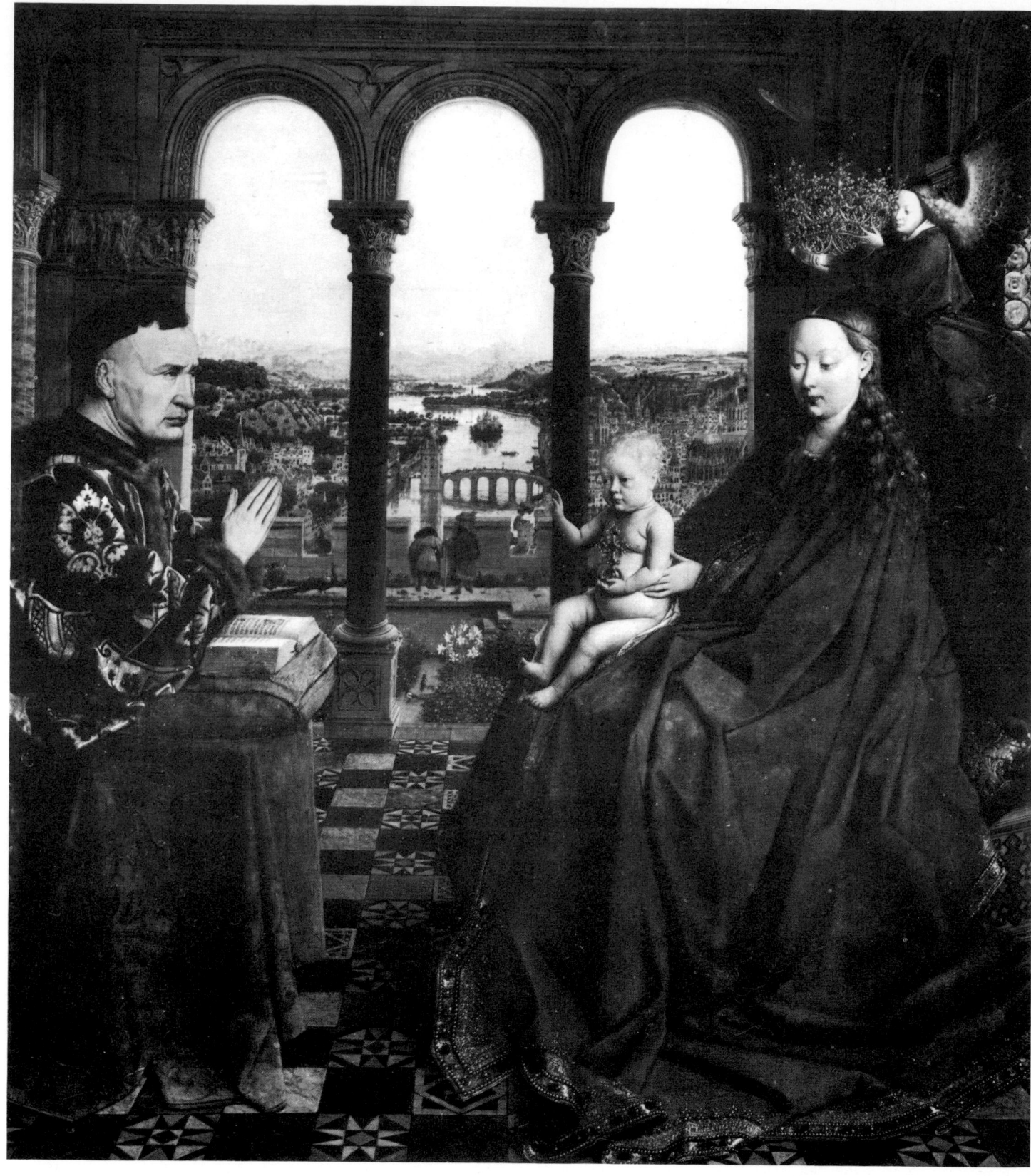

32 Jan van Eyck (*c.* 1390–1441).
The Madonna of Autun. Paris, Louvre.

3 Mirror of truth

In 1458, the townsfolk of Ghent made preparations to receive in great pomp Philip the Good, Duke of Burgundy, who was due to pay his first visit in ten years. The town's various guilds and confraternities, and especially the chambers of rhetoric, vied with each other in organizing splendid festivities and spectacles. The prince's entry was greeted by a series of *tableaux vivants* which drew upon the most glorious episodes of the history of the world. The most grandiose of these *tableaux* celebrated the mystery of the Redemption: on a three-tiered platform fifty feet long and twenty-eight feet deep, living figures re-created all the scenes depicted in the *Adoration of the Lamb* altarpiece that had been begun by Hubert van Eyck and finished by his brother Jan in 1432 for the church of St Bavon at Ghent. Thus the theatre imitated art, and life asked painting to lend it its colours. It is true that painting had never made, and would never again make, so great an effort to combine with nature, to merge into it so completely as to leave no further ambition than to be as pure an image of it as that reflected by the mirror.

The van Eyck brothers were undoubtedly the greatest innovators in the whole history of painting, conceiving a new aesthetic and then discovering, to express it, means so perfect as to remain for ever out of the grasp of succeeding generations. This secret that the van Eycks took to the grave with them was that of a stupendous technique based on a perfected process of oil-painting. This permitted the superimposition of infinitely thin, translucent layers of pigment, and thus transformed the plain, dull surface presented hitherto by the picture's glazing into a fluid of unfathomable depth capable of suggesting any inert or living matter – velvet, silk, stone, marble, jewellery, flesh, and, above all, that evanescent element, the atmosphere.

Oil-paint had existed before the van Eycks, but had been difficult to use because of the time it took to dry, a problem they partially resolved by using a siccative and also, no doubt, by improving the paint's binding quality. Jan invented a procedure which was to provide the basis for all the subsequent explorations that painting has undertaken; what he could not hand on was his genius, based as it

undoubtedly was upon an exceptional visual acuity which allowed him to distinguish the peculiar nature of things and to discern the best means of conveying their image. No amount of scientific investigation has succeeded in analysing his technique: the researches undertaken at the central laboratory of the Belgian museums, when the Ghent Altarpiece was restored there in 1950, have confirmed only that the painting was executed 'in depth', by superimposed coats, some of them in oil-based medium, others in tempera which may have been applied as scumbling, an astonishing possibility.

Means always reflect the ends that inspire them. If the van Eycks perfected a new technique which was to permit the most perfect mimesis that ever reigned in painting, it was because nature had begun to exercise a profound appeal upon the soul of Western man.

Giotto's ordered world still belonged to the universe of the cathedral, that universe in which everything was regulated by a single thought of God's. His work was deeply imbued with 'Christocentrism', that concept, defended so ardently during the thirteenth century by St Bonaventure and Robert Grosseteste, which made of the total Christ, *Christus integer*, the principle of a vision of the world through the eyes of faith. As we have seen, Giottesque humanism was a divine humanism centred entirely upon the person of Christ, and the cycle of St Francis at Assisi was itself a Christological cycle, for Francis had adopted the Pauline doctrine: 'I determined not to know anything among you, save Jesus Christ, and him crucified.' Jesus crucified was indeed the only knowledge admitted by this saint, who was so hostile to books and theologians. Giotto reflected the mainstream of thirteenth-century thought, that of Albertus Magnus and St Bonaventure, rather than that of St Thomas Aquinas (whose dialectical universe brings to mind, rather, Andrea di Bonaiuto's allegorical paintings in the Spanish Chapel in the cloister of Santa Maria Novella, Florence, works which reflect some of the abstract nature of scholastic thought). With Giotto, however, the notion of an 'external world' is absent; all creatures partake of the Creator and are meaning-

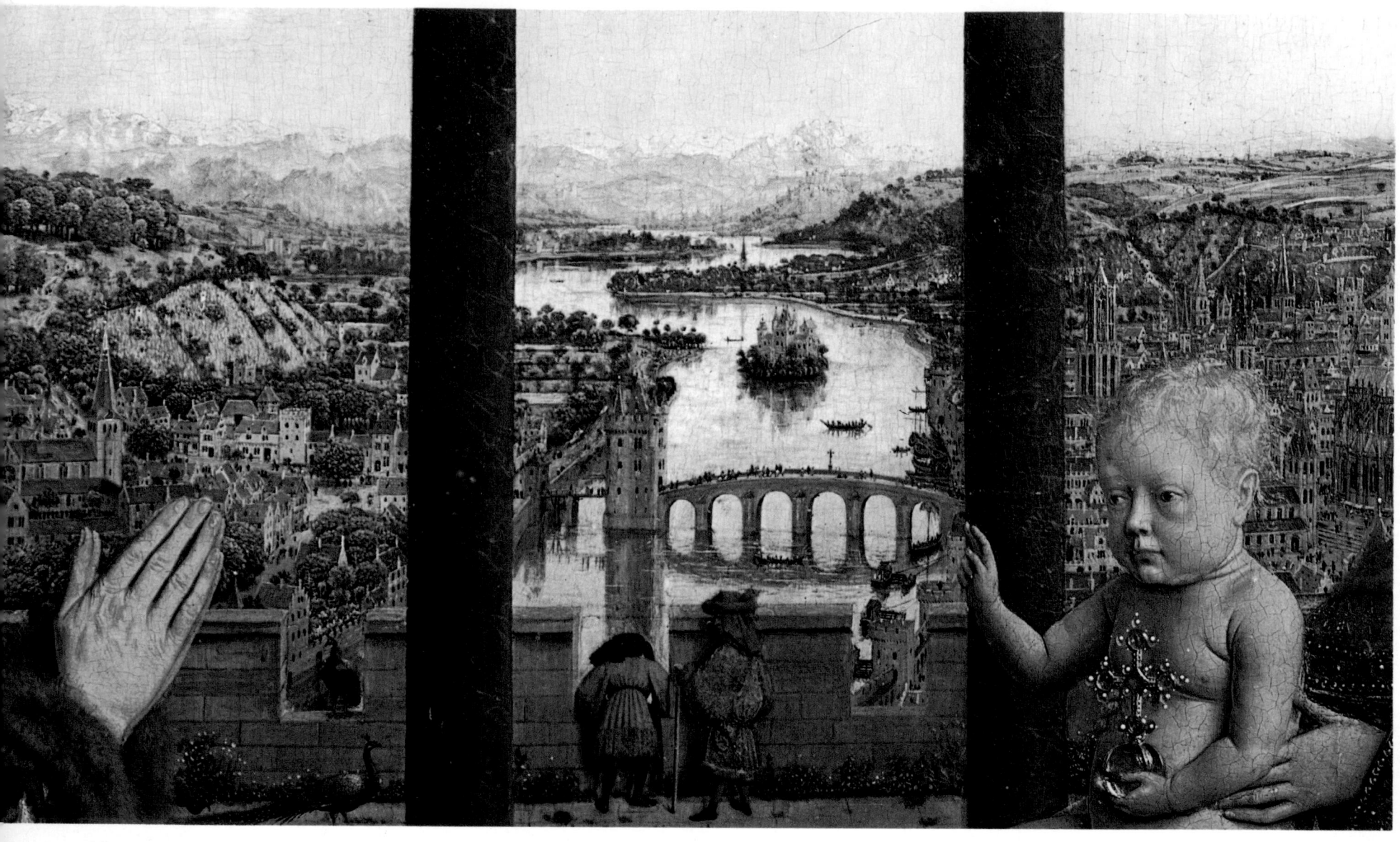

Thanks to an acuteness of visual perception which has remained unique in art, Jan van Eyck was able to concentrate a whole universe within the compass of a few square inches. At a moment when the Middle Ages were giving way to a new era, he dedicated painting to the quest for appearances.

ful only in relation to him, appearances are simply signs by which God reveals himself, the real world does not exist as an object.

A great controversy existed in the Middle Ages relative to the problem of knowledge; this was the question of universals. Those known as 'realists' granted general ideas a real existence independent of the mind and even independent of tangible objects, and considered that the universal existed before the thing, *ante rem*, either in the form of an eternal essence or as a concept of divine intelligence; the 'nominalists' claimed, on the contrary, that concrete reality existed only in individual beings, dismissing 'universals' as mere words. It is perfectly clear that Giotto, confronted with the external world, thought in terms of kinds and species, not of individual things: he painted not a tree but 'tree-as-idea', not a horse but 'horse-as-idea', not Judas but the spirit of evil. His creative imagination constantly retraced the individual thing back to the concept from which it derived; he admitted the

beings and things of nature into his work not for their own sakes but, as with thirteenth-century cathedral porches, in so far as they agreed with the idea to be expressed.

During the course of the fourteenth century, nominalism finally triumphed over realism. The empiricism natural to the English temperament manifested itself in the thought of the theologians of the school of Oxford, notably William of Occam, for whom there were no essences distinct from individuals and to whom the object to be known appeared contingent and singular. Occam proposed that an attitude of probabilism should succeed that of certitude in metaphysics, and suggested that the real should be sought after and 'tested' in nature rather than in philosophical speculation.

This gradual progress of thought, moving in the direction of the knowledge of nature as such, began to affect art during the second half of the fourteenth century. An unknown artist, perhaps Girard of Orleans, painted Western civilization's first por-

35 French school, 14th century. *King John the Good*. Paris, Louvre.

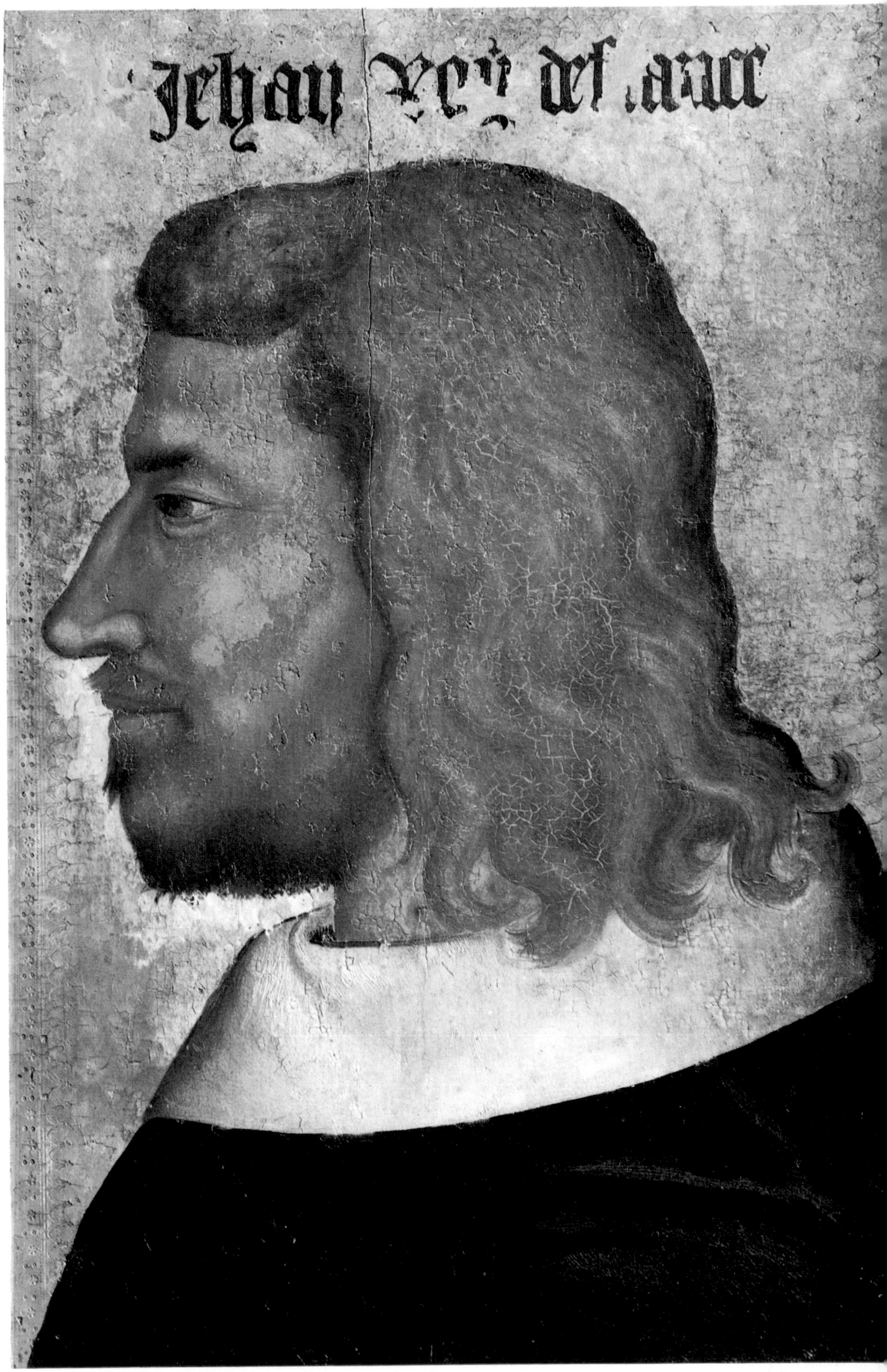

34 Jan van Eyck. *Baudoin de Lannoy*. Berlin-Dahlem, Gemäldegalerie.

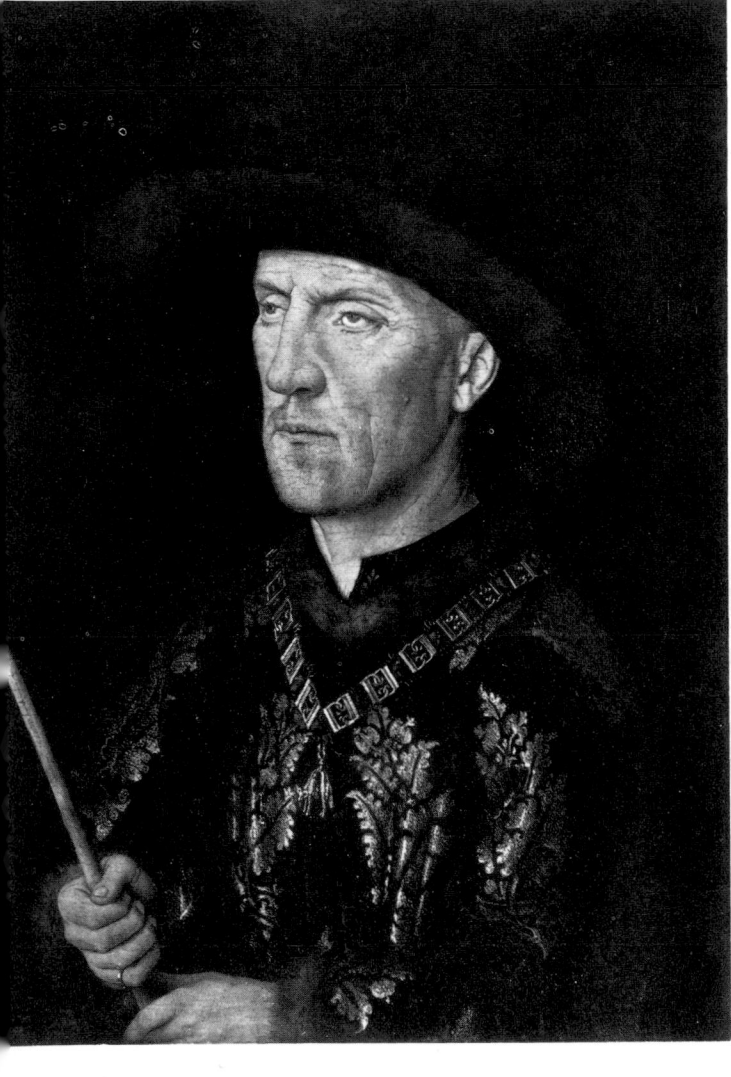

Shortly after 1350, an unknown artist, with the king of France as his model, painted the first realistic portrait in the history of Western civilization. Van Eyck took up this new idiom, and endowed the figures he painted with an intensity of physical presence which no other artist has ever been able to emulate.

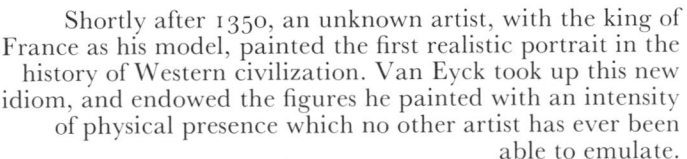

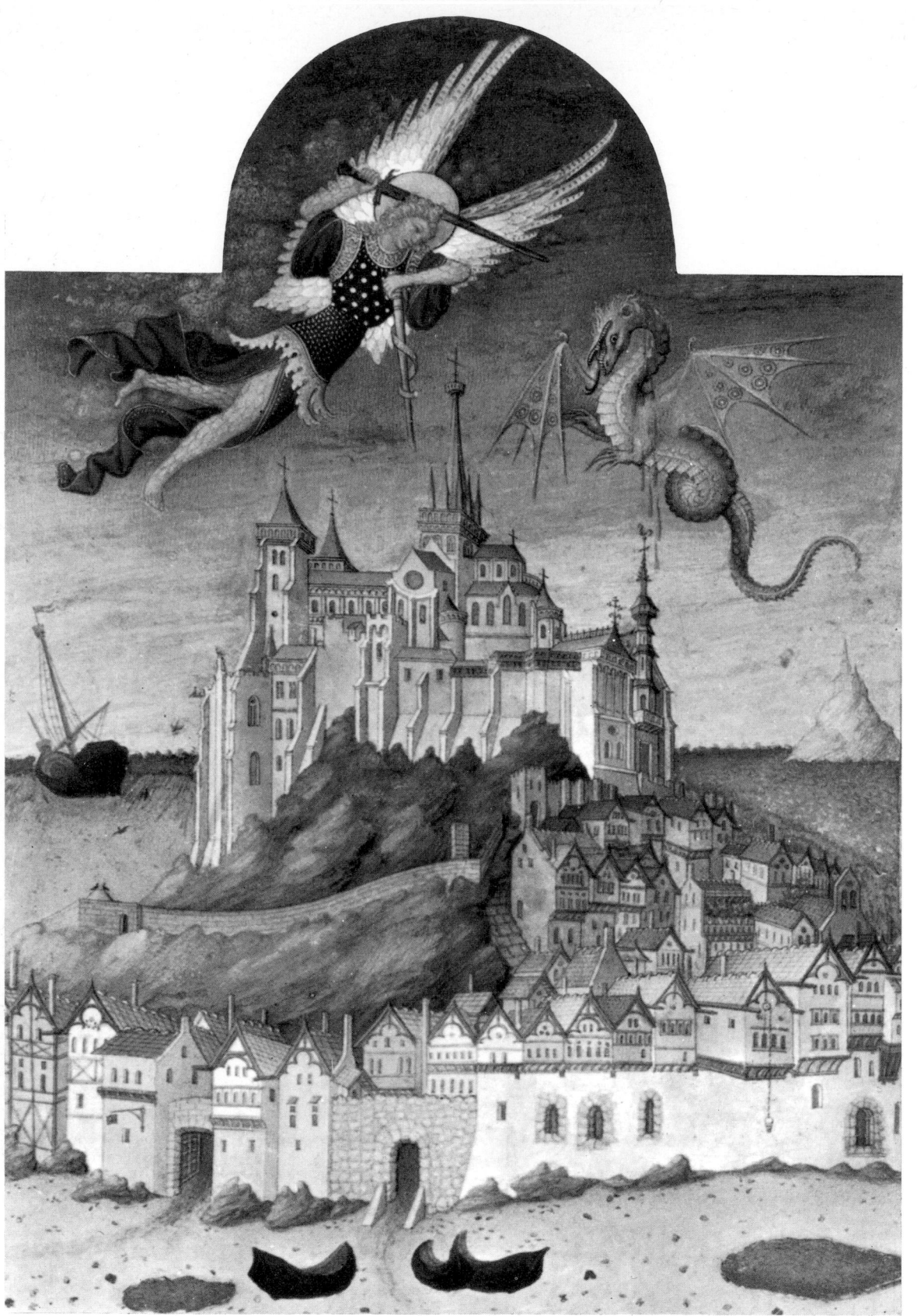

36 Pol, Hennequin and Hermant de Limbourg (active 1400; d. before 1416). View of Mont-Saint-Michel, illustration from *Les Très Riches Heures du duc de Berry*. Chantilly, Musée Condé. The Limbourg brothers were certainly the first to represent a specific building realistically.

37 Jan van Eyck. Detail of *The Marriage of Giovanni Arnolfini and Giovanna Cenami*. London, National Gallery.

Intent on apprehending space in its totality, Jan van Eyck suggests the fourth wall of a room, the one situated behind the artist, by reproducing its image on the wall facing the spectator, in a convex mirror which also reflects the backs of the figures whose portraits are being painted.

trait, that of King John the Good of France (*pl. 35*), reduced to being simply an individual, captured in his temporal reality, without embellishment and stripped of any aura of royalty. This isolated work provides evidence of the new tremor of feeling that was passing through French painting at the time. But the rest of the evidence has disappeared, in particular those visions of forests and wild life which covered the walls of castle halls and recalled to the nobility the world such as it appeared to them: a universe in which they could measure their strength against that of the wild animals. The frescoes in the Garde-Robe of the Palace of the Popes at Avignon are the only surviving examples of this art, but it is uncertain whether they are French or Italian.

Some time prior to 1348, as we have seen, Ambrogio Lorenzetti had decorated the walls of the Palazzo Pubblico at Siena with landscapes peopled by animals and peasants (*pl. 31*). In northern Italy, the vigorous advance of medical science gave rise to the need for illustrated manuals of plants, herbals or *Tacuina sanitatis*, which were executed with varying degrees of skill and all show a new curiosity in the products of nature. Fauna aroused just as much curiosity as flora, and during the fourteenth century all the princes of Europe, and especially those of northern Italy, kept private zoos and allowed the animals to wander around their apartments, including even such exotic beasts as cheetahs which it was fashionable to import from the East. Artists began to attempt to capture in their drawings the living beauty of wild and domestic animals: the library at Bergamo has preserved a 'zoological' manual compiled by one such artist, Giovannino dei Grassi, who was one of the original architects and decorators of Milan Cathedral, and this tradition was revived in the fifteenth century by Gentile Bellini and Pisanello. In France, an artist whose identity has never been established illuminated, around 1380, *Le Livre de la Chasse* for Gaston Phoebus, and the '*queste en lisière*' (beating the borders for game) of folio 62 V° already shows the lively appreciation of nature in summer which was to receive glorious expression in *Les Très Riches Heures du duc de Berry*.

This manuscript, illuminated between 1411 and 1416 by three brothers, Pol, Hennequin and Hermant de Limbourg, is the first work of art in which the seasons are represented as other than abstractions. Each artist has faithfully translated the image of nature appropriate to the particular month he illustrates in this calendar, and the miniatures in the other part of the book, still imprisoned in the Italian style of the Trecento, prove by contrast the sense of liberation that the artists must have

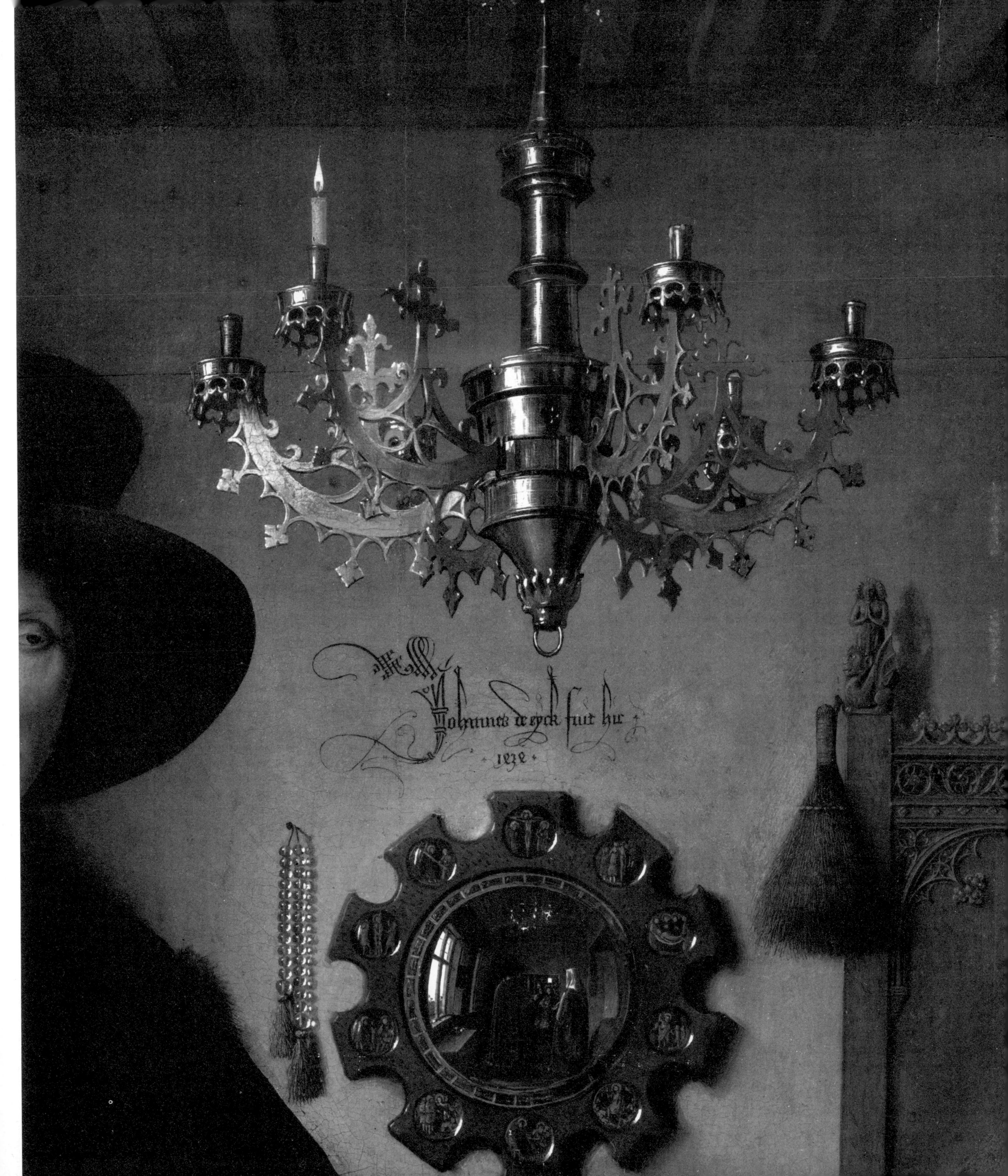

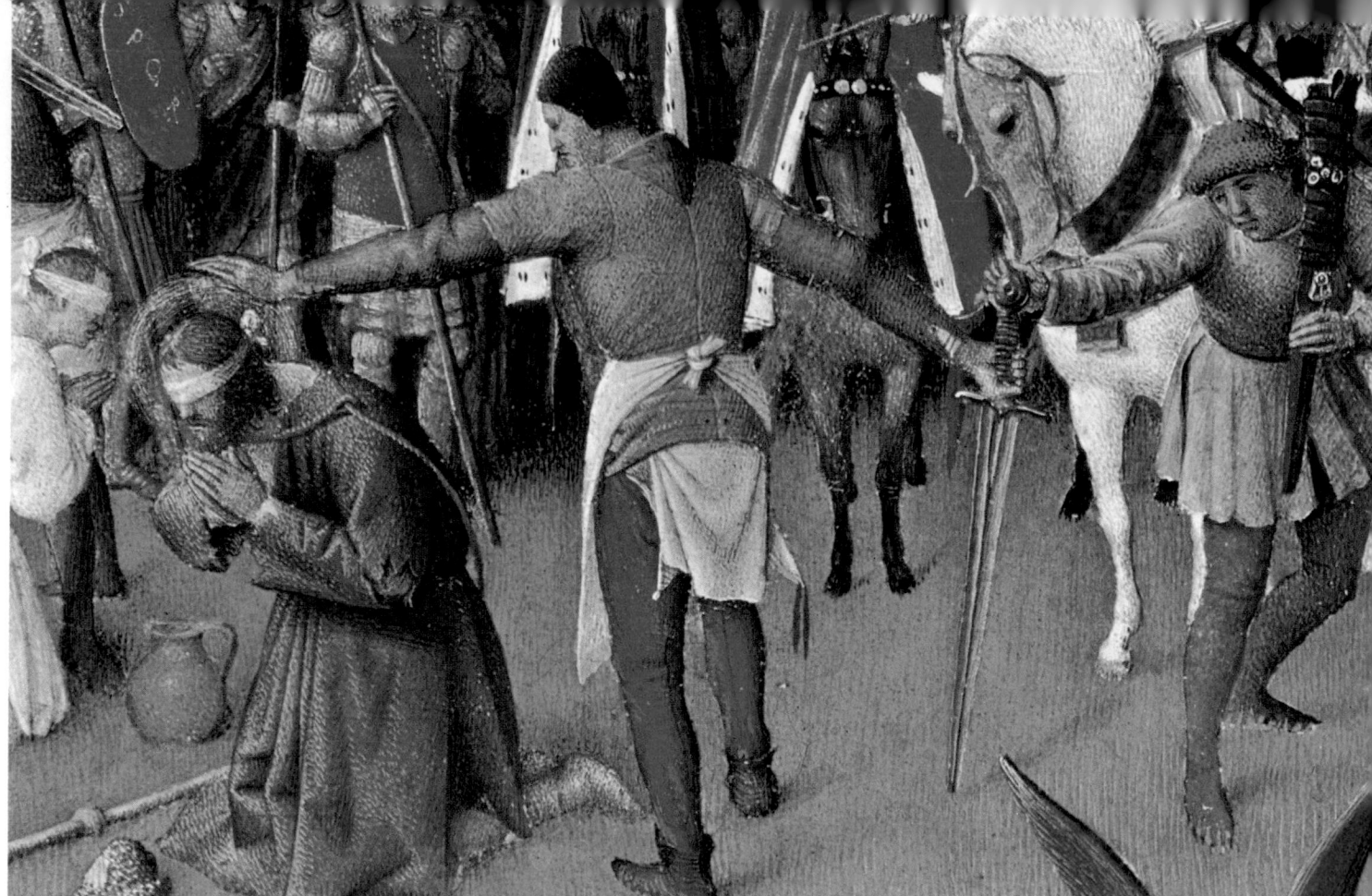

38 Jehan Fouquet (*c.* 1420–*c.* 1481). Detail of *The Martyrdom of St James*. Chantilly, Musée Condé.

Jehan Fouquet's keen visual sense is shown here by the accurately observed attitude of the executioner poising his sword so that the saint's head will be severed by a single stroke.

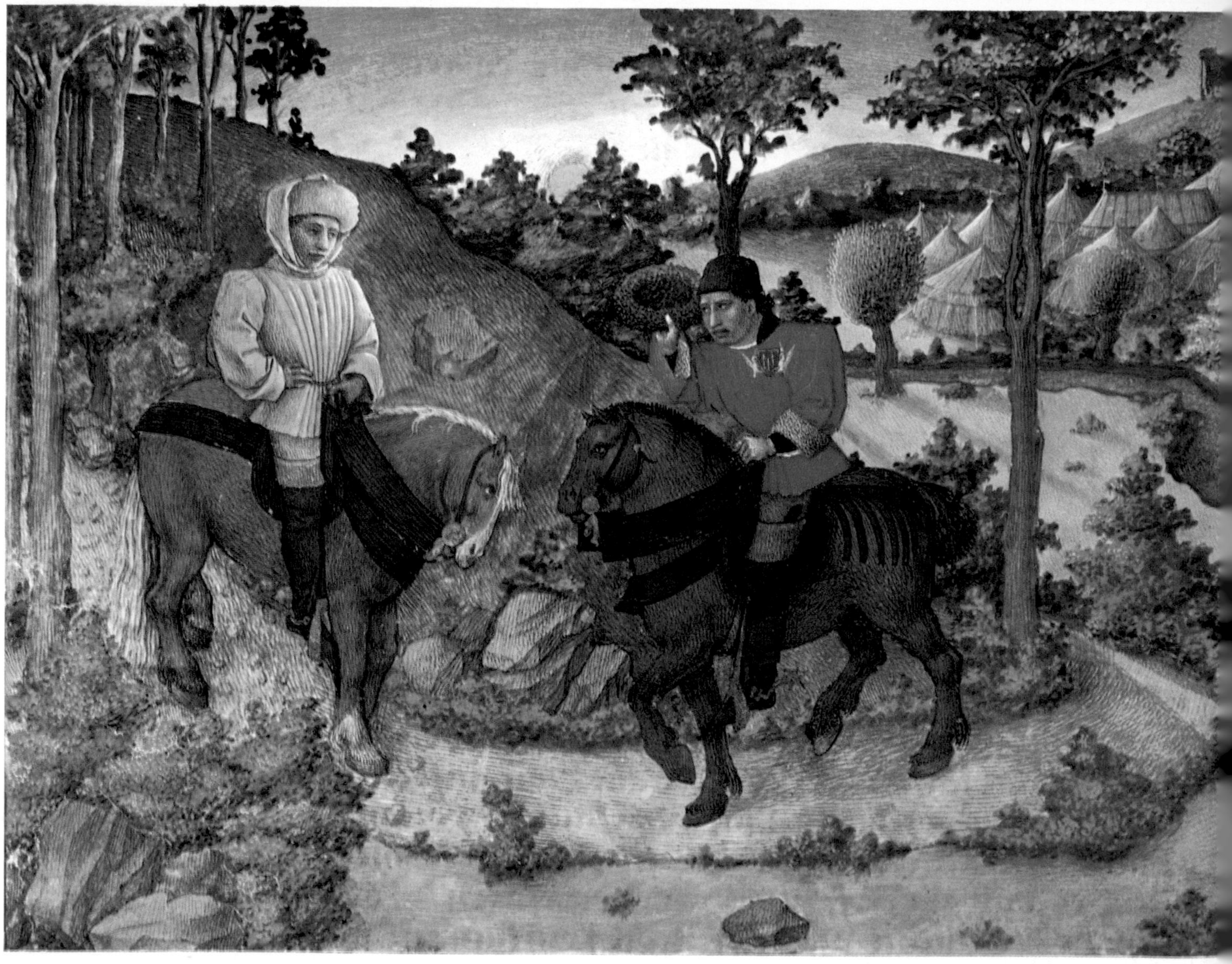

39 Vif Désir finds Requête once more, folio 31 of the manuscript of *Le Livre du Cuer d'Amours Espris*. French school, 15th century. Vienna, Nationalbibliothek.

The unknown artist (perhaps King René of Anjou) who illustrated the *Cuer d'Amours Espris* anticipated Giorgione and the Venetians in expressing all the nuances of light and shadow dictated by the sun's course.

experienced in painting a subject in which they could break new ground: their representations of castles are so accurate that an archaeological interpretation which I once formulated of the miniature representing Mont-Saint-Michel (*pl. 36*) allowed me to conclude that one of the three brothers must have made a pilgrimage there around 1390 and kept a sketch made on the spot!

The art of the van Eyck brothers may well have sprung from this intimate world of the miniature, if it is true that the so-called *Turin Hours* represents the actual work of the van Eycks rather than, as some believe, a belated emulation of their art. Tragically, part of the book perished in the fire at Turin Library in 1902. Although this disaster may have benefited the game of conjecture so dear to scholars, it certainly deepened the mystery surrounding the origins of the van Eycks. Almost everything that tradition has passed on to us concerning these artists has been challenged by now, and the very existence of Hubert, supposedly the elder of the two, has been called into doubt: rather than sifting the evidence on this point until there is nothing left but dust, it might be more sensible to put together the few pieces of information we do possess so as to draw the appropriate historical conclusions. A positive attitude of this kind is, in any case, justified by the fact that the *Three Maries at the Sepulchre* (Rotterdam) constitutes a harmonious link between a few of the pages of the *Turin Hours* and certain portions of the Ghent Altarpiece, attributable in both instances to Hubert.

It seems that Jan van Eyck developed the basis of his incomparable art during the prolonged execution of the Ghent Altarpiece, in the course of which he had to pay a visit to Portugal, one souvenir of which was incorporated into the polyptych in the shape of its Mediterranean flora. This work constitutes one of the most important iconographic enterprises of Christian art, for the role assigned to the image here represents a complete reversal of the tradition followed by Christianity since its inception. The Ghent Altarpiece remains the boldest, most paradoxical endeavour ever made to paint the supernatural world in terrestrial guise; and in it, the physical world, having asserted its presence, reveals all its individual elements for the artist's marvelling eye to explore. As in the thought of William of Occam, the universe is apprehended not as essence but as a sum of individual beings, each of which is to be approached as an independent value by sympathetic intuition acting directly. Responding to man's awakened ambition, the world opened itself up as a limitless field of experiment, suddenly entering with all its infinity into painting,

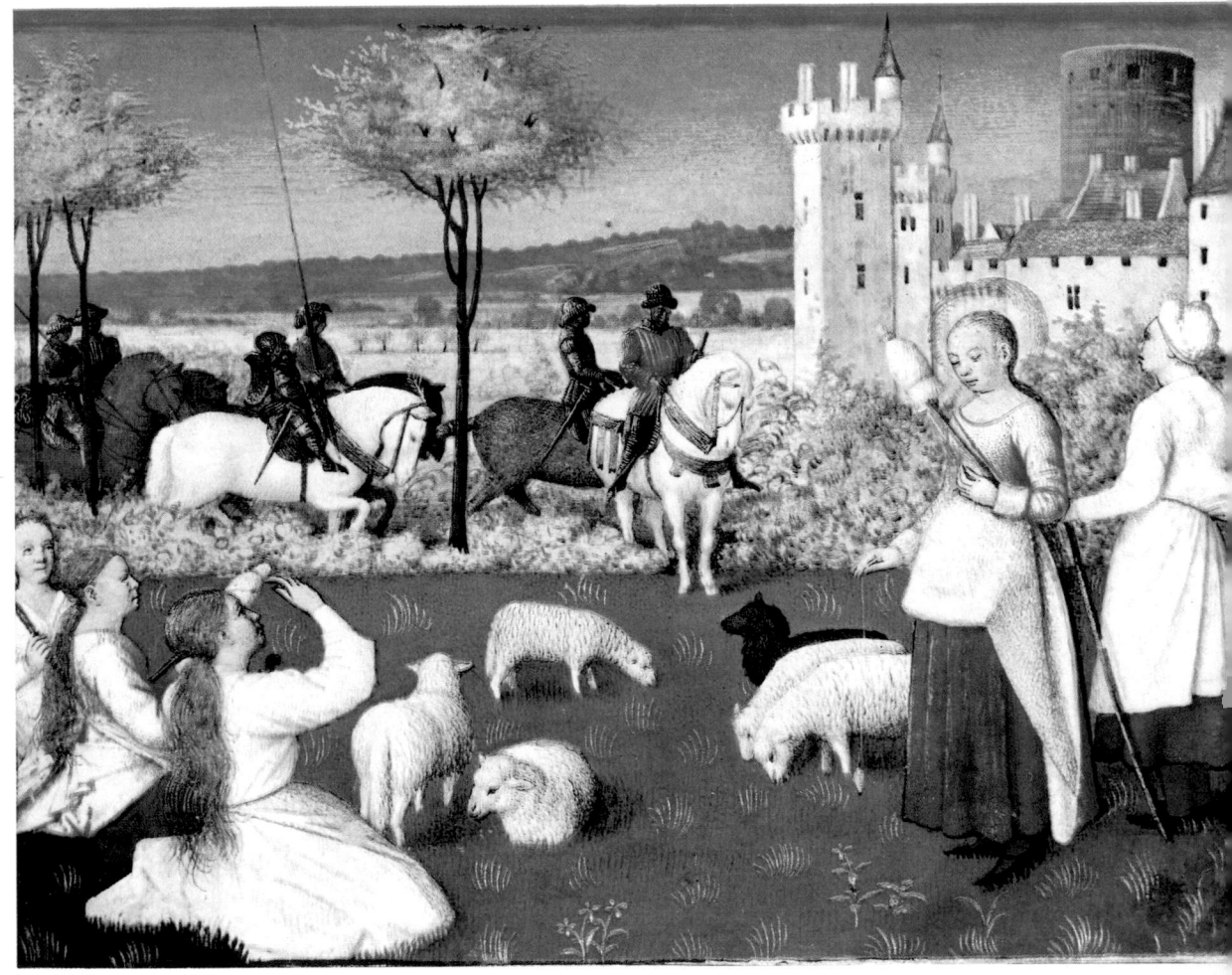

40 Jehan Fouquet. *St Margaret and the envoys of the prefect Olybrius.* Miniature. Paris, Louvre.

The peaceful countryside of France, the innocent charm of young girls, as expressed by Jehan Fouquet, spring from the same poetic vision which was to inspire Corot four centuries later.

from which it was, as it were, excluded again only in our present era. That transformation set in motion the pursuit of appearances which continued until impressionism, and also the passion for creating likenesses, the vanity of which was deplored by Pascal. Eyckian objectivism thus attained its greatest intensity at its very outset, and apart from a few Dutch painters of still-lifes, working in a far more restricted field, no artist was ever again able to endow the object with the same hallucinatory presence. In this figurative appearance, the object, finally stripped of all symbolic veneers, reveals itself to us as heavy with real significance, more so than the real itself; transposed into the 'vanity' of painting, the object enters the sphere of the intemporal.

Although the world which van Eyck reveals is apprehended in its physical truth, it is none the less experienced through the feelings of a profoundly Christian soul. A kind of inner irradiation seems to emanate from all things, as though it were light which gave them substance. In contemplating the meadows of the *Adoration of the Lamb*, I cannot help thinking of that old Augustinian doctrine – revived by Robert Grosseteste and other medieval theologians – which viewed knowledge as an 'illumination' of the soul, animated by God. In his *De Luce*, Grosseteste holds light to be *corporeity* itself, the primary form that unites with matter to constitute bodies, and it is evident that the object in a painting by van Eyck owes its whole being, its matter, its colour to the light which, rather than striking things as an external agent, appears to well up from the depths. This light originates in the brilliance which 'illuminated' the illustrated books of the Middle Ages, in which it preserved itself like a secret, guarded safely against the day, in those precious images bathed in lakes of gold. Thus, while Italian painting was originally mural, that of the northern schools was first inspired by the miniature. The advance of objective knowledge soon led to the abandonment of the theory of illumination; from the fourteenth century onwards, philosophers followed St Thomas Aquinas in believing that knowledge resided in a capacity natural to man, and that the gift of illumination was simply the gift of natural light made by the Creator to his created beings. But van Eyck, grappling with this unknown world which was slowly emerging in the closing years of the Middle Ages, seems to have conceived of truth as being created in the radiance of increate light.

The transition from the miniature to the painting involved essentially the transformation of the surface into the illusion of three dimensions. At the time when the Italian Renaissance was considered the sole repository of truth, van Eyck's failure to make proper use of *perspectiva artificialis* was put down to the awkwardness of a primitive. A profounder insight would have revealed that van Eyck's methods resulted from a different perception of space from that of the Italians, in that his aim was to apprehend space in its totality and not as a void opening out from the human eye. He takes up a hovering position from which he overlooks the world: in the *Marriage of Giovanni Arnolfini and Giovanna Cenami*, a mysterious work which certainly contains the indecipherable symbol of his art, he sets a convex mirror in the background (*pl. 37*) to reflect the side of the room whose wall has presumably been removed so that he can see through into the room. The contraction of the resulting image gathers the space together in a 'nuclear' density of quasi-metaphysical power, almost bringing to mind those modern scientific theories which calculate that, if all interstitial empty space were suppressed, the total matter of the world would be reduced to the volume of a locomotive or a box of matches. The space which the Italians of the Quattrocento enclosed within their visual pyramid is an anthropomorphic concept. In Eyckian space, the earth seems to unfold itself under the sovereign gaze of God contemplating his work (*pl. 33*). (Later, with Bruegel, this universal space became secularized and turned into a world seen through the eyes of a philosopher.) How fascinating it would be if we still possessed that 'map of the world' which Jan van Eyck once painted for the Duke of Burgundy and which must surely have embodied his conception of the universe!

Jehan Fouquet reached manhood at the moment when France was at last emerging from the anarchy and bloodshed that had afflicted her for a hundred years. His luminous work is a hymn to the joy of living in a liberated France, growing green again under the warm sun of victory. On the day of deliverance, France discovered the painter who was destined to celebrate the beauty of her reconquered lands, and the love of the native earth and sky. All the great landscape-painters of the fifteenth century painted nature. But Fouquet painted France: verdant plains watered by great majestically flowing rivers, the earth as harmonious as a goblet in which the air's liquid light is trembling, towns floating on the plains like ships with countless masts, white châteaux and manors anchored to the sides of hills. All this is truly France as reflected in the two provinces, the Ile-de-France and Touraine, which form the country's heart. The French countryside, no longer trampled, pillaged and burned, begins at last to bask in peace, though no human life peoples its lush stretches, and nature lords it there alone.

Men can indeed be seen in the foreground going about their business, which seems to consist mainly in killing each other, but they are mere passers-by, history's walkers-on crossing the proscenium of the theatre of eternal nature. It would seem that, before Bruegel, Fouquet already sensed the epic contrast between nature and man, the immutable and the ephemeral.

Fouquet's miniatures are the microcosm of nature and French society in the fifteenth century. The artist has witnessed war and peace, knows how men kill each other, how they strike blows and parry them; he perceives the organic unity of the pitched battle, that monstrous being formed of countless entangled destinies. He is Mantegna's equal in his knowledge of anatomy, and has studied the dense and beautiful volumes of the horse more closely than Paolo Uccello. He has penetrated the silent life of objects: a ray of light making the wine in a glass sparkle like a ruby suddenly fills us with an awareness of the magical proximity of the real. And he is familiar with the gestures of men at work: an impassive observer, he has watched with a careful eye the posture of the executioner calculating rather ostentatiously the strength and the correct sword angle required to sever the neck with a single painless cut (*pl. 38*); yet he is equally aware of the tender commotion surrounding the birth of the child in the warm intimacy of a room lit by the whiteness of the sheets wrapped around the woman who has been confined.

Sometimes one of these passers-by steps out from the narrow frame traced on the parchment, and his image looms out at us on the scale of the world we live in. In passing from the universe of the miniature to that of painting, these beings who had hitherto existed solely in terms of their gesture or function suddenly acquire a powerful individuality. These portraits share Piero della Francesca's monumental form and Jan van Eyck's existential intensity (*pl. 34*), but possess an added 'naturalness' which is uniquely French. The essence of Fouquet's genius lies in this search for a classicism which orders nature only so as to express its truth more clearly. Were they to spring to life from the book in which their images lie imprisoned, the personages of Fouquet's miniatures could enter our own world just as they are, so little have they been affected by the decadent stylization prevalent in the art of their time.

Thanks to Fouquet's truthful testimony, we are able to imagine the world of peasant, townsman, prince and warrior at the centre of which lived Joan of Arc. He painted the 'shepherd-maid' herself in the guise of one of the saints whose voices she heard, a girl working her spinning-wheel and keeping an

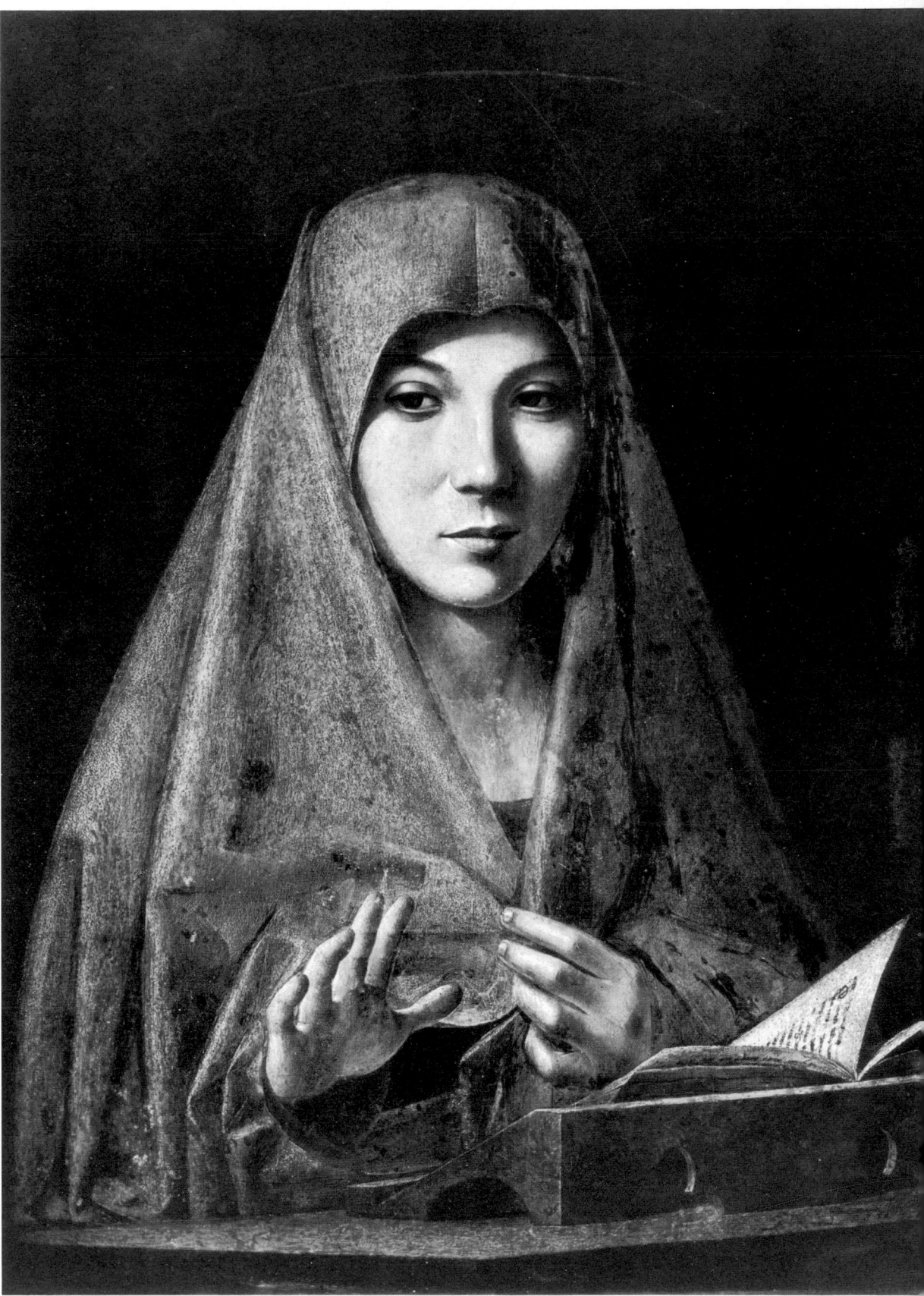

41 Antonello da Messina (*c.* 1430–79). *Virgin Annunciate*. Palermo, Museo Nazionale.

The Flemish technique of oil-painting, which he doubtless inherited from Petrus Christus, allowed Antonello to give a greater intensity to the human face.

eye on her sheep while a noble cavalcade advances towards her. In this legendary encounter in the shadow of a fortified castle (*pl. 40*), one is tempted to see, in place of the Roman prefect Olybrius approaching St Margaret, some ambassador sent by the Dauphin Charles to the Maid of Orleans to implore her to come to the rescue of the kingdom.

The country which gave birth to Joan, the most astonishing prodigy in history, simultaneously produced the level-headed genius Fouquet. This contemporary of the miracle-worker was himself so little drawn towards mysticism that he preferred to confine the invisible within the dimensions of the visible: his angels are choristers, the Virgin's features are those of the king's mistress and the figures of the Trinity are deacons celebrating the liturgy. Yet this positive character had certain traits in common with the young woman whom Alexandre Dumas called the 'Christ of France': good sense, optimism and good health. Fouquet shared the same climate as Joan, just as Rogier van der Weyden and Geertgen tot Sint Jans shared that of St Lydwine of Schiedam, and he represented a complete break with the flamboyant romanticism which was rampant throughout northern Europe as a result of the aesthetic domination of Flanders. This was the moment when the court of Burgundy, embracing all the chimeras of the Middle Ages, oppressed these ancient dreams under a vulgar display of wealth and a bombastic naturalism. In this sense, Fouquet is not a child of his century, for amid the confusion of the expiring Gothic age, his work stands out like a promontory facing a new world. His paintings have a greater affinity with the work being produced by his contemporaries in the Italian Renaissance or with that of van Eyck than with anything else of his own period. Not that one should deduce any particular influence from this fact. Fouquet's classicism, far from being a gilding laid over a medieval illumination, comes straight from the heart: it is a moment in that French tradition which, above all the vicissitudes of evolution and of styles, comprises a never-failing perception of harmony. That same tradition, which gave the Middle Ages their masterpieces of monumental sculpture, remained a royal prerogative and, during the fifteenth century, followed the monarchy from the region of the Seine to that of the Loire.

Fouquet's century was one of unparalleled instability and tragic violence, and its art translates the resulting tensions of force and anguish. It is, then, a miracle in itself that France, which was enduring greater physical and spiritual agonies than any other nation, should have given Europe this lucid genius.

Fouquet's genius found no inheritor, any more than did that of van Eyck .– a further point in common between them. However, in Provence, a mysterious and unidentified artist revealed his sensitive awareness of nature in his illuminated illustrations for the manuscript of *Le Livre du Cuer d'Amours Espris*, that strange dream of chivalry and courtliness written by René of Anjou, titular King of Naples (*pl. 39*). This unfortunate monarch, the vassal of the King of France and the companion of Joan of Arc, had preferred the cause of the fleur-de-lis to his own interests and thus lost his domains. It had been thought at one time that René, who was known to have been a painter, had illustrated this strange book himself; later, this tradition was dismissed as a legend, but now it is being revived once more, an example of the kind of merry-go-round on which historical criticism often finds itself embarked when it lacks adequate documentary evidence. Dr Paecht, examining *Le Livre du Cuer d'Amours Espris*, has recently presented fresh arguments in favour of the original legend.

This little book's sixteen miniatures present a visual poem on the theme of light that is unparalleled in painting before Claude. It celebrates all the hours of the day, from dawn to nightfall, with a marked preference for the twilight hour, when darkness and light vie for supremacy, and the shadows lengthen along the ground. The artist who created it knew that no shadows are absolute, and a dull gleam shimmers even in his nights. This love of light assorts so well with the poet-prince's purity of spirit that it is pleasant to imagine that he was in fact the artist who painted these unique works.

In Italy, Antonello da Messina was the first to develop the Eyckian technique of oil-painting that had probably been introduced into Sicily itself by Petrus Christus, Jan's immediate follower. The surviving fragments of his output (*pl. 41*) indicate that he understood how to use this new technique as a means of strengthening even more the sense of human presence which was the aim of Quattrocento art, but that he did not have an equally deep perception of nature. It was at Venice that the Eyckian world was belatedly reincarnated, the magical process having been transmitted by Antonello himself, and it was sixteenth-century Venice that was destined to carry oil-painting to its highest peak of expressive power.

Under the direct impact of Mantegna and the distant influence of van Eyck, Venice, in the person of Giovanni Bellini, freed itself from Byzantine constraint, not by rejecting it out of hand but by incarnating the object of Byzantine contemplation

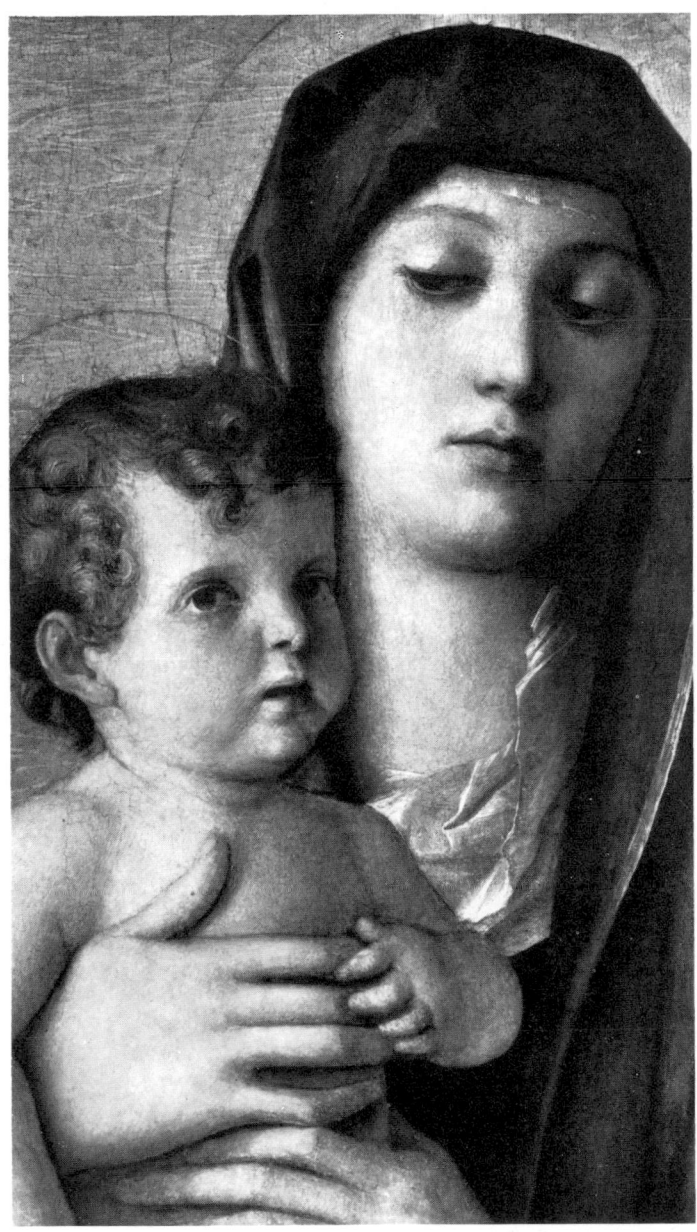

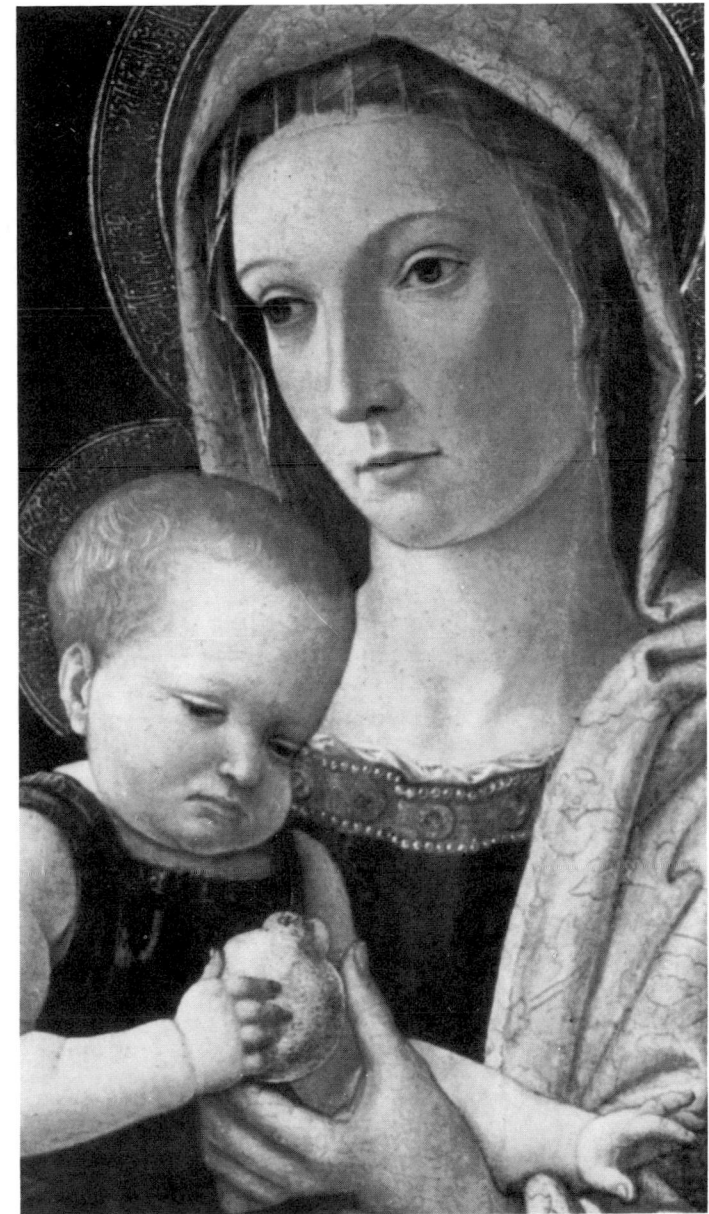

42 Giovanni Bellini (*c.* 1430–1516). *Virgin and Child*. Milan, Castello Sforzesco.

43 Giovanni Bellini. *Virgin and Child*. Venice, Accademia.

The transition from the Quattrocento to the Cinquecento can be followed in the work of Giovanni Bellini; he passes from observation to harmony, from the personal to the impersonal, from sharply defined drawing to bland modelling.

in the various guises of the visible world. Art became a mirror of the world in order to reflect eternal truth. Uniting in himself the two opposite tendencies, Bellini took as his point of departure a very strict observation of single entities which he then gradually raised to the height of concepts. This pursuit of the transcendental is particularly noticeable in his series of Madonnas (*pls 42–3*). Marian iconography had been the essential theme of Byzantine art and the one to which it had given the highest spiritual meaning. By the persistence with which he, like

Raphael, returns incessantly to the theme in order to perfect it, Bellini reveals to us that his ultimate aim is harmony, the harmony which, according to the philosopher Philolaus, is the unification of the multiple and the agreement of the discordant. But he approaches this summit gradually. At first, detecting the singular aspect of each form, he emphasizes its articulations; later, though, it is the reciprocal element within the form that he perceives. Consequently, instead of placing the accent 'harshly and crudely', in Vasari's words, on demarcations,

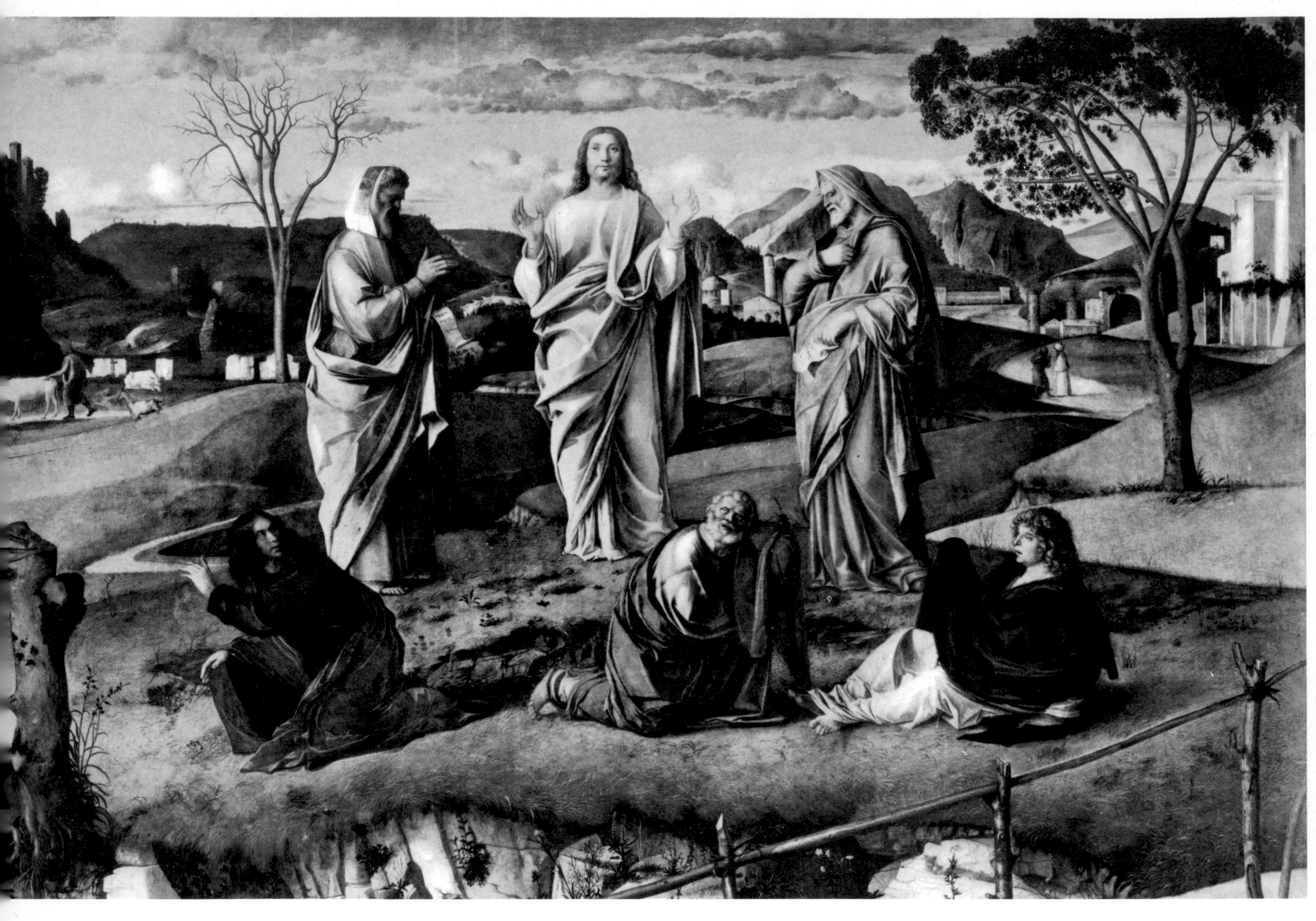

he seeks out transitions. But what relates him most closely, perhaps, to van Eyck is a comparable poetry of light; he captures its emanations in this Venetian countryside where, filtered by the moist atmosphere, it loses the sharp cutting edge it possesses in Tuscany and bathes everything in radiant clarity. Two landscapes provide particularly significant examples of his work. The National Gallery's *Agony in the Garden* (*pl. 45*), which hangs adjacent to a painting of the same theme by Mantegna, makes us spectators of the genesis of a world. In the Bellini, the atmosphere of our own planet envelops a landscape which in Mantegna's picture is a wilderness of rock and lava, and the landscape becomes an integral part of the picture; we are present at the moment when man is about to surrender himself to the musical harmony of the universe, and to abandon all thought of dissecting nature. The figures of the apostles still have something of the stiffness of statues, but one can guess that they will soon awake from their long stony sleep, to be reborn at the dawn which is breaking on the horizon, the dawn of the sixteenth century.

The Naples *Transfiguration* (*pl. 44*) is harmony

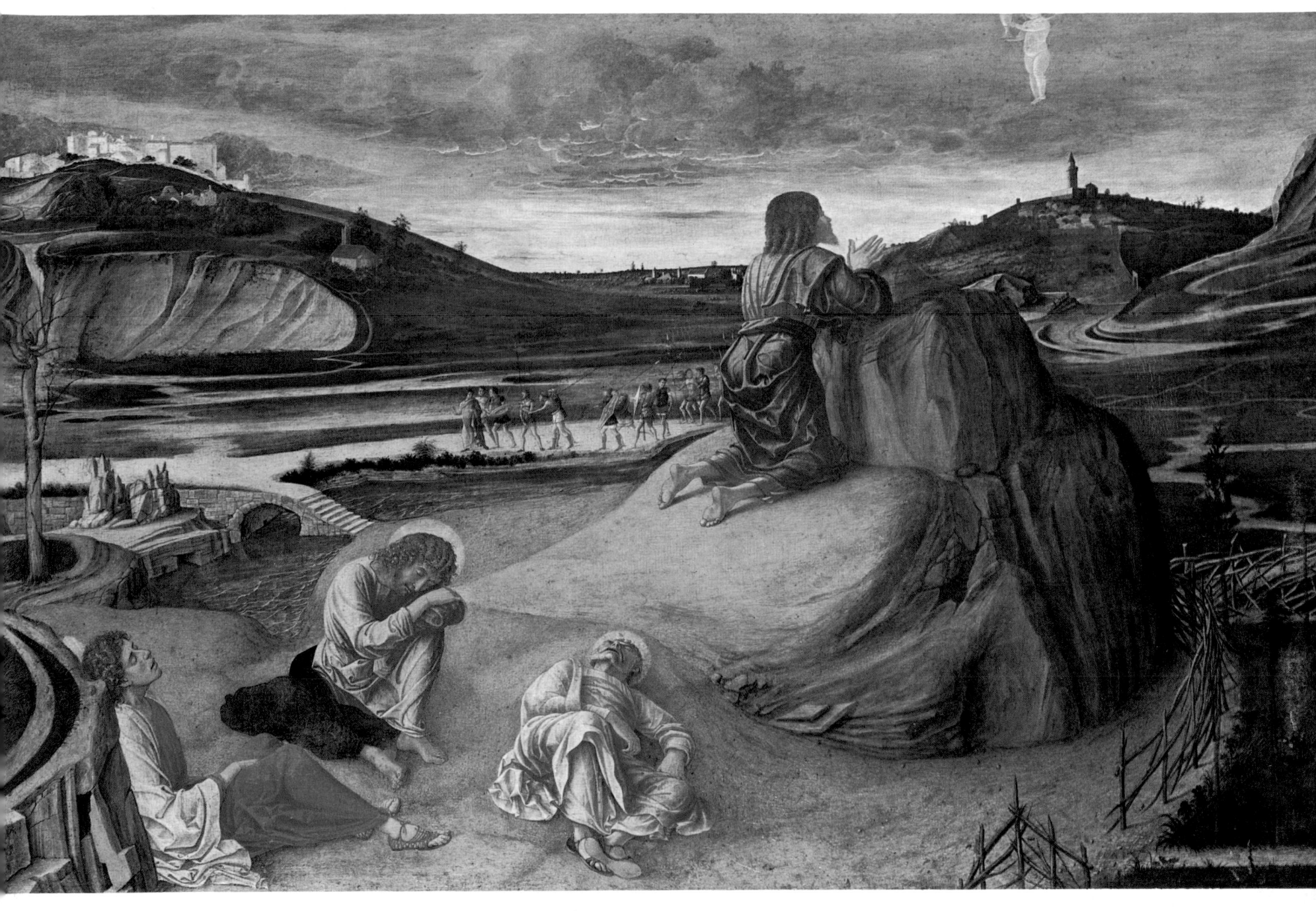

attained. This is one of those admirable late winter landscapes which Bellini enjoyed executing in the knowledge that this is the season of the year when the days are suffused by the most beautiful light. The sky, quilted with great silvery rain-clouds, is one of those hazy constructions radiating brightness which Bellini never tires of repeating and which, in nature as in his pictures, take possession of our gaze, thirsty as we are for light, and absorb us in contemplation of their splendour. In the middle ground, a passing peasant urges his cattle forward in a slow, peaceful rhythm. The motionless attitudes of the figures in this biblical scene correspond perfectly to the picture's theme, the expression of contemplation itself. Indeed, this sense of immobility, of opposition to progress, characterizes all Bellini's work, which remains as immutable as Byzantine art. For the last time, the world appears transfigured by the eternal truth which illuminates it. Both van Eyck and Bellini made this discovery of the physical world under the stimulus of an act of faith in divine creation. But the morrow was to bring Giorgione, and with him there would be the earth we live upon, and nothing but the earth.

45 Giovanni Bellini. *The Agony in the Garden*. London, National Gallery.

Giovanni Bellini heralds the modern landscape. Before Giorgione and Titian, who were his pupils, he expressed the most delicate nuances of the Venetian light; no painter after him has been able to capture the moment of dawn as he did in the London *Agony in the Garden*.

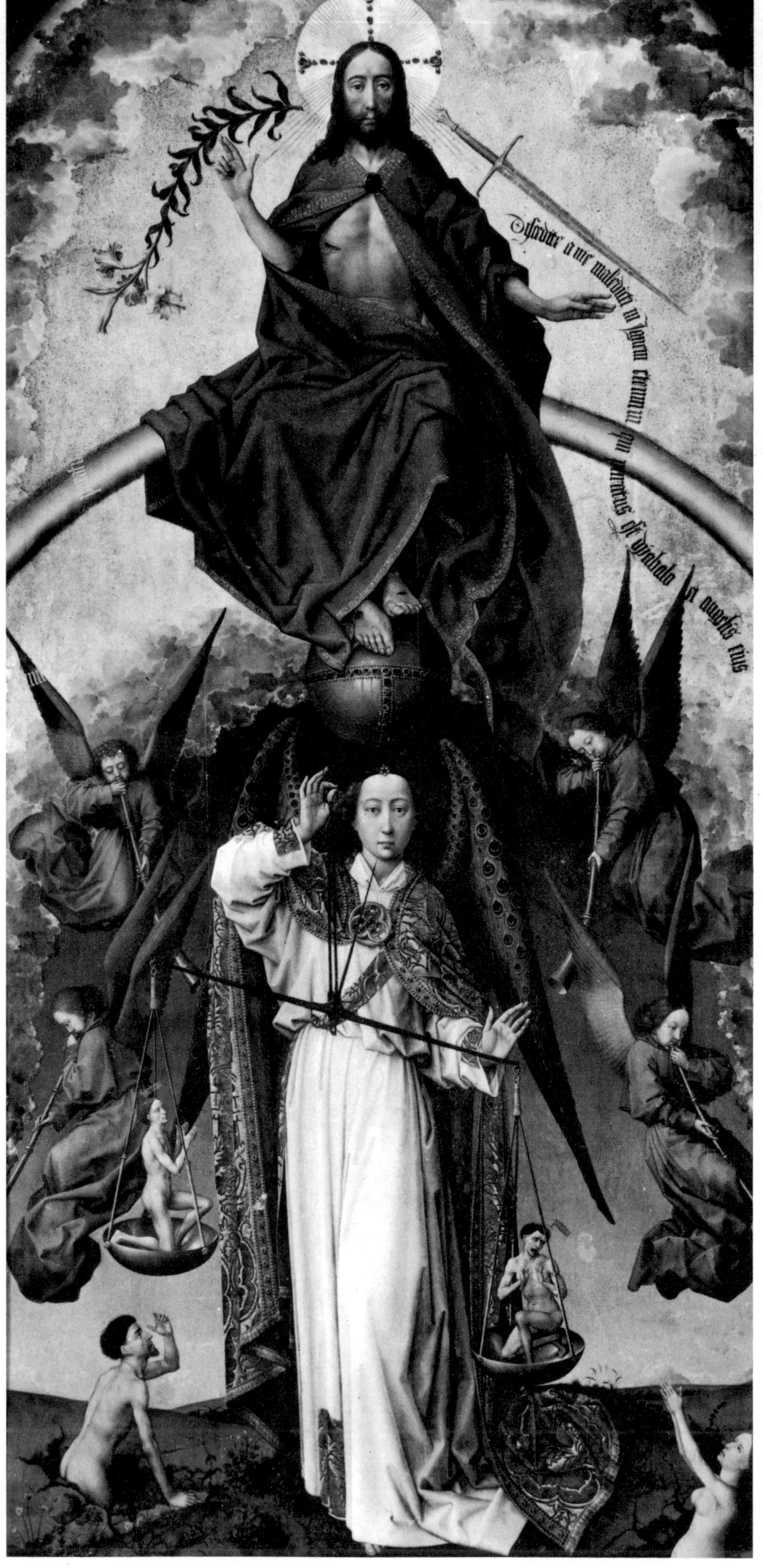

46 Rogier van der Weyden (*c.* 1399–1464). The Angel of Justice, detail from *The Last Judgment*. Beaune, Hôtel-Dieu.

4 Between heaven and hell

The polyptych of the *Last Judgment*, painted for the Hospice de Beaune by a whole workshop under the direction of Rogier van der Weyden, is, together with the *Adoration of the Lamb*, the most important production of early Flemish painting. But the world it reveals to us is quite different from that of the Ghent Altarpiece, that vision of paradise, conceived as a May festival to which the Universal Church is invited, in which peace and joy reign supreme. Van Eyck's optimism, like that of Fra Angelico, reflects the fresh breeze of the Renaissance breathing life into the world of faith, whereas Rogier's art is filled with the malaise of a civilization which feels its foundations shake beneath it. In the Beaune painting, a grimacing, terror-stricken mob of humanity jostles its way towards hell, rushing headlong of its own accord, repulsed by the light. According to the theologians, indeed, God does not damn; man condemns himself. But there is no such crowd on the opposite side of the composition, where only a few naked souls are advancing timidly and uncertainly towards a paradise whose narrow gate is guarded by a grim angel; they look back towards God, questioning his justice, as though, filled with the sense of their unworthiness, they dare not believe in their good fortune. It is true that the austere figure of St Michael (*pl. 46*) is hardly encouraging: he is holding a pair of scales in his hand, and the pan holding the vices is tipped down, thus signifying that the individual soul upon whose destiny judgment has just been pronounced is consigned to eternal torments. The twelfth and thirteenth centuries were more merciful: on the tympanums of their cathedrals, the scales were always tipped in favour of the good, despite the Evil One's cunning attempts to alter the balance. But in the paradise shown us in the Beaune Altarpiece, there are many called and few chosen. Placed originally upon the altar of the great hall of this asylum-chapel, the painting was intended to prepare the sick for a Christian death, in an era when souls were cared for more effectively than bodies. More than one dying man must have breathed his last in fearful contemplation of this scene in which hope is doled out so parsimoniously.

Throughout the fifteenth century, while the Dance of Death leered down from the walls of cemeteries, European art was filled with more or less dramatic interpretations by painters and sculptors of the theme of the Last Judgment. A softer echo of the Beaune polyptych is to be found in Danzig: this triptych, handed over by Memlinc in 1473 to the representative of the Medici bank in Bruges, was embarked for Florence the same year, but the ship was boarded at sea by the German pirate Peter Benecke, and this image of sovereign justice, the most precious treasure in the whole cargo, was offered by Benecke to the Marienkirche in Danzig. A more merciful *Last Judgment* is that by Stefan Lochner, in which the elect form a dense crowd at the entrance to paradise and are welcomed by swarms of angels. And in the composition which Fra Angelico conceived and had painted for the church of Santa Maria degli Angeli in Florence, the angels and the blest, reunited at last, dance a joyous round in the middle of the verdant celestial meadows.

During the heyday of medieval theology, Christians were entirely absorbed in the supernatural and made no clear-cut distinction between this world and the next. The faithful shared their lives with the heavenly host in a familiarity to which the piety of present-day Italian, Spanish or South American crowds still bears witness. The thirteenth century had witnessed a kind of second Incarnation in mystical art and literature. The sacred personages of Christ, the Virgin and the saints had assumed shape; the faithful lived in their presence, at a time when the sole aim envisaged for human life was the path of salvation.

This essential unity between the natural and the supernatural was destroyed in the following century. As times changed, man began to feel that his appointed destiny was no longer one of harmony but of power; his mission was to conquer the world and to conquer himself. The flow of transcendental certainties which had bathed his soul now made way for a superabundance of conquering energies which impelled him thenceforward to seek out fugitive certainties in thought and action; at the same time, the life of the individual, limited to itself, now appeared nothing more than a constant striving without ultimate reward. Man fell from the paradise of essence into the hell of existence.

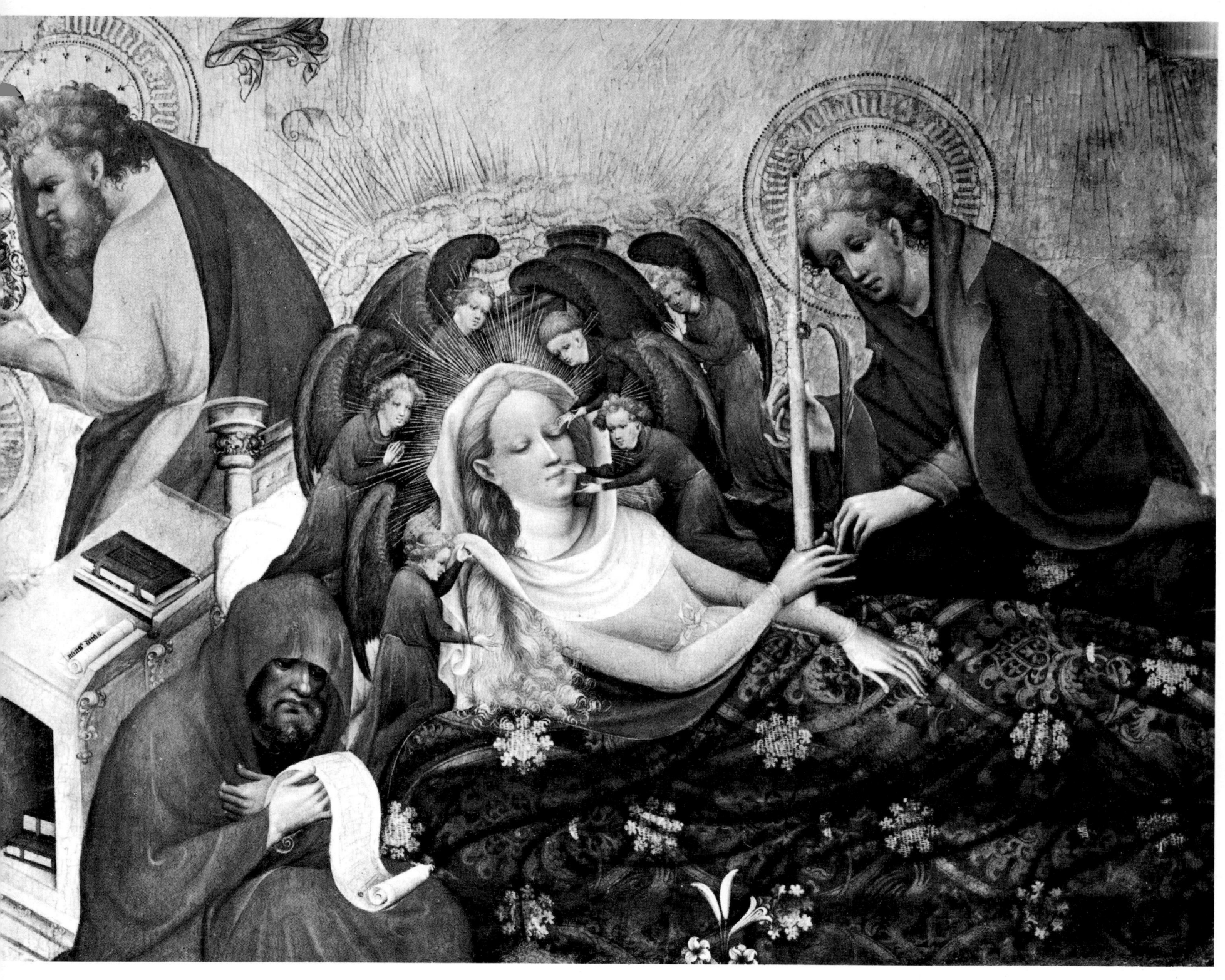

47 Konrad von Soest (active early 15th century). *Dormition of the Virgin*. Dortmund, Kunsthistorisches Museum.

The pioneers of the Italian Renaissance whole-heartedly accepted this reversal in the order of things, in which man displaced God as the centre of the world, and Konrad Witz, alone among northern European artists, affirmed man's autonomy with the same expressive force as the Italians, even adding his own note of brutal cynicism (*pl. 48*). But in general the peoples of the North, the 'Gothic' peoples, now felt themselves to be orphans of God.

Their souls were oppressed by what Jakob Boehme was to call, much later on, the 'wrath of God'.

Tormented by the anguish of being damned, some spirits sought consolation in fantasy, and dreamed of a paradise in which human beings would finally be relieved of the weight of matter. To such people, angelic nature seemed, in opposition to the humanist ideal, to be the nature closest to pure being. The Germanic mystics of the fourteenth

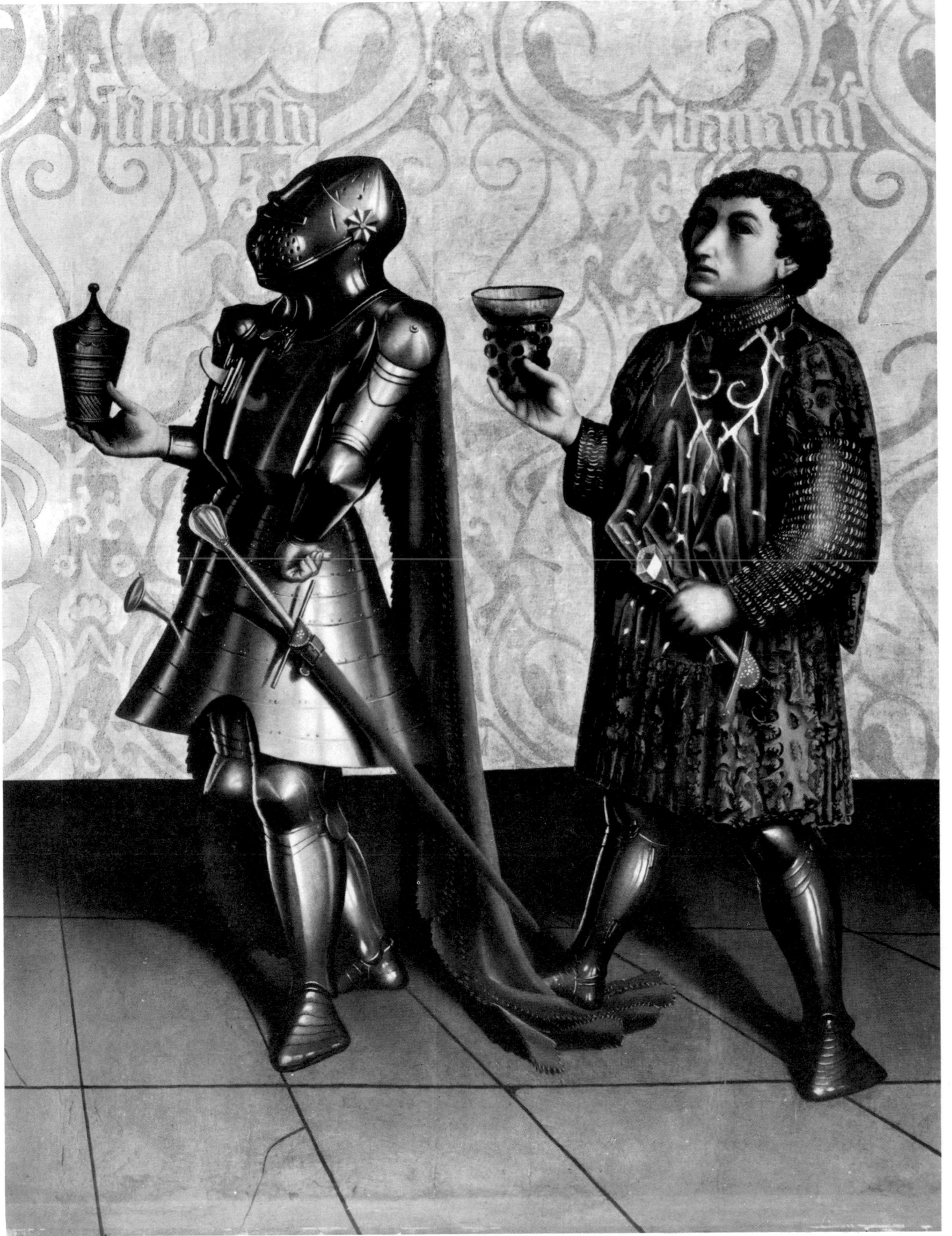

48 Konrad Witz (*c.* 1400–*c.* 1447). *Sabothai and Benaiah bringing water to King David.* Basle, Kunstmuseum.

Driven to extremes, fifteenth-century Germany either overemphasized the power of the human body or, on the contrary, dematerialized it; while the artists of southern Germany depicted steel-limbed giants, those in the north painted the most ethereal angels in the whole of Christian art.

57

century, determined to free themselves from the constraints of nature so that they might better enter into perfect union with God, prepared the way in Germany for the angelism which flourished in painting during the first half of the following century, particularly in Westphalia and the Rhineland. Konrad von Soest discovered the nature of angels in that of birds, depicting in a state of weightlessness beings whose faces were those of infants in the cradle, while unreal adolescents with tapering hands, long wavy hair and supple bodies lent their image to the supreme incarnation of purity, the Virgin Mary (*pl. 47*). The recrudescence of the Marian cult in the fifteenth century expressed the anguish of the sinful soul instinctively seeking the maternal breast as protection against divine wrath; the 'legend of Our Lady' is full of stories of the bandits, assassins and debauchees who have wormed their way into paradise thanks to some *ave Maria* recited daily or on the deathbed, a pious fraud condoned by the Virgin so as to thwart inexorable justice. Villon, poet of rogues and vagabonds, is also full of devotion for Mary. Only Chinese painters have been as successful as Konrad von Soest (and the Master of the *Little Garden of Paradise* of Frankfurt) in suggesting by means of form and colour what is essentially formless and colourless, the entities which are called – inaccurately – creations of the mind.

This angelism permeated a whole area of German painting, touched Italy with Fra Angelico and Sassetta, became vulgarized at Cologne with Stefan Lochner, and, reduced to affectation, was introduced into Flanders by Memlinc who was himself of Rhenish origin. But while a few poetic spirits abandoned themselves to such fantasy, others felt, deep in their souls, the tragedy of shattered faith.

Angel, devil and tormented man provided the three themes for northern painting during the fifteenth century. God lost his serenity and became the 'Man of Sorrows'; the August Face reflected the drama of the Passion, that terrible indictment of sinful man. Prompted by this sorrowful awareness, Rogier van der Weyden (*pl. 46*) developed a style which influenced the whole of Europe and swept the Eyckian style ruthlessly aside. He resuscitated the fourteenth-century tradition of ascetic thinness, and his vacillating, elongated, stiff and almost ataxic bodies seem exhausted by some tragic spiritual conflict; cast into hell, they become mere disjointed puppets. Nature, invoked by van Eyck in all the freshness of a world's first dawn, seems in Rogier's work to have been sterilized by some evil genius and reduced to a lifeless backcloth: space is introduced

clumsily and timidly, in depth, through oblique openings; the repeated fold marks of the draperies represent the graph of an anguish which is never permitted the relaxation of a curve or the gracefulness of an arabesque. This new yet prematurely old style infiltrated itself everywhere except into Florence, and influenced even so serene an artist as Giovanni Bellini.

One French artist, however, the Master of the *Pietà* of Villeneuve-lès-Avignon – who may almost certainly be identified as Enguerrand Quarton – was to bestow upon this style a formal grandeur worthy of the contemporaneous creations of the Renaissance, attained through a spiritual loftiness which makes this picture the noblest work that the virtue of sacrifice has ever inspired in art (*pl. 49*). Here is a perfect example of the instinctual capacity of French sensibility to internalize feelings in order to experience them in depth. The silence of the Avignon *Pietà* is more eloquent than the harrowing cries of Rogier's *Deposition* which expresses pain through the medium of its physical effects, as Rubens was to do later on. The master who conceived this 'Pity', leaving behind him the tumultuous times in which he lived, foreshadowed the introspective piety that was to characterize the French mystics of the seventeenth century. But, above all, this work is surely the supreme example in figurative art of an expressive tension finding its suggestive value in a highly perfected form; in this respect it provides a strong contrast with Rogier's imagery which, moving though it is, registers itself in an uncertain form, in a style that lacks self-confidence.

The fifteenth century witnessed the appearance in art of the spirit of Evil. Conceived hitherto as an abstraction, Evil suddenly assumed flesh and the mask of a human face. German painting, surfeited with angels, was now able to satisfy hidden urges towards cruelty and atrocity. The scene of the Passion served as a pretext: a satanic aura emanated from Christ's tormentors, while the sublime victim himself, spurned and tortured, suffered the ultimate degradation of being stripped of all human dignity. The highest image of God, that of the Trinity, grew distorted: the beautiful theological iconography of the Gothic Trinities, with its purity of conception, became transformed into a group of figures with a direct appeal to the emotions. In the case of certain Bavarian masters of the end of the fifteenth century (*pl. 50*), the intrusion into their work of this frenzied emotionalism constituted an attack upon the Godhead, injecting it with a miasma rising from hell.

Although this convulsive style was entirely alien to France, it was in the region of Paris, nevertheless,

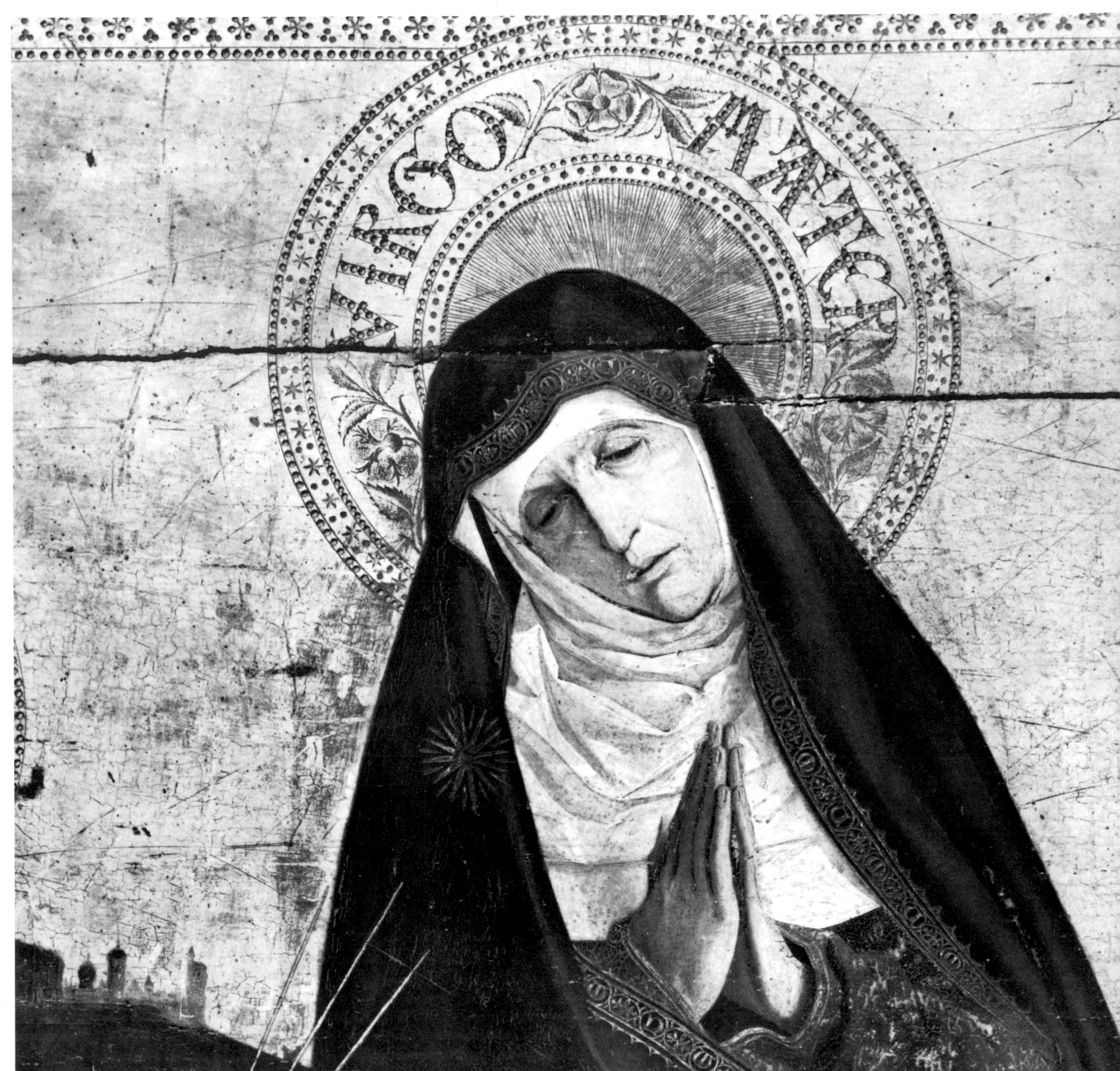

50 Bavarian Master (15th century).
The Holy Trinity. Blutenburg church.

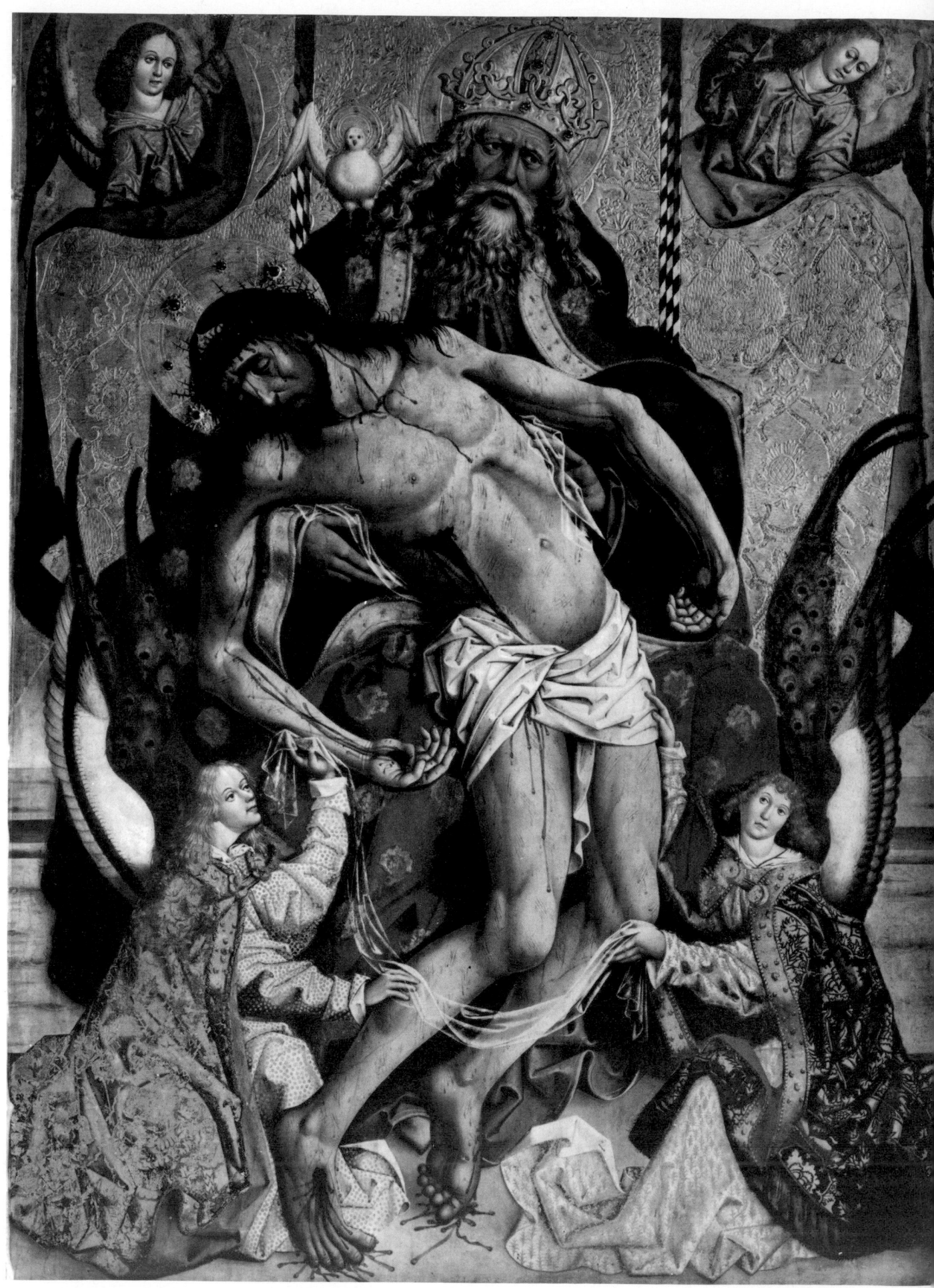

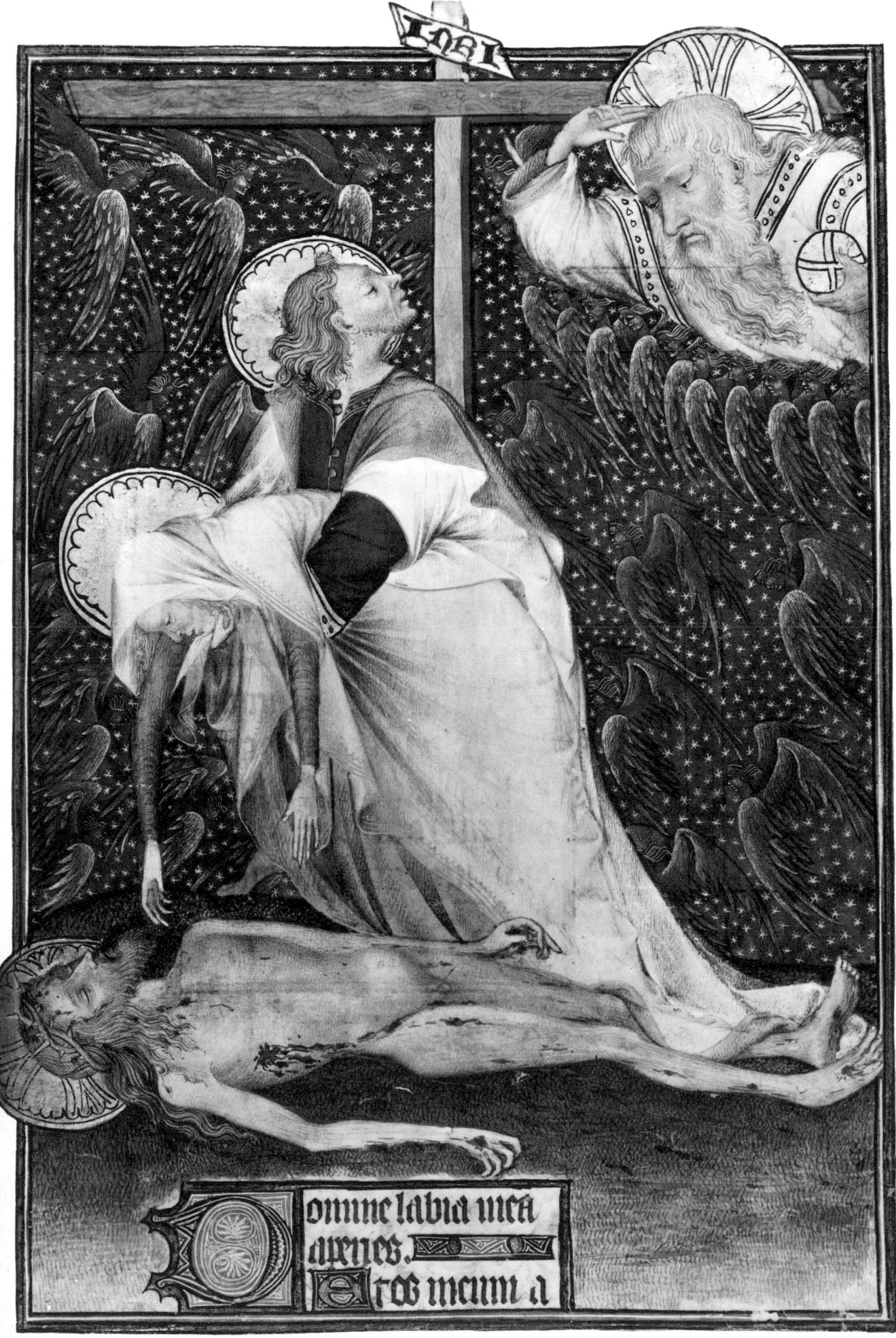

51 The Deposition, miniature from *Les Grandes Heures de Rohan* (*c.* 1418). Paris, Bibliothèque Nationale.

The intensity of the feeling of suffering experienced by certain fifteenth-century artists evoked a violence of expression which remained unparalleled until the twentieth century.

that an unknown master, perhaps of Germanic origin, illumined the manuscript known as *Les Grandes Heures de Rohan*, some time around 1418. The archaic nature of this work is emphasized by the schematic page layout, the reverse perspective, the conventional attitudes of the human figures, the Gothic linearity. Although nature is strangely absent in these paintings, they are nevertheless governed by the sinuous style of *Les Très Riches Heures*. But here that style is contorted by an anguish which shows in the grimacing faces and twisting forms, and gives a monstrously bloated aspect to certain figures that loom up on the surface of the page in menacing close-up. In the *Deposition* (*pl. 51*), St John, supporting the lamenting mother as she leans over the body, looks back towards God the Father less to implore his mercy than to admonish him who, from all eternity, had determined upon this drama. Painted in an unhappy historical period, in which the fair realm of France was dominated by the spectre of death, this work seems to have been engendered in an apocalyptic atmosphere. It is intriguing to speculate upon the identity of this artist of genius who preceded Grünewald by a century, and upon the character of Yolande d'Aragon, wife of Louis II of Anjou, who was bold enough to commission such a revolutionary work at a moment when fashion favoured the refined elegance of the miniatures produced by the workshops of the Master of *Les Heures de Boucicaut* or the Master of *The Bedford Hours*.

In Germany, Martin Schongauer assumed Rogier's mantle, evoking the same bottomless misery of lost souls in the same tortured style whose crabbed, flawed pattern he exaggerated to create the painting style of the period known in Germany as the *Spätgotik*, though the painters of the German Renaissance later gave this belated Gothic style a rhythm and breadth that considerably altered its impact. At the same time, in Flanders, Memlinc softened the style's harshness; although the faces of his Virgins or donors are not exactly wreathed in smiles, at least they no longer register disquiet. These pictures, taken as a whole, give the impression that the elect are destined to enjoy the kind of comfort appropriate to bankers and merchant drapers whose moderate religiosity has placed them in good standing with an Eternity where their pious foundations have earned them a credit balance.

Indeed, a certain relaxation of the harsh style of the fifteenth century became evident throughout Europe at this moment, in Italy (Perugino), Germany (Hans Holbein the Elder), France (the Master of Moulins) and Spain (Juan de Flandes), a calm preceding the storm which was to see the

Church rent by schism, the destiny of the Christian called into question, and man, shorn of the concept of free will, become a slave of sin.

The extraordinary art of Hieronymus Bosch no doubt expresses a premonition of this drama, an intuition of the overthrow of a whole world. Certainly, his imagery introduced an entirely new dimension of the invisible into the domain of art, and with this concern with the immediate rather than the beyond, the depths rather than the heights, the unconscious made its entry into painted imagery. In liberating all the forces of the imagination, Bosch extended enormously the scope of painting, limited hitherto to the illustration of religious or profane life, and opened the way to the endless speculations of future commentators. Unquestionably, the artist must have experienced a demiurgic satisfaction, similar to that which animated the twelfth-century Romanesque sculptor, in creating this antiworld of which the Prince of Darkness is monarch.

The weird hordes which torment the human beings in paintings such as the *Temptation of St Anthony* (*pl. 52*) are composite creatures from Satan's bazaar, the spawn of inert and living forms and even of objects invented by man; these monsters, the apostles of anti-Creation, dedicated to the degradation of the divine work, lure into their ranks sinners seized by a furious urge towards self-destruction, sinners who are mad without knowing it. At the moment when Bosch was painting his fantasies, a number of writers were seeking to find a deep meaning of some kind in dreams and in madness, and to discover in irrationality a sort of advanced point of the intellect on the road to the unknown. The fool, essential character in the medieval *sotie* or satirical farce, plaything of the court – he who is free to say anything at all – seems to have been invested with a kind of prophetic frenzy. The fifteenth century commenced with the 'Dance of Death' and ended with a 'Ship of Fools'; folly took over from death in keeping watch over human anxiety (*pl. 53*).

Historians have shown such passionate interest in Hieronymus Bosch's imaginary world that they have tended to ignore his bold technical innovations. Even though it had lost the mysterious depth of the van Eycks' process, Flemish handling continued to produce a sort of enamel-like glaze, painstakingly executed by craftsmen to capture objective definition as closely as possible. In Bosch's pictures, the figures, especially those in the foreground, are still painted 'in the Flemish manner', but in the backgrounds (*pl. 56*), the scenery, the sky and the water, the artist innovates by using a thinner handling consist-

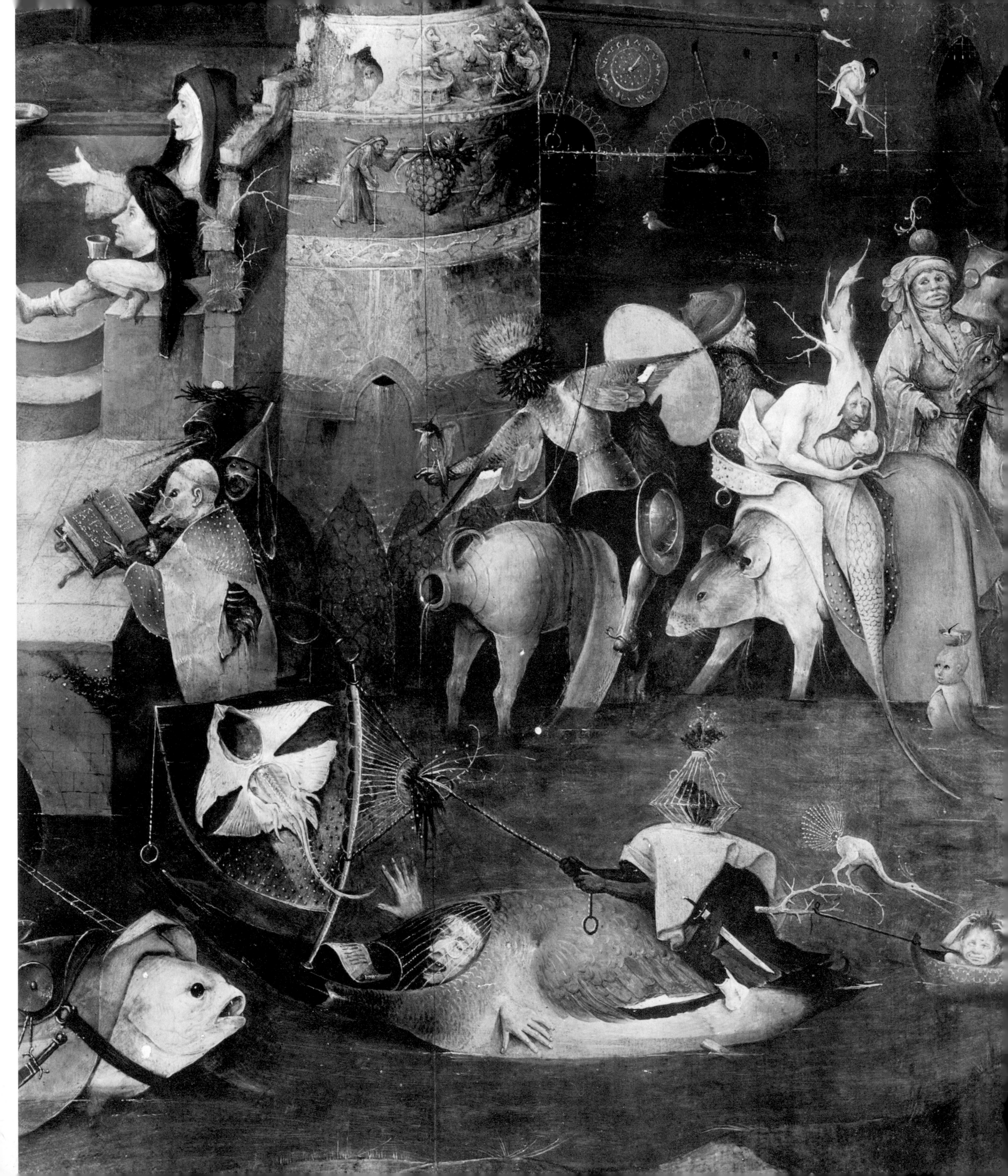

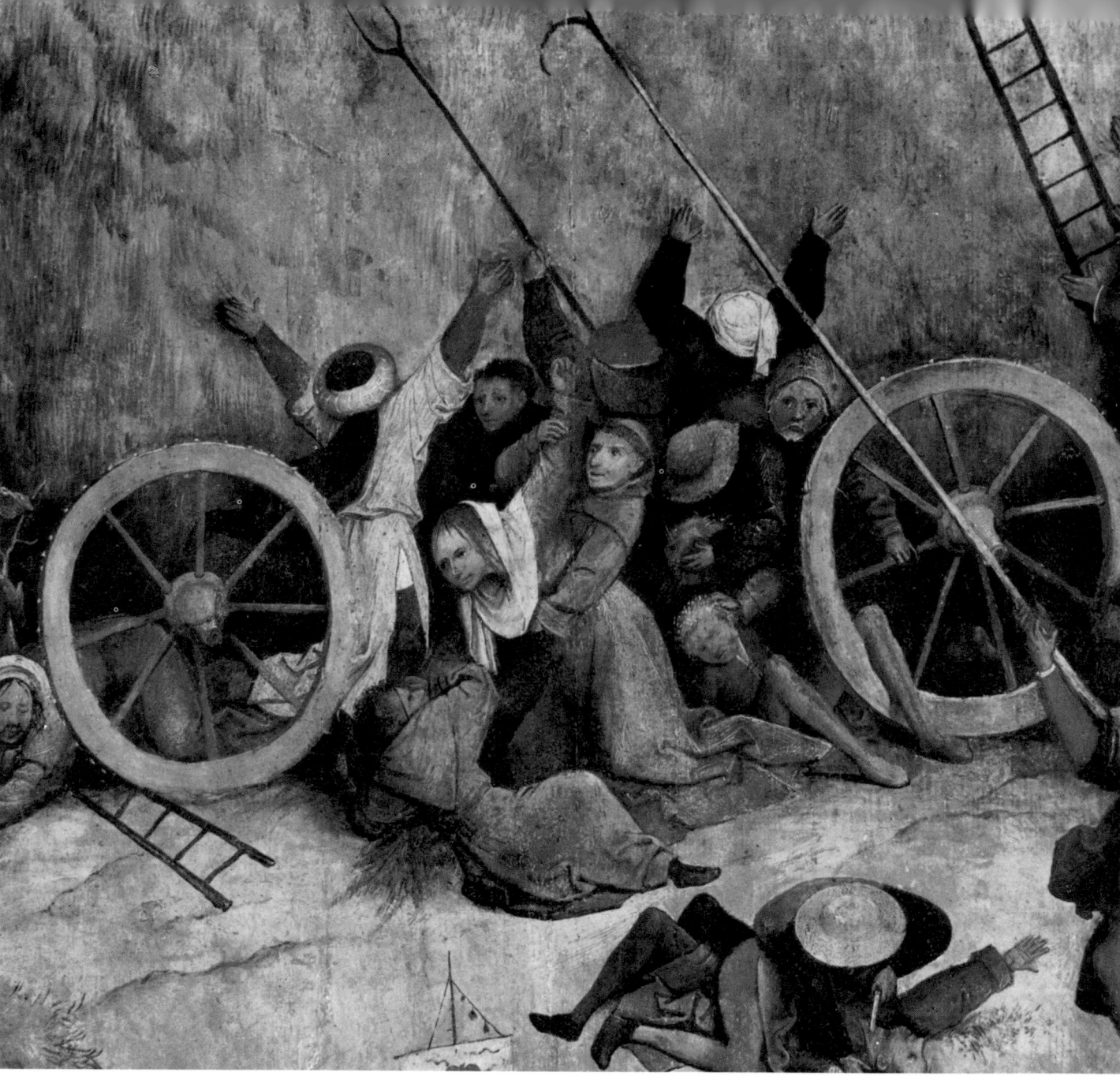

53 Hieronymus Bosch.
The Hay-wain. Madrid, Prado.

Anticipating Bruegel, Bosch invents the universe-picture, teeming with life; but beneath the appearances of reality his is a fantastic universe.

ing of very fluid tinted glazes: on these occasions, he abandons the local colour-tones, imprisoned within precisely outlined forms, that were traditional in the Flemish school, preferring broken, shaded-off, transparent, fugitive, moist tones which flow freely from the brush to blend all the elements in the picture into a harmonic unity. This shimmering brushwork was not understood by any subsequent artist except Bruegel, who seized its full possibilities.

The world of Grünewald is entirely different from that of Bosch, and the figures he painted are possessed by a different madness, that of the Cross. Since Grünewald's identification as Mathis Nithart (alias Gothart), it has been possible to glean some idea of his personality through a revealing document, the inventory of the deceased's belongings. After his death, which occurred in the Saxon town of Halle, a stronghold of the Reformation, his house was found to contain twenty-seven bound sermons by Luther, a nailed casket housing a bound New Testament, a number of Protestant pamphlets and

an Anabaptist creed. But it also contained all the costumes and regalia he had worn at the court of Mainz, where he had spent several years as official painter and artistic adviser to Archbishop-Elector Albert of Brandenburg who had manœuvred with such duplicity between Rome and the Reformation. Mathis had taken these symbols of luxury with him when his support for the Peasants' Revolt and for the Anabaptists forced him to flee from Mainz in 1526. The evidence of his life shows us an impassioned spirit, involved in the great social and religious struggles of his epoch, a partisan of the terrible Anabaptist fanaticism which shook Germany and almost plunged it into anarchy.

We owe to this man, wrongly named Grünewald since the seventeenth century, one of the most astonishing achievements in the history of painting: the altarpiece for the Antonite monastery of Isenheim, now in the Musée d'Unterlinden, Colmar. Our own era which has, at Huysmans's instigation, rediscovered this forgotten work and made it famous, has perhaps misinterpreted it in detecting

64

in it a hellish paroxysm of German expressionism. This polyptych, with alternative images provided by the folding panels, evokes neither heaven nor hell, but the terrible spiritual conflict which arises when the soul, aspiring towards God from the depths of its despair and confronted by the forces of suffering, sin and doubt, keeps a saving faith intact through all adversity; having triumphed over all temptations, the soul has conquered evil and at last attained the supreme Light, losing its identity in the bliss of divine unity. Too much attention has been focused upon the monsters depicted on these panels (*pls 57–8*) – which are certainly the most vividly terrifying monsters ever seen in a work of art – and upon the expiring Christ (*pl. 54*), a Goliath whose broken, swollen body is covered by the pustules which are a symptom of ergotic poisoning. The idea that this image represents some Germanic sadistic obsession betrays a lack of understanding of the high theological ideal that actuates it: the hideousness of this pustular body symbolizes all the ignominy of man's sins, which Christ assumed so entirely that the sheer weight of horror caused him momentarily to lose heart. Without doubt, too, the Antonites, whose mission it was to tend the victims of ergotic poisoning, specified when commissioning the altarpiece that Christ, as an example of supreme charity, should be represented stricken with the terrible disease.

This image of horror only attains its full meaning when considered in relation to his Christ of the Resurrection (*pl. 55*), which shows the metamorphosis of a human body into a glorious body, a metamorphosis which the chosen will be called upon to emulate. In the words of Huysmans: 'We are witnesses of the resumption of divinity as it blazes up together with life, and of the formation of the glorious body which vanishes in an apotheosis of flames of which it is both the source and the focus.' Grünewald's light is not the radiant limpidity that illuminated van Eyck's idyllic meadows, for it is not of a visual order: it emanates from fire, that primordial element from which God forged the worlds, as some medieval theologians believed. For man, it flows from the depths of the soul, from those depths where the divine example remains lodged, deaf to all incitements from the senses and the intellect, to rise again only at the call of the Word.

If the aim of Western painting was to express everything which had haunted man's mind and imagination throughout the ages, there remained one arena of thought into which it was powerless to penetrate: lofty mystical speculation, that ontological state of ecstasy which has always possessed a few individuals who, in their quest for pure Being, have groped through the shadows in search of light. Grünewald alone (and not El Greco, as has generally been suggested) has succeeded in crossing this boundary and suggesting in forms and colours something of the struggle which the human soul undergoes as it wrestles with the Invisible. Grünewald's work, in all its strangeness, can best be understood in relation to the whole literature of medieval mysticism, mainly Germanic in origin, in which the soul of the visionary, hounded down by the demon, endures nameless physical and psychological trials that leave it at the doors of death, whence, having purified its own essence, it emerges ready to unite itself with the divine essence. Not surprisingly, medieval Christians had found these mystical experiences impossible to express in terms of art, except by symbols so obscure as to conceal their true significance, or else by even less 'significant' exercises in tenderness and affectation.

In providing the artist with a certain distance between subject and object, the spirit of the Renaissance allowed him to objectify the mystical phenomenon, and thus to interpret it in paint. Anabaptism, carrying to its furthest conclusion the Lutheran idea of justification by faith, taught a kind of illuminism, claiming that the believing soul was inspired directly by God, manifesting himself through apparitions and dreams. No doubt Grünewald sensed the mystical element suffusing the burning faith of this other-worldly sect. In any case, he fashioned an intensely personal aesthetic with which to express his feelings: agitated drawing which plunged away from the object rather than defining it, combined with a marvellously rich colour of unparalleled brilliance. To furnish this rainbow palette of his, he engaged in alchemy, as is attested by the inventory carried out after his death: the expert called upon by the Frankfurt magistrate to itemize his belongings on behalf of his adoptive son found, among the stocks of colours in the studio, extraordinary powders and stones which he was quite unable to identify.

With a nervous brush, Grünewald spreads shifting colours, in films as flowing and transparent as watercolour, which form a kind of iridescent veil over the surface of the paint. And yet this artist who dares give shape to the unknowable is equally capable of lingering delightedly to paint a rose, a wash-tub, a doe, the tall pine-forests climbing the mountain sides. His virtuosity excels equally in 'representing' the visible world and in suggesting the invisible world, and in so doing developing the brush's potentialities more thoroughly, perhaps, than any subsequent artist: and yet it would seem that he exerted no influence on his contemporaries.

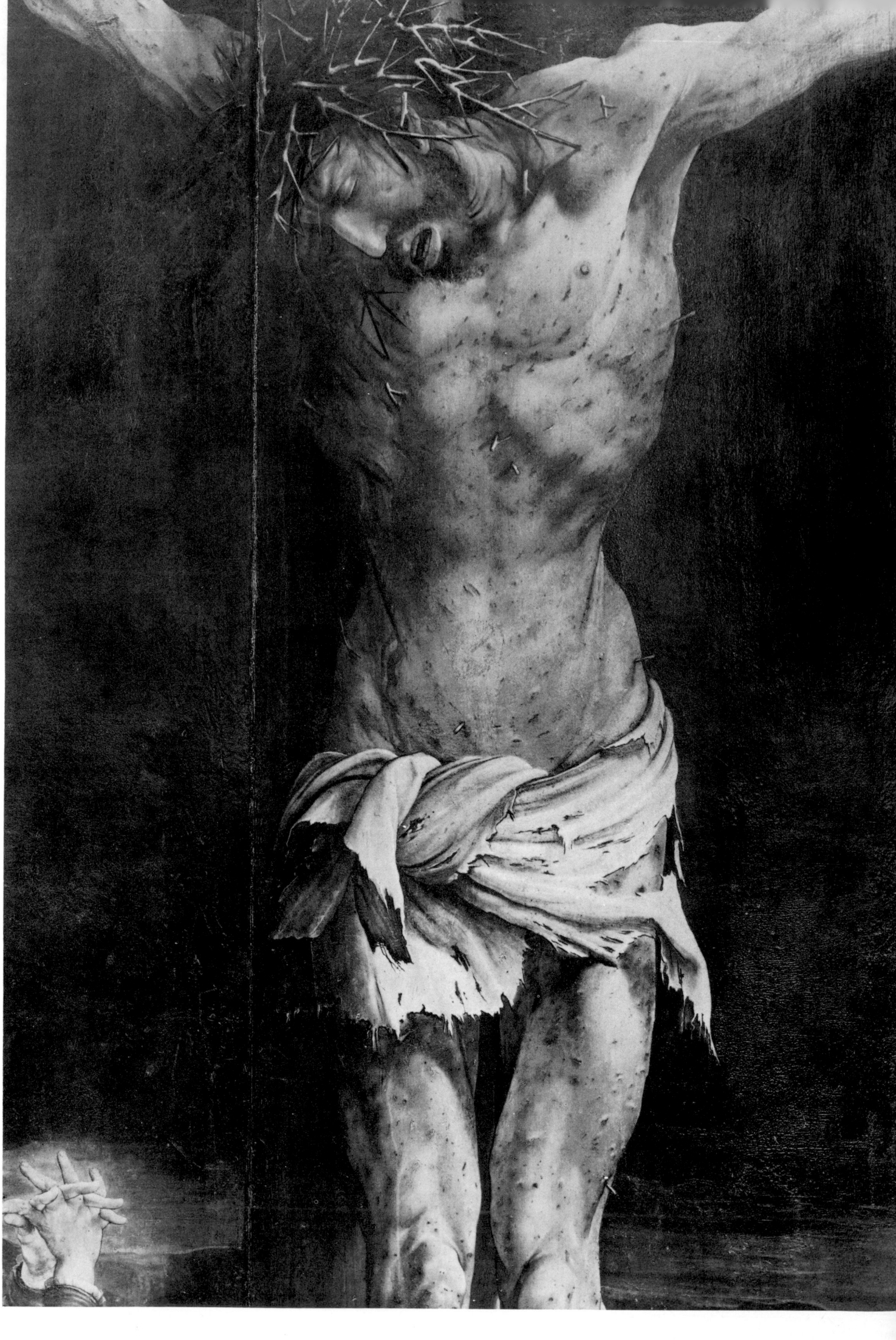

54 Grünewald (before 1480–1528).
Christ on the Cross, central panel of
the Isenheim Altarpiece. Colmar,
Musée d'Unterlinden.

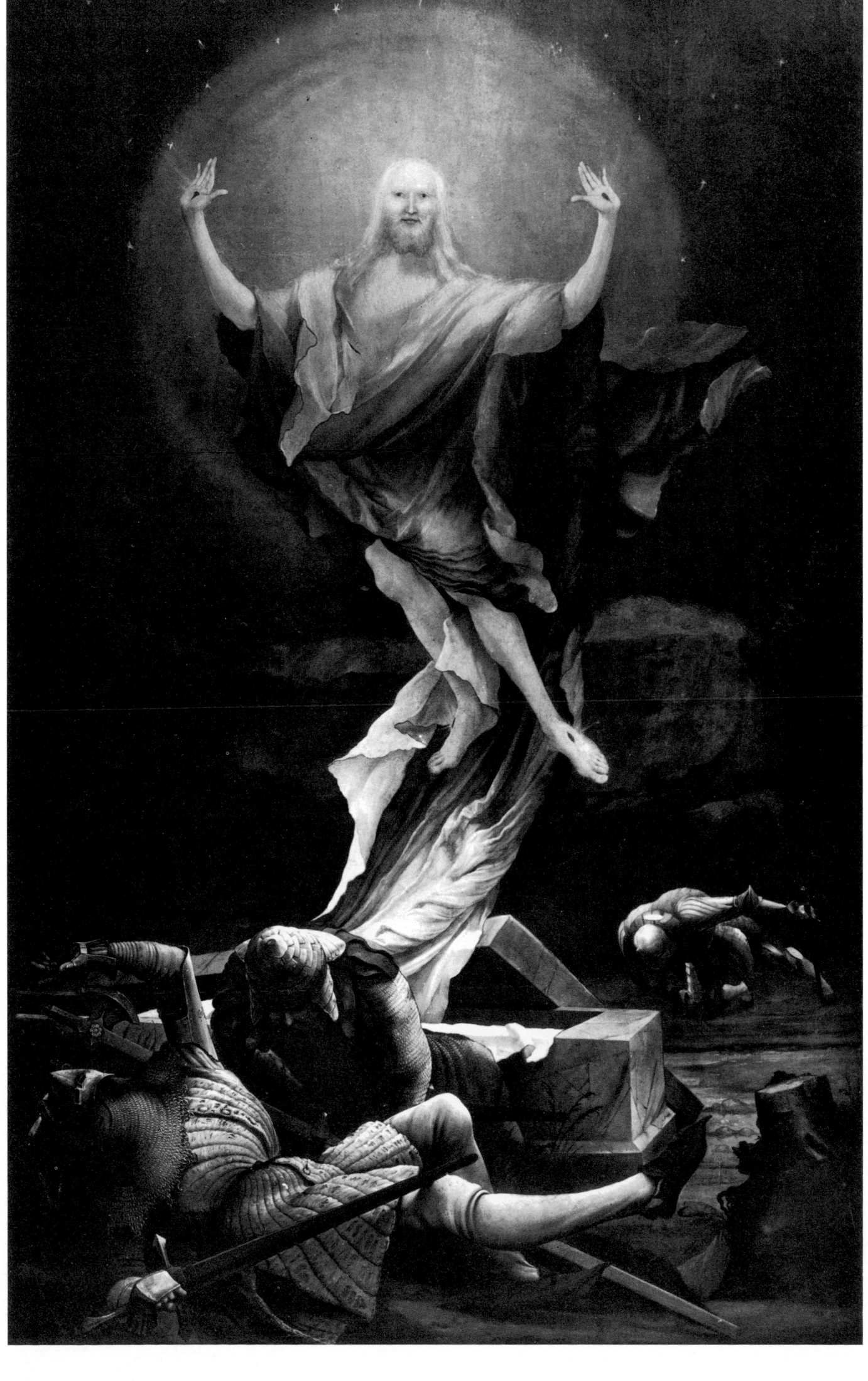

55 Grünewald. The Resurrection, volet of the Isenheim Altarpiece. Colmar, Musée d'Unterlinden.

Metamorphosed by sin into a tortured and hideous figure, the body of Christ is transformed into light, in the Resurrection. Endowed with a visionary genius and able to call upon a prodigious technique, Grünewald expressed, more effectively than El Greco or any other painter, the mystical soul at grips with the invisible.

67

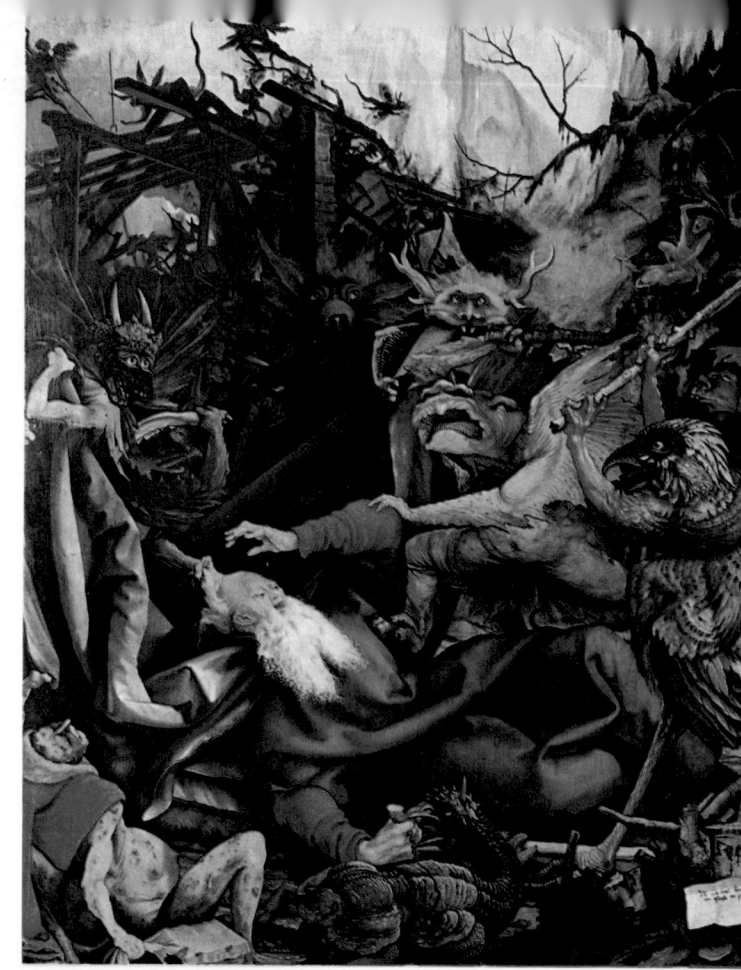

56 Hieronymus Bosch. Conflagration, detail of *The Temptation of St Anthony*. Lisbon, Museu Nacional de Arte Antiga.

Perhaps it was inevitable that so extraordinary a body of work should have been doomed to temporary oblivion. What is surprising is that there actually existed someone prepared to subsidize this genius's audacities, a patron in the person of a certain Italian, Guido Guersi, Preceptor of the Antonites, who commissioned the Isenheim Altarpiece and doubtless specified the iconographic programme. Grünewald must have found himself inspired, at the Isenheim monastery, by some special current of mystical awareness; certainly, none of the other rare surviving works by his hand possess the same degree of transcendent spirituality and artistic excellence. The Isenheim Altarpiece shares with many of the greatest works of art the quality of having originated in a providential encounter.

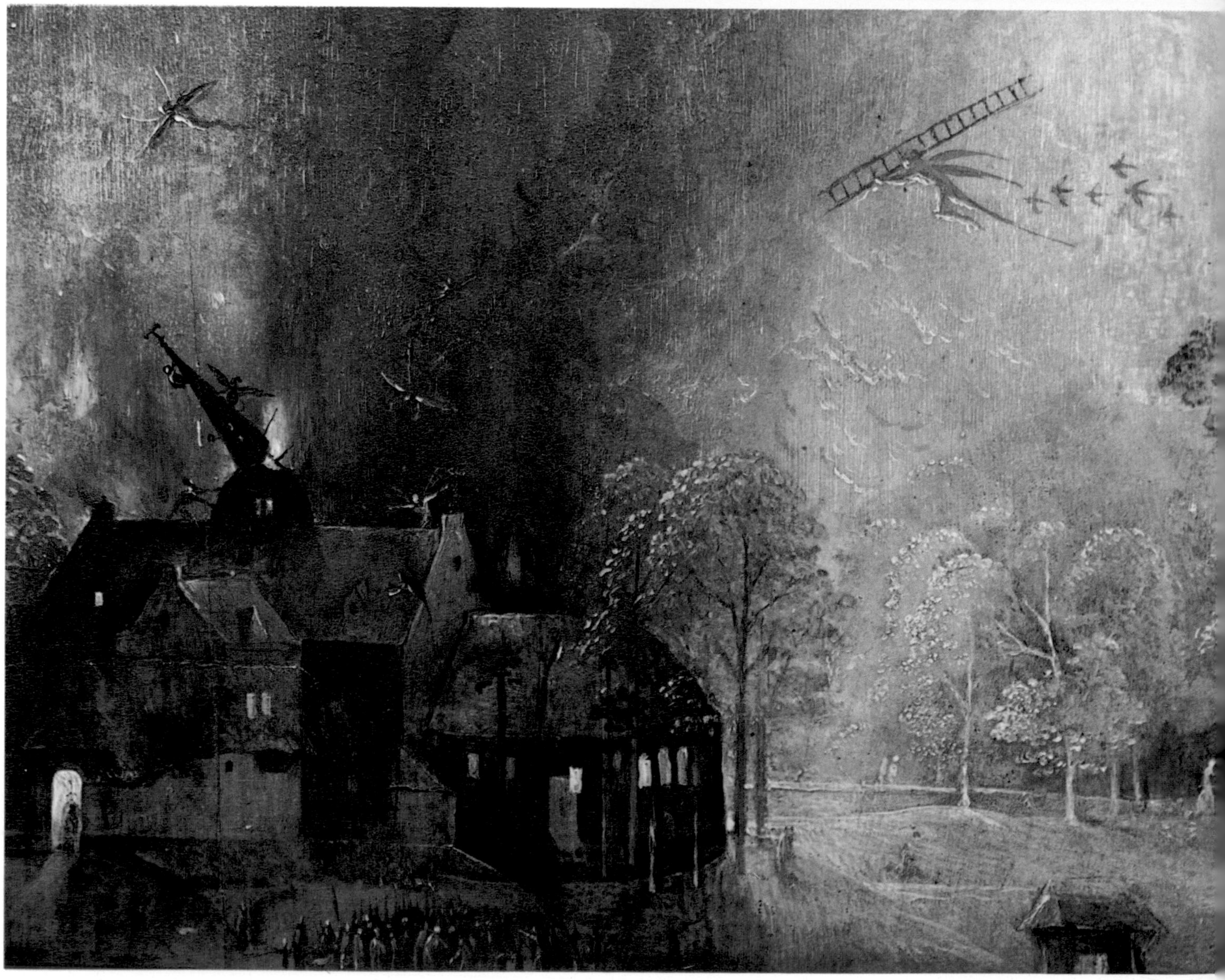

To paint his nightmare visions, Hieronymus Bosch freed himself from the objective technique practised in the Flemish school since van Eyck and invented a transparent handling, fluid and supple, the possibilities of which were understood, after him, only by Pieter Bruegel.

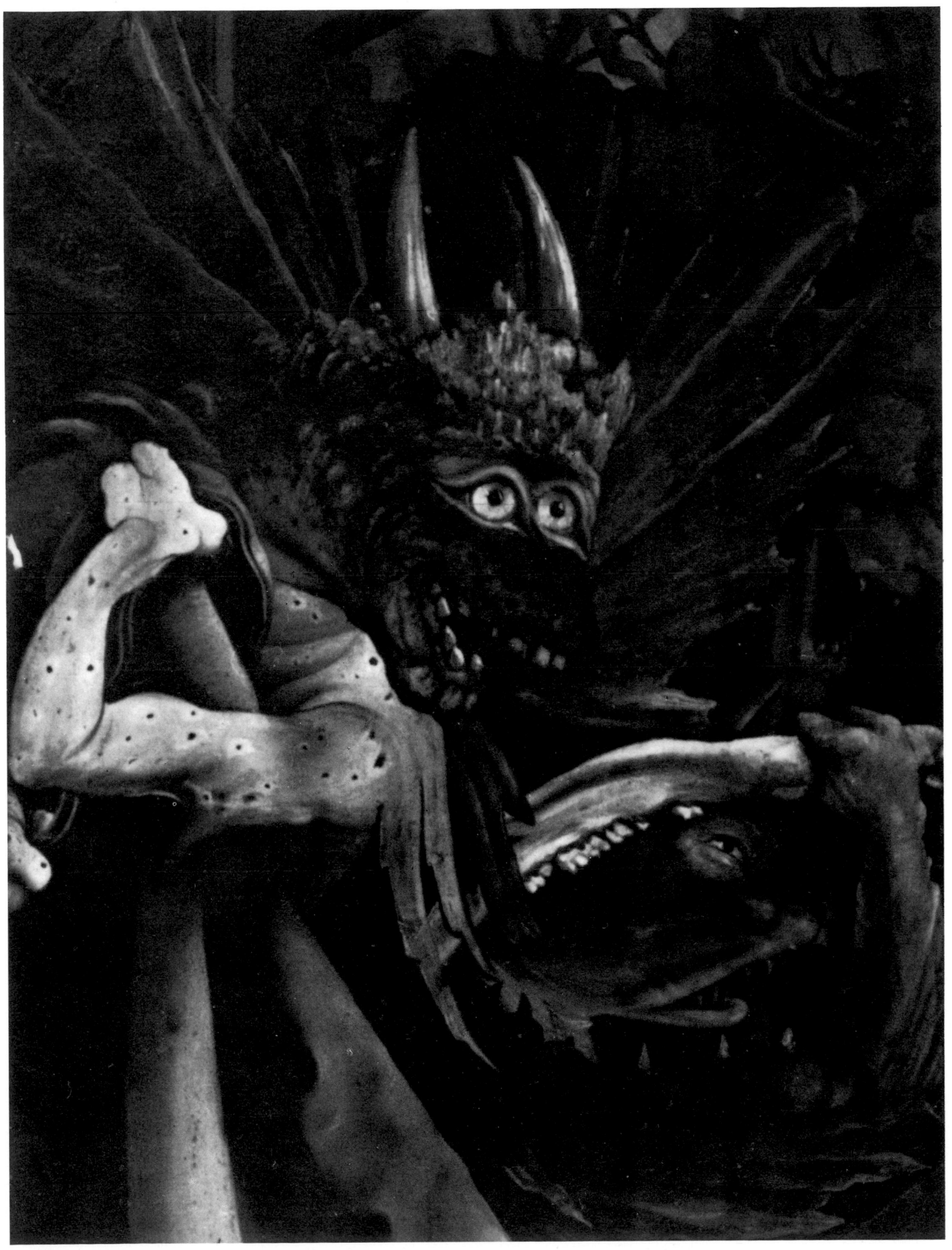

57–8 Grünewald. The Temptation of St Anthony, panel and detail of panel from the Isenheim Altarpiece. Colmar, Musée d'Unterlinden.

Far more vivid than those of Bosch, which seem to have emerged from some kind of surrealist trick shop, Grünewald's monsters are the most frightening ever produced by Western art.

59 Antonio Pisanello (1397–1455). Drawings of *Hanged men*. London, British Museum.

5 The primitives of the intellect

While van Eyck, in Flanders, eliminated the subjective aspect of the object as far as possible, some Italian artists were following the opposite course. Having become acutely aware of the unique position in nature granted him by his faculty of acquiring knowledge, man was no longer content to see himself as a mere component of the universe created by God, for whom all things are as one; he wanted, rather, to distinguish himself from the world by using his intellect to objectify the rest of creation. The dream that consumed Quattrocento man was many-faceted: to conceive a thing by integrating it into himself, making of it an 'object' reducible to the dimensions encompassed by the mind; to force the infinite to inscribe itself within the limits set out by intelligence; to imprison the universal within the pure geometry of thought; to make matter subservient to ideals; to reduce the organization of the world to an architecture based upon numerical relationships.

This era witnessed an heroic endeavour to remould the world on a human scale; and, as with the sharply receding perspective in the pictures of that time, everything converged towards the horizon of thought. Space, too, became plastic: ceasing to be synonymous with extension, space itself became measurable and thus architectural, arranging itself into a perspective that directs the eye towards its depth with the strictness of a reasoned argument. The statue, that is to say a completed, enclosed space independent of its environment, became the ideal formula among this generation of pioneers who had finally broken with the Middle Ages; the sculptors now constituted the avant-garde, preceding by at least a quarter of a century the painters who, in their turn, began to envisage their pictures as a construction of strict volumes, thus rejecting painting's traditional concern with the modulation of values and colours.

Masaccio, who died at the age of twenty-seven, stood out from among his fellow artists, perhaps by virtue of that mysterious faculty which sometimes endows with a prophetic vision those doomed to die young, as though some law of life demanded that every man should fulfil himself within an allotted time span. Masaccio attained by instinct the aims that the Italian school was to achieve only after more than a half century of research. Renewing Giotto's ideal of concentrated strength, he anticipated the sixteenth century: his feeling for harmonious composition foreshadowed Raphael, and in his conception of the human body as being powerful and broad, filled with a dramatic intensity, he preceded Michelangelo. During his short career, Masaccio elaborated bodies which seem made from the rock's very substance, surrounding them with a contracted space, a kind of condensation of a universe from which they appear to remain aloof (pls 60–1).

The notion, fostered by Berenson, of an essential antagonism between the Middle Ages and the Renaissance, and of a consequent division of Italian artists into clear-cut categories, is untenable. Certain painters seem to hover between the two worlds: Fra Angelico, Paolo Uccello and Masolino in Florence, Pisanello in Verona, Sassetta in Siena. A few prophetic geniuses such as Masaccio delivered their message as though deaf to the voices of the world, but for the most part the motivating factor lay in a resolution of the contradictions which are the natural elements of a human life. The drama was forged from the confrontation between an individual and an 'environment' which continually presented ambivalences resulting from the gap between generations, the disparity of social systems and the incompatible aspects of a dying civilization and one in the process of birth.

Long considered Italy's most characteristic representative of international Gothic, and the last exponent of medieval civilization, Pisanello is known to have left his native city to execute commissions in Rome and Naples, and appears to have been fully acquainted with developments in Florence. The extraordinary subtlety of his art results from a tension between the medieval civilization that had moulded him and the humanist aspirations with which he sympathized. This tension is revealed in his drawings, which bear witness to an exceptional, and often cruel, acuteness of vision (pl. 59).

Nor was Fra Angelico necessarily a man of the Middle Ages simply because he was a monk and a model of piety. Not only was there as yet no overt

60 Masaccio (1401–28). *The Crucifixion*. Naples, Museo Nazionale.

61 Masaccio. Fresco of *The Expulsion of Adam and Eve from Paradise*. Florence, Santa Maria del Carmine.

After the Giottesque style was finally abandoned by painters about 1400, Masaccio revived it, re-creating, in terser terms, its expressive power based upon the power of the human body, and thus foreshadowing the dramatic art of Michelangelo.

contradiction between faith and the new ways of thought but, on the contrary, the humanists fondly imagined that all problems could be resolved in agreement: St Antoninus, Bishop of Florence from 1446 to 1459, even went so far as to quote Ovid from the pulpit! Combining within himself the lofty theological intellectualism of the Dominicans and the emotional intensity of the Franciscans, Fra Angelico was nevertheless an entirely modern painter, concerned to establish a scheme of relationship between the figure and its environment, and to discover the correct principles of relief in defining bodies (*pl. 62*). He was just as fascinated by questions of perspective as was Uccello, but he preferred curved spaces, symbolizing harmony, to the dizzy

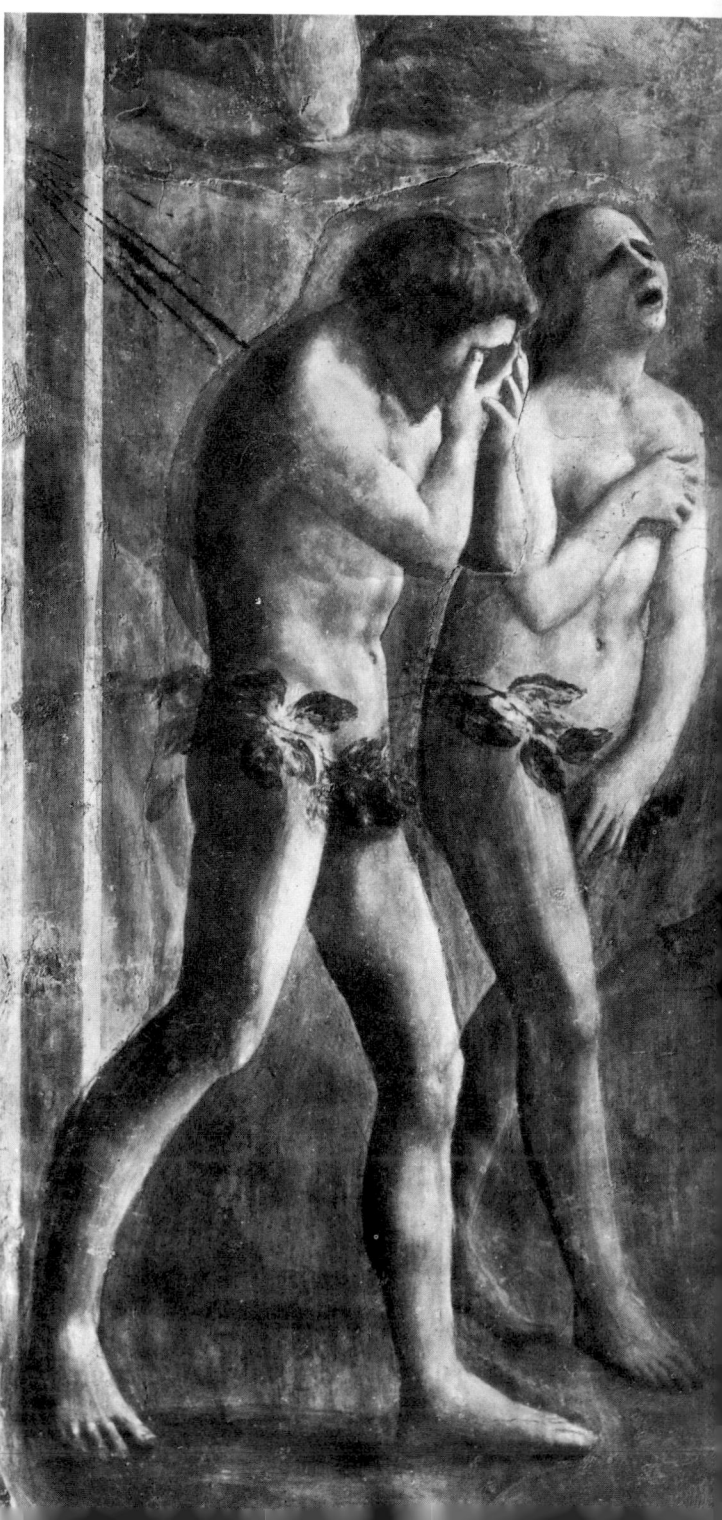

rectilinear vistas of which the latter dreamed. And this great Christian was the first to paint a realistic paradise in which the ring of angels and the chosen were arranged in depth in a true space.

As for Paolo Uccello, he was perhaps the most tormented of all these artists, suffering from a fundamental dualism that resulted from a critical conflict within himself between the ethical standards of the Middle Ages and those of the Renaissance. Not that Uccello was a 'transitional' artist, but, although he was deeply attracted by the new values, he rejected any idea of subservience to them; his work constitutes a final salute to the dying Middle Ages, to the decadent world of chivalry and hagiography (*pl. 63*). The contradictory feelings about the relationship between man and God which troubled him are reflected clearly in his work, engendering two forms of religious art, one narrative and poetic, the other austere, biblical and grandiose. Purely humanist speculations upon form and space appear on the fringe of this religious faith, and the resulting tension, assuming dramatic overtones, makes Uccello, who defended his independence fiercely, one of the most attractive artists of his century.

The second generation of the Florentine school found itself faced with a crisis. Knowledge was identified with creation: for the Quattrocentro, the technical procedures which the Middle Ages had considered to be the essential feature of the work of art were now viewed merely as an 'application' of the creative process, which was in itself a strictly mental elaboration. The search for knowledge replaced the acquisition of skill as man's chief mental objective, and with this new supremacy of the intellect, perception was now identified with conception. The automatic intellectual process of converting anything perceived into a concept meant that nothing remained obscure, in a mental world in which light reigned as evenly and as brightly as it did in certain paintings of the period. The dark forces of the human psyche were to remain ignored in art for four hundred years. Quattrocento man was essentially a conscious man, and the art he created lacked lyricism, except when a self-centred intelligence became intoxicated with its own virtuosity. This quality endowed the Florentine artists with the freshness of primitives: they may be called the primitives of the intellect.

Alesso Baldovinetti, with his cold rationalism, confronted this problem very directly, as Leonardo was to do later on; for Baldovinetti, beauty could only be attained through the application of rigorous laws. His *œuvre*, like Leonardo's, was small and entirely experimental. Like Leonardo in relation to his *Mona Lisa*, he attempted in a series of closely

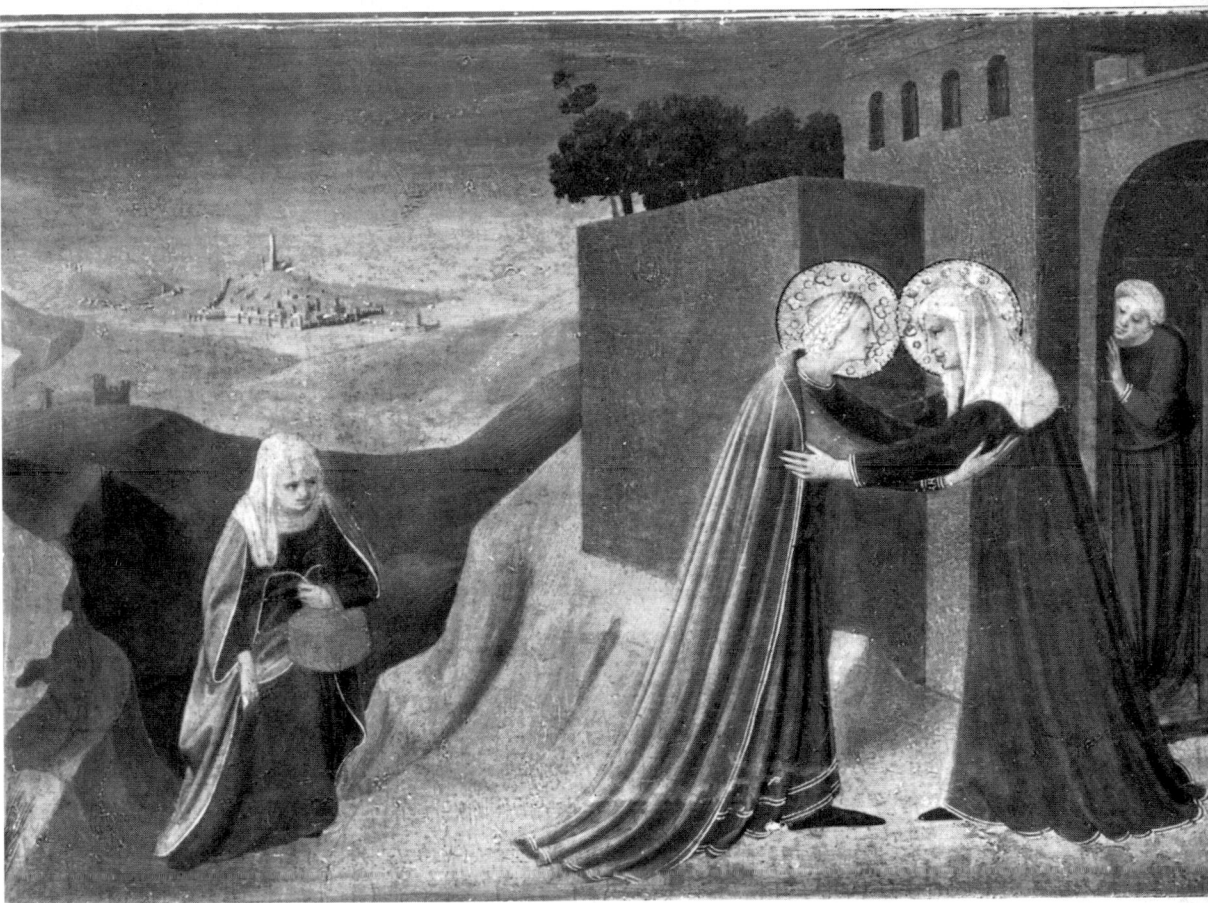

related pictures to match the perfection he had achieved with his *Virgin and Child* (the Louvre), not only his masterpiece but one of the chief glories of Florentine art. And he anticipated Leonardo's landscapes with his vision of the universal, schematized in a cartographic projection (*pl. 65*).

The whole of the Quattrocentro must be placed under the sign of energy. Man in this epoch had an insatiable desire to understand, and the intellect's power of exploration seemed limitless to him. The sole limit to a concept was deemed to be the one immediately above it, embracing a larger generality. Increasingly sharply defined intellectual experiments evolved from each other with implacable logic, following a quickened rhythm which testifies to an enormously energetic mental activity in these artists' workshops. However there were inevitable limitations to this craze for causality. Intelligence, transmuting everything it touched into abstraction, devoured the world without satisfying its hunger, and was soon reduced to feeding off itself. The immediate intellectualization of perception stifled intuitive inspiration at its source. Compared with genuinely open-minded creators such as Fra Angelico and Paolo Uccello, Andrea del Castagno appears as a dry calculator, imagining that he can simplify the problem of humanism by

62 Fra Angelico (*c.* 1400–55). The Visitation, predella of *The Annunciation*. Cortona, San Domenico.

Fra Angelico was not, as has been suggested, an artist attuned belatedly to medieval feeling but, on the contrary, a pioneer. Like Masaccio, he rediscovered the expressive value of the human body, adding to this a new perception of landscape.

63 Uccello (1397–1475). *The Rout of San Romano*. London, National Gallery.

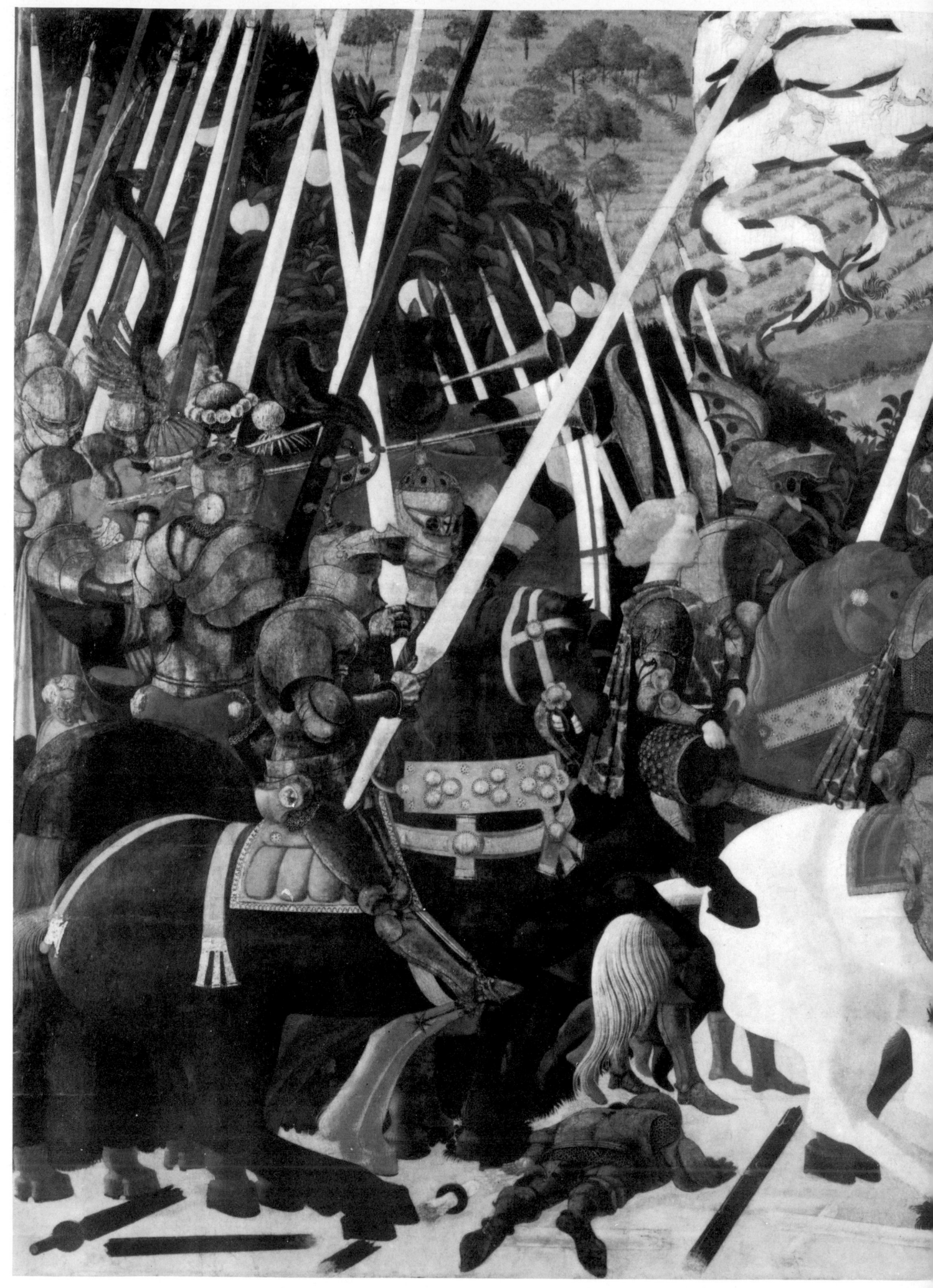

Through the theme of battle, Uccello affirmed the power of the human body in action, reduced by its armour and weapons to a geometrical concision.

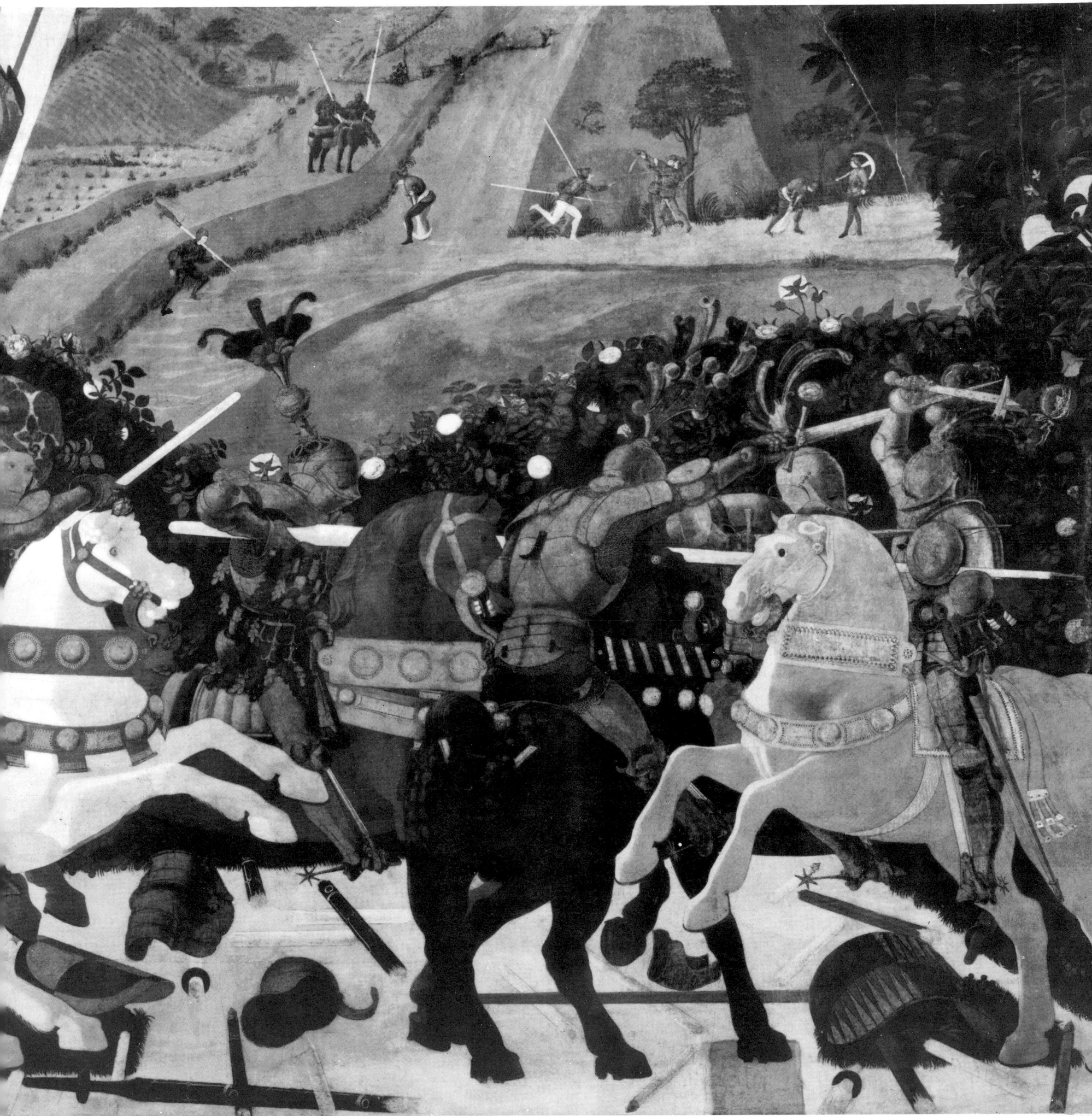

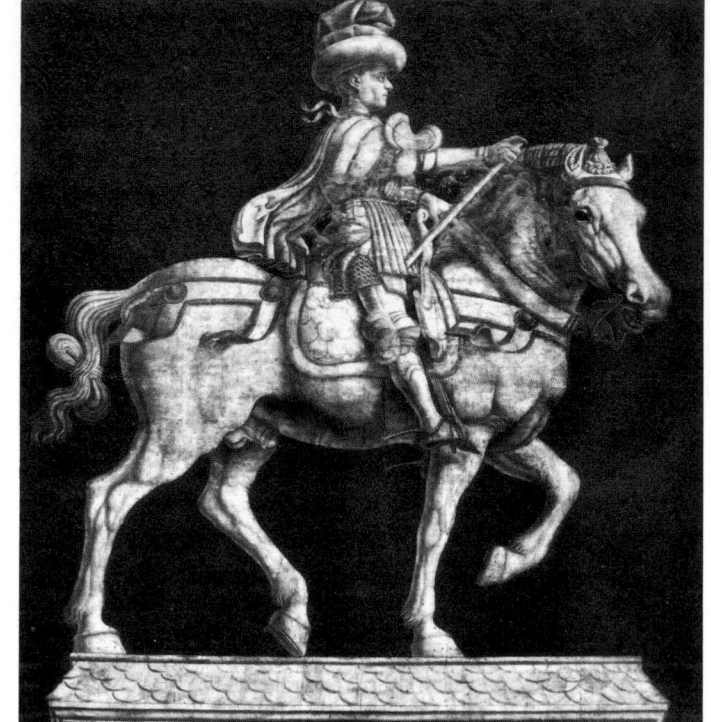

reducing the image of the world to man's dimensions, and hoping to increase man's presence by using paint to construct facsimiles of statues (*pl. 64*).

The Florentine school died of anaemia through granting exclusive rights to the intelligence and ignoring the virtues of the imagination. The amiable and facile eclecticism of Filippo Lippi, Pesellino, Gozzoli and Ghirlandaio is to some extent a phenomenon of academicism. The case of Botticelli typifies the intellectual sickness which was gnawing at the soul of Florence. This mystical spirit, attracted by lyricism and, to an even greater degree, by harmony, found himself condemned by this intellectualism to a state of constant agitation. The languid sadness of his Madonnas, the nostalgia of his portraits, the nervous style which gives a spasmodic rhythm to his compositions and exacerbates the sharpness of line and the leaping contours of the figures, reflect the death throes of Florentine art. Botticelli is like a man who discovers the charms of the world too late and reaches out to seize them just as they fade away.

To trace the later development of the Quattrocento's great voyage of discovery it is necessary to move away from Florence and examine other schools which owed their emancipation to that city. In Umbria, Piero della Francesca inherited Paolo Uccello's passion for perspective and Masaccio's sense of grandeur. No one affirmed the pride of Quattrocento man with loftier dignity than this strange artist.

The Quattrocento's pride in its conquest of the intellectual process endowed it with a sense of godlike superiority over the forces of nature which found particularly appropriate expression in the equestrian statue: this image, the century's obsession and Leonardo's despair, symbolizing intelligent power taming brute force, represented the human demiurge and exercised a powerful influence over the sculptors of the period. A few painters, such as Uccello and Castagno, were also attracted by the subject, but others, including Masaccio, Piero della Francesca and Mantegna, preferred the image of man to stand alone, as though proud of the privilege of verticality. Piero's man, a statue planted in the ground, seems to revel as much in his *stasis* as medieval man did in his *ecstasis* (*pl. 67*). The *Annunciation* in the Perugia polyptych (*pl. 66*) offers us two statues petrified by pride, lost in the contemplation of their wholly autonomous existence, separated by an unbridgeable gulf of space. The instinct for relationship no longer inhabits these opaque bodies, cut off as they are from a nature which is, nevertheless, more realistic than that of Masaccio. But this nature, having ceased to possess an intrinsic value, has become nothing more than an object of domination. The will to power now permeating individual consciousness provided the impetus for the passionate belief in progress which was to dominate humanity, separating the individual from each object as soon as its conquest was achieved, excluding any possibility of sympathy between the thinking self and things.

The intellectual ferment of Florence worked on a powerful imagination to produce the greatest painter of the Quattrocento in the person of Mantegna. This precociously brilliant artist was only sixteen when he started work on the fresco cycle for the Eremitani Church in Padua which included four scenes from the *Life of St James*, destroyed together with the church during the Second World War. It would seem that in order to gain recognition for his genius the young man had to surmount opposition, starting with that of his adoptive father and master Francesco Squarcione, with whom he quarrelled in 1448, the same year that he signed a contract for the Eremitani commission, and whose house he promptly left in his urge for independence. The spiritual son of Donatello, whose living tradition he perpetuated in Padua, Mantegna was well acquainted with the scientific preoccupations of the Florentine painters, but, although enriched by their knowledge, he treated all the problems of foreshortening and perspective as a virtuoso, resolving them intuitively. To the Florentine discoveries he added a new concept which carried within it the seeds of the future in painting.

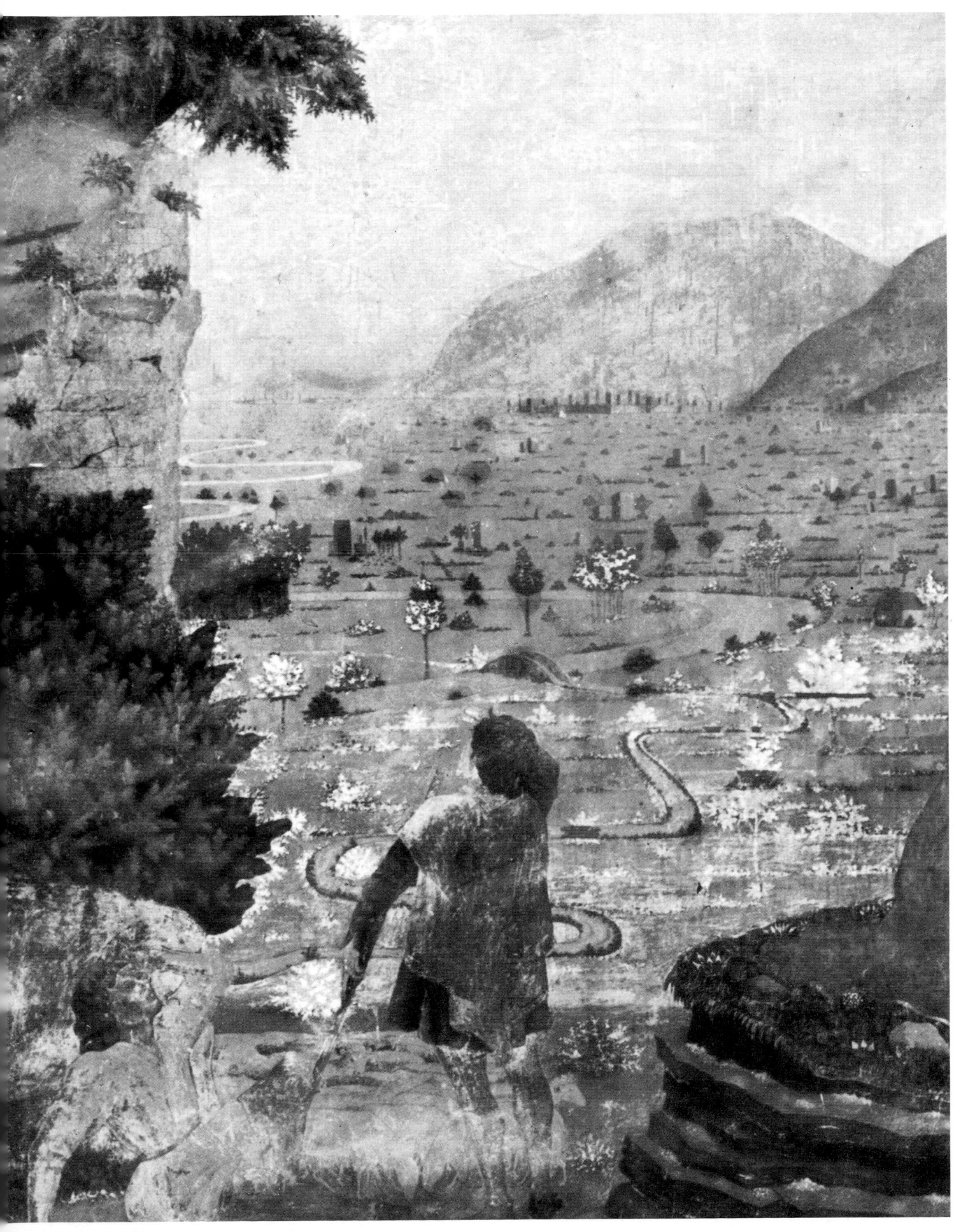

Baldovinetti and Piero della
Francesca invented the cartographic
landscape, a sort of panoramic view
of the universe, which Leonardo was
to make use of in his *Mona Lisa*.

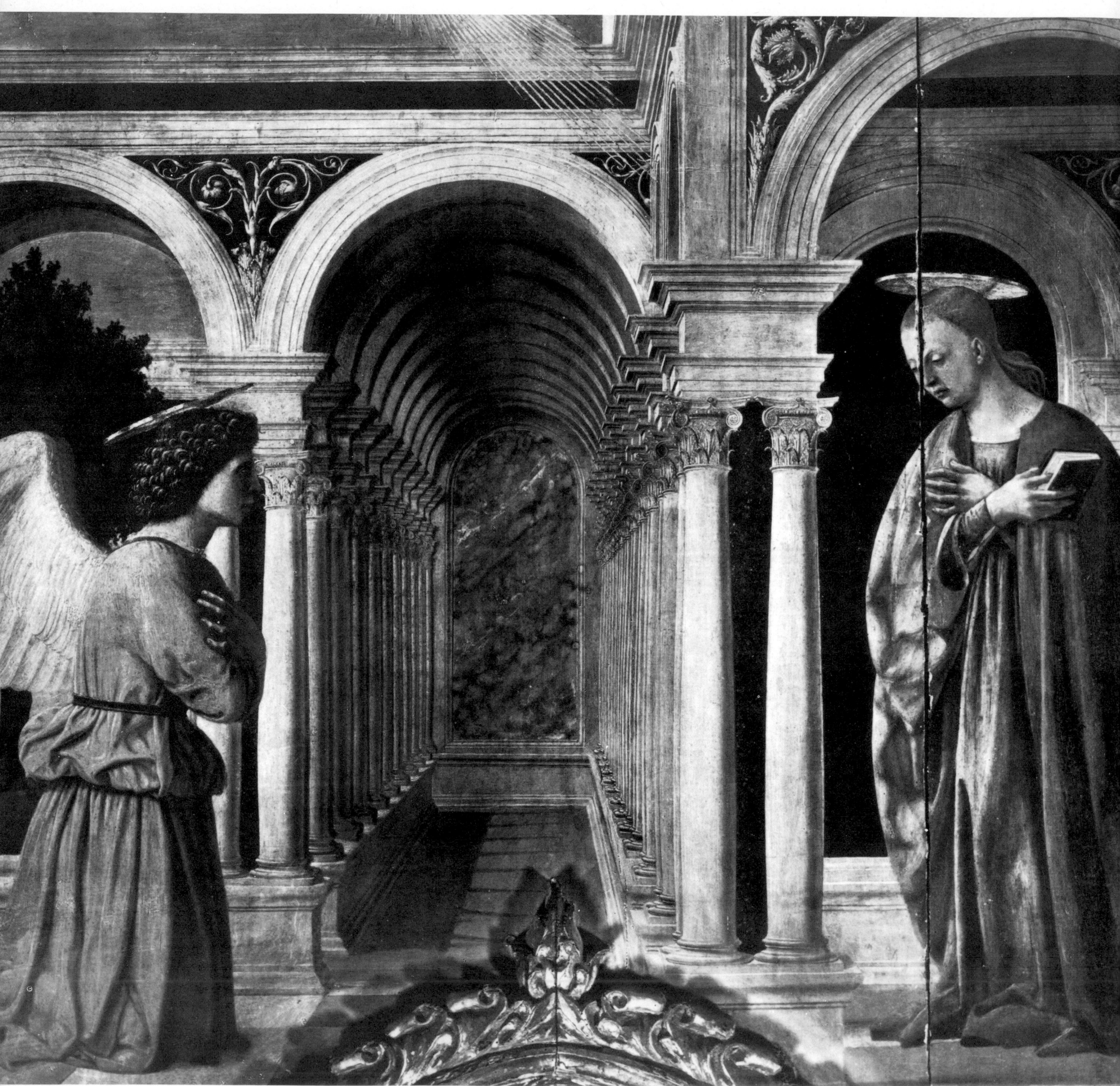

The Florentines' intellectualism made them visually adept at perceiving form (the soul of substance, as the body is its matter), for vision is the most intellectual of our senses: the operation of seeing transforms itself of its own accord into the operation of conceiving, and is always preceded to a greater or lesser extent by that of foreseeing. Mantegna, a northerner whose intelligence had not stifled his instinctive faculties, perceived beyond form the presence of the mysterious world of matter. He added to the spatial values of the Florentines what Berenson has called 'tactile values'; not content with the visual appearance of things, he set out to convey the illusion of material texture. Matter, which painters thenceforward applied themselves to evoking in all its subtle variations, first appeared to Mantegna in the guise that was nearest his own geometric vision of the world, that of mineral. Looking at a picture by Mantegna, one can almost feel the smoothness of the marble surfaces, the coldness of the metals, the hardness of the corals (*pl. 68*).

The use made by Mantegna of all these visual data went far beyond the stage of experimentation, for he achieved a synthesis of all the discoveries of the Quattrocento, creating a logical universe rich in varied forms and possessing laws to control the relationships between beings and things. Mantegna lived in intimate association with the natural world, as the backgrounds of his pictures reveal: a Lilliputian human and animal world teems there, all its gestures and attitudes accurately recorded. The man who painted the rabbits in *The Agony in the Garden* (*pl. 69*) is a poet sensitive to bucolic charm. With Mantegna we are very far away from the urbane painters of Florence, living in a world that is a pure mental abstraction. All forms perceived by this artist undergo a strange mutation and become lapidary. Mantegna's imagination is a spring which turns everything to stone.

The latinization which Mantegna attempted to impose upon the world he depicted provided an additional stimulus for the imagination to travel back in time. Obsessed with antiquity, he achieved in paint Alberti's dream of re-creating in modern society the institutions of the ancient world. No other painter except Poussin has possessed such a highly developed sense of history.

Even with these passionately lucid men of the Quattrocento, it was inevitable that eventually the obscure forces of the unconscious should reappear. Towards the end of the century, artists were often visited by the spirit of the bizarre. The satirical mythologies of Piero di Cosimo (*pl. 70*) and the senile inspirations of Giovanni de Paolo beckon us

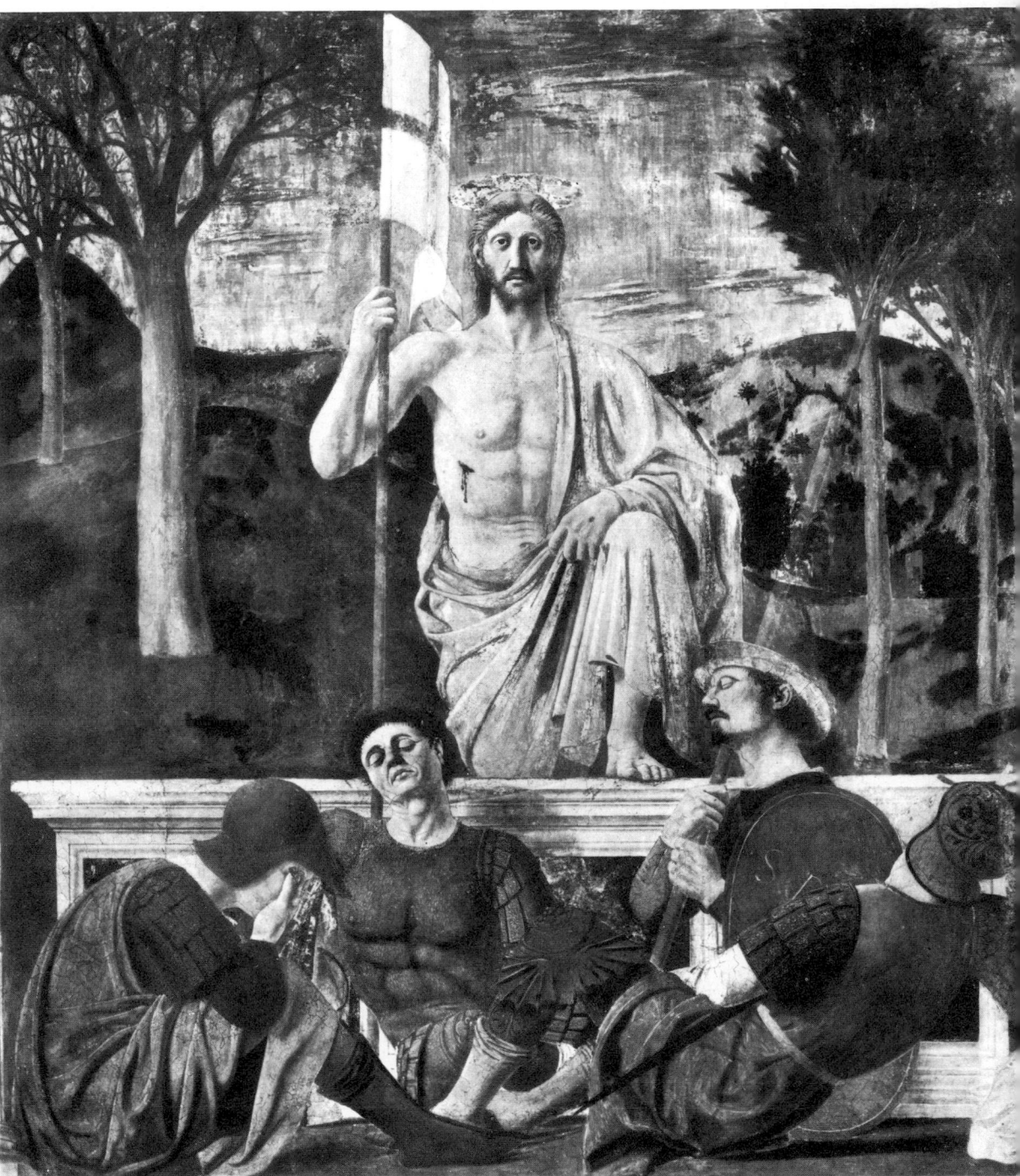

67 Piero della Francesca. *The Resurrection*. Borgo San Sepolcro, Palazzo Pubblico.

Piero della Francesca preceded Michelangelo in celebrating the power of the human body. He portrays his revived Christ as a Hercules.

66 Piero della Francesca (1410/20–92). *The Annunciation*. Perugia, Accademia.

Filled with the loftiest sense of humanist pride, the figures of Piero della Francesca stand as though petrified in the solitude created by their will to power.

79

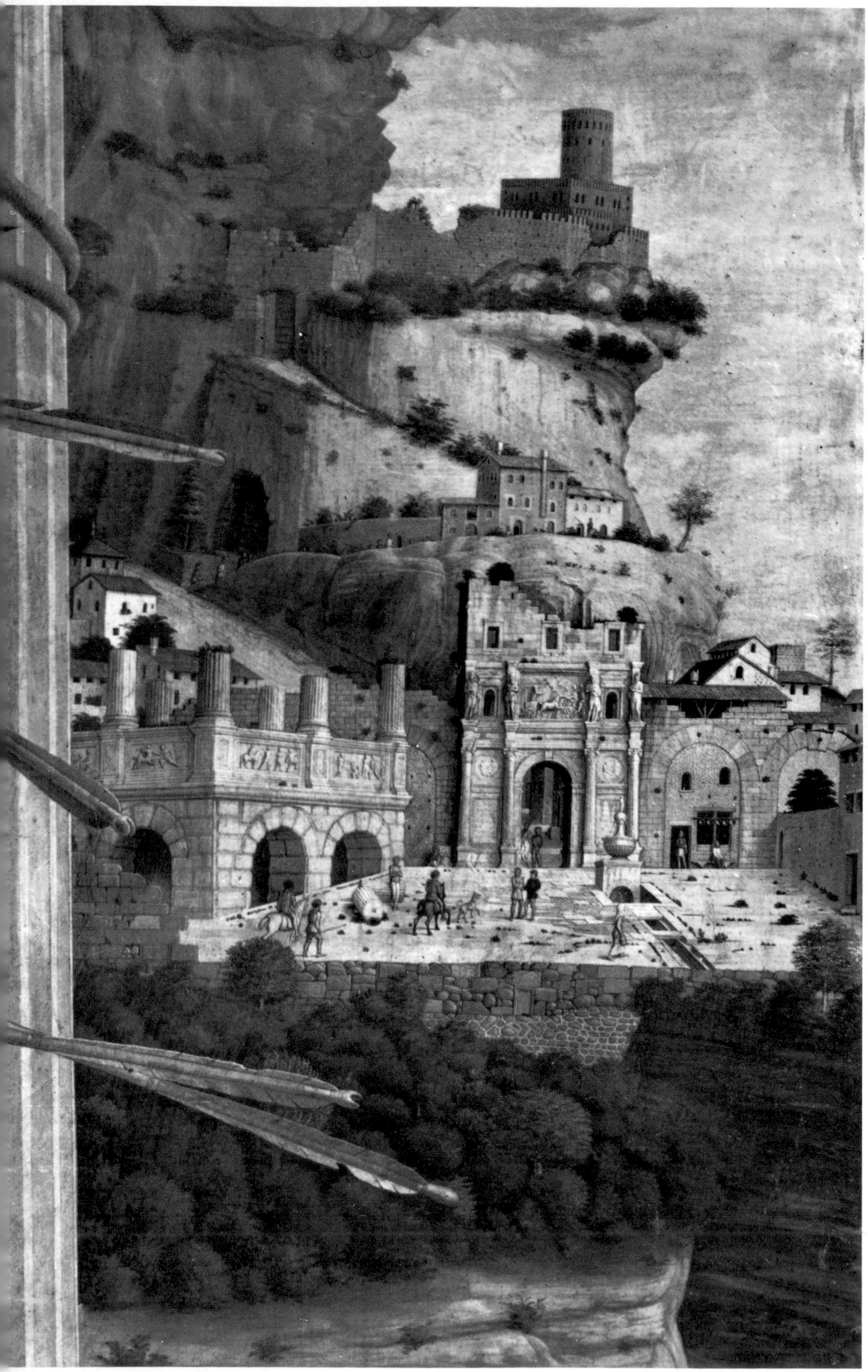

into an inverse world for which Piero della Francesca's spectral impassiveness has already prepared us. The fantastic exercised a particularly strong influence in the schools of northern and central Europe. These regions, while still under the spell of the legends of the Middle Ages, found themselves suddenly exposed to an art created by surveyors and geometers. The imaginations which for centuries had been perfectly attuned to the supernatural transformed the precise world of Florence into a chimerical universe. The school of Ferrara, which produced Cosimo Tura (*pl. 71*), Ercole dei Roberti and Francesco del Cossa, surpassed itself in this predilection for the fantastic. The impression of unreality conveyed by this art resulted from the skilful use of means going beyond the senses' normal perceptions: exaggerated foreshortenings and tactile values, extravagant projections, soaring architectures, impossible rocky constructions, human figures with convulsive gestures or paralysed limbs. The surrealist movement, which has promoted a return to favour of these strange painters, helps us to understand their neurotic psychology.

This strange phenomenon affected the whole of northern Italy to a greater or lesser extent, including Mantua and Venice. The cause of this uneasy passion may perhaps be traced to the German influence which penetrated northern Italy far more profoundly than the rest of the peninsula. Italy was not exempt from the flamboyant Gothic which had swept the whole of northern Europe at that time, and the tense, jerky style of the Ferrarese recalls that of certain Bavarian painters. The artists of Ferrara have the same relationship to those of Florence that Milan Cathedral has to the architecture of Michelozzo.

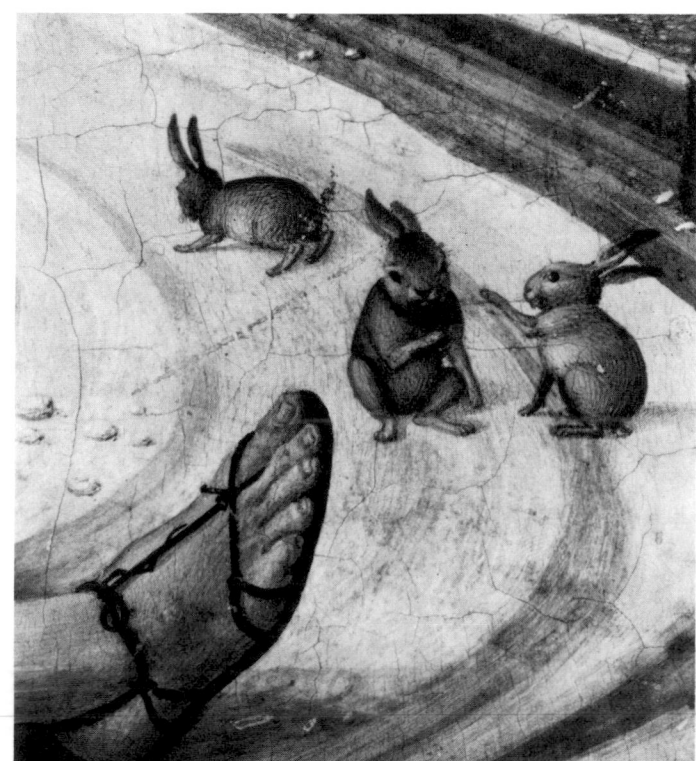

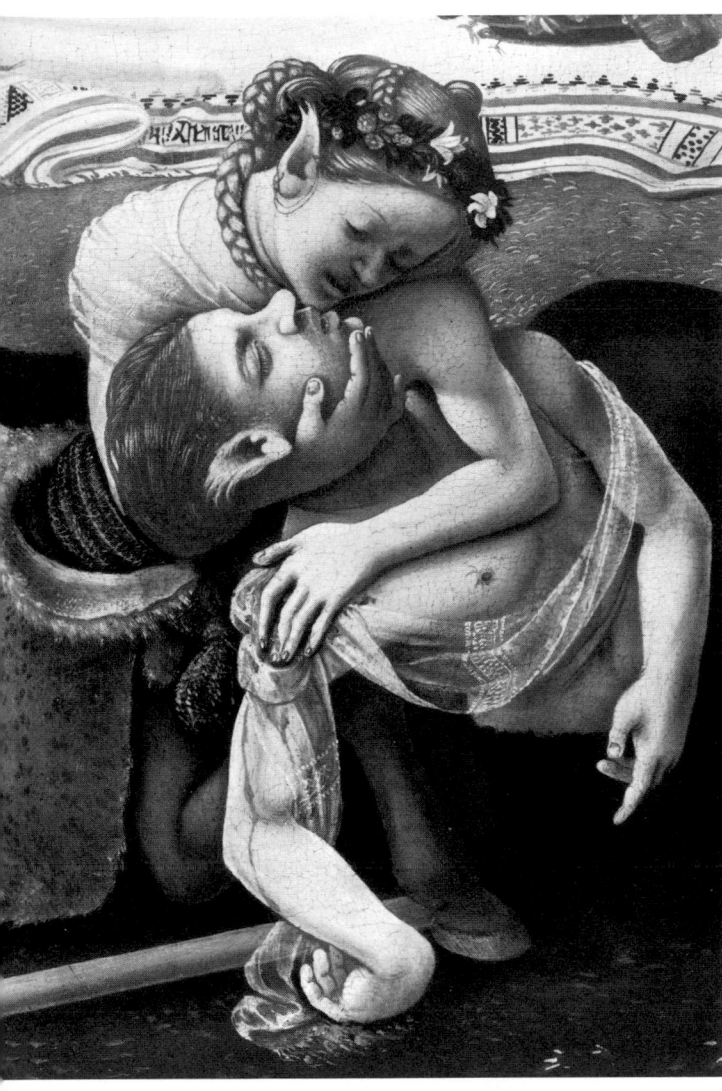

70 Piero di Cosimo (1462–1521). Detail of *Battle of the Centaurs and the Lapiths*. London, National Gallery.

71 Cosimo Tura (*c.* 1430–95). *St George and the Dragon*. ▶
Ferrara, Cathedral Museum.

In a spirit of protest against classicism, certain Italian artists imagined a fantastic world freed from its restrictive rules.

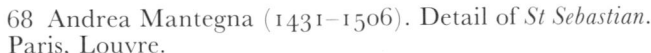

68 Andrea Mantegna (1431–1506). Detail of *St Sebastian*. Paris, Louvre.

69 Andrea Mantegna. Detail of *The Agony in the Garden*. London, National Gallery.

Mantegna is the first universal painter, including in his work not only an imaginary world inspired by a re-creation of antiquity but also nature in its most familiar details.

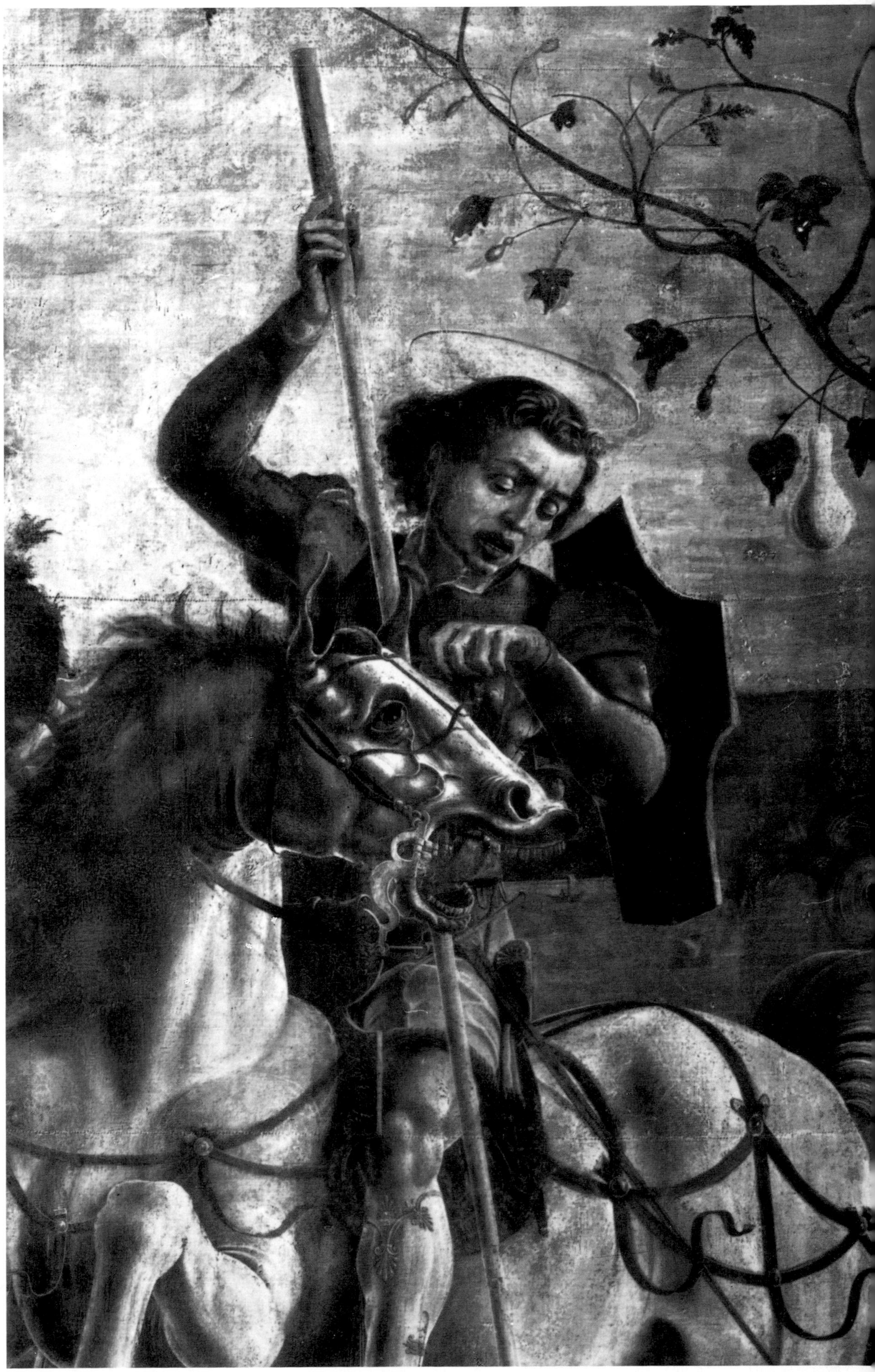

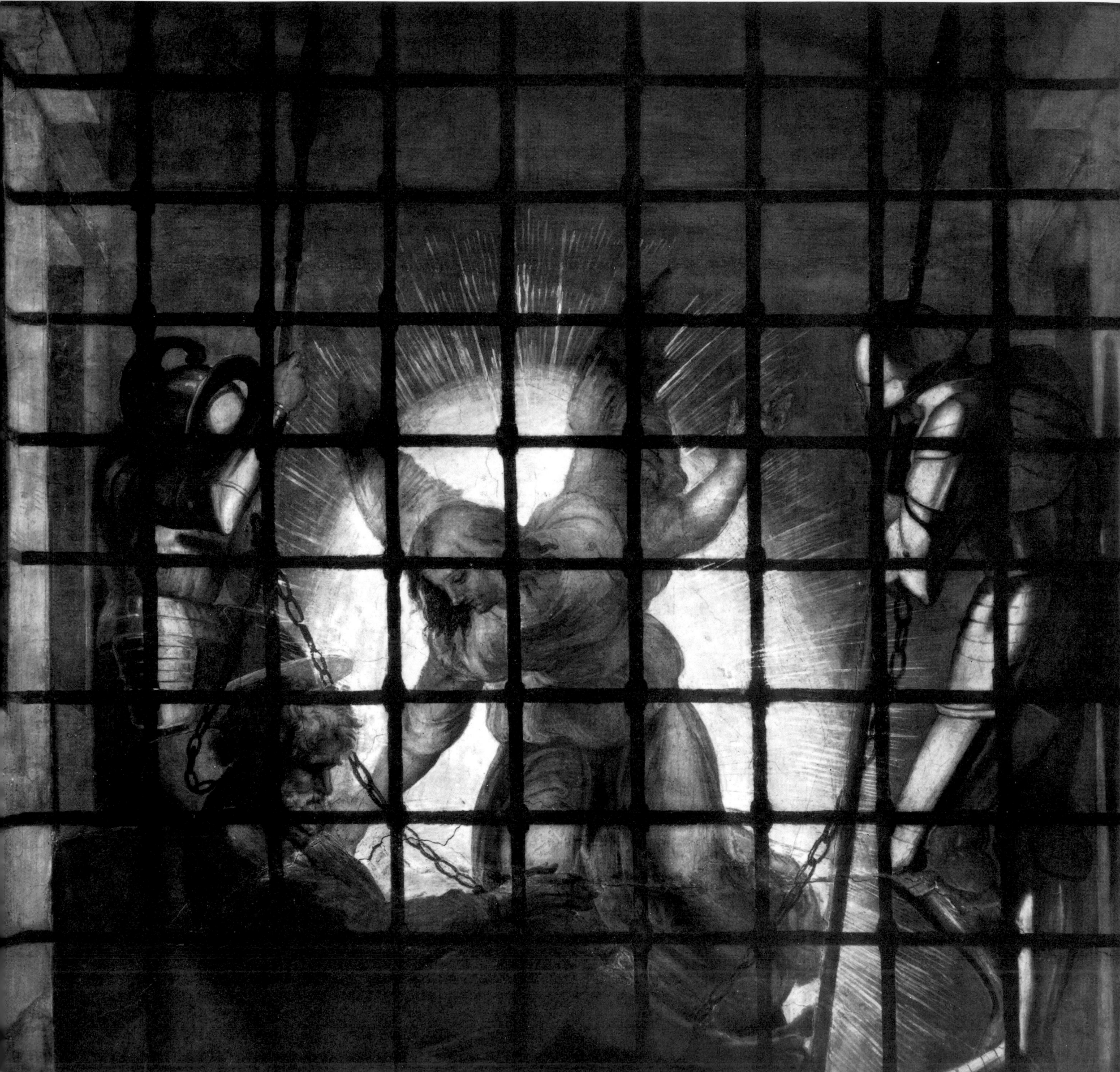

6 The creators of classicism

72 Raphael (1483–1520). The angel of light, detail of *The Liberation of St Peter*. Vatican, Stanza d'Eliodoro.

The moments of classicism are always brief, but certainly none can have been so fleeting as the Italian classicism which reached its creative peak between 1508 and 1512, when Michelangelo and Raphael were both working within a few yards of each other at the Vatican. The history of art has never paid sufficient tribute to the few patrons who have just as much right to be considered pioneers as the artists they sponsored. Whether or not Julius II was in fact as uncouth as he has been made out to be, his cultural awareness clearly extended to a sense of grandeur and an intuition for what might best serve his glory, and it is to his credit that he allowed each artist to accomplish his artistic destiny. One can only imagine the bewilderment that would have overcome Michelangelo had he been called upon to undertake the apotheosis of peace in the Stanza della Segnatura, or Raphael's dismay at having to interpret the sombre universe of the Old Testament on the ceiling of the Sistine Chapel. The pope's confidence in Michelangelo was so great that he allowed him to choose his own themes, thus initiating a revolutionary change in the status of the artist, who was thenceforward held in esteem as a creator of ideas as well as of forms. The Old Testament terrors which were to become one of the most powerful ingredients of the Protestant revolt snarl down from the ceiling of the Sistine Chapel solely by grace of Michelangelo.

The modern movement has based itself upon a hostility towards the aesthetic principles set out by Raphael and transmitted through three centuries as far as Ingres; when the fauves consigned all museums to the flames, it was above all Raphael's pictures that they had in mind. In André Malraux's *Les Voix du Silence*, Raphael rates only two illustrations, against fourteen for El Greco. (And there were none at all in the first edition, published as *La Psychologie de l'art*.) On the other hand, at the beginning of the twentieth century Salomon Rienach, in his *Apollo*, had allotted eighteen reproductions to Raphael and not a single one to El Greco. We should not allow ourselves to be guided by either of these extreme attitudes, but rather consider dispassionately whether Raphael brought anything really new to the art of painting. It can

be affirmed quite objectively that he was more of an innovator than Leonardo.

Leonardo's supreme genius sought to crystallize in one simple formula the relations between the figure and its frame. The *Mona Lisa* (*pl. 73*) is already contained in Baldovinetti's *Virgin and Child* (*pl. 74*), a hieratic image of perfection, strictly circumscribed and standing out against a cartographic landscape which is in effect a plan of the universe. In the *Mona Lisa*, the figure and landscape lose this abstraction. The blandness of the modelling gives spiritual warmth to the figure and atmospheric moistness to the elements of nature; but this animation is still obtained in the Florentine manner, by *sfumato* blending of light and dark, and thus invariably through the medium of drawing rather than, as is the case with Giorgione, through the living quality of the colour.

In his aim to release the inexhaustible resources of painting, Leonardo, basing his technical researches on principles developed more or less directly from Pliny, made heroic efforts to perfect the means he had acquired in the workshop of Verrocchio, only to reach a deadlock which compromised the very future of his pictures. He might possibly have bent destiny to his will, had his mind not been so thirsty for knowledge in every field. Leonardo made painting the supreme gesture of a philosophy aiming to achieve understanding of nature through its re-creation, giving a new vigour, in terms of profane expression, to the ancient beliefs in the equal validity of the image and its double; the fascination still exercised on the public mind by the *Mona Lisa* is proof enough of his success in this aim. But for Leonardo painting was simply one mode of investigation among many, and one to which he devoted only a very small part of his time.

The four years during which Raphael and Michelangelo were both engaged in painting projects at the Vatican, working warily in concert, constitute one of the privileged moments of history: these two artists together assumed at this time an archetypal value in the future development of forms, achieving the ideal of humanist culture in the totality of its ambivalence.

Raphael's reputation has suffered because his

impressionable nature allowed itself to be inspired by the successive environments in which he lived. Such virtues of sociability are now considered reprehensible in an artist; in our own age genius is visualized as frowning and sullen, and is therefore more readily recognized in Michelangelo's instinct for revolt than in Raphael's conformism. Yet Raphael's creative genius was the equal of Michelangelo's; it is in means of expression rather than in quality that they differ.

Michelangelo was passionately attached to the city of his birth, anguished by its decline from power, deeply frustrated in his unrequited patriotism, his republican convictions unsatisfied, his religious hopes deceived. His withdrawn personality (which is revealed, incidentally, by a morphopsychological analysis of his face) could only exist in terms of defiance of his environment and rejection of the external world, leading eventually to an obsessive assertion of his self in essential conflict with the non-self. On the other hand, Raphael's profound nature, combined with the influence of the cultural atmosphere of his native Urbino, allowed him to find self-accomplishment in the harmony between self and non-self, seeing in things those aspects which might draw them together rather than separate them; in this he was aided by his affectionate temperament, perhaps intensified by the loss of his mother who died when he was eight.

During the first twenty years of the sixteenth century, the Rome of Julius II and Leo X was one of those places which, like the Athens of Pericles, were capable of provoking the spark of genius; and so a Roman miracle occurred in the same way that a Greek miracle had once occurred. It is difficult to imagine Raphael's destiny without Rome. At the moment when he was about to be summoned by Julius II he had progressed no further than had Leonardo, bringing his own style to the Florentine cantilenas of the Virgin, and already experimenting, on this restricted theme, in those melodic sequences of which he would later show himself the master in Rome. But his 1507 *Deposition*, painted on the eve of his departure for the eternal city, showed that the procedure was unproductive when applied to an expressive scene composed of several personages.

By the autumn of 1508 Raphael was in Rome, and Julius II had commissioned him to paint the Stanza della Segnatura. The decorative theme of this room (whose original purpose remains uncertain, though it almost certainly started out as a library) was entirely one of concord, and celebrated the reconciliation of ancient Wisdom and revealed Truth. This syncretism must have been familiar to Raphael who would have seen its realization, in an even bolder context perhaps, in his native city, in the castle of Urbino where a pair of 'chapels' bear the inscription: 'Behold these twin sanctuaries, scarcely separated. One is sacred to the Muses, the other to God.' No doubt the programme of the Segnatura was laid down by some cultivated person; nevertheless, in all times (except our own) the summits of culture have been attained when an artist has come forward who is capable of incarnating the spiritual life of his epoch. In the same sense as the great theological complexes of the thirteenth-century cathedrals, the Parthenon or the Buddhist grottoes, the Stanza della Segnatura is one of those fortunate instants when thought takes shape, thanks to the visual eloquence towards which Italian art since Dante had been tending.

A comparison between the Segnatura paintings and the Old Testament frescoes in the Sistine Chapel, in which the first Florentine painters of the late fifteenth century had striven in vain to achieve a monumental style, makes Raphael's originality strikingly apparent. The eye wanders and the mind becomes perplexed when confronted by such confused aggregations; indeed, the impasse reached by Quattrocento Florentine art is well illustrated by these vastly enlarged easel-paintings, conceived independently of the space destined to house them, their cartoons prepared with reference to a workshop's visual angles and transferred to the wall surface without any modification. With one's first steps into the Stanza della Segnatura, on the other hand, the mind, guided by the eye, is immediately transported into a lucid world where there reigns a harmony derived from moderation. The compensated gestures of Plato and Aristotle in the *School of Athens* (*pl. 75*), answered by those of the two saints standing on either side of the altar in the fresco wrongly called the *Disputa* or 'Disputation concerning the Blessed Sacrament' (*pl. 77*), express that law of equilibrium through which the human being achieves total self-accomplishment. Leonardo, deeply troubled by the problem of gestural expression, had already employed this compensated gesture in his *Virgin of the rocks* (*pl. 76*), in which the angel's dynamic gesture is balanced by the Virgin's static gesture. Raphael gives these two movements to the two philosophers who dominate classical culture, but the compensation here is stricter, since the movements interpret the oscillation of the pans of a pair of scales seeking a just weight: each movement expresses the essential doctrine of the two masters of Greek thought. We are concerned here, then, with a key gesture.

The lunette of the *Virtues* yields us another key, that to Raphaelesque art: a melodic liaison between

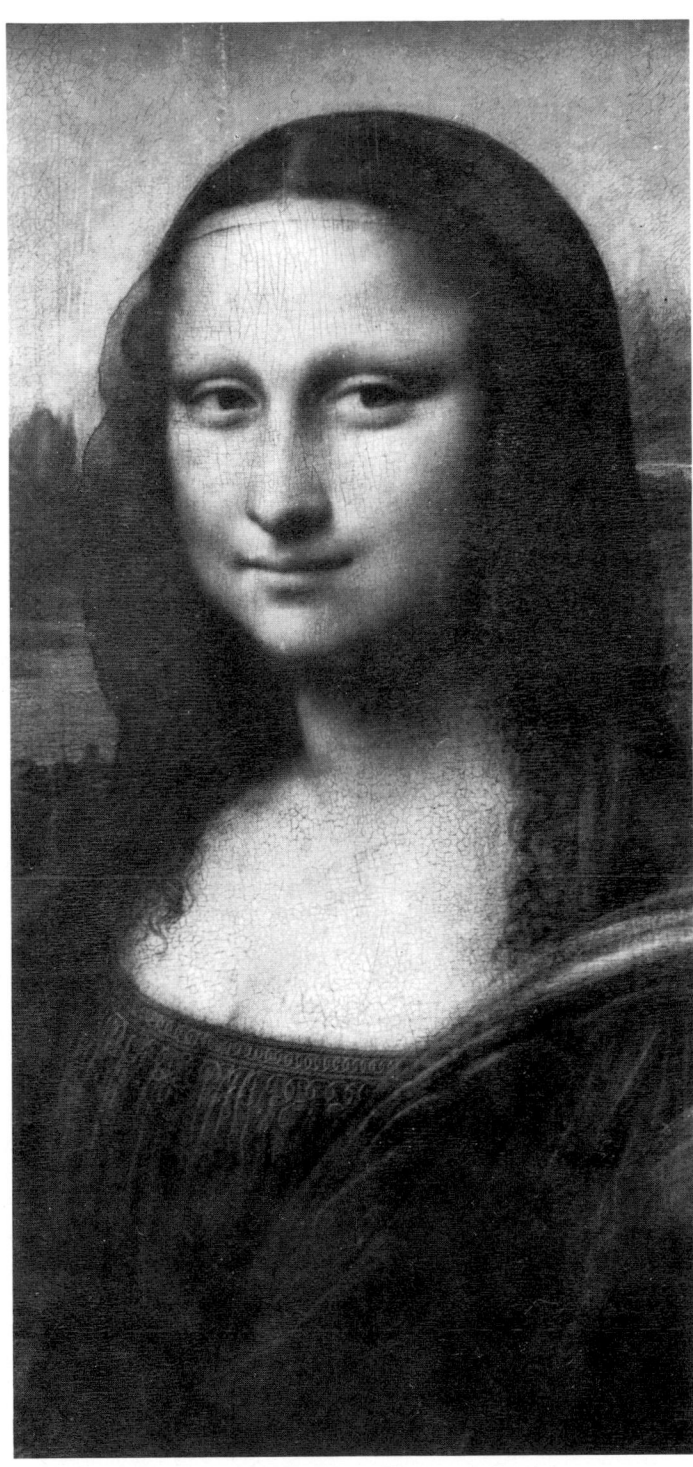

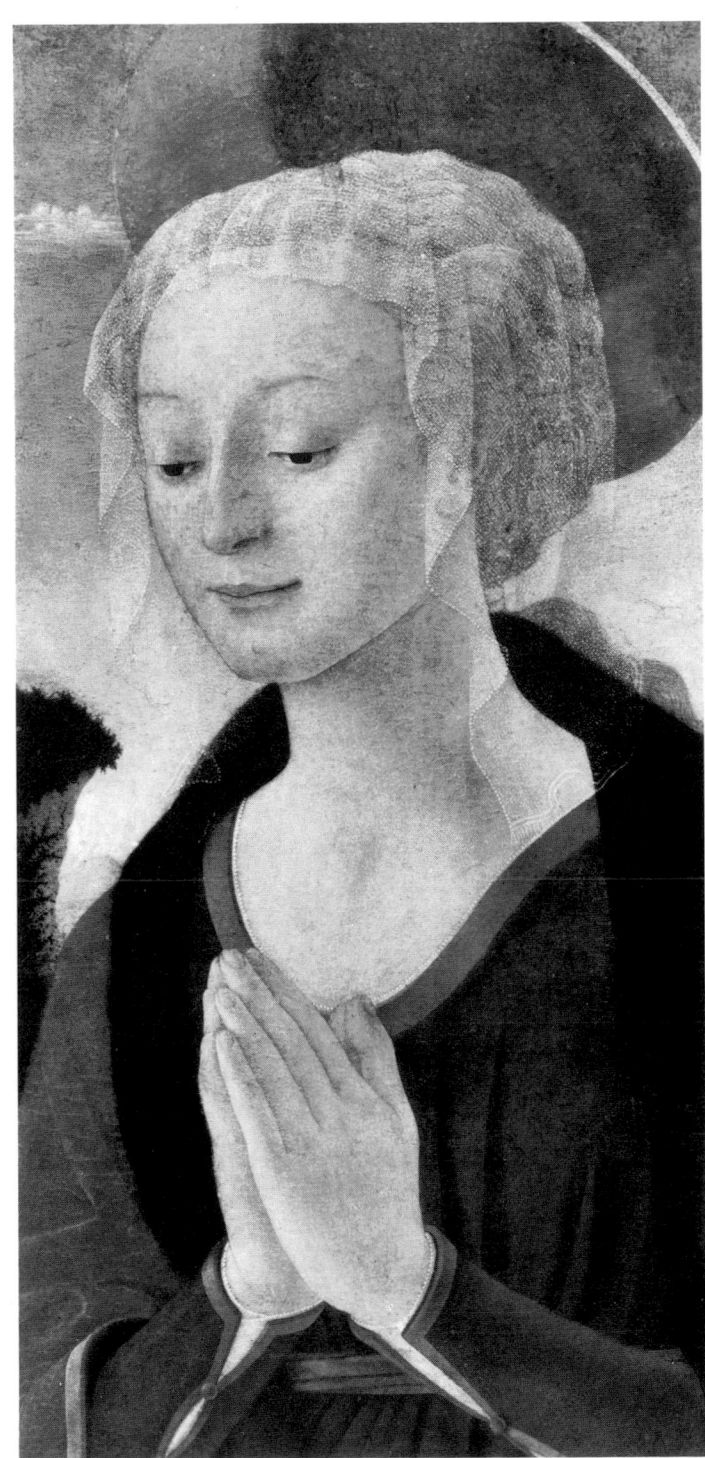

73 Leonardo da Vinci (1452–1519). Detail of *Mona Lisa* (*La Gioconda*). Paris, Louvre.

74 Alesso Baldovinetti. Detail of *Virgin and Child*. Paris, Louvre.

The profoundly humanist ideal for which the painters of the Quattrocento sought expressive form in the type figure of the Madonna was restated by Leonardo in terms of the profane world, by incarnating that ideal in a living model.

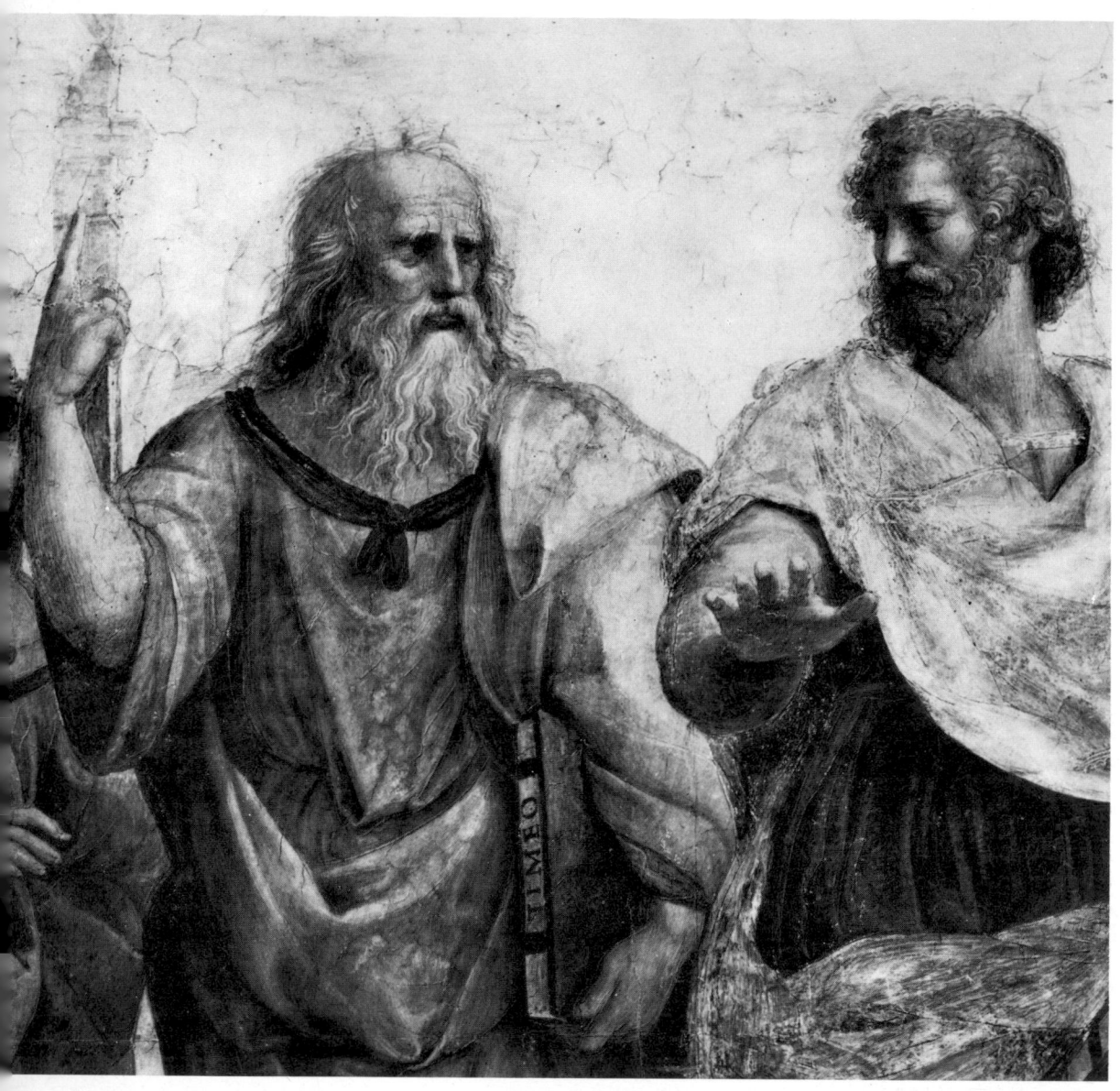

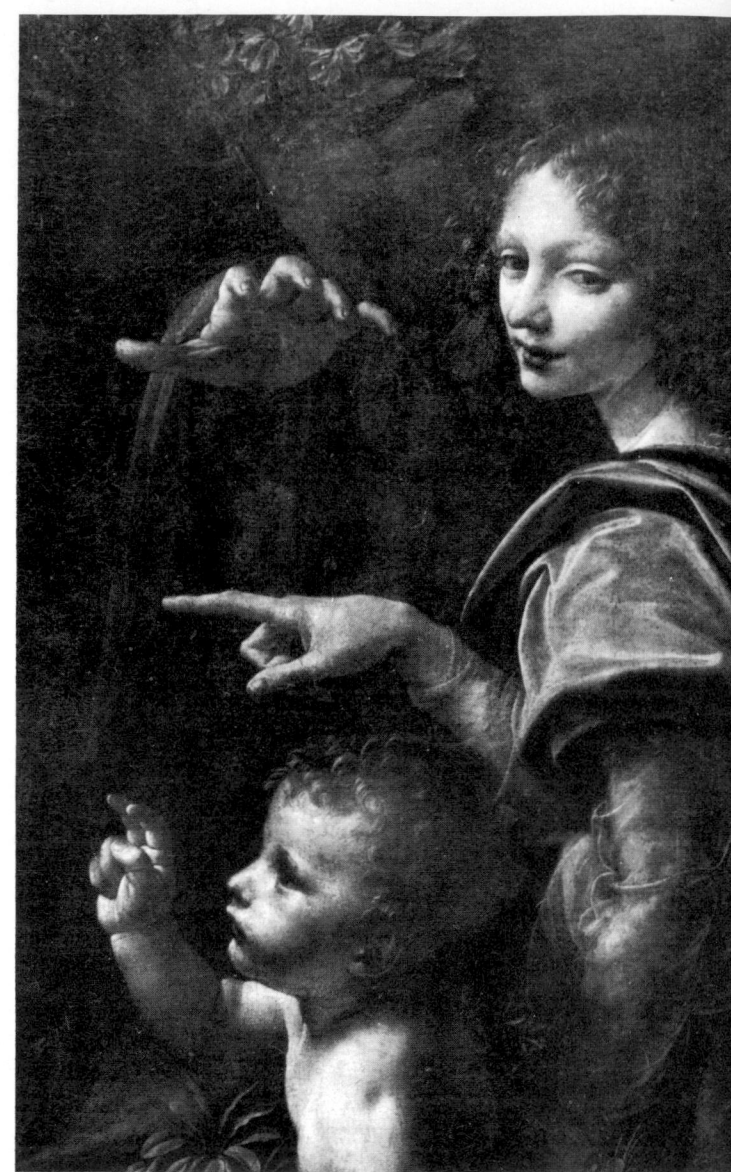

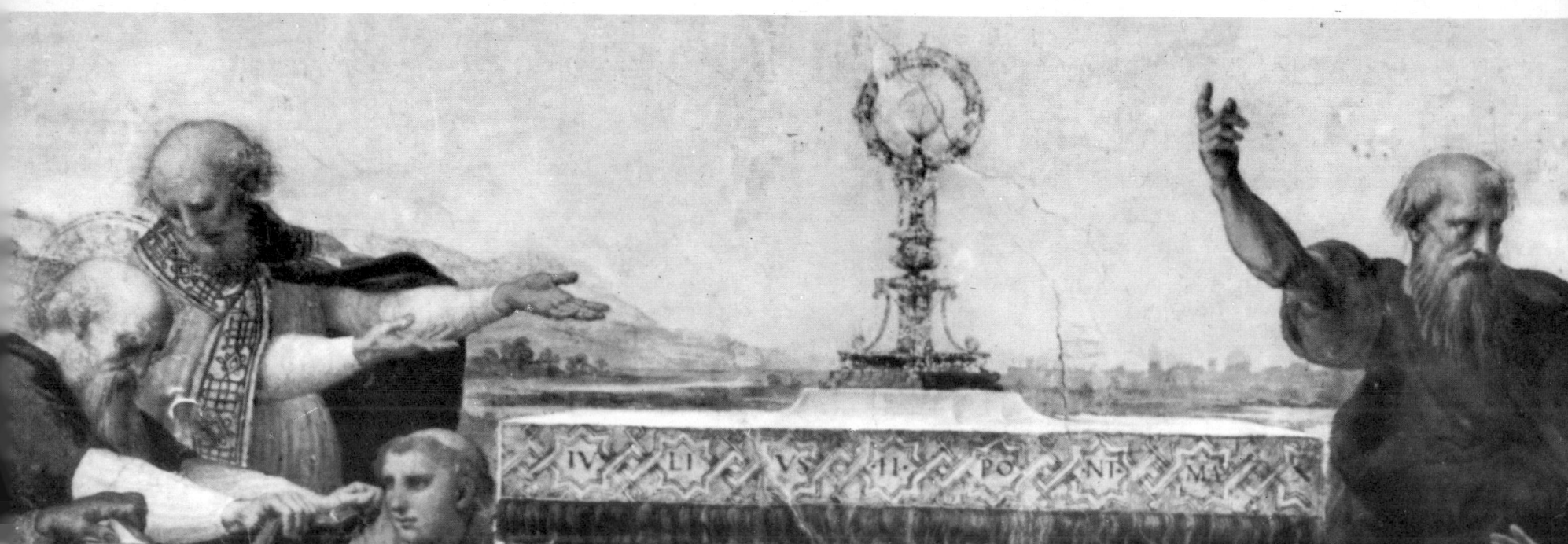

figures whose gestures, attitudes and inflexions, although gratuitous in appearance (at least as regards their expressive value) are in fact motivated by the desire to achieve a perfect continuity between the counterbalanced forms. The homogeneity of the forms throughout the room produces a consonant space in which the rhythms spread from one wall to the other. At a moment when the art of painting showed signs of becoming moribund, Raphael rejuvenated it through means similar to those of Giorgione, by enriching it with musical principles. What the latter found in chromaticism, the former obtained through harmony. Raphael went further, by creating a 'scenic' spatial vision long before the invention of opera and the rise of stage design. Rejecting the yoke of linear perspective within which Quattrocento man had dreamed of imprisoning things, Raphael expanded space by means of curvature. In the *School of Athens*, as in the *Triumph of the Church*, he created for the spectator a scenic space so new that it remained for long undeveloped by others, and it was not until the eighteenth century that the theatre itself rediscovered it.

We know that in 1518 Raphael organized the performance in Rome of Ariosto's *I Suppositi*, building a theatre and designing the setting. We do not know what this setting was like, though it probably conformed to the elementary scenographic principles of the time; in fact, a letter from a contemporary, describing the spectacle, says of the stage setting that 'it was a fine vision of entrances and perspectives that were highly praised'. At the end of the sixteenth century, the permanent setting of the Teatro Olimpico at Vicenza, designed by Palladio and Scamozzi, still brought the spectator's vision up sharply against the wall of the setting, the *frons scenae* in which a few perspective vistas provided the sole visual relief. It was essentially as a working painter that Raphael conceived this flight into space which was to constitute the future for both painting and the theatre.

His boldness may be appreciated by a comparison of the *Disputa* (*pl. 80*) with the *Paradise* painted by Orcagna at Santa Maria Novella a century and a half previously (*pl. 78*). The vision of the Trecento artist is theologically more correct, since the concept of paradise is that of a world no longer governed by the distance and hierarchy appropriate to our own. But Raphael conjures forth a possible paradise as seen by a spectator sitting in the 'royal box' of an ideal theatre, substituting a human point of view for the divine concept. Fra Angelico had first pointed the way when he arranged the ring of angels and the elect around Jesus and Mary in the

perspective of a diagonal movement (*pl. 79*), a fact which is in itself sufficient to refute those who would deny Fra Angelico his place in the Renaissance and make of him a mere mendicant wandering in the fusty aftermath of the Middle Ages.

In the *Foligno Madonna*, and, even more, in the *Sistine Madonna* now in Dresden, Raphael created the theatrical typology of appearance which for the next three centuries was to provide the model for the representation of the supernatural. The *Sistine Madonna*, which Augustus the Strong, while Elector of Saxony, bought for an enormous sum, had such intense transcendental significance for post-Renaissance man that its form was passed on intact as far as Ingres. Although the painting may have lost some of its powers of fascination for us today, it has throughout its history inspired an ever-renewed chorus of admiration (to which Goethe contributed some verses). Even in our own days, the view of this image aroused such mystical emotions in the breast of the Marxist Sergei Bulgakov that he was converted to Christianity; later, after he had been ordained and become a distinguished exponent of Orthodox theology, a newly acquired passion for Russian icons turned his love of the picture into hatred!

One non-conformist school of thought holds that the decadent phase of Raphael's art commences with the paintings executed in the other Vatican Stanze, after the completion of the Stanza della Segnatura, but it would seem unfair to reproach the artist for failing to reproduce the harmony of the Segnatura frescoes in themes which were not in themselves harmonious. Having descended from the lofty regions of the ideal, Raphael entered into contact with the human drama. Although his temperament found the clash of battle uncongenial, he succeeded in adapting his melodic system to the expression of tumult in the *Fire in the Borgo*, as he did in the *Liberation of St Peter*, where the angel of light (*pl. 72*), a sun of justice, stands out against a night scene worthy of Tintoretto. In these paintings he achieved a loftiness of spirit that only Rembrandt was to rediscover. Whereas in the Stanza della Segnatura he had delighted in giving classic expression to all ages of humanity, from the ideal beauty of adolescence to the majesty of old age, he now became attracted by the realism of individuated expression, as in the *Miracle of Bolsena* with its memorable portrait of the indomitable Julius II (*pl. 82*) and its depiction of the rugged soldiers of the Swiss Guard. It is true that the prejudice of the anti-Raphaelites has declared Sebastiano del Piombo to be the creator of these figures, but then this same faction has even gone so far as to attribute the

75 Raphael. Plato and Aristotle, detail of *The School of Athens*. Vatican, Stanza della Segnatura.

76 Leonardo da Vinci. Detail of *The Virgin of the rocks*. Paris, Louvre.

77 Raphael. Detail of the *Disputa* (*pl. 80*). Vatican, Stanza della Segnatura.

Both Leonardo and Raphael sometimes convey the classical ideal of equilibrium through a subtle balancing of gestures. A particular significance attaches to the gestures with which Plato and Aristotle express their essential philosophy: Plato, the idealist, points at the sky, whereas Aristotle, the explorer of nature, seems to wish to embrace the earth.

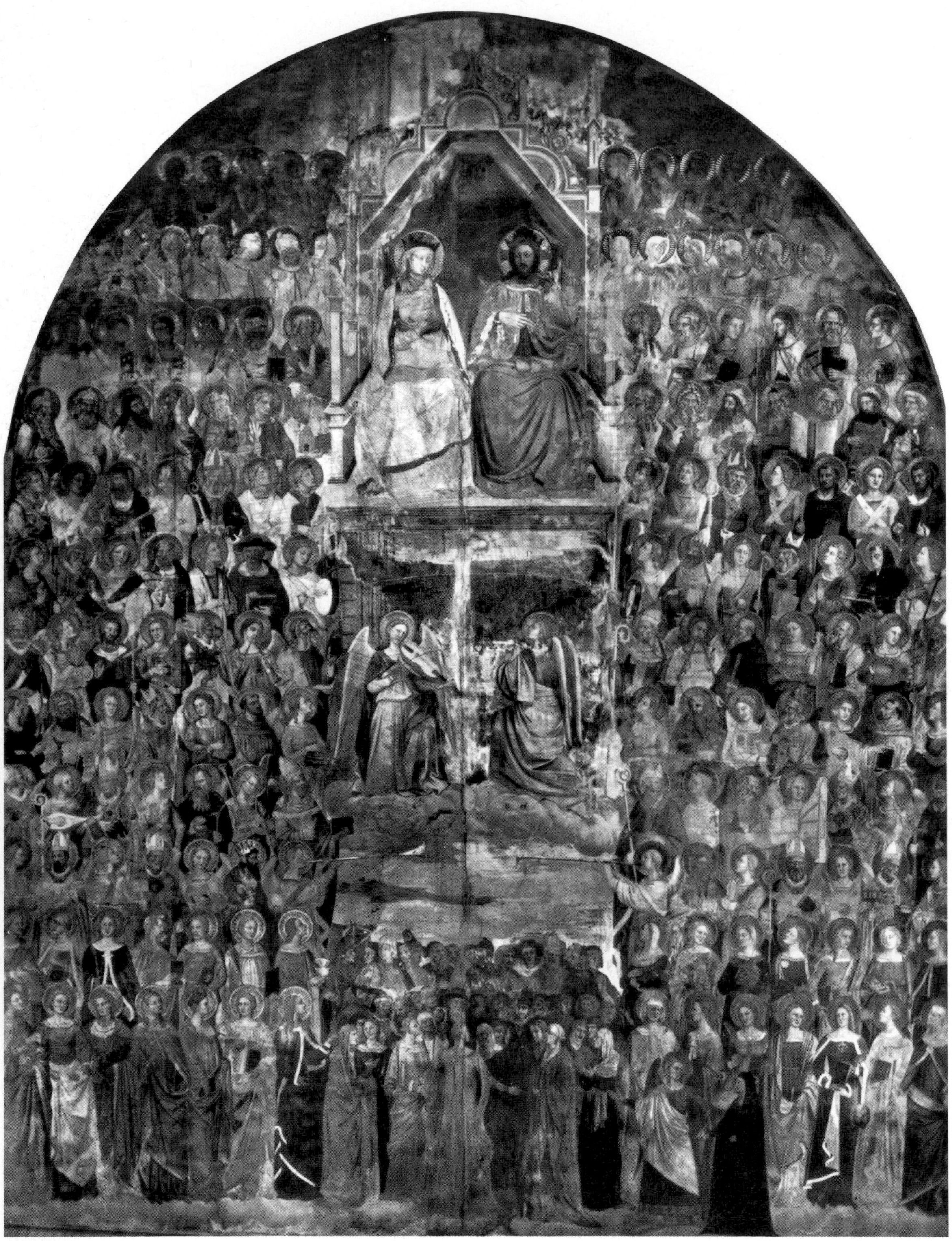

extraordinary Giorgionesque landscape of the *Foligno Madonna (pl. 83)* to Dosso Dossi!

Overwhelmed by commissions and entrusted with various architectural and archaeological projects, Raphael became in his last years a sort of painting contractor, designing cartoons which were converted into frescoes by a whole team of apprentices led by Giulio Romano as foreman. Although this procedure led to some diminution in the composition's formal strictness, its quality remained intact: in any case, the new manner provided fresh sources of inspiration for the future. The *History of Psyche* (Farnesina) opened the way to the Olympian cadences of the baroque world, while the cartoons of the *Acts of the Apostles* and the biblical frescoes of the Stanze later inspired Poussin. Moreover, Raphael's love of antiquity provided the positive stimulus for the humanist adoption of the ornamental devices known as *grottesche* (grotesques), inspired by the Roman paintings found in places such as the Golden House of Nero. The superb decorations that he himself executed in the *stufetta* of Cardinal Bibiena and in the recently rediscovered Vatican *loggetta*, and those created by Giovanni da Udine under his supervision in the Vatican *loggie* and the Loggia della Farnesina, all incorporate the elements of modern still-life and realistic depiction of animals, based on the principles of this ancient form of decoration. Raphael demonstrates such incessant powers of renewal and so animated a creative faculty that all attempts to represent him as being the prisoner of academic formulas must inevitably fail.

78 Andrea Orcagna (active 1343; d. 1368). Detail of *Paradise*. Florence, Santa Maria Novella.

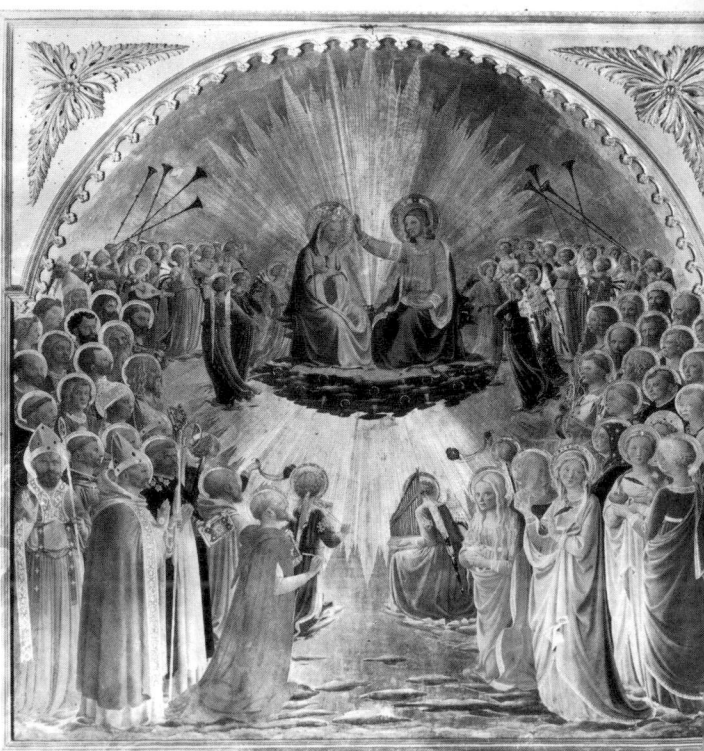

79 Fra Angelico. *The Crowning of the Virgin*. Florence, Uffizi.

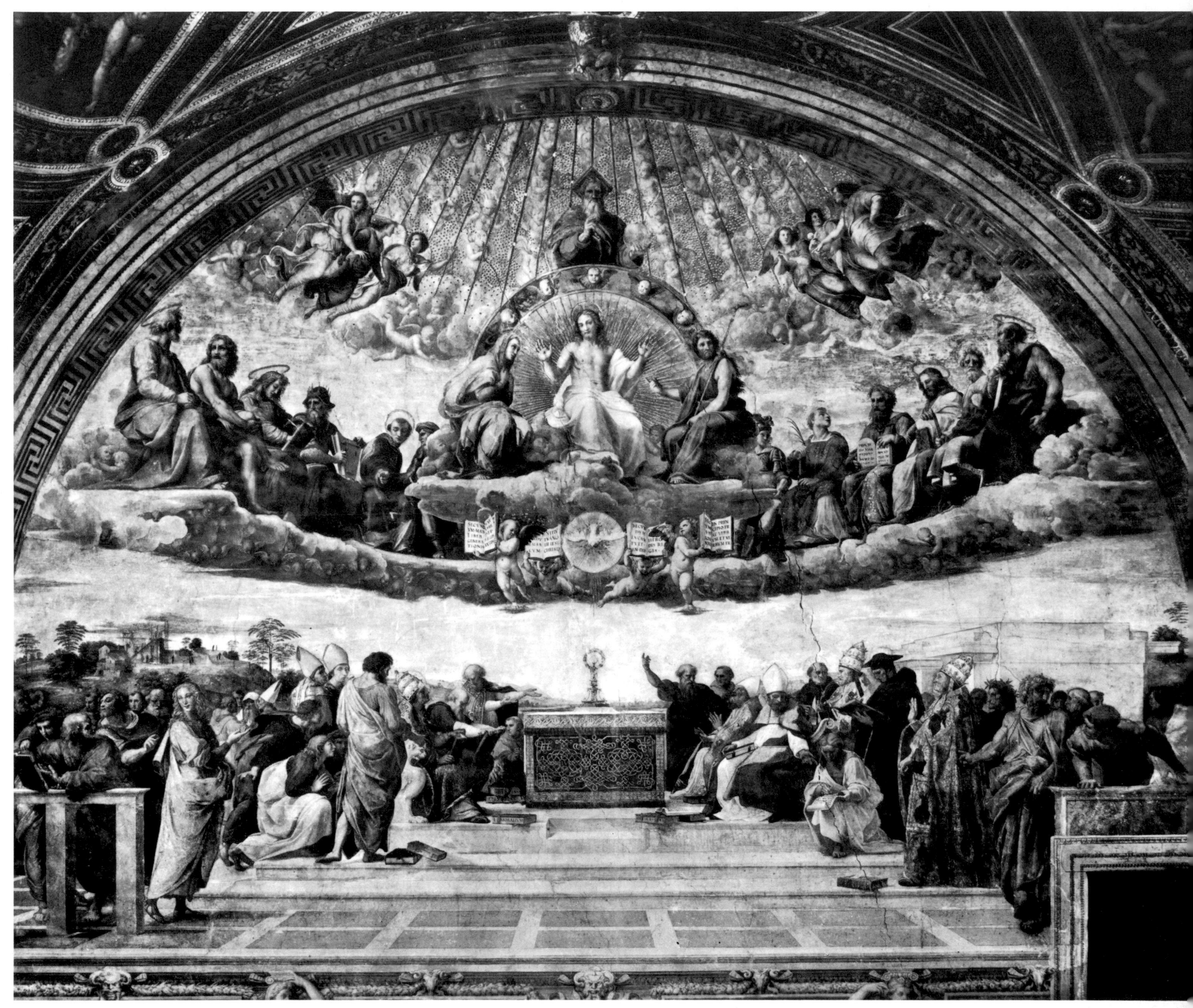

80 Raphael. The *Disputa*. Vatican, Stanza della Segnatura.

The conquest of space achieved by Raphael in the *Disputa* contrasts with Orcagna's *Paradise* which belongs to the heavenly world where the notion of distance is unknown. Fra Angelico's *Crowning of the Virgin* marks a step forward in a definition of curved space which was to present an entirely new solution in relation to the perspective-oriented ideas of the Quattrocento.

In fact, in the domain of painting at least, the scope of Michelangelo's art is by no means as great as that of Raphael. He is supposed to have been more conscious than Raphael of his creative urge, and yet he, too, was indebted to Rome for the revelation of his genius. The sculptures he executed prior to his arrival in Rome were essentially Donatellesque variations: even in the case of certain Madonnas, that of Bruges, for instance, or the *Pitti Madonna* (a *tondo* or large medallion), he may be said to follow Raphael. And what a peculiar hybrid is his *David*, with Michelangelo's artificial muscles grafted on to a Donatellesque anatomy. The strange crucifix of painted wood, recently discovered and now in Santo Spirito, Florence, confirms (if it is indeed by Michelangelo's hand) that the artist's direction during his Florentine youth gave no hint of the powerful nature of the work that he was to accomplish in Rome. This epicene *Christ* has a distinctly mannerist quality about it, and one's natural inclination would be to date it at around 1550 rather than the years preceding 1500. The *Holy Family* (or *Doni tondo*) – the one easel-painting which art historians credit unanimously to Michelangelo – would make one suspect that it was the art of painting which rescued this sculptor from his complexes. What would he have been had not the ceiling of the Sistine Chapel offered to his imagination an inexhaustible field of forms to create, liberating him from the craft limitations of statuary? Since Michelangelo never completed any work of art except his paintings, it is permissible to suggest that he was essentially a painter, possessed of an urge to create sculptures which he never had the heart to finish.

Simultaneously, Raphael at the Segnatura and Michelangelo at the Sistine Chapel were rediscovering classical antiquity's profound vision of the human body as the very substance of art, thus bringing to fruition a concept that the Quattrocento had sought hesitantly to express. But Michelangelo went much further than Raphael in this direction, for he dreamed of an impossible world populated solely by human beings: the self liberated from the non-self, but subject to the will of God.

In the Sistine Chapel, Michelangelo created the first true painted ceiling, covering the vault with painted architectural settings upon which he posed his personages. Rather than visualizing these figures in foreshortening, as seen from below, he applied them in apparent bas-relief or in the round to the vault's concave surface, treating it as though it were a partition-wall (*pl. 84*). He was not bold enough to suspend them above the head of the spectator, as Correggio was shortly to do. For Michelangelo, as for Raphael also, form was an *image* giving expression to an idea; it is an extraordinary chance that brought these two together, to work a few paces apart in an atmosphere of mutual jealousy, the one painting a world in revolt, and the other an idea of concord.

Two instincts vied for supremacy in Michelangelo's soul, the cult of beauty and the passion for drama. Some of his figures are constructed according to the strictest principles of classicism, while others, on the contrary, evoke the exuberance of the Hellenistic period of antiquity and foreshadow the baroque forms of the seventeenth century; this dualism was almost certainly intentional, since the artist sometimes combined the opposing principles in his *ignudi*, nude adolescent figures (*pl. 85*). Michelangelo bequeathed to his age a power of corporeal expression which enraptured a very great number of artists, though none of them ever came near to achieving the same effects. But despite his immediate influence, he must be considered to have diverted painting from its true course by running counter to the impetus bestowed upon it by Raphael. The future of painting lay in spatial expression, in the exploitation of its resources for the purposes of discovering nature and exploring the soul's feelings. Michelangelo checked this advance by re-emphasizing mural painting and by limiting it to the one theme, that of the human body, which was to obsess the mannerists to the point of frenzy.

Michelangelo and Raphael alone bear the responsibility for Roman classicism, although Michelangelo himself fostered the anti-classicism which sprang up after Raphael's death. The future of classicism lay elsewhere, in Venice, a city preserved from both spiritual and political adventures, where a natural sensuality tended to soften the rigours of Florentine-style neoplatonism by discerning greater reality in the world of appearances than in the world of ideals. Titian exemplifies this attitude. When he paints a nude (*pl. 91*), he reduces Giorgione's Venus to the status of a simple courtesan; his art as a whole seems to lack the element of discovery. Having inherited Giorgione's means, he used them to increase the register of human and natural expressions available to painting, aided in his ambition by his extraordinary longevity. But if he attempted with doubtful success to transcend the technique handed on to him by Giorgione, it is certain that he did not invent that technique any more than he invented Giorgione's poetics. However, before his death he experienced a sudden rejuvenation and with it a belated access of boldness.

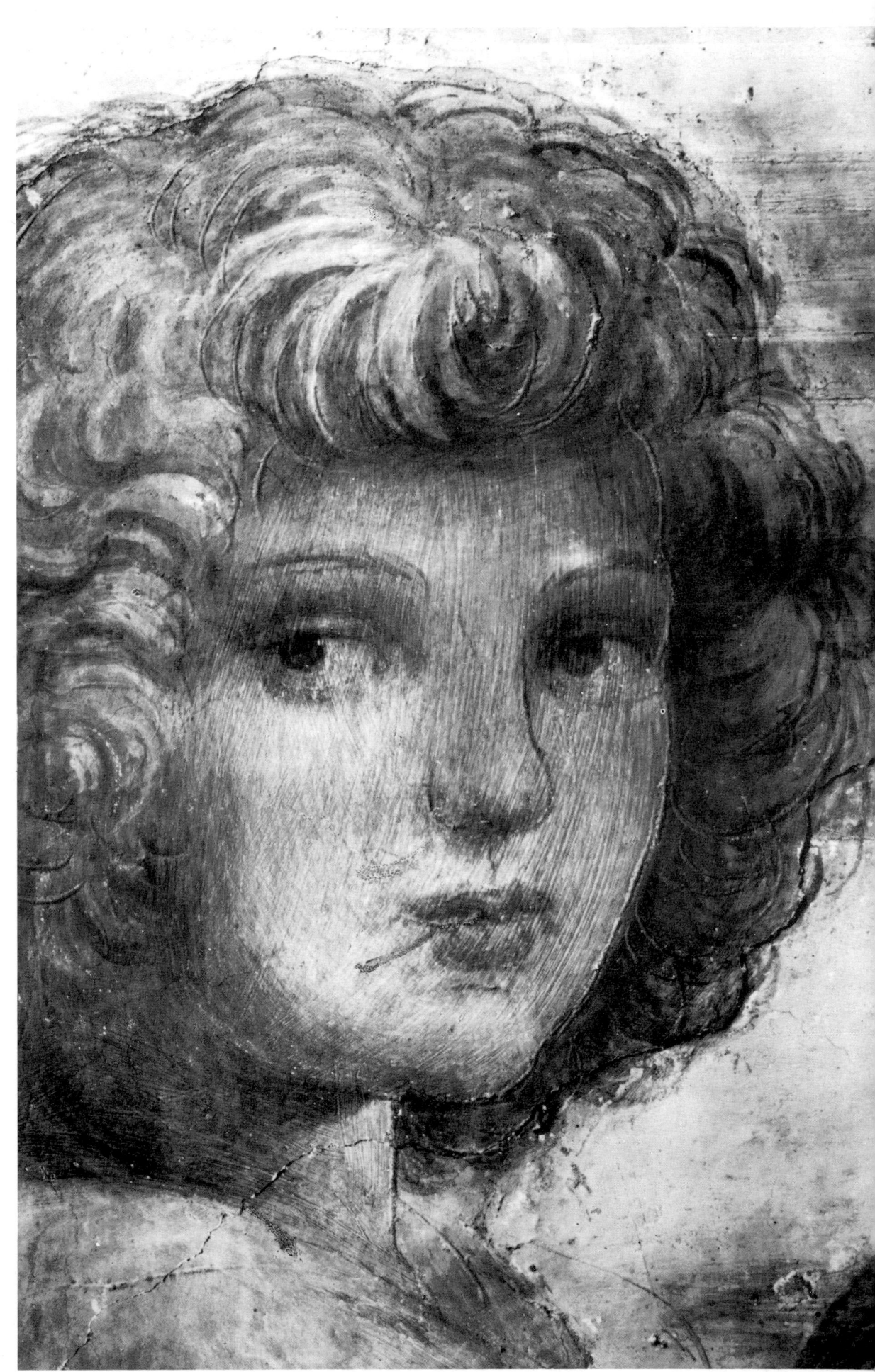

Only the conformist prejudice of anticonformism could blind anyone to the rhythmic elegance of Raphael's brushwork, even in figures, such as this, in which he is most closely inspired by antiquity.

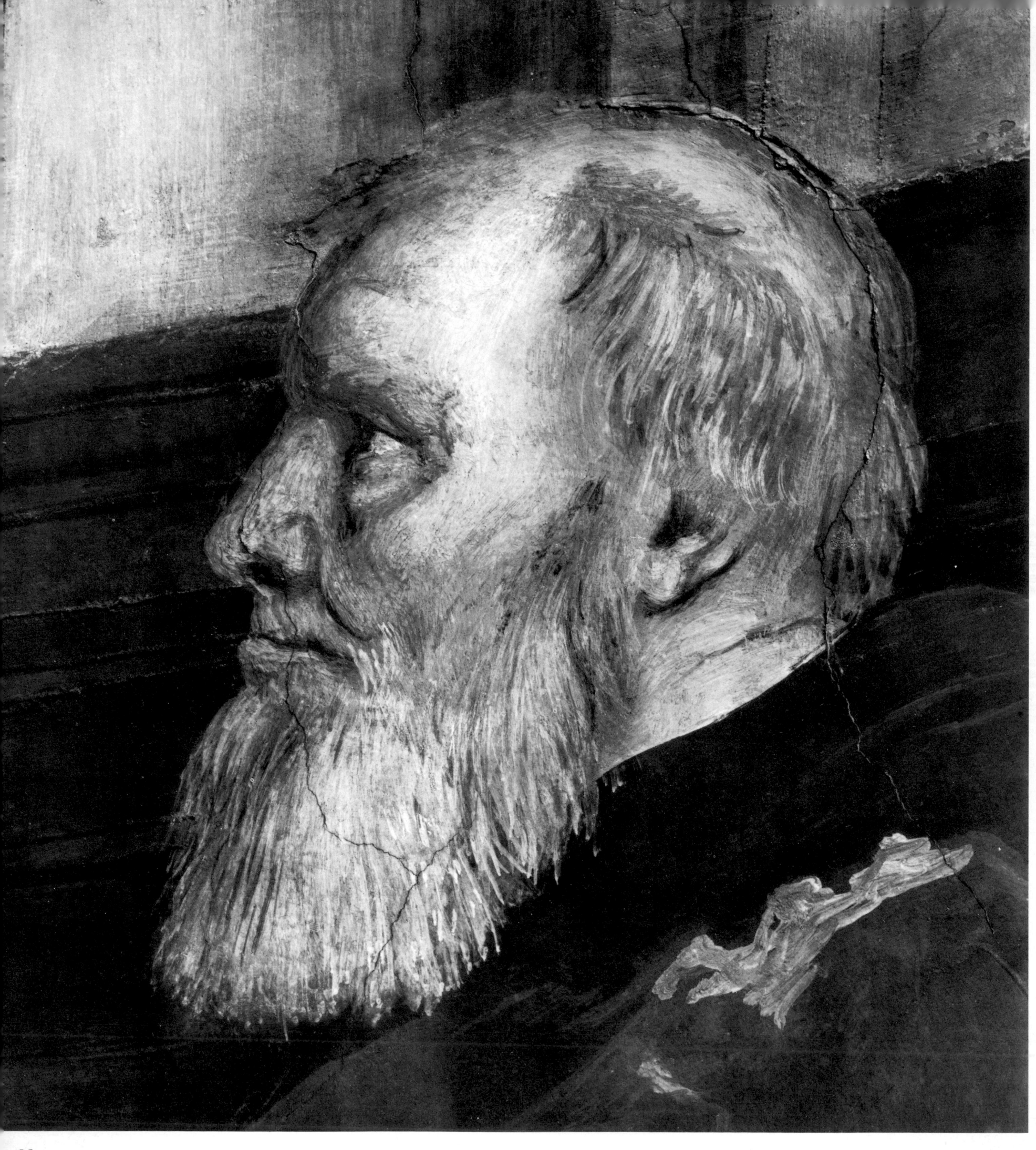

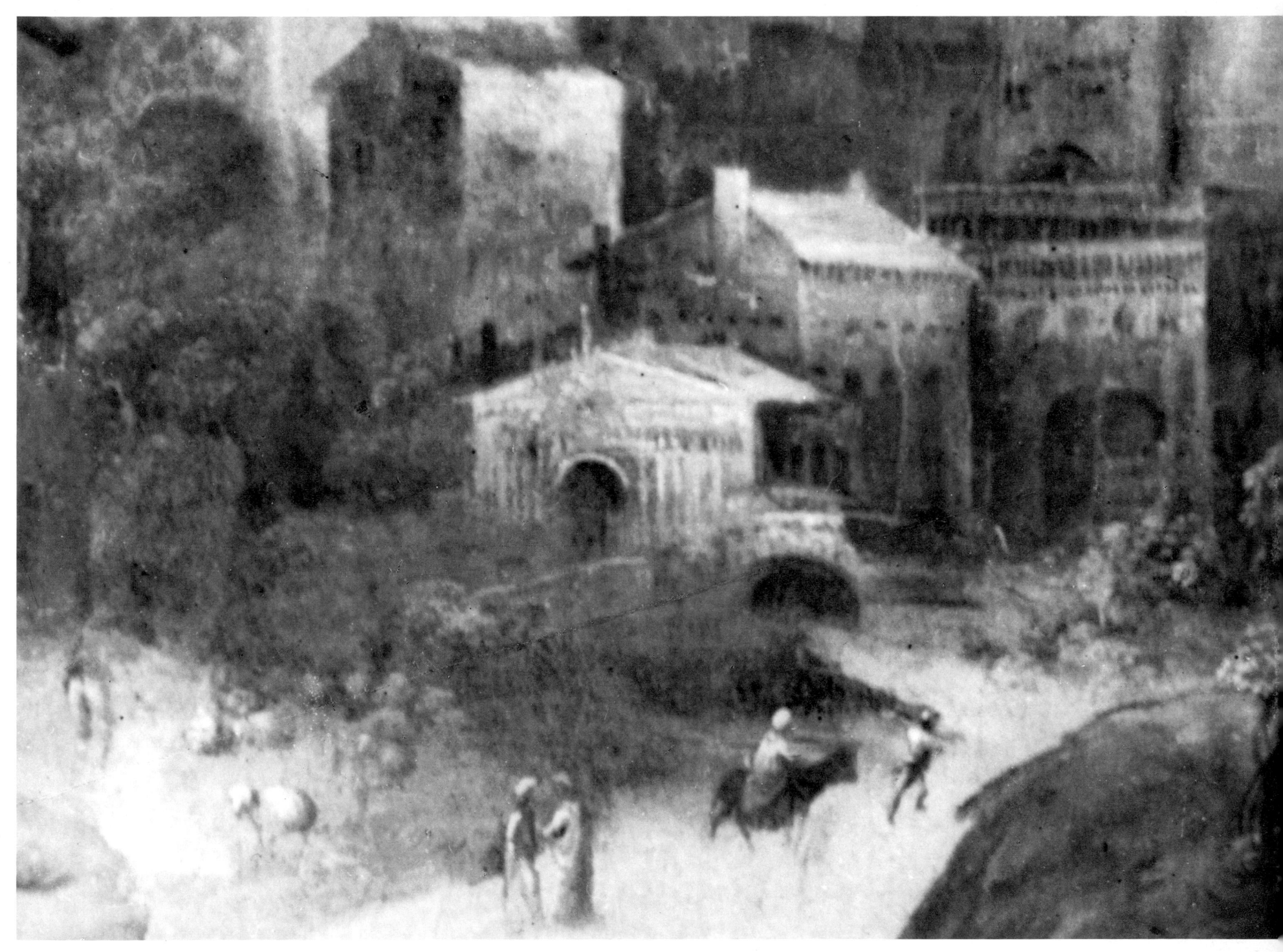

82 Raphael. Head of Julius II, detail of the *Miracle of Bolsena*. Vatican, Stanza d'Eliodoro.

83 Raphael. Landscape, detail of the *Madonna of Foligno*. Vatican, Pinacoteca Vaticana.

The evolution in Raphael's painting towards an increasingly free treatment can be clearly traced in the transition from the *School of Athens* to the *Miracle of Bolsena*, the *Liberation of St Peter* and the *Madonna of Foligno*.

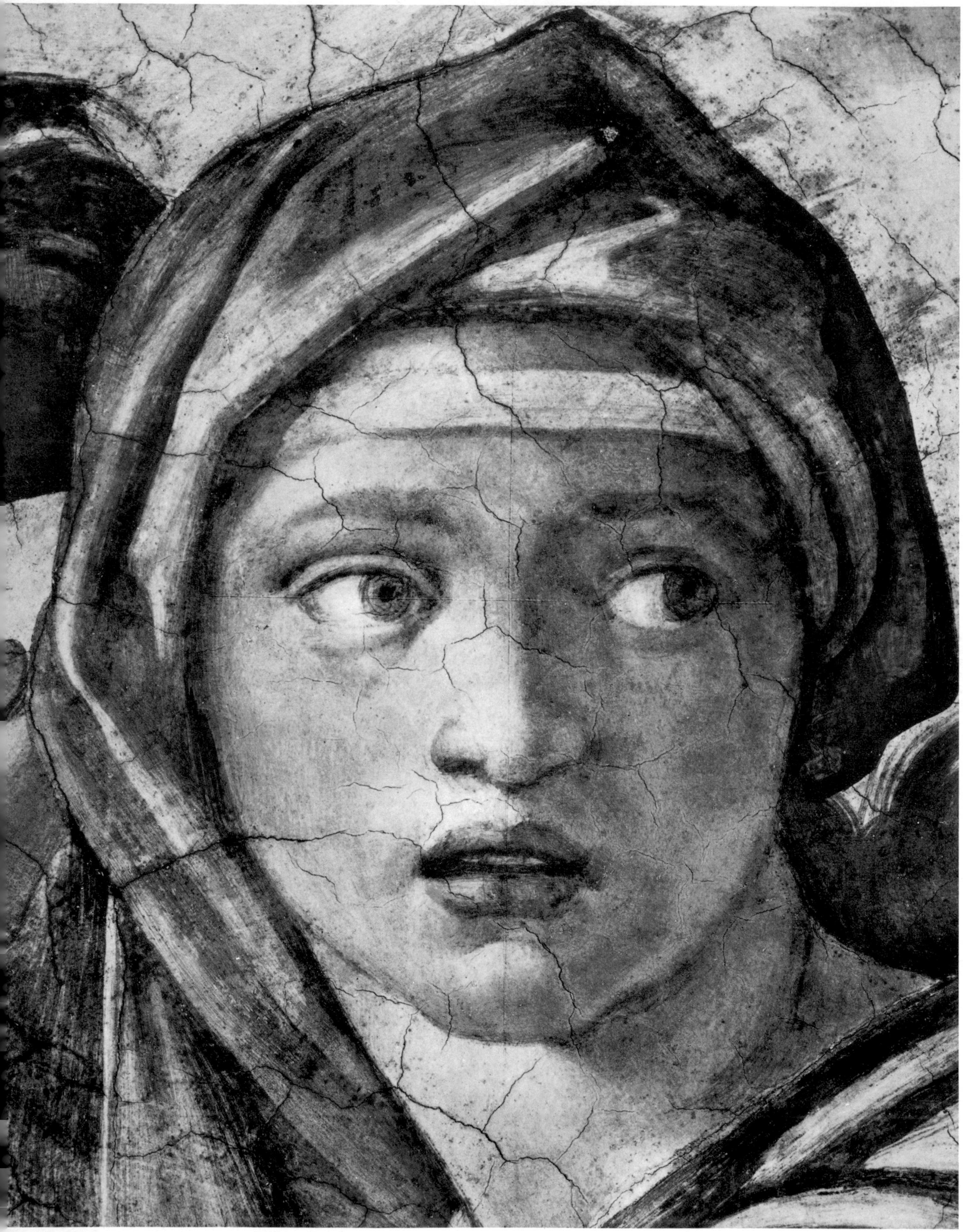

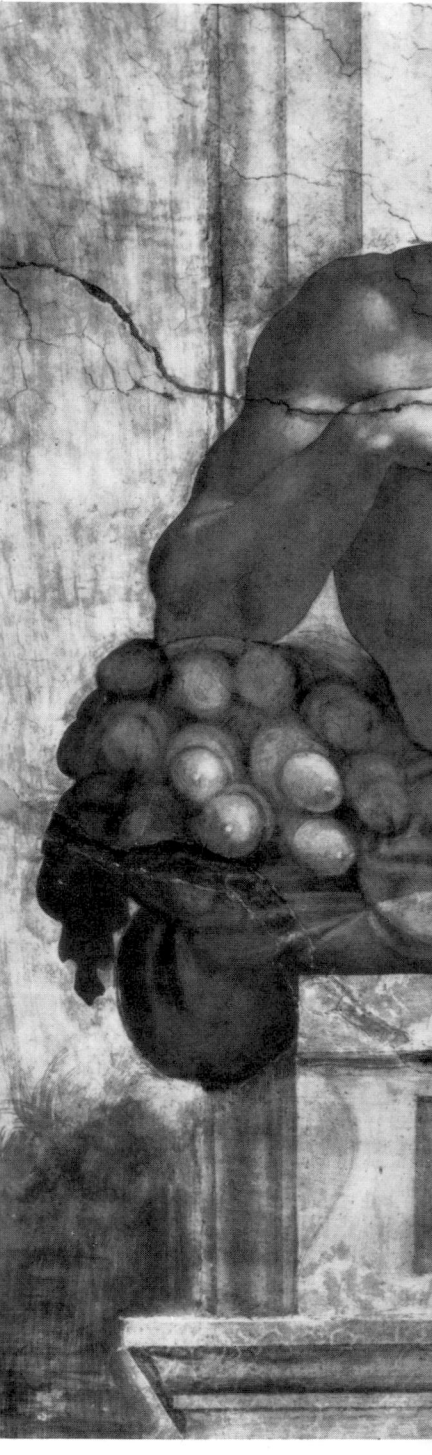

84 Michelangelo (1475–1564). *The Delphic Sibyl*. Vatican, ceiling of the Sistine Chapel.

Michelangelo endows with expressions of passion these faces whose beauty is inspired by classical antiquity. In terms of historical precedent, Michelangelo's outlook resembles that of Scopas, while Raphael recalls Phidias.

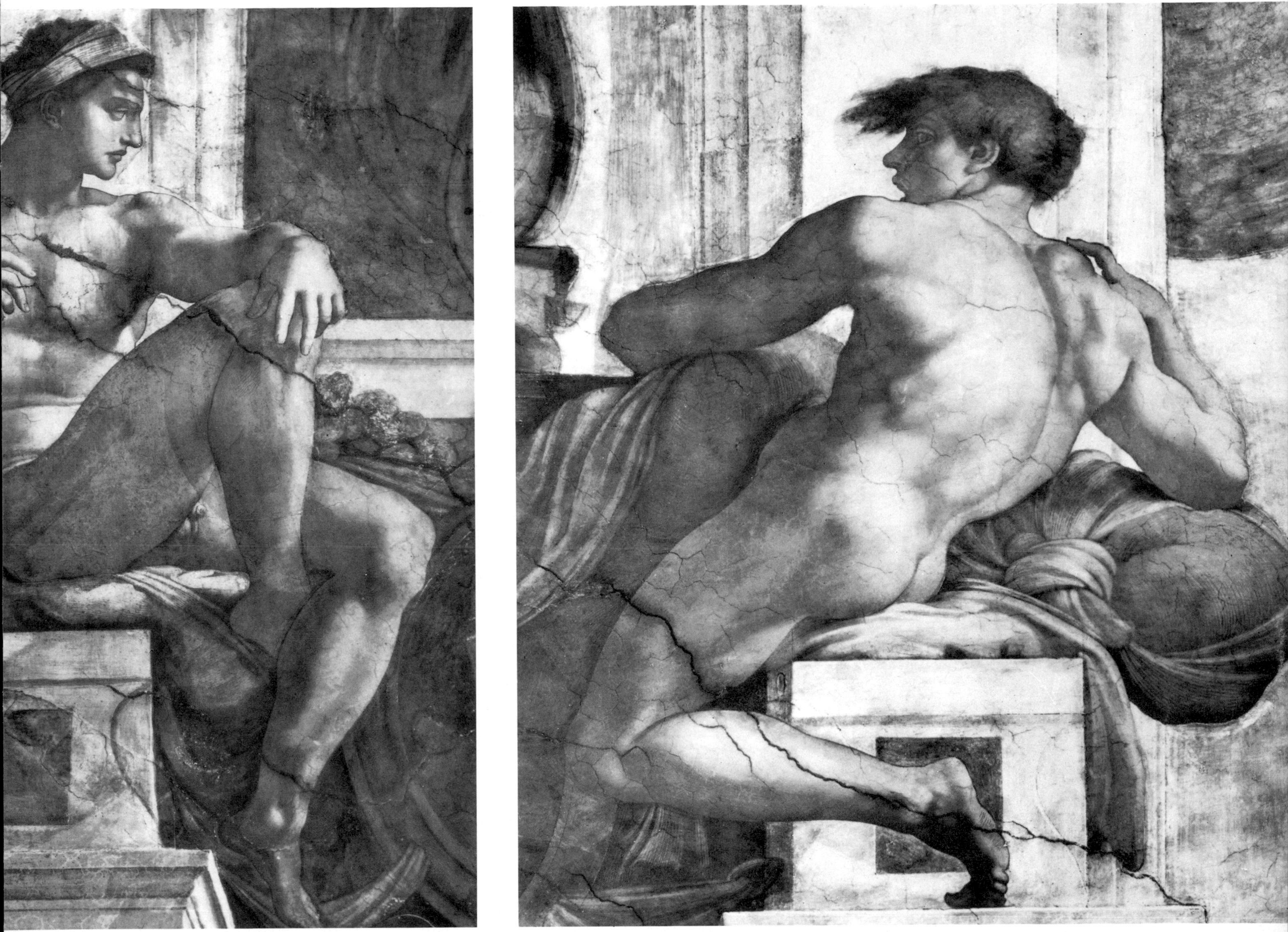

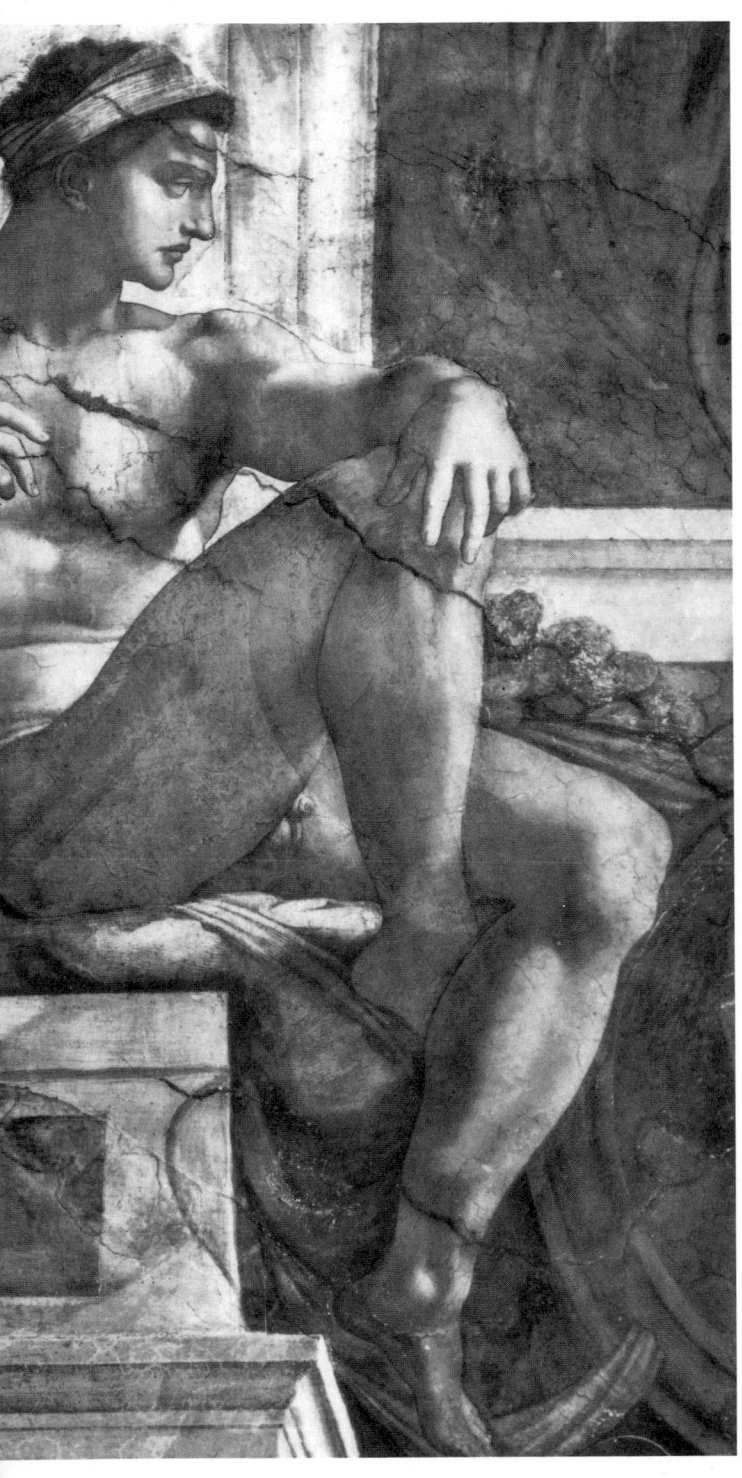

85 Michelangelo. *Ignudi*. Vatican, ceiling of the Sistine Chapel.

In the *ignudi*, Michelangelo was able to experiment with all the attitudes of the human body, and it is from these that classic and baroque form descended.

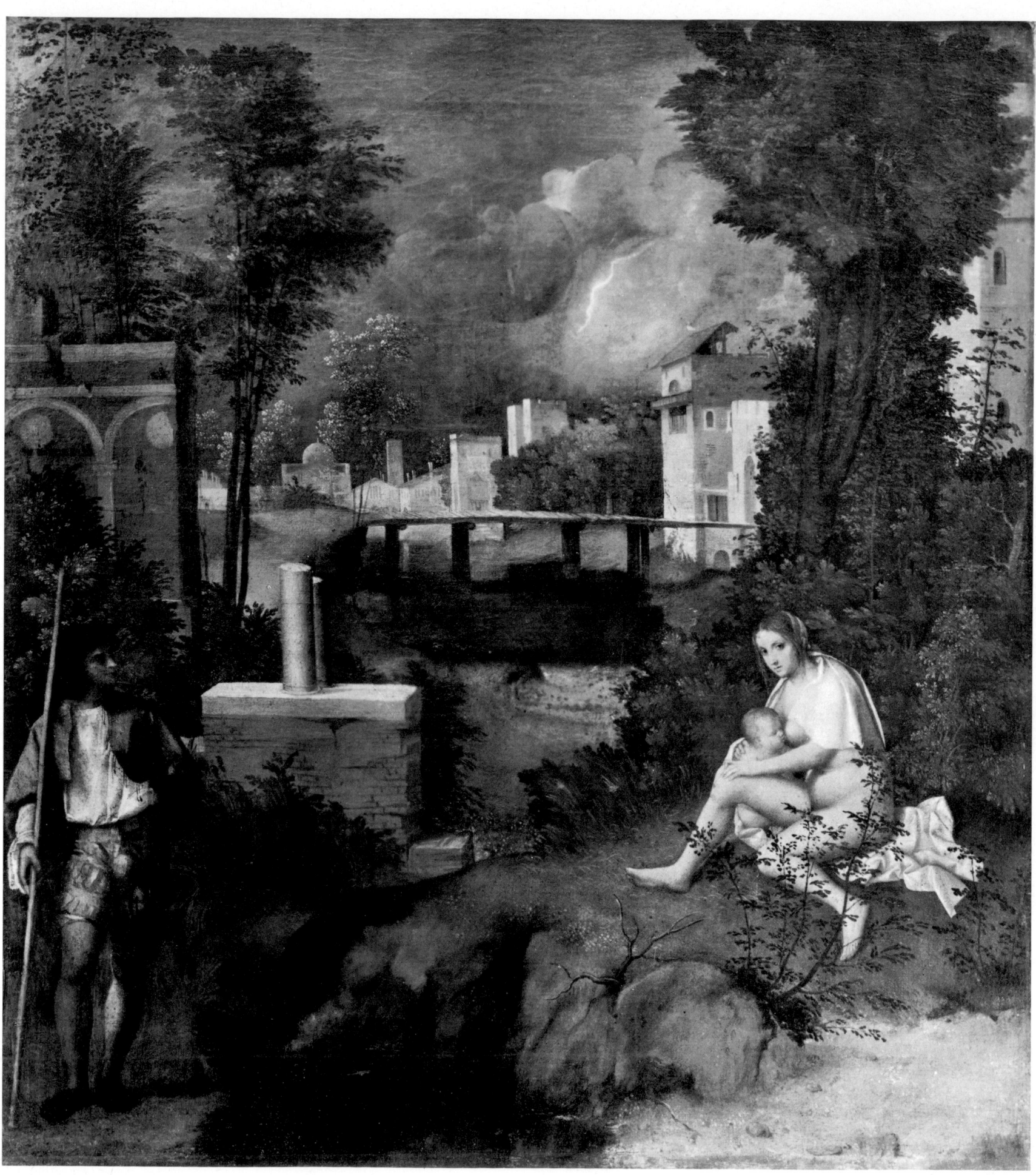

7 Elusive Giorgione

86 Giorgione (1476/8 1510). *Tempesta*. Venice, Accademia.

We know too little about Giorgione to trace a biography, but can glean enough to visualize a passionate life with a tragic destiny, of a kind which is popular today with those who are no longer capable of perceiving human interest except in a dramatic context. This young patrician endowed with genius, 'drawn towards romance and delighting in the lute, sang and played this instrument so divinely that he was often called upon to exercise these talents at the concerts and social gatherings arranged by the Venetian nobility'. One can picture the carefree life of this child of pleasure, a golden existence cut short brutally by an atrocious death. At the age of thirty-four, Giorgione was carried off by the plague after, it is said, having witnessed the death at his side of a woman with whom he was at that moment engaged 'in the delights of love'.

From all this, however, the exacting historian can retain only the single fact that Giorgione died a victim of a plague epidemic; the proof for this is provided by a letter dated 7 November 1510 and addressed to Isabella d'Este who was seeking to acquire a painting by the late master. We are not even certain that Giorgione was a member of the noble family of the Barbarelli, since Vasari describes him as being of humble origin. The nickname Giorgione appears to be a distortion of the Venetian-style appellation by which he is referred to in contemporary documents: *mistro* Zorzo, Zorzou or Zorzi da Castelfranco. His birthplace, Castelfranco, is a pretty town lying at the foot of the fore-Alps, surrounded by what is perhaps Europe's best-balanced countryside, where all the elements – water, mountain, sky, tree and human habitation – combine in easy harmony. The only surviving documentary evidence relating to his works concerns sordid negotiations with the Fondaco dei Tedeschi (the German Exchange) in Venice over payment for the frescoes which he had painted there. Unfortunately, nothing remains of these frescoes but faded fragments. A few references to works of his in Venetian collections, including lists drawn up fifteen years after his death, attest to his posthumous fame. And that is all.

The mystery of Giorgione has been further obscured by the very efforts which have been made to clarify it. The uncertainties surrounding the man and his work offer a fertile field for art critics to indulge in their favourite exercises, and they have seized the opportunity to the full: the study of Giorgione has almost succumbed beneath the weight of *giorgionismo*.

Of the few works recorded by Marcantonio Michiel as being in Venetian collections shortly after Giorgione's death, it has been possible to identify three: the *Tempesta* (Venice), the *Sleeping Venus* (Dresden) and the *Three philosophers* (Vienna). The *Concert champêtre* (*Rustic Concert*) in the Louvre, which has frequently been attributed to Titian, is not mentioned until the seventeenth century, but it fits in well with the *Judith* in the Hermitage, and also with the *pala* or altarpiece known as the *Castelfranco Madonna*, which, although not mentioned in any document, is, by some miracle, accepted unanimously as being by Giorgione's hand. To these we may add the Vienna *Laura*, authenticated by an inscription which does not appear open to doubt, the *Man with the arrow*, also in Vienna, and the *Christ carrying the Cross* in the Scuola San Rocco (Venice), although this last work is now no more than a ruined remnant. It is reasonable to think that the two pictures in the Uffizi attributed to Giorgione, the *Judgment of Solomon* and the *Ordeal by fire*, are in fact early works. Finally, we may possess an indirect reflection of Giorgione's own face in the Brunswick *Portrait of a man*, which may be a partial copy of a *David* mentioned by Vasari, the composition of which is known to us through an engraving.

There is no doubt that there emerges from this small group of paintings a personality that is well defined psychologically, artistically and technically. During 1955–6, I was able to see almost all the pictures attributed to Giorgione, even those not included in the exhibition at the doge's palace in Venice, notably the Hermitage *Judith*, that essential painting which provides the central link between the Castelfranco *pala* and the Louvre *Concert champêtre*. I have acquired one conviction as a result: Giorgione is not susceptible to proof, only to feeling, and must be approached with the heart rather than the mind. A certain poetic charm which is quite unique emerges from his works.

Giorgione's almost undefinable poetry is slightly

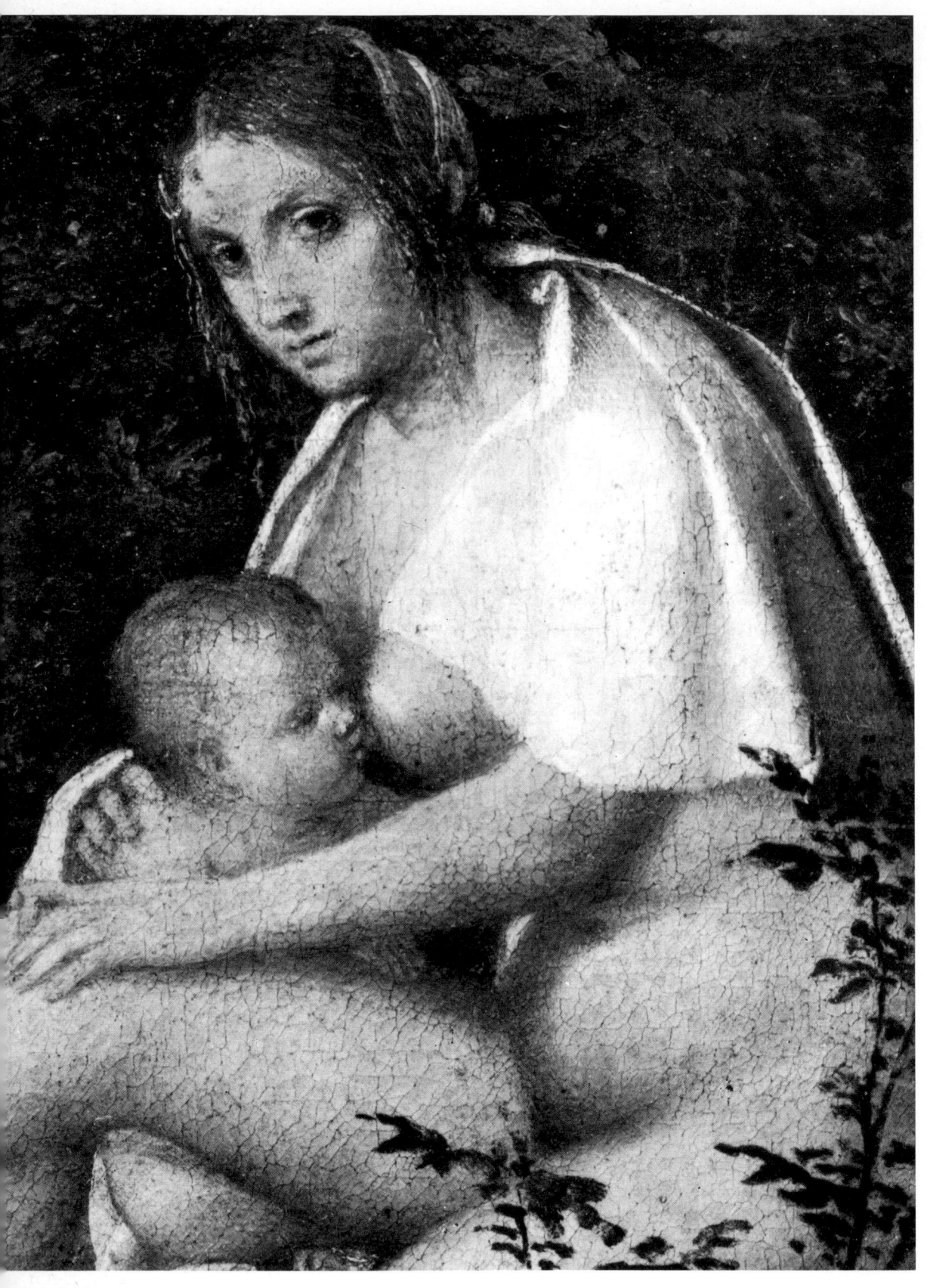

87 Giorgione. Detail of the *Tempesta*. Venice, Accademia.

different from the dark, 'saturnine' romanticism upon which so many authors have expatiated since the thesis set out by G. F. Hartlaub in *Giorgiones Geheimnis* (Munich 1925). The subject of two of Giorgione's pictures, the *Tempesta* (*pls 86–7*) and the *Three philosophers*, whose meaning has been lost to us, has been interpreted by this historian as signifying the existence in Venice of an occultist secret society, of which Giorgione is presumed to have been a member. According to this theory, the *Three philosophers* symbolized the three masonic orders and the picture was made to be hung in the society's meeting-room. There is no bridling the imagination once it is freed from the constraints of history; however, the truth here is doubtless simpler. The *Three philosophers* probably symbolize the three forms of wisdom. As for the *Tempesta* (which is not, in fact, stormy at all), X-ray examination has revealed a female nude beneath the young man at the left: there seems no reason to disagree with Eugenio Battisti's opinion (in *Rinascimento e Barocco*, Milan 1960, p. 151) that the picture represents the nymph Io, impregnated by Jupiter manifesting himself as a streak of lightning, and protected by Mercury in the form of a shepherd. This explanation tallies with a particular passage in Ovid's *Metamorphoses*.

I would add that the Castelfranco *pala*, too (*pls 88–9*), may well contain a hidden meaning. The reduction to two attendant personages – a warrior and a monk – of the usual *sacra conversazione* which in the work of followers of Bellini is usually more heavily peopled, may indicate the artist's intention to symbolize the two choices open to man at the moment of embarking on life: action and contemplation. But this is unimportant. The true mystery of Giorgione lies elsewhere than in a question of the more or less hermetic meaning of his paintings or the frenzied romanticism of his imitators. It is possible, even probable, that artists such as Savoldo, Dosso Dossi and Pordenone profited from his inspired example, but the element of emotionalism in their treatments is contrary to Giorgione's outlook, profoundly foreign to that chaste reticence of the soul which can be apprehended only by allowing oneself to become slowly steeped in it in complete inner silence. This salutary process was rendered more difficult at the great 1955 exhibition at the doge's palace by the necessity of making oneself deaf to the false notes struck by so many attributed pictures, all clashing with the divine violins of the master.

It is at this point that Titian appears in his true light: he uses feelings to flaunt them and catch beautiful reflections from them. Titian is not only an artist but a man of the world as well, and occasionally even something of an orator. His virtuosity contrasts with Giorgione's spontaneity, which is compounded of hesitation, irresolution, modesty and even timidity; these feelings imbue the face of the woman giving suck in the *Tempesta*, of the *Laura*, of the *Man with the arrow*, of the two saints and the Madonna of the Castelfranco *pala*, of the *Christ carrying the Cross*. A certain gentle melancholy contributes a hint of bitterness to the *Portrait of a man*. But this is as far as one may go: any hint of emotionalism can only derive from Titian, not Giorgione, and this is why I hesitate to ascribe to the latter the *Concert of chamber music* in the Pitti (Florence). The old man and the youth would marry well into the Giorgionesque family, but at the centre there is an adult who possesses feelings, who is well aware of the fact and shows it too openly; his sidelong glance and rolling eyes have found part of the traditional repertory of emotional expression in art since the sculptures of Scopas, and already foreshadow Rubens.

It has been claimed that a comparison of Titian's *Sacred and profane love* and Giorgione's *Concert champêtre* (*pl. 90*) would reveal their respective authors simply through the joyous atmosphere radiating from the first painting, in contrast with the sadness impregnating the second. Giorgione's sadness, however, is never a lamentation. It is, rather, a profound gravity that emanates from his works, and this gravity is specifically Venetian, a heritage from Byzantium. The same nuance is apparent in Giovanni Bellini's grieving figures, mostly saints, in whom one senses the melancholy of the divine being transported to earth but still dreaming of heaven; immured in his own self, he is unable to become part of the world whose beauties the artist has spread around him. But Giorgione succeeded in secularizing painting, and his sublunary beings, no longer remembering heaven, live upon earth. A wall is suddenly broken down, that wall of contour within which Bellini enclosed his human figures. The soul pours forth through this breach, and, for the first time in painting, contact is established between the soul and the world: the universe ceases to be a spectacle whose marvels the painter enumerates and contemplates without being able to participate except intellectually. Now the soul, burdened with the weight of the world that has invaded it, tends to withdraw into itself, and this withdrawal expresses itself through a perfectly controlled silence. Herein lies the quality that may truly be called Giorgionesque. It is this quality, too, that binds Giorgione to Vermeer, to whom he is akin as a painter through his intimist feeling for light,

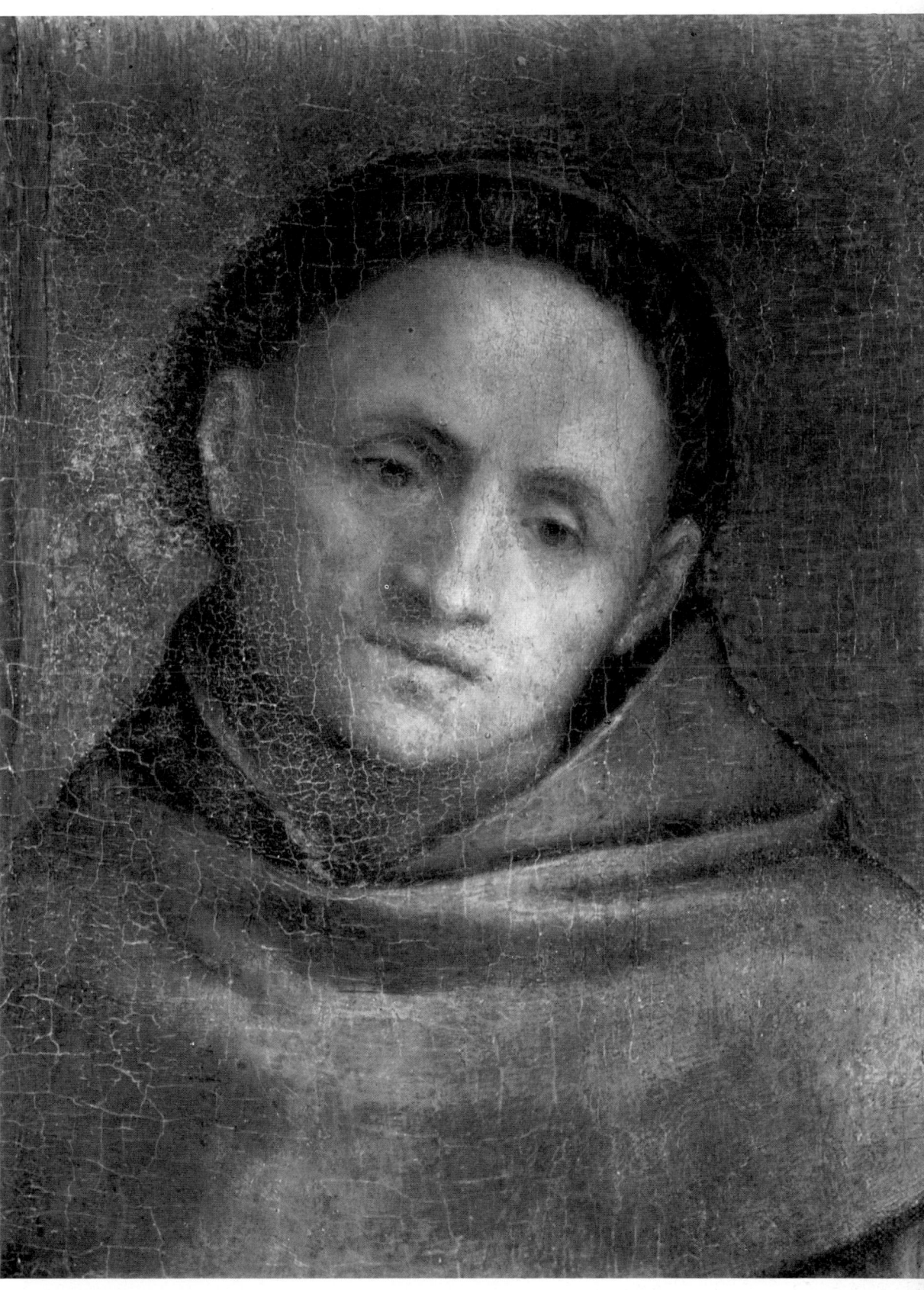

especially the way he spreads pearls and diamond-bright needles along the edges of shadows.

The *Castelfranco Madonna* (*pl. 89*), more than any other painting by Giorgione, gives an insight into this immersion in nature of figures enveloped rather than delimited by their contour. Because, in this

88 Giorgione. St Francis, detail of the *Castelfranco Madonna*. Castelfranco, San Liberale.

The melancholy look of Giorgione's personages provides painting with a new direction, that of the expression of sentiment.

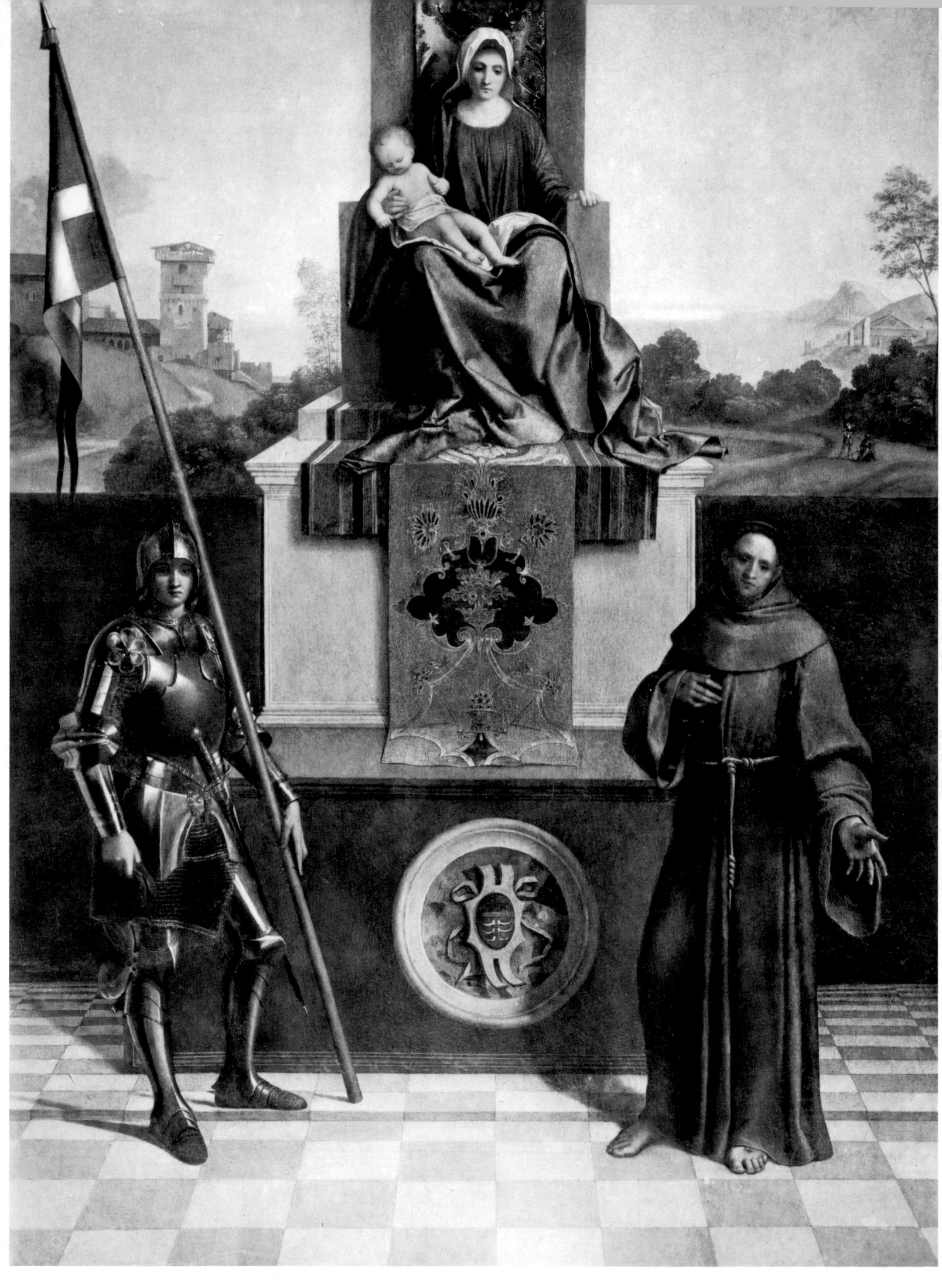

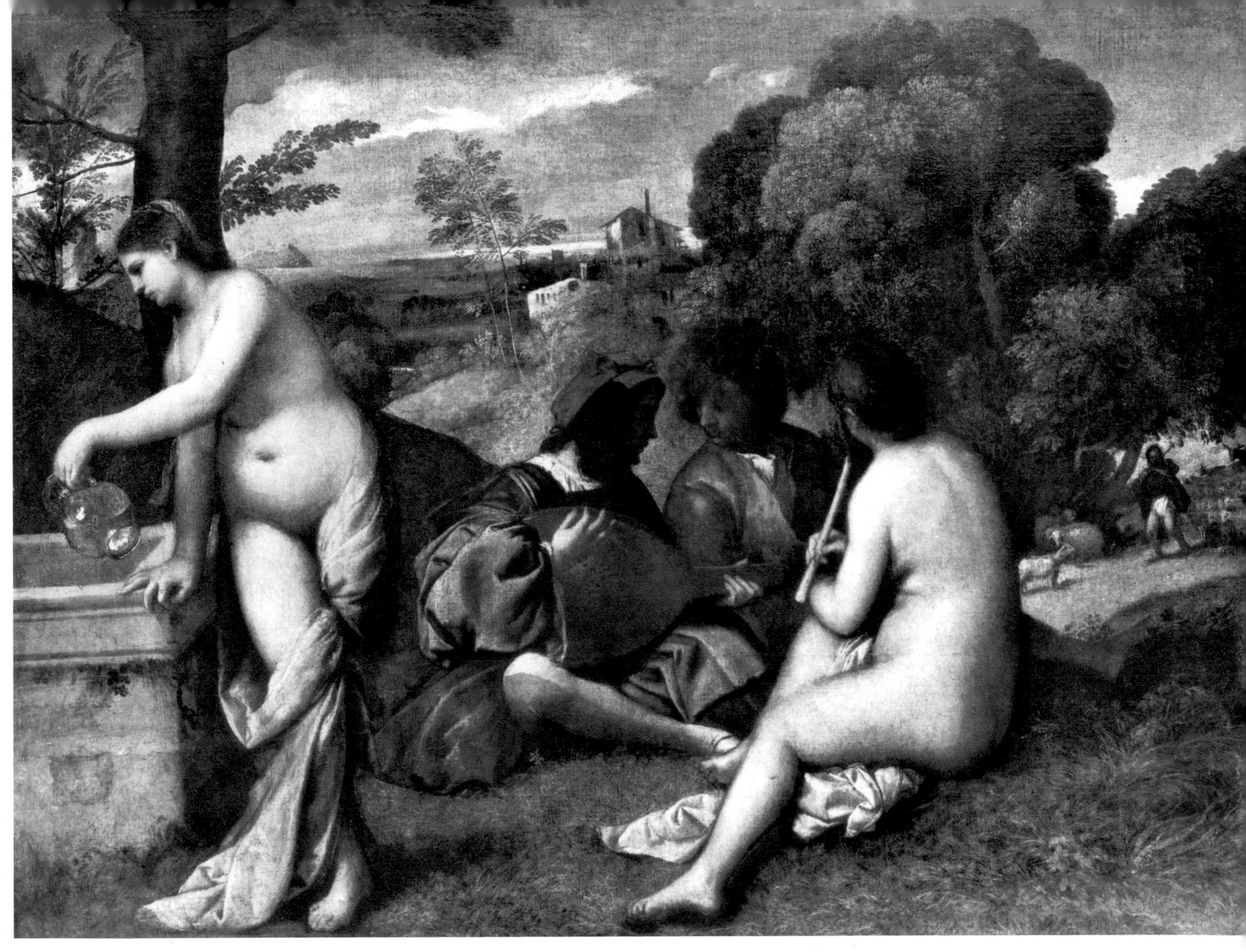

sacra conversazione, the personages have their backs turned to the landscape, it is easier to appreciate what they owe to it. Every aspect of them reflects their surroundings: their deeply reflective faces whose features are blurred by a soft shadow, St Liberale's armour which is a mirror of light, the moist drapery of the Madonna's robe. Enamoured of music – which in his time was essentially polyphonic – Giorgione invented symphonic painting. An identical fluid circulates throughout the picture: each colour contains some echo of the nearest and most distant colour; the light does more than envelop things, it seems to give them life, assuming an infinity of subtle variations in response to the tonalities of the colours and substances which absorb it, diffuse it gently and reflect it in bright flashes.

Bellini, Giorgione's master, spreads his colours evenly over the whole surface of his paintings,

making each of its tones homogeneous. Giorgione, on the other hand, employs a richer pigment which he wields freely according to the requirements of the object to be painted and the intensity of the light. He inaugurated the modern handling in which paint thickness varies in direct proportion to light intensity, and the layers of paint are progressively thinned, to a point of transparency, in order to represent the shadow whose mystery shows hollow on the surface of the canvas, while the light accents are thrust towards the eye by thick impasto. Titian was the first artist capable of making full use of the new processes created by Giorgione. The difference between them is that Titian practised the technique as a virtuoso, whereas for Giorgione it was a means rather than an end.

Prior to Giorgione, a picture was thought out before being painted. Giorgione's method of pro-

◀ 89 Giorgione. The *Castelfranco Madonna*. Castelfranco, San Liberale.

90 Giorgione. *Concert champêtre*. Paris, Louvre.

Giorgione plunges man into the heart of nature; it is present everywhere in the form of light and atmosphere enveloping beings and things, even when, as in the *Castelfranco Madonna*, it is still only a backcloth.

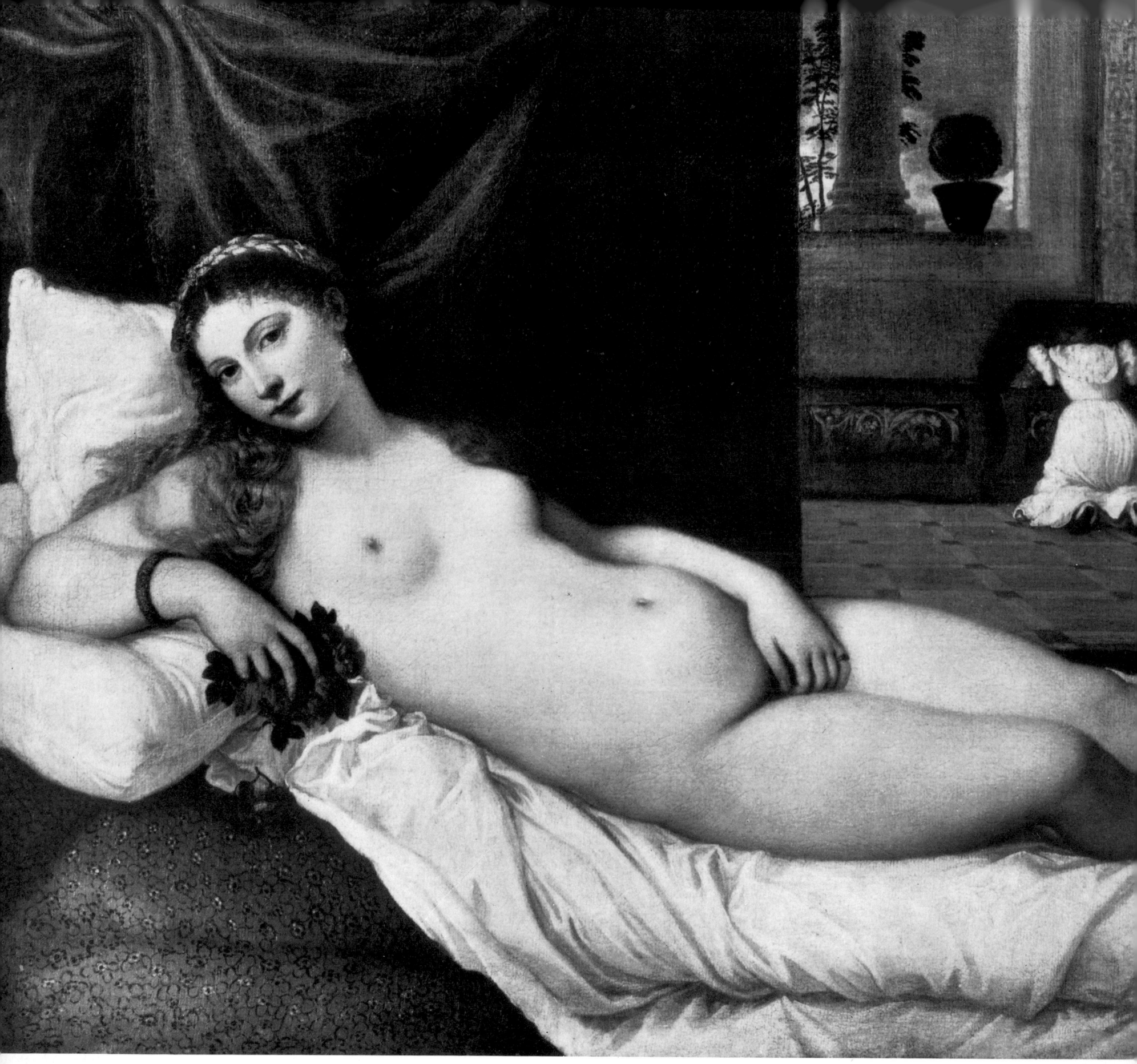

cedure was absolutely revolutionary. Vasari's comment on his supposed predilection for drawing is the sort of conventional formula which this Florentine artist, for whom painting was *l'arte del disegno*, applied to all the great masters; if Giorgione had really completed so many drawings, it is surprising that none of the great private collections, which vied so eagerly for drawings by the masters, contained any

at all by him. On the contrary, Giorgione gives the impression of having attacked his canvas directly, placing his faith in pure improvisation. Indeed, composition is by no means the strongest element in his painting: the *Tempesta*, a work of his youth, is very badly planned, with its complicated system of *coulisse* foreshortening; the dissection of the landscape in the *Three philosophers* is eccentric, with

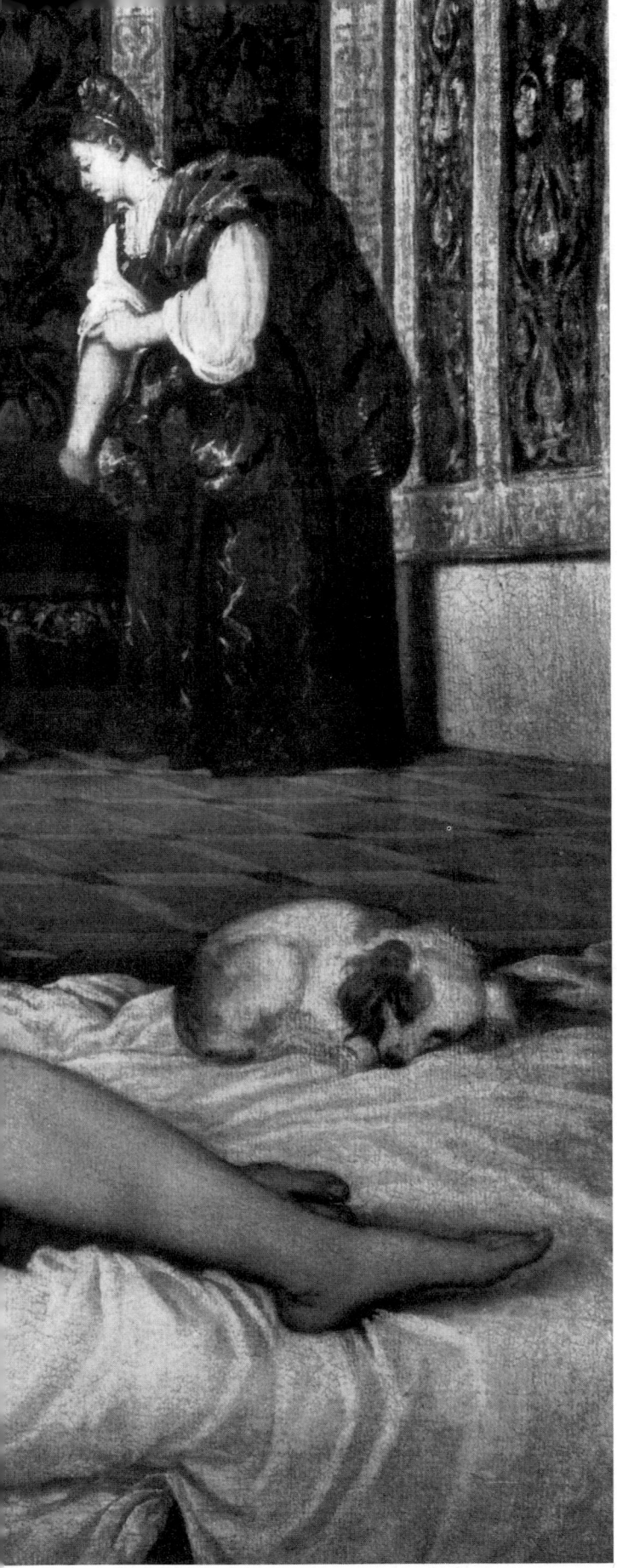

a third of the canvas swallowed by shadow; as for the *Castelfranco Madonna*, in which he had to conform to current conventions, he adopted a pyramidal arrangement which was totally commonplace. The *Concert champêtre*, which is certainly his last work, is better balanced, but still forms juxtaposed compartments. Titian was to show a far greater facility in the distribution of planes and figures. What brings

unity to a picture by Giorgione is the immersion of all the forms in a single fluid, a single atmosphere. Painting, as he did, according to spontaneous impulse, Giorgione sometimes hesitated, and recent X-rays of three of his paintings have revealed to us the ghosts of these uncertainties. It even seems that he sometimes abandoned a canvas because of his feelings of dissatisfaction or despair: two of his paintings were completed by others, the *Three philosophers* by Sebastiano Veneziano and the *Sleeping Venus* by Titian.

Several factors combine to suggest that Giorgione may well have been the first artist to paint for his own pleasure. The silence of the archives proves that he received few commissions (one only is recorded, that of the decoration of the Fondaco dei Tedeschi). In addition, he is known to have painted only one religious picture, the *Castelfranco Madonna*. F. Saxl has argued (*Lectures*, London 1957) that the *Sleeping Venus* seems to have been inspired by the description of the sleep of a nymph in the *Hypnerotomachia Poliphili* of Francesco Colonna, a book which reflected the literary imagination in Venice in Giorgione's day. But this description is itself certainly based on some antique statue of Ariadne. And in any case, Giorgione cannot have been illustrating the *Hypnerotomachia*, since he turned the nymph into a Venus, a fact proved finally by the presence of Cupid, overpainted subsequently but recently revealed by X-ray examination. The artist's imagination, aroused by his reading, drew an ideal image from the subject in the process of transposing it. The theme of closed eyes also constituted an innovation in painting; the pure face expresses latent being, closed shut upon its mystery.

It is curious that most of the pictures by Giorgione of which record has survived, whether landscapes or figures, represent unexplained subjects. But this fact does not necessarily make Giorgione a hermetic painter, creating enigmatic variations on obscure themes. It would seem, rather, that (as Venturi has claimed in his rebuttal of Hartlaub's thesis) he was the first painter to dispense with a subject, that is to say the first of all modern painters. It is easy to imagine the contrast between Giovanni Bellini, who had never in his life created a work which had not been commissioned in advance, and his independent-minded young pupil disinclined to paint for churches or monasteries, or to amuse his colleagues in the *scuole* with the kind of picture-books that Carpaccio was turning out at the time. Here was an artist impatient to express his feelings, thinking of painting in terms of a passionate quest for a new universe, the universe of the soul. He was fortunate to have the encouragement of a circle of aristocratic art

91 Titian (1485/90–1576). *Reclining Nude*, known as the *Venus of Urbino*. Florence, Uffizi.

The *Venus of Urbino* is the first naturalistic nude in the history of painting. Giorgione, who inspired Titian's theme, had painted a goddess; Titian, on the other hand, posed a living woman in the pose of Giorgione's Dresden *Venus*.

lovers who bought his work, and when the connoisseur Marcantonio Michiel prepared his notes on Venetian collections in 1525 it was in the *palazzi* of the Vendramins, the Grimanis, the Veniers, the Loredans, the Corners and the Rams that he discovered Giorgione's paintings.

Here was a veritable revolution, a major turning-point in the history of painting: a picture ceased being merely an appendage to a monument, dependent upon a social structure for its existence; it became an autonomous object, a *work of art*.

This new concept of a picture as a glorious message springing straight from the depths of the soul also gave it scarcity value, and soon wealthy art lovers were vying with each other to acquire these unique objects at any price. On 25 October 1510, Isabella d'Este, Marchioness of Mantua, who was always on the lookout for precious objects to add to her collection, wrote to Taddeo Albano of Venice asking him to try to obtain for her a *Notte* (nocturnal scene) which she described as *molto bella e singolare*, and thought must be among the effects of 'Zorzo da Castelfranco'; as far as the price was concerned, she authorized him to pay any sum necessary, 'for fear that the work should be bought by someone else'. This proves that Giorgione did not work to order, and that there were pictures in his studio for sale. Isabella, who had been frustrated in her repeated efforts to obtain a picture from Leonardo da Vinci, had no better luck with this *Notte*; we know from Taddeo Albano's reply that there were two pictures, but that neither of these was available. However, he may possibly have negotiated successfully for the *Concert champêtre* on her behalf, since that painting was later in the collection of the Gonzagas of Mantua.

The vague nature of the landscapes in Giorgione's paintings adds weight to the argument that he is a 'pure' painter, that is to say, one who seeks to fulfil his inner yearnings by composing pictures in which he is not obliged to interpret a given theme. Only the *Tempesta* lends itself to description, and even here the enumeration of its constituent details is soon exhausted (supporters of the thesis of hermetic intention have tried to see in it the four elements), whereas the elements that make up the topographical universe of a picture of Bellini's such as the *St Francis* (New York, Frick collection) are endless. The landscapes of the *Three philosophers*, the *Concert champêtre* and the *Castelfranco Madonna* are so featureless that they cannot be related to any actual site, and the fairly precise landscape of the *Sleeping Venus* is by Titian. For Giorgione, nature is not a spectacle unfurled for the eye's contemplation, and he avoids depicting panoramic landscapes; from his

vantage-point in a single meadow, whose small space surrounds him, he creates the 'motif', the unified subject, as painted by the modern landscape painter. Since for him nature is one and indivisible, it can be perfectly expressed in any single one of its aspects, in a small corner of the Venetian countryside where he was born, for instance.

At one time, Giorgione was hailed as the first artist to paint the *tramonto*, the hour tinged with the sadness of the setting sun, described by Aretino and so dear to Venetians, especially Titian. This opinion was based upon the *Concert champêtre*, but its twilight shadows were in fact the product of the progressive discoloration of the glazes, and the cleaned surface eventually revealed full daylight. The landscape of the *Castelfranco Madonna* is imbued with the clear light of morning. And in the *Three philosophers*, the sun is rising, not setting.

Until Bellini's time, painting had been a search for harmony between God, man and the world, but for post-Bellini Venetians the dialogue was reduced to the last two terms. Giorgione transformed painting into the expression of an emotion, the confidential message of a soul. The beauty of the *Concert champêtre* has tended to draw attention away from the essential peculiarity of this themeless picture. It would be difficult to attribute any symbolic meaning to this gathering of nudes and young musicians disporting themselves freely in natural surroundings. Yet this is a unique instance in Venetian painting. Although attempts have been made in the past to attribute the *Concert champêtre* to him, Titian never painted so *gratuitous* a picture: the Bridgewater House *Diana and Callisto*, which might be considered similar, symbolizes the three ages of man, while the three Ferrara *Bacchanals* are evocations of the golden age. Titian is in fact a true theme painter, an 'illustrator' seeking motivation for his inspiration in a literary subject. Palma Vecchio was the only Venetian to imitate Giorgione, and the clumsiness of his efforts are only too apparent in his *Concert champêtre* (Uffizi). Giorgione's whole concept was so modern that it inspired Manet three centuries later. The enigma of the *Concert champêtre* is the enigma of Giorgione himself: in its magnificent isolation, this work, certainly the last that the artist completed, is his supreme message.

During the sixteenth century, painting in the north of Italy was fed by the two contrary streams of Giorgionism and classicism, but all these currents can be traced back eventually to Giorgione. If he had never lived, it would have fallen to Titian to lead the rebellion against the heritage of Bellini, and himself invent the free handling which abandoned the definition of forms in favour of a subtle moulding of shades of expression. In the event, it sufficed for him to borrow this handling from Giorgione and develop its possibilities, although along the lines of a different creative method. As with Giorgione, his primary concern was painterly quality, but he differed in that he first carefully led up to the work itself through a whole series of drawings; in this way, while using a visibly improvised handling, Titian in fact progressed unerringly towards a meticulously calculated composition. Throughout his long life he never ceased to multiply the resources of this free handling, incorporating extensively into his pictures blends of colours which have, unfortunately, lost their true values over the years. Titian also owed to Giorgione the sense of intimate harmony between man and nature which favoured the expression of his sensuality and which allowed him, for example, to evoke the twilight in the *Entombment* (Louvre) simply through its reflection on the faces of the participants. Furnished with all these techniques, he became the poet of Venetian painting, creating forms derived from the contemplation of pagan or Christian literary sources. Up to the moment when, in extreme old age, a new fire began to course in his veins, he always remained centred on this art of averages that depended upon a harmonious relation-ship between the artist and his social surroundings.

Without going as far as Berenson, who called Titian the Augustus John of his time, one can say that he preceded van Dyck (who was greatly influenced by him) in the role of the aristocracy's favourite portraitist, eager to furnish a flattering image of his sitter; no one excelled him in expressing the soul of Venice with its voluptuous inclinations. The three Bacchanal paintings, commissioned by Alfonso d'Este, Duke of Ferrara, for his alabaster chamber, contain a sensuality which bursts out like a fanfare at the beginning of Titian's career; but this freedom in fact justified itself as an evocation of antiquity. Similarly, the *Feast of the gods* which Bellini painted for the same room, and the landscape of which was later repainted by Titian, derived the inspiration for its scenes from Ovid, Lucian and Philostratus respectively. This expansiveness of a life without restraints was the prerogative of the gods, not mankind, and was situated in a world of myth rather than reality. Titian showed far greater boldness when he painted the picture, incorrectly called the *Venus of Urbino* (*pl. 91*), which in 1538 in a letter from Guidobaldo II of Urbino is designated simply as a 'nude woman'. This was the first time that a woman had displayed her naked charms to a painter without the pretext that she was simply there to conjure up the beauty of some immortal in the artist's mind. Here we are entering the world of

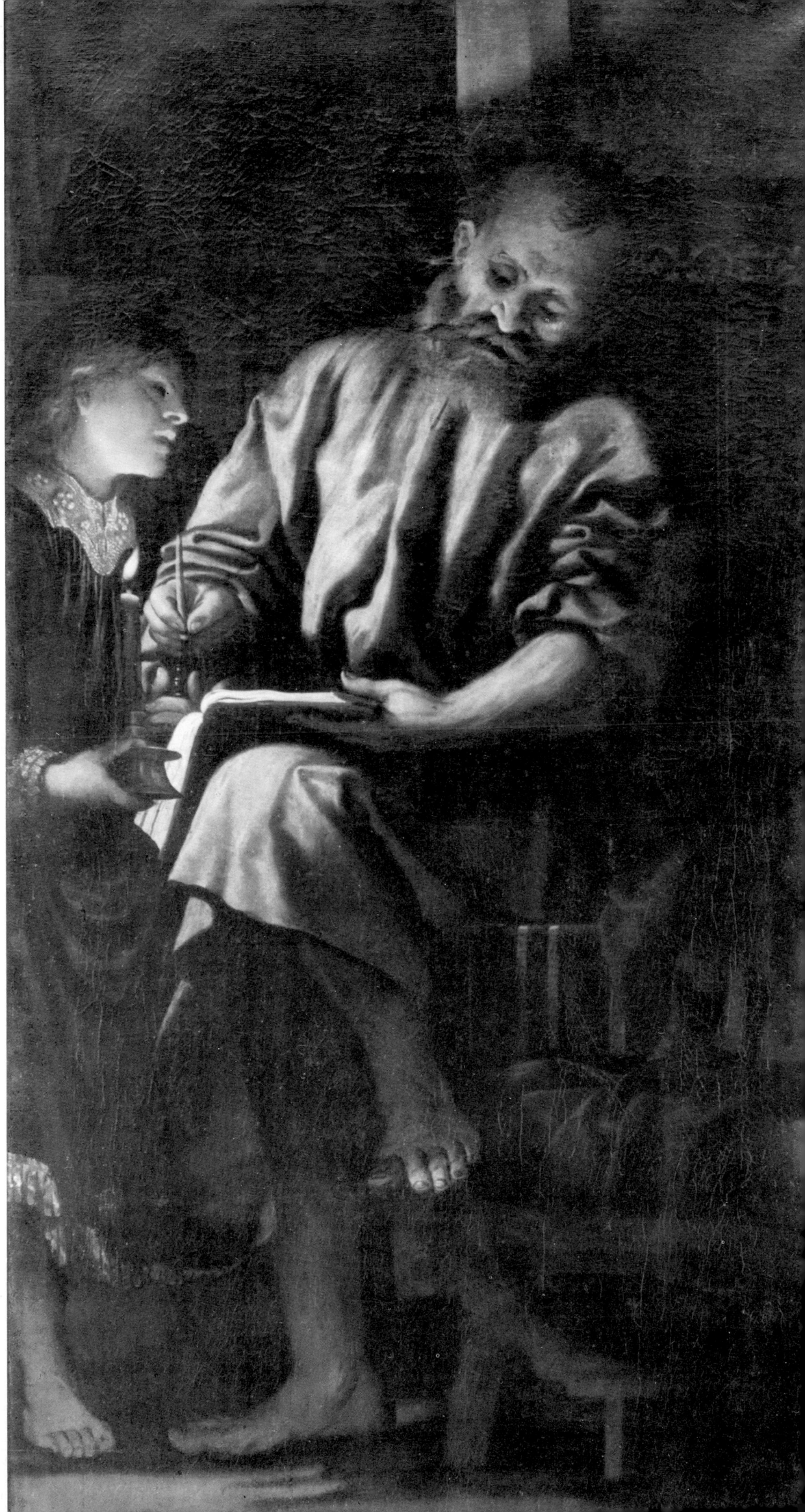

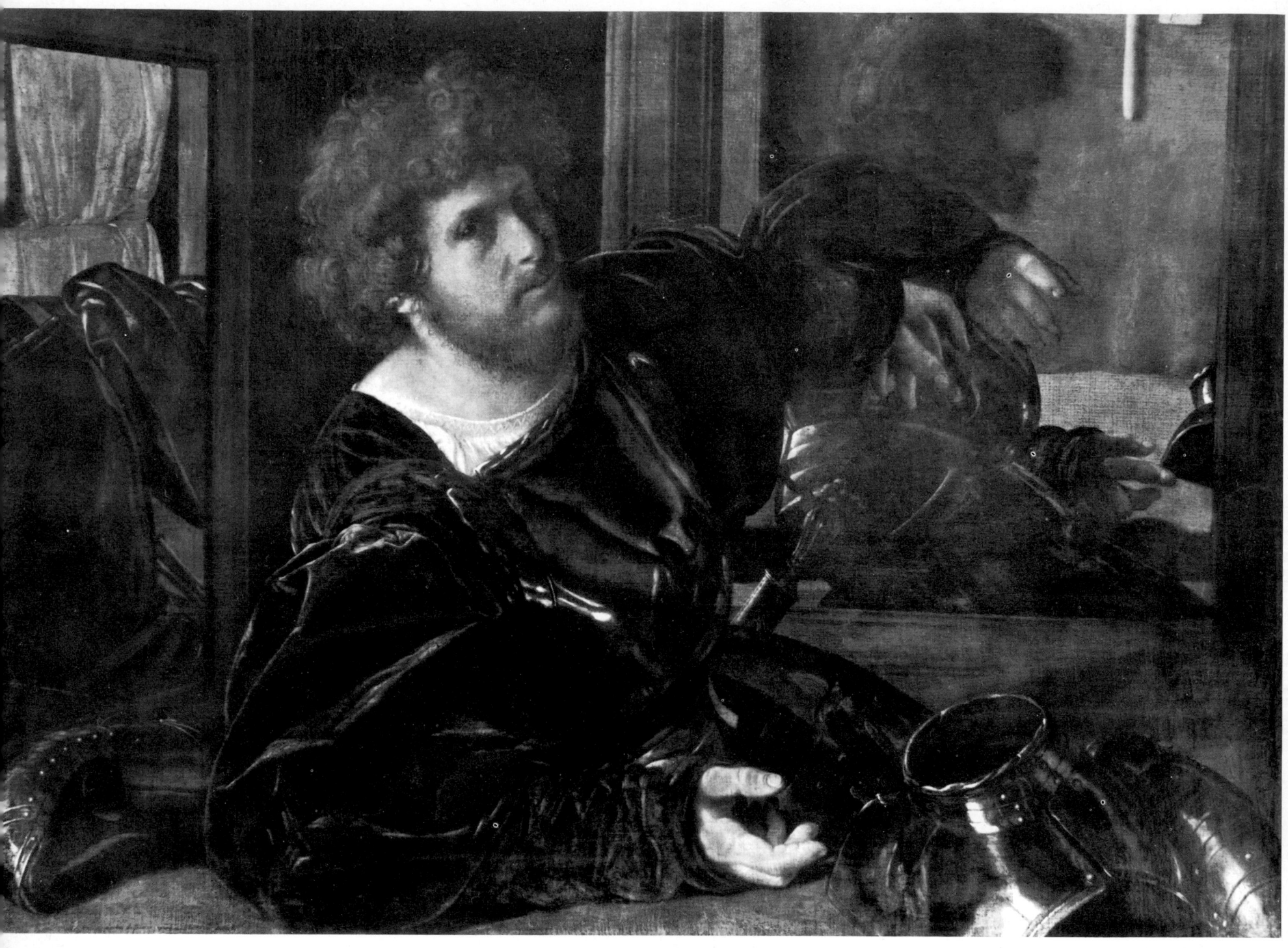

93 Giovanni Girolamo Savoldo (c. 1480–after 1548). *Man at arms*. Paris, Louvre.

The bold composition of Savoldo's *Man at arms* is doubtless inspired by a lost picture by Giorgione, mentioned by Vasari.

modern painting; this nude study, which does not represent Leonora, Duchess of Urbino, as was once thought, but, as the duke's correspondence establishes, a studio model, initiates a long line of descent that passes through Velázquez, Boucher, Fragonard and Manet, to end with Renoir.

Classicism had hardly begun to establish itself at Rome, in the pontificates of Julius II and Leo X, when a reaction against it began to set in. The most astonishing aspect of this reaction is that Raphael himself anticipated it in the last Stanze of the Vatican. In Florence, this ferment was already brewing in 1520. In northern Italy, though, the

situation was more complex. There, anticlassicism did not have the character of a reaction, since its first vigorous impulse was synchronous with the classicism whose principles were established by Titian in Venice itself; it was, rather, a spontaneous movement which sprang up in the provincial schools of Brescia, Cremona and Ferrara, and which in many ways foreshadows romanticism. The precocity of this form of romanticism is all the more remarkable if one thinks that already in 1521 Moretto and Il Romanino were commissioned to paint the chapel of the Blessed Sacrament in San Giovanni Evangelista at Brescia, and that in 1520

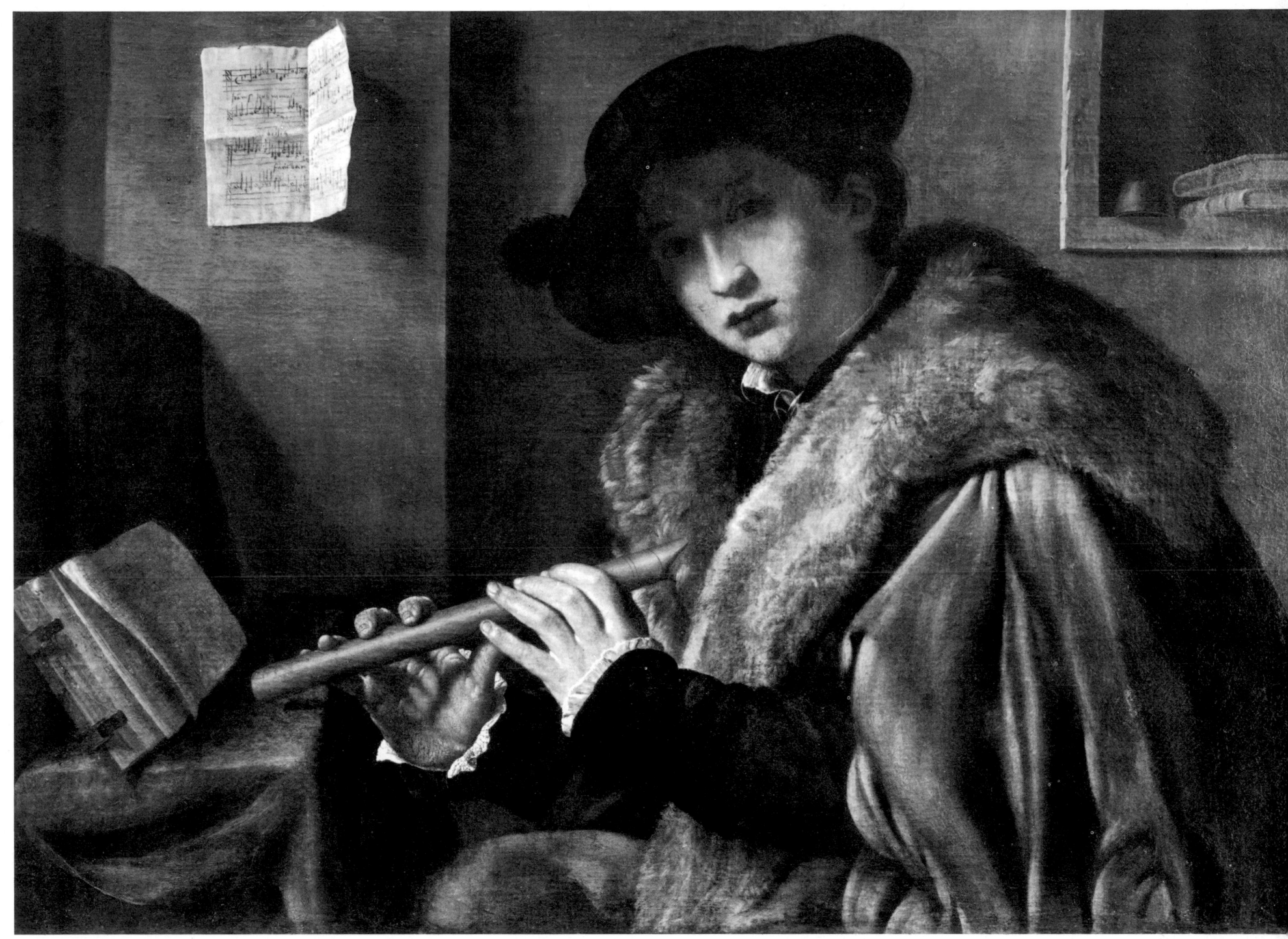

the administrators of the cathedral of Cremona cancelled their contract with Il Romanino, so that the decorations for the dome should be completed by the extravagant Pordenone, whom they considered more 'avant-garde'.

This romantically oriented movement has been called 'Giorgionesque', although attempts have also been made to discover local roots for it, especially in Brescia, and so to identify a 'pre-Giorgionism'. The idea of a link with Giorgione rests mainly on a certain form of portrait, with a melancholy expression, which was supposedly inspired by a few figures formerly attributed to Giorgione but now

generally considered to be copies of lost originals. But even if one were to make an exception in the case of the Brunswick portrait, and treat it as a faithful image of a lost portrait of Giorgione, it would still remain a very fragile base upon which to erect this whole edifice. What is more probable is the Giorgionesque derivation of the romantic interpretation of landscape indulged in by Savoldo and Dosso Dossi, for all the painters in and around Venice must have been struck by the novelty of Giorgione's particular feeling for nature.

As regards the question of whether Giorgione may be considered the inventor of chiaroscuro,

94 Giovanni Girolamo Savoldo. *Flute-player*. Florence, collection Contini-Bonacossi.

To plunge the face in a portrait in semi-darkness, as a way of expressing the mystery of the soul, was a singularly audacious notion at that time.

nothing in his extant paintings lends weight to such a supposition. We have, it is true, documentary evidence that he painted two *Notti*, one of which was so fine that, after his death, Isabella d'Este made every effort to obtain it. On the other hand, it has been pointed out that in the sixteenth century the term '*Notte*' applied to this kind of picture always designates a Nativity, whether it is a night-piece or not. It has even been suggested that Giorgione's *Notte* might be the Allendale *Nativity* now in the National Gallery, Washington, in which the lighting effect is of broad daylight. As far as present historical knowledge is able to determine, the two earliest *tenebrosi* pictures in Italy are by Savoldo and Il Romanino; their great originality lies in the fact that, whereas in Correggio's *Notte* (about 1530) and two other night-pieces by Savoldo the illumination is a supernatural light emanating from the Infant Jesus, in these two pictures the lighting is produced by an artificial source. They both represent the apostle St Matthew visited by the angel and writing under his inspiration, either by the light of an oil-lamp (Savoldo's version, in the Metropolitan Museum) or a candle (Romanino's version, in San Giovanni Evangelista). Raphael had used chiaroscuro in his composition at the Vatican depicting St Peter delivered from prison (*pl. 72*), where a supernatural light emanating from the angel floods the whole prison, while outside the soldiers are lit by their own torches in a moonlit landscape. But the chiaroscuro of Il Romanino's *St Matthew* (*pl. 92*), as also that of Savoldo's picture, is of a quite different nature: the feeble glimmer of the lamp or the candle produces a complex play of violently contrasted lights and shadows which expresses the pathos of the inner life, as in the nocturnal scenes of the followers of Caravaggio. Indeed, there is such a family likeness between Il Romanino's *St Matthew* and the first St Matthew painted by Caravaggio for San Luigi dei Francesci, Rome, that it seems hardly possible that the latter should not have seen the earlier composition. The theme of the apostles, ordinary humans transfigured by the Holy Spirit, was to become one of the favourite motifs for seventeenth-century artists concerned to evoke the depths of the human soul. The paintings created by Il Romanino on the four pendentives of the cupola of the chapel of the Blessed Sacrament at San Giovanni Evangelista constitute the work of a genuine precursor.

The situation in the provinces was particularly favourable for avant-garde painting. The history of painting abounds in examples of provincial artists inhibited neither by the dogmas nor the traditions laid down in the great art centres. These blind creators often showed greater foresight than the masters who lent their lustre to the schools. An imagination unbridled by conformist patterns, a hand never subject to automatism, a blissful ignorance of technical rules, sometimes combined to produce artists of genius who instinctively anticipated future developments despite the apparent disadvantage of isolation.

In antiquity, classical aesthetics, although reigning supreme in the large cities, gave way, in the outer limits of the Roman world, to a feeling for forms which constituted a profound influence in the formation of the sculptors, and anticipated that of the Middle Ages. In a later age, while the learned speculations of official theological art held sway in Byzantium, monks in the rock-monasteries of Cappadocia, caring little about dogma and following their inclinations in their paintings, evolved an emotionally charged religious idiom which became known to the West through intermediaries and provided inspiration for the artists of the Dugento and Trecento. In the extraordinary creative ferment of the Renaissance, Italy, the country most subject to the orthodox rule of the established schools, nevertheless offers us examples of provincial painters whose work was created without reference to tradition despite the fact that they sometimes lived in the immediate vicinity of a great centre. Within more or less easy reach of Florence or Venice there were 'provincial' centres in which painters gave free expression to their temperament.

The Lombard Duchy of Brescia, conquered early in the fifteenth century by Venice, had been a war-like city famous for its arsenals, and still knew how to bear arms when occasion warranted. By the sixteenth century, it was no longer one of those places in which history is made, but it continued to dream of past glories, and Il Romanino painted on its walls plumed warriors who, with all their swashbuckling airs, betrayed some sense of uneasiness. To have one's portrait painted in Venice by Titian was a guarantee that it would radiate health and serenity, whereas a Brescia painter would bring some inner torment to the surface. The painter most faithful to the spirit of Giorgione was the Brescian Savoldo. In his *Man at arms* (*pl. 93*), reflected in a play of mirrors, he was certainly imitating a picture by Giorgione described by Vasari and now lost. The people Savoldo shows us seem lost in thought, plunged in an anxious and heartfelt self-questioning. The *Flute-player* (*pl. 94*) may be listening to the last echo of his instrument or else dreaming of as yet unplayed melodies; his face is half in a shadow, a boldness which Titian, whose models expected their likenesses to be well lit, would never have got away with. The figure is swathed in a soft, fine, ash-grey shadow which colours the face, explores the greys of the fur and caresses the delicate hands.

It is difficult to tell whether a picture such as the *Flute-player* was done as a portrait or simply for the artist's own pleasure, as must have been the case with the *Peasant*, who had obviously not commissioned it. In any case, it seems extremely probable that, apart from the works he completed for the great and for churches, Savoldo painted for the sake of painting, in the spirit of Giorgione; Titian, pre-eminently the 'painter of his age', never permitted himself this luxury. Savoldo was far more interested than Titian in experimenting with colours. The intensity of Titian's colours is flattened by their fusion in a tonal unity; the true colourists, Lotto and Savoldo, were outside Venice, outside Titian's orbit, at least, and it would seem to be from these that Veronese was to derive the brilliance of his colour. Savoldo's work shows his fondness for unusual colours: blue-greys, silvery greys, garnet-reds, pinks, pure whites, deep blacks, greenish blues, purplish violets, oranges, bright yellows. On one occasion, in the *Mary Magdalen approaching the Sepulchre* (*pl. 96*), he produces a great burst of violent yellow which drenches the whole picture: such a bold stroke was not to be repeated again until the advent of Tiepolo. Usually, though, what unifies all his colours and prevents them from being discordant is a chiaroscuro which envelops them in a soft shadow, or sometimes adulterates all the tones by converting them into the hues of a night-piece, thus anticipating El Greco's effects. Savoldo was, indeed, an extraordinary precursor, anticipating not only El Greco, but also Veronese, Caravaggio, Tiepolo. To this list one might add Bassano, whose landscapes he foreshadows in his liking for rustic settings; he must have been the first to include the portrait of a farmhand in a picture; and in his *Nativity* he gives St Joseph the furrowed features of a man of the people.

Although Savoldo knew what was going on in Venice, having worked there on several occasions, he did not allow himself to be diverted from his purpose. Moretto, on the other hand, wavered between a belated Bellinism and the seductions of Titian, although these proved rather too sophisticated for his provincial timidity. But he loved the subtle hues of Brescia, especially the greys. The soul of Brescia came alive in his portraits, in which, as in certain portraits by Savoldo, the hands are open and stretched out towards the spectator, as in expressionistic portraits of the baroque era.

Il Romanino, who worked at Brescia, Cremona

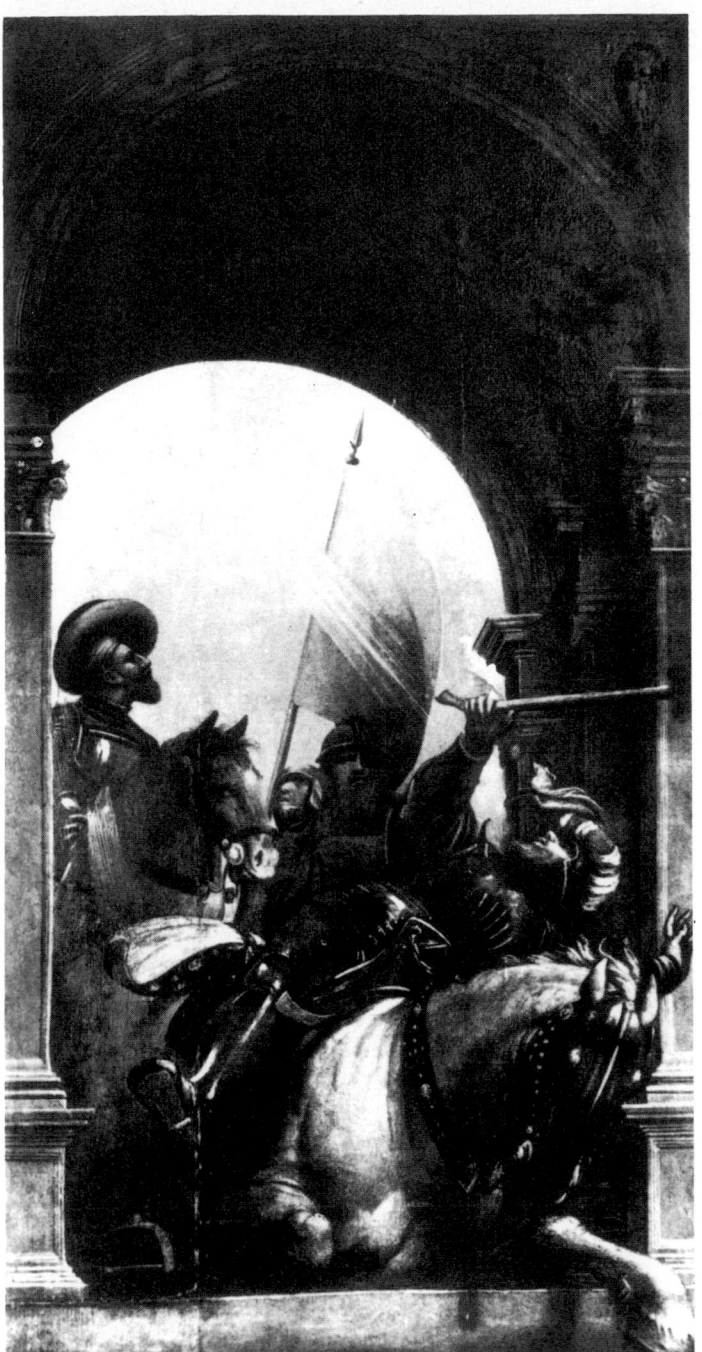

95 Pordenone (*c.* 1484–1539). *The Conversion of St Paul*. Spilimbergo, Cathedral.

Breaking away from classicism, Pordenone was the first artist bold enough to 'break' the surface of his painting by making the figures seem to be moving towards the spectator.

and Trent, was avowedly provincial and brashly self-confident. Whether fresco or oil, each painting was for him a bravura piece in which he sought to astonish, by any one of a number of means: indifference to the subject, off-handedness, not to say impudence, the use of airless compositions packed with human figures, squat bodies surmounted by bullet heads, slipshod treatment, exaggerated foreshortening, caricatured expressions. His *Last Supper* (church of Montichiari) accumulates two clusters of unprepossessing characters. And yet, to show off his knowledge, he painted one of the most beautiful still-lifes that Italy has produced, a composition that can stand comparison with the best seventeenth-century Dutch work in that idiom.

The proud city of Cremona, prosperous thanks to the fertility of the surrounding countryside, was too far from Venice to arouse her cupidity, and tended

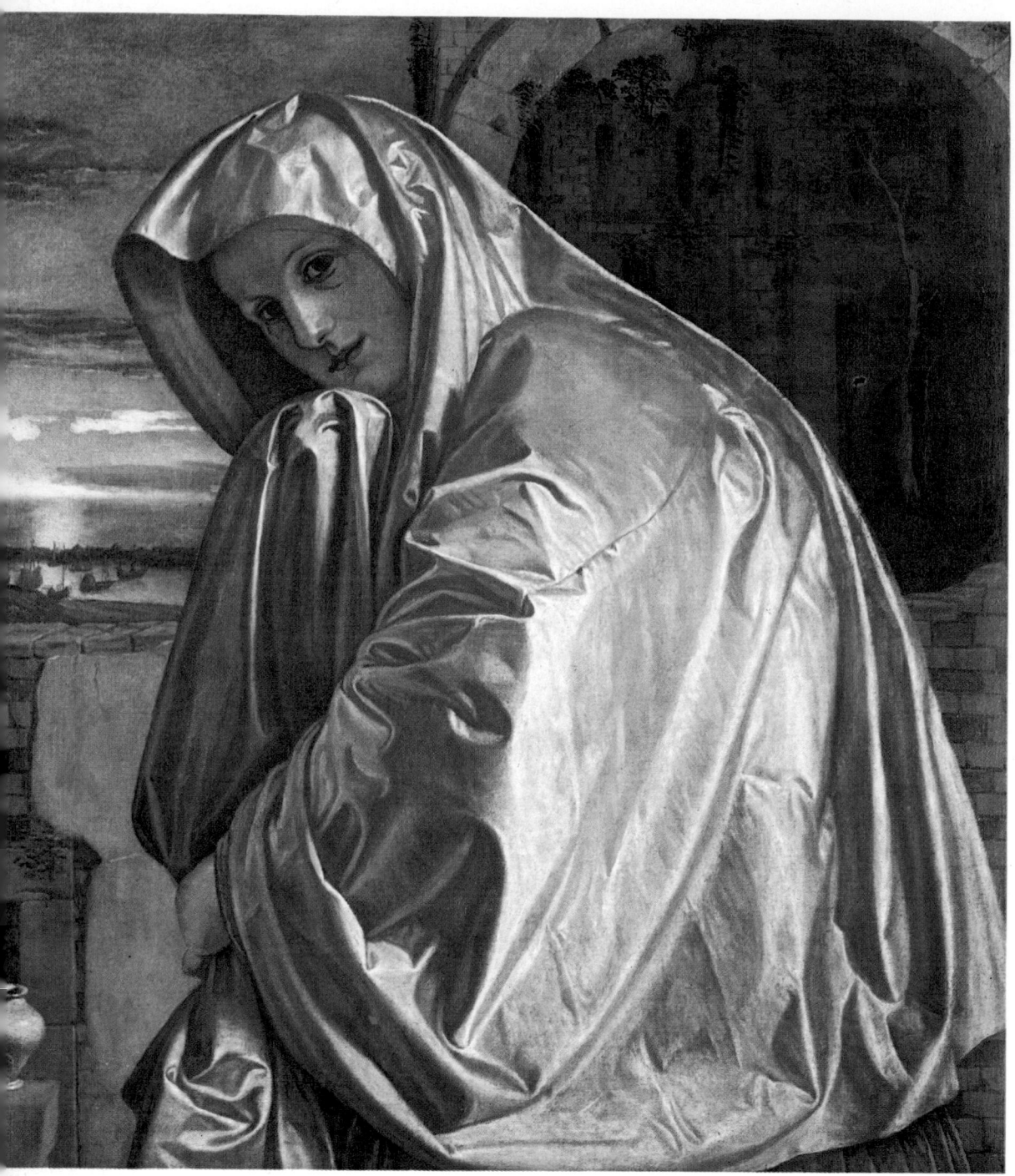

ing eight frescoes, he was replaced in 1517 by Altobello Melone, another Cremonese painter who 'thawed out' the Bellinesque immobility and brought to graphic language a new freedom which Il Romanino was to draw upon when he took over the project in 1519. This was Il Romanino's first important commission, and in the four frescoes of the Passion which he painted in the nave he indulged in every whim that his imagination could conjure up, filling the compositions with the extravagant costumes of which he was so fond. But this did not seem audacious enough to the people of Cremona, and in August 1520 the cathedral's newly appointed administration grievously wronged Romanino by cancelling the contract that their predecessors had made with him. They replaced him with Pordenone, whom they qualified as a *magister summus et pictor excellentissimus* (supreme master and most excellent painter), and from whom they expected miracles just because he had been to Rome.

Emboldened by this expression of confidence, Pordenone took every conceivable artistic liberty, and turned the cathedral into a veritable experimental laboratory for his spatial and expressionist researches, filling the dome with frenzied crowds and convulsive figures. These innovations must have proved perfectly acceptable to his patrons, since a bill of payment to him qualifies him as a *magister modernus*. Without a question, the avantgarde was in favour in Cremona!

Pordenone anticipated Caravaggio by sixty years, resembling him in his life as well as in his art. He appears to have been a violent man, and ready to cross swords at the slightest provocation. While at Venice, he is supposed to have incurred the enmity of the all-powerful Titian, for daring to enter into competition with him to win a commission from the doge, and actually winning the commission; after that, while painting at Santo Stefano there, he always kept a sword and buckler within reach. Although this story may be apocryphal, it fits in with what we know of his character from legal documents of the time. When his father died in 1533, he sued his brother Baldassare over the division of the inheritance. He was denounced by his brother for having abstracted some of the unapportioned goods, and after the ensuing brawl Baldassare lodged a complaint against Giovanni Antonio, with the Podestà, for having tried to lure him into an ambush. Pordenone's name, like that of Caravaggio, must have featured frequently in police reports. He came to a miserable end, under circumstances similar to those that attended, later, the death of Caravaggio, dying alone of a mysterious illness, in

96 Giovanni Girolamo Savoldo. *Mary Magdalen approaching the Sepulchre*. London, National Gallery.

In this picture Savoldo has painted a Venetian woman dressed up as Mary Magdalen, and invented a bold use of colours that was later imitated by Veronese and Tiepolo.

to gravitate in the orbit of Milan, where an insipid Leonardesque manner still prevailed. Cremona's success in resisting this tendency was doubtless due to the fact that she had been exposed to the eccentric influence of Ferrara. At the beginning of the sixteenth century, her school of painting had provided the meeting-point for various different tendencies which the cathedral's decoration emphasizes. Boccaccio Boccaccini, born in Ferrara of Cremonese parents, started work on it in 1514, in a spirit inspired by Peruginesque and Raphaelesque classicism, though not without bringing to these influences a personal accent that presaged the Emilian charm of his later work (*Nativity of the Virgin*). After paint-

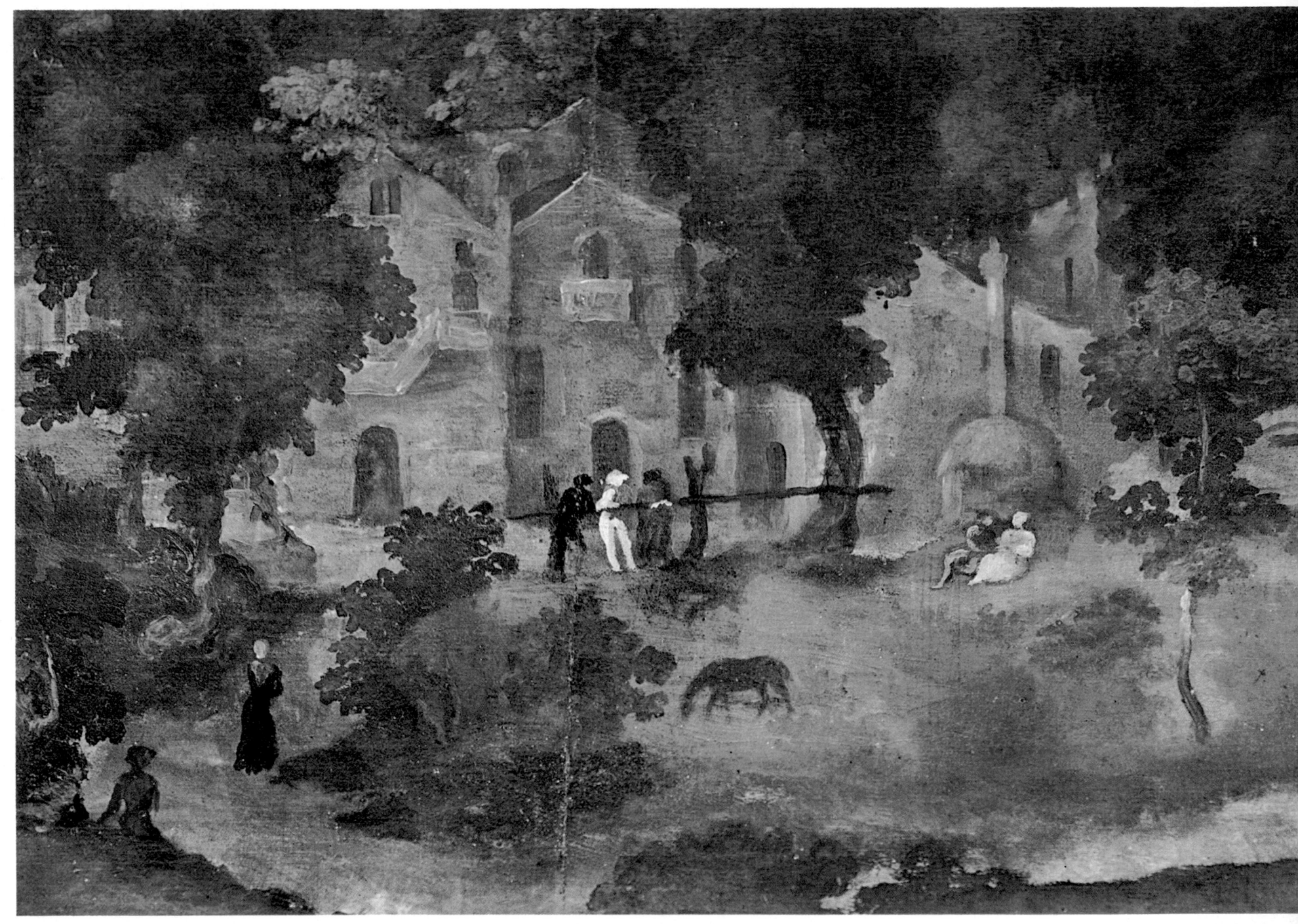

a Ferrara inn. He was probably poisoned; at least, that was the opinion of the dismayed duke who had invited him to Ferrara.

Pordenone was among the first painters to break down the barrier separating the spectator from the actors. Well before Caravaggio – in 1520 in Cremona, in fact – he directed the movements of his figures backwards, and in the *Christ nailed to the Cross* not only pointed the foot of the Cross towards the faithful but made it protrude beyond the cornice which edges the picture, while one of the thieves, his hair gripped by a soldier, is teetering in space, one arm hanging down over the same cornice. In the *Crowning with thorns*, a horseman is depicted as though in the process of springing into the nave; and the artist repeats this leap into space in an even more audacious manner in the *Conversion of St Paul* in Spilimbergo Cathedral (*pl. 95*). In the Scuola San Rocco, Venice, he hurls down on us the infirm who are supposed to jump into the *Pool of Bethesda*; the pool itself, rather than being painted, is suggested in the space between the spectator and the picture.

Even Caravaggio never went so far as Pordenone in producing effects of foreshortening seen from close up. There is, too, an aggressive quality in Pordenone which forces the spectator to take part in the confused mêlées he sets in action on the inner

97 Il Romanino. Landscape, detail of *The Visitation*. Brescia, Cathedral.

In painting this fragment of nature, Il Romanino seeks to communicate an impression rather than to describe.

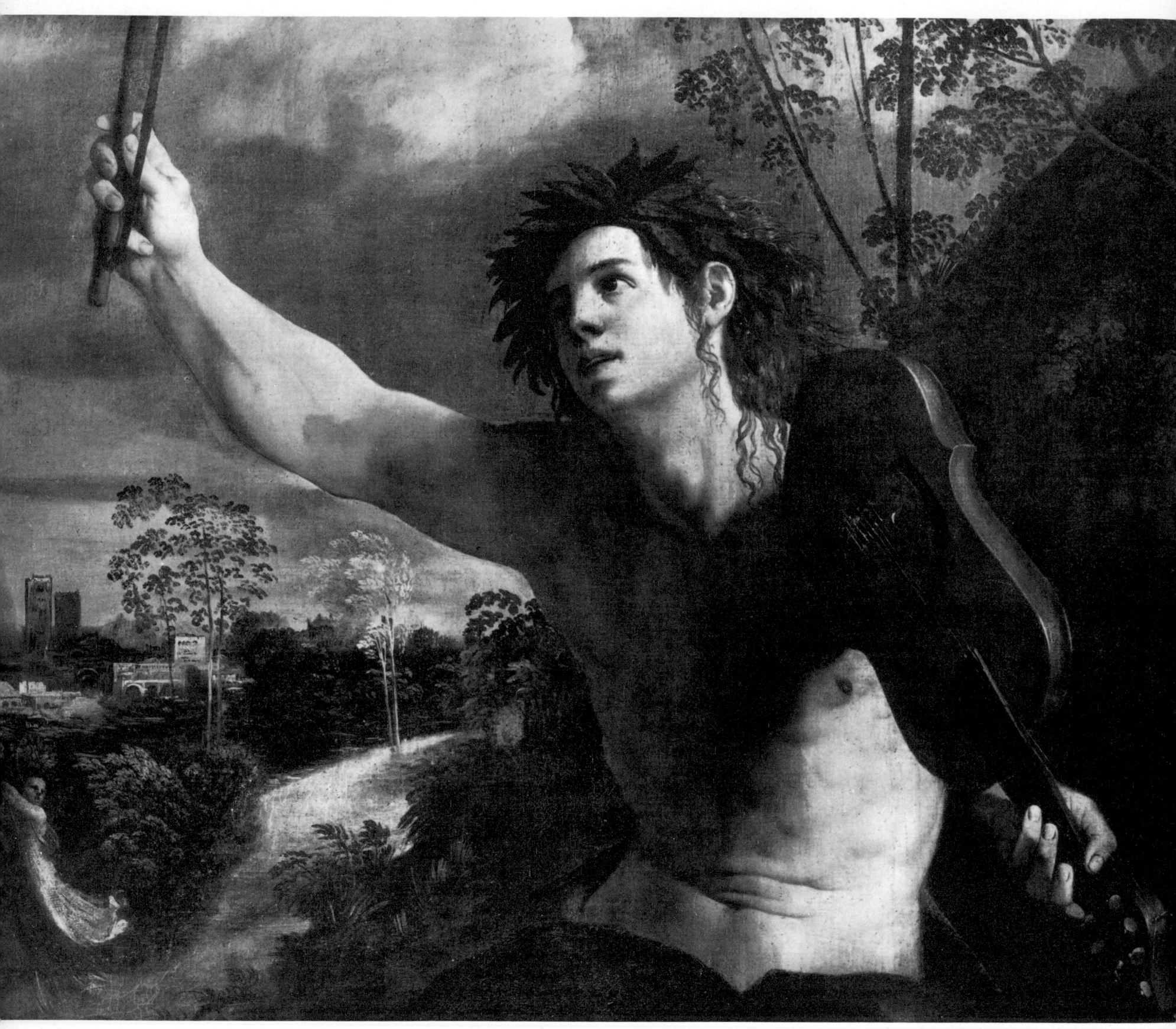

98 Dosso Dossi (*c.* 1479–1543). Detail of *Apollo and Daphne.* Rome, Galleria Borghese.

Dosso Dossi paints wild visionaries, such as this Apollo, which is as different as it could be from the serene figure of another violin-playing Apollo, that depicted by Raphael in the *Parnassus.*

99 Dosso Dossi. Landscape, detail of *Circe.* Florence, Uffizi. ▶

Dosso Dossi's views of nature, outlined boldly in a splash of touches of colour, are mirages rather than landscapes; they foreshadow Rembrandt's dream landscapes.

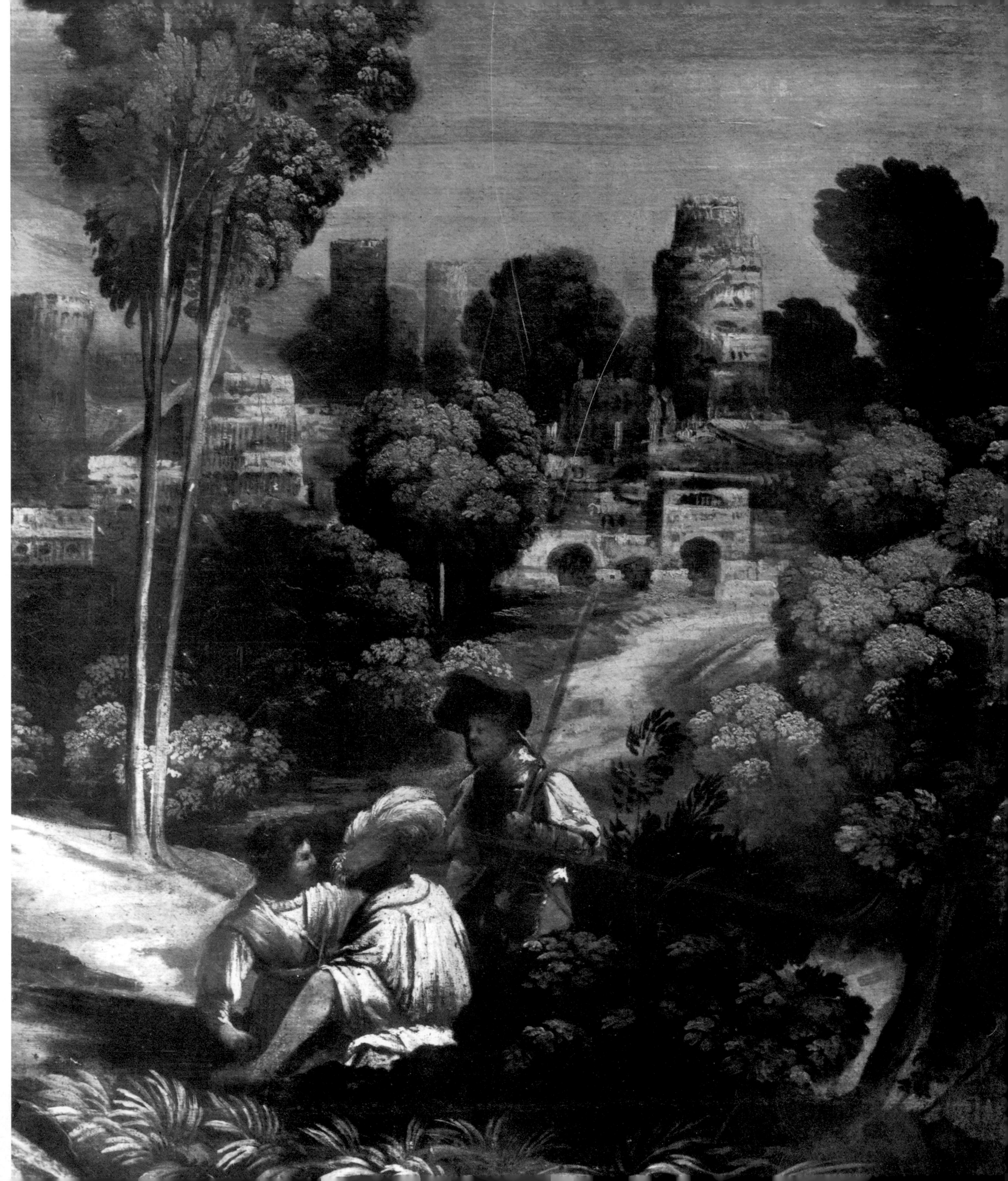

100 Dosso Dossi. *St John the Baptist*. Florence, Pitti.

This spectral image of *St John the Baptist* is doubtless a self-portrait of the artist.

walls of churches. The spectator ceases being a witness and becomes an actor in these battles of vagabonds; they are compulsively lifelike, because Pordenone went down to the slums to find his models, and re-created their violence in his hasty treatment, his slapdash drawing and his sketchy Daumier-like relief. On the wall of the façade of Cremona Cathedral, a colossal fresco showing a yelling mob in an apocalyptic storm turns out to be a *Crucifixion* acted out by footpads. All the participants in this drama, from the Christ to the thieves, from the holy women to the soldiers, are persons possessed. This vision of horror is all the more extraordinary if one bears in mind that by this date Michelangelo had not yet painted the *Last Judgment*. At Rome, Pordenone could only have seen the calm visions of Raphael or the intensely moving monumental frescoes of the Sistine ceiling.

Although the sheer power of biblical fervour emanating from the Sistine Chapel must have had an enormous effect in liberating this simple provincial from the constrictions of the style of Bellini, the sight of German engravings must have played some part too. These engravings had had such a success in northern Italy that Dürer journeyed to Venice specially to prevent his own from being counterfeited.

On the dome of the Malchiostro Chapel in the cathedral of Treviso, Pordenone imitated Michelangelo by painting the Creator of the world. But, with a boldness that was to remain unparalleled until the advent of the eighteenth-century Italian and German ceiling painters, he suggested movement by shifting the composition off-balance, propelling the cherubs towards one side of the concave surface. He repeated this composition, later, in the Franciscan church at Cortemaggiore, and here the group of cherubs comes tumbling down over the edge of the cornice in the direction of the altar picture which depicts the Immaculate Conception. In both these domes, the sky seems literally to be tipping over on to the earth. Pordenone is the first painter to have filled the enclosed space between a church's outer walls by projecting images beyond the partition-walls on which they are painted, thus creating that life of forms in space which the baroque art of the seventeenth and eighteenth centuries was to rediscover. This animation of the interior through mural decoration was later to be controlled by the baroque painters as though they were harmonizing a ballet or concerto; but Pordenone achieved the effect in terms of confusion and anarchy. One cannot but admire the sheer power of imagination that drove this passionate artist to launch himself upon his frescoes at Cremona Cathedral at the moment

in time when Raphael was breathing his last, and when, in neighbouring Ferrara, Titian was just completing, in the *camerini d'oro*, his voluptuous visions of the golden age.

Dosso Dossi had also had a part in decorating these *camerini d'oro*, having collaborated with Titian in painting the *Feast of Cybele* there. This is one of Dossi's only two classical works, the other being *Circe* (a theme he treated twice: Uffizi, Florence, *pl. 99*, and National Gallery of Art, Washington). The unfounded suggestion that Ferrara's spirit of rebellious independence had died with Cosimo Tura and Ercole Roberti was disproved, not only by Lodovico Mazzolini (died before 1530) with his *Massacre of the Innocents* (Uffizi), but by Dossi himself. Perhaps it was his love of parallels that inspired Vasari to provide Dossi with the same year of birth as Ariosto: there is no doubt that the two were twin geniuses, in any case. The epic of *Orlando furioso*, which has continued to fire the imagination of painters including Delacroix, was born in the court of Ferrara, with its poetic, dream-like atmosphere. It would be fascinating to know how it came about that the ancient magical world dear to the Celts achieved expression in this city of the Renaissance: there is no more astonishing literary creation than this poem in which farce alternates with tragedy; in which the heroes fight and struggle surrounded by the powers released by wizards, or in thrall to enchantments woven by the sorceresses who are their lovers; in which the living and the inanimate constantly exchange their forms; in which Roland, the wisest of knights-errant, pursues love fruitlessly while sowing it along his path, and finally loses his reason. A topsy-turvy world, where mirage succeeds mirage in an endless chain, where the very concept of man breaks down in the seething swirl of a nature in perpetual creative gestation.

It is the reflections of this poetic world which illuminate with their lightning flashes Dosso Dossi's strange pictures. We know little about the man himself, except that his sense of the bizarre was not always appreciated, if we are to believe the story of his setback at the Este palace, where Girolamo Genga is supposed to have gone so far as to have Dossi's frescoes obliterated. Apparently he was on bad terms with his brother, Battista, although the latter collaborated with him on most of his pictures. Even in his run-of-the-mill religious pictures, he made every effort to adapt the required details to his whims; but without any doubt he preferred court-commissioned secular pictures, in which his imagination had freer rein. Some of these themes were clearly inspired by a poet: *Jupiter, Mercury and Virtue* (Vienna), for example, the *Nymph Calypso*

(Galleria Borghese), the *Departure of the Argonauts* (Washington), and the doubtful mythological subject known as *Antiope* (Marquess of Northampton). Dossi painted the magician Circe twice, the first time sweet and simple as a Giorgione nymph, the second time, ten years later, a figure fully conscious of her power. His most expressive painting is undoubtedly the *Apollo and Daphne* (*pl. 98*); its divine violinist could not be more distant in spirit from the peaceable musician who conducts the singing and dancing of the Muses in Raphael's *Parnassus*. Brandishing his bow, the delirious Apollo conjures up on the horizon impetuous storm winds from which a puny figure of a woman, usually considered to represent Daphne, is fleeing in terror. Set off by brilliant splashes of colour, Dossi's landscapes reveal to our eyes a russet ground burnt by the passage of some meteor, or hovering in the mists of a dream, like the landscapes of Rembrandt. In the midst of these enchanted castles and blazing forests, lit by the blood-red rays of the setting sun, live a hazily defined race of people born of water, fire, tree or wind, ready at a single wave of the magician's wand to revert to the elements. With his portraits, Dossi occasionally makes a real effort to follow the model, but at other times he seems to have re-created one of those dream beings who inhabit his distant provinces. It is perhaps not unduly fanciful to imagine that his own face may be reflected in that of the *St John the Baptist* whom he painted twice, a spectral countenance with melting features which seem ready to fade away altogether, so faintly are they delineated on the canvas (*pl. 100*).

Among all the painters of this period, Dosso Dossi is, with Savoldo, the one whose affiliation to Giorgione is the most evident. Savoldo's figures are clearly members of the same family as the saints of the *Castelfranco Madonna*. For his part, Dosso Dossi derived his feeling for landscape from the *Concert champêtre* and, even more, from the *Tempesta*. He sensed the impulse, common to man and nature, that quickens Giorgione's paintings, but he went even further: in his landscapes (*pl. 99*), man abandons his soul to nature. Lost in an evolving cosmos, man is reduced to the status of a furtive apparition, condemned at the very moment of his birth.

Thus, *giorgionismo* dissipates the mystery around Giorgione at the same time that it proves his worth. During his short life, the master of Castelfranco fashioned the most profound of all truths, that of the soul as prime mover. All the painting accomplished in Venice and within Venice's field of influence radiated this truth for a long time to come.

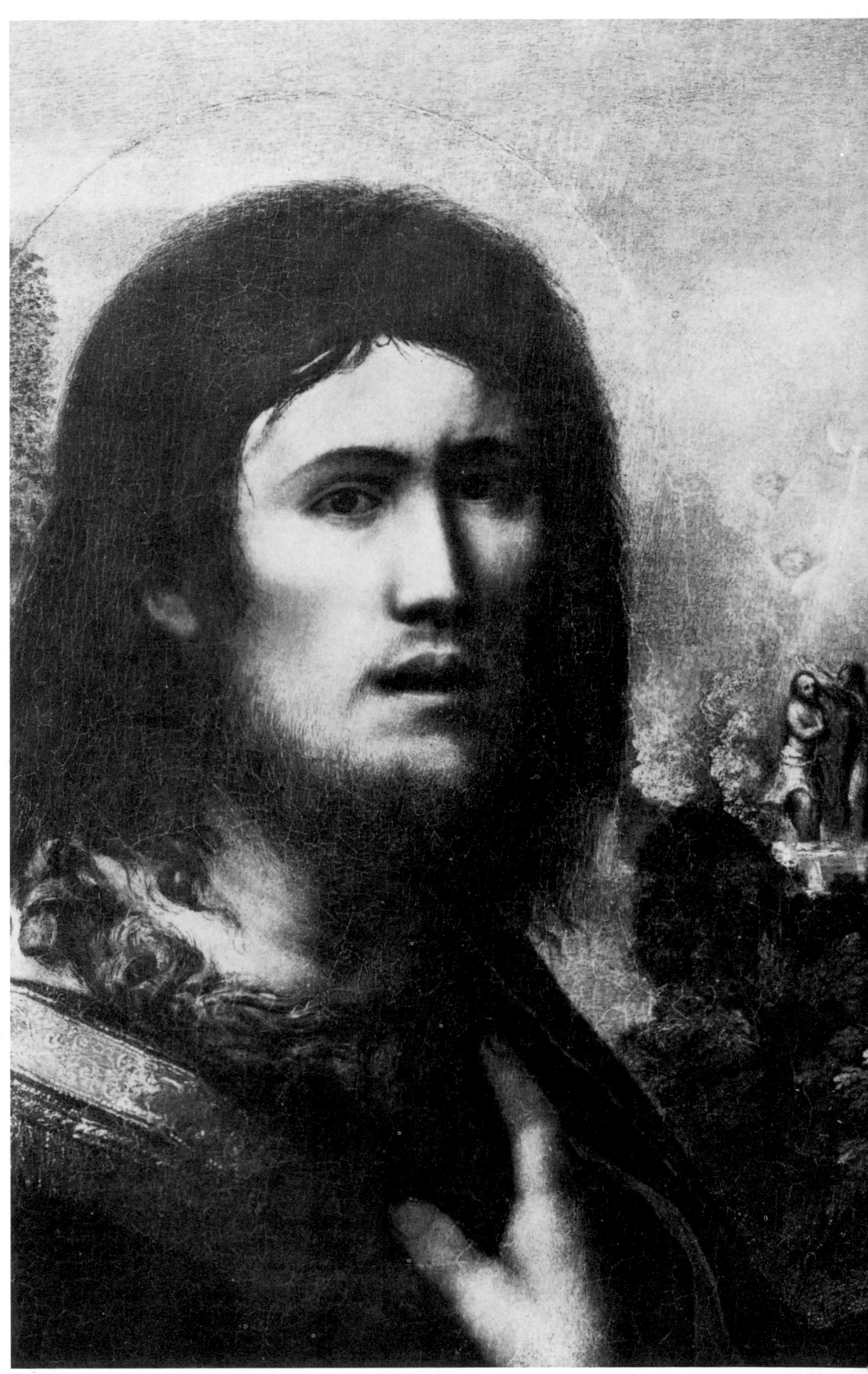

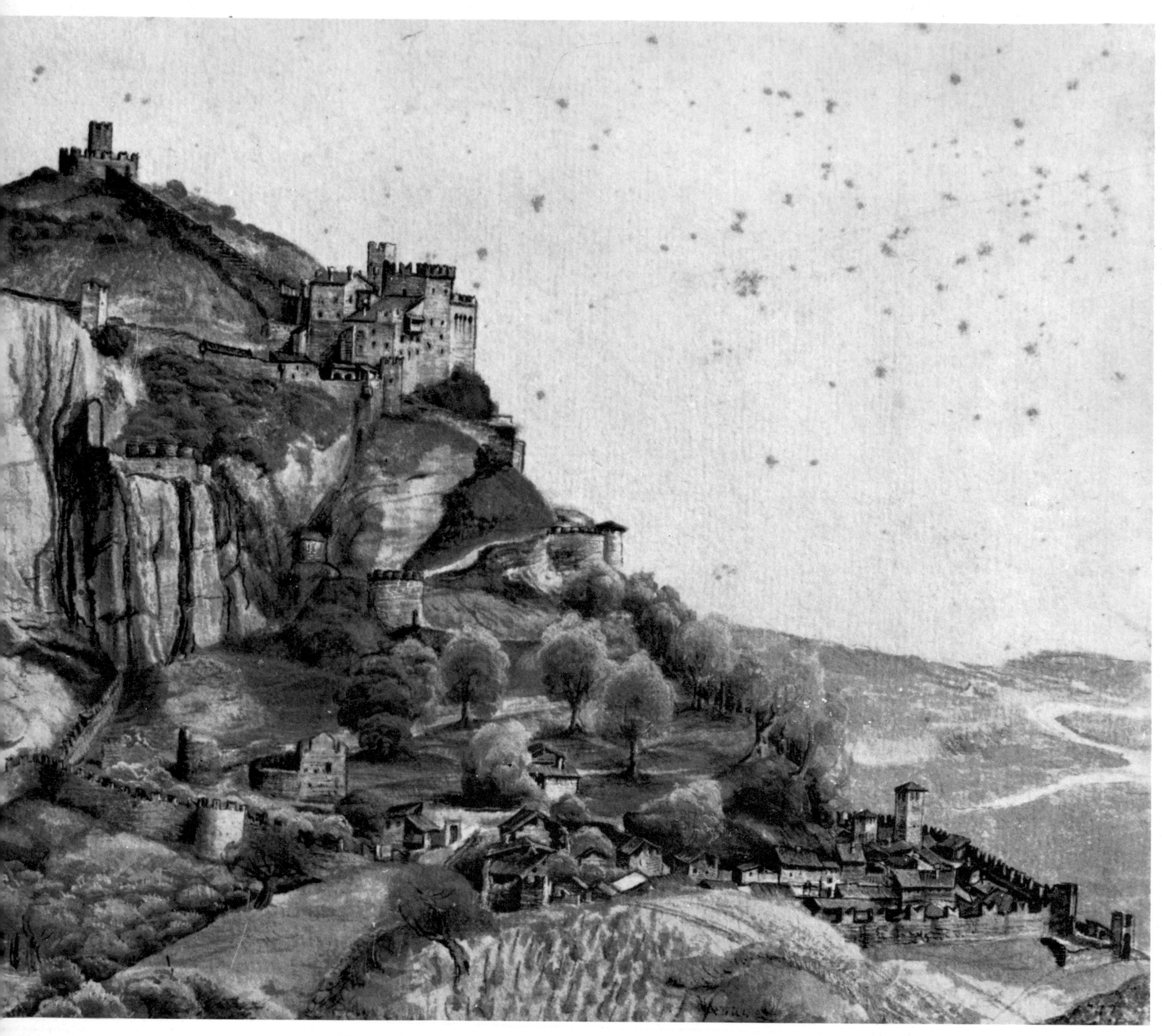

101 Albrecht Dürer (1471–1528). Arco, detail of *Mountain landscape*. Paris, Louvre (Cabinet des Dessins).

8 Northern humanism

Drawn during Dürer's first visit to Italy, before he was twenty, this self-portrait reveals his remarkable analytical faculty; in his hands, the line is as expressive as colour as a process of observation and introspection.

The German Renaissance was anticlassical. Politically and spiritually, it expressed itself through the Reformation which divided the Church with its proclamation of the rights of God as against those proclaimed by humanism. The first quarter of the sixteenth century, which saw Luther's revolt, was also the period during which German painting sparked into a brilliance which very soon burnt itself out and was not to be revived until our own century.

In his eagerness to assimilate the Renaissance, Albrecht Dürer attempted vainly to squeeze through the strait gate of forms and principles the immensity of the German soul with all its repressed desires, for which the only outlet hitherto had been an often confused mysticism. The Germanic need to embrace the world in its multiple aspects was stimulated by the phenomenological spirit of the Reformation, which brought back to earth human curiosity about the Beyond.

In order to remain master of the hunger for knowledge that devoured him, Dürer tried to make himself as objective as Leonardo, whom indeed he resembled in many ways; but, unable to assuage this fever, he ended up as a Faust, filled with a deep yearning for the infinite. Like Leonardo, he perfected a marvellous analytical instrument with which to carry out his experiments: drawing. Drawing had been an indispensable auxiliary for the painter's researches since the end of the fifteenth century, but its significance as a method for Dürer was the opposite of what it had been for Leonardo or Raphael. In his preliminary sketches, Leonardo stylizes the impression of the real or the flow of thought, while Raphael is able, with a few strokes of the pen, to project on to paper the rhythm of the form his mind has envisaged: this manner of drawing, intended to express a form in its unity by means of a single flowing line, postulates a pre-existing idea. Dürer's procedure, on the other hand, is one of pure analysis (*pl. 102*). Confining himself to the object, he first reproduces the appearance of one of its terminal points, then proceeds by degrees until each segment has been brought forward to constitute a whole; the form which presents itself to his eyes is broken down into its articulations,

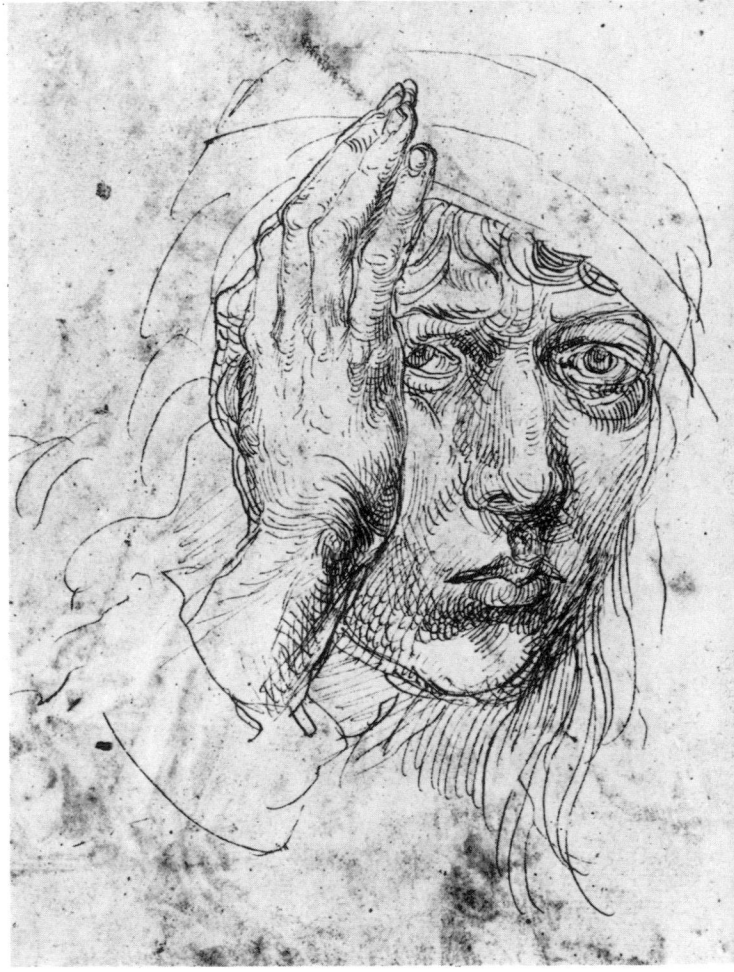

explored in its various facets, reduced to the state of a skeleton, and endowed with an astonishing but essentially soulless verisimilitude. During the nineteenth century, van Gogh was to practise the same style of drawing. It is only the watercolours, in which Dürer notes down travel impressions (*pl. 101*), or sketches features of some animal or plant, that retain a spiritual quality not yet sterilized by analysis.

Drawing, which for the Italians had remained a means, was transformed by Dürer into an end in itself. By transferring the image to wood or copper

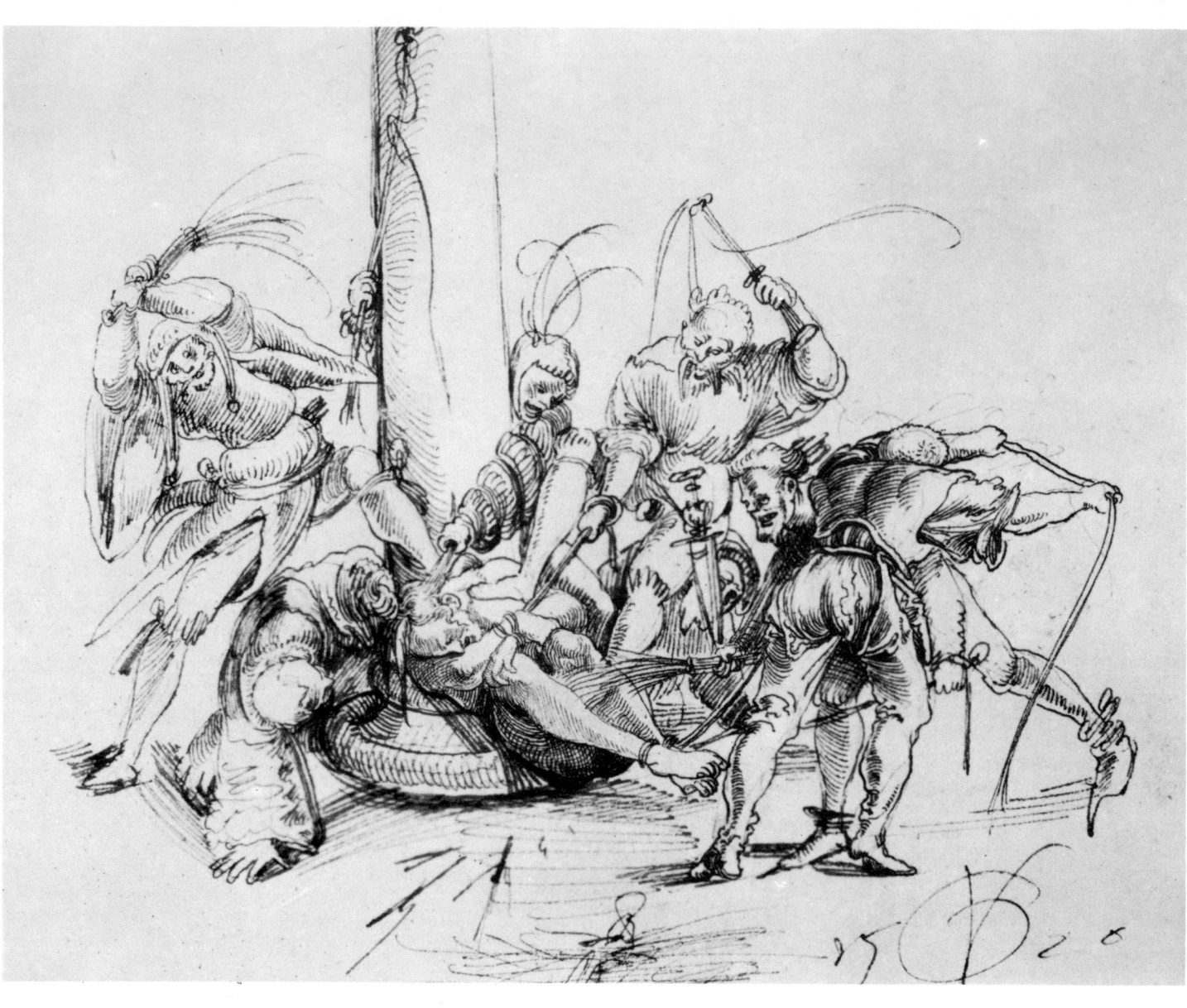

With lines as violent as strokes of a
whip, Urs Graf flagellates the
pitiful victim who may perhaps be
Christ.

104 Nikolaus Manuel Deutsch
(1484–1530). *Death disguised as a
soldier embraces a young woman*. Basle,
Kunstmuseum.

This soldier-painter had no
compunction in deriding the idea of
death by depicting it in terms of
violently erotic gestures.

by engraving, he assured it a distribution as extensive as that which printing was simultaneously
providing for human thought. The engraving process liberated Dürer from all the petty restrictions
that working to order imposed upon him in his
painting; in this new medium he was free to express
his aspirations in objects possessing an excellent
commercial value. Engraving was so much an
autonomous art for him that, to celebrate the glory
of the Emperor Maximilian, he raised a triumphal
arch which consisted of ninety-two printed woodcuts and was over eleven feet high.

Dürer's virtuosity in handling a gouge or a burin
has never been equalled. Although in the woodcut
his line is synthetic, in copper engraving it lends
itself ideally to the exploration in depth and the
enumeration of the infinite which haunted him so.
It was this latter medium that he chose for expressing his philosophical thought (*Nemesis, The Knight,
Death and the Devil, St Jerome, The Sea Monster and
the Prodigal Son, Melencolia, Adam and Eve*), while the
woodcut served him for the speedier production of
the religious series which sold so well.

Dürer proved that black and white had just as
many resources at its command as colour. His
engravings earned him world-wide fame during his
lifetime, and remained models for the future,
especially the copper engravings in which the line
is more modern, less Gothic, than in the woodcuts.
Rembrandt was greatly in his debt.

The marvellous tool created by Dürer to allow
him to carry out his methodical investigations
served others to explore the realm of the imaginary.
Albrecht Altdorfer and Wolf Huber produced convulsive landscapes which spring up in a sort of
pyrotechnic display of lines. The boldness of the
linear composition in the engravings of Urs Graf
and Nikolaus Manuel Deutsch redeems the otherwise intolerable realism of their licentious images.
These two Swiss painters took part, as mercenaries,

in the Italian wars, Deutsch as a field clerk, Graf as a soldier, and seem to have retained from their soldiering the feeling that the whole world is depraved. Their drawings describe the life of the foot-soldier, his bragging and indiscipline, his coarse manners, his cruelty (*pl. 103*), his encounters with love and death (*pl. 104*). The work of these two represents the first echo in art, since Hieronymus Bosch, of a feeling of revolt against human idiocy.

However, when Dürer took up a paintbrush it would seem almost as though his inspiration froze. Avant-garde in drawing, he remains archaic in his painting, in which the predominant influence remains Bellini, through whom, in fact, he first discovered the Renaissance. His paintings are the exact opposite of his engravings: the teeming world of his woodcuts and engravings suddenly congeals when interpreted in colour. This man, capable of including the infinite in the few square inches of a plate, in his paintings succeeds only in producing juxtaposed images painted in strident colours which make them clash violently rather than blend together. Even the prodigious visions of the universal contained in the *Nemesis* (*pl. 105*) or the *Small Passion* are transformed into a somewhat inert landscape background. This failure is nowhere more apparent than in the *Martyrdom of the Ten Thousand*, a seething composition coiled in upon itself like a form which has failed to erect itself in space. His finest picture is the 1511 *Adoration of the Trinity* (*pl. 106*). At the same moment as Raphael, he conceived the idea of a composition in space being arranged like a floating ring seen in perspective in depth. But whereas in Raphael's fresco, the figures are actors playing to the spectator, in Dürer's picture their thoughts and their faces are turned towards God; there is even a promise, in this painting, of the soaring grace of the baroque and rococo ceilings of eighteenth-century Germany.

Painting is fluid, and made to unify matter. Drawing separates matter. Dürer's obsessive anguish, resulting from an inhibition of the faculty of attraction, found in drawing an outlet which painting refused. In his immediate circle, the gift for painting flourished among masters of more modest ambitions. Even if Lucas Cranach, with his belated style, was basically an image-maker, the profound romanticism of the German nature inspired certain other artists, especially Albrecht Altdorfer, Wolf Huber and Grünewald, with a creative power that allowed them to break through the constraints which paralysed Dürer. A new feeling for nature flourished among the painters of the Danube school, Altdorfer and Huber, a vision of subjective nature which was able to express the soul's impulses

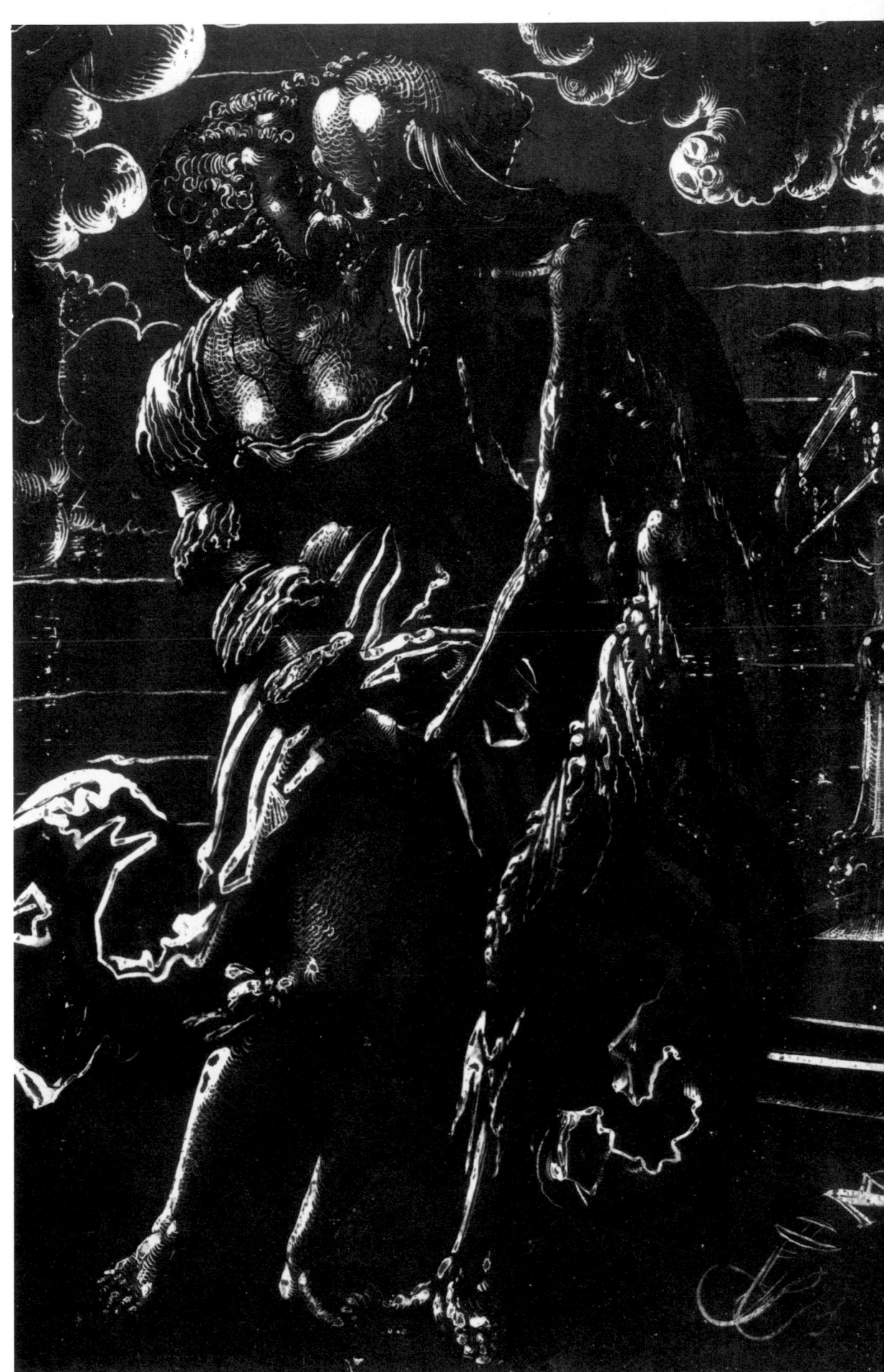

105 Albrecht Dürer. *Nemesis*. Engraving on copper. Paris, Bibliothèque Nationale.

By means of line alone, Dürer creates an imposing universe which seems somehow to be dominated by the absurd.

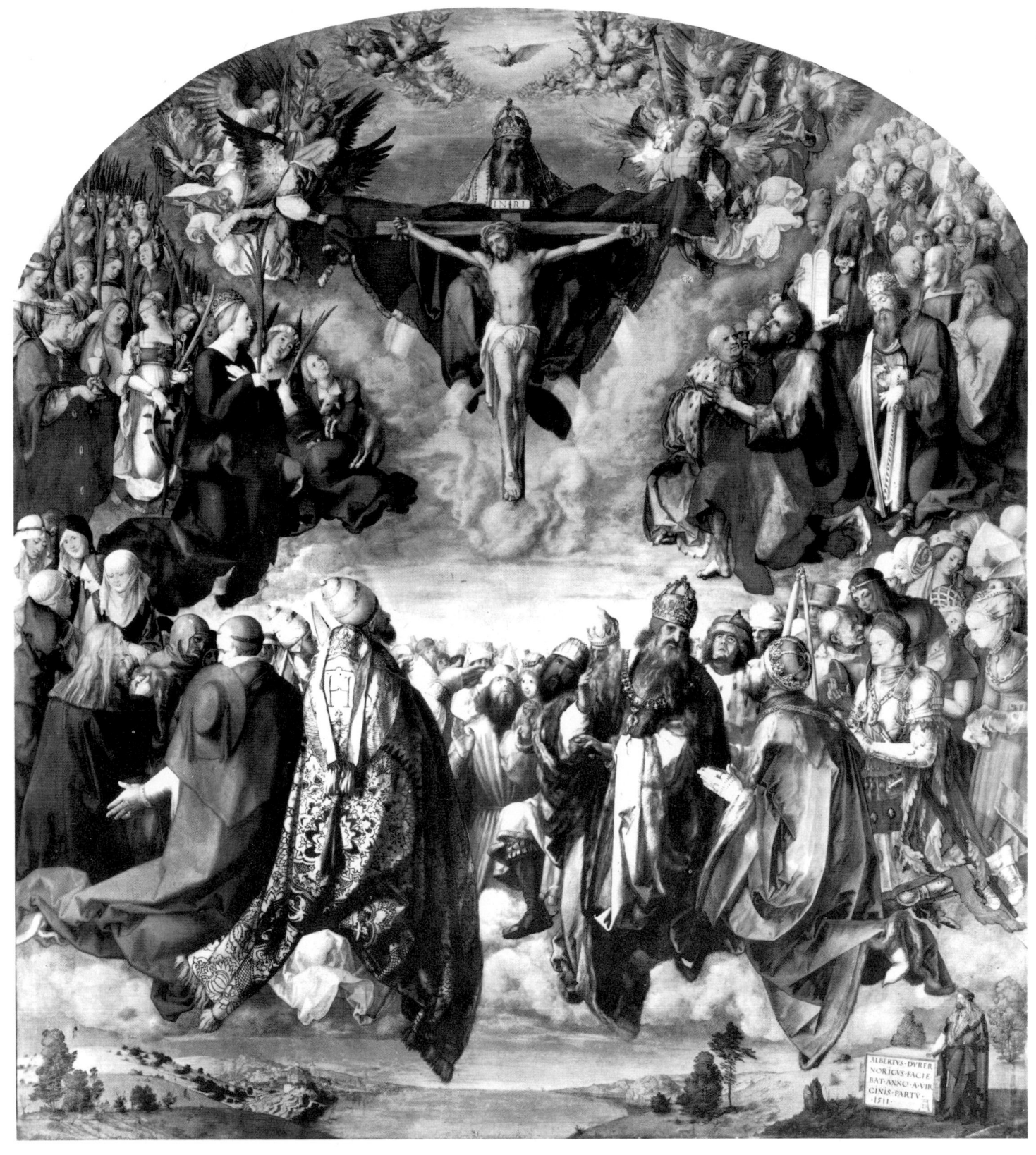

106 Albrecht Dürer. *The Adoration of the Holy Trinity*. Vienna, Kunsthistorisches Museum.

With its hovering figures making a semicircle facing the front of the picture, this composition constitutes a bold spatial vision.

107 Wolf Huber (*c.* 1490–1553).
View of Feldkirch. Pen-and-ink
drawing. Munich, Alte Pinakothek.

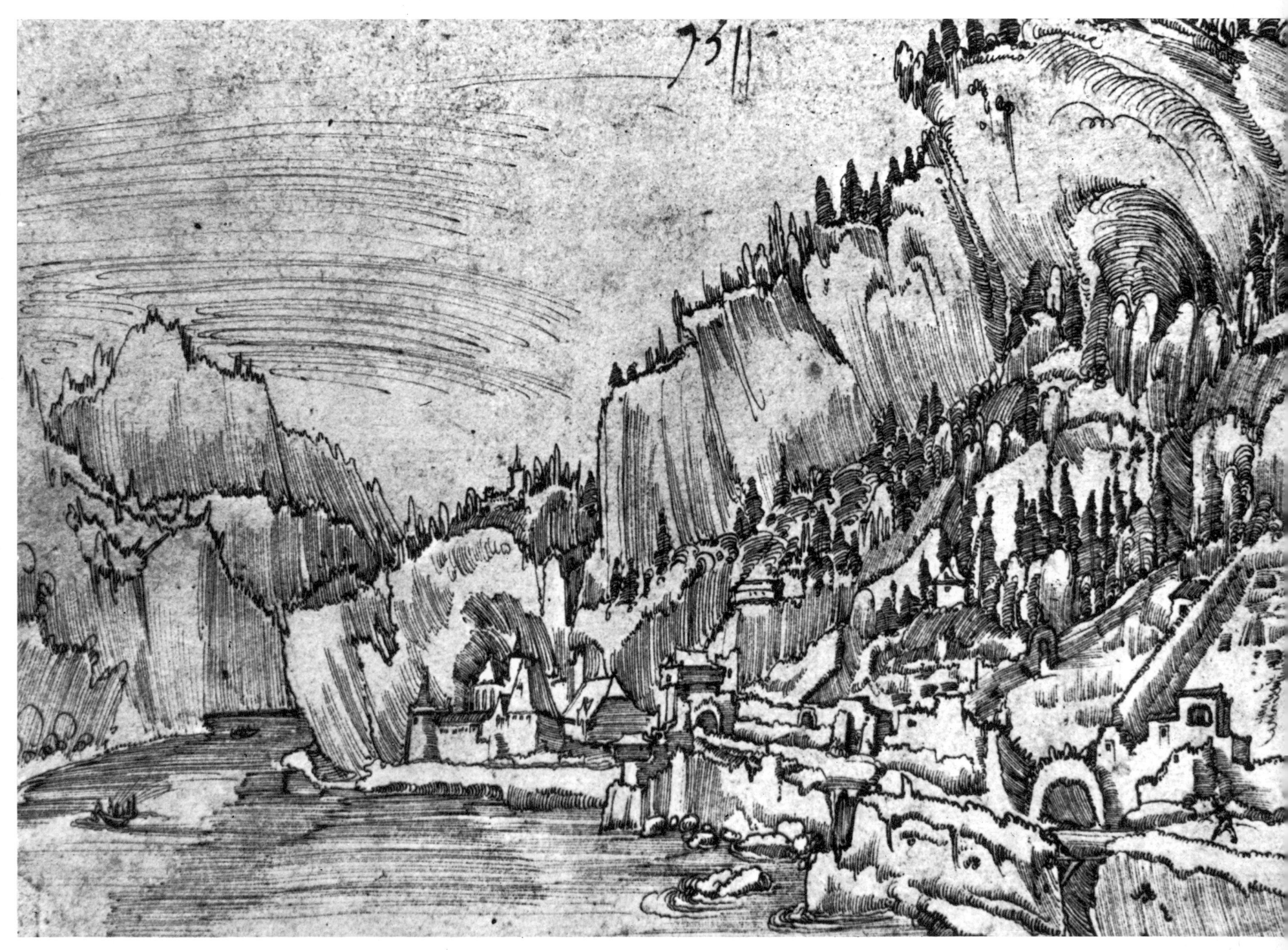

(*Stimmung*) in terms of paint, and thus bring it closer to the spiritual essence of things. This fusion was achieved through light, an iridescent light in permanent process of transformation, passing ceaselessly from shadow to brightness and from brightness to shadow, moulding beings and things alike, enclosing them in the same living tissue, making them participants in the same drama. Although Altdorfer's artistic output consisted mainly of altarpieces, together with a few more personal pictures, including pure landscapes (the first in the West), a chance commission resulted in his producing a

painting which ranks with the Isenheim Altarpiece as the greatest masterpiece of German painting.

In 1529, Altdorfer executed for William IV of Bavaria *Alexander's Victory* (*pl. 109*), which is now in the Munich Pinakothek. In contemplating this marvellous picture one calls to mind the words of Heraclitus: 'War has begotten the world, war reigns over the world.' The universe is a conflict of forces which create and re-create worlds, and man himself finds himself implicated in the perpetual flux of phenomena; the cosmos is a vast theatre in which man, activated by his own conflicts, makes history.

108 Albrecht Altdorfer (c. 1480–1538). *River landscape.* Pen-and-ink drawing. Budapest, Museum of Fine Arts.

Abandoning Dürer's strict objectivism, the graphic artists of the Danube school created visionary landscapes which expressed their pantheist feelings.

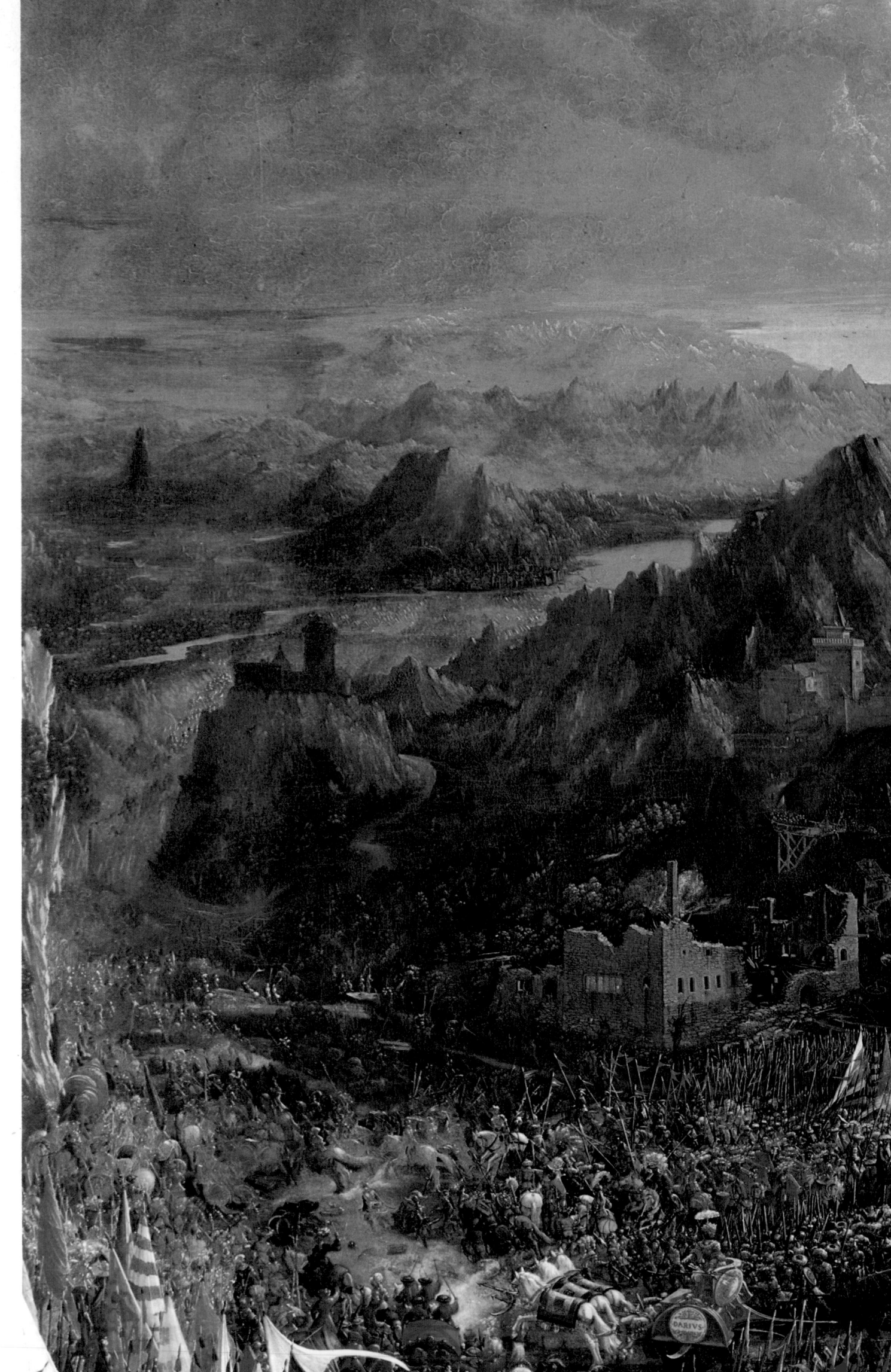

109 Albrecht Altdorfer. Detail of *Alexander's Victory* (*The Battle of Issus*). Munich, Alte Pinakothek.

No painting has ever contained a greater expressive power than this pictorial microcosm in which the human drama takes place in the context of a cosmic vision.

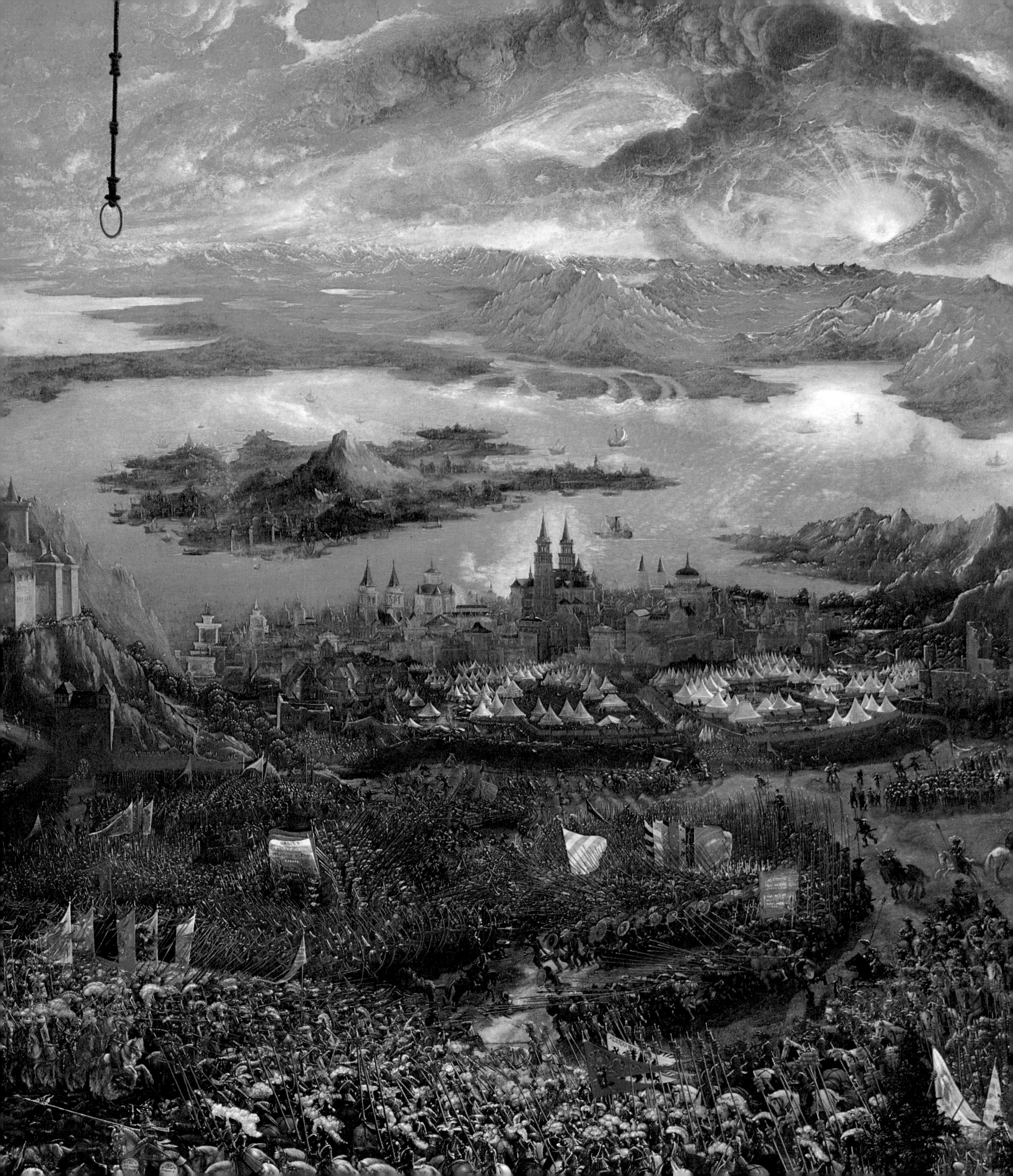

A vast plain, seen from a high mountain and bordered by the estuary of a great river, is filled to its edges by the massed forces of two rival armies. Nature seems to be associating itself with the human drama by staging a drama of its own, that of the sun setting behind thick clouds, while at the opposite side of the picture, the moon rises in the sky; the movements of the two heavenly bodies, representing the alternation between day and night, symbolize the unfolding of time, the cosmic time in terms of which the time of history is recorded. Even Bruegel never carried painting further in its creative capacity than does this universe-picture.

The Italians had created a rectilinear space – the world seen through the window of the human intellect – but the Germans preferred this hovering vision, which was already tempting a few Florentines at the end of the fifteenth century and had been adopted by Leonardo. One can almost see the globe, covered by its horde of murderous ants, rotating in front of one's eyes. Oil-painting, this mirror which van Eyck had invented, no longer reflects the calm, paradisaical visions so dear to the men of the Middle Ages, for whom the whole of nature was a garden; now, images of murder and glory are reflected in its limpid water, as though they had been conjured up by some sorcerer. Nature is no longer a thought emanating from God; being thought out by man, it has become the cosmos.

This vision should be correlated to the great geographical and cartographical movement which was just then refashioning the appearance of the earth. *Perspectiva artificialis*, rectilinear perspective, had been invented by city men used to the plunging vistas of streets. An alternative vision, as expressed in the work of certain Florentine artists such as Baldovinetti and Pollaiuolo in the second half of the Quattrocento, derives from a cartographical conception. The first maps showing the world in two hemispheres date from the end of the fifteenth century. The battle in *Alexander's Victory* is being fought over ground that represents a spherical projection, a portion of a planisphere, and when Altdorfer painted this picture in 1529 his was an absolutely original perception.

Twenty-five years later, this bird's-eye view, contemplating a projection of the earth's orography and planimetry, had become unexceptional. Bruegel spent part of his life in Antwerp, the most cosmopolitan city of the sixteenth century and at that time the great centre of mapmaking under the leadership of Mercator and Abraham Ortelius. The latter, the author of a *Theatrum orbis terrarum*, wrote proudly of his friendship for the man he called 'the greatest artist of his century', and it is not surprising, perhaps,

that in his paintings Bruegel drew inspiration from the art of cartography.

At the moment when Bruegel appeared on the scene, the Flemish school was mired in the endless complications of a crisis produced by the inability of painters to assimilate the new relations between space and figure that had been imposed upon them by the Renaissance. With the coming of Bruegel, all these problems were resolved as though by magic. He borrowed from Hieronymus Bosch a few elements of his symbolic system. But, more important, he revived Bosch's handling of paint, freeing colour from the obligation, imposed upon it by the Flemings, of serving strictly to complement form, and transforming it into a light fluid, circulating through all the parts of the picture like blood in an organism. Despite the frequently repeated claim that his short stay in Italy between 1552 and 1553 left absolutely no mark on him, the fact is that he gained from this visit something far more profound than the imitation of a style: he gained a principle. For there seems no doubt that it was the contact with Italian art that gave him the organizing genius to resolve multiplicity into unity. He achieved, in fact, what was later to be Cézanne's ambition: to be classic in terms of nature. In his majestic composition, *Winter* (*pl. 110*), the line of four trees, following the same direction as the hunters, guides the onward movement of the space which the flight of a bird of prey is pursuing through the air as far as the distant mountains. This bird in space is sufficient on its own to defy the eye's attempt to calculate the immensity in which it is gliding. The gyratory composition of the *Land of Cockaigne*, inspired perhaps by the idea of the wheel of fortune, makes the men so real that we can almost touch them. The diagonal direction of the *Blind leading the blind* drags us down with them in their headlong fall, while in the background the tiered roofs of the calm village church teach us that the wisdom of the species withstands the folly of individuals. And then we are made dizzy, in looking at the *Magpie on the Gibbet* (*pl. 112*), by the way the space swirls around the gibbet upon which is perched that legendary bird whose pranks are recorded in so many popular tales, transformed here into the point around which the universe revolves. In *The Bearing of the Cross* (*pl. 111*), the event is dispersed over a vast plain until the details become blurred where the plain's distant reaches drop behind the horizon.

No painter ever explored space as thoroughly as Bruegel. In comparison, Rubens merely passed through space. Bruegel achieved a synthesis between the Italian vision of perspective and the innate Flemish predilection for large dimensions,

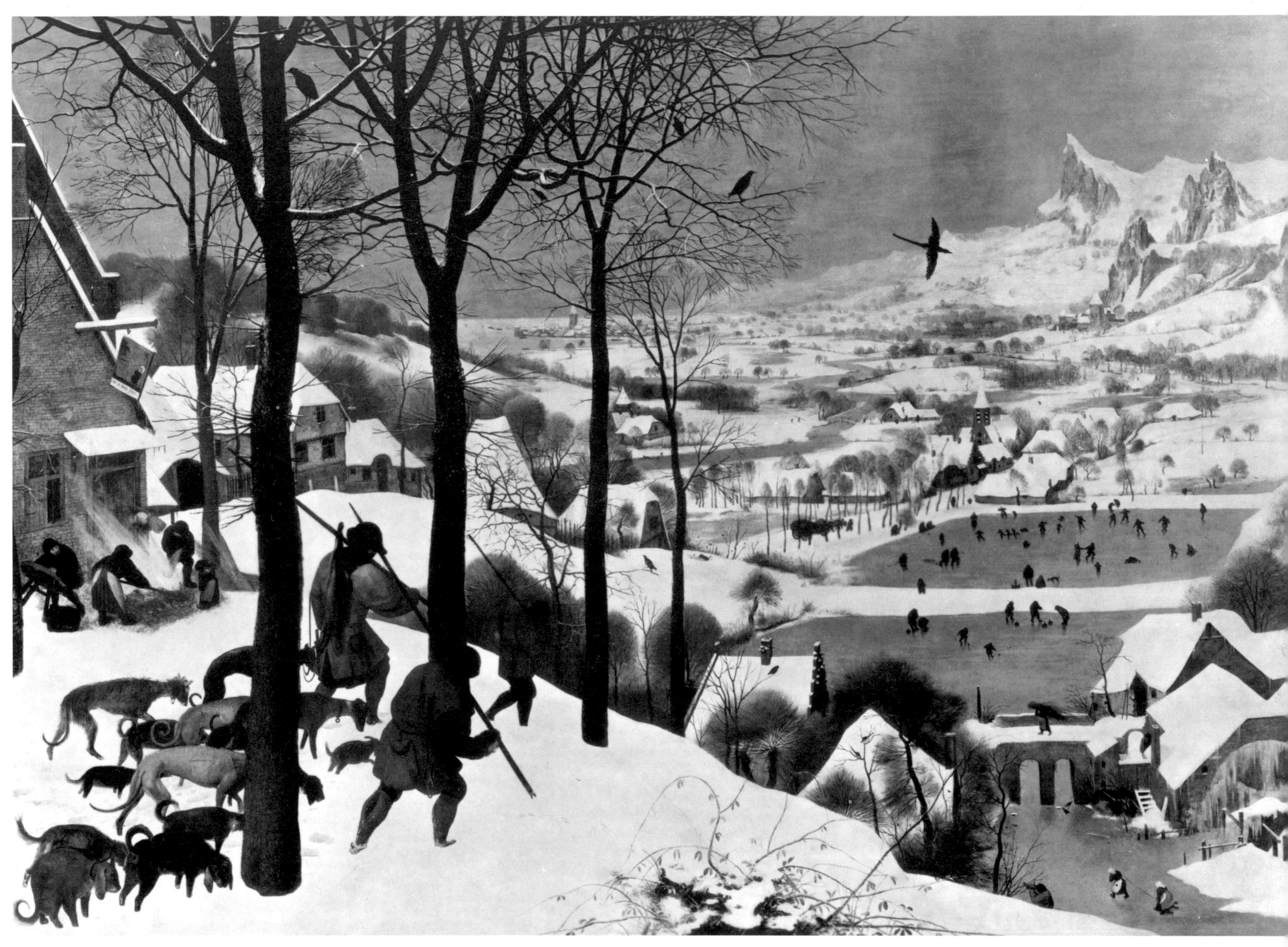

by blending broadness and depth in the vastness of a world of infinite perspectives. If one were to seek an appropriate emblem for Bruegel, it would surely be the eagle: alternately soaring through the air while the universe races away like a film beneath his wings, and swooping vertiginously down to earth to seize his prey. Perhaps no other artist has ever delved so deeply into the predicament of man, forced to witness the unfolding of his destiny on the surface of this earth while longing for deliverance from his terrestrial yoke. Even though confining himself within the borders of his provincial scene,

Bruegel retained the memory of the mountains and seas he had seen during his Italian voyage, and lived in his imagination through the great adventure which, during his lifetime, impelled men to cross oceans in search of new territories to conquer. He was neither a historian nor a moralist, but an anthropologist; he took as his subject for analysis the human phenomenon at its most elementary, at the point where it lies outside the scope of history, hoping that a study of the instinctual life of the common people would reveal something of the mechanism of human existence. Following a theory current

110 Pieter Bruegel (*c.* 1525–69). *Winter*. Vienna, Kunsthistorisches Museum.

Bruegel resolved the crisis of the mannerism which had enmeshed the Flemish school, by creating a universe the natural appearance of which conceals a profound strictness; he re-established the living relationship between figures and space which had been neglected by the previous generation of painters.

127

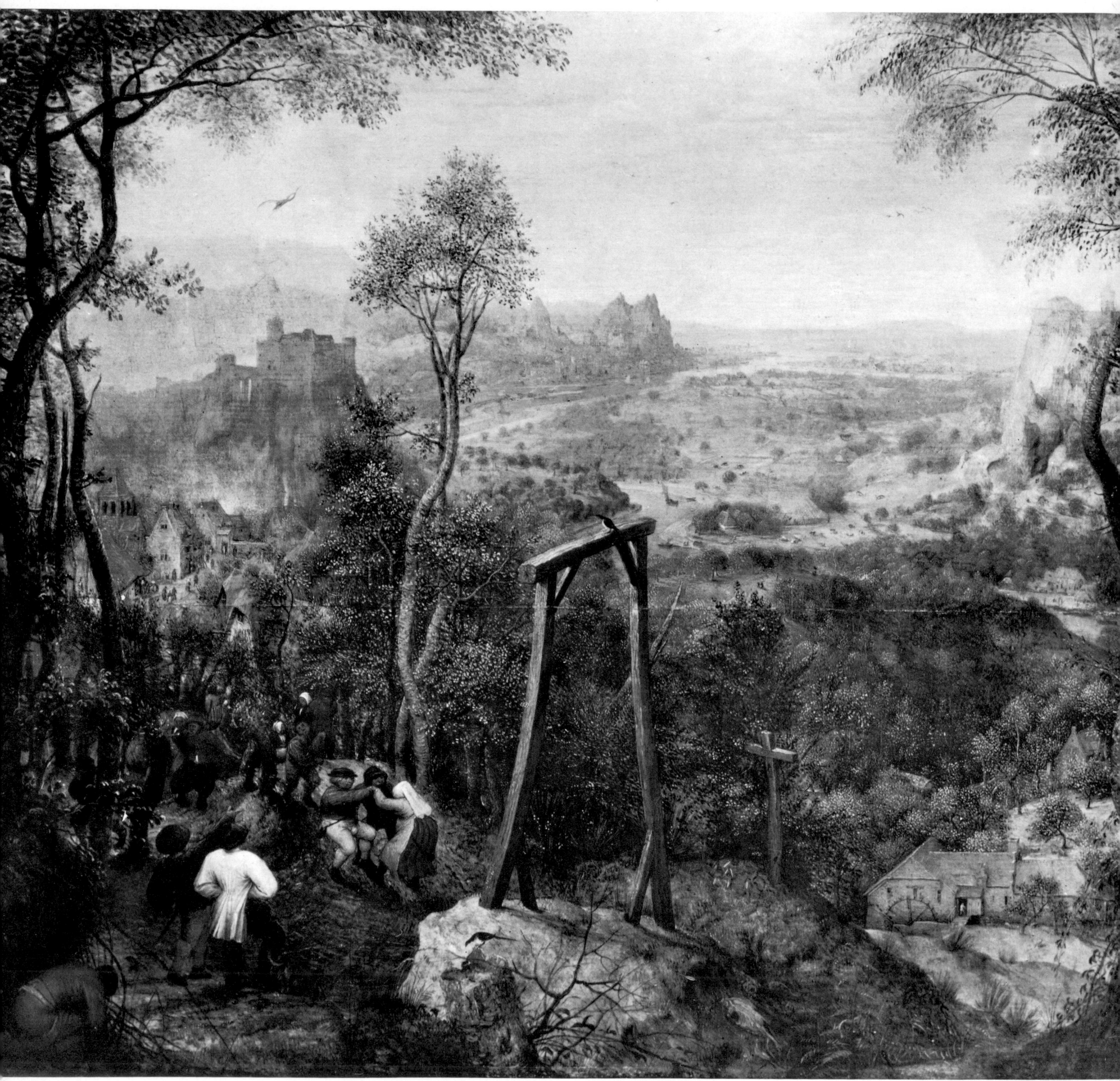

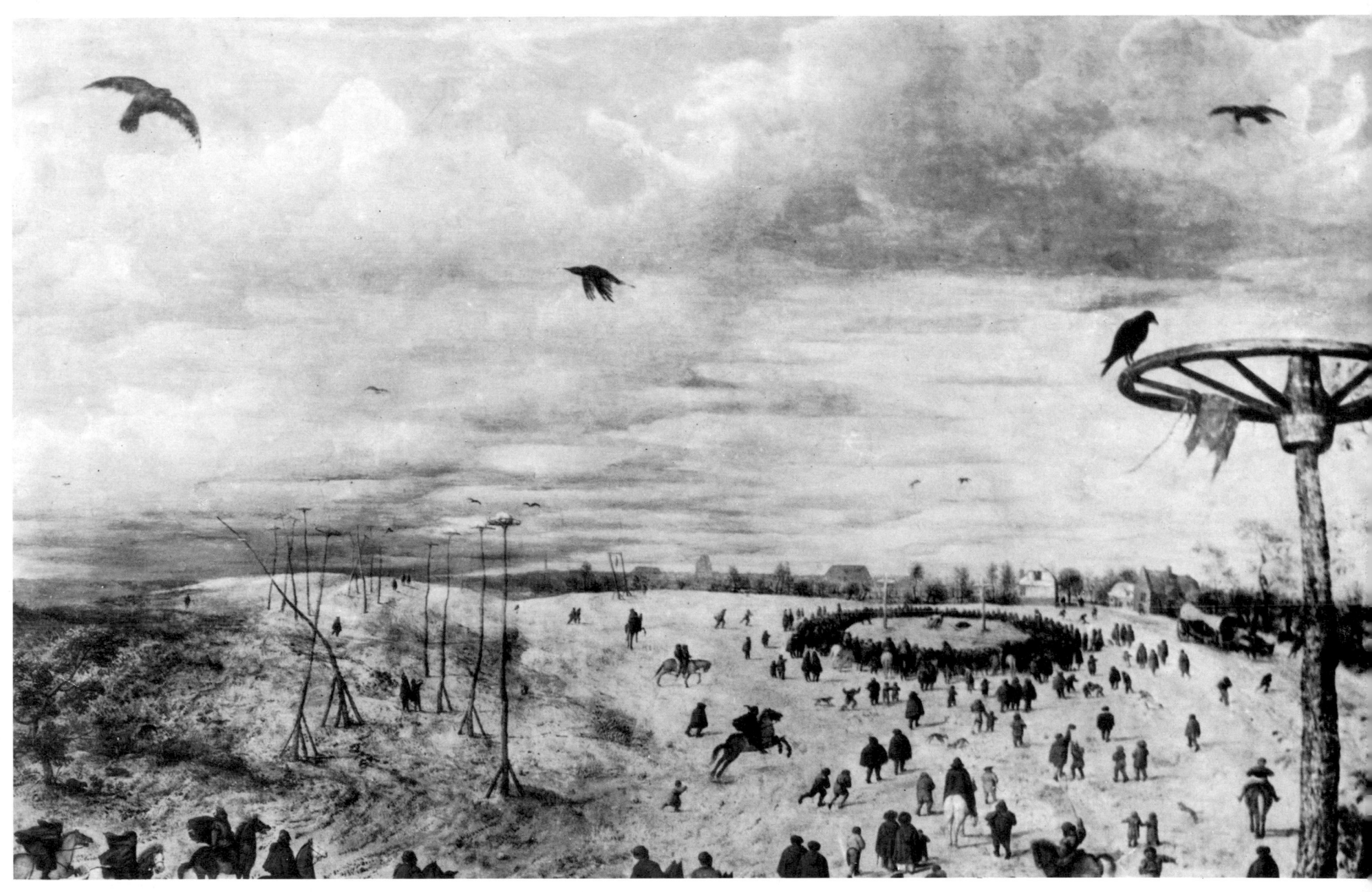

in his time, he saw in human folly a sort of negative image which would reveal the truth of the soul. Bruegel's 'drollery' may appear to be nothing more than picturesque amusement, but in reality it is a manifestation of humanism.

All Bruegel's compositions are based upon principles which are so simple that they appear perfectly natural; yet the sheer genius required to extract this 'natural' element from nature's multifarious spectacle can best be appreciated by comparing it with the works of an artist such as Patinir, which are no more than puzzle pictures. By regulating the universe, Bruegel achieved the dream of sovereignty that had tormented the painters of the Quattrocento, especially Leonardo. Bruegel is one of those poet-painters in whose art

form flows fully moulded from the idea that engenders it. And yet there are still some who see in him nothing more than a jester, wily peasant, great drinker and womanizer. Others, again, suppose his painting to be charged with hidden significance deriving from symbolic initiations and humanist inspirations. Bruegel is certainly a philosopher, but one who thinks in forms; nothing could be further from the spirit of the *rhétoriqueurs* than his highly allusive art. His work might be summed up by this phrase from Cicero which his friend, Abraham Ortelius, chose as the epigraph of his *Theatrum orbis terrarum*: 'The horse is created to carry and to draw, the ox to plough . . . but man to consider and contemplate with the eyes of understanding the disposition of the universal world.'

111 Pieter Bruegel. Detail of *The Bearing of the Cross*. Vienna, Kunsthistorisches Museum.

◀ 112 Pieter Bruegel. *The Magpie on the Gibbet*. Darmstadt, Landesmuseum.

Certain paintings by Bruegel suggest a view from a height; during the sixteenth century, this bird's-eye view was enjoyed, in their imagination, by the geographers and scholars who, in the wake of the navigators, were drawing up maps of the earth.

113 Giuseppe Arcimboldo (1527–93). *Head composed of the faces of animals*. Graz, Joanneum.

9 The labyrinth

In 1895, in a Latin thesis presented at the Sorbonne, Romain Rolland argued that Italian painting after Raphael had been in a state of decadence, produced by the estrangement from nature and the substitution of the principle of the authority of antiquity, by admiration for Michelangelo and by the scholastic system imposed by the Carracci brothers. Opinions have changed considerably since that date. The classicism elaborated at Rome during the pontificate of Julius II was of short duration, as are all classic forms, resting as they do on a delicately balanced structure. But what followed it was something more complex than a mere 'decadence': it was a crisis in the art of painting, a new style. This style has been called 'mannerism', a name derived from the term *maniera*, used by Vasari in his *Lives of the Artists* to designate the style of a particular master.

The first attempt to rehabilitate mannerism, which was long regarded (and Rolland's attitude was entirely typical) as the decay of the Renaissance, came in 1920 with the appearance of Hermann Voss's study of sixteenth-century Roman and Florentine painting (*Die Malerei der Spätrenaissance in Rom und Florenz*). And between the two wars the surrealists added their voices in favour of this world which seemed to have emerged from the twilight zone of the human conscience. The path followed by the painters of that era has been compared to the one traced by strollers lost in a maze, that favourite adornment of gardens since the Middle Ages when it was known as the 'house of Daedalus'. If one were to equate inventive power with nonconformism, the mannerist painters could all be labelled avantgarde; but our own era has taught us that nonconformism nurtures its own conformism, and audacity its own academicism. Thus the Italian courts of the second half of the sixteenth century, deprived of the distractions of war, were constantly seeking relief from boredom, and the court painters had no option but to provide such relief; there was therefore no particular merit in being audacious, since it was taken for granted that the artist would be a constant source of original, and preferably wildly eccentric, ideas.

With this in mind, I would prefer to apply the term 'anticlassicism' rather than 'mannerism' to the initial avant-garde stage of the revolt against classicism; this has the advantage of pinpointing the originality of the early work of Pontormo and Rosso, and of including painters, such as Correggio, whom historians of mannerism have tended to regard as isolated figures, but who, unlike so many mannerists, were genuine creative innovators.

Anticlassicism was born in Florence, the city abandoned by Leonardo, Raphael and Michelangelo. Its first ferments may be discerned in the struggle which pitted Leonardo against Michelangelo in the competition for the decoration of the Sala del Gran Consiglio of the Palazzo Vecchio in 1503 and 1504. Since the idea of competition and the desire to outbid the opposition inevitably go hand in hand – Leonardo was over sixty and his rival only twenty-eight – each did his utmost to demonstrate his virtuosity. The wriggling masses of bodies in Michelangelo's cartoon of the *Battle of Cascina*, far from prefacing the noble cadences of the Sistine ceiling, heralded the fall of the damned in the *Last Judgment*.

The workshop of Andrea del Sarto, a painter whose disturbing *morbidezza* was already challenging the serenity of classicism, may be said to have provided the basis for the reaction against it, since his pupils included Pontormo and Rosso. They both made their first appearances as artists by his side, working in the precincts of the Annunziata between 1513 and 1517. Pontormo's *Visitation* and Rosso's *Assumption*, while showing the care exercised by pupils to follow their master's rules, give a hint of some indefinable sense of uneasiness. Rosso really hit home in 1521 with the famous *Deposition* (*pl. 114*), a veritable manifesto of anticlassicism, in which the tragic is expressed plastically by the aggressiveness of the volumes, stylized into a kind of cubism, and of the strident colours. This picture may almost be considered the *Demoiselles d'Avignon* of mannerism. We do not know how this strange work was received, although such eccentricity cannot have passed unnoticed in the traditional atmosphere of early sixteenth-century Florence. Vasari relates that a *Sacra Conversazione* (*pl. 115*) painted by Rosso in 1518 provoked lively criticism; no sooner had Monsignor Buonafede, administrator

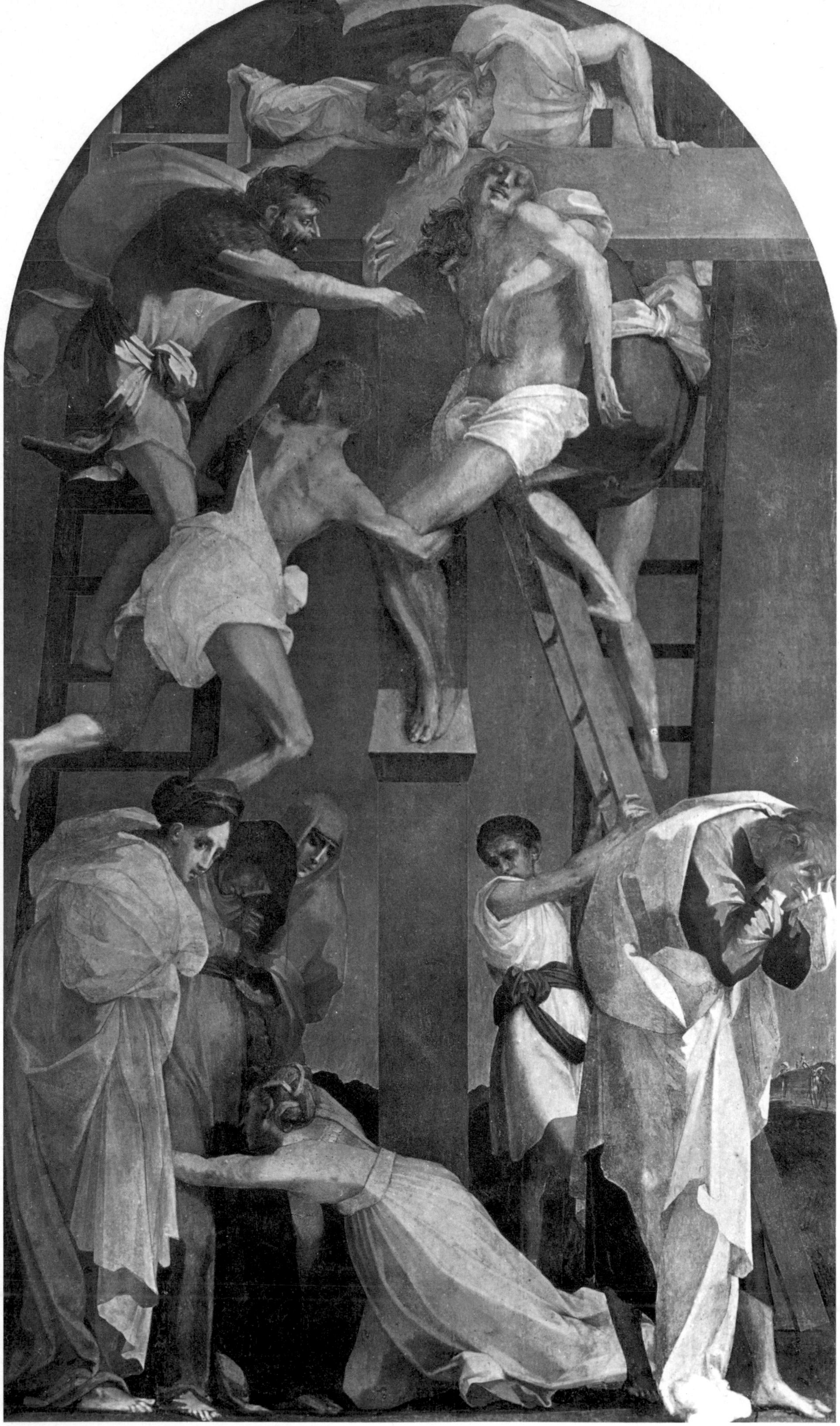

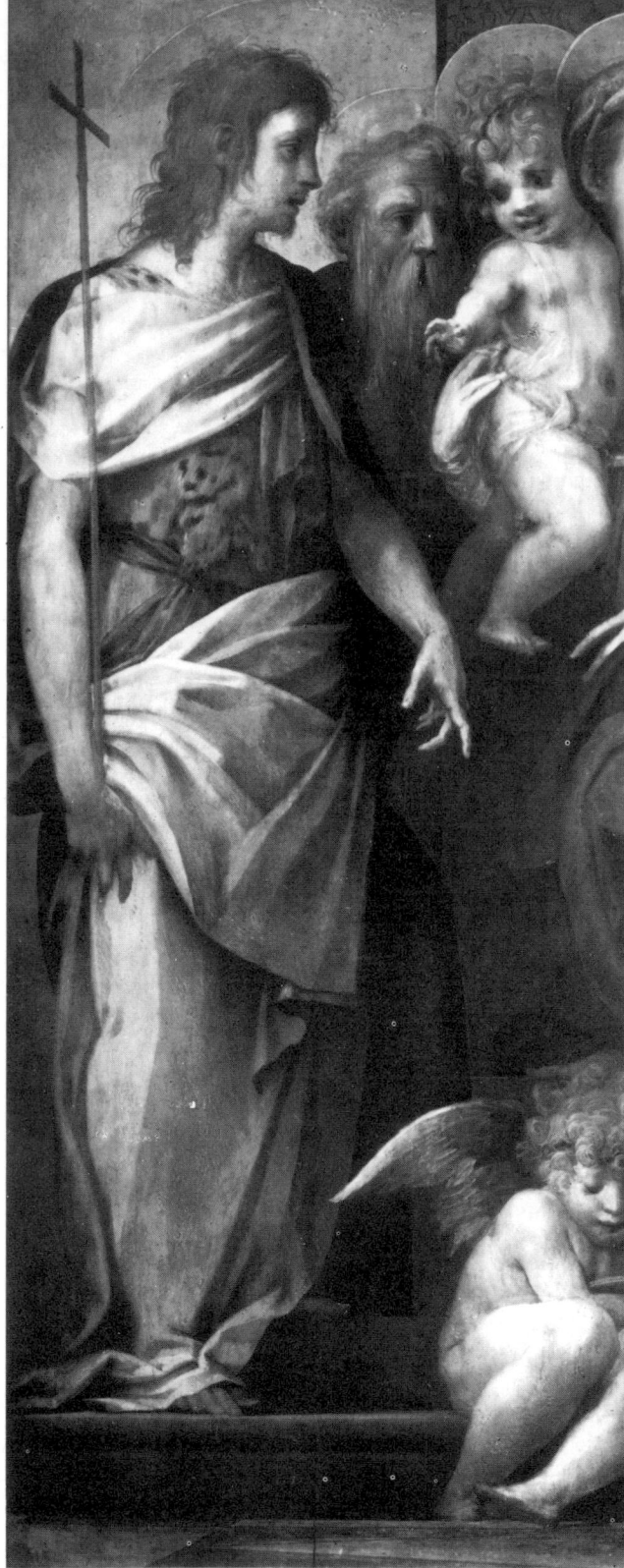

◀ 114 Giovanni Battista Rosso (1494–1540).
Deposition. Volterra, Pinacoteca.

The reaction against classicism originated in Florence
just at the time when Raphael had established its
principles in Rome. Certain pictures were judged so
scandalous that they were refused by those who had
commissioned them; this was the case with Rosso's
Sacra Conversazione (*pl. 115*) painted in 1518 for Santa
Maria Novella.

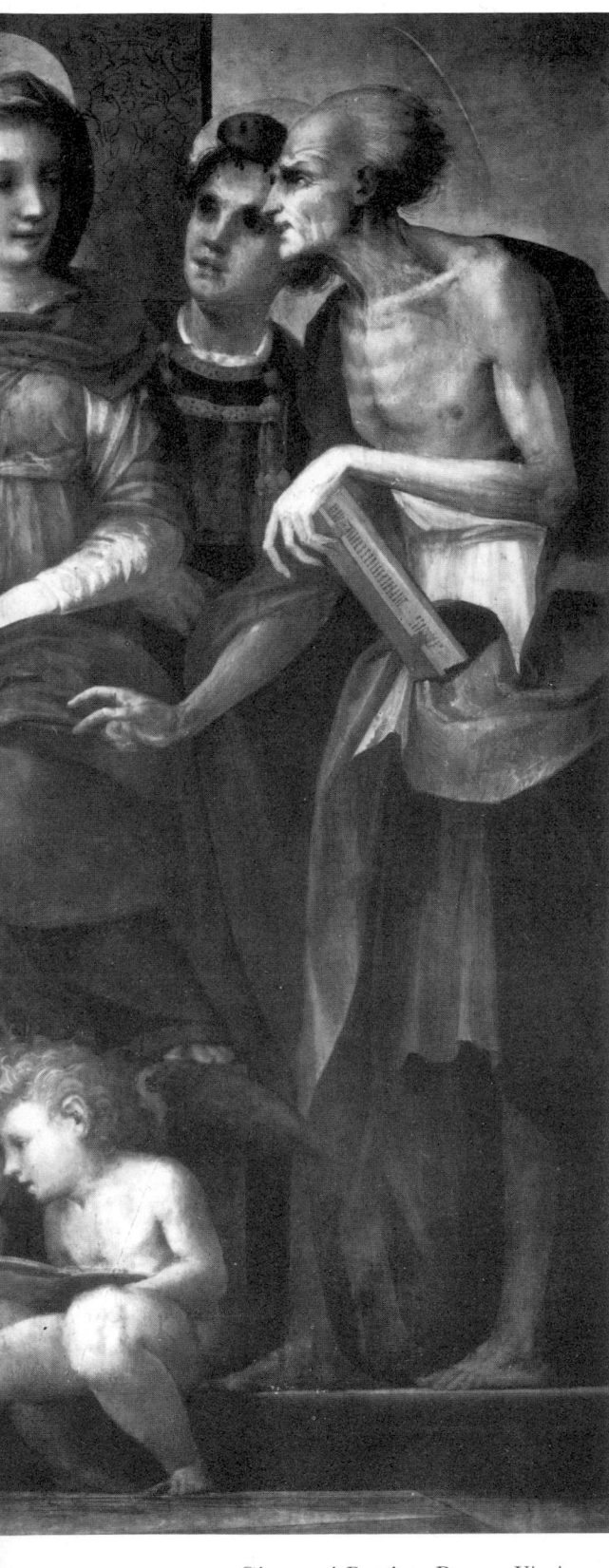

115 Giovanni Battista Rosso. *Virgin and Child enthroned with four saints*. Florence, Uffizi.

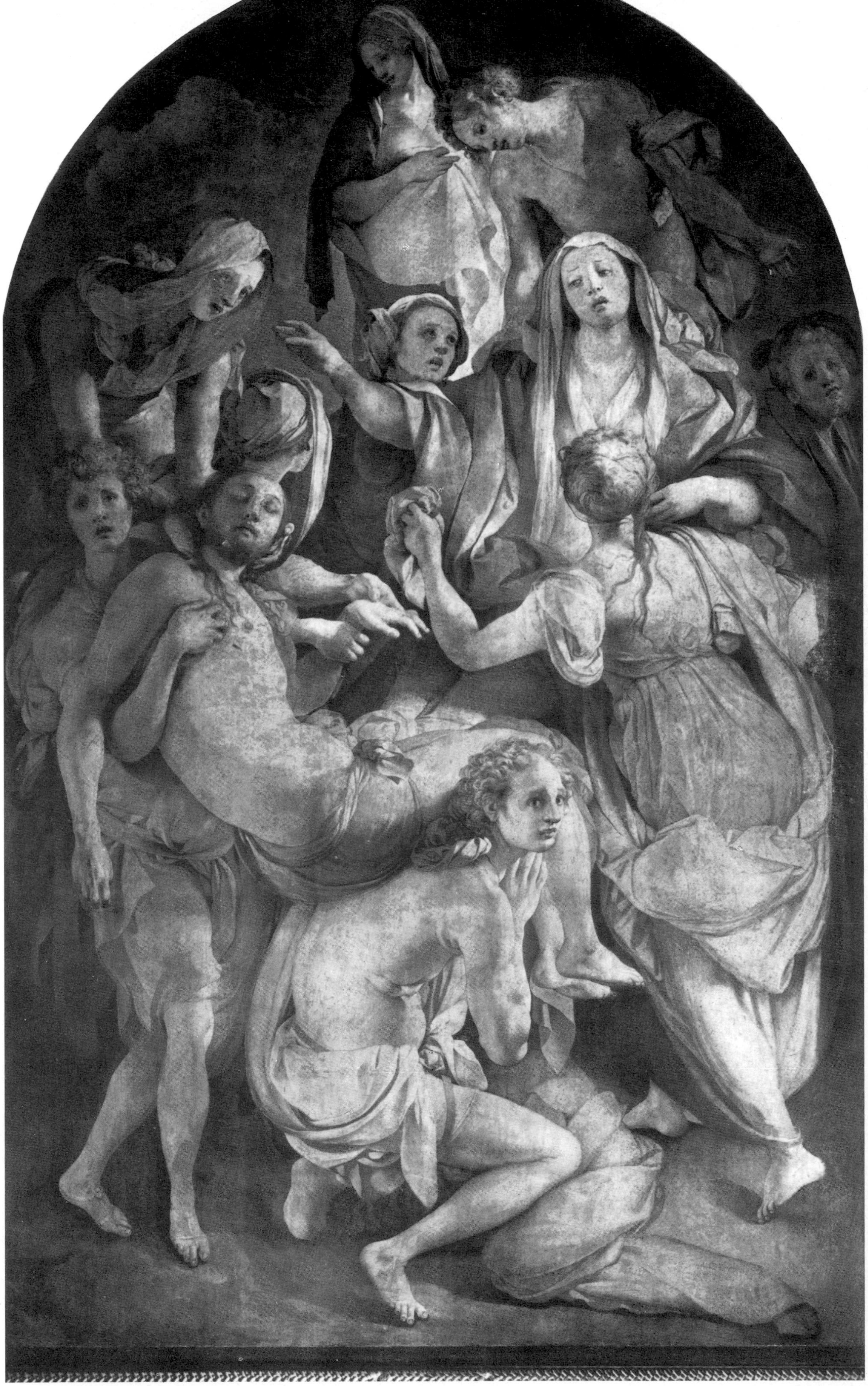

116 Jacopo Pontormo (1494–1557). *Deposition*. Florence, Santa Felicità.

of the church of Santa Maria Novella, who had commissioned the painting, seen 'all these diabolical saints, Rosso being accustomed to depict certain cruel and desperate expressions in his oil sketches, ... than he fled from the house and refused to accept the panel, declaring that he had been cheated.' This, then, was the first picture in the history of painting to create a scandal. The idea of outdoing others in extravagance was born, and five years later Pontormo painted his own *Deposition (pl. 116)*, a blasphemous work which, in a tottering composition, piles up tiers of androgynous wild-eyed creatures, one of whom, in the foreground, has adopted an indecent stance. A strange feeling of vengeful zeal seems to suffuse this work by a hypochondriac whose diary reveals him as being obsessed by his digestive processes and haunted by a terror of death, a man who ended by barricading himself in his house, drawing up the ladder which gave access to his studio like a drawbridge.

During this time, at Parma, a painter was producing work which showed that it was possible to reject classicism without necessarily adopting a revolutionary attitude. The anticlassicism of Rosso and Pontormo was based upon a negation, while that of Correggio was purely creative.

Risking the disapproval of a certain school of modern critical thought, I have no hesitation in saying that Correggio was one of the great creators of modern painting. Even his earliest works show how his use of movement disturbs the precepts of classic composition; in the *Rest on the Flight into Egypt* (Uffizi), painted around 1516, the composition has a diagonal flow, in the manner of Rubens. Then in 1518 he paused, and seems to have surrendered himself to the delights of humanism in the Camera di San Paolo of the Parma convent; here, for the abbess, who would appear to have led a far from monastic life, he painted a mythological cycle which is among the most pleasing of those created during the Renaissance.

In 1520, however, he was awarded the commission for the decoration of San Giovanni Evangelista. The only surviving painting is the *Ascension (pl. 118)* on the cupola, a work of astonishing boldness. Only a visit to Rome on his part can explain his successful assimilation of the morphology of Michelangelo and Raphael. But although he may have borrowed his *ignudi* from the Sistine Chapel, here he launches them into mid-air, and this *Vision of St John at Patmos* really is suspended above our heads. This was the first use in history of a *trompe-l'œil* effect to produce the illusion, exploited so brilliantly later by baroque artists, of nude figures floating in space.

Five years later, Correggio repeated this *tour de force* with his *Assumption of the Virgin (pl. 119)* for the octagonal dome of the cathedral, but with this painting he went even further, and his hordes of interlaced bodies whirling round in space almost obscure the Virgin in their midst. The pictures of the last period of his brief life are increasingly regulated by the rhythm of movements. The confused grouping of the *Madonna with St Sebastian*, with its mannerist overtones, is an exception. The *Martyrdom of St Placid and St Flavia (pl. 117)*, the *Deposition*, the *Madonna with St Jerome*, the *Madonna with St George* are all composed according to a system of counterpoint, with alternately advancing and retreating movements travelling diagonally, so that the painted surface becomes a centre of intense activity, suggesting to the beholder a snapshot of a moment in time. In addition, to emphasize his great spiritual tenderness, Correggio creates a sort of mime in which facial expression plays an important role, suggesting a unity of feeling among the characters; St Placid and St Flavia, for example, awaiting their martyrdom, gaze passionately towards heaven. All the elements of the baroque were invented by Correggio: spatial vision projected on to the curvature of cupolas, composition in terms of movement, the rhetoric of expression. But these qualities were not to be appreciated until half a century later, when Barocci and the Carracci had succeeded in taming the exuberance of mannerism.

During the seventeenth century, Correggio was one of the most widely imitated artists of the Renaissance, and Pietro da Cortona, Guido Reni, Eustache Le Sueur and Rubens were all in his debt. His influence continued to be felt in the eighteenth century, by Pellegrini and Boucher, for example, and was of the utmost importance for Prud'hon in the dawn of our own era. Indeed, no other artist, with the possible exception of Raphael, has exercised such a lasting influence. Yet during his lifetime he received the treatment which has been meted out to so many innovators. In an age of arrogant self-advertisement, he appears to have been timid by nature and to have led a discreet existence wholly devoid of the glamour that attached itself so easily to the lives of celebrated artists. His decoration of the dome of Parma Cathedral provoked violent criticism: labelled a 'hash of frogs' legs', it so upset the cathedral authorities that they broke their contract with the artist, thus preventing him from painting the apse. Yet Titian, when contemplating the dome, declared that even if it were to be turned upside down and filled with gold the value of its paintings would still not have been approached.

The calm of the Venetian school was broken by the appearance of a painter who was even more precocious than Correggio, and who shared his anti-classical instincts. But Lorenzo Lotto never knew Correggio's posthumous fame, until he was finally dragged from obscurity by Bernard Berenson, who in 1895 devoted an enthusiastic book to him. Although a Venetian, and one of the rare artists to be born on the lagoon, Lotto worked mostly outside his native city, in the surrounding area and as far afield as the Marches, Treviso, Bergamo, Jesi, Recanati, Ancona and Loreto. There is a mystery here which can only be explained by some incompatibility of humour between Lotto and Venice; no doubt its artistic circles, attuned to the classicism of Bellini and Titian, were little inclined to appreciate his odd temperament, his inventive curiosity, the small attention he payed in his painting to polite custom. Lotto was one of those 'provincials' who, like Pordenone, Romanino and Savoldo, found that remote towns gave them a greater freedom to develop their critical approach to art. He seems to have enjoyed working in Bergamo, where he spent the most fruitful years of his life. Berenson remarks that there would appear to have been a close bond between the artist and the people of this town who, according to contemporary accounts, themselves tended to be of a capricious and moody disposition.

His background as an artist remains obscure. The three giants of Venetian classicism, Bellini, Giorgione and Titian, made only a superficial impression on him in his early years; on the other hand, he seems to have been marked by a mysterious northern influence, illustrated by indubitable affinities with Jacopo dei Barbari, Albrecht Dürer and even Holbein, to whom the *Youth before a white damask curtain* (Vienna) was once attributed. Apart from the impact of Il Perugino, with whose work he may have become acquainted while working in the Marches, the paramount influence on him was Raphael, an influence established during the stay he made between 1508 and 1512 in Rome, where he had been summoned to execute paintings in the Vatican. The works of the Bergamo period, the frescoes of Trescore (1524) and San Michele al Pozzo Bianco (1525), the cartoons for the stalls of Santa Maria Maggiore (1523–32), are all full of reminiscences of the Stanze and even of the Sistine Chapel.

During this same period, Lotto produced his three finest altarpieces, which are also the most personal and the freest from outside influence, those of San Bartolomeo (1516), San Bernardino (1521, *pl. 120*) and Santo Spirito (1521). In these, he reveals the full power of his compassion, vivacity and unforced tenderness, to which is added an entirely new sense of composition in space and a taste for saturated colour differing radically from Titian's symphonic variations. (The latter, incidentally, have been affected by the passage of time, whereas Lotto's colours have remained intact.) Between 1530 and 1540, on the other hand, he seems to have come entirely under Titian's sway. These deviations from his natural path probably explain the element of slackness which can be detected in his last paintings, apart from the portraits. But, in fact, nothing could have been further from Titian's calm sensitivity than Lotto's temperament, tormented by a curiosity and impatience which impelled him to refashion his approach ceaselessly, like Picasso in our own century. Titian's society portraits, in which the individual reveals himself beneath the mask of convention, are serene effigies. Lotto's portraits, on the contrary, relate him to the northern painters; each figure posing before him becomes the subject of a character study, and these psychological portraits retain a truly modern accent (*pl. 121*). The remarkable aspect of his religious pictures is that the male and female saints, and even the roguish choirboy angels, are individuals, and if the Virgin is a beauty, hers is a living beauty (*pl. 122*).

Lotto is an independent, the indocile scion of a school which insisted that all progressive tendencies should be founded upon a respect for tradition. There has been some attempt to represent him as a precocious mannerist, but the few points he has in common with them are largely superficial. His unstrained sincerity and spontaneous genius set him apart from the anxieties and sophistications of mannerism. He stood equally distant from the Venetian classicism which unfolded with the majesty of a dogma; as a painter of temperament, Lotto constituted a scandalous exception to the Venetian rule.

It will be seen that the anticlassical reaction commenced as early as 1520–5, and so may be considered to have preceded mannerism properly so called rather than to have emanated from it: the expressive force of Pontormo's and Rosso's first works goes beyond mere *maniera*. Mannerism spread throughout Italy between 1525 and 1530 as a result of the scattering of the Roman artists, and continued into the rest of Europe; Rosso and Primaticcio, for example, went to Fontainebleau to create the basis for a new court art.

Rather than a style, mannerism is a pattern of imagery, as is surrealism today; and all the freer because there was no longer a *regola d'arte* to exercise a restraining influence on those painters who seemed

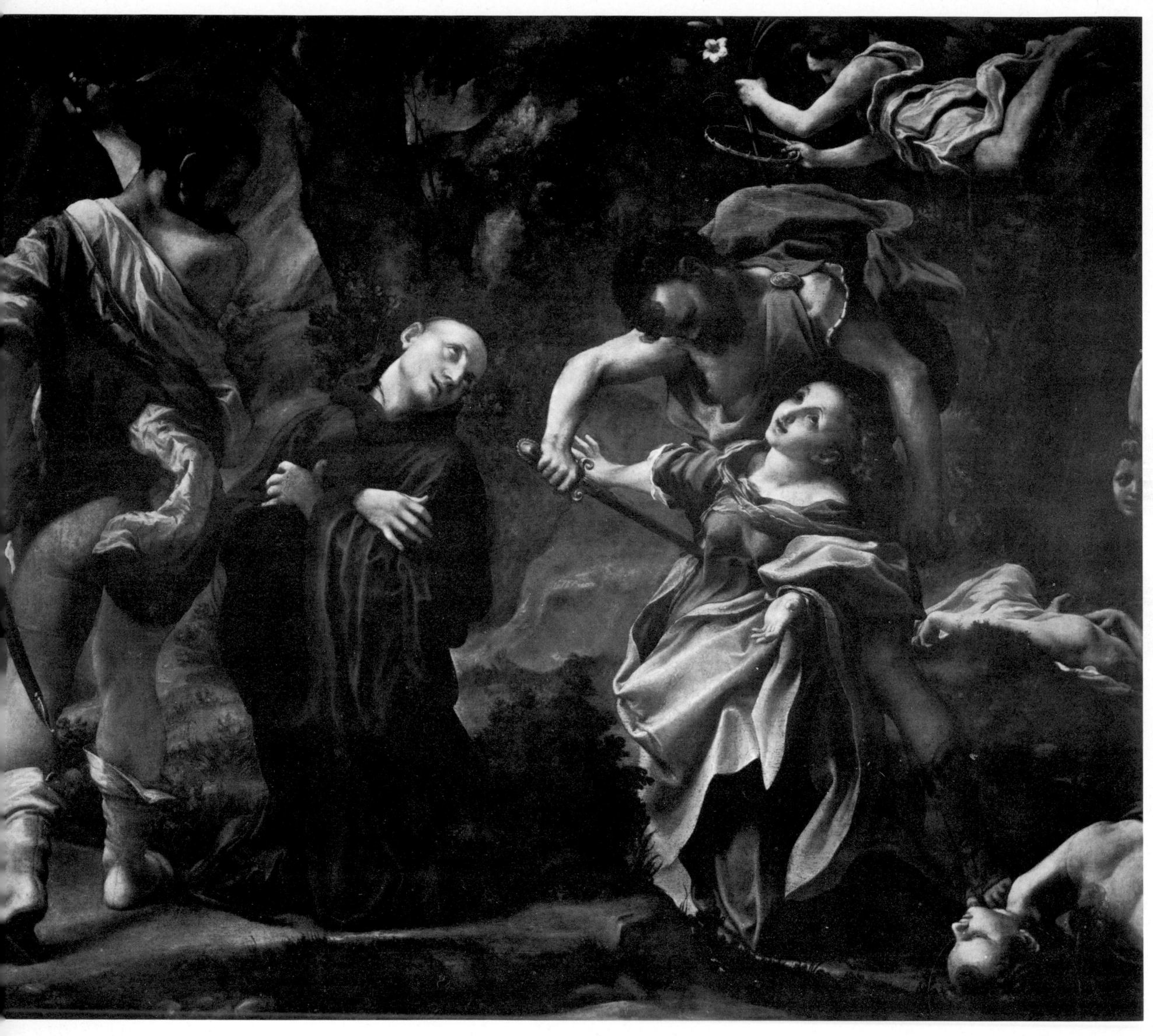

117 Correggio (*c.* 1489–1534). *The Martyrdom of St Placid and St Flavia*. Parma, Pinacoteca.

118 Correggio. *The Ascension of Christ in the midst of his apostles*. Parma, San Giovanni Evangelista.

Correggio detaches Michelangelo's *ignudi* from their supporting walls and suspends them in mid-air. These spatial researches dominate the contrasting movements of the figures in his easel-paintings.

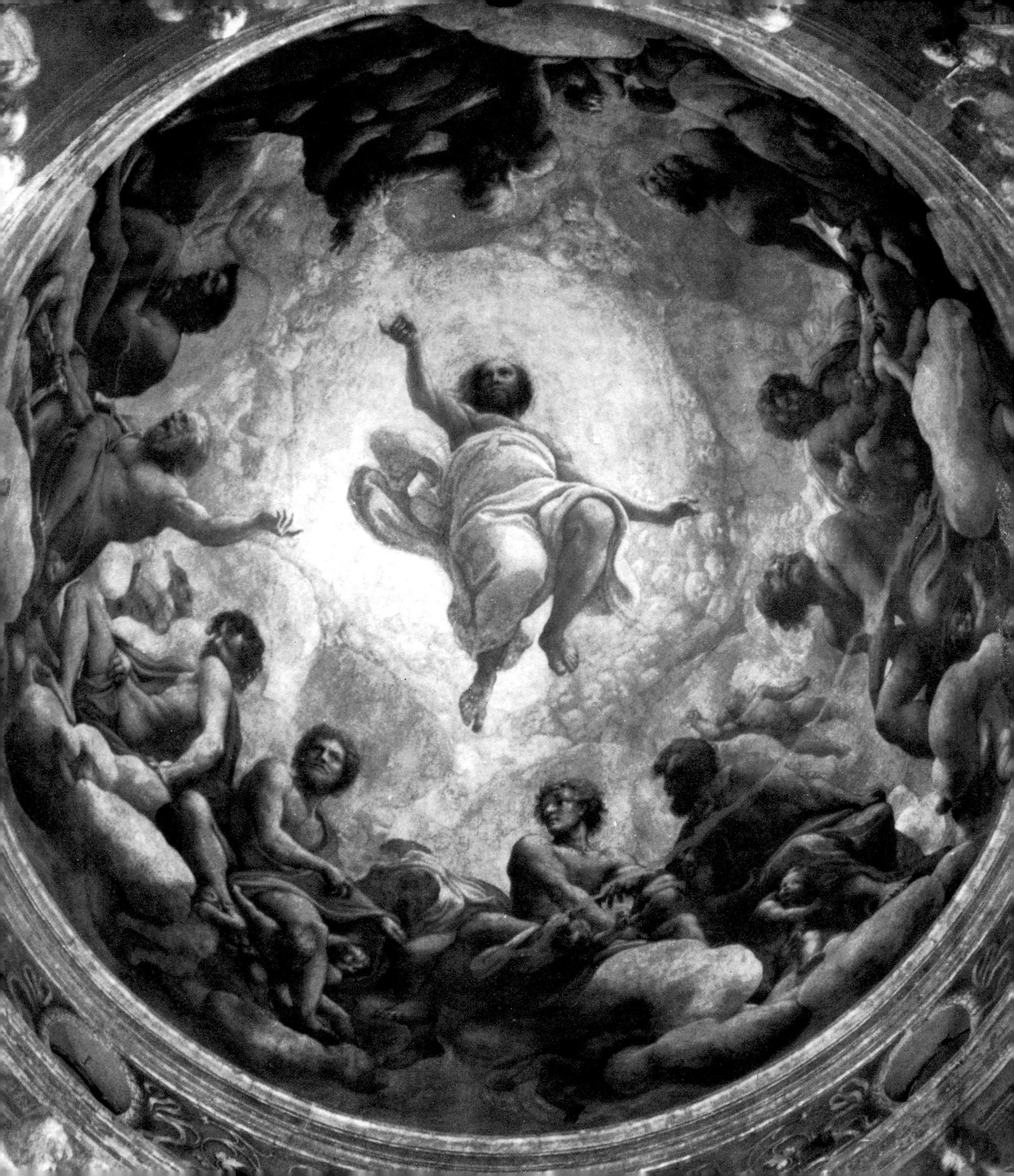

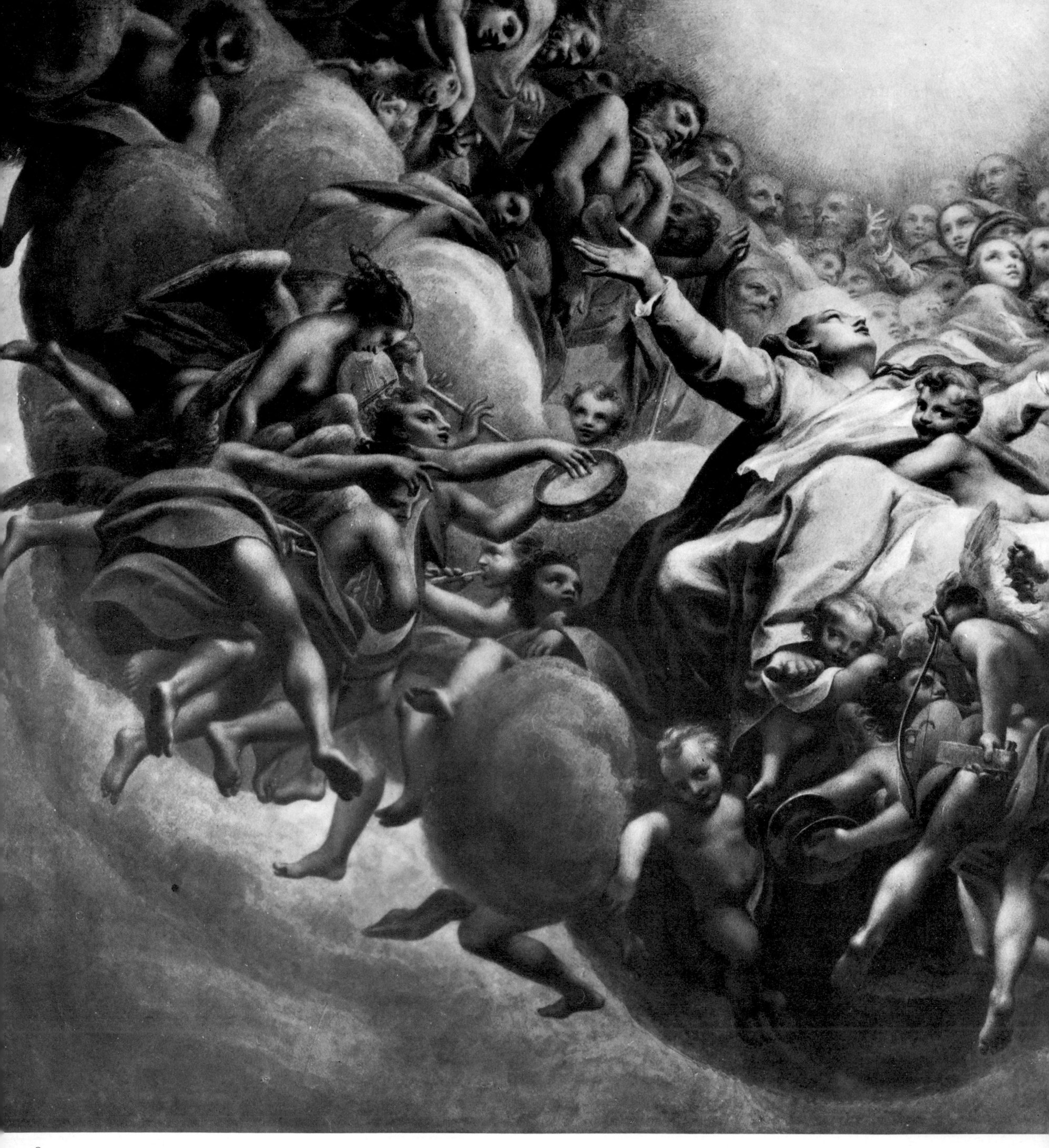

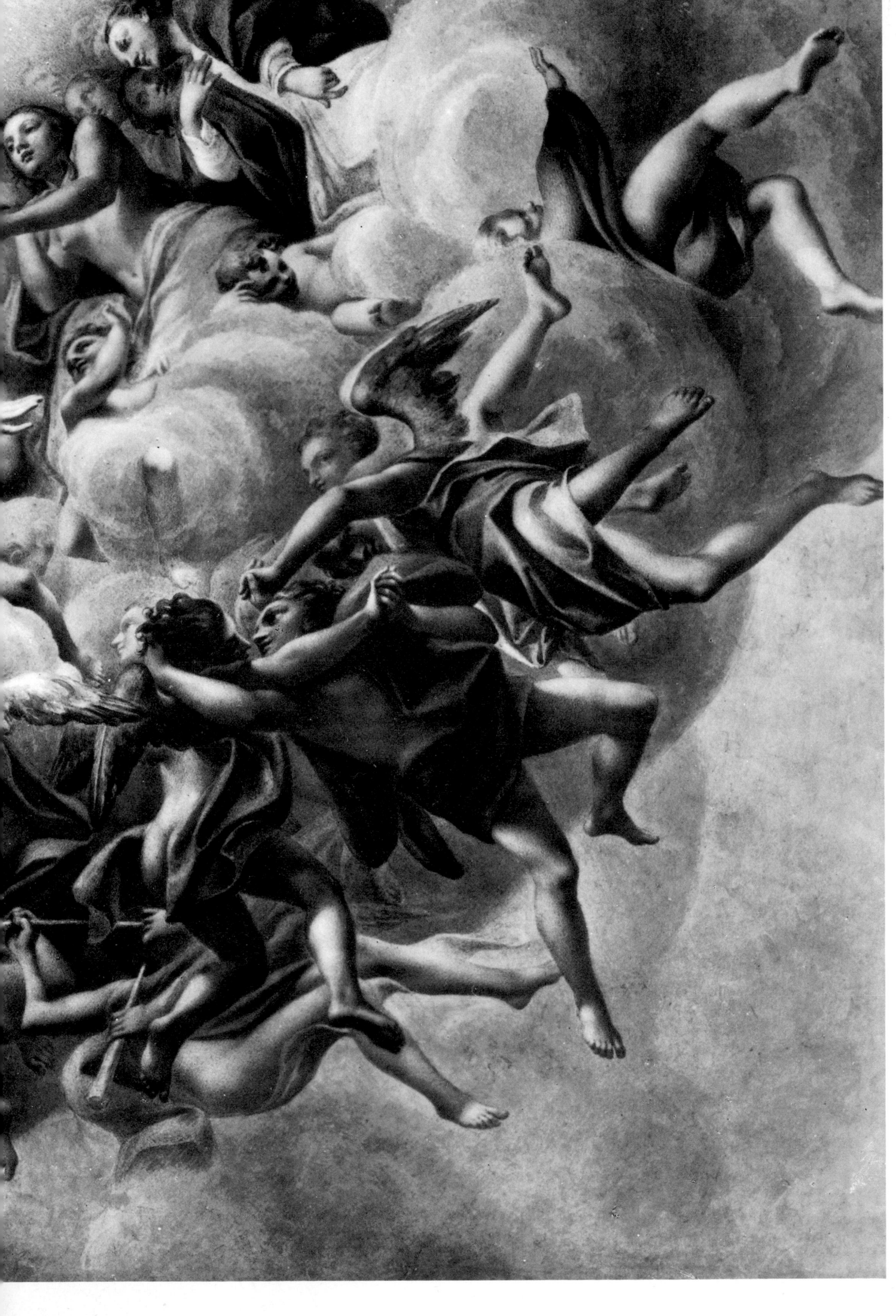

119 Correggio. Detail of *The Assumption of the Virgin*. Parma, cupola of the Cathedral.

This ceiling composition seemed so audacious to Correggio's contemporaries that the commission for the decoration of the choir, which was to have followed the decoration of the cupola, was withdrawn from the artist.

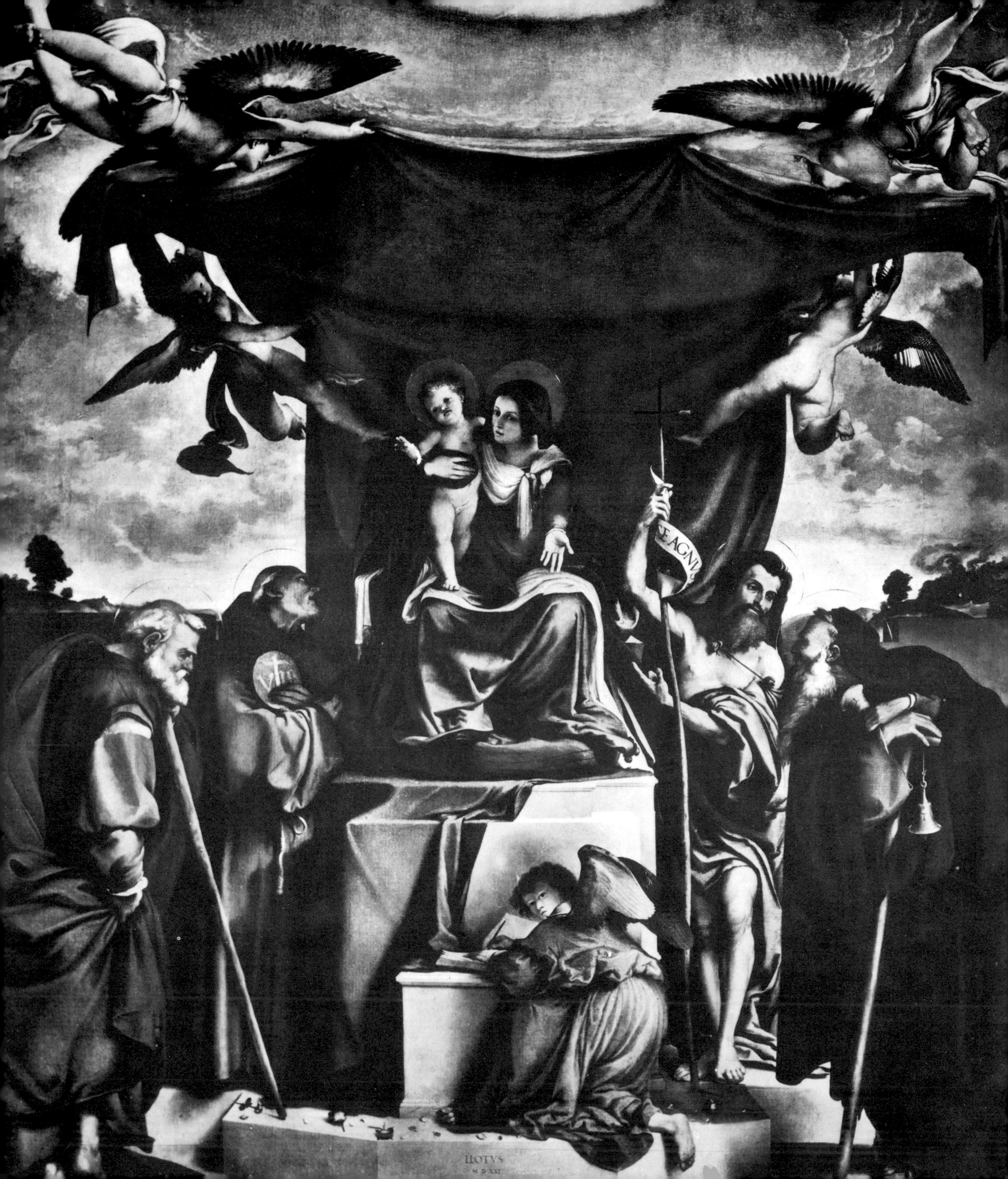

LOTVS
M D XXI

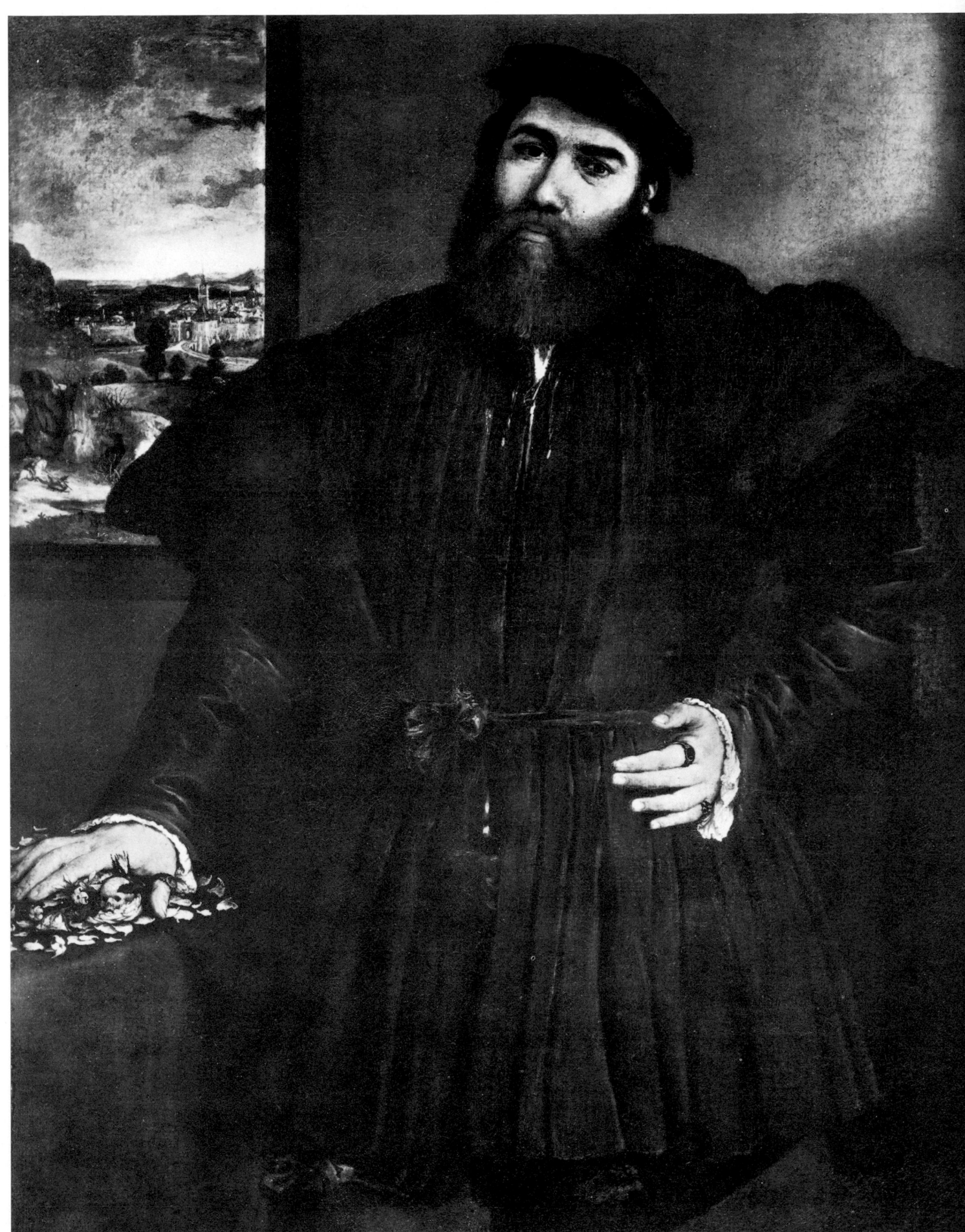

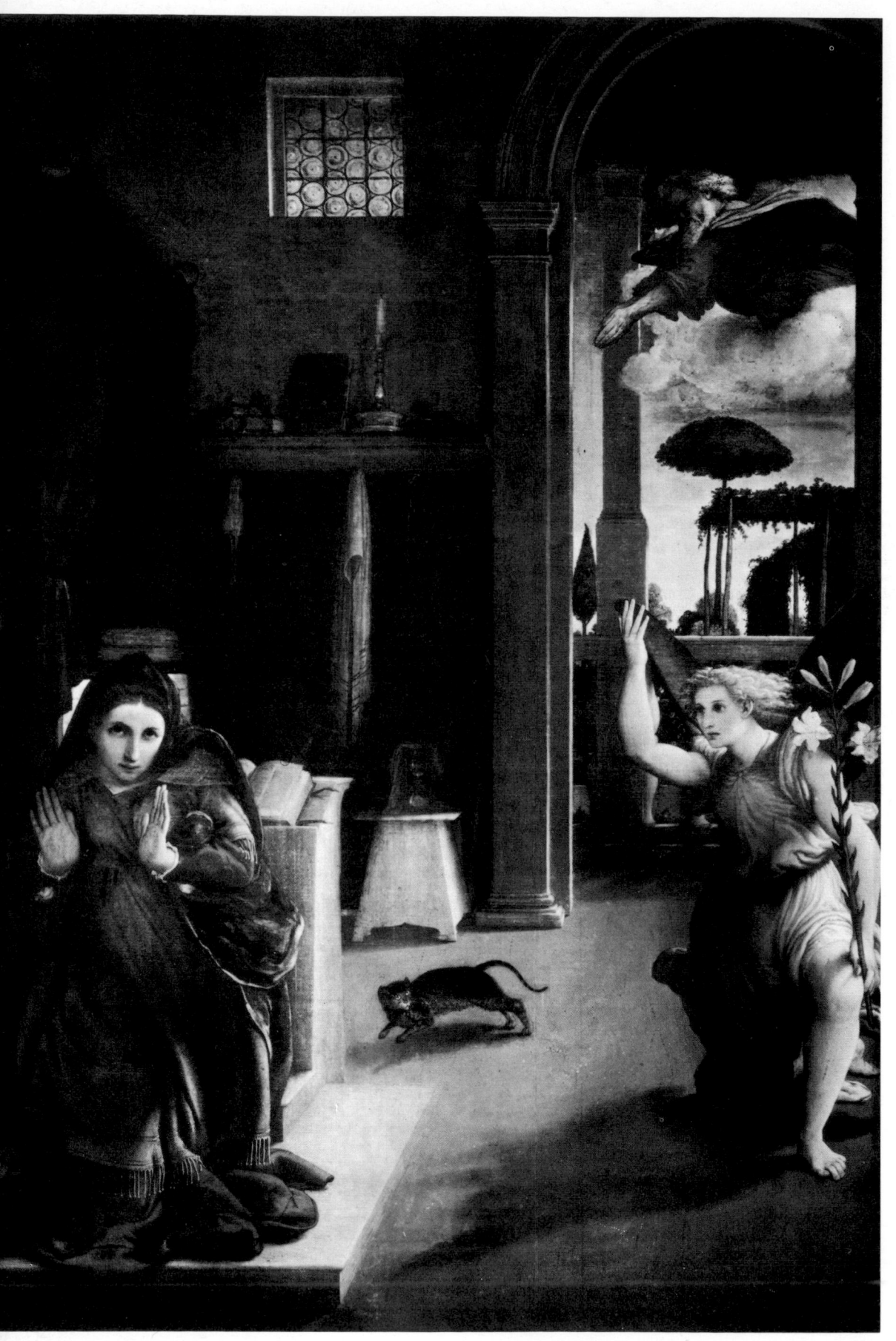

122 Lorenzo Lotto. *The Annunciation*. Recanati, Santa Maria Sopra Mercanti.

In this extraordinary composition, Lotto sweeps aside all the conventional ideas surrounding such a traditional subject, turning a religious scene into a theatrical drama.

to have been suddenly 'abandoned by the gods', by those gods who had watched over Italian art for three centuries. Very few of them possessed the genius to transcend their self-imposed limitations. Among these few was Parmigianino, whose manneristic variations on Correggio contain refinements that are absolutely foreign to his model, being the product of artifice. This excessively self-conscious art produced painting such as the *Madonna with the long neck* (*pl. 123*), in which elongation and an exaggerated foreshortening that projects the bust towards the background turns her into some kind of precious object of a hard, gem-like perfection. It is understandable that this undisciplined manner of painting, its peculiarities given sanction by the occultism that was all the rage at the time, should have spread freely throughout Europe. Prague, under the reign of Rudolf II, was one of its most active centres; there, the Milanese Arcimboldo amused the court with portraits in which the faces are composed of flowers, fruits, objects, even animals (*pl. 113*) or flames.

An opposite effect of anticlassicism was seen in a devoted application to reproducing nature with a mimetic exactitude, renouncing all aesthetic considerations and directing skill solely towards the scrupulous re-creation of the object, plant or animal. This taste for painting flora and fauna originally found expression within grotesque ornaments, as though this irruption of gratuitous matter could not be tolerated by the classical spirit unless caught up in some decorative rhythm. Flowers, plants and animals were detached from nature and reproduced on their own. The insatiable curiosity about nature which filled seekers such as Aldrovandi prompted them to make 'copies' of natural objects and creatures and build up collections of them. Dürer had provided an example of this mimetism, and at the beginning of the sixteenth century, Joris Hoefnagel had practised it for the courts of Munich and Vienna. Italy, versatile as ever, did not lag behind in this field. The finest of all naturalist painters is a Veronese, Jacopo Ligozzi, who painted for the Grand Duke Francesco I de' Medici some admirable plates of plants and animals which are now in the Uffizi collection.

On 31 October 1541, Michelangelo finally revealed to the eyes of his disconcerted admirers the fresco of the *Last Judgment* in the Sistine Chapel, above the altar where, the following day, Paul III was due to celebrate high mass for the eve of All Saints' Day. The artist had been working there since the spring of 1536, preparing to deliver in this form his personal Christian message. No doubt Michelangelo's concept was influenced by an

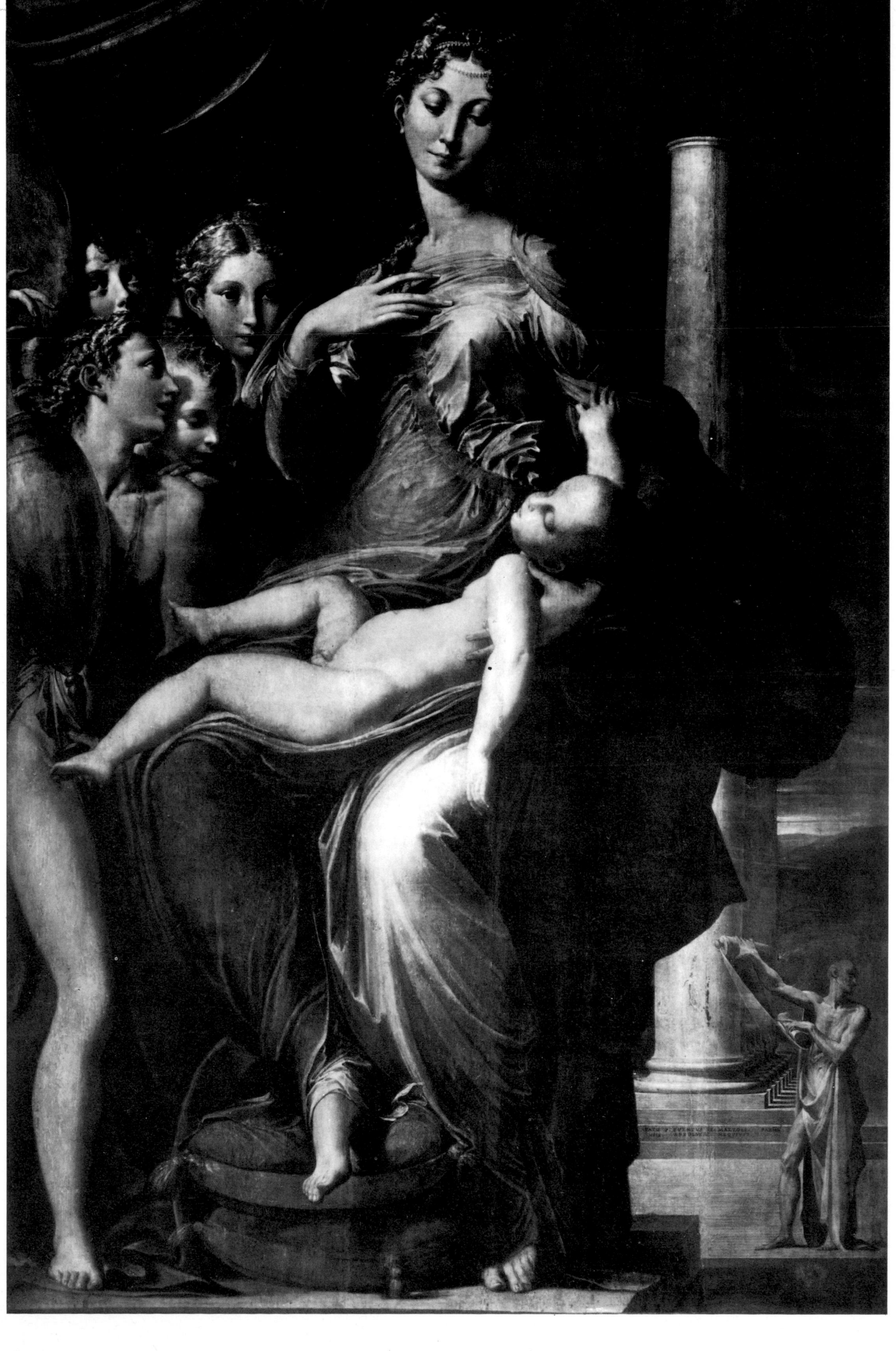

123 Parmigianino (1503–40). *The Madonna with the long neck*. Florence, Pitti.

Parmigianino's researches are the affectations of an aesthete unconcerned with the moral content of a picture and interested only in making it a vehicle for intellectual speculation.

143

original project, which had been to paint a Resurrection above the altar and a Fall of the Angels above the entrance. The intention of this scene would have been to show above the altar, where the sacrament effecting salvation is administered, the terrible face of supreme Justice which would appear at the end of time.

According to Charles de Tolnay (*Michelangelo*, Princeton, 1947 etc.), several myths can be detected at work in this colossal image, for which Michelangelo found inspiration not only in a careful reading of the Bible but also in a profound knowledge of antiquity: the myths of the revolt of the Titans and of the wheel of fortune, the heliocentric cosmology which the artist may have drawn directly from the sources of antiquity, and which may have had a symbolic value for him, the Pythagorean myth of celestial attraction projecting the souls of the chosen towards the stars, while the damned are committed to the souls of animals. The Sun-Christ, centre of an orbital gravitation, is both Zeus and Apollo, and in fact borrows certain traits from the Apollo Belvedere. The most surprising aspect of this syncretism is the indisputable fact that the pose of the Virgin (*pl. 125*) has been borrowed from a rather lascivious antique statue, the squatting Venus (*pl. 126*); there seems no reason to doubt that Michelangelo, remaining faithful to Florentine neoplatonism, intended to suggest a fusion between the Virgin and the platonists' Venus, who represented the guardian principle of Humanity saved by Love. This conception of a mystagogy uniting Christianity and paganism is entirely appropriate to the world of the Renaissance. But the religious significance of the fresco is impregnated with the spirit of the Reformation: at the time that he painted it, Michelangelo, together with his close friend Vittoria Colonna, was frequenting a religious circle in which Juan Valdés played the role of spiritual adviser, and which, like the Protestants, professed a belief in salvation through faith alone. This circle was broken up by the Inquisition, and if Michelangelo escaped the attentions of the authorities it was doubtless because of the almost princely status he enjoyed in Rome.

However, it was not this heretical atmosphere that shocked his contemporaries but, rather, the indecency of this display of colossal nude figures in a church, for Michelangelo had not veiled any of the anatomical characteristics of his personages. Even before the work was finished, the pope's master of ceremonies, Biagio de Cesena, had condemned it as being a fit decoration for a bath-house or a tavern, and Michelangelo had revenged himself for this remark by giving this official's features to Minos, king of the underworld. Michelangelo's most

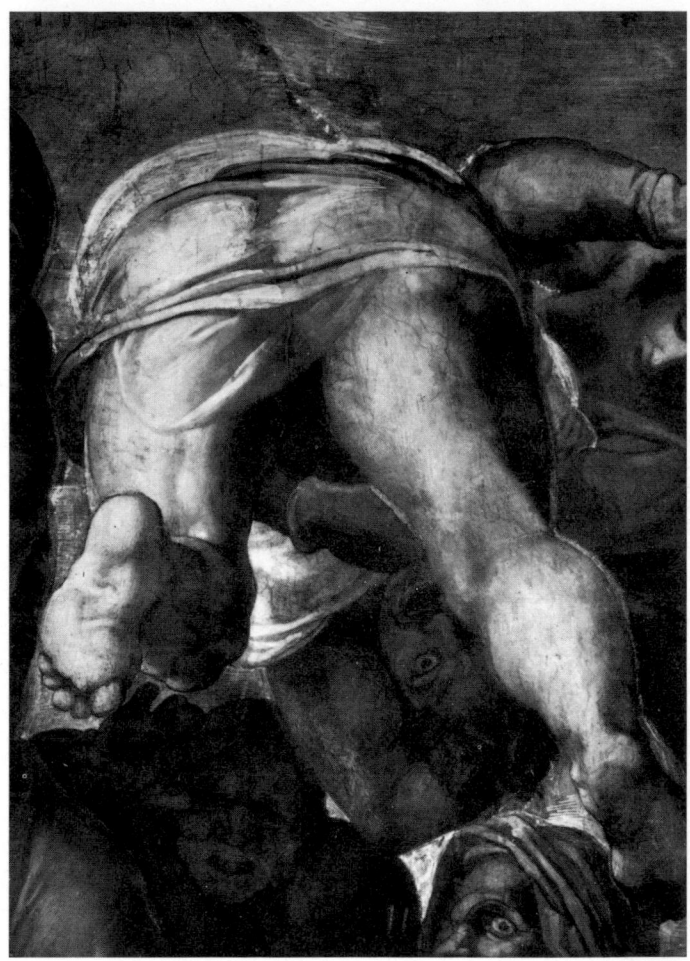

124 Michelangelo. Damned soul, detail of the *Last Judgment*. Vatican, Sistine Chapel.

violent critic was Aretino, who resented the former's avowed lack of respect for him, and in a letter which he made public, as a 'baptized Christian', this blackmailer and apologist for vice set himself up as the defender of morality.

Paul III, who was still activated by the spirit of the Renaissance, came to Michelangelo's defence. Paul IV was on the point of ordering the fresco destroyed, but contented himself in the end with having the genitals veiled (*pl. 124*) by Daniele da Volterra, who thus gained the nickname 'Il Braghettone'. Pius IV had yet more draperies added. The question of the work's continued existence was

125 Michelangelo. The Virgin (inspired by the statue of *Venus and Cupid*), detail of the *Last Judgment*. Vatican, Sistine Chapel.

126 *Venus and Cupid*. Hellenistic period. Roman copy. Naples, Museo Nazionale.

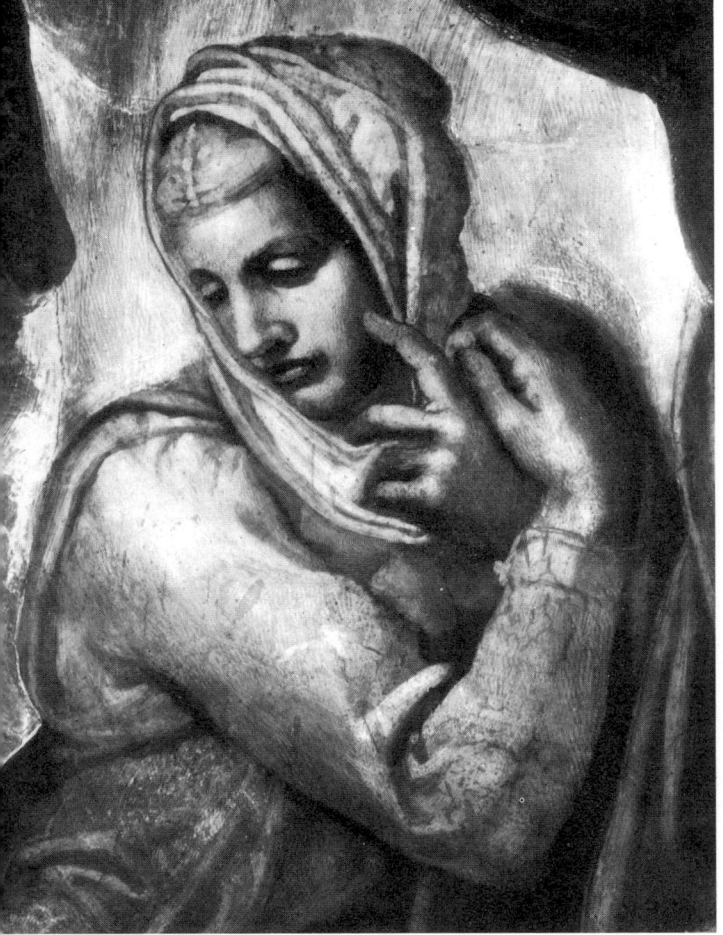

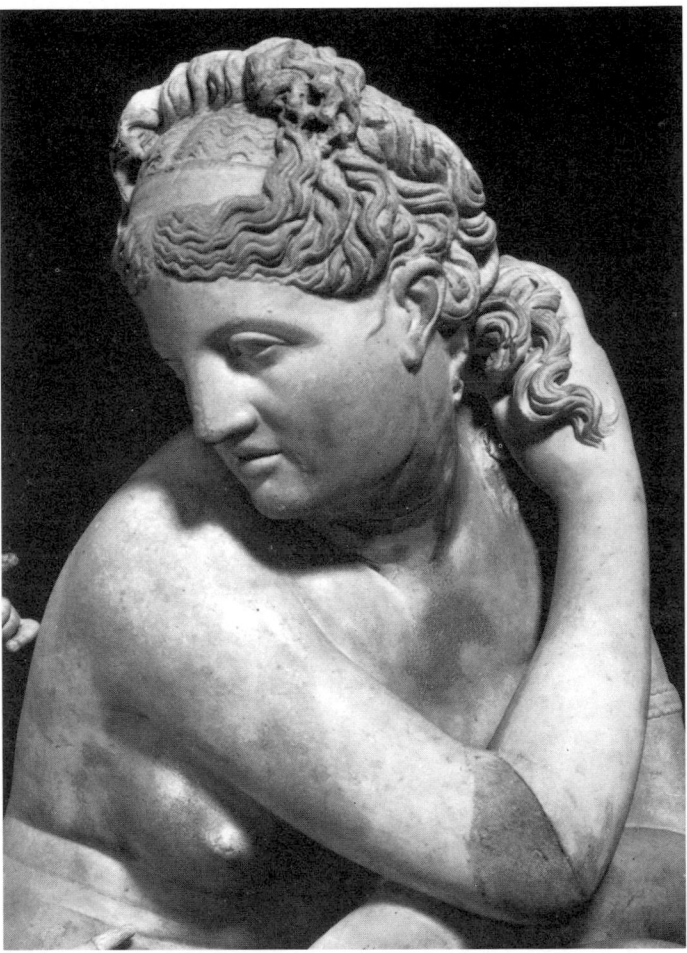

Despite the veneration in which Michelangelo has always been held, the innovations of the *Last Judgment* have continued to provoke bitter criticism from the moment of completion of the composition until the present day.

again raised under Pius V: El Greco, who was in Rome, urged its destruction, proposing to replace it by a fresco that would be 'modest and decent and no less well painted than the other', but the saint did not dare efface the sacrilegious decoration and limited himself to having certain bodies repainted. Clement VIII, finally, decreed its suppression, but had to retreat in face of the protests of the Accademia di San Luca. In 1762, Clement XIII ordered more veils still to be added, and in 1936 rumours circulated that Pius XI had expressed a desire to see this covering-up process continued.

Until the end of the sixteenth century, writers on art, even those most favourably disposed towards Michelangelo, such as Vasari, all criticized the *Last Judgment*, at least in the name of decorum or the appropriateness of the image to its subject. As we have seen, the scandal of the *Last Judgment* has not yet died down. Many Catholics continue to veil their faces in front of it, and many lovers of art continue to find it 'in bad taste'. Aesthetically, Michelangelo was ahead of his time and can be considered an immediate forerunner of the baroque: and the audacities of baroque art are today still an object of scandal for lovers of classicism as much as for lovers of modernism.

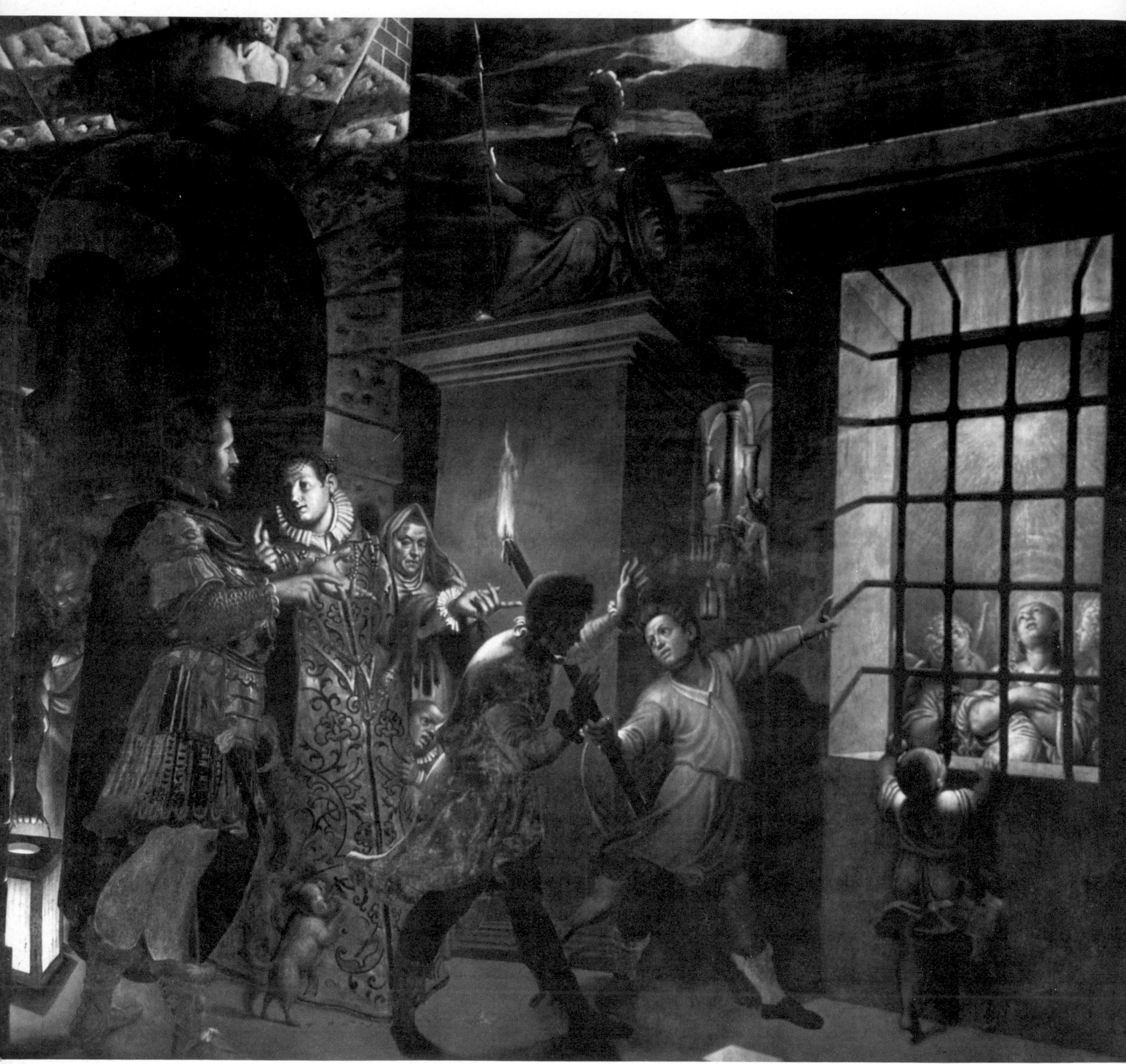

127 Antonio Campi (*c.* 1514–87 or after 1591). *The Empress Faustina visiting St Catherine in prison*. Milan, Sant'Angelo.

10 Difficult victories

Some time around 1580, the Italian painters finally came down from the clouds and regained contact with concrete reality. Rather than involving a return to classicism, this reaction against mannerism engendered the baroque. In 1585, the Carracci founded in Bologna the teaching academy known as the Accademia degli Incamminati. Although aiming at renovation, their approach was essentially scholastic and was based, additionally, on a careful study of nature, as is shown by the huge number of drawings they made and by Annibale's few realist paintings. Other artists, however, who did not belong to this Bolognese circle with its traditional faith in the idea that anything could be learnt, overcame mannerism through more genuinely progressive personal efforts. Antonio Campi of Cremona, for example, anticipated Caravaggio's night-pieces by twenty-five years in his 1580 painting *The Empress Faustina visiting St Catherine in prison* (*pl. 127*). And he was not the only one, at that time, to seek from the night those deep sources of inspiration which would make the artist aware once more of the human drama. The few night-pieces painted by Luca Cambiaso in Genoa approach far closer to the feeling of the seventeenth century. Georges Isarlo was the first to point out how closely Cambiaso's *Madonna with a candle* (Palazzo Bianco, Genoa) foreshadows Georges de la Tour; as for the *Workshop of St Joseph* (*pl. 130*) Cambiaso preludes not only La Tour but the Rembrandt of the *Holy Family* (the *Carpenter's family*).

Isolated in the distant school of Genoa, which lacked any indigenous tradition, Cambiaso sought to create the basis for a new art. His originality is less evident in his paintings, where the treatment is slack and conventional, than in his admirable drawings, which often possess Rembrandt's visionary spontaneity. Each time Cambiaso set his marvellously agile pen to paper he embarked on a voyage of discovery; in front of his easel his enthusiasm seemed to cool. Clearly, the process of painting bored this impatient artist, and it was no doubt this, rather than a desire to show off, that prompted him to paint with both hands at the same time, as though he were a pianist. His researches led him in two opposite directions: realism and abstraction. He attempted to prise religious subjects loose from the iconological shell within which they were trapped, and to breathe into them a new vitality, that of the human drama. Thus, the *Visitation* (*pl. 128*) takes place on a flight of stairs, its landing crowded with children and with seated women, one of whom is working her spinning-wheel; at the curve of the steps, the bemused Virgin observes the approach of St Elizabeth, exhausted by her exertions in climbing the stairs. It was Cambiaso who initiated the popular, evangelical approach which guided religious painting until Rembrandt's time, and for which Caravaggio is generally given credit.

Cambiaso's cubist drawings (*pl. 129*) have received great attention in modern times, but far from being the 'bizarre' product of a mannerist imagination, a suggestion recently revived by Jacques Bousquet (*Mannerism: the Painting and Style of the late Renaissance*, translated by Simon Watson Taylor, New York 1964), they reveal an attitude which is the exact opposite. The artist was seeking to rediscover the principles of the construction of the human body, principles that had become lost in the platitudes of mannerism. He was not the inventor of the process known in Italy as *quadratura*; Dürer, for one, had employed it occasionally for the same reasons. Lomazzo, writing in 1584, traced this system of schematizing the human body to a Lombard tradition, claiming that Vincenzo Foppa had already used it, and that Bramante had made a book of models which was known to Raphael and which had passed into Cambiaso's possession. But Soprani, writing a biography of Cambiaso in 1674, protested violently against this assertion, which he considered a plot to tarnish the glory of his hero. Whatever the facts may be, Cambiaso's cubism is based upon absolutely opposite motives from those of twentieth-century cubism, since his whole aim was to discover the visual reality of the body, while the cubists set out to destroy it.

The study of another artist, Federico Barocci, will allow us to perceive the passage from mannerism to baroque, a passage which in his case resulted from an internal effort showing proof of great creative

128 Luca Cambiaso (1527–85). Detail of *The Visitation*. New York, collection Bertina Suida Manning.

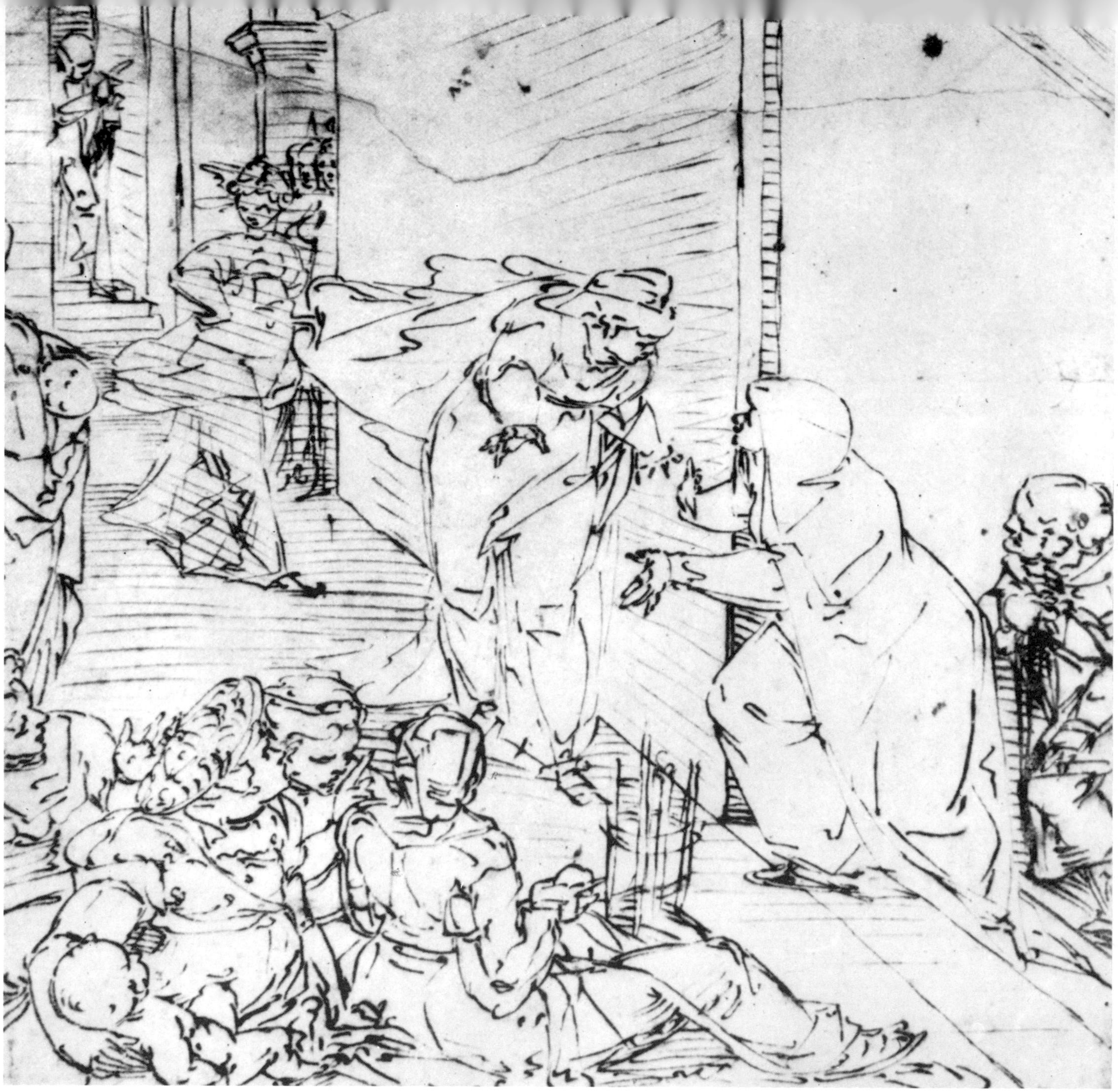

129 Luca Cambiaso. *The Resurrection of Christ*. Frankfurt-on-Main, Städelsches Kunstinstitut.

Although as a painter Luca Cambiaso often shows himself to be still influenced by the conventions of his time, his drawings express an untrammelled creative imagination. He sometimes makes use of a cubist procedure to define his forms more effectively.

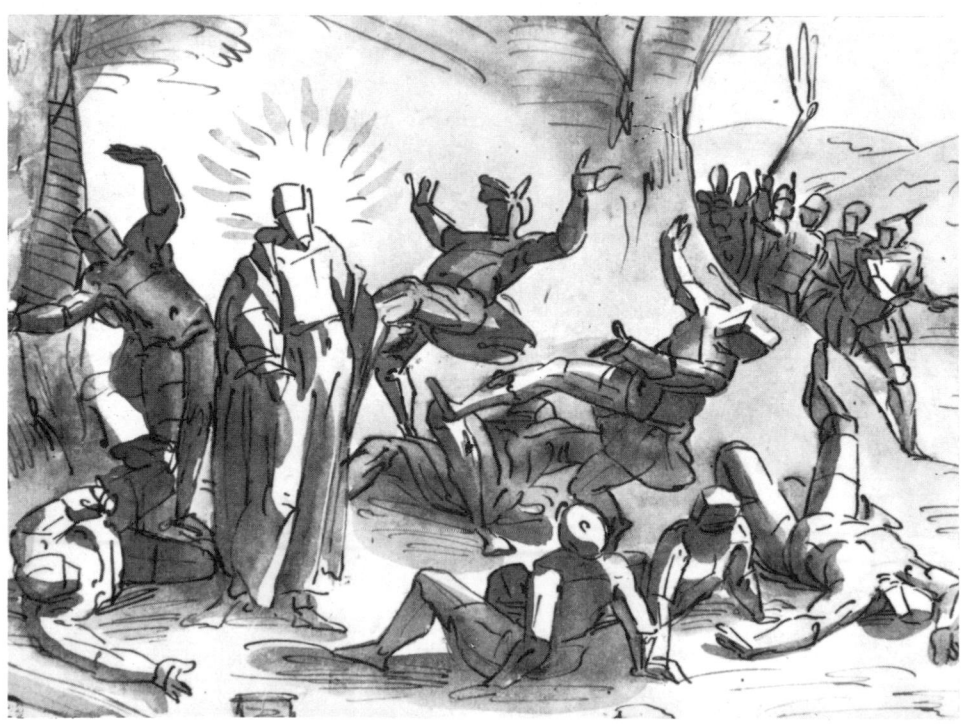

130 Luca Cambiaso. *The Workshop of St Joseph*. Wilton House, collection Earl of Pembroke.

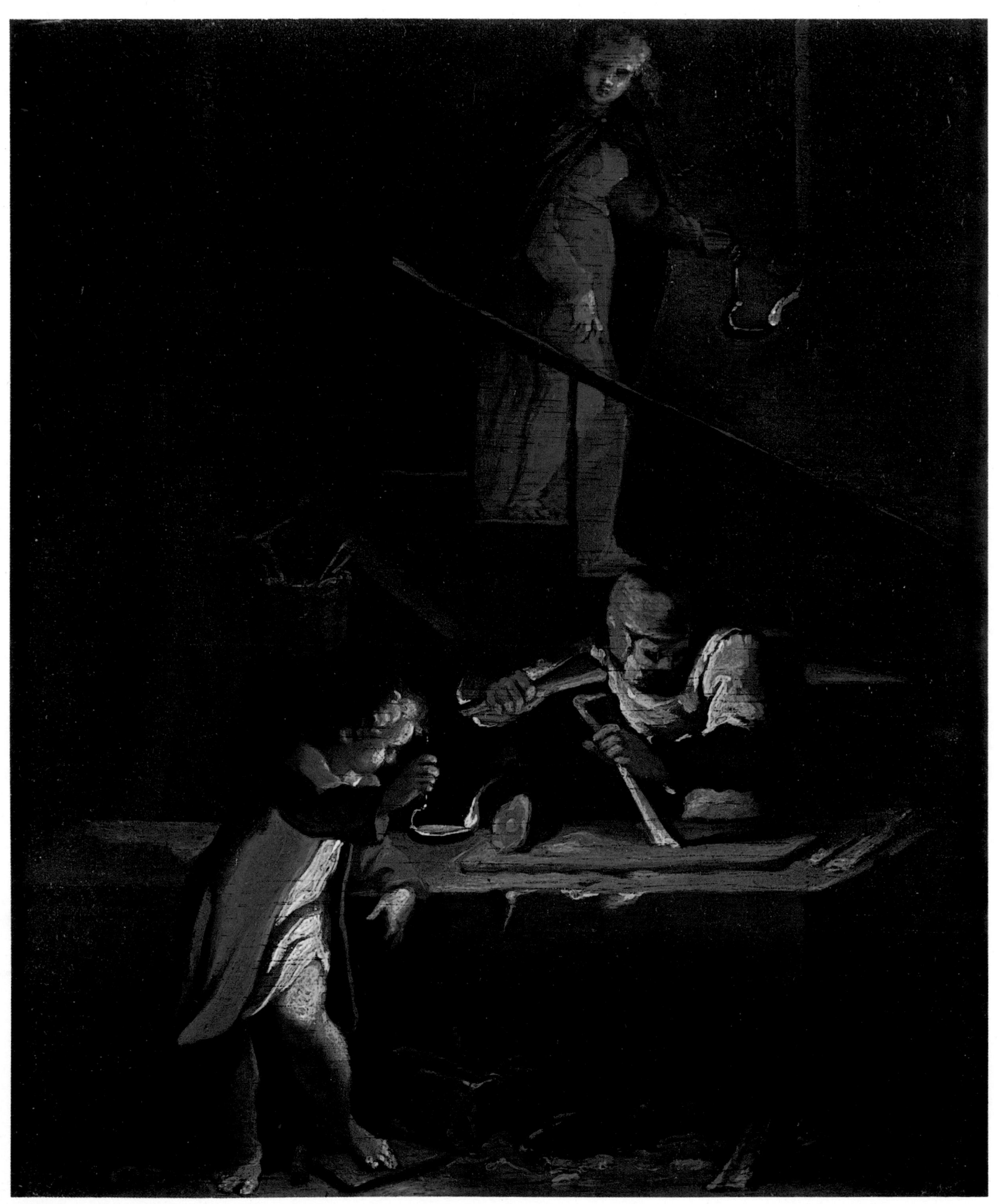

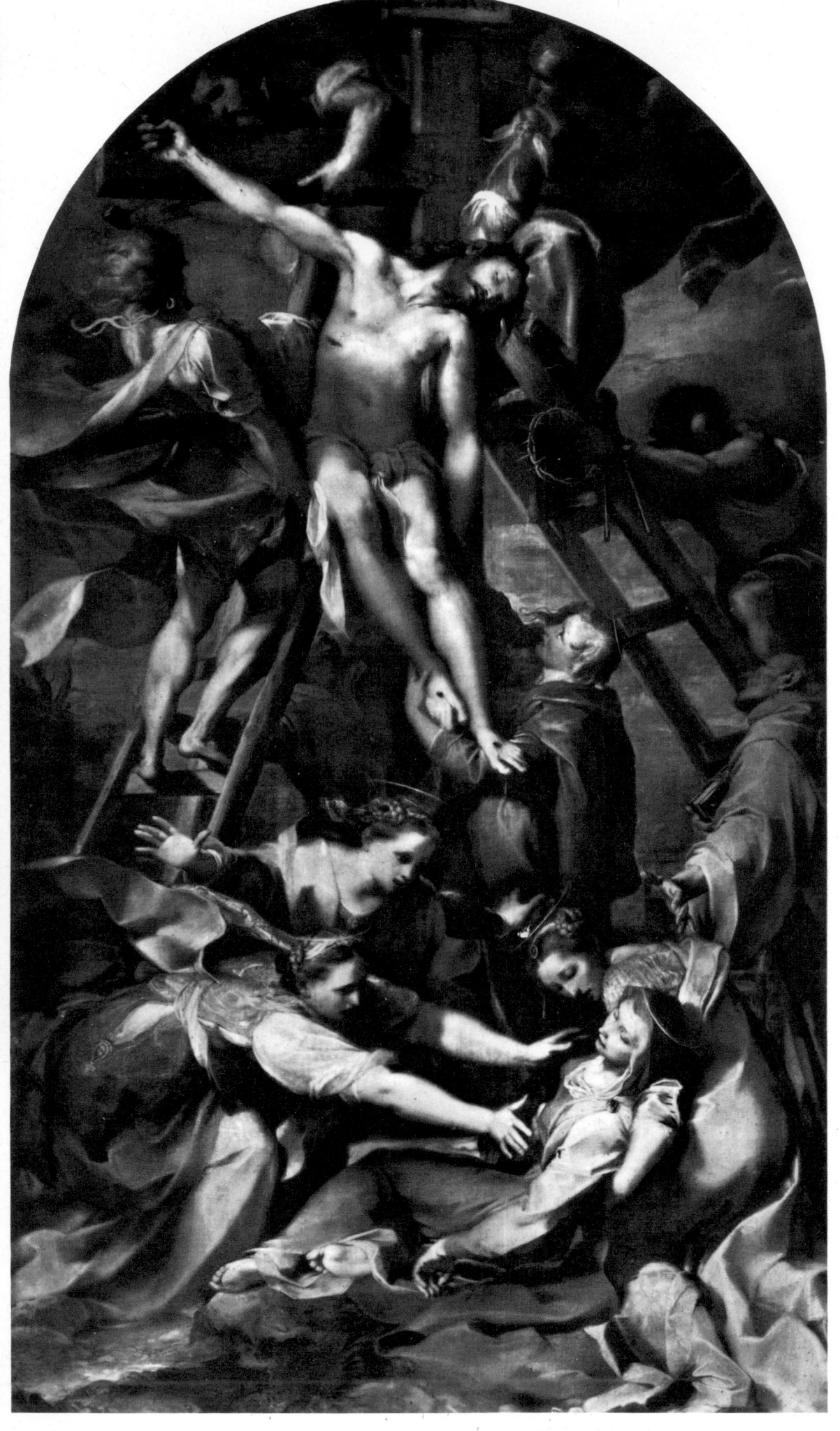

power. His *Deposition* of 1567 (*pl. 131*) is a typically mannerist composition, comparable to the celebrated 1521 *Deposition* by Rosso (*pl. 114*). Yet some ten years later, in 1579, his *Madonna of the People* (*Madonna del Popolo*) (*pl. 132*) demonstrated that he had succeeded in eliminating mannerist complications and creating a composition in which spatial balance is achieved by subtle modulations of form, thus anticipating the baroque. In this respect, he went beyond the Carracci, whose forms always remained heavy and even awkward; he achieved that definition of human figures in space which was to be a characteristic accomplishment of the baroque painters of the following century. The sources from which he drew his principles were Raphael and Correggio; fortunately he had remained uninfluenced by Michelangelo's *terribilità*.

Barocci derived his style directly from Correggio who, from his position astride mannerism, was the true initiator of the baroque. Bellori, in his *Lives*, tells us that Barocci was much impressed by a few pastels by Correggio which a painter returning from Parma showed him. But it seems clear that the influence must have been far deeper; indeed, to understand Barocci's art at all one must suppose that he had been to Parma himself and seen Correggio's masterpieces there, so close a knowledge of them is revealed by his own pictures. Among those artists who were seeking to detach themselves from mannerism, drawing was practised as a discipline, and Barocci was as assiduous in this respect as the Carracci and Cambiaso. We know from Bellori that Barocci's beautiful paintings were the fruit of methodical preparatory work, and hundreds of surviving drawings bear witness to this fact. The recent biographer of Barocci, Harald Olsen, in a painstaking inventory of these, lists no less than eighty-seven preliminary studies for his masterpiece, the *Madonna of the People*.

So great an effort on the part of an artist who was partially disabled must arouse one's admiration. Bellori's account of Barocci's life paints a grim but not untypical picture of those times, when it was perfectly normal to make use of the sword or poison to rid oneself of a rival. In this case, it seems that a group of painters who were jealous of Barocci's precocious talent invited him to a banquet at which they contrived to have him eat a poisoned salad. Although he survived, he contracted a disorder of the digestive tract which could not be cured even by the physicians called to his bedside by Cardinal della Rovere. For four years he was unable to paint, and then was able to paint only two hours a day, remaining in constant suffering night and day. It was in order to recover his health in his native

131 Federico Barocci (*c.* 1535–1612). *Deposition.* Perugia, Cathedral.

132 Federico Barocci. *Madonna of the People (Madonna del Popolo)*. Florence, Uffizi. ▶

climate that he is supposed to have left Rome and returned to Urbino. In any case, this provincial environment favoured the development of an art whose apparent ease is in reality a conquest, based upon profound meditation. By renouncing the lax Roman atmosphere in this way, Barocci was able to find his affinity with the aesthetic of religious intuition recently developed in Emilia on Correggio's initiative, which had allowed this region to avoid the mannerist confusion then reigning at Rome and which Bologna escaped only through the academicism of the Carracci.

Preserved by its very backwardness from the crisis in the arts that, originating in Florence, had spread its mischief throughout Italy, sheltered by its geographical situation and political position from the disquiet that filled men's minds elsewhere, Venice found itself spared for a long time from mannerism and its anguished obsessions. While Florence exerted its saturnine influence over the rest of Italy, Venice produced Veronese, one of the greatest but one of the least inventive of painters, who depicted life in the hedonistic style favoured by Venetian artists from Bellini to Titian. Capitalist stability allowed Venice to outlive its era of political glory and maintain the illusion of a power which now derived solely from its revenues.

The torment which afflicted the other artists of Italy did touch one Venetian, a painter enamoured of grandeur but sapped by a congenital weakness: Jacopo Robusti, called Tintoretto. This strange genius has provoked the interest of Jean-Paul Sartre, who has endowed him with the romantic stature of a *peintre maudit*, 'the prisoner of Venice'; and before that, Jules Villemin attempted to apply to him the methods of psychoanalysis. Sartre's study of Tintoretto does throw some light on his subject, but the personality that emerges from his investigations is more credible as a literary creation than as an historical figure. As for Villemin's thesis, it results in some extremely bold extrapolations, such as the suggestion that the artist's cycle of the Scuola di San Rocco was inspired by St Ignatius of Loyola's *Spiritual Exercises*; a prudent historian can only accord limited interest to such exercises in a still inarticulate field of experimental psychology.

It will doubtless be more fruitful to look at the pictures themselves rather than their subjects, which in that era were still not a matter of free choice for the artist, and to examine those subjects only in relation to the manner in which the artist has interpreted them. It will be worth while to recapitulate briefly the few anecdotes which provide the basis for the fictionalized view of Tintoretto. To begin with, he is supposed to have been so precocious

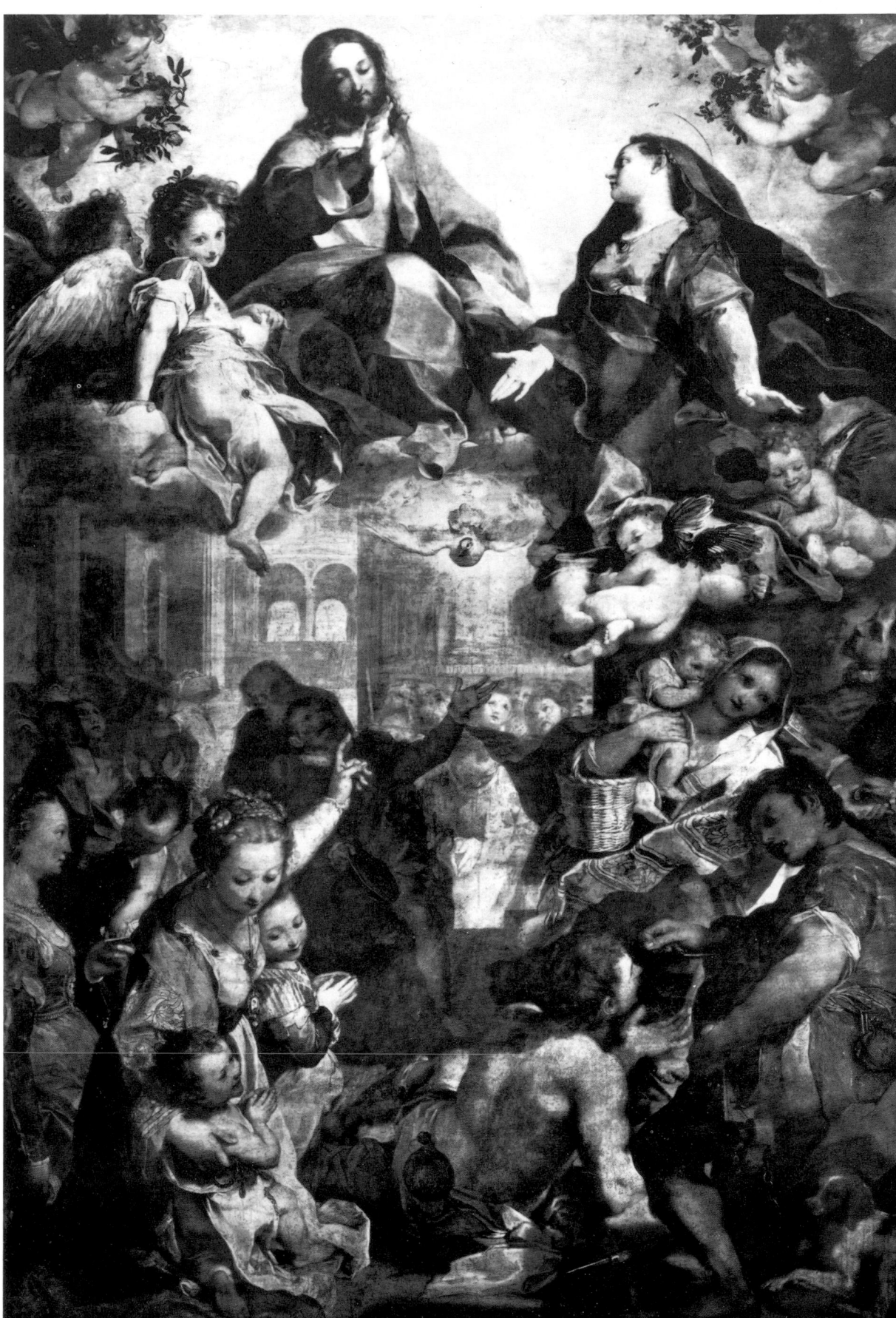

A comparison between the *Deposition* of 1567 and the *Madonna of the People* of 1579 shows how Barocci was the first to be able to put an end to the confusion of mannerism and create a new order, that of baroque composition.

that Titian grew jealous of him when he was still only twelve, and expelled his new pupil from his workshop; this early experience of Tintoretto's has allowed certain interpreters to discover in him neurotic tendencies typical of 'the child abandoned by his father'. However extraordinary young Jacopo's gifts may have been, it is unlikely that they could have aroused Titian's hostility at that early stage; it seems far more likely that the expulsion – if it occurred at all and is not simply a myth – resulted from youthful misbehaviour. In any case, we have no idea who taught the rudiments of painting to this young prodigy who in 1539, at the age of twenty-one, was already in possession of his full artistic powers. It is certain that he was energetic in securing commissions for himself, using such business methods as making gifts of his pictures, or selling them for nothing but the cost of the materials, or securing advantage for himself in competitions by producing a finished work where his colleagues had only sketches to show. This pushfulness may well have been interpreted as impatience to impose his own style of painting, an idea well calculated to shock right-thinking people in a Venice reigned over by the all-powerful Titian who, in the words of Sartre, 'was a whole academy in himself'. In any case, it is difficult to visualize this painter, the recipient of so many official and private commissions, as a recluse and misanthrope. He undoubtedly forced the hand of the Scuola di San Rocco when, at the 1564 competition, he unveiled before the astonished members of the confraternity his own completed painting, already in the place designated for the winning picture. This ruse succeeded admirably, since during the next thirty years, until 1594, the Scuola offered him its walls as a vast field for the exercise of his imagination. No doubt the confraternity was initially tempted by the favourable prices that the artist must have quoted them, since the sample he gave them of his talent in the 1564 picture was mediocre. But the fact that he worked for so many years on this one commission must mean that some genuine attachment existed, based on mutual sympathy.

Although Tintoretto may occasionally have imitated Titian, or assimilated the style of Veronese (who repaid the compliment by borrowing from Tintoretto), his whole art was nothing less than a manifesto directed against the classicism which Titian had elevated into a dogma in Venice. The confusion in his compositions, his love of river imagery, the feverish nature of his eternal quest, all bring him close to mannerism. But the rapid, spontaneous touch which is his most original characteristic contrasts strongly with the elegant, even affected treatment typical of the Florentine, Emilian and Roman mannerists. He transcends mannerism, too, in his consciousness of the drama that motivates him.

It is a matter of controversy as to whether Tintoretto ever saw Michelangelo's frescoes in the Sistine Chapel, particularly the *Last Judgment*. We are too ill-informed about his life to know if he travelled, or if he really was the 'prisoner of Venice'. Personally, I can detect no direct influence of Michelangelo in Tintoretto's art, and if he has anything in common with Michelangelo it is his constant preoccupation with the idea of the end of the world. But whereas for Michelangelo the end of the world is a matter affecting mankind alone, it assumed with Tintoretto the nature of a cosmic upheaval. It is perfectly natural that an inhabitant of Venice, that floating city eternally menaced by some fresh invasion by the sea, should imagine the last day as a diluvial cataclysm. Tintoretto's *Last Judgment* in Santa Maria dell'Orto is a flood in which the bodies of the damned are swept away by cataracts. The artist constantly showed his predilection for themes in which water forms an integral part of the drama; indeed his whole artistic output resembles some kind of river of flowing shapes. It is relevant that the mainlanders Titian and Veronese were classicists; with the Venetian Tintoretto, mobility is the principle of his composition, just as fluidity is the essence of his treatment. Once the earth has been swallowed up by the waters, the universe reverts to the primordial space from which the earth originally sprang. Many of Tintoretto's bodies (*Origin of the Milky Way*, *The Three Graces*, *Bacchus and Ariadne*) float in the ether, weightless, just as the bodies carried away by the flood float on the waters. Tintoretto, who painted a Paradise of elliptic orbs suggesting the idea of heliocentric gravitation, was the first artist to feel that lure of infinite space which in those days affected only a few scholars and which, a century later, made Pascal tremble at the brink of the abyss of heresy. This premonition probably resulted from instinct rather than any conscious reflection of Copernicus's recently formulated theories, although it is normal that at any given moment of time a particular vision of the world should motivate the creative expression of artists as well as thinkers.

Tintoretto employed a further method of breaking down forms: the explosion of light and shadow. His famous *St Mark rescuing a slave* (1548) inaugurated this kind of explosive composition, in which all the elements are dispersed along the many axes of a space that is literally split open, and the process is used in conjunction with an aquatic

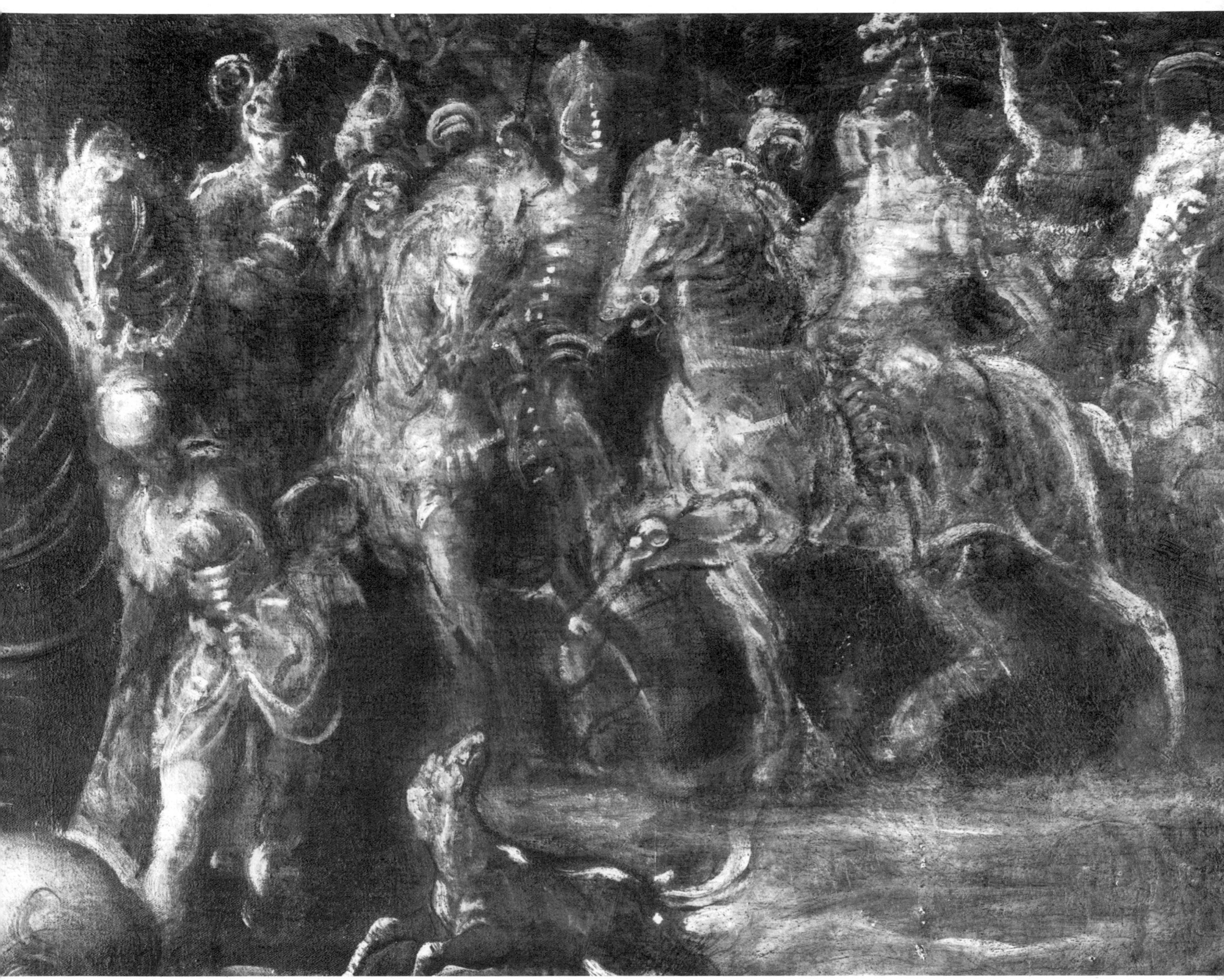

133 Tintoretto (1518–94). Detail of *The Adoration of the Magi*. Venice, Scuola di San Rocco.

Contrary to the principles of classical execution, Tintoretto inaugurated an abbreviated, rapid, allusive treatment which suggested rather than described forms.

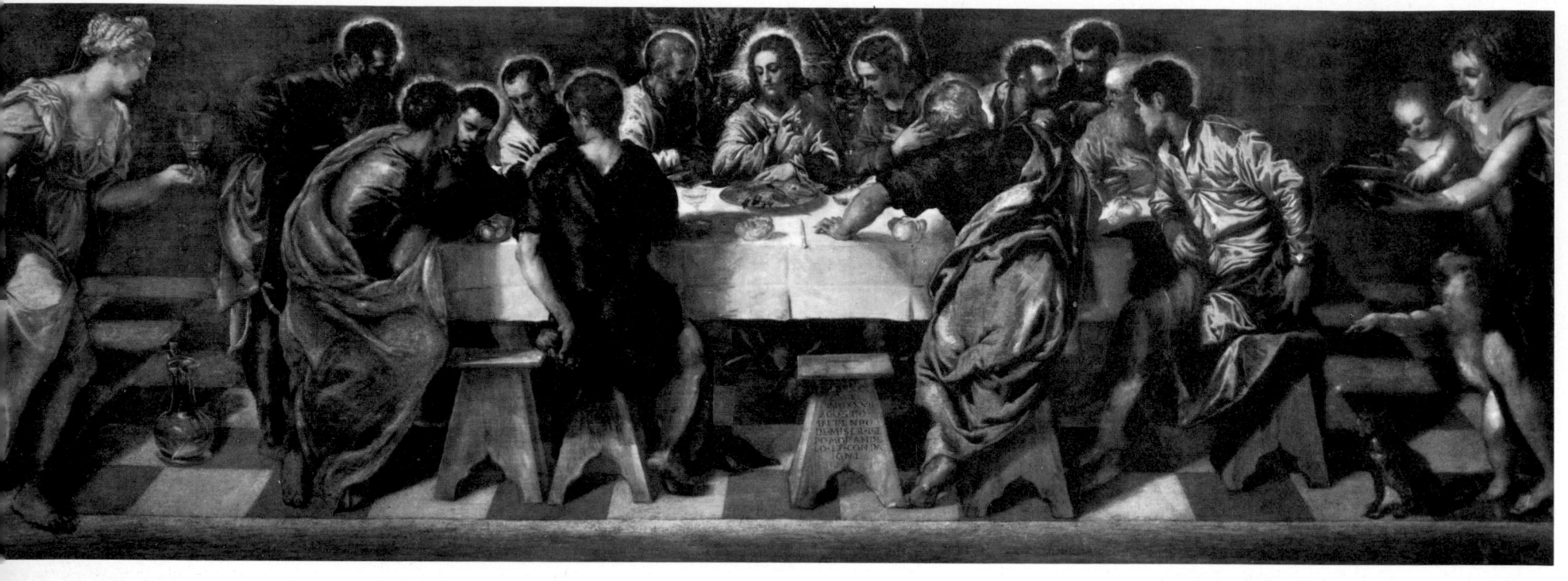

134 Tintoretto. *The Last Supper* (1547). Venice, San Marcuola.

135 Tintoretto. *The Last Supper* (*c.* 1560). Venice, San Trovaso.

136 Tintoretto. *The Last Supper* (*c.* 1580). Venice, Scuola di San Rocco.

The numerous *Last Suppers* which Tintoretto painted show a gradual development in the direction of drama and spatial exploration, but also increasing mastery of technique.

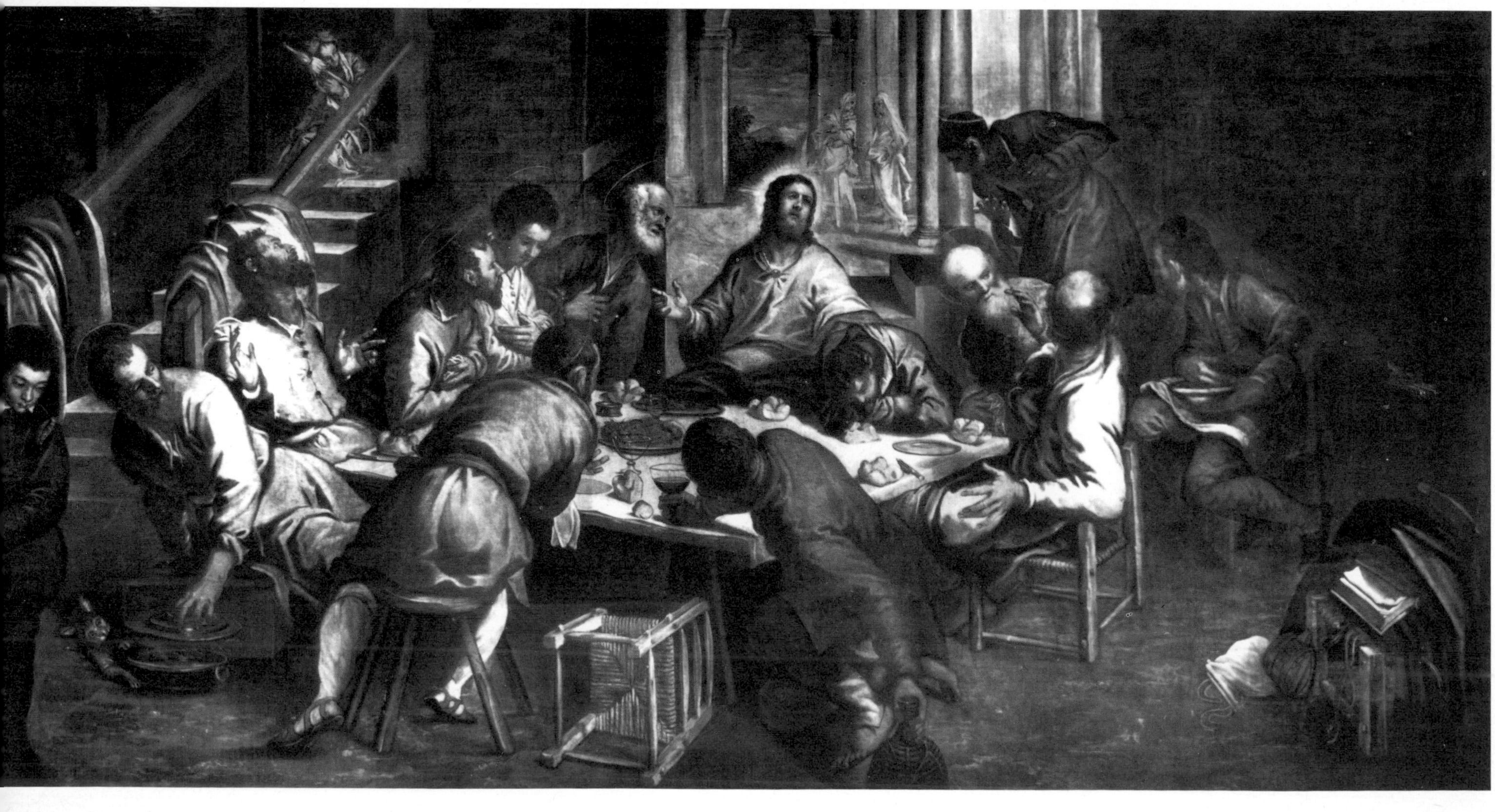

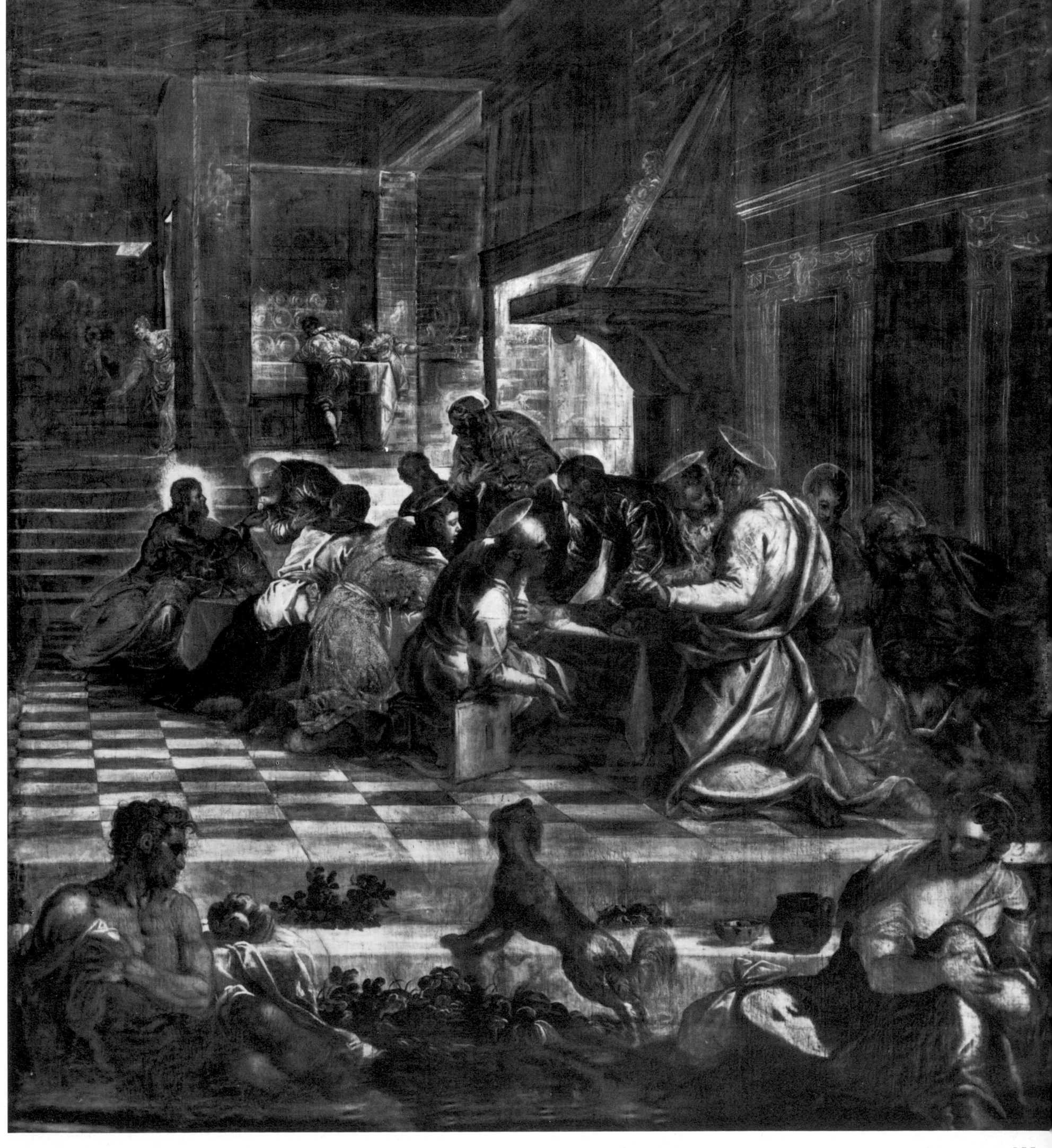

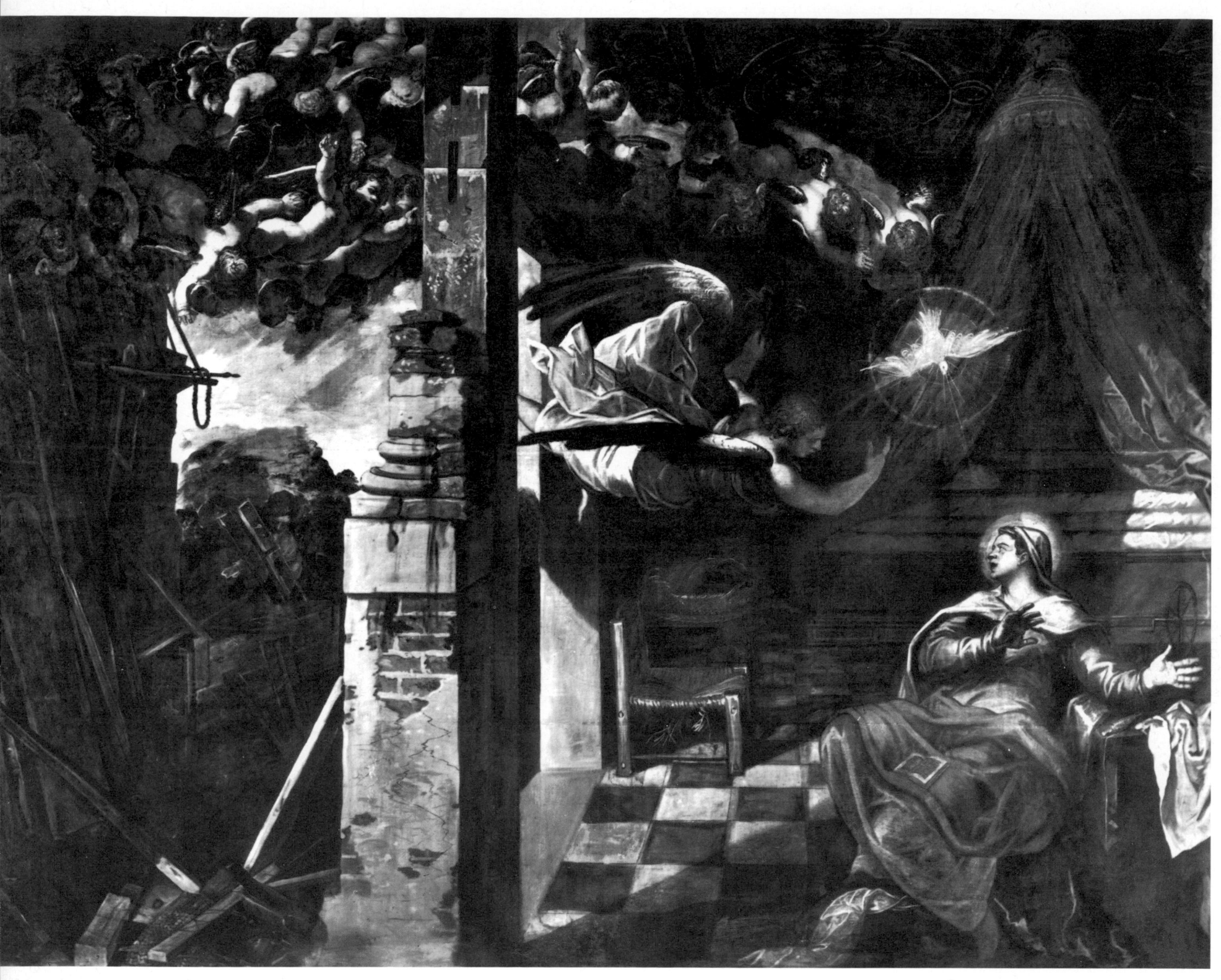

137 Tintoretto. *The Annunciation.* Venice, Scuola di San Rocco.

In a sort of cosmic drama, Tintoretto confronts the natural world with the supernatural world.

fluidity which makes the forms stream uncontrollably from the brush. Becoming aware of this anarchic exuberance, he strove to bring it under control; the study of one particular subject, which he painted ten times during his life, the *Last Supper,* will serve to illustrate this progression in his art.

He first tackled the theme of the *Last Supper* in 1547 at San Marcuola (*pl. 134*), with a soberly

classic composition arranged broadways, following the larger dimension of the working surface, and given solid equilibrium at both sides by two figures. By 1560, in the San Trovaso version (*pl. 135*), this liturgical celebration had been turned into a drama which projects the distracted actors in all directions. This drama reaches a peak of frenzy in the San Polo version composed between 1565 and 1570,

156

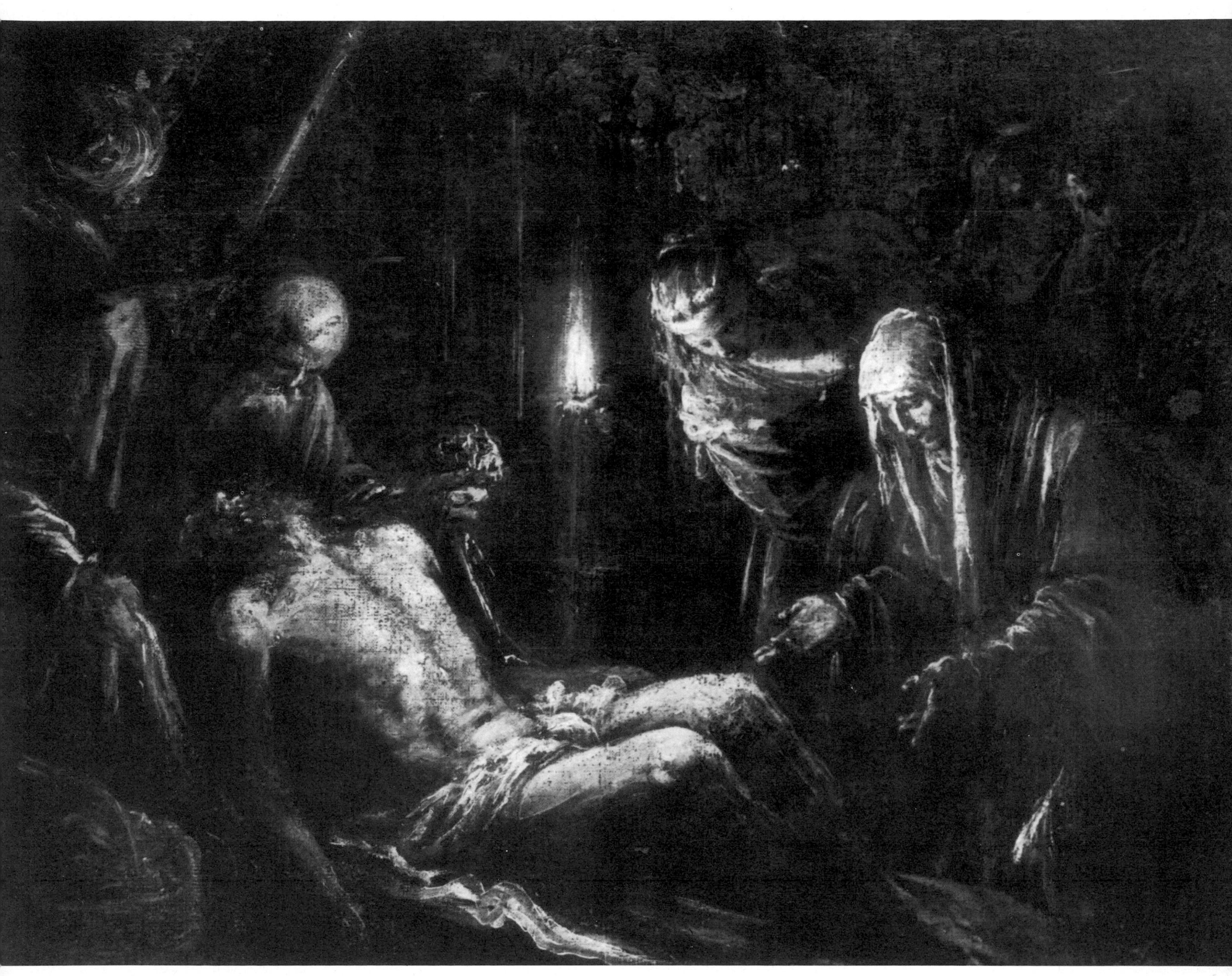

where the composition totters despite the efforts made to hold it in balance. Towards the end of his life, however, around 1580, in paintings of the same theme at the Scuola di San Rocco (*pl. 136*) and at Santo Stefano, Tintoretto succeeded in canalizing this movement within the diagonals of space, inventing a method of composition which was to be used very frequently during the baroque era. At the same time, so as to counter this tendency of the composition to spill over towards the viewer, he wedged it securely along a step, thus showing unmistakably his desire to rediscover the solidity of the earth's contour. At Santo Stefano, figures seem to have positioned themselves at the four corners of the picture as though to enclose the painting surface more effectively, while at San Rocco the vast hall

138 Bassano (1510/18–92). *Deposition.* Lisbon, Museu Nacional de Arte Antiga.

Bassano is the true initiator of a handling which was to be that of Rembrandt, and which involved working the pigment in depth.

157

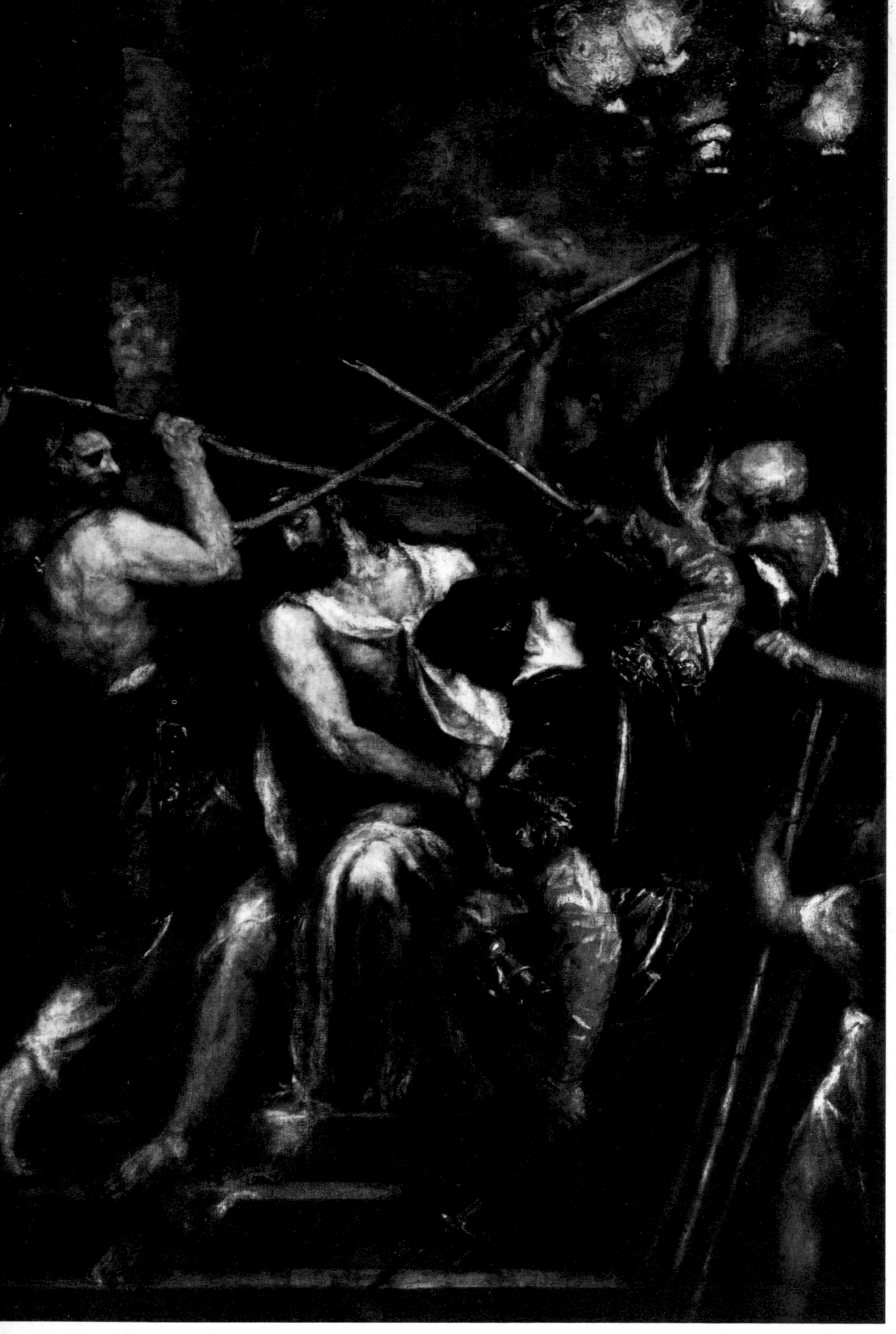

139 Titian. *Christ crowned with thorns*. Munich, Alte Pinakothek.

Towards the end of his life, Titian abandoned the Venetian technique of transparent painting, and, like Bassano, adopted the method of working pigment in depth which Rembrandt was later to revive.

which houses the composition imprisons the restless space within its quadrature. The artist had no need of this stratagem in the *Last Supper* at San Giorgio Maggiore, painted in 1592–4, shortly before his death; here, he achieves unity between the natural and supernatural worlds through the simple interplay of gestures in the context of a structural space, making the symbolic event a drama of universal significance.

This brief survey of Tintoretto's career gives some indication of his complex nature. Once he had realized that Titian's painting could not be developed except by the artist himself (and, in fact, Titian's longevity allowed him to achieve that development), he was seized by a creative fever. Enjoying a facility that led him astray as often as it served him well, his breathless approach produced a world of forms constantly in the process of being swept away by a hurricane. Perceiving intuitively that beyond this universe lay another that would open itself up to mankind's imagination, he nevertheless struggled to stem this process of disintegration by inventing new structures. He finally achieved this ambition in the Scuola di San Rocco, which remained for so long a laboratory for his artistic experiments. Here, during a great part of his life, he conferred with his own soul, and the hospice became for him a retreat for meditation, where he painted from a sense of inner necessity rather than pride. The real Tintoretto, the Tintoretto true to himself rather than to others, is to be found in this great cycle of images. The huge *Crucifixion* of 1566 is still chaotic, but the *Christ before Pilate*, the *Carrying of the Cross* and the two versions of the *Life of St Roch*, belonging to the same sequence of paintings, are organically controlled. The later compositions such as the *Adoration of the Magi (pl. 133)* and the *Temptation of Christ* (1576–81) and, above all, the last ones, the *Annunciation (pl. 137)*, the *Flight into Egypt* and the *Holy Family* (1583–7), are 'accomplished' works in which the majestic rhythms of the baroque find orderly expression. Mellowed by age, the artist at last discovered the path of nature that had remained hidden from him previously, but which now provided a revelation that allowed him to transform cosmic drama into landscape, as in *St Mary the Egyptian* and *St Mary Magdalen*.

Despite Tintoretto's reputation as a 'wild' painter, he should rather be considered as one of the most marvellous examples of creative energy, a man who tamed a turbulent temperament and guided his tremendous energies throughout his life towards a final and complete triumph. In this way he avoided the sense of failure that cast a shadow over Michelangelo's last years and made it impossible for that artist to complete many of his projects.

One painter who was briefly influenced by Tintoretto, despite the provincial isolation in which he lived at Bassano, was Jacopo da Ponte, known as Bassano. The reputation he enjoys today is somewhat disproportionate to his talent, and doubtless results from the great honour that befell him of having inspired the youthful El Greco. The 1957 exhibition of his work at the doge's palace in Venice allowed us to judge him as a painter of rather poor imagination, sticking to traditional compositions to which he gave a fresh and mannerist flavour through his liking for popular scenes and animal life. His novelty lies in a happy way of wielding a brush that is very different from Tintoretto's passionate approach, a sketched style that allowed him to work rapidly and also provided a means of avoiding structural problems. In this, he resembles Luca Giordano, and might equally well have merited the seventeenth-century painter's appellation 'Fa Presto'. Giordano, though, entirely lacked the kind of caprice which, in Bassano's work, was to open up new perspectives for painting in the seventeenth century. Bassano's paintings are full of such felicities of expression, and in this respect he must be considered further ahead of his time than Tintoretto and closer to the Titian of the last period (*pl. 138*).

Titian was constantly tormented by technical problems; and, unfortunately, his experiments to increase the seductive power of the sensual colour-values he had inherited from Giorgione had a deleterious effect on the lasting quality of his paintings. No doubt the reservations expressed by certain critics (Berenson, Isarlo, Sartre) about his genius result from the fact that many of his pictures really have lost their original flavour, and, strictly speaking, if an artist's work should always be considered as a whole, it follows that any failure is no less unfortunate for being a technical one.

Towards the end of his life, however, tired of these fruitless researches and of the classic formalism which he had maintained for nearly half a century, Titian allowed his brush to move with greater freedom over his canvas. Attaching less importance to keeping form subservient to reality, he listened to inner voices; in a few paintings, such as the *Descent from the Cross* (1559, Prado) or the *Christ crowned with thorns* (1560, *pl. 139*), he gave a foretaste of Rembrandt's sublime handling, with a sort of thick, viscous pigment in which the forms have become nothing more than manifestations of an inner life. This transformation can be seen in the *Marsyas* (Prague), the *Tarquin and Lucretia* (Vienna), the *Virgin and Child with SS. John and Catherine* (National Gallery), the *Nymph and Shepherds* (Vienna), the famous *Pietà* which was finished after his death by Palma Giovane, and the admirable *St Sebastian* (Hermitage).

It is not impossible that Titian, at a certain point, may have cast an interested glance in the direction of Bassano and Tintoretto. He was certainly acquainted with the latter's work, as can be seen from 1550 onwards in paintings such as the *Diana and Callisto* (Bridgewater House) which seethes with life as vigorously as does Tintoretto's *Nine Muses* (Hampton Court), where the nine seem numberless. Thus the two enemies, taking entirely opposite paths, ended up by meeting each other.

The figures at the base of El Greco's *Christ driving the traders from the temple* (Minneapolis version), painted during his stay in Rome, include portraits of Titian, Michelangelo, Raphael and a further unidentified person. The reason for this remains obscure, although the insertions may well have been made at the request of whoever commissioned the work; in any case, we have no reason to interpret it as a gesture of respect by the artist to his masters. Certainly he owed something to Titian, but Raphael contributed nothing to his development, and his attitude towards Michelangelo was, as is well known, extremely disrespectful. During his Italian period, El Greco was a close follower of Tintoretto and Bassano, and would doubtless have remained so had he not for some unknown reason decided to move on to Spain. The case of El Greco highlights one of the sources of creative inspiration: the 'dialogue' between an artist and his environment, the decision to accept or reject that environment. El Greco discovered his true artistic nature in Spain, although the kind of painting that he formulated there went completely against the grain of the Spanish school's evolution.

Uprooted from his Venetian surroundings, El Greco's thought turned inwards. The intense mystical speculation sweeping Spain at that time oriented him towards a religious exaltation which nothing in his Italian period would have allowed one to foresee. Establishing himself in Toledo, he completed for the cathedral the painting *El Espolio (Disrobing of Christ)* which provoked such lively controversy at the time. After this, he offered Philip II a picture made especially for him, the *Adoration of the Name of Jesus (Dream of Philip)*. The king, who was well aware of the futility of the Spanish school of painting of his time, would seem to have wished to put this unknown artist to the test; in any case, he commissioned El Greco to paint a large picture, the *Martyrdom of St Maurice and the Theban Legion*, for a chapel in the Escorial. The artist worked on the

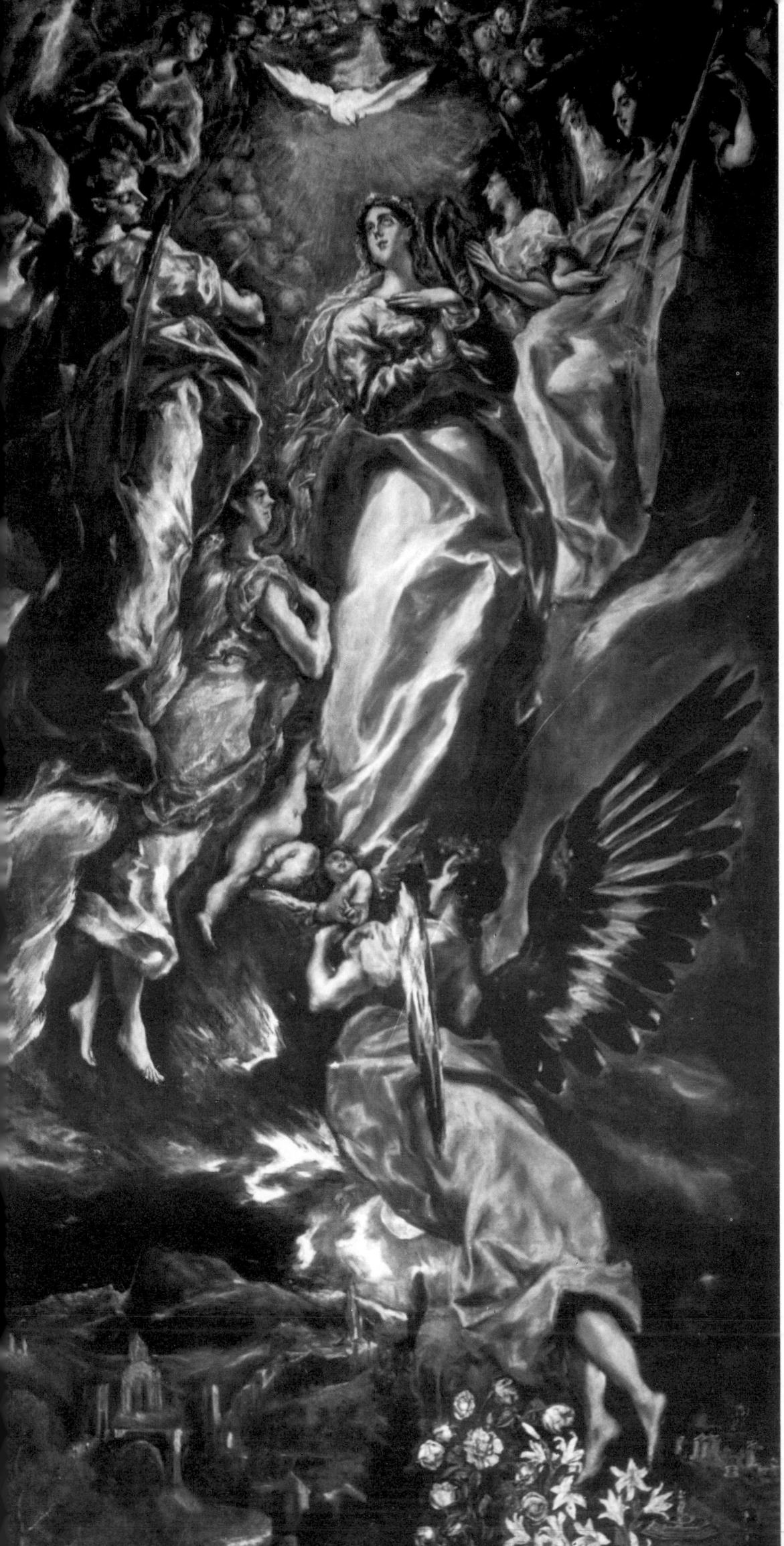

painting for two years and in 1582 delivered it to the king, who was not pleased by what he saw and did not hand it over to the prior of the monastery until 1584. The prior, in his turn, hesitated to install the painting in its allotted position in the chapel; finally, the king commissioned a substitute from an obscure Italian, Romulo Cincinnati. Nevertheless, the difficulties must have arisen from some question of iconographic orthodoxy rather than aesthetic considerations; the superiority of El Greco as a painter was sufficiently acknowledged by the fact that the king awarded him 800 ducats for a work judged unsuitable, while Romulo received only 500 ducats. The *St Maurice* was, in fact, deprived of its sacred function rather than refused; it was given a home in the rooms of the Escorial set aside for a museum.

The peculiarities of the *St Maurice* are, to some extent, the gratuitous revelations of an artist in search of himself. His self-discovery came a few years later, with the *Burial of Count Orgaz*. El Greco ultimately benefited from his rejection by the court and his consequent withdrawal from the Madrid scene, for it was in the overheated atmosphere of Toledo that the forty-five-year-old artist was able gradually to give full expression to his genius. Isolated as he was in a foreign country (he never learnt to speak Spanish well), his thoughts naturally went back to his Cretan heritage, and the ancient Byzantine tradition rose to the threshold of his conscious mind. The change he was about to impose upon the art of the Renaissance was comparable to that which the Byzantine art of the fifth and sixth centuries had imposed upon the art of classical antiquity. El Greco had no love for the human body celebrated so untiringly by the Renaissance and glorified by Michelangelo: his whole aim was to torture the body as though plunging it into an inferno, forcing it to expiate some gross excess of pride. This elongation of proportions, with the consequent dematerialization of human forms, is typical of the aesthetic expression of every civilization which recognizes the primacy of the spirit over the senses: the Christian East, Chinese Buddhist art, the Gothic, and even mannerism in so far as it calls into question the positivism of the Renaissance. El Greco exaggerates this tendency to the point where his human figures are transformed into long flames writhing in that lacerated space which Tintoretto had taught him to create (*pl. 140*).

Some years ago, at a time when it was fashionable to explain genius by physical blemishes, an attempt was made to show that this elongation resulted from the artist's defective vision, based on the assumption that he had suffered from astigma-

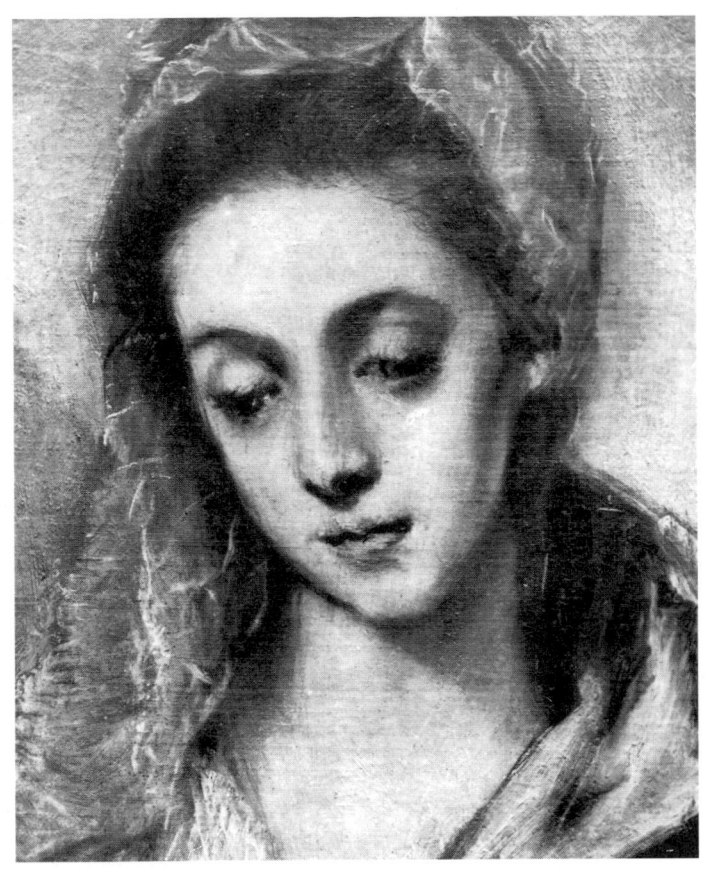

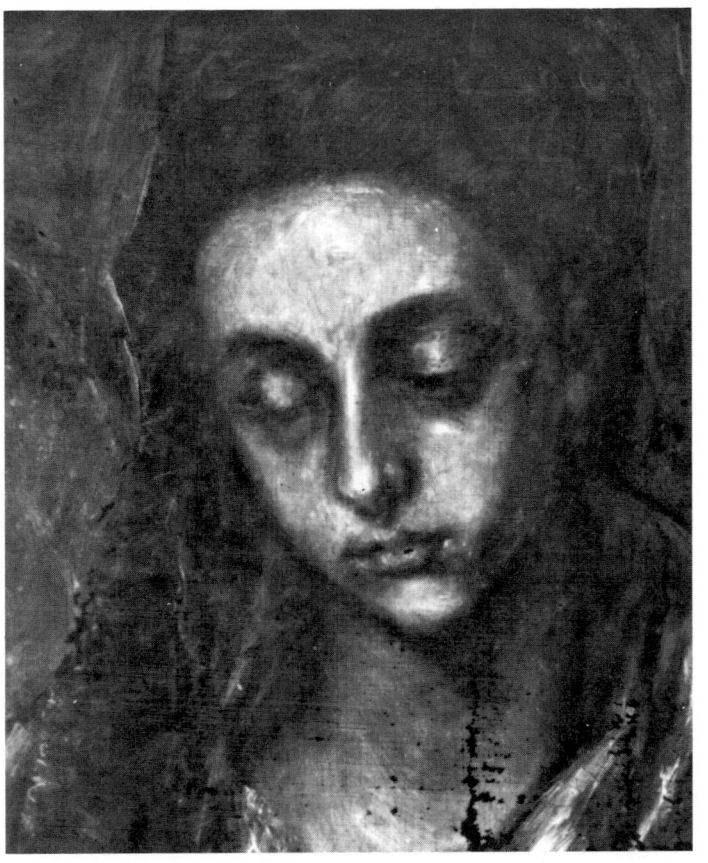

tism. But laboratory tests soon put paid to this tendentious nonsense: X-ray photographs reveal that certain faces in El Greco's paintings conceal other far more realistic faces. It was no doubt his mistress Doña Jerónima who posed for the *Holy Family* of the Hospital Tavera, in which the model's face is hidden beneath that of the Virgin, as though behind a mask *(pls 141–2)*. El Greco's instinct was served, in fact, by a consciously directed will.

Although the many examples of pious imagery supplied by El Greco and his studio prove that this aspect of his painting had a certain success, it was not really Spanish in spirit, and remained very distant in feeling from the mystical flights of his contemporaries, St Teresa and St John of the Cross, despite the affinities which have been alleged. The visions of these saints embraced a world of light in which they imagined themselves living in happy familiarity with the beyond, an attitude which, during the following century, helped to spread religious realism. El Greco's human beings, however, do not live in paradise: they aspire to it. They are not the elect of heaven but souls in purgatory consumed by a burning desire for God and bitterly aware of all that still separates them from him.

On more than one occasion El Greco found himself at loggerheads with the ecclesiastical authorities who commissioned pictures from him, although this fact does not imply that his talent was not appreciated. He found himself in a similar position to Caravaggio, his audacities being as highly appreciated by enlightened art lovers and fellow artists as they were frowned at by the clergy. He was proud by nature, too, and conscious of his dignity as an artist. The lawsuit he engaged in against the confraternity of the Hospital de la Caridad, Illescas, when it contested the price of the altar he had painted and sculpted for the hospital, demonstrated his indomitable nature. The confraternity fought him tooth and nail, but throughout the years that the case dragged on, from one appeal to another, the successive experts that were summoned all came down on his side in the dispute. Only after the Council of the Archbishopric of Toledo had seized all their church's precious objects, including the Virgin's mantles and jewellery, did the Caridad brothers finally admit defeat and decide to make their peace with the artist. The outcome of this case had considerable repercussions throughout Spain. At the beginning of the eighteenth century, the biographer of the Spanish painters, Palomino, who was no admirer of El Greco's, said that 'all artists are indebted to him for having defended their rights so honourably, in that he was the first one ever to put up a good fight'. In fact, the final resolution of the lawsuit, in May 1607, remains a landmark in the history of the social emancipation of artists.

◀ 140 El Greco (1541–1614). *Assumption of the Virgin*. Toledo, Museo de San Vicente.

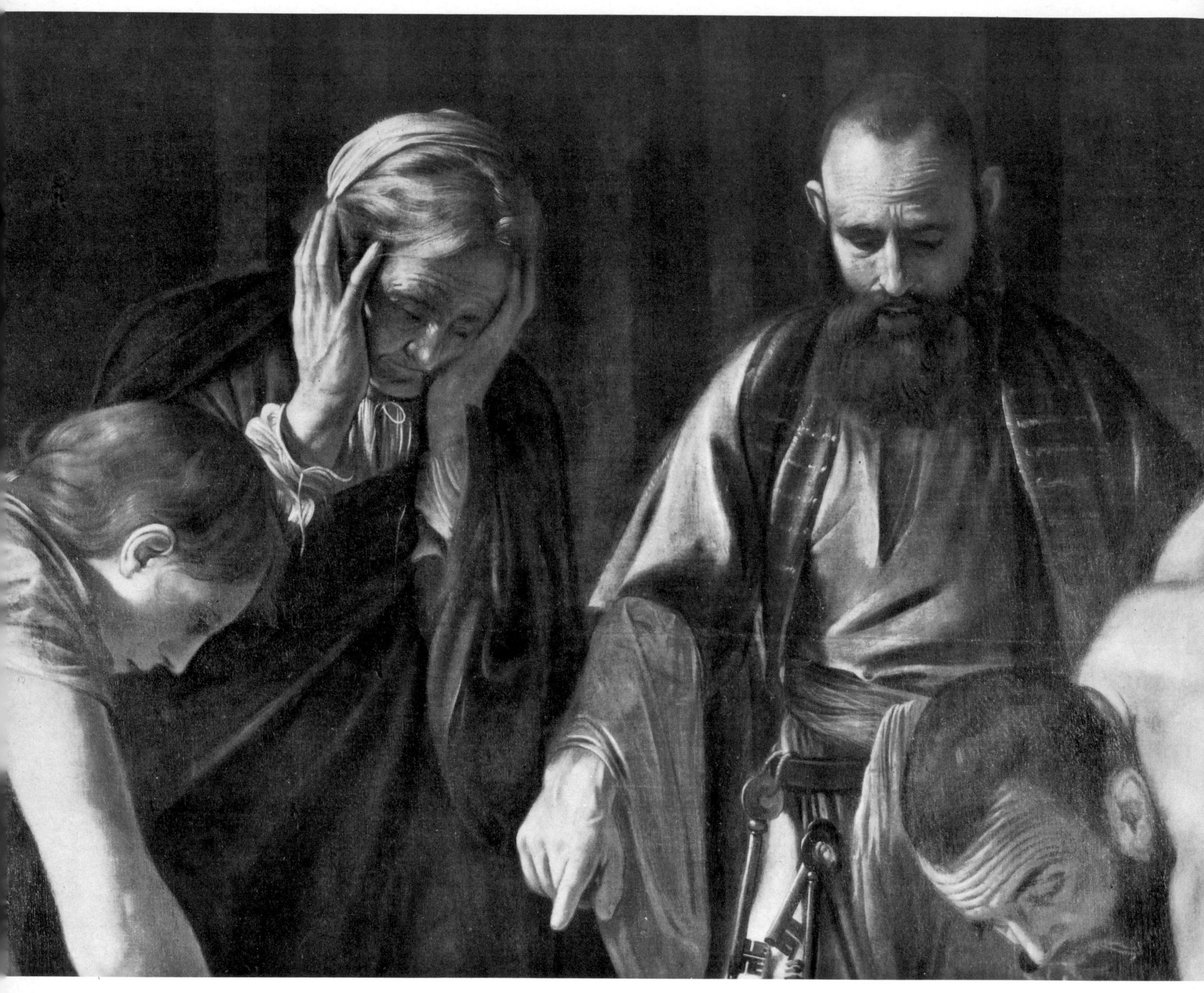

143 Caravaggio (1573–1610). Detail of *Beheading of St John the Baptist*. Valletta, Cathedral.

11 The weight of the soul

Caravaggio is a painter after the heart of our own epoch. His frantic existence provides all the excitement demanded by those who prefer to reduce artists to the level of their own human foibles. He must seem a hero to all those for whom creation is synonymous with disruption.

In fact, the story of Caravaggio's life is so utterly at variance with his art that it is of little use to us in approaching the paintings except in terms of analysing his unconscious psychological motivation. Caravaggio was a man who could not even eat artichokes in an inn without picking a quarrel with the server. He was a heartless wretch who refused to recognize his brother. He was a troublemaker who spent his nights in low haunts and was constantly arrested for brawling. One such quarrel, over a game of cards, ended fatally, with his adversary dead and Caravaggio himself wounded: on this occasion, he succeeded in escaping after hiding in the Sabine hills. Reaching Naples, he later embarked for Malta, where the Order of St John was in search of artists. Here, after assaulting a knight justiciary, he was thrown into prison, but managed to escape to Sicily where he went from one town to another seeking refuge. Returning to Naples, he tried to reingratiate himself with the Grand Master of the Order by making him the gift of a painting; but once again he got involved in a brawl, and this time suffered a severe head wound. According to Bellori, he then left Naples for Rome, having learnt that Cardinal Gonzaga's intercession with the pope on his behalf had secured him a pardon. But the strange direction he took makes it seem more likely that he was heading for Tuscany and avoiding the papal states. He disembarked at Porto Ercole in the Maremma, which was at that time a Spanish possession; here he was arrested by the Spanish guard in mistake for someone else, and imprisoned. Released after two days, he found that the felucca which had brought him had sailed away, taking all his baggage and, no doubt, his pictures too. In despair he wandered about the swamps of Porto Ercole under the terrible July sun, *il sol leone* as Baglione calls it, searching for his lost possessions. He caught malaria and died miserably in a hospital, at the age of thirty-seven, perhaps without even knowing that a pardon was awaiting him in Rome.

This is one side of his biography, but there is another. At an age when others are just starting out, Caravaggio was already acknowledged in Roman circles as a great artist, and receiving important commissions that made him the envy of the other young artists. Although the Church authorities were shocked by his new kind of realism and turned down some of his altarpieces, he invariably found a wealthy patron to buy them at huge prices. When the *Death of the Virgin* was rejected by the church of Santa Maria del Popolo, the rumour soon went round that a masterpiece was on the market. Rubens, who was then court painter to Vincenzo Gonzaga, Duke of Mantua, urged him to acquire it, advice backed up by the duke's representative at Rome who wrote that its author was 'among the most famous modern painters of Rome, and this picture is considered one of his best works'. The duke promptly bought the painting; the Romans were dismayed at losing this unique work, and the duke's representative wrote to him that to satisfy the unanimously expressed wish of the city's painters he had been obliged to delay its despatch by one week so that it could be viewed by the public. And the whole of Rome filed past the admirable and scandalous picture.

When Caravaggio fled from Rome after slaying the young Ranuccio Tommasini, it was Duke Martio Colonna who afforded him protection in his palace. Going on to Naples, Caravaggio found that his fame had preceded him, and here, as elsewhere in his constant search for refuge, he was given painting commissions. In Malta he was treated with great honour; the grand master, Alof de Wignacourt, was so pleased with his portrait that he gave him a gold chain, and two slaves to look after him; the Order created him a knight. These favours indicate that Caravaggio was not basically anti-social and that his rages probably came over him in sudden fits. It seems safe to assume, too, that he was by no means irreligious. There could have been no greater triumph for him than this elevation to the same rank as his rival, the Cavaliere d'Arpino, in whose studio he had worked during his early years, and whom he had supplanted at San Luigi de' Francesi; protected by the Order, he was now in a position to obtain a pardon and return to Rome.

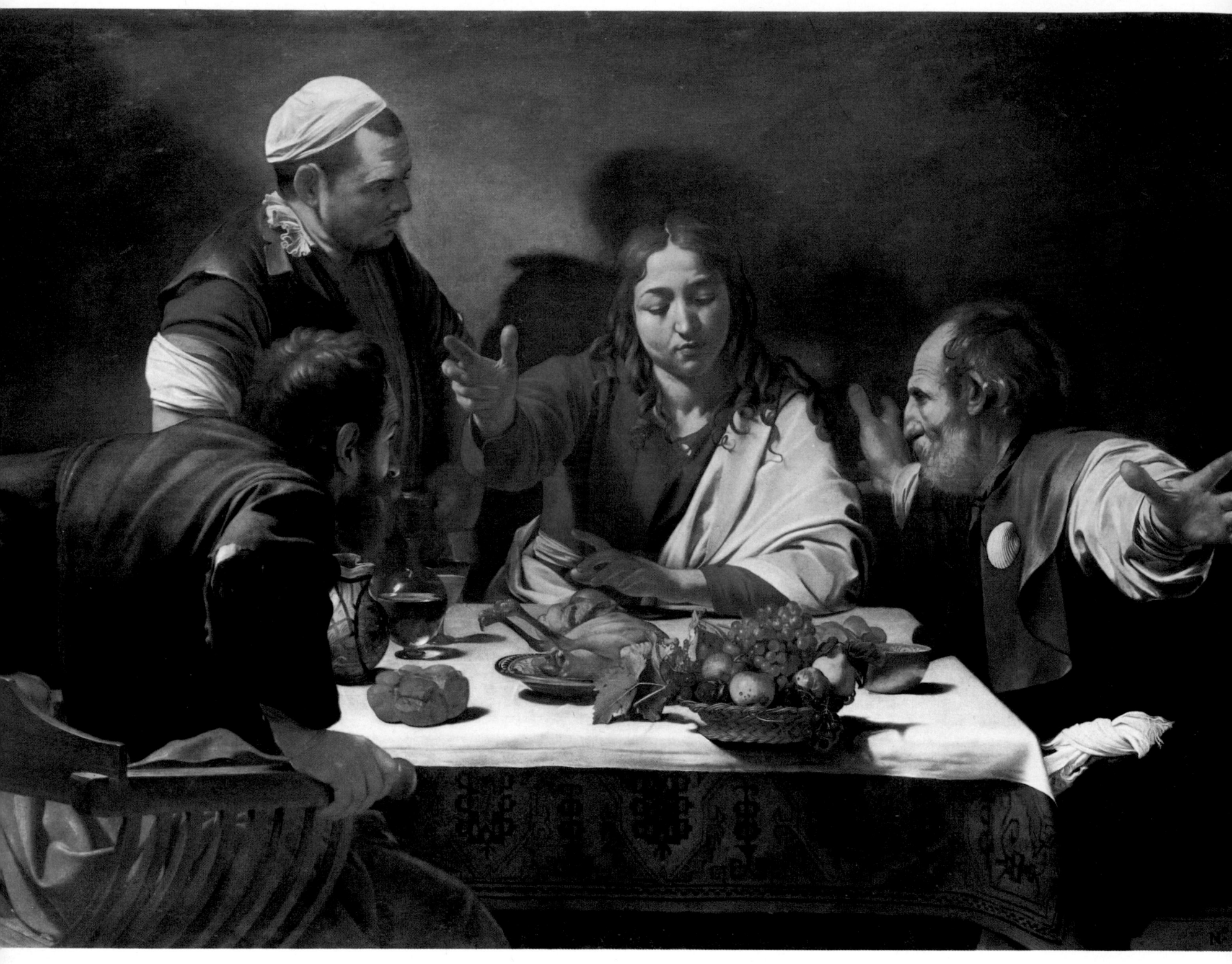

144 Caravaggio. *The Supper at Emmaus*. London, National Gallery.

He compromised this marvellous success immediately by becoming involved in a quarrel with a knight justiciary, a nobleman whose rank was higher than his own. And there he was, an outlaw once again. We shall never know what lay at the root of his psychological disturbance, but Caravaggio was truly a victim of what the psychologist Jules Laforgue has called 'the failure complex'.

The development of Caravaggio's work during his turbulent life passes through several phases. He first appears as a gifted and wayward artist, painting pleasing studies of equivocal young men, such as the *Bacchus* (Uffizi), the *Concert* (Metropolitan Museum) and the *Lute player* (Hermitage), or scenes of low life, such as the *Fortune teller* (Louvre) and the *Card players* (formerly Sciarra collection). Then, suddenly, a commission from San Luigi de' Francesi to decorate a chapel with a series of pictures of the life of St Matthew changed his whole life, bringing about a veritable conversion. X-ray examination has revealed two preliminary sketches under the surface of the *Martyrdom of St Matthew* which show

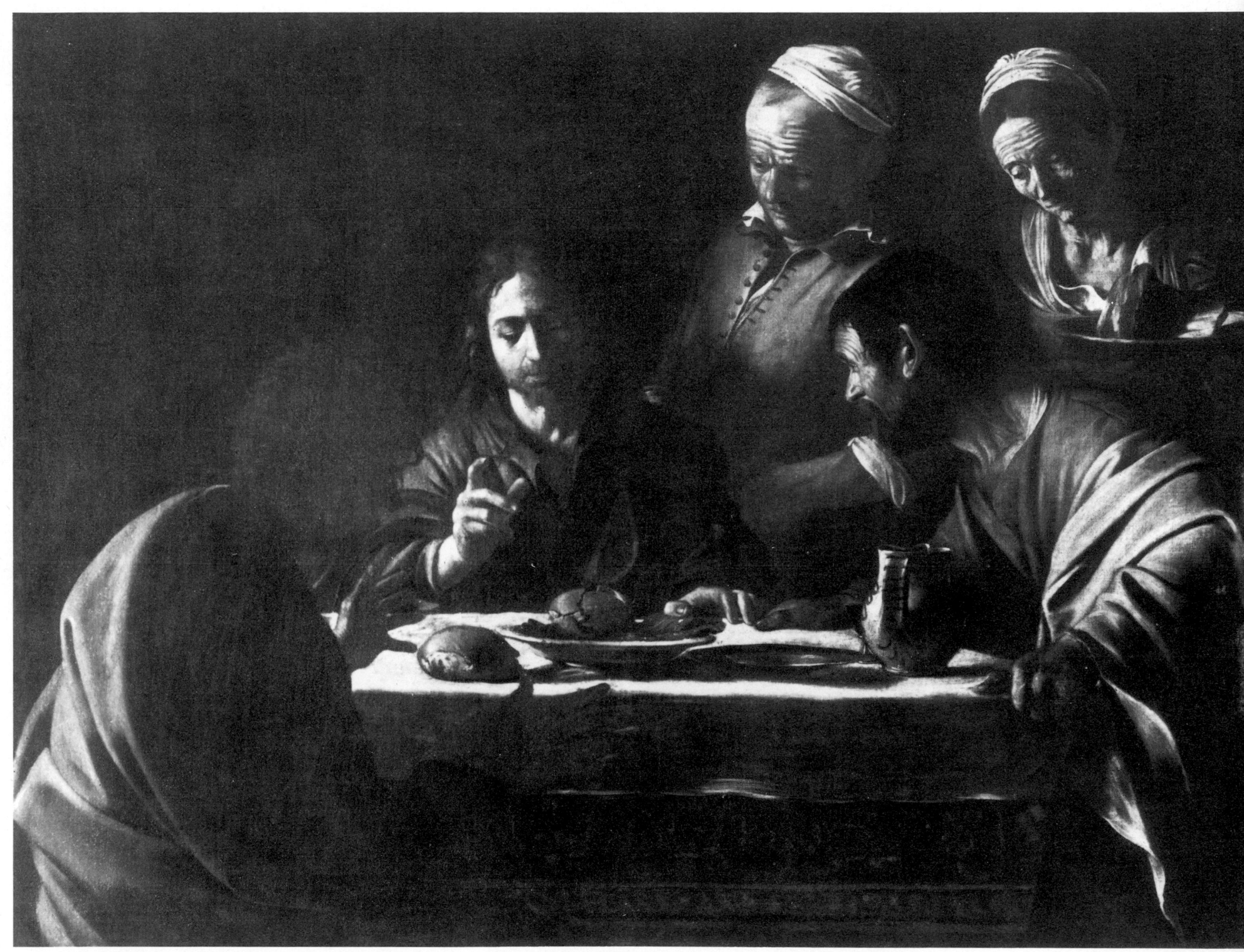

145 Caravaggio. *The Supper at Emmaus*. Milan, Brera.

how bitterly the artist had struggled against his mannerist tendencies during the execution of the painting. He finally put youthful frivolity behind him in the *Calling of St Matthew*, where, as Giotto had done before him, he dared confront the human drama in all its naked truth.

From that moment onwards, and until the end of his life, this human resonance filled Caravaggio's paintings ever more profoundly. One subject that he treated twice at a few years' distance shows the extent of the transformation that had taken place in

him. The National Gallery's *Supper at Emmaus* (*pl. 144*), with its marvellous still-life and the exaggerated posturings of its human figures, is profane not only in the sense of being secular but even in the sense of being sacrilegious. The pilgrims' gestures would almost be appropriate to the sort of ale-house argument in which the artist so often became embroiled; indeed, these pilgrims seem about to come to blows. The Christ is a village dandy, with a sensual, vulgar face. In the later Brera version (*pl. 145*), on the other hand, the Christ is

A comparison of these two pictures shows Caravaggio's progress towards a deeper understanding of the inner life; the earlier version is a somewhat blasphemous *genre* scene, whereas the later one possesses a genuine sacramental value.

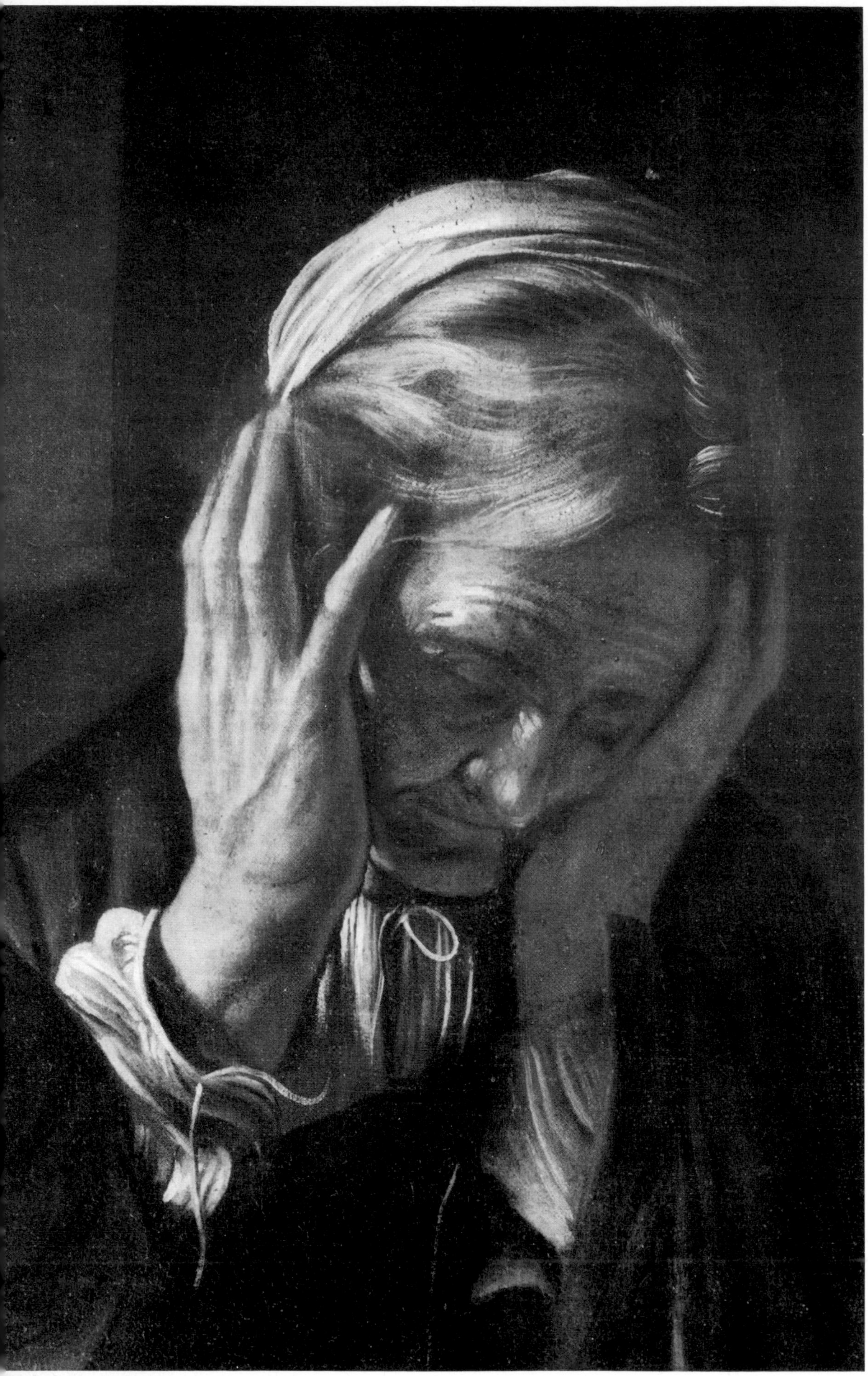

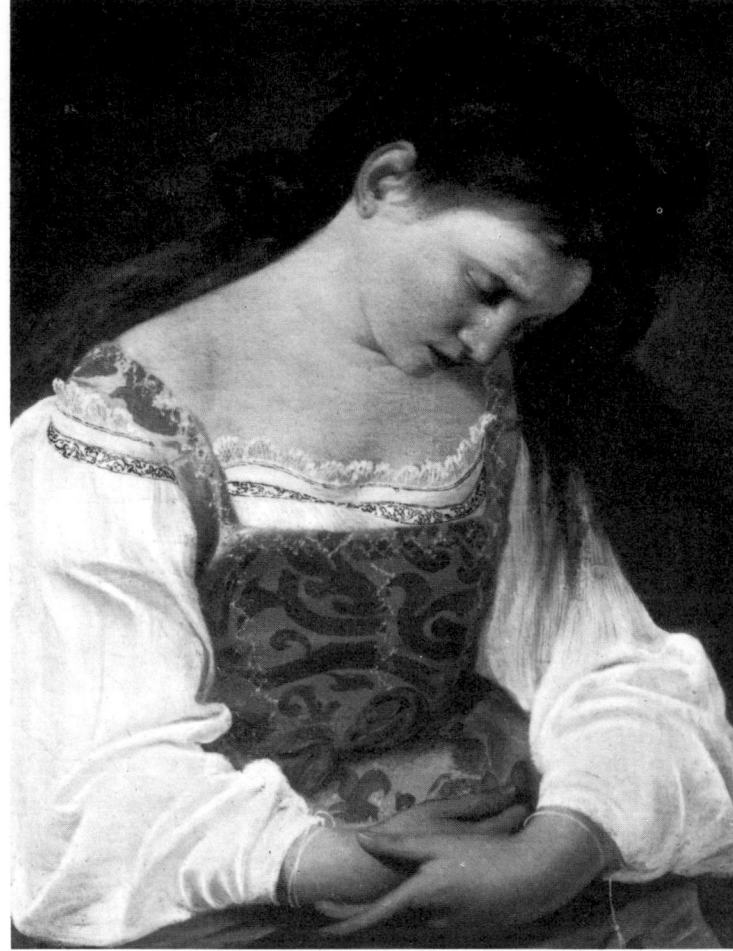

portrayed with traditional gravity of features, and the explosive violence of the London composition is replaced by an inner concentration. The actors in this drama are silent, filled with awe at the mystery they are witnessing. An old woman with a gnarled face brings the humble testimony of a being who has lived and suffered uncomplainingly. Caravaggio was fond of depicting this type of old woman; the most poignant of such representations is in the *Beheading of St John the Baptist* (*pl. 146*), where the woman looking on has the same expressive power as the Virgin in the Avignon *Pietà* (*pl. 49*) or the old women of Le Nain.

An interesting comparison may be made, too, between the *Magdalen* of Caravaggio's worldly period (*pl. 147*), a young maiden tearful at having to renounce her finery, and her counterpart (a picture known only by copies), painted in the Sabine hills when he had fled Rome after his homicidal duel: the later Magdalen (*pl. 148*) is bent backwards as she sends her terrible cry into the night. It is hard to imagine that the same man painted two such different works.

It is curious to note that Caravaggio's early conventional period left no breath of scandalous conduct. Only when drama entered into his art did

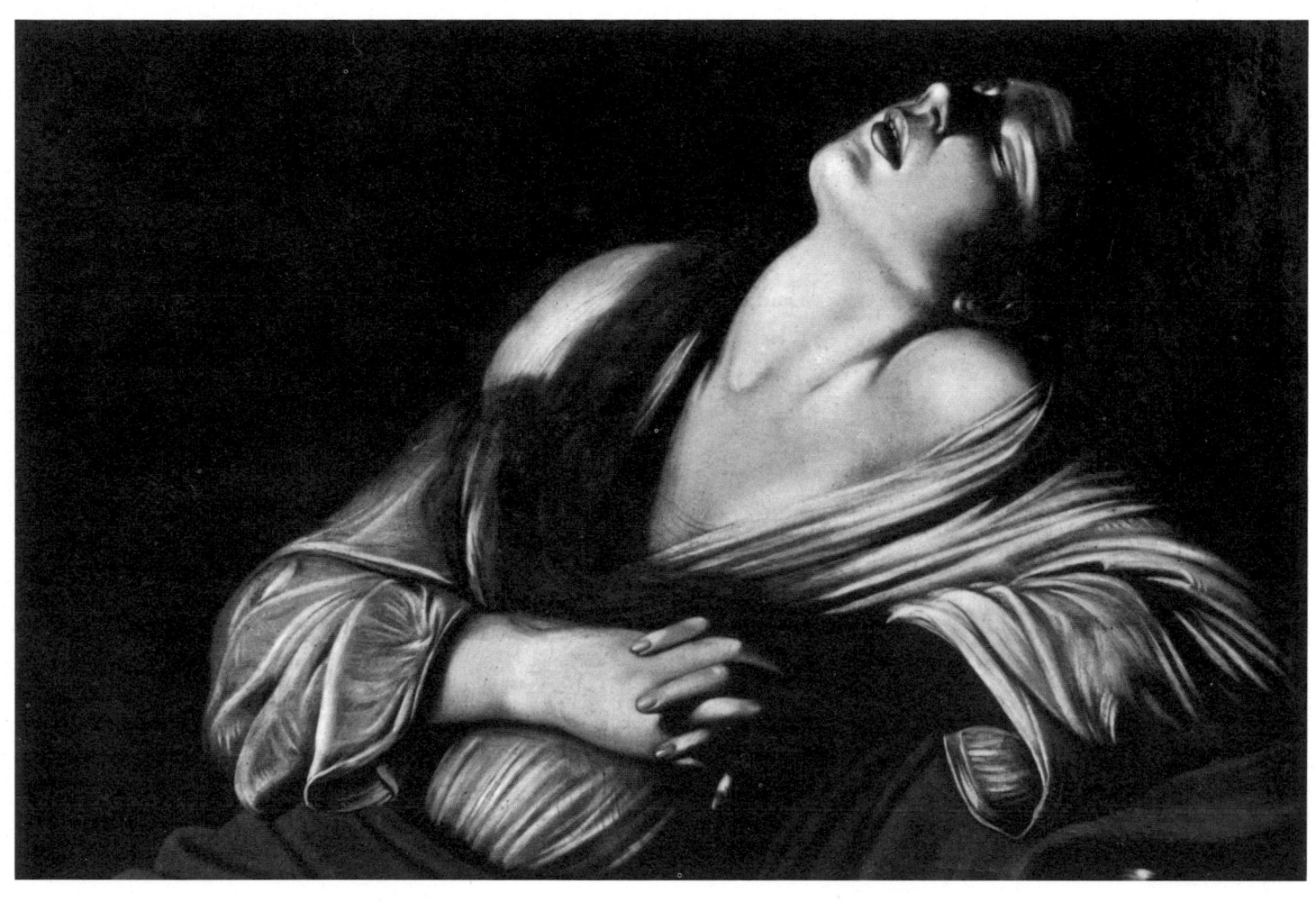

it also, apparently, irrupt into his life. The police dossier begins at the time of his first masterpiece; it is almost as though violence invaded his soul at the same time that his painting became inwardly directed and impregnated with silence.

Caravaggio was a giant among painters; and his far-reaching influence on the evolution of form was more benign than that of Michelangelo. Indeed, it may be said that whereas the latter initiated the most meretricious of the various currents of mannerism, Caravaggio blocked its way, exposed its tricks, guided painting back to its natural sources and restored the human content. He was a new Giotto, as Masaccio – to a less important extent – had been at the beginning of the fifteenth century. Italian art has shown an occasional tendency to stray into formalism, which has always needed to be corrected by the appearance of a Giotto to reaffirm that the fundamental basis for painting in that country is the human body. To rediscover the body's innate energy, Caravaggio swept away all the posturing puppets of mannerism and made his ideal the *uomo qualunque*, the man in the street, for whom he sought models in the Trastevere district of Rome. At the same time, he found human dignity in poor people, for whom the business of living and dying was a grave matter. Men, women, children, the aged, assumed the burden of fate by accepting it body and soul, having never been granted the intellectual means to discriminate, to avoid responsibilities or to indulge in self-glorification.

Bellori reproached Caravaggio for having visualized things only in their accidental, contingent aspect, but the opposite is true: it is the peripheral that he eliminates, reducing his compositions to a few essential figures who live the moment of passion with burning intensity. They communicate very little with each other; each follows his own pre-destined role. But occasionally the night is rent by the purity of a naked cry, and the harsh gesture that accompanies it is part of a vital rhetoric entirely characteristic of the Italian soul. With equal willingness, executioners and martyrs do their duty (*pl. 143*), because their destiny lies within them. Living, for them, is a religious act, and this artist, expelled by timid clerics from their churches, produced some of the most spiritually sublime paintings of the whole century.

The Madonnas of Caravaggio (*pl. 150*) are possessed of an inner strength that makes them impervious to the blows of fate, like the Virgin of

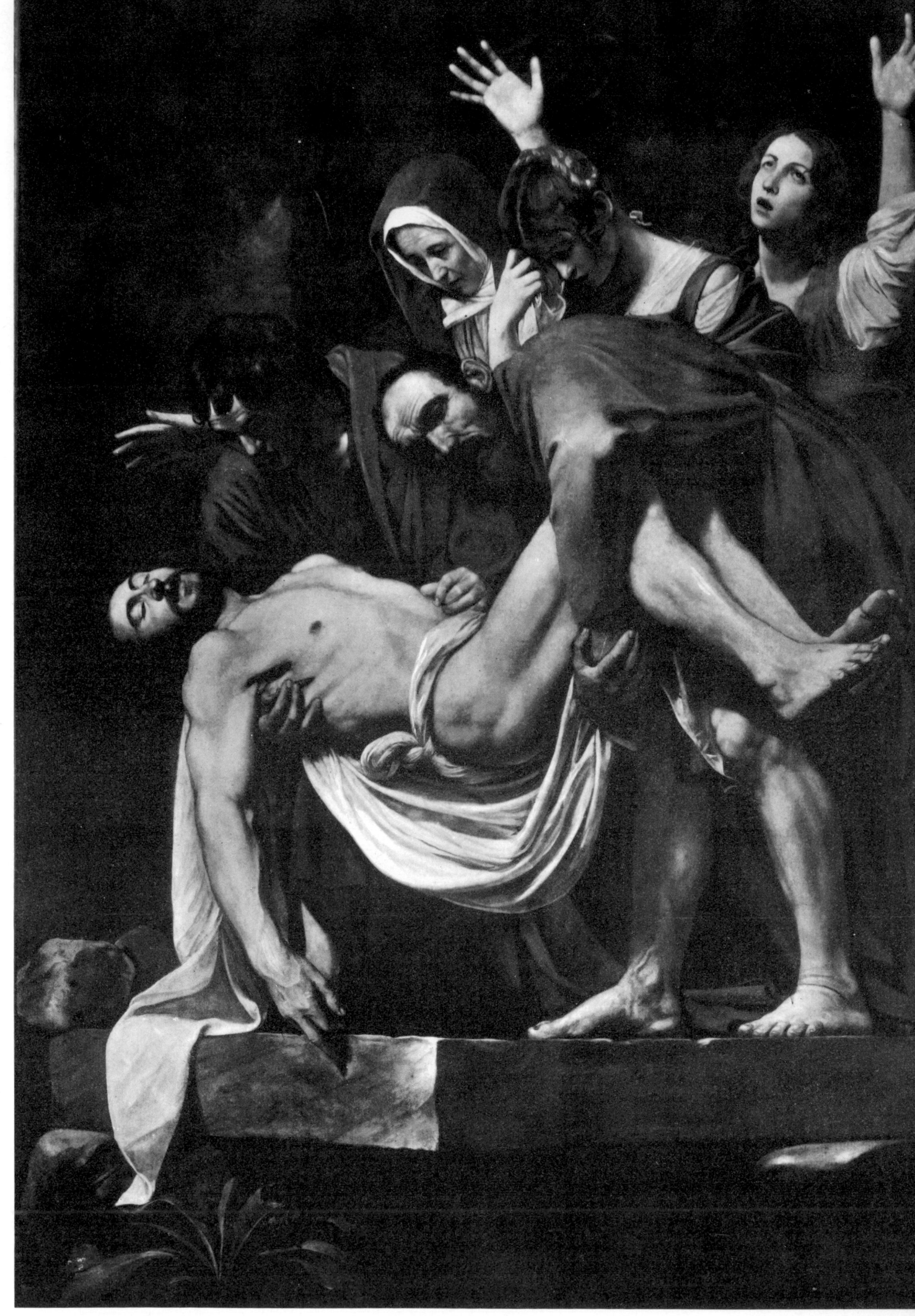

149 Caravaggio. *Entombment*. Vatican, Museum.

Anticipating the discoveries of the modern cinema, Caravaggio often places the line of the horizon (i.e. the eye level) in his pictures below the line of the earth.

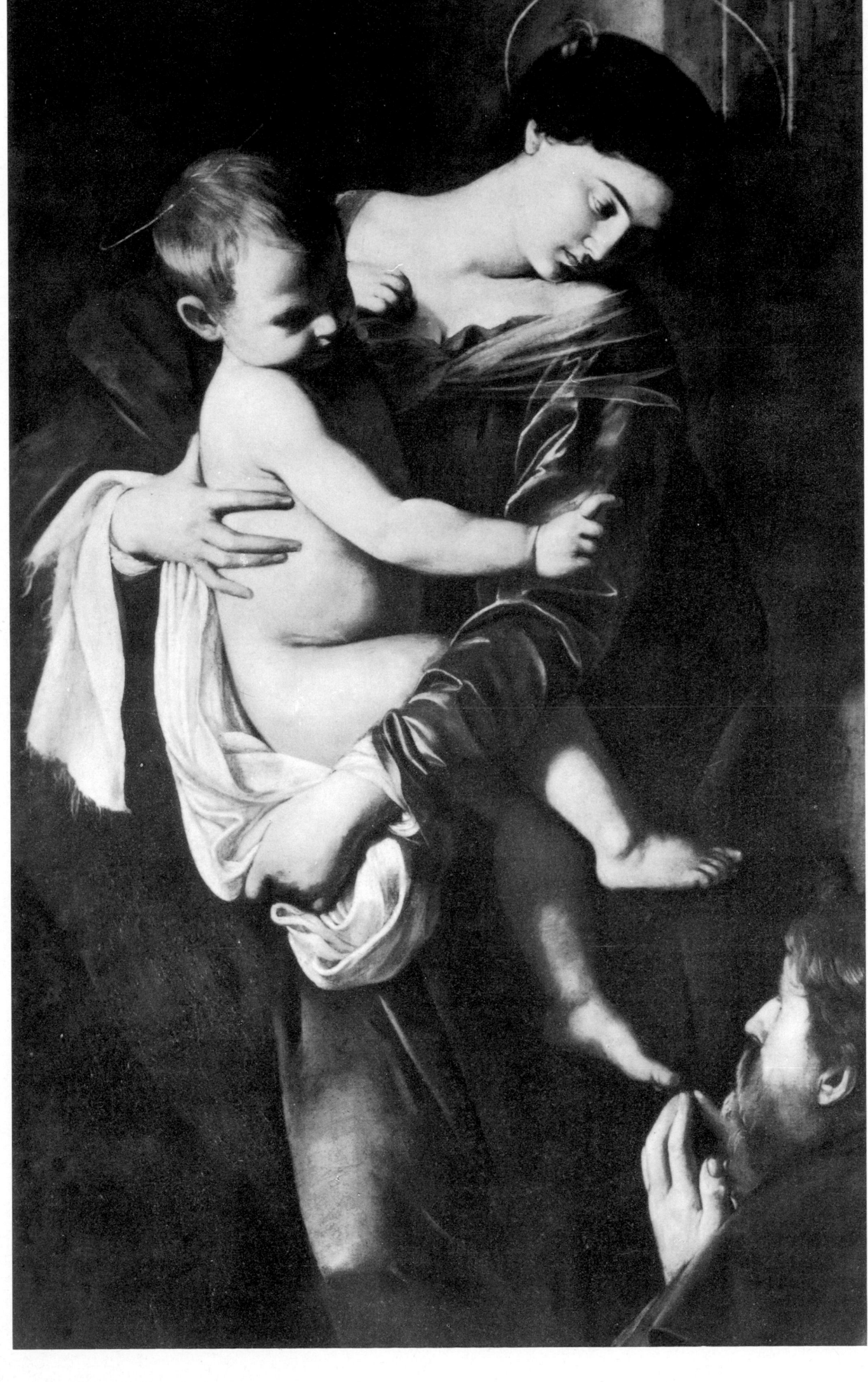

150 Caravaggio. Detail of *The Madonna of the Pilgrims*. Rome, Sant'Agostino.

This picture alone would suffice to show how wrong was the traditional opinion that Caravaggio only painted what was ugly.

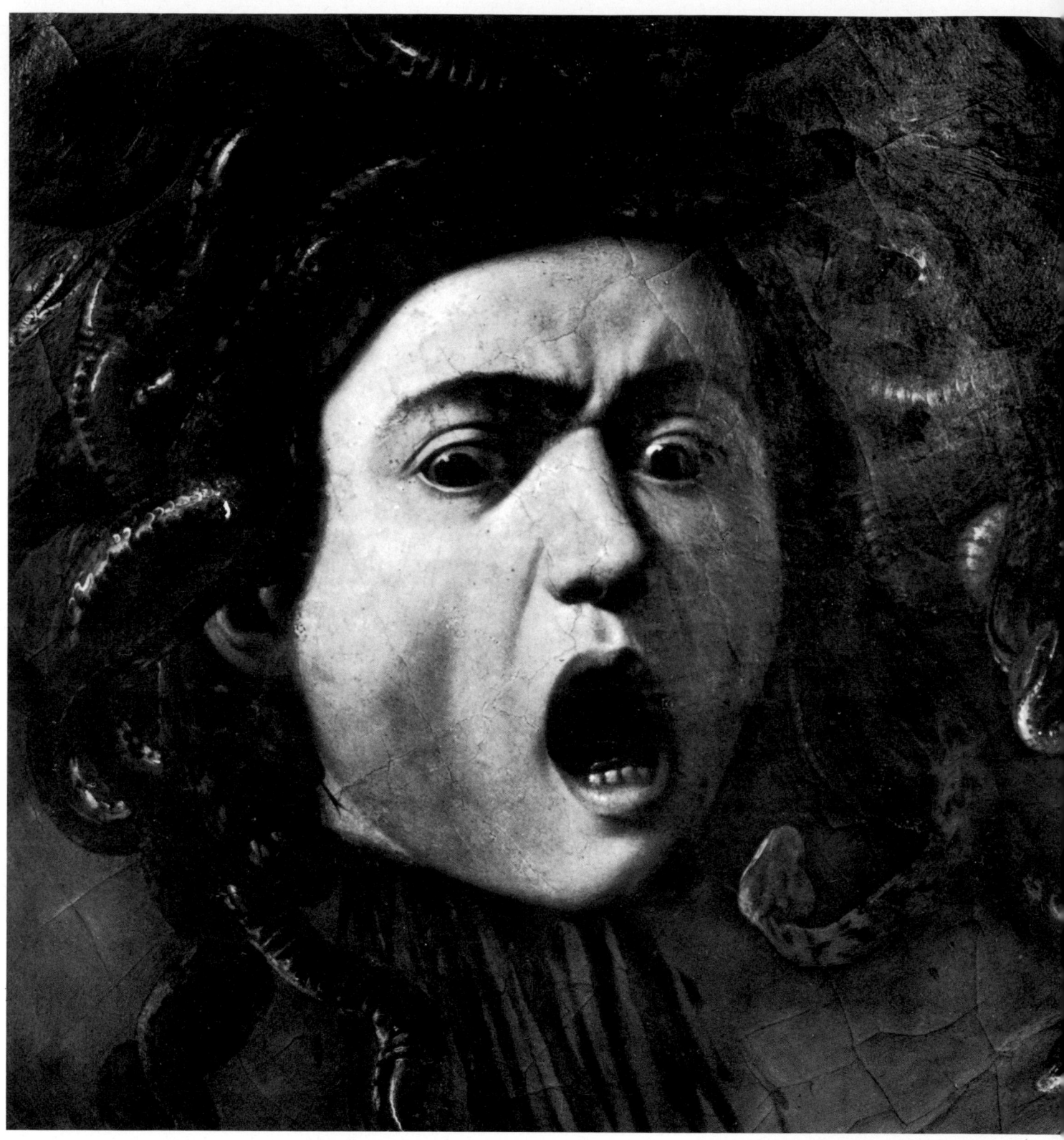

Giotto's *Annunciation* (*pl. 20*). Caravaggio borrowed the features of his Madonnas from the young peasant girls of Latium, Junos whose severe beauty and chaste gracefulness were to make them the favourite models of Roman painters of succeeding generations down to the nineteenth century. For this man with the reputation of a brute was susceptible to feminine charm. He elevated the image of woman in painting, by establishing that to be worthy of an artist's brush it was no longer necessary for her to be a goddess or a duchess; thus he fulfilled Savonarola's express wish to see painters take a woman of the people as a model for their Virgin. What attracted Caravaggio was, precisely, the pure outlines of those peasant faces which, in all their sane simplicity, seemed to have been freshly modelled by the Creator.

Having dedicated painting to man and man alone, Caravaggio suppressed the world by shroud-

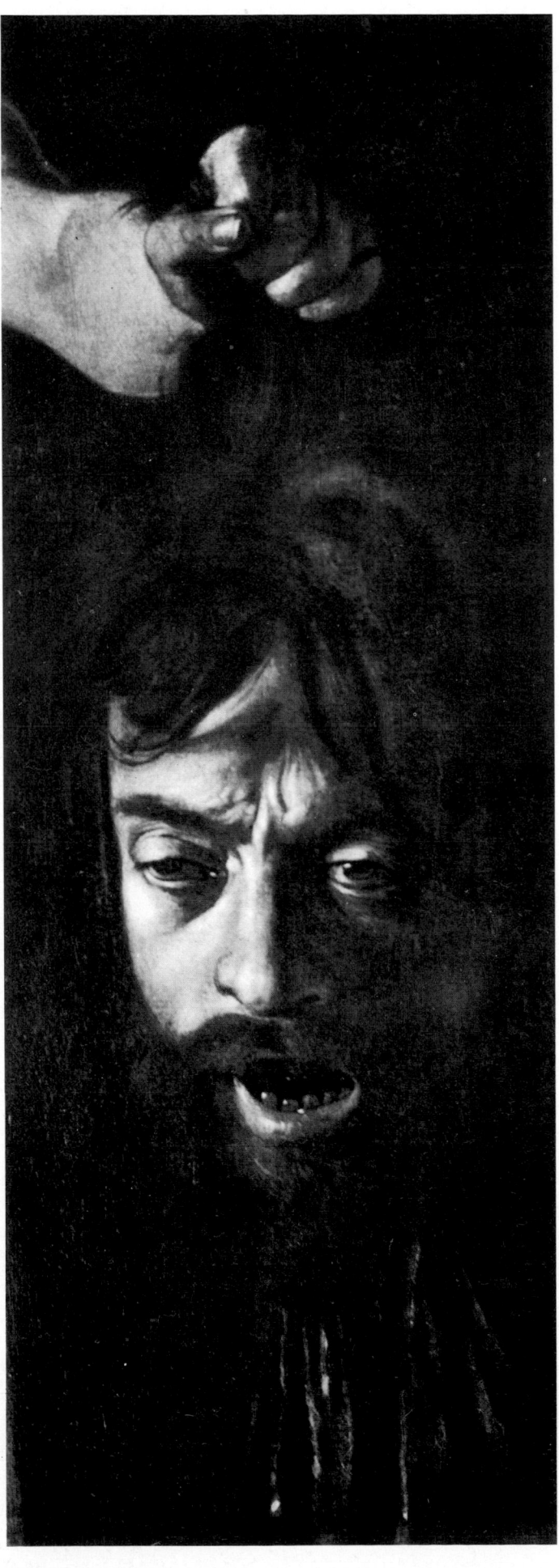

ing it in night. He was not the first to appreciate the resources which darkness offered to the painter, but with him darkness was a principle, not an effect. He put an end to a century of the kind of studio lighting which, by wrapping itself round forms so as to define them more effectively, ended by stripping them of their substance. The oblique ray of light which enters his compositions penetrates the night like a scalpel and, creating great contrasts of shadow and brightness, asserts the presence of the bodies with powerful modelling of their volumes. He is careful not to attenuate this sculptural strength through the effects of brushwork; his handling is entirely traditional in its concentration on the definition of forms, and colour is for him always the servant of volume.

It was the Spaniards who understood most clearly, as early as the seventeenth century, that the very essence of Caravaggio's art was *relievo*, the sense of relief projection from a flat surface. Velázquez's father-in-law Francisco Pacheco suggested this indirectly in his book *El Arte de la Pintura*, and in the eighteenth century Palomino said so, unequivocally, in his *Museo pictórico*. In Caravaggio's last works, though, shadow takes on a more tragic hue, and in paintings such as the *Raising of Lazarus* and the *Martyrdom of St Lucy* becomes as fine as ash, turning into a shroud which veils the faces in twilight. The shadow of death stretches over everything, and in the *Beheading of St John the Baptist* (*pl. 143*) the night becomes an abyss in which the world is swallowed up.

To give the human body the greatest possible presence, Caravaggio simplified composition. By erecting statuesque groups in the foreground of the picture and propelling the gestures of these figures forward from the rear, he invited the spectator to participate in the scene (*pl. 149*). Breaking the old conventions of perspective in this way, he invented the technique of close-up which all the *tenebrosi* made use of subsequently, and which foreshadowed the innovations of the cinema. This accretion of physical presence diminishes in his last paintings, where the bodies seem to have become shadows moving in darkness.

Was Caravaggio a deliberate revolutionary who sought to draw attention to himself by adopting an eccentric attitude, and who, with this in mind, determined to make a complete break with the past? This is the traditional theory, going back to the seventeenth century; it was the view held by Poussin, who considered Caravaggio's intentions to be entirely destructive, and by Velázquez's rival Bartolommeo Carducci (Carducho), who called Caravaggio 'Antichrist'. Faithful to the classical

152 Caravaggio. Head of Goliath, detail of *David holding the head of the giant Goliath*. Rome, Galleria Borghese.

Caravaggio projected his rage into the head of Medusa; and, in an unconscious desire for self-punishment, gave his own features to the decapitated head of Goliath. These pictures thus became projections of his own inner drama.

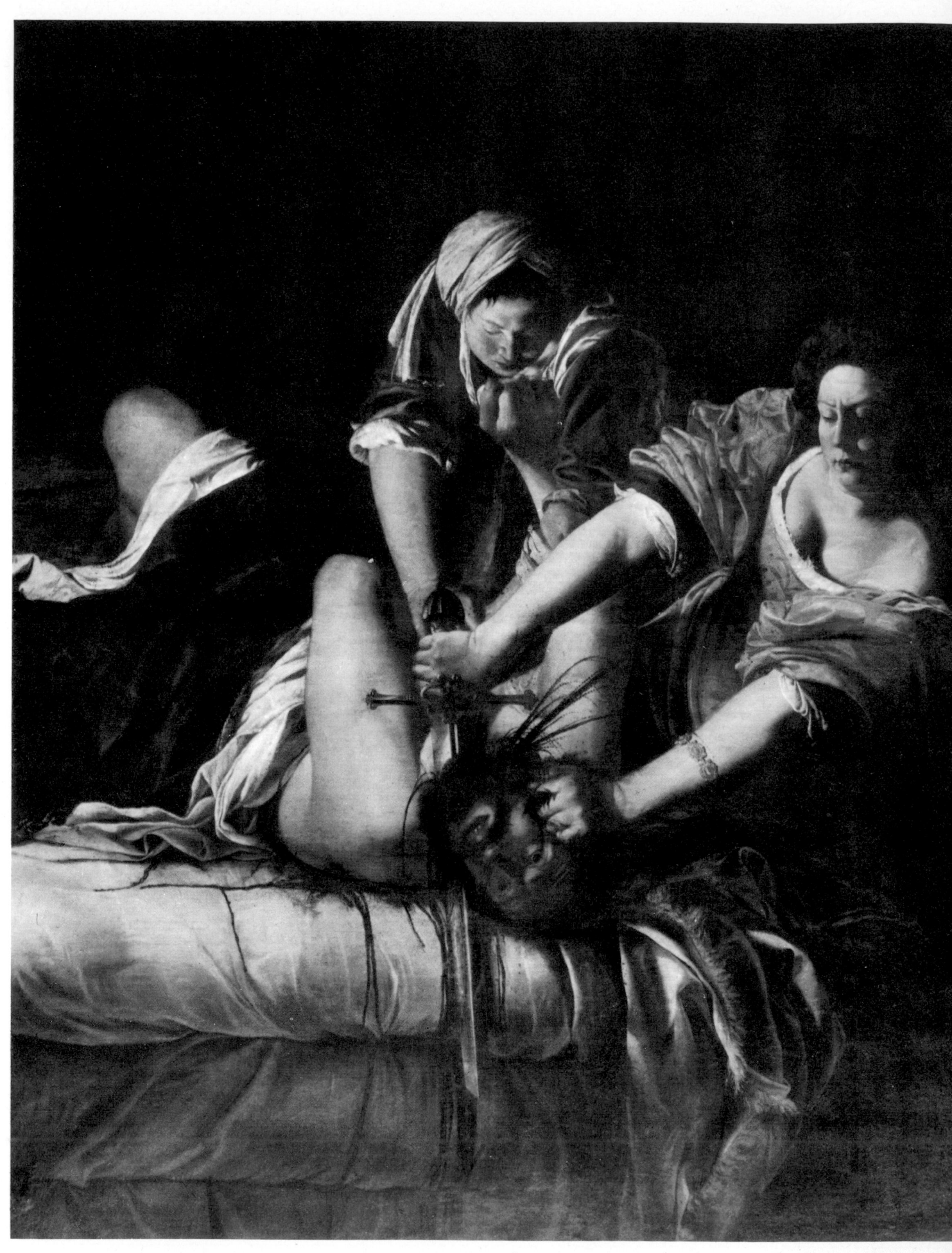

The appearance of sadism in art in the late sixteenth century is a manifestation of a profound spiritual malaise.

aesthetic in a century which had rejected it, Bernard Berenson refurbished this theory towards the end of his life, and so aroused the wrath of the devoted sect of Caravaggists. But this hypothesis of a desire to break away at all costs must be considered untenable in view of Hugo Wagner's demonstration (in *Caravaggio*, Berne 1958) of the extent to which Caravaggio borrowed from Michelangelo, Raphael, Correggio, Savoldo, Titian and the statuary of classical antiquity. Even the Carracci absorbed fewer influences than this. It would be nearer the mark to view Caravaggio as an heir of the Renaissance who restored its true values.

The mystery of Caravaggio has preoccupied a number of critics in the last few years. The Italian critic G. C. Argan sees him as a precursor of existentialism who possessed a tragic awareness of the total strangeness of the real, of the impossibility of a harmonious relationship between the two realities constituted by the self and the other; in Argan's view, the raw reality which Caravaggio constructs outside time and space is unreal, an attempt to discover 'the point of fracture between an equally problematical inner and outer experience, the moment at which the fury of being subsides into the absolute immobility of non-being'. In Caravaggio's poetics, death is thus the natural end of existence, a death which is not the transition from one life to another but a full-stop; the artist himself is thus, according to Argan, an unbeliever (see *Scritti di storia dell'arte in onore de Lionello Venturi*, Rome 1956). Mauro Calvesi goes even further, seeing in Caravaggio an adept of the pantheistic theories of Giordano Bruno, who was burnt as a heretic at Rome's Campo dei Fiori in 1600 (see *Trésors du Vatican*, Geneva 1962). For Walter Friedländer, on the contrary (*Caravaggio Studies*, Princeton 1955), the profound influence in Caravaggio's life was the mysticism of St Philip Neri who, in his passionate love for the poor, went to preach in the slums and was greatly beloved by humble folk.

Rather than pursue such contradictory theories, it is better to return to the evidence: the forty surviving paintings, and what we know about his life. The discrepancy between these two sets of information must surely indicate that this vigorous personality suffered from a sickness of the soul, a neurosis, which at certain moments plunged him into all the horrors of paranoia. Some of his pictures are filled with symbolic significance: he expressed his aggressiveness, for example, by painting a head of Medusa (*pl. 151*) – an unusual subject for an artist of that time – and giving it the tragic grimace of the demented youth in Raphael's *Transfiguration*. Self-punishment found an outlet in the painting in

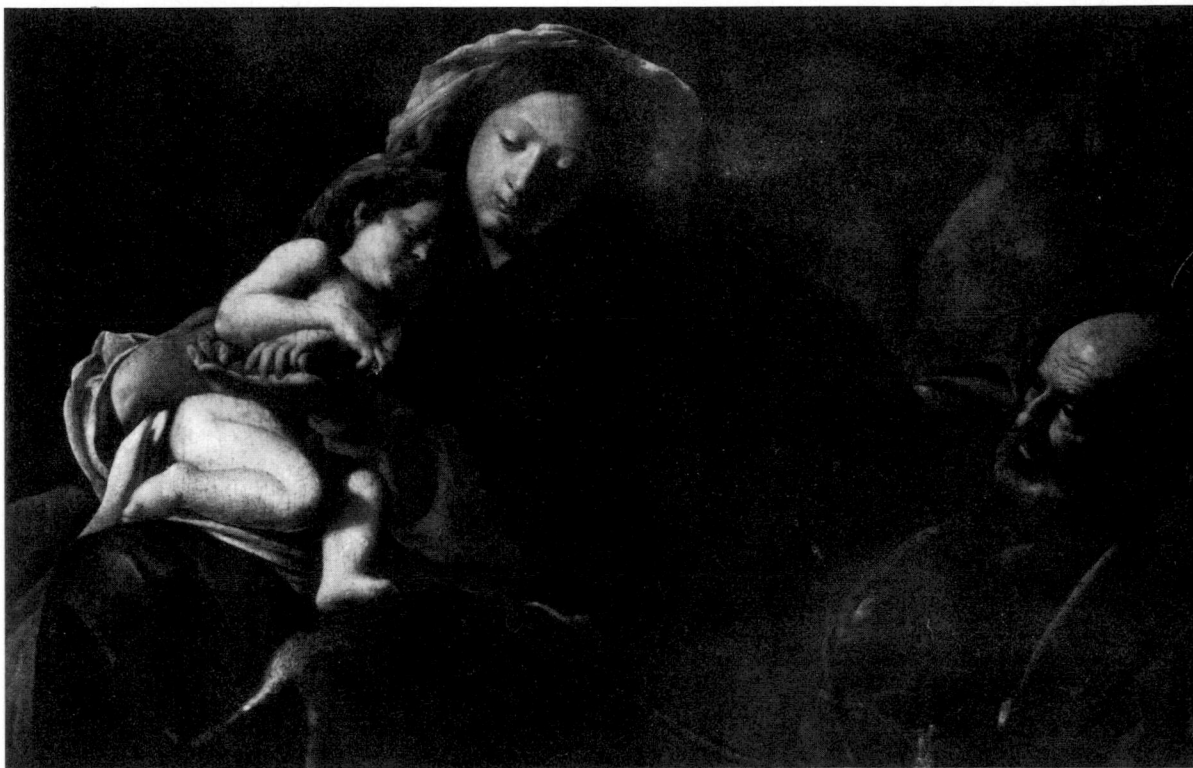

which he has given his own face to the horrible severed head of Goliath brandished by David (*pl. 152*). He could escape this fury only when, under the spell of artistic creation, he felt himself a demiurge, soaring above his own being, his dark impulses 'sublimated'. He had the merit of being equally ignorant of the hedonist ethic which finally stifled the Renaissance, and of the kind of aristocratic disquiet cultivated by mannerism as an elegant attitude, a refinement of court life. For Caravaggio, life was a drama resting upon the essential discord between man and the world. The tragic pathos which resulted from this realization contained within it a creative, heroic principle which forced him into a perpetual confrontation with all that was, and could only be, contrary. Caravaggio, like Giotto, recaptured the grandeur of classic tragedy, but Giotto is Sophocles, while Caravaggio is Aeschylus.

Caravaggio's discoveries continued to exercise immense influence throughout the seventeenth century. Far from engendering any kind of conformism, they aroused a sense of freedom by offering artists a new means of exploring the hidden recesses of the soul. At Rome, certain painters were his disciples, if not his pupils: Baglione, for example, who later took him to court for slander, and Orazio Gentileschi, who was a witness for the defence at the trial of the action.

Gentileschi, too, was a man of contradictory temperament. His paintings tend either to add an element of poetic tenderness to Caravaggio's art or

154 Battistello (*c.* 1570–1637). Detail of *The Flight into Egypt*. Naples, Museo Nazionale de Capodimonte.

Battistello, in his few Caravaggesque paintings, maintains the profoundly human emotional content of Caravaggio's work, adding to it a particularly delicate touch of his own.

to accentuate its popular feeling to a point of triviality. The work of his daughter Artemisia was even more personal, for her pictures reveal a lascivious eroticism and an instinctual cruelty pushed to the point of sadism. These two tendencies are united in the theme of Judith and Holofernes, which formed the subject for several of her paintings (*pl. 153*). She often used the rays of light from a candle to shred the shadows, a method of cutting light and shadow into strips for dramatic effect which is contrary to the spirit of Caravaggio, whose chief aim was always to emphasize volumes. Indeed, he never made use of candlelight, with which the mannerists had already experimented and which was to become one of the trademarks of the second-generation Caravaggists, such as the Dutchman Gerrit van Honthorst who, during his stay in Italy, gained the nickname of Gherardo delle Notti.

Caravaggio's stay in Naples left a deep mark. His most faithful disciple there was Giovanni Caracciolo, called Battistello. Of all the throng who imitated Caravaggio, it was this admirable artist who assimilated most closely his art, his poignant human gravity, his pensive melancholy, and the religious solemnity which the master discovered in the life of the common people, that eternal reservoir of great primal feelings. To all these elements he added a personal accent of sentimental poetry and quickened tenderness (*pl. 154*). Trained as an academic painter, he employed chiaroscuro to obtain the solid definition of forms which was his master's great concern. Il Battistello provided the solid foundation for Caravaggism in Naples.

Giuseppe (José) de Ribera gave a new direction to Caravaggism in steering it towards a romanticism which was to become the distinguishing feature of the Neapolitan school. Although Naples became the great centre of the *tenebrosi*, the 'shadowy' followers of Caravaggio, these deviated increasingly from the spirit of the master; Caravaggio would never have recognized the sort of soupy nocturnal atmosphere in which they bathed their figures as deriving originally from his own researches.

In their enthusiasm at discovering a second Michelangelo, modern critics have made Caravaggio responsible for 'tenebrism' throughout Europe, but a more profound knowledge of seventeenth-century painting must modify this opinion. The examples furnished by Caravaggio served, rather, to reveal a tendency which was achieving more or less conscious expression in the north as well as in the south. Recent criticism has been able to enumerate the pictures by Caravaggio which had reached Spain by the beginning of the seventeenth century and which may therefore have exercised an influence on the development of the Seville school at the threshold of Spain's 'golden century'. As a result, it is no longer possible to view Zurbarán's tenebrism as derived from that of Caravaggio. Plastically, it derives from the Seville tradition of sculpture which was then at its highest point of inspiration, and psychologically the existential nothingness which envelops his human figures relates to the spiritual and monastic currents of his time. On the other hand, it is certain that the Velázquez of the first period, the so-called 'period of the *bodegones*', was directly influenced by Caravaggio. This is confirmed by Pacheco, who, after speaking of Caravaggio's naturalism, adds: 'My son-in-law follows this path.' Velázquez's painting soon took other directions, but he retained from his youthful admiration for Caravaggio the absolutely sure sense of form which never deserted him even in his most impressionist manner.

Utrecht became the furthest outpost of Caravaggism in northern Europe. Honthorst, returning from Italy in 1620, soon abandoned the spirit of the master, preferring to give a bourgeois rhetorical veneer to the popular themes he treated. The well-behaved soldiers and courtesans he included in his pictures to please his customers are very different from the male and female vagrants featured by the other Utrecht Caravaggist, Hendrik Terbrugghen. Terbrugghen genuinely deserves the appellation of pioneer, for he succeeded in producing a new Caravaggism based on clarity rather than darkness, a transformation that the admirable painter Serodine had already accomplished in Italy. Terbrugghen had trod in Caravaggio's footsteps, having arrived in Rome while the latter was still alive. In the pictures which he painted on his return to Holland in 1620, Roman Caravaggism and northern expressionism intersect, with sometimes one and sometimes the other tendency predominating. Thus, his *Crucifixion* (New York, Metropolitan Museum) has the tone of a Grünewald, whereas other works of his are linked with Roman or northern tenebrists, Elsheimer, Saraceni, Gentileschi, Pieter Lastman, and even show affinities with Serodine. The connection with Serodine poses problems, since the latter was not in Rome during Terbrugghen's stay in that city. But these analogies between artists who were sometimes working at a distance from each other can be explained by the simple phenomenon of the convergence of effects flowing from a single cause.

In 1625, Terbrugghen, who like Honthorst was a Catholic, abandoned religious themes for genre scenes, perhaps for commercial reasons, perhaps because profane subjects gave more freedom to a painter with an experimental frame of mind. In his final years, Terbrugghen gradually abandoned tenebrism for a 'luminism' which led him to researches which were in a sense the very opposite of Caravaggism proper, namely the study of the coloration of shadows. His last works, such as the *Jacob and Laban* (National Gallery), the same theme at Cologne, the *Lute player and female singer* (Louvre), the *Annunciation* (Diert) and the splendid *Concert* (Palazzo Barberini, Rome) painted in the last year of his life, 1629, are executed with a brush which is sensitive to delicate nuances, to the transitions of light and shadow, to the unctuous quality of thick pigment. Abandoning the strict delimitation of local tone values which had characterized his previous work painted in the Roman manner, Terbrugghen evolved a richer colour which he endowed with an atmospheric, 'impressionist' value; certain of his still-lifes make one think of Vermeer and Chardin, others evoke Monet. But, even if he went beyond Caravaggio, he never betrayed his principles. The solidity of his forms remained faithful to the spirit, if not the letter, of the master's work.

The importance of Terbrugghen in the evolution of Dutch painting was apparent in 1935 on the occasion of the Vermeer exhibition which inaugurated the Boymans Museum in Rotterdam. That same year, I showed, in my essay on the exhibition in the periodical *L'Amour de l'art*, how Vermeer's luminism may have flowed from Caravaggio's tenebrism through the agency of Terbrugghen. The school which flourished in Utrecht around 1620–30 was a great laboratory in which the blending of Roman tenebrism and northern tradition produced new directions which proved of lasting value for Dutch and European painting.

As for the 'tenebrism' of Georges de La Tour, it would now seem that its sources should be sought in Utrecht rather than in Rome. The Roman archives, and in particular the registers of Easter communion, all of which have been preserved intact, allow us to know the names of the artists who frequented the eternal city during the seventeenth century. There is no trace here of La Tour's name, although several other French artists journeyed to Rome to learn the value of darkness in painting.

During the fifteen years of his stay in Rome, Simon Vouet showed himself one of Caravaggism's most faithful adepts, and when he renounced this influence he lost his humanistic quality. His compatriot, Valentin, on the other hand, was so determined to remain faithful to the master's spirit that he spent his life in Rome and died there. When Vouet returned to the court of France he had no choice but to betray Caravaggio, confronted as he was by the French school's great tradition of bright, clear painting, a tradition which stretches without interruption from Fouquet to David.

Georges de La Tour was not really an exception to this rule. It should be remembered that he did not live in French surroundings but in the rather isolated atmosphere of Lorraine, at that time part of the Holy Roman Empire, in the provincial town of Lunéville. The drama of man's solitude in an empty, meaningless world became, for La Tour, that of the soul at grips with the terrible problem of grace. La Tour's humanism renounced the light of the sun, even those few rays which still penetrate into Caravaggio's cellars. His human beings live in catacombs by the gleam of candles and torches. Monumental figures project fantastic shadows on to the walls, while the brutal, lurid light of the candles picks out the faces and bodies in sharp relief. Acting out their whole lives in these dark, bare underground places, these cave-dwellers are born and die there, pray to God and nurse the sick there; soldiers play dice, a child helps its father who is a carpenter, a little girl learns to read among these shadows, in the flickering light of a torch, under her mother's watchful eye. And in one corner a bandy-legged, gouty, blind beggar plays a hurdy-gurdy.

All these scenes are, in fact, illustrations from the New Testament. La Tour went even further than Caravaggio in the way he costumed his characters. While Caravaggio still depicted the toga occasionally, even if it was in tatters, La Tour clothed them all in the popular dress of his time, grey, red or blue frieze; even the angels were condemned to the same drab uniform. These individuals all seem to belong to some monastic confraternity which has made a vow of penitence to lead a subterranean life, like those Egyptian hermits who chose to live among the tombs. Apparently vowed to silence, their lips are sealed. They make few gestures, and these are usually to clasp their hands together. A race of troglodytes, it consists entirely of old men ravaged by darkness (one of them is blind), sleeping children, women chastely veiling their glances behind half-closed lids (*pl. 155*). This renunciation by a whole people of the lusts of the flesh has a grandeur about it that is worthy of Pascal. Dead to the world of appearances, they are dedicated exclusively to the life of the soul. The object upon which these beings constantly meditate is revealed by one of the women: the Magdalen who gazes fixedly at her two faces reflected in a mirror, the face of today, so young and so pure, and the face of tomorrow, a skull resting on a book which she is holding in her hand.

And yet La Tour is not an avant-garde painter. His imagination is extremely limited, and he seems

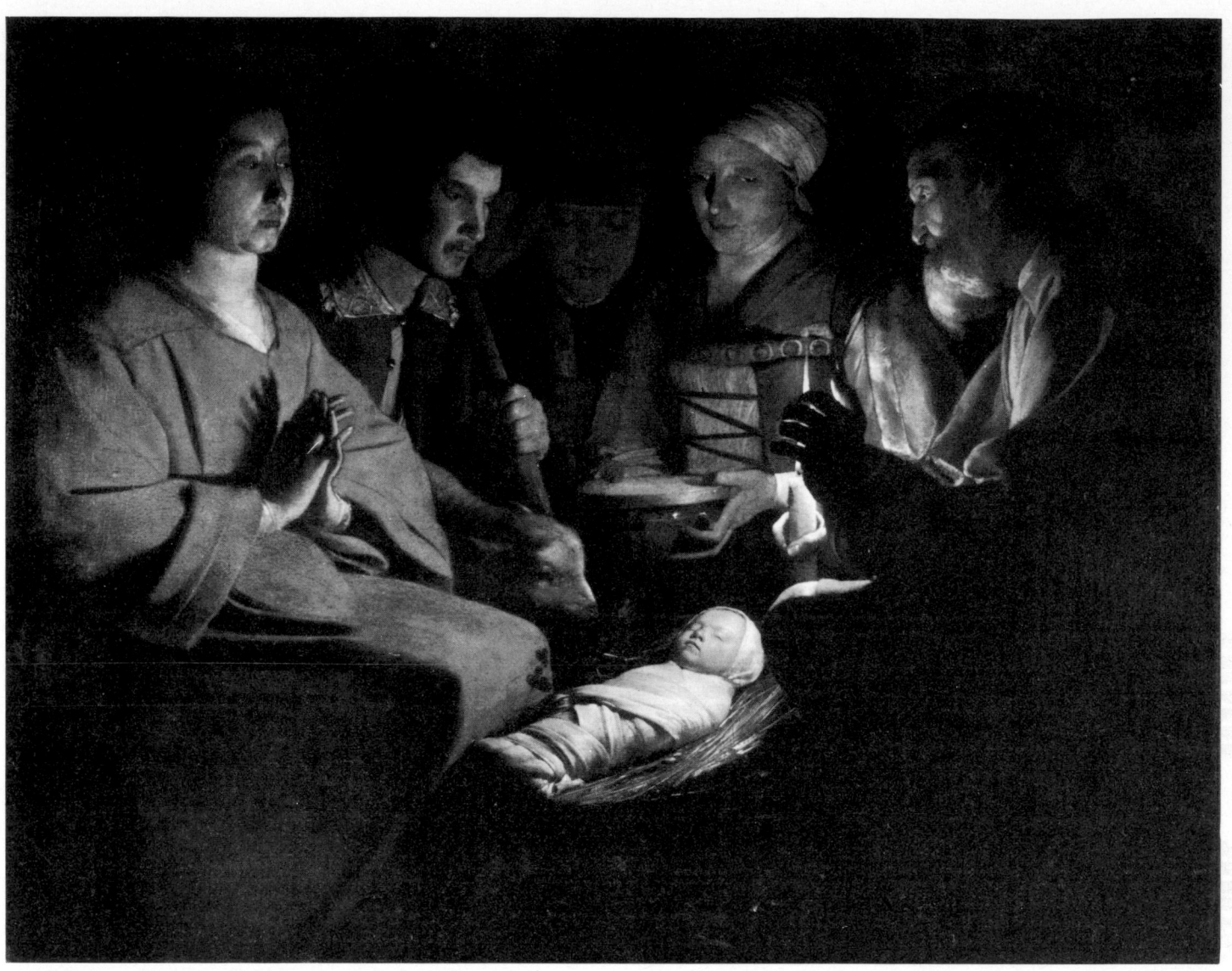

to have relied entirely on a morphological repertory established in his youth. Moreover, his plastic idiom is certainly borrowed from the international language of Caravaggism, with Terbrugghen and Honthorst acting as intermediaries. No further proof is needed of the immensity of the revolution sparked by Caravaggio than the fact that it could contain within its ranks both La Tour and Vermeer!

There is nothing ascetic about the human beings depicted by La Tour. Like those of Zurbarán and Rembrandt, they are the descendants of Caravaggio's athletic plebeians. Their bodies seem to be bowed beneath the weight of their inner life. During the seventeenth century, the most profound spirituality was transmitted not through ethereal entities such as saints and angels but through the gravity of human bodies. The image of the athlete symbolized the sheer weight of the overcharged soul that the body had to carry. The life of the soul was lived as a drama of earthly life, rather than as an aspiration to the Beyond. It was only the Christians whose

minds were on this world who saw God come to life from the ceilings and altars of the churches and appear among them, surrounded by His chosen. Those Christians who rejected this life never enjoyed these dreams; bent low beneath the stern gaze of the 'God of Abraham, of Isaac and of Jacob', to whom they dared not raise their eyes, they experienced Christianity as an ethical system rather than a theology.

Speculation concerning the possibility that mere being might attain access to pure Being through the transforming power of the union with God reached its culmination with St John of the Cross and St Teresa of Jesus. Whether they were driven by charity (St Vincent de Paul, St Francis of Sales, Rembrandt) or by the egoism of an individual ascesis (Duvergier de Hauranne, La Tour), the seventeenth-century mystics lived the spiritual life in action. What tormented these men enamoured of God was less God than human destiny. There was a great deal of stoicism in Jansenism, just as there

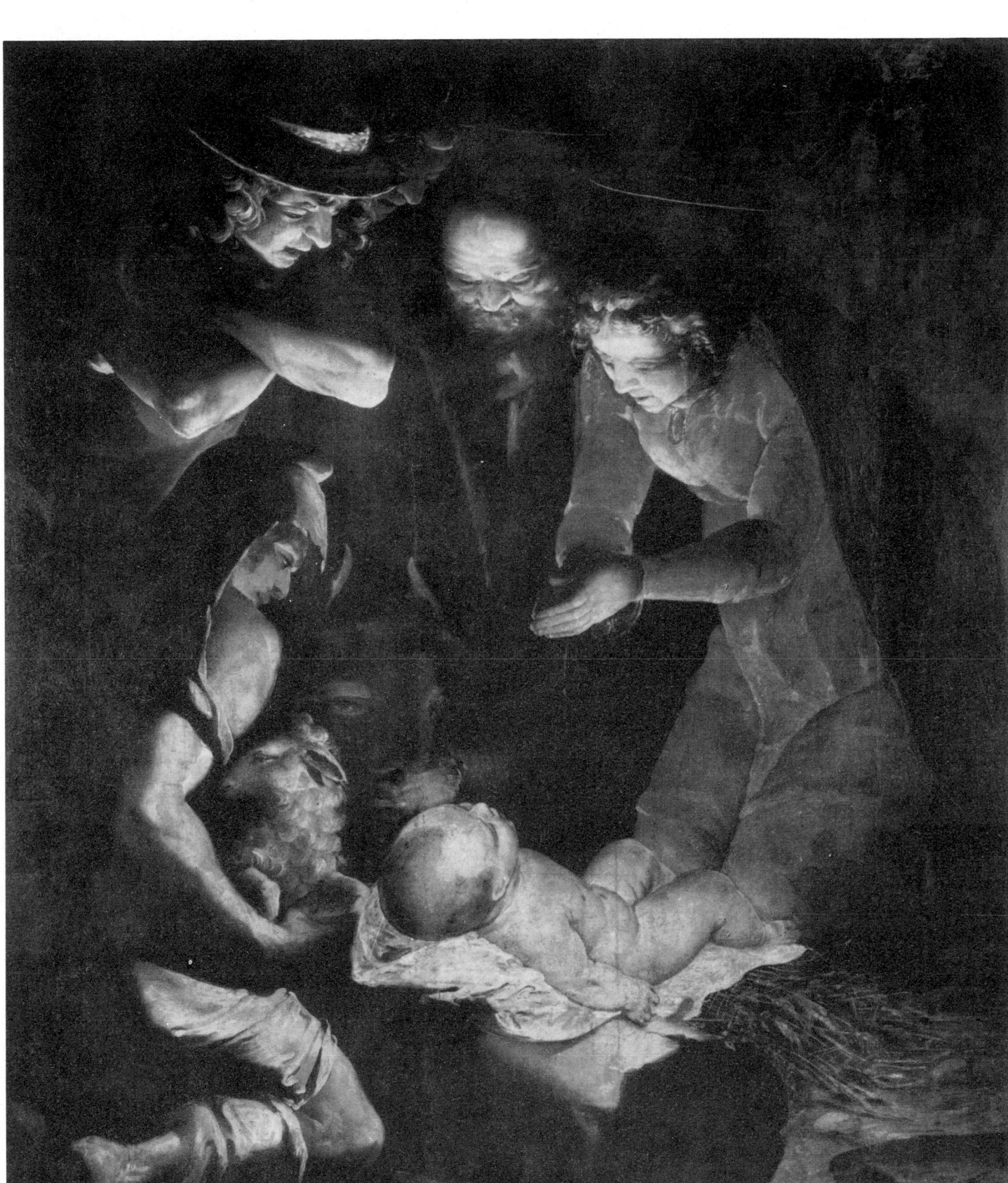

156 Luca Cambiaso. *The Nativity.* Milan, Brera.

was in the art of Caravaggio. Perhaps the clerics who rejected Caravaggio's altarpieces felt dimly that this religion was humane, too humane, inspired by man's innate dignity, a pre-eminent dignity circumscribed by God alone. Between the great eddies of the Renaissance, the Reformation and the Counter-Reformation, *virtù* had become Christianized, while sainthood had become humanized: the meeting-point was virtue. Christianity had become a humanism.

The dramatic possibilities of night effects in the *Nativity* had been explored well before Georges de La Tour, but in his case the darkness is a manifestation of the inner life.

177

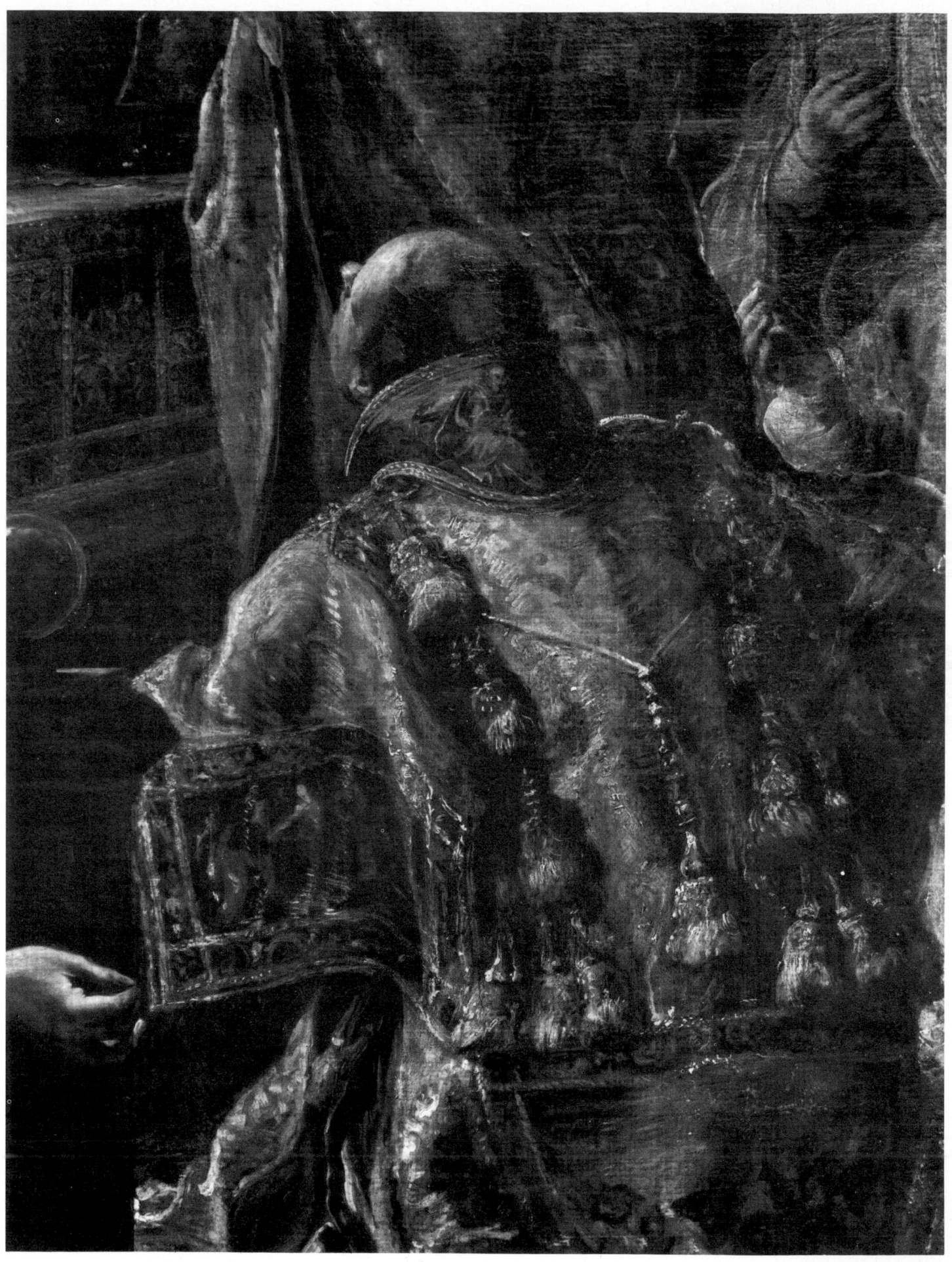

157 Juan Carreño de Miranda (1614–85). Detail of *The Foundation of the Order of Trinitarians by St John of Matha*. Paris, Louvre.

12 A new language

In 1627, Francisco Herrera the Elder, painter of Seville, received from the college of San Bonaventura a commission for a decorative scheme designed to celebrate the life of the 'seraphic doctor', St Bonaventure. He painted four of the pictures of this cycle (*pl. 158*), but for some unknown reason failed to complete it, and the task was confided to Francisco de Zurbarán. Herrera was both temperamental and hot-tempered, and it has been surmised that he abandoned the project as a result of some quarrel with the monks. It would seem, though, that aesthetic differences were more likely to have been at the root of the trouble. Herrera's romantic, passionate, allusive manner corresponded to a strain of bravura in Spanish art which must have dismayed a city in which, since the beginning of the century, the sculptor Martínez Montañés had imposed the concept of a proper classical balance in place of the exacerbated mannerism of the sculptors of the *bajo renacimiento*. Zurbarán had inherited this tradition of formal, sculptured severity, together with the lofty spirituality of Montañés. One can guess that the monks of San Bonaventura must have preferred to see their patron honoured by Zurbarán, whose solemn brush gave to the saintly figures that mystical presence which the religious mentality of the time demanded, rather than by Herrera whose caricatural figures foreshadowed those of Goya.

The altarpiece in question has long since been dispersed. Separate acquisitions, spaced over a century, have allowed the Louvre to group together four paintings, two by Zurbarán and two by Herrera, which can confidently be regarded as having originally formed part of it. Side by side, these silent witnesses of opposing aesthetic outlooks allow an immediate insight into the nature of the great debate which divided the seventeenth-century art world.

For the painters of the Renaissance, the picture was a composition of individual forms; they had inherited the aesthetic of classical antiquity, renovated by Giotto, which had based art upon the representation of the human body. Around this body, all the physical elements of the world were themselves apprehended as independent objects in their corporeity, and thus painting turned itself into

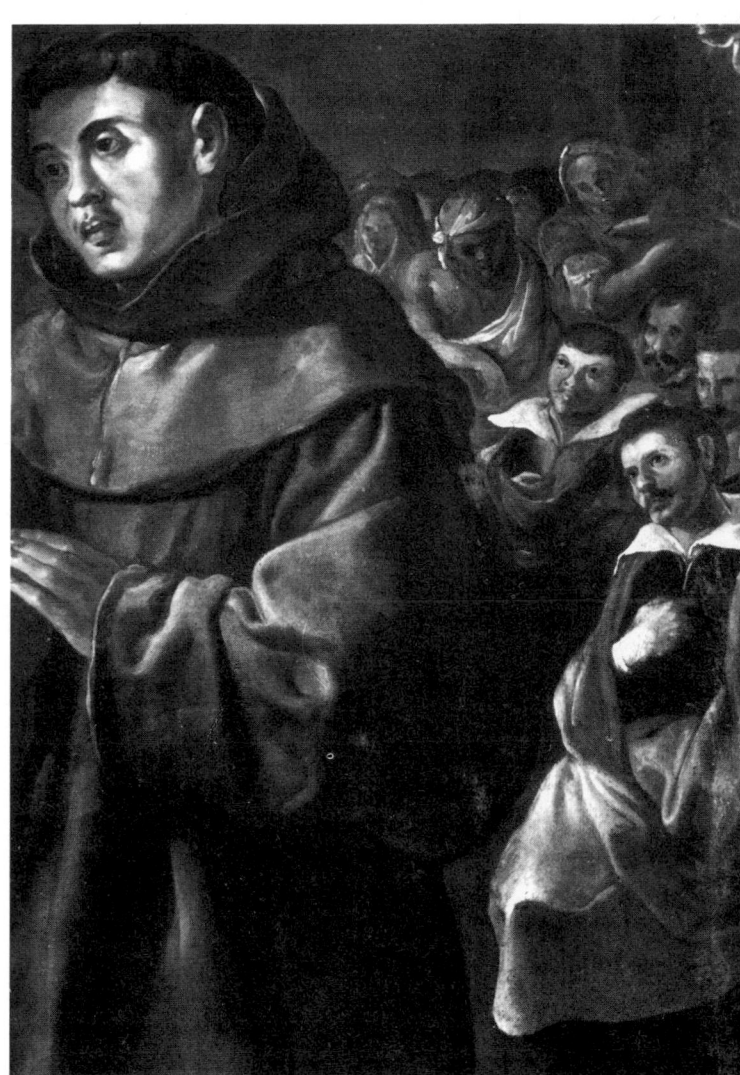

158 Francisco Herrera the Elder (1576–after 1657). Detail of *The Communion of St Bonaventure*. Paris, Louvre.

Herrera's bold treatment of his figures anticipates Goya; it is understandable that the monks of San Bonaventura in Seville should have preferred the style of Zurbarán who completed this commission.

the servant of sculpture. Raphael and Michelangelo, in the Stanze and on the Sistine ceiling, gave the sanction of classicism to this aesthetic. Mannerism itself, especially in its second phase, respected these positions; never before had pictures been 'finished' with such care, and those of Bronzino, for example, seem to be made of some hard gem-like substance.

Venetian art alone, exploiting the discoveries of Giorgione, had employed the atmosphere as a means of reuniting these separate bodies without breaking the unity of the composition. Towards the end of the sixteenth century, Venice saw a confrontation between the rival principles in the persons of Veronese, who endowed forms once again with Bellini's limpidity, and Tintoretto, who dissolved them in shadows.

Although Tintoretto pointed the way forward towards the new painting, there was no immediate response. At the beginning of the seventeenth century the centre of attention was not Venice, which had to wait for Poussin to rediscover it, but Rome. Rome, faithful to its traditions, upheld the principles of statuary form, in a conventional manner in the case of the Carracci, and by direct recourse to nature in the case of Caravaggio. The sway exercised by these artists was so great that Italy was inhibited for some time from developing the new pictorial form.

The Flemish school joined Italian tradition in one respect: it also, although adhering more closely to the real, had conceived each form as a corporeal object, all the resources of dextrous handling being applied to the definition of that object's substantial significance. So, apart from the isolated example of Tintoretto, there was nothing to suggest at the beginning of the seventeenth century that a new concept of painting as painting was taking shape. The formal Italian tradition continued throughout the century, while the Netherlands experienced a magnificent revival of objective painting. Most French painters sought inspiration from both these tendencies and remained deliberately insulated from the current of innovation: Poussin and Claude, however, were wise enough to maintain a distance between themselves and the Parisian scene, where art was becoming increasingly subordinated to the fashionable requirements of the court.

Within a few years of each other, Peter Paul Rubens in Antwerp and Frans Hals in Haarlem had turned tradition upside down and created the new language of painting.

For Rubens it was the renewed contact with his native soil, made possible by his return from Italy in 1609, that allowed him to set aside the disciplines to which he had adapted himself while in the south,

and to conquer his own individual craft. He was to become the most painterly of all painters, with the possible exception of Velázquez and van Eyck. The evolution of Venetian painting, from Giorgione to Titian, and from Titian to Bassano and Tintoretto, had been in the direction of an ever-increasing use of thickness in paint. At the outset of his career, Rubens preferred to knead the impasted paint finely, as in the *Philopoemen* sketch (*pl. 159*) and the *Adoration of the Magi* (Groningen). On his return to Antwerp, however, he revived the van Eycks' transparent technique, sketching out a grisaille which allowed the white undercoating to show through and then superimposing thin glazes or half-tints. But whereas van Eyck gave the greatest thickness to the shadowed parts and a delicate thinness to the light parts, Rubens followed the example of Bassano and reversed the process, keeping the extrusions of paint for the eye-catching bursts of light, and giving the shadows a mysterious depth by brushing them in with faint tints.

This was to be the very basis of modern painting: light expressing itself in relief. Rubens created a supple technique which held together all the assembled elements in a single fluid; it was like a generous sap circulating in the beings and things of this world, an all-embracing, eternal force manifested in short-lived individual beings, as in the *Battle of the Amazons* (*pl. 160*). His handling was amazingly rich and completely adaptable to his different needs. Rubens had no set technique; rather, he created one for each picture. Although in his sketches he allowed himself the delicious pleasure of improvisation (but only after prudent graphic meditations beforehand), he was capable in his medium-size works of giving the illusion of 'finish', of caressing forms slowly and amorously, giving them voluptuous fullness with his brush, as van Eyck would have done (the *Christ on the straw* and *Virgin with the parrot* in Antwerp, the *Self-portrait with Isabella Brandt* in Munich). For larger-scale works, he used a more summary, more opaque technique involving fewer layers of glaze (the sequence of paintings of the Medici Gallery, Louvre).

Towards the end of his life, during the period of domestic bliss resulting from his marriage to Helena Fourment, his manner became even freer and more spontaneous. Putting aside his tendency towards a somewhat overpronounced handling, he allowed himself a sort of relaxed informality which brought him close to Velázquez, abandoning compositions half-way through their execution to endow them with the charm of improvisation. Unfortunately, the balance of colour-values in these pictures is necessarily so subtle that often it has succumbed to

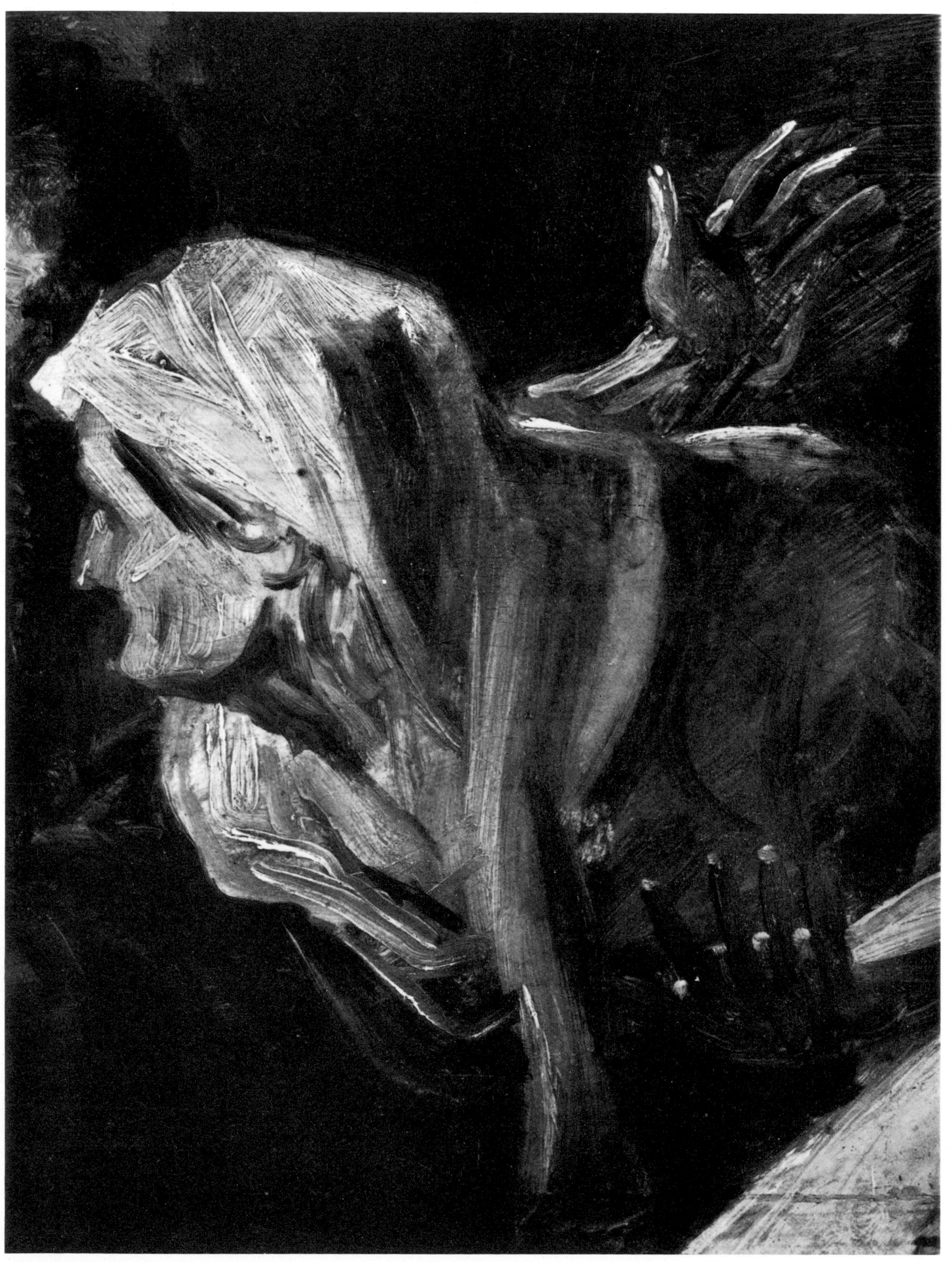

159 Peter Paul Rubens
(1577–1640). Detail of *Philopoemen
recognized by an old woman*. Paris,
Louvre.

This flowing and impasted paint
provides the means for the youthful
Rubens to express freely his sensual
temperament.

181

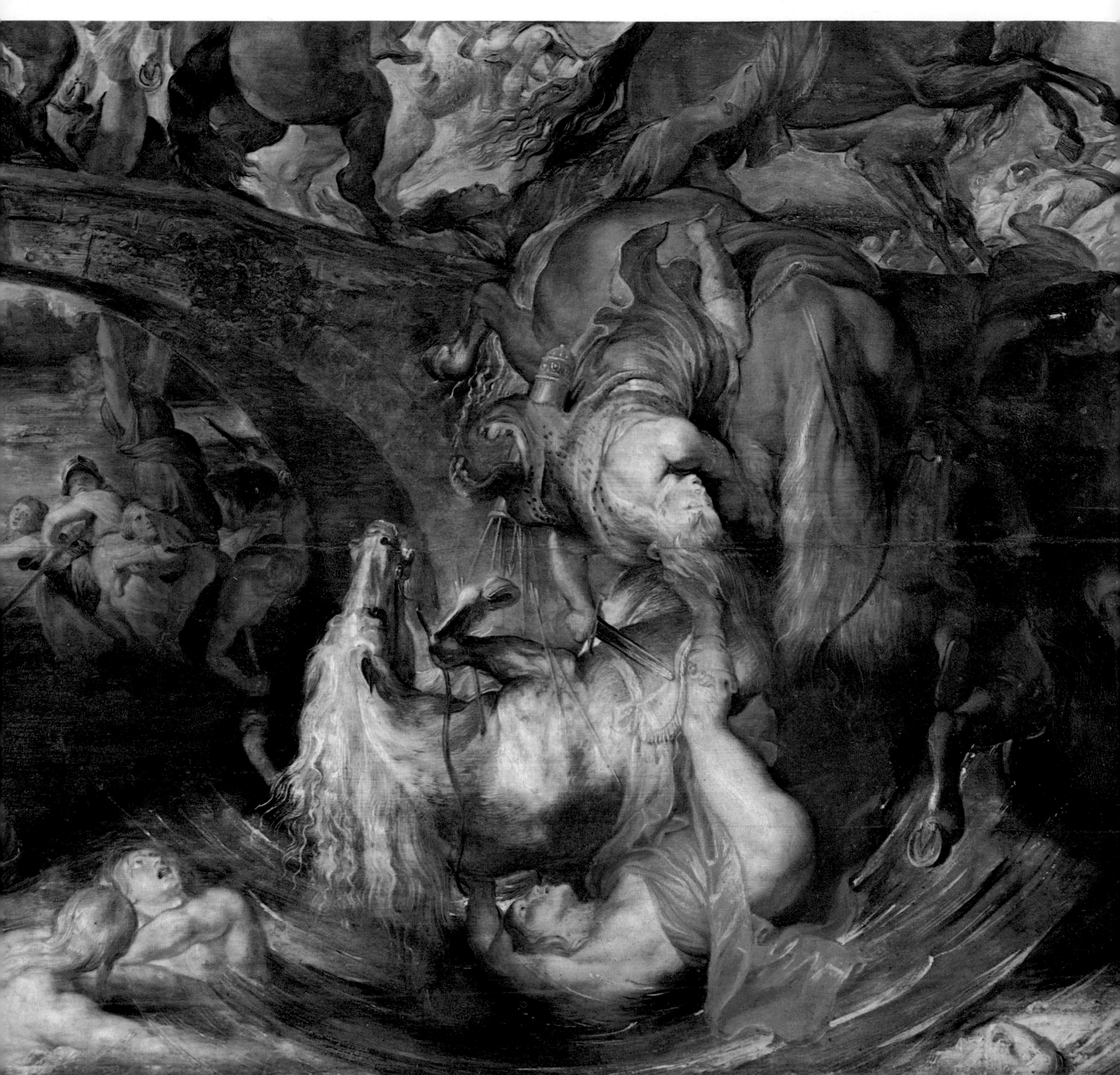

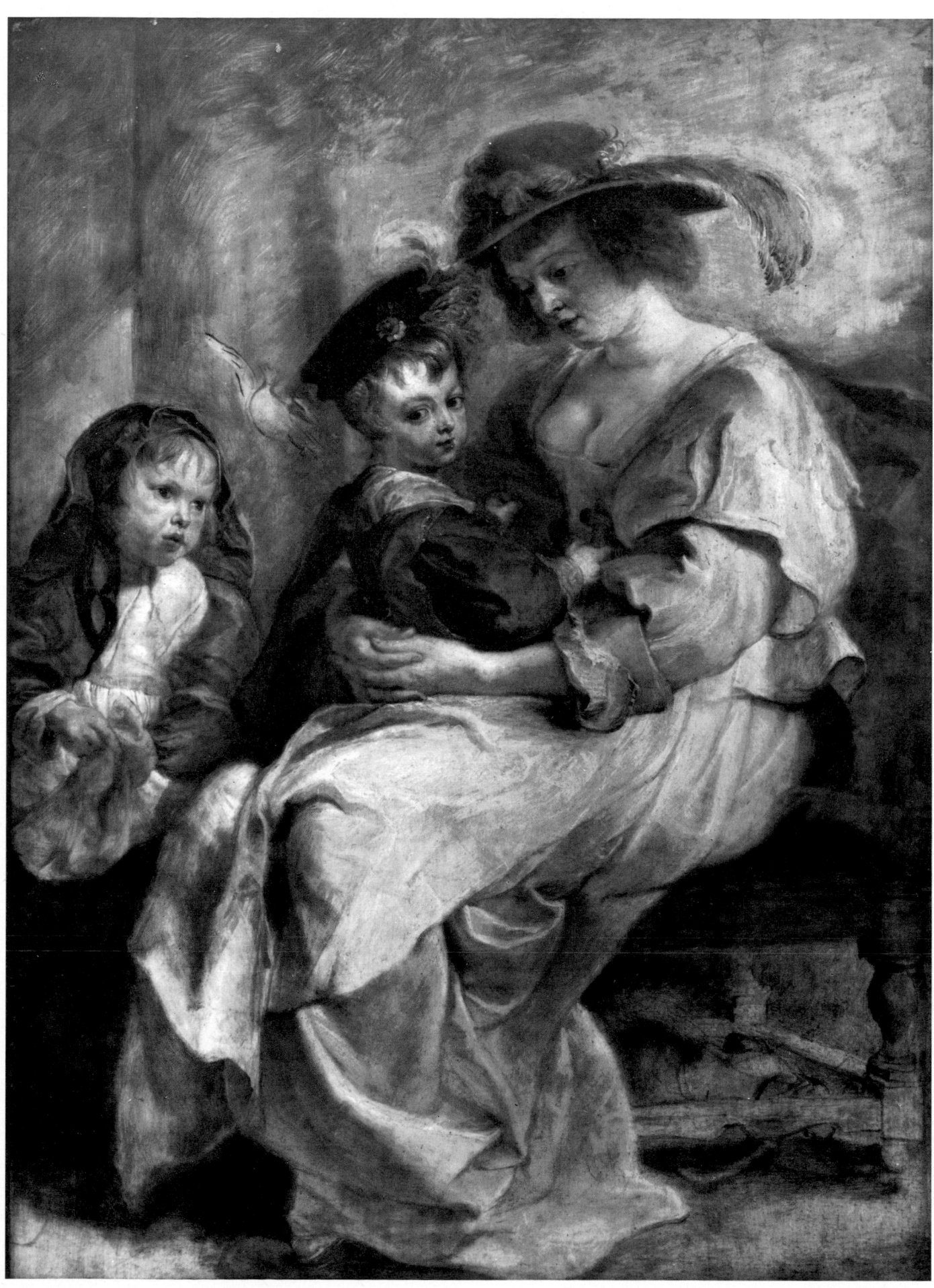

160 Peter Paul Rubens. Detail of *The Battle of the Amazons*. Munich, Alte Pinakothek.

161 Peter Paul Rubens. *Helena Fourment and her children*. Paris, Louvre.

Rubens handled transparencies, impastos and *demi-pâtes* with equal virtuosity; no subsequent painter has been able to match the genius with which he made use of all the resources of the brush.

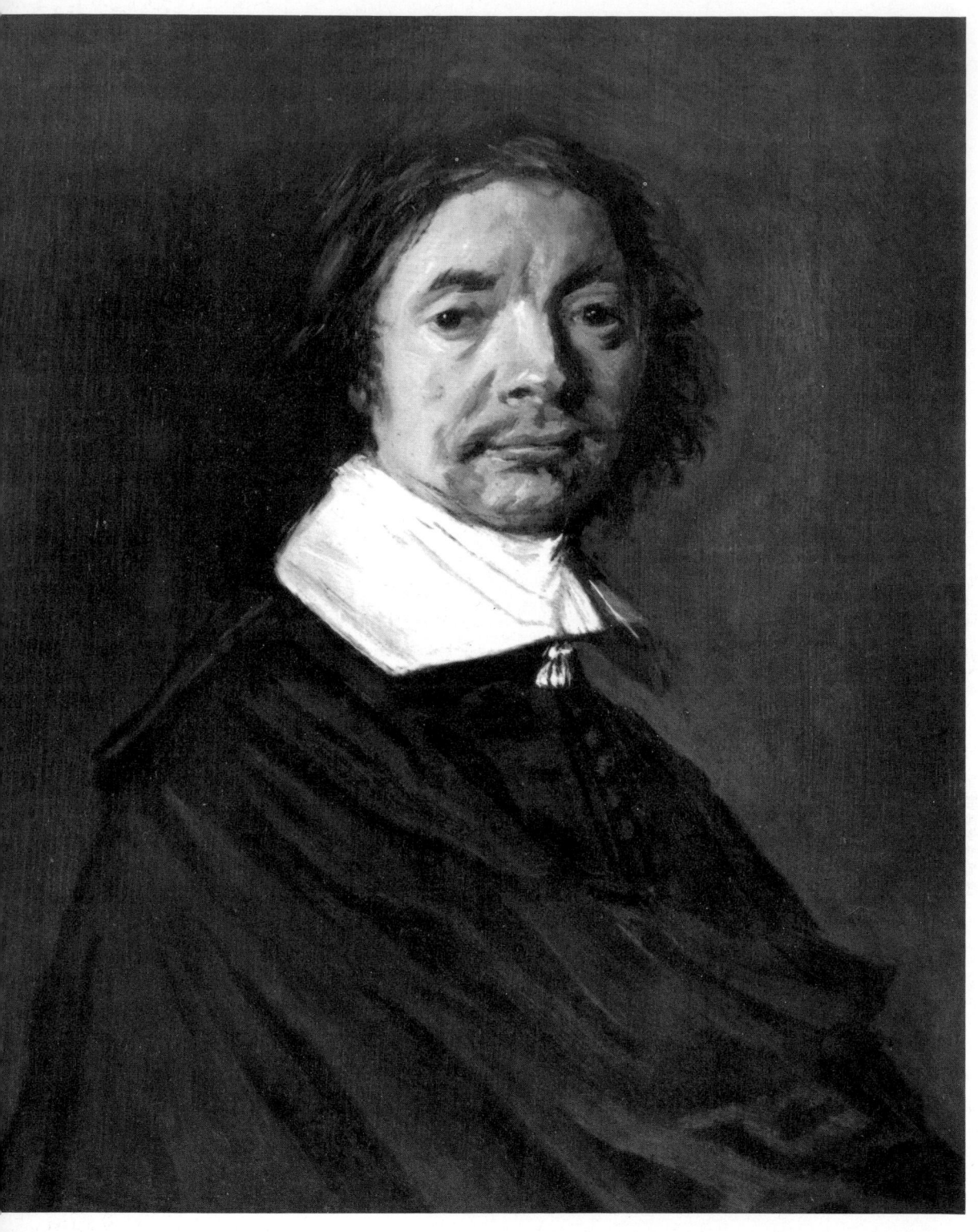

162 Frans Hals (1585–1666). *Portrait of a man*. The Hague, Mauritshuis.

tion with other artists. His splendid handling is evident only in those paintings where, although he had assistants working for him, he remained personally in charge of the whole operation; where he allowed the entire scheme to be executed by pupils, the resulting paintings are like lifeless corpses through which the blood is no longer circulating (for example, the cartoons of the *Triumph of the Lord's Supper*, or the *Chase* of Marseilles). Only that delightful painter Jan 'Velvet' Bruegel successfully assimilated, on a smaller scale, this beautiful transparent handling, although he was considerably older than Rubens: but then Bruegel also had the example of his own father's pictures. The fact that it proved impossible to pass on the benefit of Rubens's craft of handling paint, however simple the process of transmission might seem, tends to refute Michelangelo's dictum that 'one paints with the brain, not the hand': genius does lie partly in the hand.

It is the hand, indeed, which seems to govern seventeenth-century painting, that hand which the artists took such pleasure in painting, often making it the bravura piece of the composition, the place where the message is concentrated. Its action is nowhere more evident than in the work of Frans Hals. His earliest group portrait, the *Officers of St George's Company of Archers* (Haarlem), dated 1616, shows a technique that is already mature, although it was to evolve towards the end of his life, in the expressionism of the *Governors* (*pl. 163*) and *Women Governors*. Yet expression was not Hals's aim. Probably no other painter allowed himself to be so carried away by the desire to suggest the operation of artistic creation; one has the sensation of witnessing a feverish battle in which the painter wrestles with appearance, and one feels able to measure its stages as though they were successive phases of a piece of music. Made of hatchings, slashes, spurts of colour, sometimes scarcely accentuated by a glaze, Hals's technique seems to be a transposition of drawing into painting: the brush never pauses for a moment, the frantic manipulation never stops.

Hals's pictures do not all show the same boldness, though. Working, as he did, in that most demanding of arts, portrait-painting, he was obliged to come to terms with the model's desire to be provided with a faithful likeness. He is said to have explained his manner in the following terms: 'I paint for the honour of my name. A painter must conceal the humble, arduous labour of exactitude which portrait-painting demands.' Often, having to restrain his impatience while modelling faces, he achieved compensation in his approach to the accessories, the clothing and the hands, making

the attentions of restorers (*The Little Pelisse*, Vienna). But the paintings of this period that have remained intact, such as the Louvre's *Helena Fourment and her children* (*pl. 161*), allow the spectator to participate in the miraculous creation of a work still in process of development, and indulge in the pleasure of imagining all the possible completions.

The most surprising aspect of Rubens's technique is that it remained incommunicable. Yet one cannot speak of a jealously guarded secret, since Rubens had several disciples, and often worked in collabora-

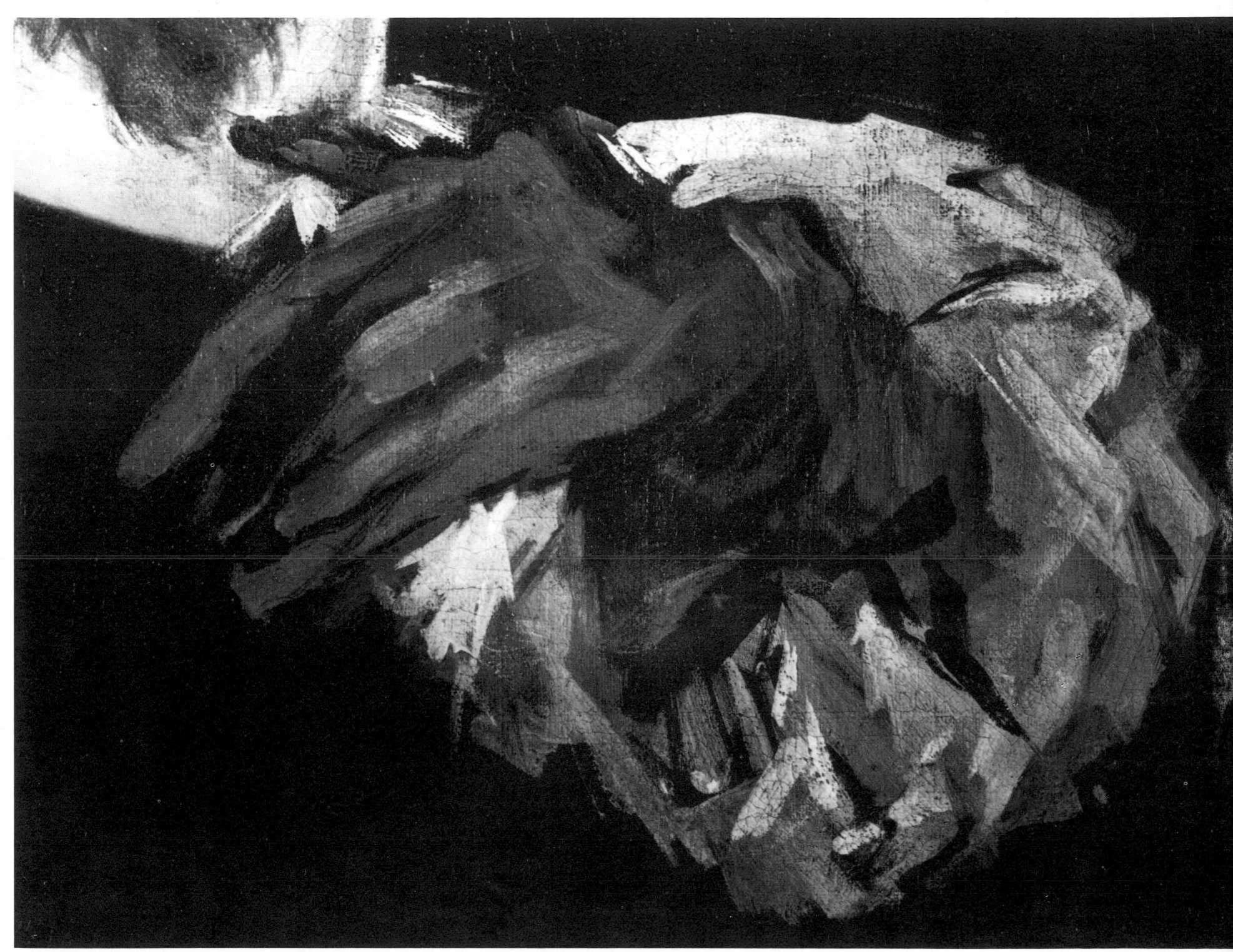

them the outlets for the joy he took in painting. In his final period he swept away all barriers and even gave faces (*pl. 162*) the same perfunctory treatment that he had previously reserved for hands.

To 'paint for the honour of one's name' was a sin in bourgeois Holland, where the artist was an artisan, neither more nor less so than a cabinet-maker from whom one ordered a piece of furniture. Hals was made to pay dearly for his pride: burdened with a large family, he spent his whole life plunged in endless law-suits with the baker, the shoemaker,

the milkman, even the canvas supplier. Fate decreed, too, that his large family should include an idiot son and a daughter who became a prostitute. However, at least part of the hardship and disorder of his domestic existence must have been due to his own flawed character. It is true that painters were badly paid in Holland, and Hals is recorded as having refused to complete a group portrait in Amsterdam because the stay there would have cost him more than the fee he would have got for the work. But he received many commissions, especially from the

163 Frans Hals. A hand, detail of *The Governors*. Haarlem, Frans Halsmuseum.

Frans Hals attacks his picture with furious energy, wielding his brush as though it were a sword.

corporations, and succeeded in transforming these wooden *doelenstukken* into jolly banquets in which the collective soul of the participants shines through. It is the impassioned movement of his brush that allows such a suffusion of warmth to pass through these figures. These commissions would have allowed a more economically minded person to live comfortably; but Hals was by nature a Bohemian, living for the moment and improvising his life as he improvised his art. No other painter produced work that was more subjective and yet less expressive. There were, for Hals, no depths to plumb; except in his last paintings, where poverty awakes a sympathetic echo in him, his work is soulless. He painted. He painted for pure pleasure, never tiring of seeing his inspired hands generate the miracle of the image suddenly taking shape on the canvas. He left behind him not so much a body of work as a splendid series of fragments.

When, in 1627, Francisco Herrera received the ill-fated commission in Seville for the San Bonaventura cycle, Diego Velázquez had been gone for more than five years, leaving behind him in that city of monasteries the sculptured style of his first manner, which Zurbarán was to take over and develop as the fashionable kind of painting there. At the beginning of his career, Murillo himself adopted this style in the cycle he began in 1646, when he was twenty-six, for the Franciscan monastery in Seville. Here, his *Miracle of St James* (the *Cuisine des anges*) and *Charity of Brother Juniper* (both now in the Louvre) represent this first manner, while the *Death of St Clare* (now in Dresden) from the same series is a harbinger of his mature style, compounded of suavity and unctuousness. Soon the sculptural style, even in Seville, became so out of fashion that Zurbarán abandoned it and made a desperate and remarkably unsuccessful attempt to imitate Murillo's prettiness and fluidity.

Velázquez's first master was Herrera, but it is doubtful whether this brief apprenticeship at a tender age left any lasting impression, since by the time he was eleven, in 1610, he had become a pupil of Francisco Pacheco who was to become his father-in-law. Pacheco, the chief representative in Seville of the academic conception of a belated variety of mannerism, had no influence whatsoever on the young man's temperament. According to Pacheco himself, Velázquez imitated Caravaggio, whose work was known in Seville through a few paintings which had recently arrived from Italy; but the artistic influence of his native city may well have sufficed for him to follow the local manner of depicting night scenes in crisp, plastic modelling.

The example of Herrera, who was opposed to this style of painting, may have been a factor in his change of course. In any case, he found his true direction as soon as the royal court beckoned him and so released him from the stifling atmosphere of Seville. His first portraits executed at the court of Philip IV aroused great enthusiasm and ensured him the protection of a monarch who was unfortunate in politics but fortunate in his artistic taste. Velázquez now had honours showered upon him, and was even awarded a coveted knighthood which relieved him of the necessity of working for commissions. From now on he had only to satisfy a king who admired him and a chief minister who protected him against court intrigues: he became the first artist to free himself from a relationship with 'customers'. He made this independence a point of honour, and when the enquiry took place which was to determine his worthiness to be received into the Order of Santiago, he persuaded several witnesses to testify that he had never received money for a painting (a claim belied by a number of receipted bills), a condition of entry into the nobility being that one must never have drawn profit from the work of one's hands.

Velázquez must have been the least mystical painter of the seventeenth century. In Madrid he was the master of his fate; freed of the importunities of the monks, he could paint men. His work includes few religious pictures, and even these seem devoid of divine inspiration; indeed, it is permissible to detect an actual element of profanation in the *Crucifixion* he executed for the nuns of San Placidio (*pl. 164*). He half masks the Holy Face, that eternal object of the ardent meditation of Spanish sculptors seeking to penetrate the mystery of the divine in human nature, using the pretext of the flowing hair. By depriving the God-man of all expressive value, he automatically avoids the most difficult problem in the art of portraiture: a strange reticence in the most versatile of painters! No doubt this effacement of God was not a deliberate gesture, since Velázquez certainly had sufficient Christian faith to live in the court of a Catholic king and is known to have possessed at least a degree of religious conviction. But *instinctively* he drew this curtain of oblivion over the divine features. One can only suppose that he felt himself to be abandoned by God, by a God whose estrangement had already begun to cast a pall of solitude and silence over the human effigies he painted.

By 1630, Velázquez's technique seems to have been fully developed. (His meeting with Rubens in 1628 must have been very useful; it certainly taught him the use of glazes.) The great problem in attempting to describe Velázquez's technique is that it defies definition and renounces principle. Although it seems improvised, one senses that it results from a process of deep reflection; its air of spontaneous inspiration conceals a slow process of secret maturation.

His painting consists of a very diluted flowing impasto accentuated by sparse glazing, fairly dense and yet impalpable, traced by a brush which never hesitates and seems to touch the canvas as lightly as it is held in the artist's hand. This rather opaque pigment, which nevertheless has a diaphanous quality about it, tends to swirl back upon itself in an unhurried, even nonchalant, movement: a handwriting showing no sense of passion on the part of its author, but rather an attitude of complete authority over the object.

Velázquez accepted the supreme challenge in painting, that of evoking appearances so as to deny their reality and make them return to the nothingness from whence they came. Conjured up to the surface from the depths of the soul, these images retain scarcely a flicker of life: they are still-born phantoms symbolizing man's ephemeral existence. Velázquez uses his magical brush to call forth these appearances for the pleasure of showing his complete detachment from them. The Catholic Spain of Velázquez, and of Zurbarán too, seems to acknowledge the physical presence only of those things relating to God: everything emanating from man is doomed to oblivion.

Creating his apparitions only to deny them the right to exist, Velázquez dismisses the tangible world as an empty spectacle. The only trace of emotion that this misanthrope betrays is when he paints themes of childhood, that secret world in which the still innocent soul trembles at the surface of appearance, before perishing entombed in the prison inhabited by those sad individuals, wedded to the misery of their mediocre personality. Sometimes the light that gleams in these children's eyes seems all the more touching for representing the thin thread of life that preserves these graceful little bodies from the inexorable approach of death (*pl. 165*).

The Spaniards of this era were obsessed by this sense of the evanescence of things and of beings. Quevedo, the contemporary of Velázquez, celebrated the memory of the artist in a sonnet which contains the lines:

> *From the painting's frail support*
> *The colour flees like a shadow*
> *Denying the relief that the hand thinks to find.*

It is difficult to tell what kind of a man Velázquez may have been. The few references to him by his

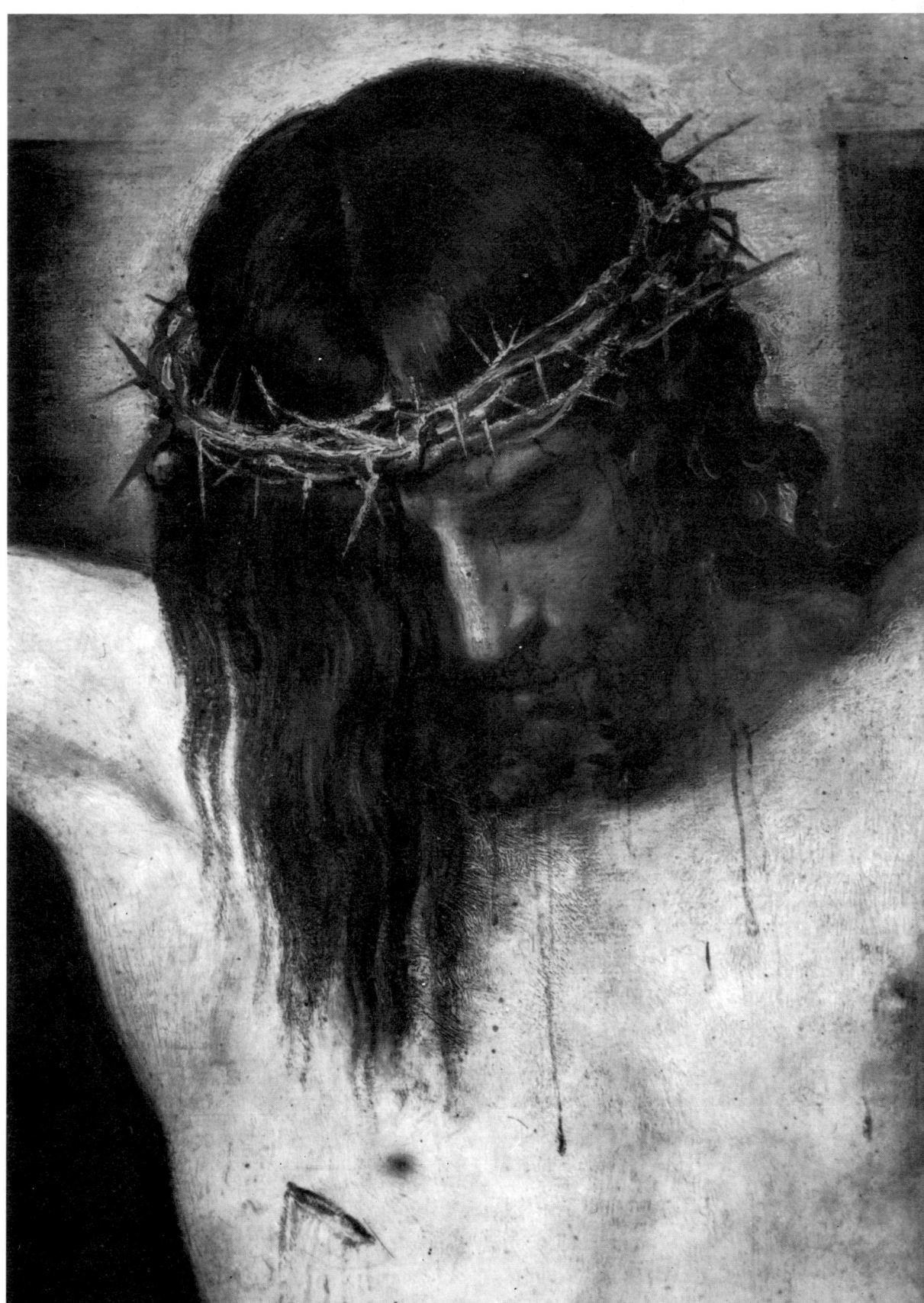

164 Diego Velázquez (1599–1660). Detail of *The Crucifixion*. Madrid, Prado.

How is one to interpret the unparalleled audacity with which Velázquez half masks the face of Christ on the cross?

Diego Velázquez. *Portrait of the Infanta Margarita in a pink dress.* Vienna, Kunsthistorisches Museum.

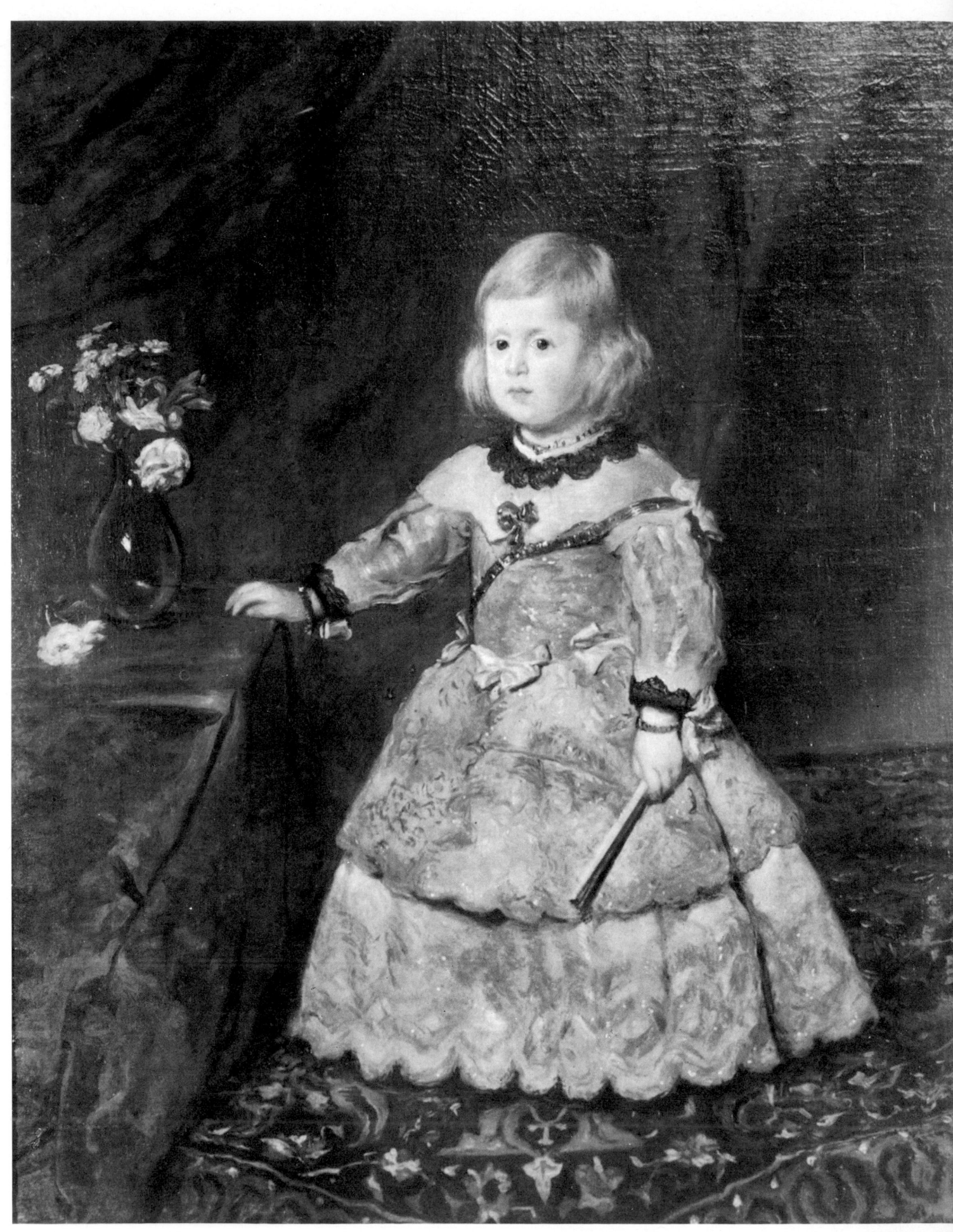

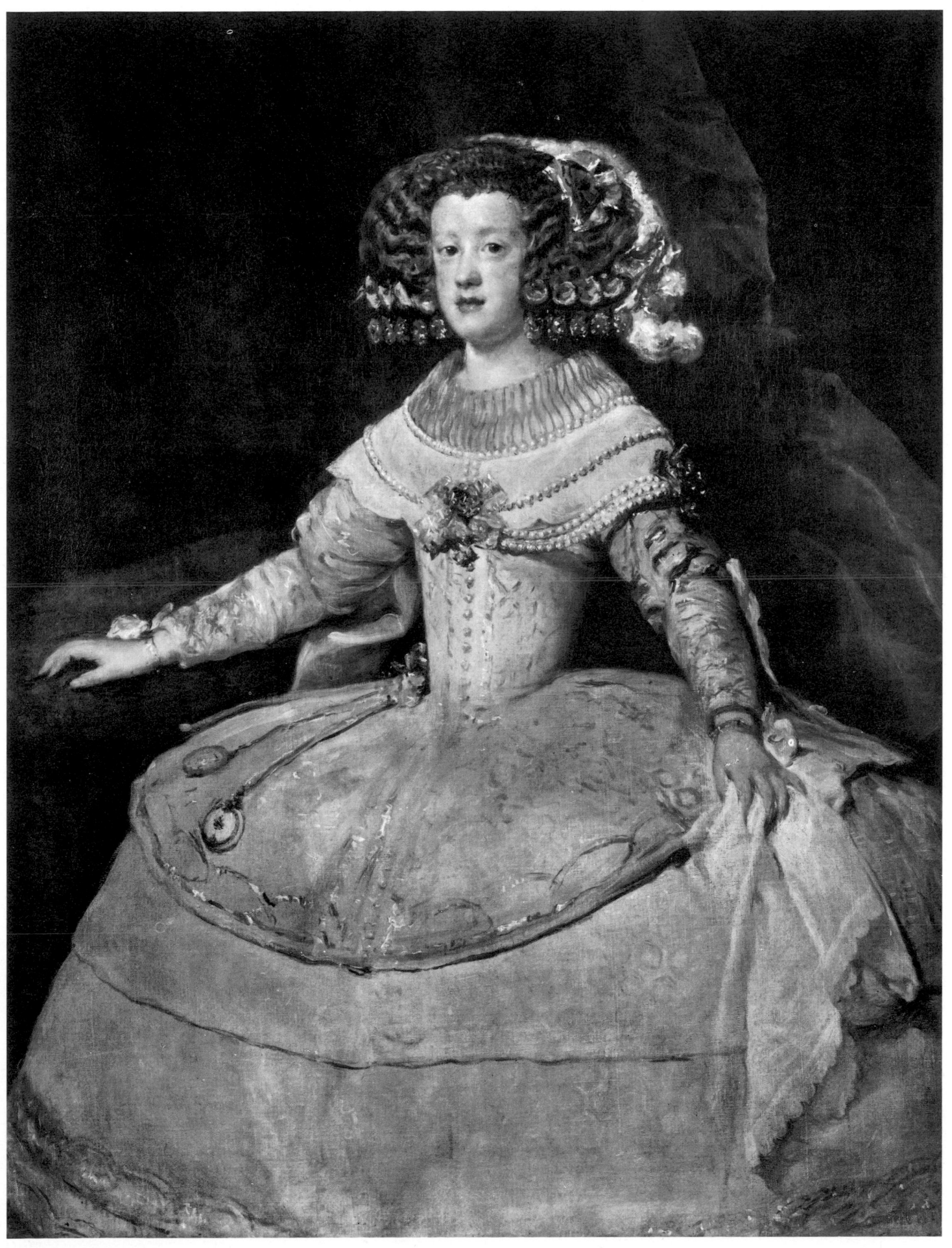

166 Diego Velázquez. *Portrait of the Infanta Maria Teresa.* Vienna, Kunsthistorisches Museum.

The art of Velázquez, the exact opposite of that of van Eyck, coaxes appearances which are as shimmering and as fleeting as a mirage.

189

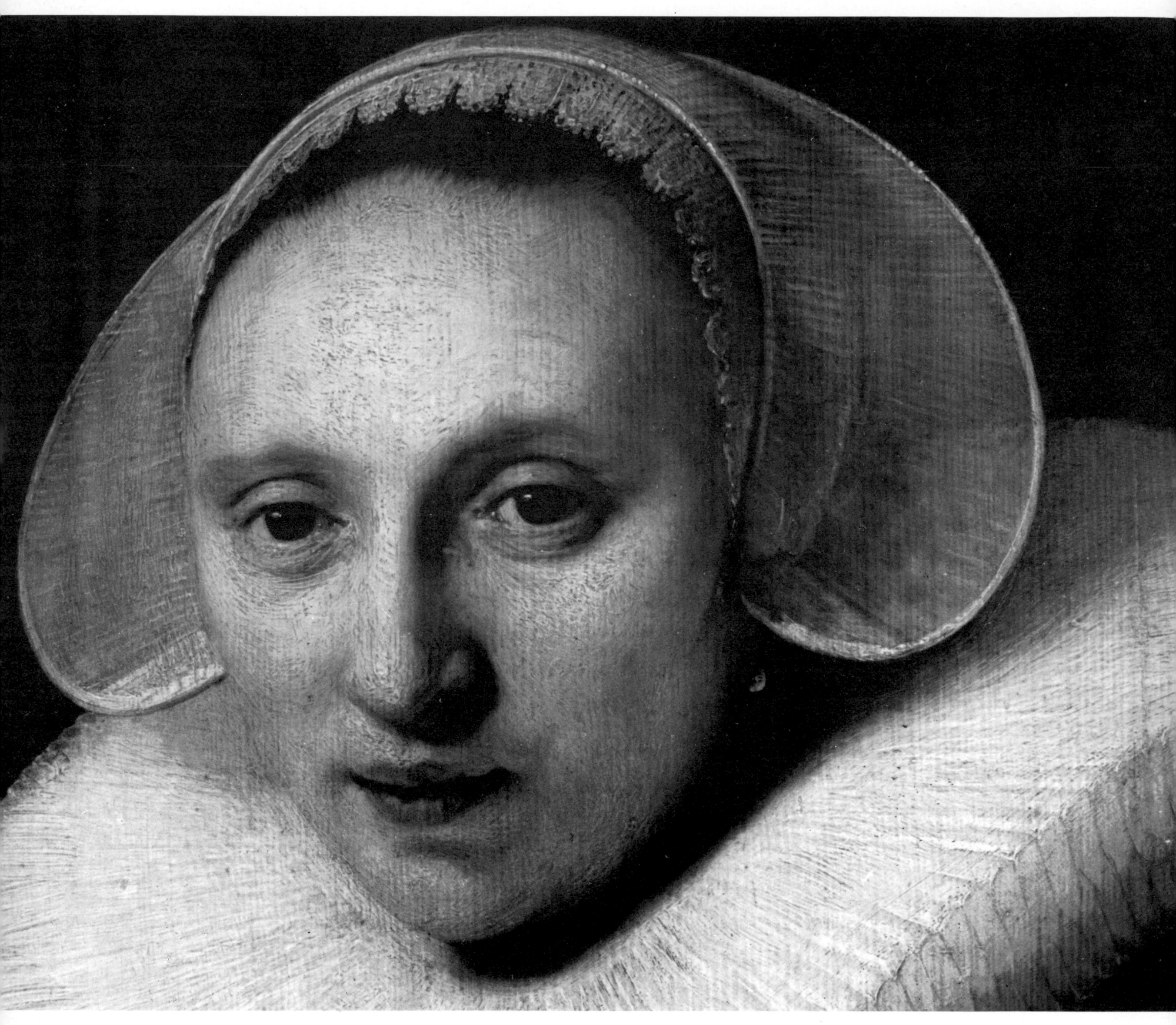

167 Rembrandt (1606–69). Detail of *Portrait of a woman*. Paris, Louvre.

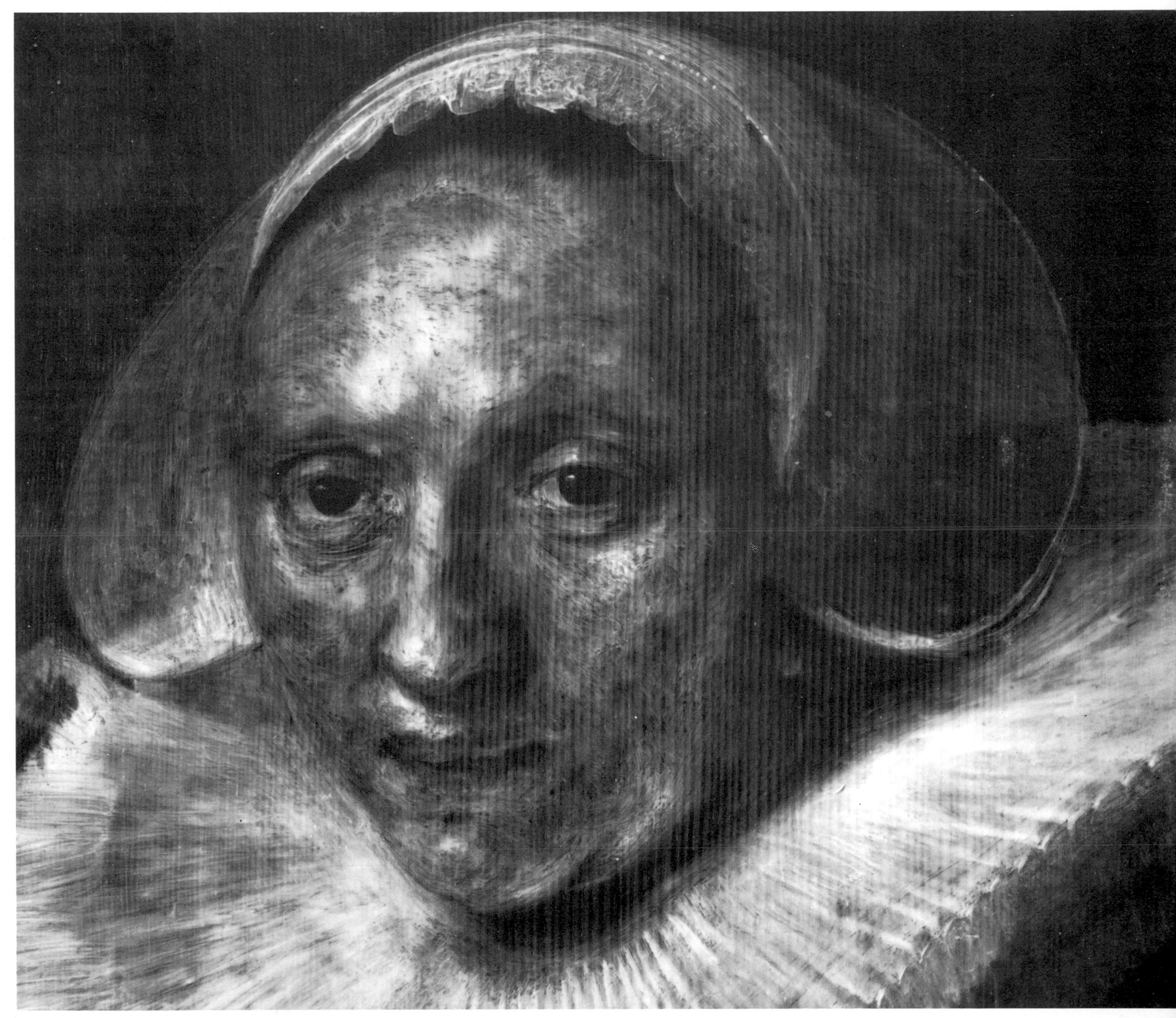

168 Rembrandt. Detail of *Portrait of a woman*. X-ray photograph. Paris, Louvre.

During his period which one might call 'worldly', Rembrandt, especially when painting portraits, concealed the impetuosity of his technique behind a surface appearance of 'bourgeois' handling.

Spanish contemporaries give us fewer clues to his character than can be gleaned from a study of his pictures. One such comment, though, describes him as a 'knight in grand style,' and it not difficult to imagine him infatuated by the idea of nobility, and rendered all the more eager to climb the social ladder by the conviction that he was an aristocrat by nature.

An ambiguous remark about him by Philip IV has continued to provoke discussion. On an occasion when the king had sent him to Italy to buy paintings, and he had lingered there longer than seemed necessary, the king, writing to his ambassador in Rome urging him to persuade his court painter to return home, said that he was fully aware of the latter's 'flema'. Some have interpreted this word as meaning that Velázquez was of a stable, 'phlegmatic' temperament; others see it as an accusation of selfishness and thoughtlessness. Each is a facet of the probable truth. A non-committal attitude suited the artist very well; during that era, it was an aristocratic characteristic, signifying a refusal to commit oneself, a disinclination to emerge from a state of silence, that 'sanctuary of prudence' as Baltasar Gracián called it in El héroe, adding that 'one should, then, imitate the procedure of God who holds mankind in suspense'. Velázquez assumes the role of demiurge, setting up brilliant appearances above the abyss of nothingness, deigning to confer on them existence of a sort but not true being. The duel between subject and object, which at one moment had appeared to have reached a solution, ends in the annihilation of both.

At the other end of Europe, in the newly created 'United Provinces' which were diametrically opposed to Spain both politically and culturally, another artist was developing a method of handling paint that was as uniquely his own as was that of Velázquez. But whereas Velázquez mastered his style so rapidly that in the absence of documentation it is difficult to classify his works chronologically, Rembrandt continued throughout his life, until the very end, to invent new means of expressing more effectively his creative desires, and the body of work he produced certainly represents the richest fund of technical experimentation in the history of painting. From the very beginning he created his own style through the way he worked his paint. Although the handling in his earliest paintings is very clumsy, he quickly acquired an astonishing virtuosity, painting small-scale pictures in which the pigment, treated minutely but in thickness, with a fine brush, contains a concentrated force (*The Artist's mother*, Amsterdam; *Saskia as Flora*, Hermitage).

Rembrandt soon entered his baroque period, during which he set himself the task of painting large-scale dramatic compositions of a boldness unparalleled until the advent of the cinema (*Blinding of Samson*, Frankfurt; *The man with the bittern*, Dresden; the *Company of Captain Frans Banning Cocq*, better known as the *Night Watch*, Amsterdam). Until 1648, the date when he painted the admirable *Pilgrims of Emmaus* (Louvre), his handling was powerful and calm, displaying progressively all the riches of the most generous impastos combined with the subtle use of glazes; he innovated ceaselessly, sometimes using – particularly for landscapes – sized mahogany panels, allowing the fruity tone to show through the brown tints, sometimes tracing the image on this foundation by scratching in the colour with the back of the brush.

Between the years 1630 and 1645 Rembrandt painted a series of far more conventional portraits of dignified burghers, but even here X-rays have revealed that the evenly spread blandness of this artificial impasto conceals the battle of brushstrokes which preceded the conquest of the image (*pls 167–8*). In his final period, Rembrandt expressed himself entirely in terms of this impassioned movement, and the paintings took shape just as they came, throbbing, from his imagination. During the last ten years of his life, pigment became as malleable in his hands as clay is for the modeller, and he abandoned the spatial researches of his baroque period to concentrate entirely on the ductility of matter.

The *Flayed ox* of the Louvre, painted in 1655, displays to us the splendour of its blood-streaked flesh and fat. This extraordinary work should be viewed as a kind of anatomy lesson: it springs from the same desire to explore the depths of carnal nature, but apprehended at a stage beyond analysis, as a kind of primordial matter forming the basis of life. This particular work is, in a sense, the antithesis of the cubist drawings of Dürer, Cambiaso and Poussin, who all responded to the spirit of the Renaissance in seeking truth beyond rather than within appearances. Rembrandt accomplished his boldest feat of all in his immense *Conspiracy of Julius Civilis* (*pls 170–1*), commissioned for Amsterdam Town Hall and then rejected by the municipal council who failed to understand that the vastly exaggerated handling allowed for the fact that the picture was due to be positioned at a considerable height and viewed from a distance.

Rembrandt had, for many years, manipulated his paint with palette-knife as well as brush; in his last works, he even worked the thick impasto with his fingers, as though he could not bear any intermediary to come between his hand and the pigment

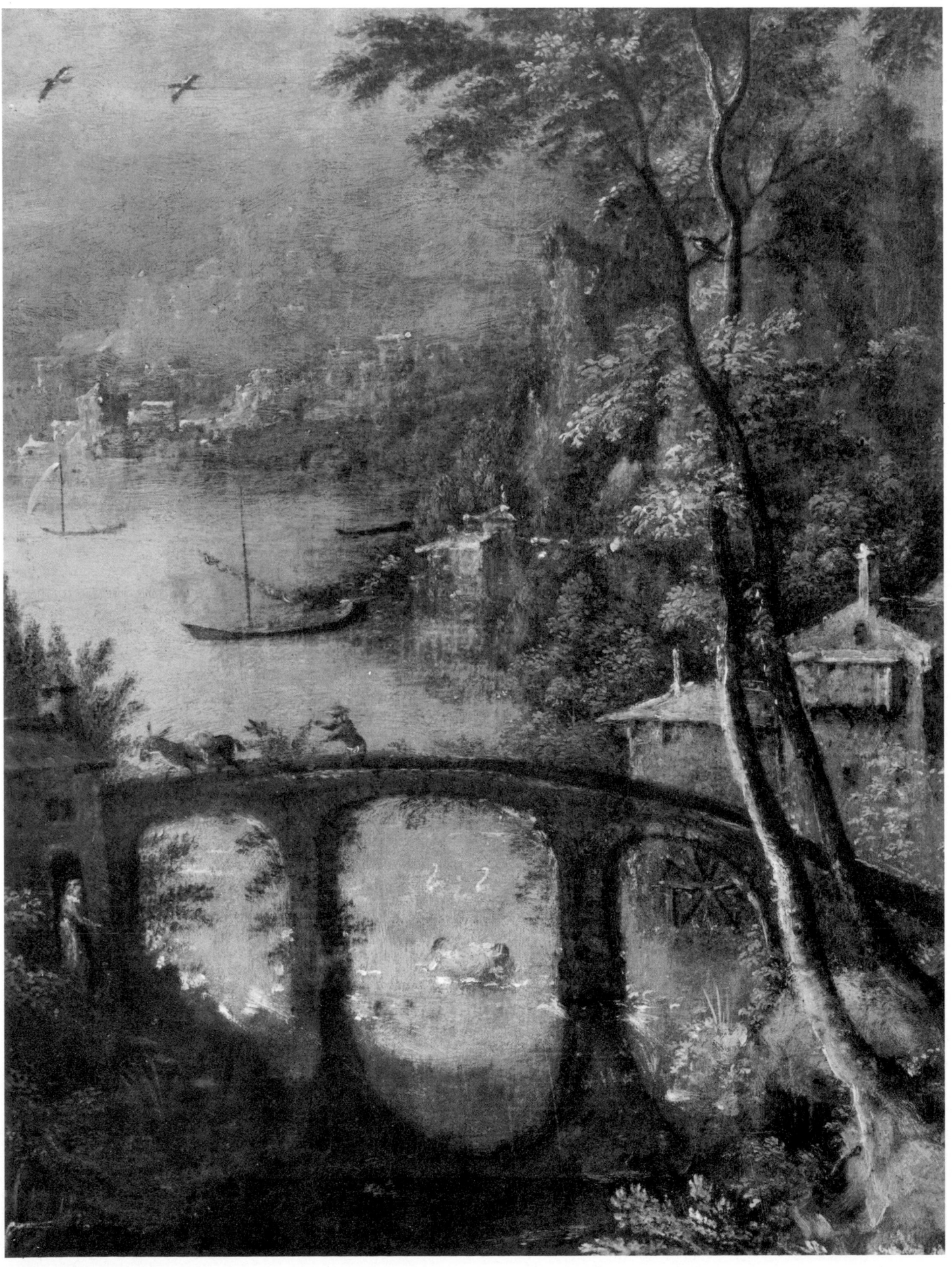

169 Gillis van Coninxloo (1554–1607). Detail of *Elijah fed by the crow*. Brussels, Musée Royal d'Art Ancien.

Anticipating Rembrandt, the Fleming van Coninxloo gives the impression, in his landscapes, of wishing to probe into the material substance of things.

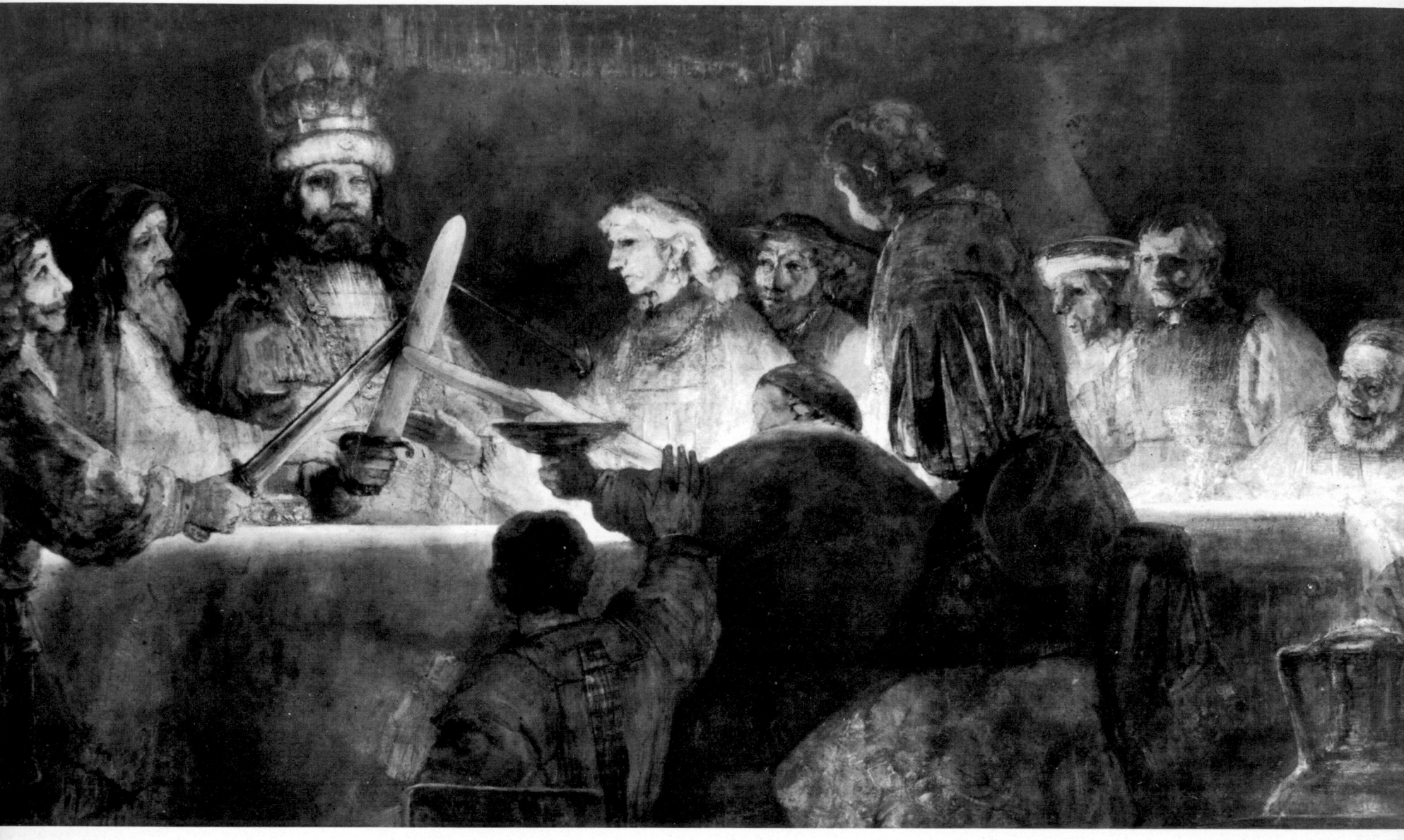

he loved to knead (the *Jewish bride*, Amsterdam; *Family portrait*, Brunswick; *Tobias*, Hermitage). Released from all descriptive servitude, this colour-drenched paint possesses an astonishing evocative force that is all the more suprising in that, truly transfigured, it no longer expresses anything but the infinite capacity for love of an old man overwhelmed by the blows of fate and condemned by bereavement to face death alone.

In his passion for the expressive virtue of matter, Rembrandt was preceded by a strange artist who lived like a hermit, Hercules Seghers. Rembrandt himself owned examples of the work of this painter, whose aim seems to have been to transcend the purely visual aspect of nature which had been all that interested landscape painters, and so to penetrate, in all its mineral density, the very matter of which the world is made. He expressed himself in etchings, in which he did not hesitate to work in negative, and to invent entirely new biting pro-

cedures to render the appearance of the earth's crust. His rare paintings reveal similar preoccupations, and these fantastic visions, rendered with finely worked pigments, certainly inspired Rembrandt's landscapes. A Flemish painter of the previous generation, Gillis van Coninxloo, may be considered the pioneer of this approach to landscape: all the elements in his marshy forests appear to blend into a kind of primordial matter, an aqueous substance which evokes the Amazonian jungle rather than Europe's orderly vegetation (*pl. 169*).

Another painter who undoubtedly influenced Rembrandt was Adam Elsheimer, a curious man whose researches into light effects also inspired that very different artist, Claude Lorrain. As Willi Drost has pointed out (*Adam Elsheimer als Zeichner*, 1957), Rembrandt made a close study of Elsheimer's work; he seems to have been particularly struck by the latter's drawings which he may have seen

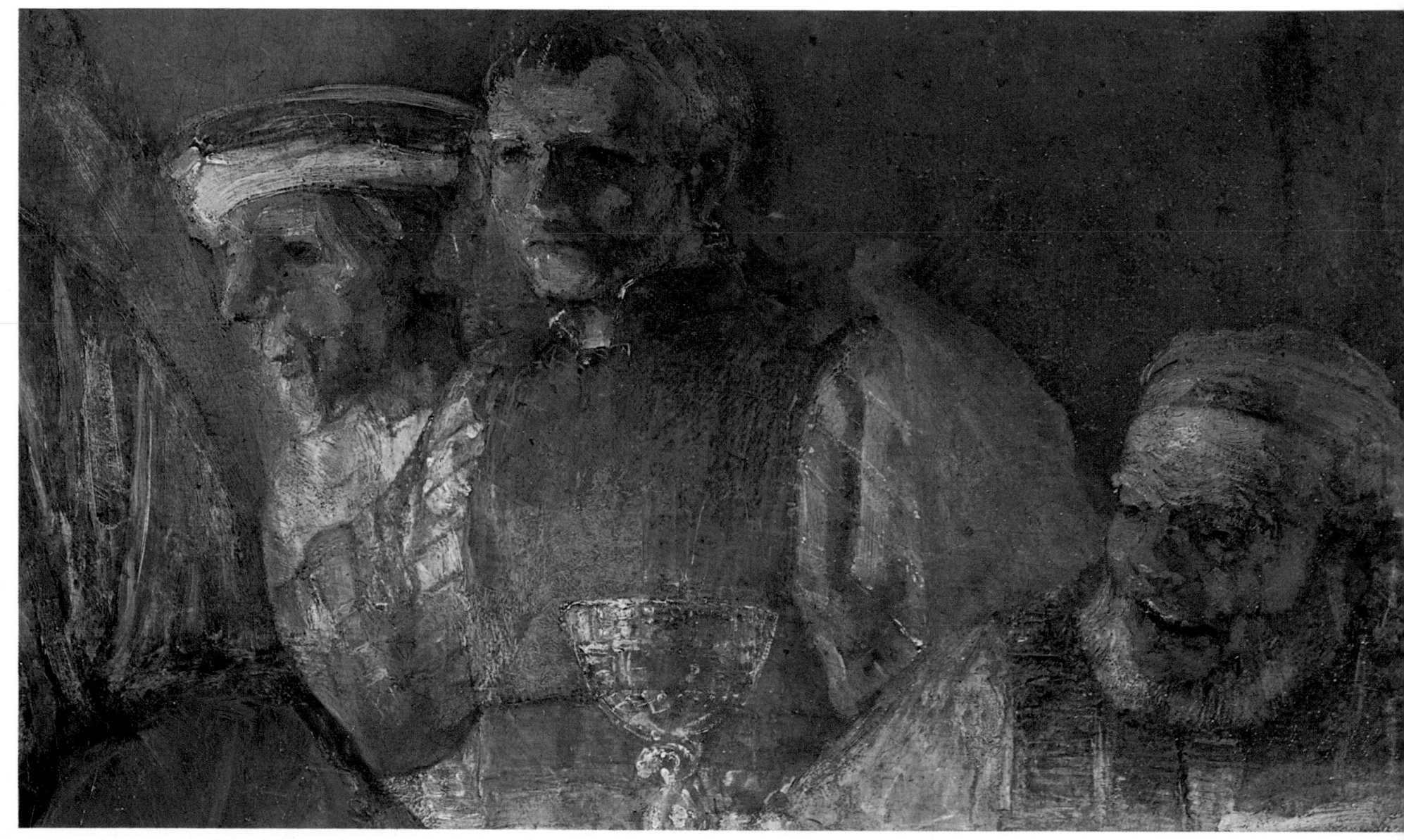

at Leyden, or else at Amsterdam, where the sister of Elsheimer's pupil Hendrick Goudt had had to sell those which had belonged to her brother. The young Rembrandt must have been deeply impressed by Elsheimer's brilliant manner of coaxing forms from the depths of the imagination and revealing them by means of a swirl of forcefully applied strokes often executed in wash-tint (*pls 172–3*).

The aesthetic theories of the seventeenth century are so impoverished that it is pointless to turn to the writings on art of the period for enlightenment about this new attitude on the part of artists. Seventeenth- and eighteenth-century aesthetic opinions were far less subtle than those of the sixteenth century, which had benefited greatly from the refinements of neoplatonism. It is a strange paradox that at the moment when painting was abandoning the literal imitation of nature, the pundits who wrote about art insisted ever more

vehemently that its aim was to imitate nature! If these authors went beyond the Aristotelian concept of *mimesis*, imitation of nature, it was only to advocate a different sort of imitation, that of antiquity. Pacheco could think of no better way of bragging about his son-in-law Velázquez than to praise his talents as a perfect imitator. So no useful purpose would be served by consulting these dusty theses. Since artists have always agreed secretly with the major intellectual developments of their own time, it may be more profitable to examine the ideas of seventeenth-century philosophers.

In addition to the importance, which I have already emphasized, of the heliocentric theory, other contemporaneous scientific investigations are relevant to an understanding of the vision of seventeenth-century painters. Certainly, the expansion of the human horizon to infinity, made possible by Copernicus, Galileo and Kepler, is reflected in the fascination with space experienced

171 Rembrandt. Detail of *The Conspiracy of Julius Civilis*. Stockholm, Nationalmuseum.

Towards the end of his life, Rembrandt produced marvellous transfigurations of colour and texture from the pigment that he explored so deeply.

195

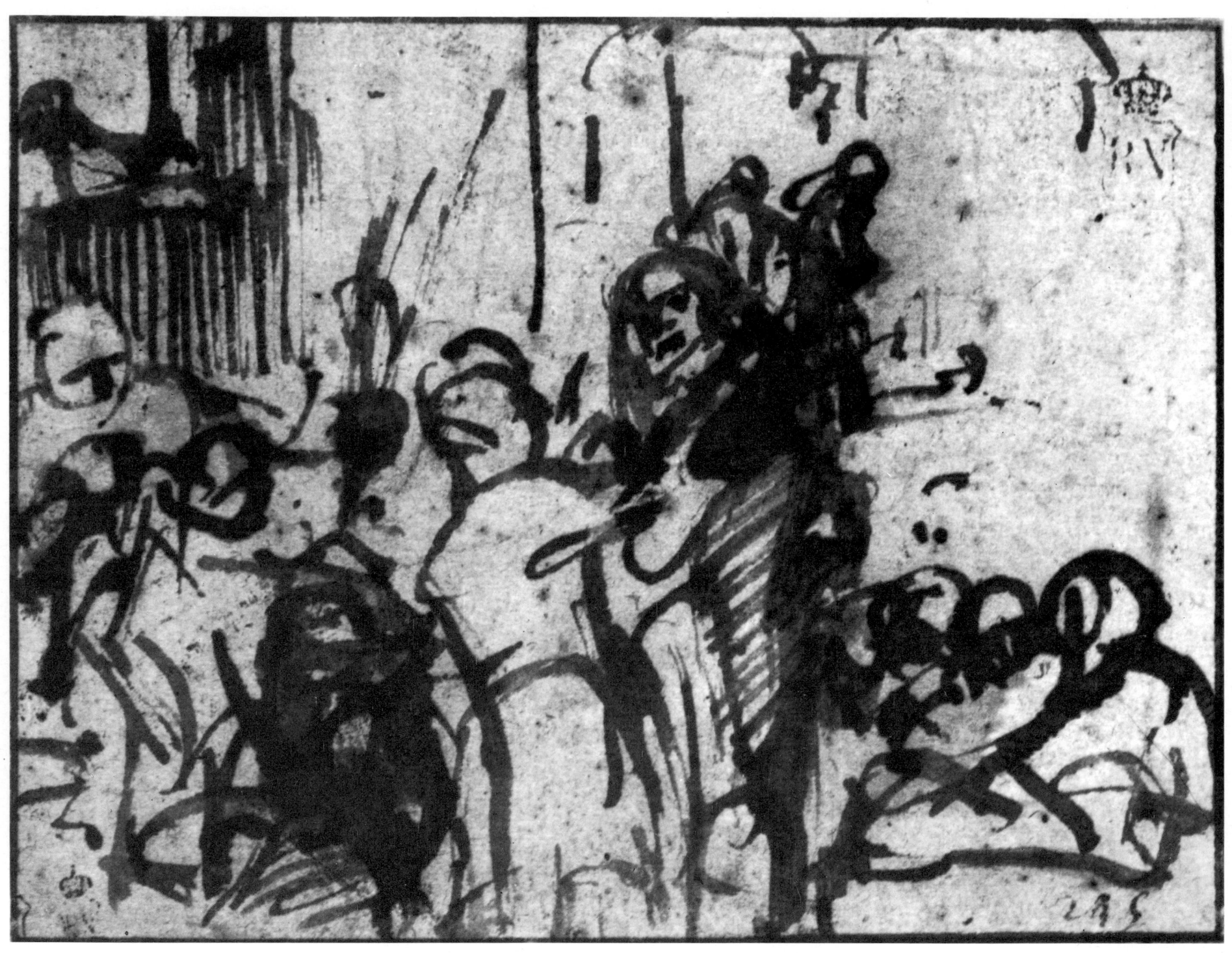

172 Rembrandt. *The Denial of St Peter*. Madrid, Biblioteca Nacional.

by the painters of that era. But, as we have seen, these spatial aspirations degenerated into a sort of intellectual equivalent of angel-worship, resulting in a withdrawal of interest from this earth, which now appeared to be nothing more than a speck in the vastness of space.

Parallel with advances in cosmology, the seventeenth century gave fresh impetus to geological research. A number of scholars sought to determine the history of the earth; it was at this point in time that the Dane Nils Steensen, making a study of Tuscany, succeeded in describing the structural evolution of this region and founded the science of stratigraphy, noting his observations in a short treatise which he published in 1669 and the title of which started significantly with the words *De solido*. This conception of the world as a play of forces had previously attracted Descartes, whose strange cosmogony had attempted to explain the formation of universal matter by postulating forces acting by means of vortices, contacts, shocks, pressures, tractions: this cosmic malaxation conjures up the image of Rembrandt kneading the pigment on his picture surface.

But the dividing line between the Renaissance and the seventeenth century may perhaps be

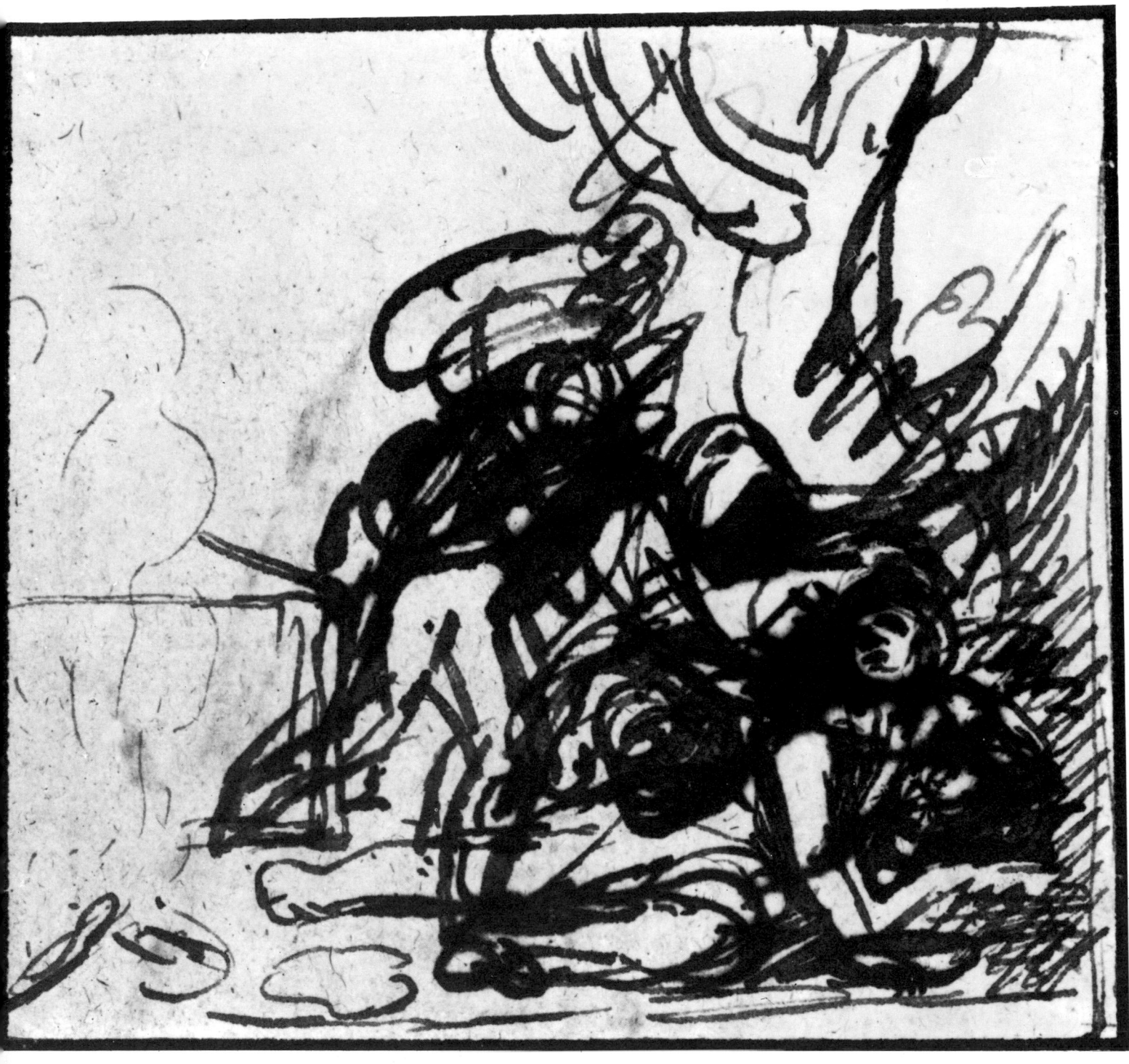

located more precisely. However incompatible they may seem to us today, aristotelianism and platonism had finally converged in an abstract conception of the world. It was not by chance that Raphael united the opposite but complementary gestures of the two masters of Greek thought at the centre of his *School of Athens*. In a stabilized intellectual universe, Plato's Idea and Aristotle's Essence, both deprived of substance, had merged as pure concepts. From the Middle Ages to the end of the sixteenth century these philosophical abstractions had resulted in the supremacy in painting of a purely visual world. Sight being the sense which is most easily amenable to intellectualization, the speculations of the artists of the fifteenth century had bestowed a geometrical framework upon this world; although the mannerists had succeeded in smashing this framework, they had allowed the forms thus released to drift aimlessly.

The creation of new structures was to be accomplished in the seventeenth century in a different direction. The great victory was the destruction of the hegemony of aristotelian and scholastic causality, which was replaced by a *Novum Organon* based upon direct experimentation with phenomena. Since scientific knowledge no longer derived from

173 Adam Elsheimer (1578–1610). *The Murder of Abel*. Frankfurt-on-Main, Städelsches Kunstinstitut.

Elsheimer was an experimentalist who influenced painters as different as Claude and Rembrandt. Rembrandt was particularly impressed by the forceful line employed by Elsheimer in his drawings.

197

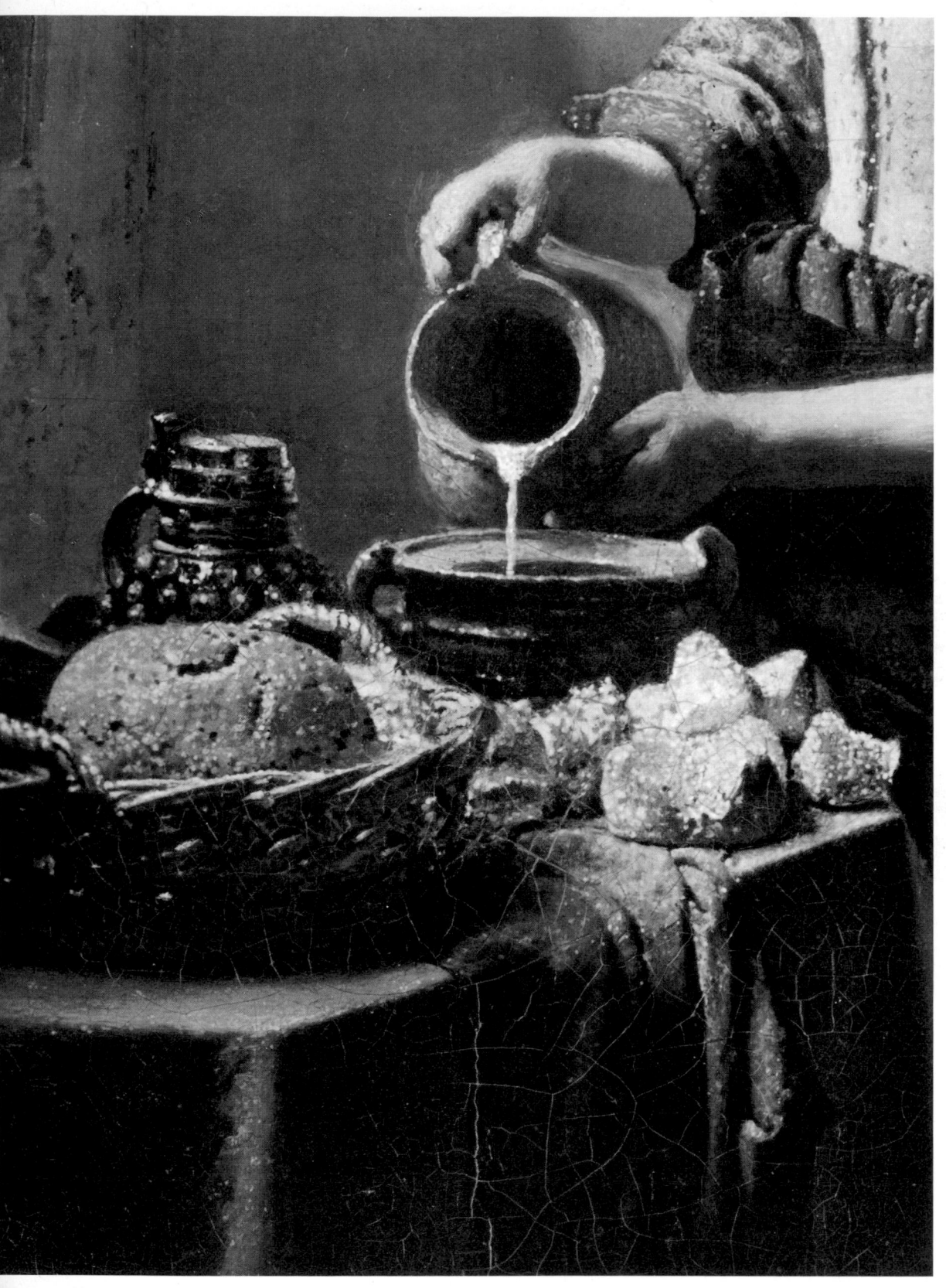

174 Jan Vermeer (1632–75). Detail of *The Milkmaid*. Amsterdam, Rijksmuseum.

In Vermeer's paintings, pigment is a luminous fluid which turns that ideal of the Dutch, the mirror-picture, into a mirror of the soul.

the *formal* and the *efficient*, the former being absorbed eventually by the latter, which was more immediately responsive to experimental data.

Seventeenth-century science was less concerned with setting up systems than with studying the properties of things and so enabling man to act upon them. In this way, things were analysed in terms of their matter and substance, their differential and specific qualities. Once the human mind had been liberated from the old classifications of the four elements, chemistry received its initial impetus and the list of known elements continued to grow throughout the century.

During the seventeenth century, philosophy, like science and painting, represented a devastating attack upon *form*, the category which had imprisoned minds for centuries, had impeded the advance of the sciences, but had inspired the masterpieces of art of the Renaissance era.

The painter, like the scholar, no longer sought for the transcendental reality behind appearances. Appearances were sufficient for him, but he was able to apprehend them only through his senses. His motto became 'I paint as I see' (not 'as one sees') and his vision therefore grew essentially subjective, addressing itself likewise to the spectator's subjectivity. The generalized objective aspect of things ('as one sees') was no longer evoked except as a framework of reference, serving, for the spectator, to evoke memories of which he would seek to grasp the proper meaning. Painting, no longer form but symbol, had become a dialogue between individuals.

The things of this world take an unconscionable time to die. While free thought sprang to life in the seventeenth century, scholastic thought continued to be taught at the Sorbonne until the eighteenth century, and in that era Père Castel was still at pains, in the Jesuit *Journal de Trévoux*, to refute the theories of Leibniz and Newton. The same sort of situation existed in painting: the formalist conception crossed the barriers of the baroque, came to terms with it, and continued its career throughout the seventeenth century, parallel with the tendency which one might call 'phenomenalist' or materialist.

France remained more obstinately faithful to artistic formalism than any other European country, and even in the eighteenth century Watteau's and Chardin's efforts to break away remained unsupported. In Holland, on the other hand, it is possible to understand how the aesthetic of image-as-form, evolving from a tradition established solidly on the basis of bourgeois taste, finally produced its antithesis in the person of Vermeer. Vermeer made use of the same fund of images, soul-

logic but from observation, it came within the field of sensibility and so became, in a sense, subjective: throughout the century, man invented instruments to supplement his inadequate senses. Descartes, Spinoza and Leibniz destroyed scholasticism's system of the four causes, retaining only two of them,

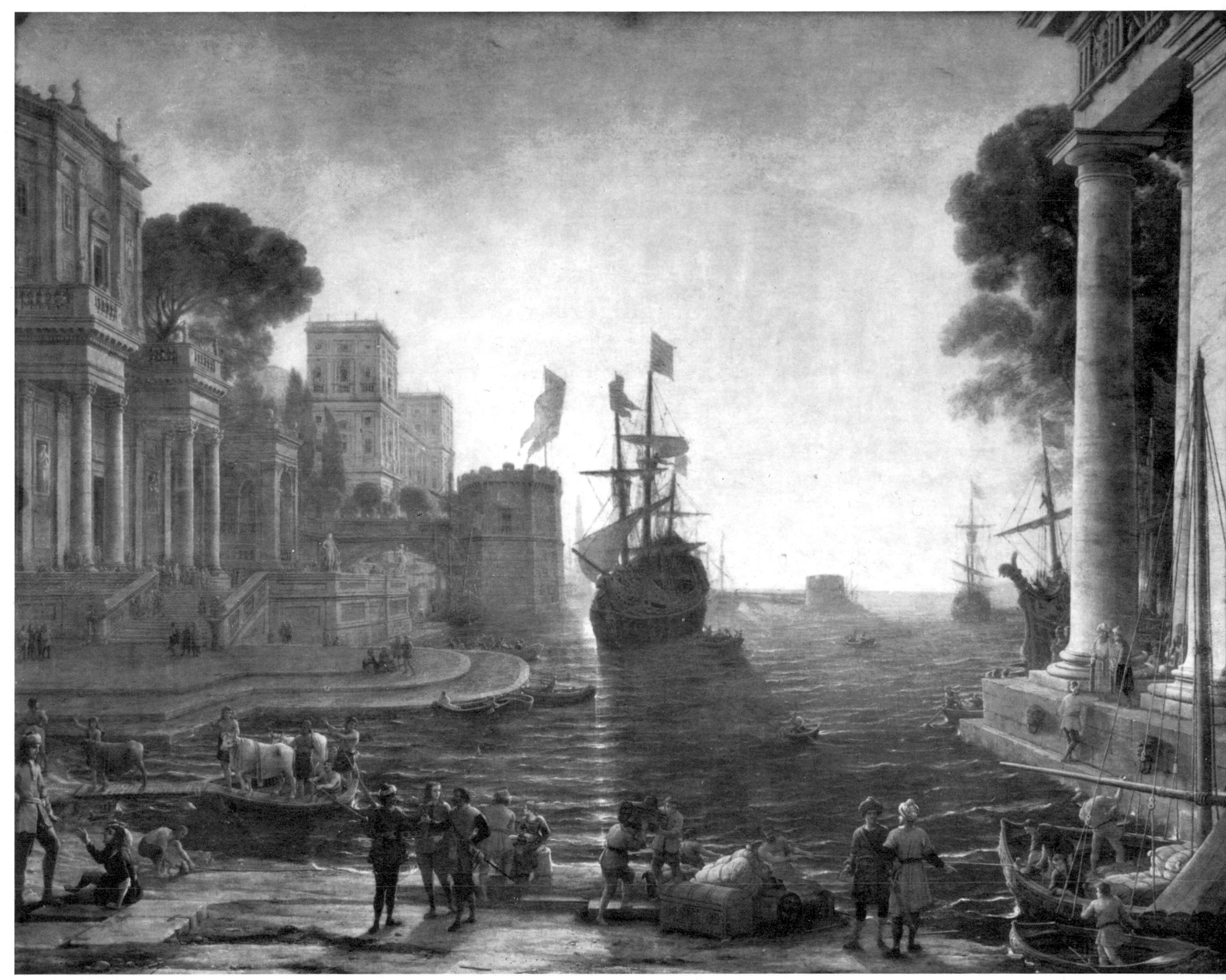

less reflections of everyday life, as the run-of-the-mill society painters of his time, but transformed them through his magical handling of paint. He breathed life into this inert substance, this thin film of colour, working the paint in depth, disintegrating it into pin-point elements, 'pearls of colour', which made it vibrate. He was able to express the nature of the soul through this living quality of his paint.

Vermeer's lack of success among his contemporaries proves how deeply engrained was their attachment to what one might call 'scholastic painting'. The same innovations which they were just able to accept, reluctantly, when used by Rembrandt in developing themes of the imagination, must have seemed intolerable when applied to their own daily life (*pl. 174*).

175 Claude Lorrain (1600–82). *Ulysses restores Chryseis to her father.* Paris, Louvre.

Claude foreshadowed the impressionists in the way he made light the very substance of things.

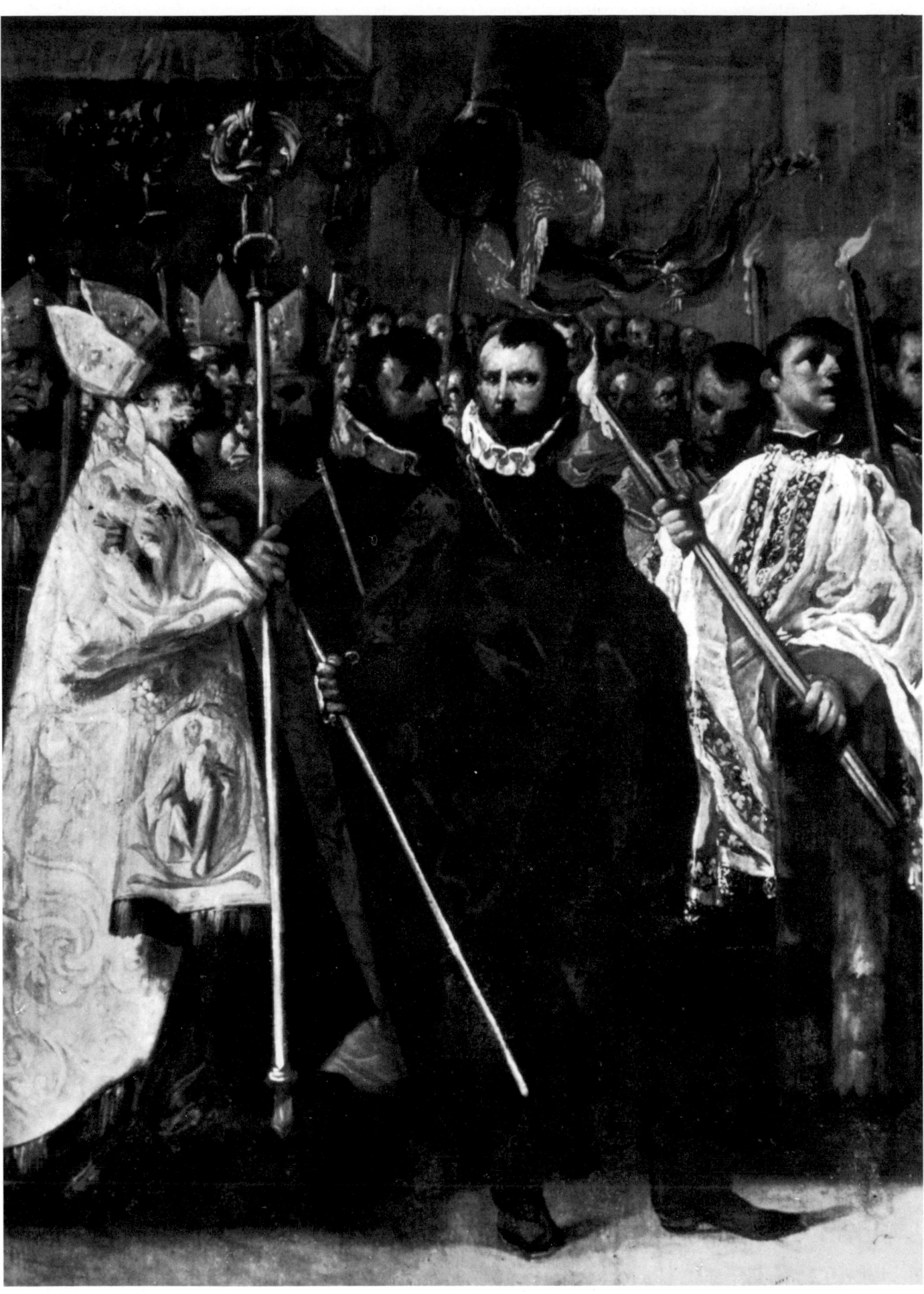

176 Francesco Maffei (active 1620–60). Detail of *The Translation of the bones of the saints of Brescia.* Brescia, Duomo Vecchio.

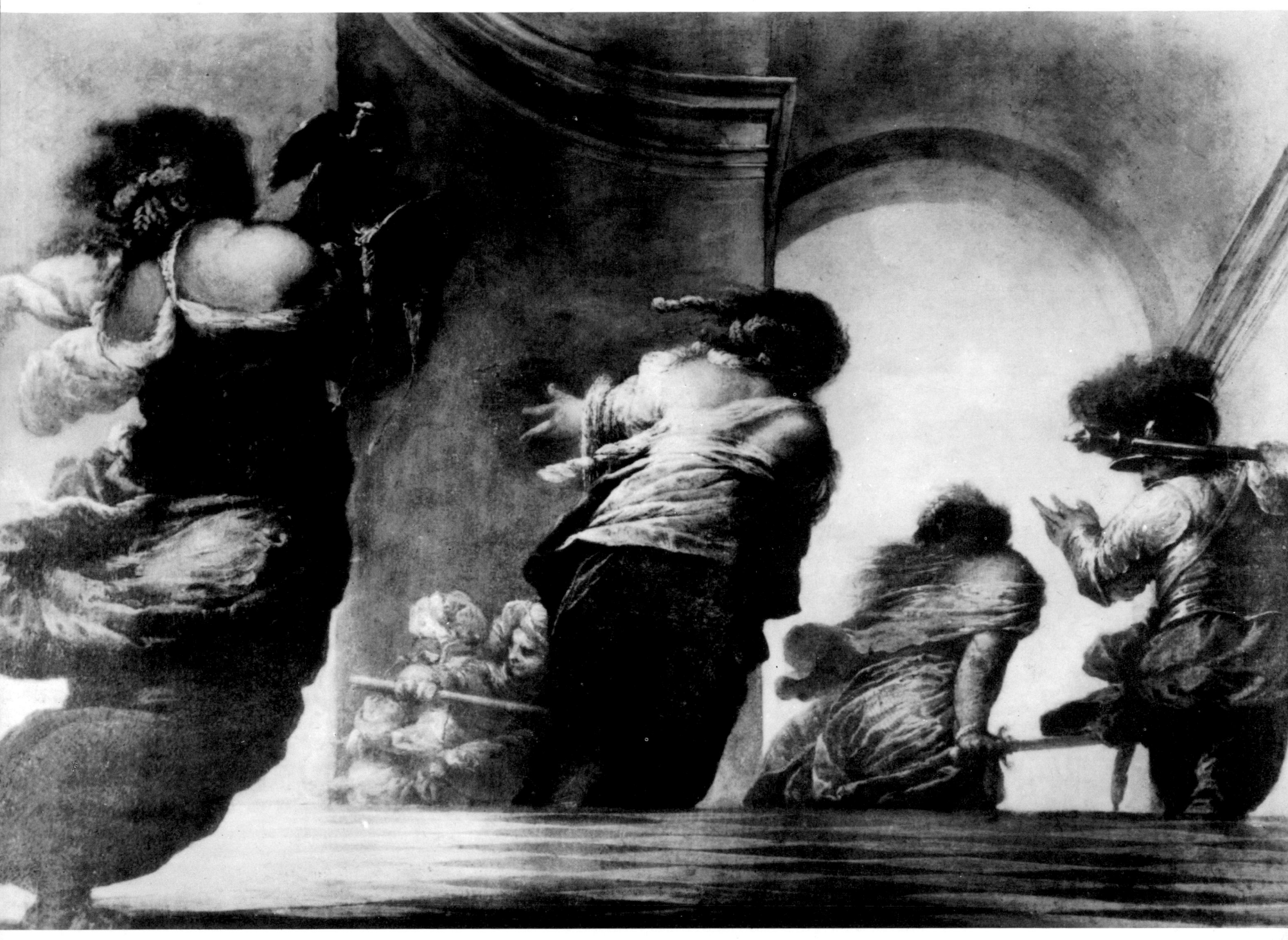

In Spain, it was Velázquez who put an end to 'scholastic painting'. Those who inherited his discoveries – his son-in-law Juan Bautista del Mazo, Claudio Coella, Juan Carreño de Miranda – thought themselves competent to handle paint with an equal freedom, but this over-confidence led them, more often than not, into confusion. One of these, however, Carreño de Miranda, drew from his brush effects of such richness that they anticipate Goya's generous use of colour. Carreño de Miranda sometimes collaborated with Velázquez, and it seems that he must have been somewhat inhibited by the latter's greatness, since it was only after the master's death that he painted his first great works. One of them is an immense altarpiece, painted in 1666 for the Trinitarian monks of Pamplona, representing *The Foundation of the Order of Trinitarians by St John of Matha* (*pl. 157*). The splendid movement of the heavens which animates its upper part makes this picture undoubtedly the supreme example of baroque in the art of Spain, a country whose traditions in painting have always run counter to the baroque depiction of the supernatural world by means of free-flowing forms.

177 Sebastiano Mazzoni (*c.* 1611–78). *The Temple of Janus.* London, collection Lady Aberconway.

The provincials of seventeenth-century Italy, especially the Venetians, countered the classical or baroque formalism of Rome and Bologna with a romanticism characterized by free treatment and colour and by bold layout.

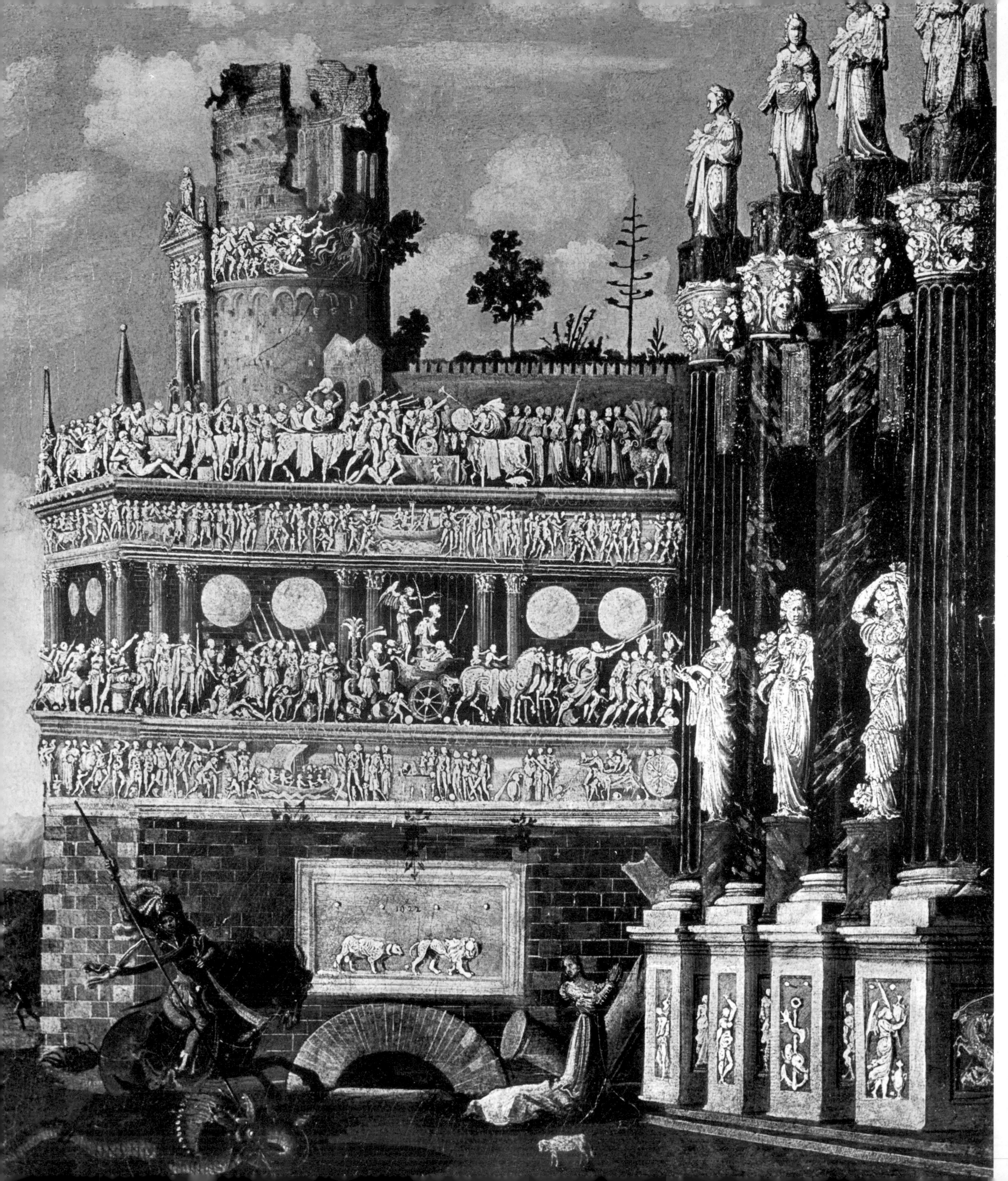

The treatment of this work was so bold that the Trinitarians of this remote provincial city, not at all accustomed to such novelties, were quite scared by it. Palomino relates that 'when the monks saw the picture close up they disliked it so much that they were reluctant to take delivery of it, and it was only the approval of the picture by Vicente Berdusan (a well-known painter of this region) that induced them to accept it'. Carreño de Miranda's treatment is much more subjective than that of his master. However free it may be, Velázquez's handling never violates the duty of 'likeness' incumbent on the portrait-painter; Velázquez's intention is not to transgress appearances but, rather, to render them as subtle as a mirage. A picture by Velázquez remains an image, an image about to vanish, crossing our field of vision for a single moment, borrowing from some form of the real its own evanescent appearance.

For Carreño de Miranda, on the other hand, the act of painting simply represents an opportunity to create a fictional world. Individual forms disappear in the rich brew; swirls of colour give birth to a miraculous universe drawing its essential unity from the original matter of painting. This masterpiece, unique of its kind in the Spanish school, belongs to the baroque lineage of Rubens. We know, in fact, that its author had been profoundly impressed by the work of Rubens, many of whose pictures had entered into the Spanish royal collection. It does not seem unreasonable to suppose that Carreño de Miranda, frustrated by the stiff portraits his post as court painter obliged him to produce, welcomed this commission from an obscure monastery in a distant province as a splendid chance to display a greater freedom of expression. And so, in one stroke, he invented this magnificent handling which, after an eclipse of more than a century, was to be rediscovered triumphantly by Goya in his frescoes for the church of San Antonio de la Florida, Madrid.

In Rome, even Poussin, who had continued to apply the principles of form established by Raphael and Titian, allowed himself to be won over by the new current during the last twenty years of his life. It was when he started painting landscapes that, by a plastic use of paint, he, too, sought to suggest some cosmic substance. The preference of French painters for landscape has always provided them with the best field for experiment and research. It led Claude Lorrain to conceive of the different aspects of the world as being produced by the infinite motions of light, thus anticipating the impressionists (*pl. 175*).

While the Roman school, rooted in the Carracci and Caravaggio, maintained aesthetic formalism

during the seventeenth century, the other Italian schools allowed themselves to be tempted by the idea of experimenting with the substance of paint. However, this approach to painting was so foreign to the Italian temperament in art that artists went no further than the destruction of formal texture, accomplished in a twilight atmosphere; they remained incapable of re-creating substance *from within*, as Rembrandt and Velázquez had done. Only a few isolated painters, Giovanni Serodine, Francesco Maffei, Sebastiano Mazzoni (*pl. 177*), really succeeded in penetrating the secrets of substance. In Verona, Maffei, inheriting the Venetian tradition, created for himself a subtle technique, animated by an iridescent colour, which can be compared to that of Velázquez (*pl. 176*). In Naples, two painters from Lorraine, whose works have been jumbled together under the single name Monsù Desiderio, worked a livid pigment into stucco-like texture to produce visions of the end of the world (*pl. 178*).

The eighteenth century, in France as well as in Italy, witnessed a strange retrogression. Formalism reassumed its supremacy. Tiepolo's technique, for example, was no more than a method of rapid execution, a *fa presto* which was still based on a principle of formal composition. Francesco Guardi was alone in being able to express the atmosphere of the lagoon through vibrating colours; Gian Paolo Panini remained a precise and accurate recorder of images. As for France, artists seem to have decided finally to confine painting within the traditional limits of academic technique, exemplified by Jean-Baptiste Oudry's masterpiece, the *White duck*, which is a *tour de force* of academicism. There was nothing to indicate that in the following century the future of painting was destined to lie in France's hands.

In England, Sir Joshua Reynolds was obsessed by technical problems, copying the masters, especially Rubens and Rembrandt, and even, allegedly, destroying some of their paintings in order to discover their secrets (there exists a so-called Rembrandt *Self-portrait*, withdrawn from the 1950 Katz sale, which might well be a pastiche by Reynolds). However, whereas objective treatment is perfectly transmissible, the same is evidently not true of subjective style, which obliges the painter to create a personal technique. Delacroix was to make the same error; and Reynolds's imitative paintings already anticipate certain aspects of the romantic painter's work. Goya, on the contrary, although formed in the classical aesthetic, was capable of freeing himself by personal effort and so creating his own handling.

Monsù Desiderio achieved his fantastic effects by treating paint as though he were working in stucco, moulding it in depth.

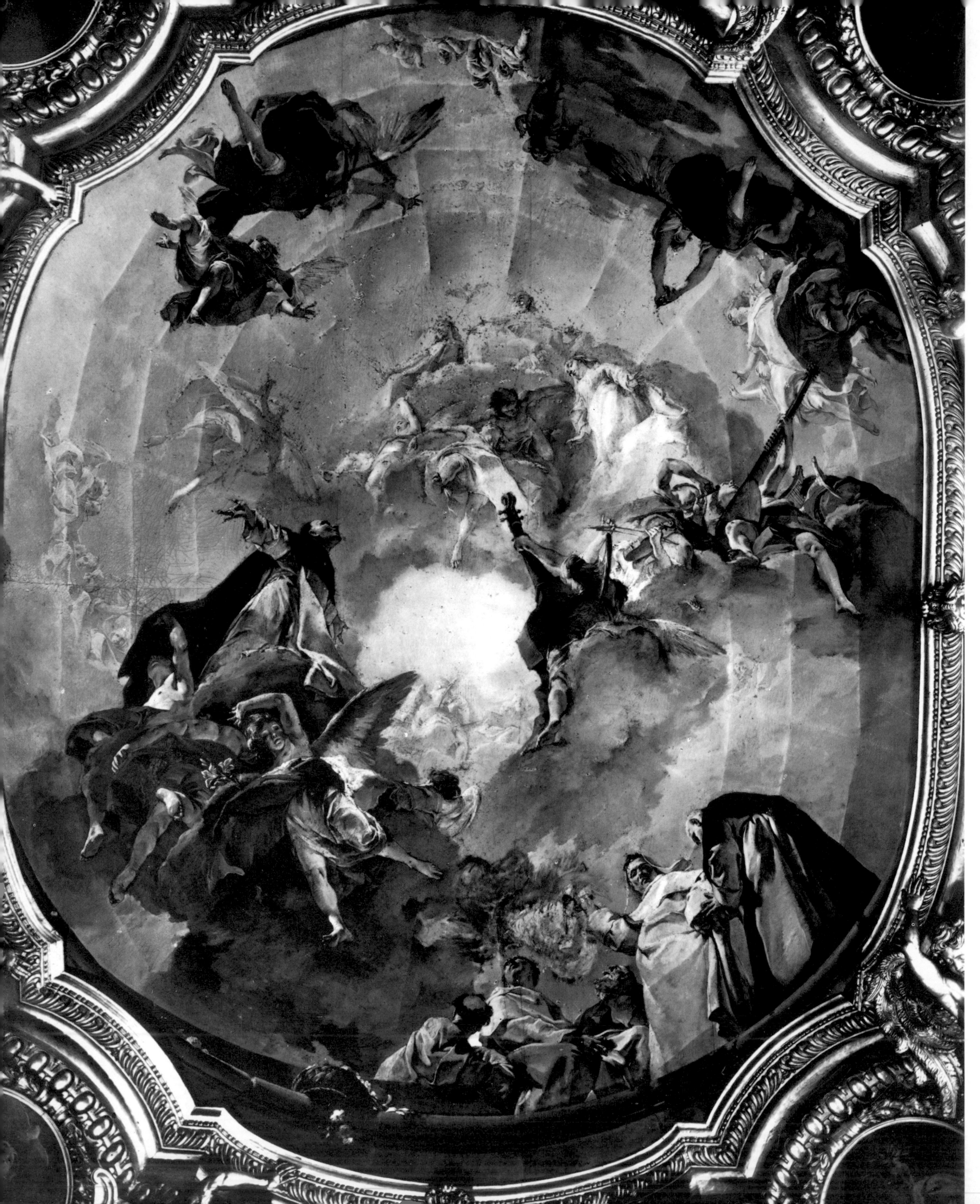

13 Conquest of space

179 Giambattista Piazzetta (1682–1754). *The Glory of St Dominic.* Venice, Santi Giovanni e Paolo.

Long convinced that *perspectiva artificialis* was based upon a scientific truth, art historians have at last come to realize the relative character of this conception of vision which could not, in fact, be real except for a one-eyed man whose eye is not only immobile but equipped with a flat retina. Until recently it was considered unthinkable to question the validity of a theory, and a practice, which were founded by Brunelleschi and Alberti and taught for three centuries in the schools and academies.

Erwin Panofsky was the first to challenge the dogma: in 1924–5, he demonstrated that this famous geometric perspective which imposed on the picture a single point of sight – that of the individual – expressed the spatial perception of fifteenth-century Italians and was not applicable to other artistic civilizations. It would be going too far to deny all objective reality to this *perspectiva artificialis*: although it does not correspond exactly to the physiology of vision, it does provide the greatest possible approximation to it, relative to the two dimensions of a picture. Certain artists – principally those who specialized in decorative schemes – were conscious of the artificiality of this single point of sight offered to the eye for the exploration of these painted surfaces. Their solution was to use more complex systems with several secondary sources which were nevertheless adapted to a general point of sight: Raphael took this approach in the *School of Athens*, and so did Veronese in the *Marriage of Cana*.

The treatment of space by painters of the modern age certainly involves a far richer approach than could be obtained simply by the application of the *perspectiva artificialis* to which nineteenth-century artists returned, and the complexity of these problems is only now receiving belated recognition. The facilities offered by numerous museums and illustrated art books may, indeed, be held partially responsible for the backwardness of art history in this field, since they tend inevitably to reduce the object to its image and cut off the spectator from direct contact with the work of art. Those paintings in which the idea of space is expressed most effectively, namely those executed in buildings and preserved *in situ*, remain largely unknown to art lovers today except in the form of flattened miniatures which deprive them of all substance. Curved surfaces, in particular, lose their natural qualities in photographic reproduction. Baroque art, which is essentially the modulation of spaces, cannot, in fact, be appreciated except in the countries which created it, and even then it would require more than a single glimpse to appreciate the full significance of these works: the sensations they provoke cannot readily be fixed in the memory except as a result of repeated examination.

Photography can produce only inaccurate results: a photograph of a church interior, such as Vierzehnheiligen near Bamberg, for instance, would give this complex, multipolar structure an axial appearance. And it would be impossible to photograph the ceiling of the staircase painted by Tiepolo at the Würzburg Residenz except in separate units, which would completely destroy the work's significance. This is one reason why the monumental paintings of the modern age, apart from Michelangelo's frescoes in the Sistine Chapel and those by Raphael in the Vatican Stanze, have not yet taken their place in the imaginary museum of our times. Another reason, no doubt, is that, in the case of ceiling paintings in particular, the many marvels they display can be appreciated properly only at the cost of a degree of physical effort which the impatient visitor is seldom willing to expend.

Leaving aside antiquity, about which the experts differ, one can say that the awakening of spatial feeling coincides with the reinvigoration of Western civilization after a period of several centuries when man's relations with the external world seemed to have been reduced to a sort of groping for immediate values. During those centuries, values had been apprehended by a series of discontinuous sensations, analogous to those through which a small child discovers the existence of objects around him. The co-ordination of these perceptions, from which sprang the concept of a multidimensional environment as the framework for human life, did not affect all the arts simultaneously; and the two great thirteenth-century civilizations, the French and the Italian, applied the new thinking in different areas of experimentation.

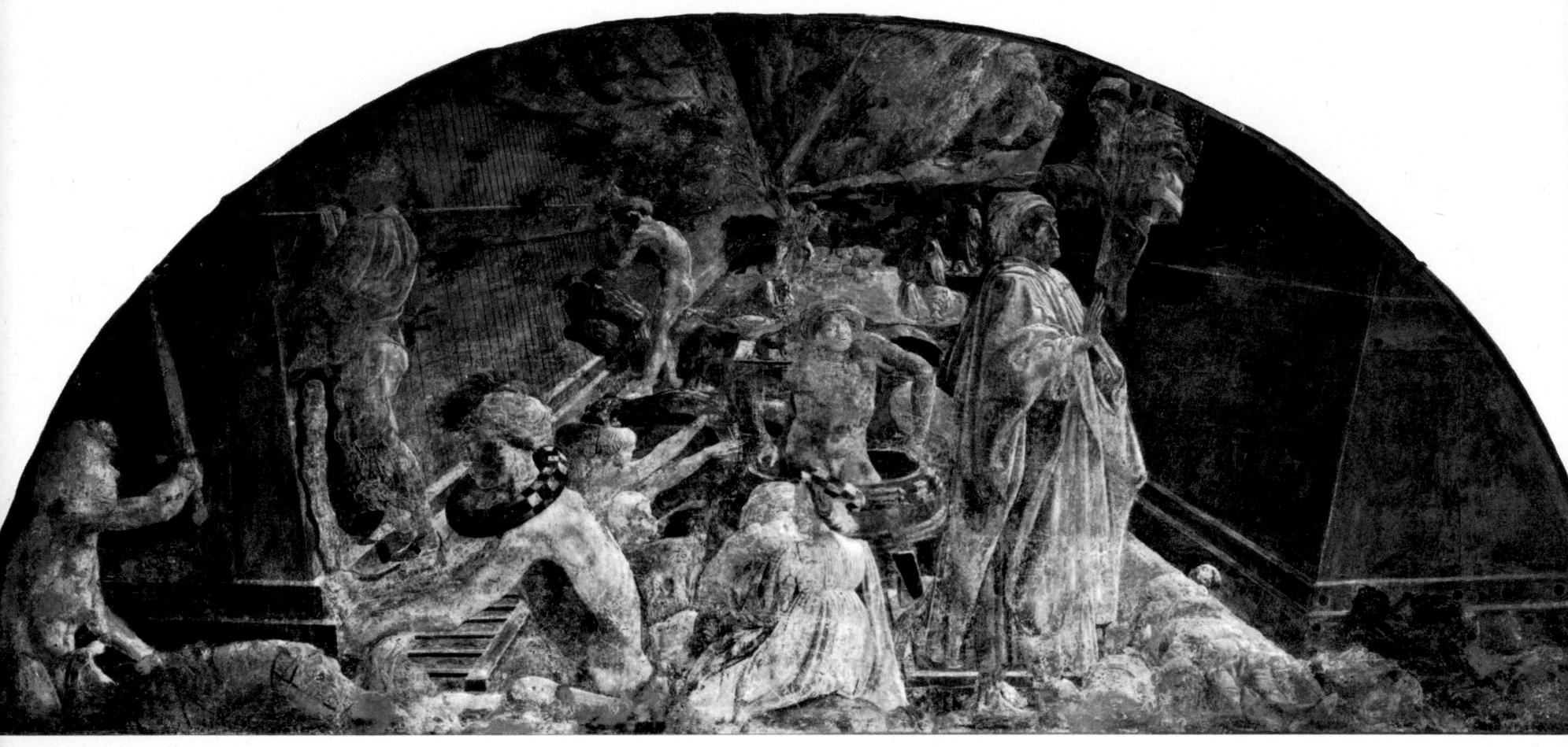

Sacrificing all verisimilitude to his passion for perspective, Uccello shows Noah's ark twice in the same composition, aligning it like two walls so as to obtain an effect of depth through the convergence of horizontals.

The first speculations on space were those of the architects of the Gothic cathedrals. They achieved in their naves the effects of perspective from which the Italians of the Quattrocento were to deduce the theoretical principles in order to apply them to painting. These architects were fully conversant with all the virtuosities of spatial design, including slowed-down and accelerated perspectives; but if the central nave provided a concrete demonstration of the thrust towards the future symbolizing the progress of Western man, the secondary effects of perspective obtained by a multiplication of aisles, tiers and columns expressed a confused aspiration towards a multidimensional space. During the same era, in France, all the arts apart from architecture remained the slaves of platitude and of superficial imagery.

The problems of pictorial space were to be born with painting itself, that is to say with Giotto. He succeeded in organizing empirically the shallow, horizonless space bequeathed him by the Middle Ages, and peopling that space with the actors of the sacred drama. In the fourteenth century the Italian painters tried to break out of this partitioned space, but could find no solution to the problem of how to deal with the horizon. The problem was solved simultaneously by van Eyck in Flanders, thanks to the observable process of aerial perspective,

and by the Florentines using the intellectual method of geometrical perspective. The medieval prison cell, from which the only escape had been by supernatural means, was opened up by the removal of one of its walls; now, Renaissance man, in his yearning for the Beyond, was able to see terrestrial horizons, luring him on to explore his existence here below. This geometric perspective which allowed the gaze to travel along the surface of the earth reflects the first action of space upon an earth which had hitherto been regarded as motionless and the centre of the universe. Now that the earth's boundaries were known, man's gaze was lifted above the horizon and into the heavens.

The century of great geographical discoveries was succeeded by the astronomical explorations of the sixteenth, seventeenth and eighteenth centuries. In 1543, the publication of Copernicus's system forced man to look beyond his terrestrial limitations; then, Tycho Brahé, Kepler, Galileo, Gassendi, Herschel, Newton, Laplace all proposed that men should face the challenge of infinity, either through observation or through calculation. It was perfectly normal that, in their own sphere of action, painters should have been eager to explore space, too. It is interesting to note that this quality is entirely absent from nineteenth-century painting, when the preoccupations of artists reverted to terrestrial and

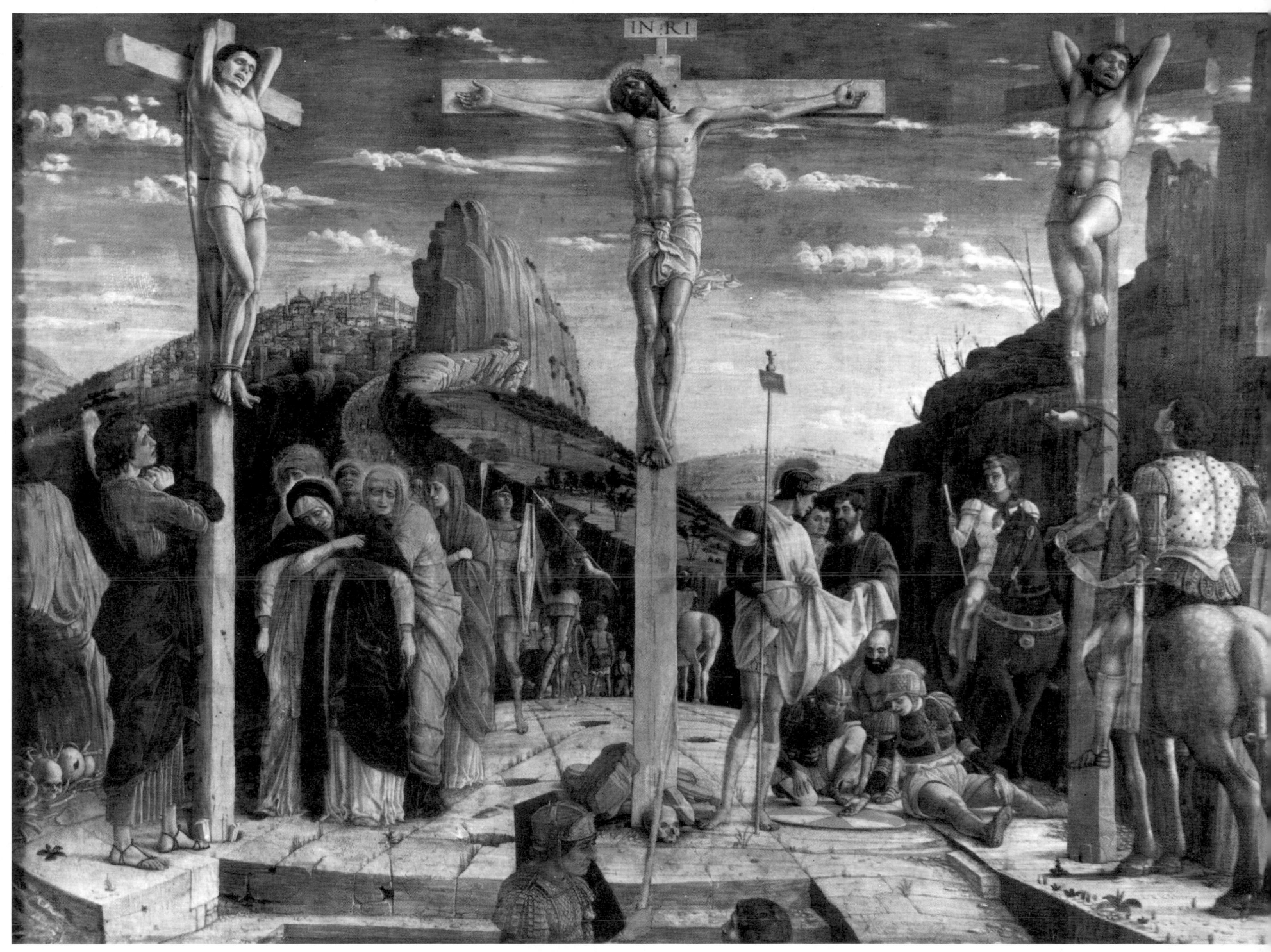

human horizons; their century was a great era of progress and discovery in the fields of geography, biology and psychology rather than in that of astronomy.

The most significant example of the intoxication with perspective to which the Florentines of the Quattrocento succumbed is the *Deluge* in the Chiostro Verde of Santa Maria Novella (*pl. 180*). In this composition, Uccello, at the risk of making it incomprehensible by juxtaposing two moments of a single action, conjures up two Noah's arks with walls

battlemented like castles and from which fleeing figures are streaming towards the horizon.

The virtuosity with which Mantegna applied the Florentine principles in order to derive completely original effects, especially in making the point of sight vary, went as far as situating that point below the level of the horizon. These innovations were symptoms of new processes of self-questioning, through which, following Leonardo and Fouquet, he achieved an understanding of the theoretical principles of *perspectiva communis*, based upon retinal

181 Andrea Mantegna (1431–1506). Detail of *The Crucifixion*. Paris, Louvre.

Mantegna is one of the very few painters who seem to have had a presentiment of the true principles of human vision, involving the appearance of a curved space.

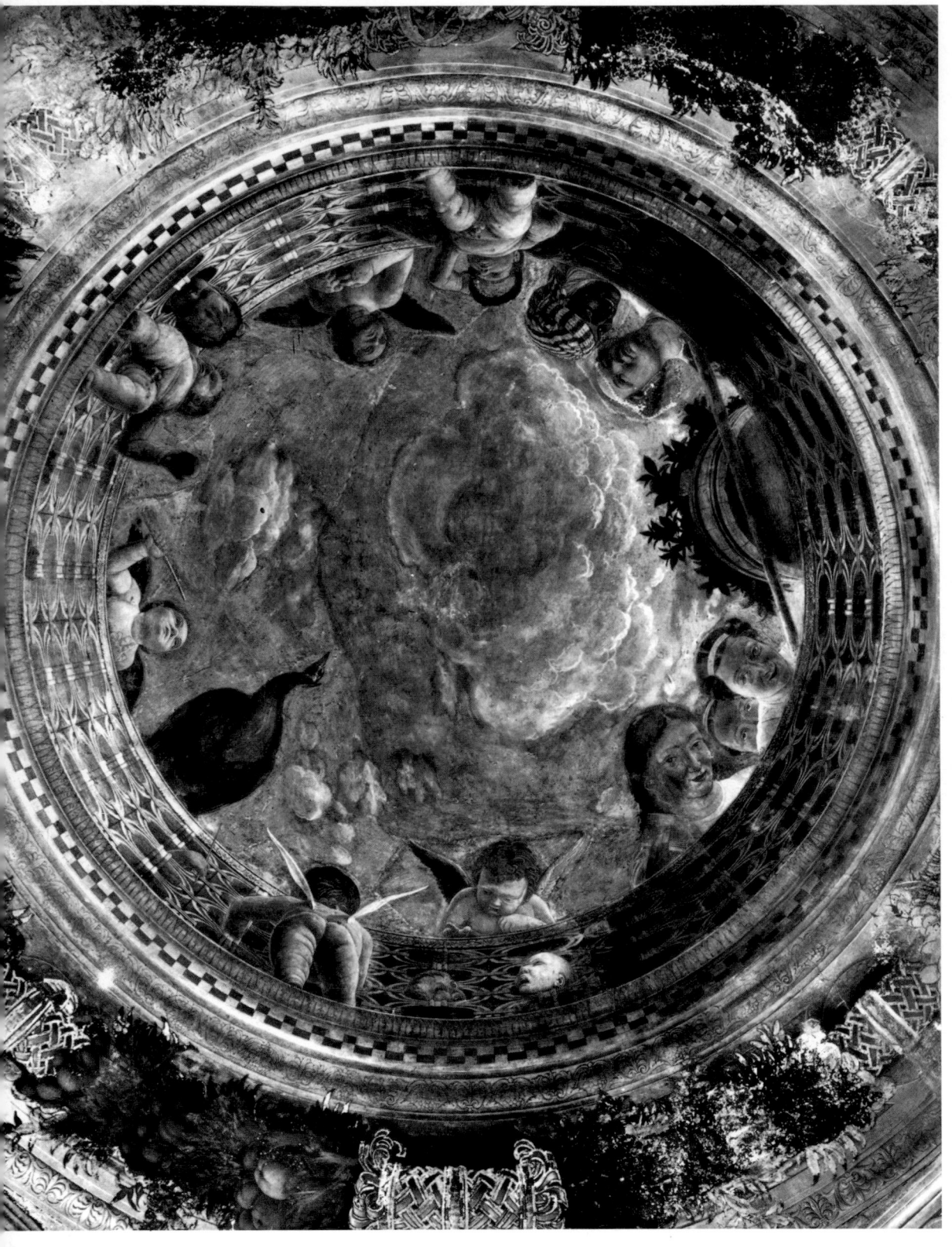

182 Andrea Mantegna. Lunette of the *Camera degli Sposi*.
Mantua, Palazzo Ducale.

Mantegna was the first painter to conceive the bold idea of
showing figures upright and looking straight down on the
spectator.

curvature (*pl. 181*). In 1474, Mantegna took a
giant step in freeing the painter from his bondage
to terrestrial surroundings: in the Camera degli
Sposi of the Gonzagas' Palazzo Ducale at Mantua
he turned his gaze vertically upwards and had the
audacity to conceive the first *sotto in sù* illusionistic
perspective in the history of painting, decorating the
dome in the ceiling with figures looking straight
down from behind a simulated balcony on to the
spectator below (*pl. 182*).

Mantegna, using *perspectiva artificialis* in a vertical
context, had demonstrated that architecture was the
indispensable adjunct to this approach. Correggio
was the first who dared to show figures floating in
mid-air on the concave surface of a cupola, without
making use of any of those architectural lines of
perspective which help to direct the eye through
space towards some imaginary vanishing-point.
This *Ascension*, painted on the cupola of San
Giovanni Evangelista in Parma (*pl. 118*), provided
an ideal theme for Correggio's imagination, which
thus envisaged a celestial orbital motion long before
Copernicus published his *De revolutionibus orbium
coelestium*.

Until the end of the eighteenth century artists
used one of two methods of ceiling painting, either
geometrical perspective expressed in architectural
terms, or spatial perspective in which hovering
figures are seen through the dome's hollow base.
The first of these two methods is known as *quadratura*.
This was first perfected during the second half of the
sixteenth century by mannerists such as Pellegrino
Tibaldi in Bologna and the brothers Cristofano and
Stefano Rosa in Venice; later, it became the preserve of specialists who were called in to provide
the backgrounds for painters of figures who had
been commissioned to decorate ceilings.

The greatest of all the *quadraturisti* was the Jesuit
lay-brother Andrea Pozzo; he achieved the masterpiece of illusionist perspective with his painting,
the *Glory of St Ignatius*, on the ceiling of San Ignazio
in Rome (1691–4), celebrating the founder of his
Order. In this theme, fictive architecture continues
the actual architecture so cunningly that the eye is
unable to discern the transition, and is prolonged
into a limitless sky which is a true vision of paradise.
The heavenly purpose of this triumphant monument
soaring up into the clouds is revealed by the successive arcades, which house a variety of allegories,
saints, angels and *putti*, a countless host filling with
its swirling flight this ideal space suggested by the
curvature of what once constituted a kind of lid,
confining the faithful within the sacred precincts.

The dizzy perspective of the ceiling of San
Ignazio is rigorously centred on a single point of

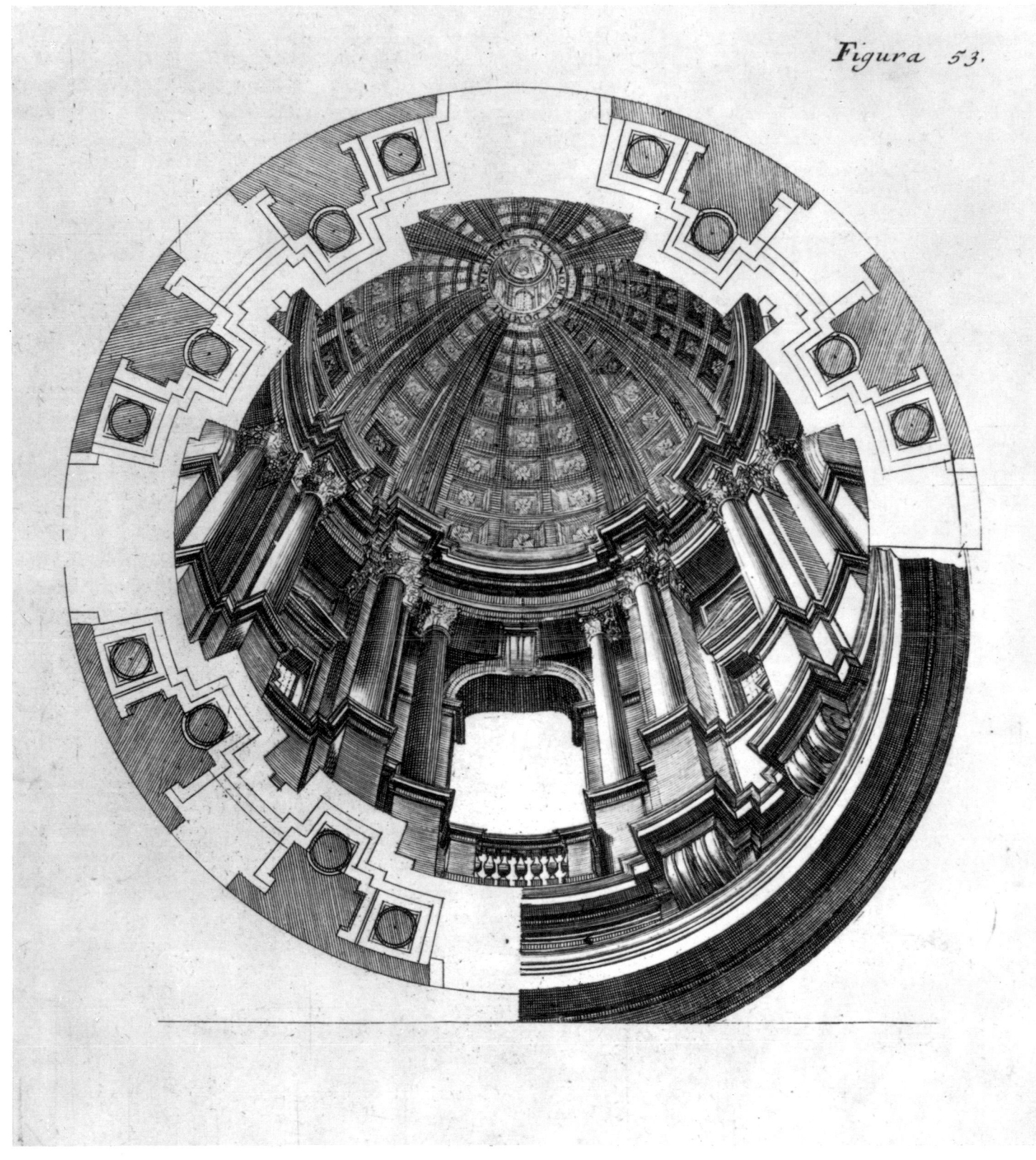

Figura 53.

sight situated in the centre of the nave at a spot marked by a circle of white marble. Padre Pozzo had gone even further in 1676, at San Francesco Saverio in Mondovi (Piedmont), where he had depicted on the curved surface of the central cupola the interior of an octagonal edifice opening up on

to the sky, seen in oblique perspective from the nave of the church. But his *tour de force* as a *quadraturista* was accomplished at San Ignazio where the fathers, wanting to save themselves the expense of constructing a cupola, had asked him to simulate one, seen from the nave, on a canvas stretched above the

To suggest on a horizontal surface the curve of a cupola seen in perspective, as Pozzo did in San Ignazio, must be considered one of the great masterpieces of *trompe-l'œil*.

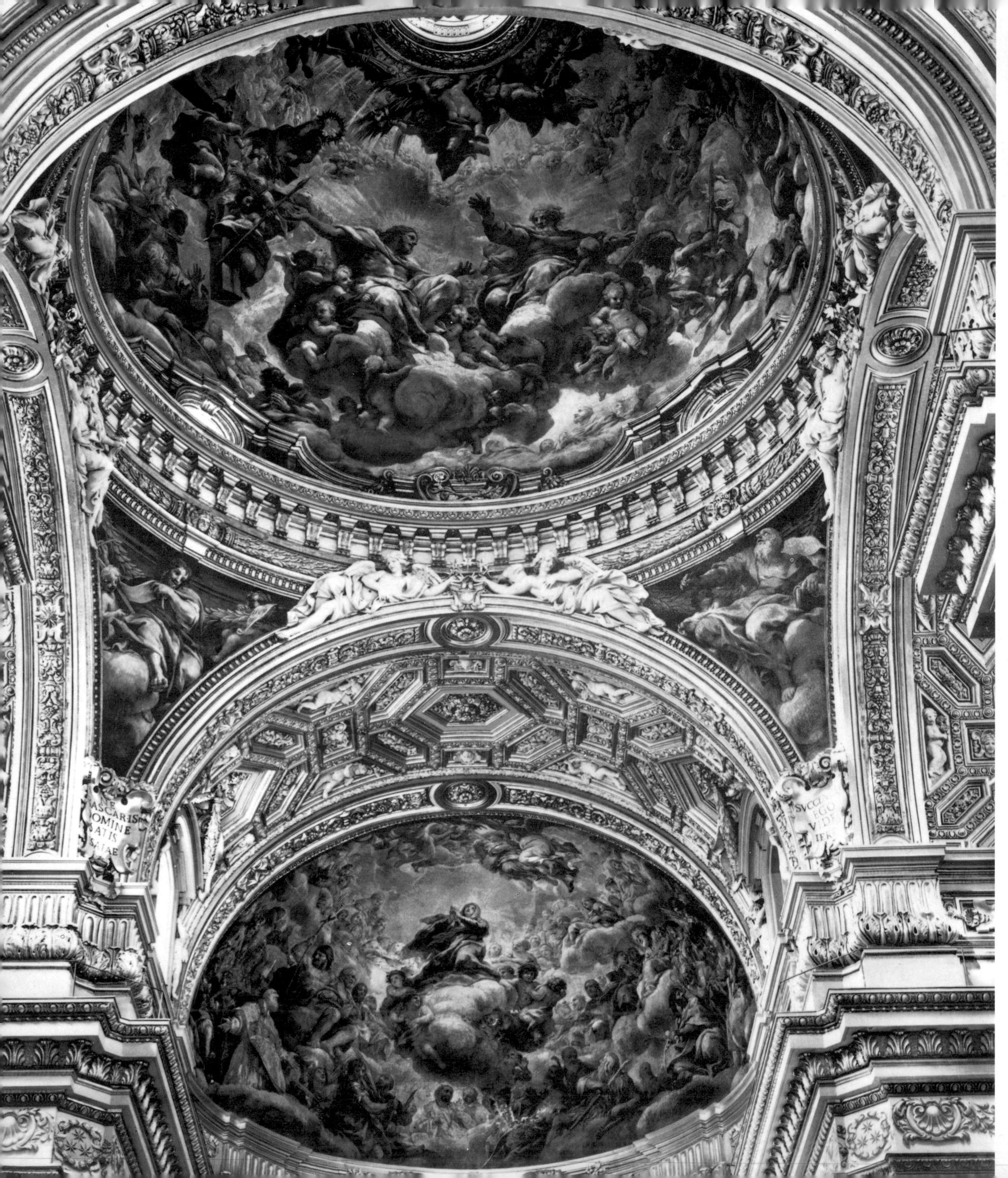

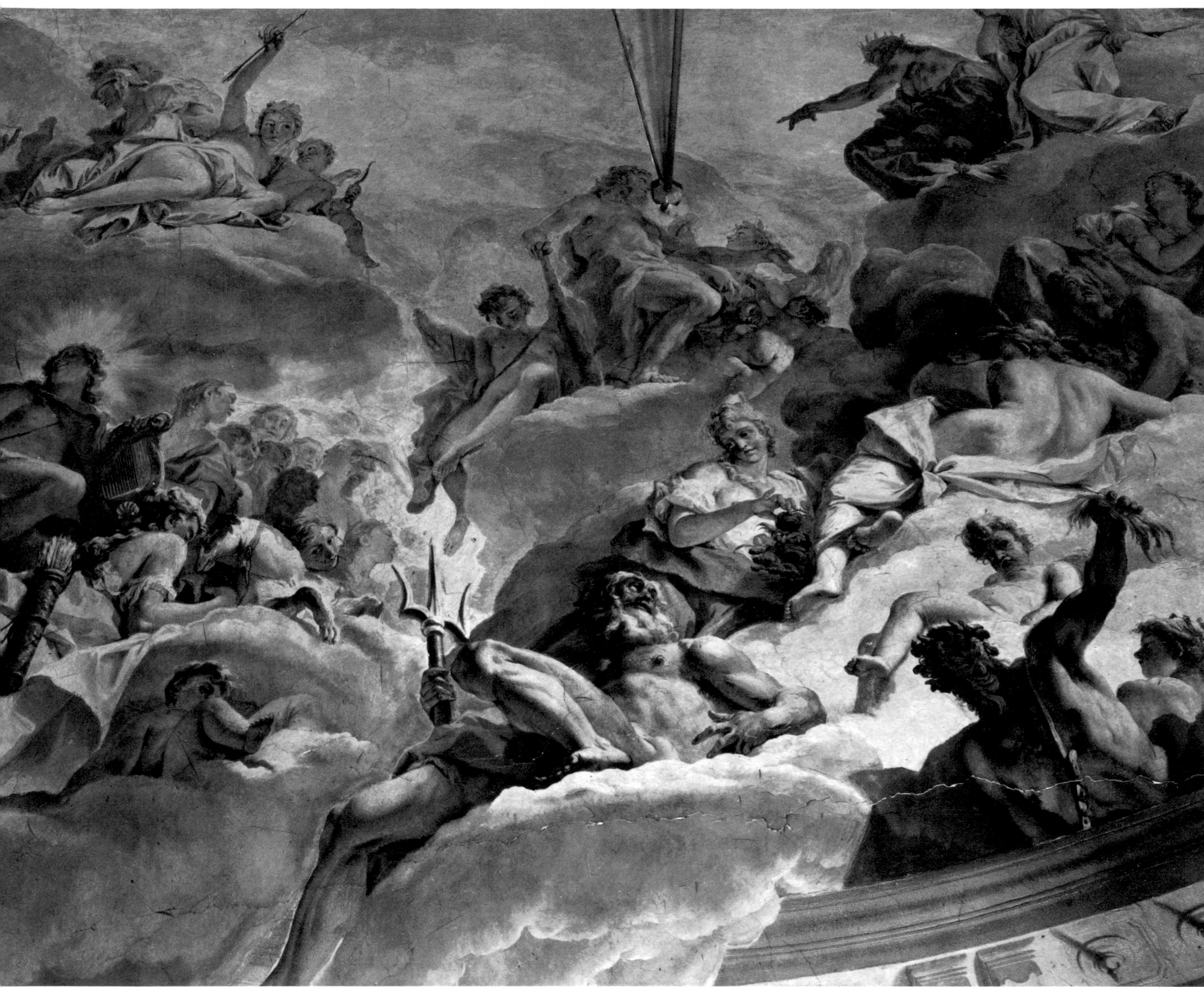

184 Pietro da Cortona (1596–1669). Frescoes in
Santa Maria in Vallicella, Rome.

185 Sebastiano Ricci (1659–1734). Detail of *Hercules
received on Olympus*. Ceiling in the Palazzo Marucelli,
Florence.

While Andrea Pozzo was making use of architectural
devices, Pietro da Cortona was following Correggio in
making his figures seem to float in mid-air.

Together with Piazzetta, Sebastiano Ricci introduced to
Venice the audacious innovation of an apparent gap in a
ceiling composition, through which a whole world can be
seen swirling around in the clouds.

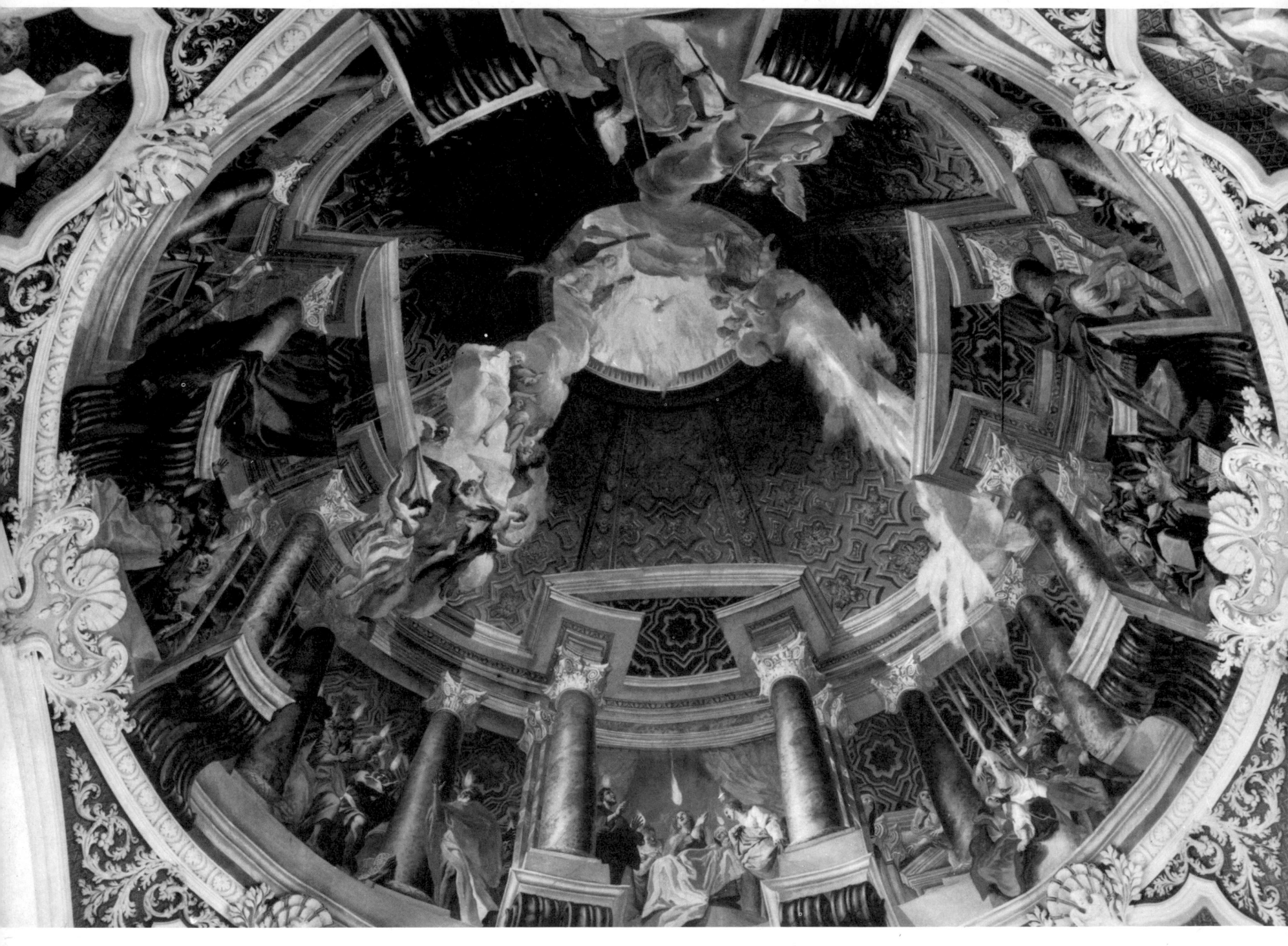

transept. This astonishing example of Pozzo's virtuosity, which has always attracted great admiration, was at one time damaged by fire, but has recently been restored and is now back in place again (*pl. 183*).

German artists of the eighteenth century were to achieve surprising effects from this soaring perspective, producing vertical illusions of simulated architecture which, when looked at from a particular vantage-point, seen *sotto in sù*, appear to be resting upon the ceiling (*pl. 186*).

At the same time as Padre Pozzo, a Genoese painter, Giovanni Battista Gaulli, known as Il Baciccia, obtained very fine effects by letting his hovering figures be seen through an apparent gap in the vault, a form of spatial expression which had already been used in Rome by Pietro da Cortona (*pl. 184*), Giovanni Lanfranco and Domenichino. This manner had the advantage of being less rigid than *quadratura*, deformations of bodies being far less apparent than deformations of architecture when viewed from a point other than the obligatory one; the whole spatial scaffolding evolves from anatomical foreshortenings, and this style of ceiling

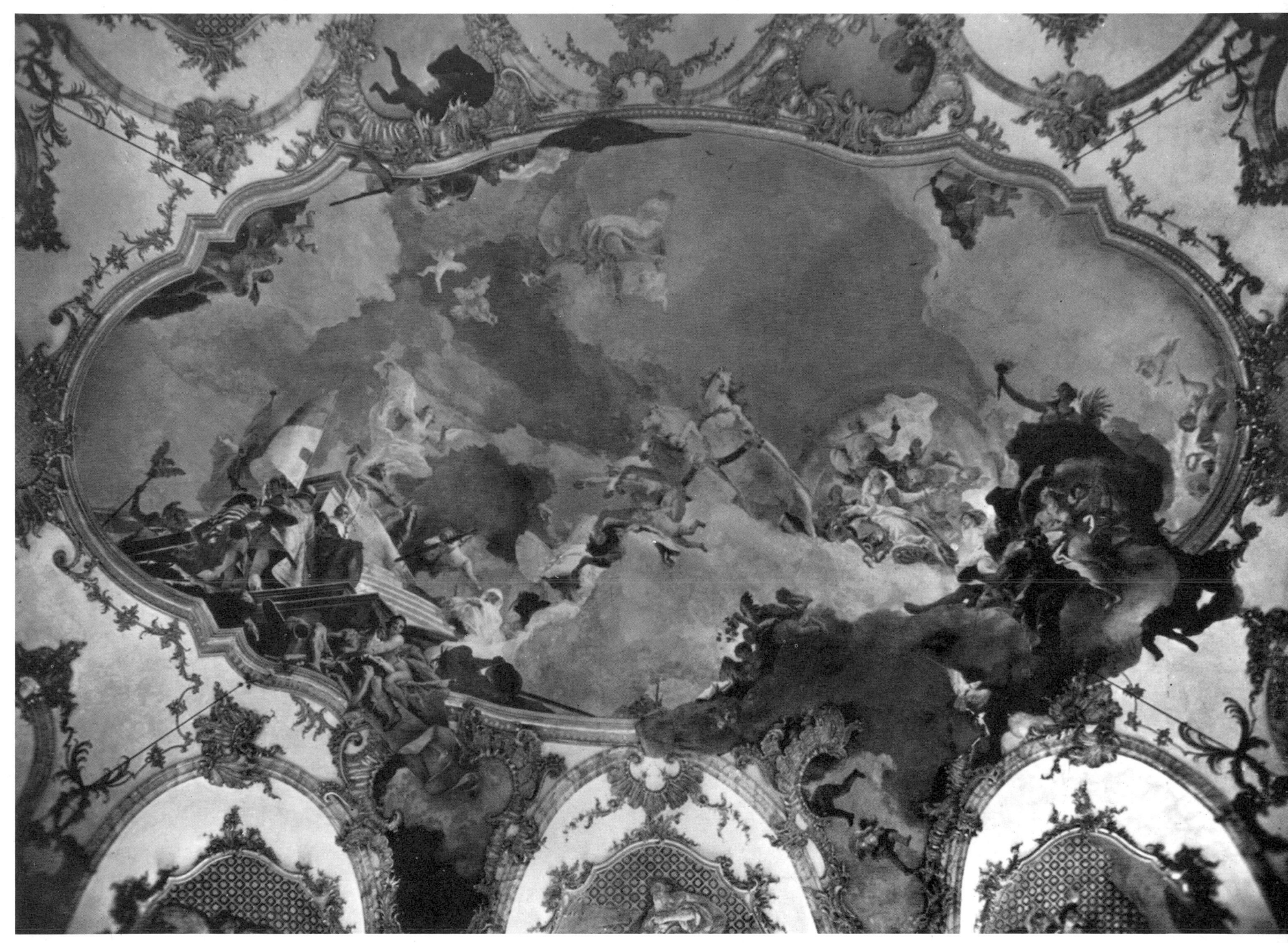

painting thus descends directly from Michelangelo's Sistine frescoes.

Pozzo's *quadratura*, like Il Baciccia's figural foreshortenings, demonstrated the inability of the Rome-based artists to conceive space in terms other than those defined by human attributes, living figures or works of architecture. It was left to the Venetians, traditionally responsive to atmospheric values, to express flight in pure space. Sebastiano Ricci, Giambattista Crosato and Giambattista Piazzetta reinforced the resources of perspective with those of colour and light; by firmly eliminating all architectural references they allowed the spectator's imagination to soar away from the ground and hover in space (*pls 179, 185*). An effect of spatial depth is obtained by gradation of light, the lightest parts of the composition being the most distant, while shadows are extended over the nearest parts, around the rim of the opening where gesticulating figures, silhouetted against the background, serve as a foil for the distant figures. The sky, in which clouds with dark under-sides and luminous crests are floating, is traversed in breadth and depth by oblique streams of flying figures; these figures grow increasingly

187 Giambattista Tiepolo (1696–1770). *Apollo leading Beatrix of Burgundy to her betrothed, Frederick Barbarossa.* Fresco in the dome of the great hall of the Würzburg Residenz.

It was in the ceilings which he decorated at Würzburg that Tiepolo gave expression most happily to his cavalcades of forms apparently vanishing into luminous clouds.

disembodied with distance, becoming finally transformed into impalpable forms blending into the play of luminous light.

In his *Glory of St Dominic* at Santi Giovanni e Paolo in Venice (*pl. 179*), Piazzetta, by using a diagonal point of sight, situates the foregrounds on the part of the ceiling which is furthest away but first to come into view, whereas the distances loom up gradually on the nearer part of the ceiling as the spectator moves forward. In this way, the worshippers are immediately confronted by the vision as they enter the church. German artists were to exploit this illusionistic procedure with great virtuosity.

Throughout Europe, Venetian painters were called upon to enliven palaces and churches with their visions. Tiepolo, the greatest of all these magicians of spatial enchantments, painted his masterpiece on the ceiling over the stairway of the Würzburg Residenz (*pl. 187*). No architectural setting could have been more appropriate for the expression of this spatial theme of ascension. At San Ignazio in Rome the spectator contemplates the Almighty as from the bottom of a well, symbolizing the condition of the Christian plunged in the darkness of his terrestrial existence, for whom the light appears as an ideal vision of the after-life. At Würzburg, on the other hand, the spectator's soul is seized by a kind of intoxication as he mounts the steps leading to the empyrean. This cinematic unfolding of space is made possible by the combination of several successive vanishing-points. The depiction of the four quarters of the world around the rim of the opening leads the spectator's imagination towards the limits of the earth's horizon before projecting it into the glittering light in which the gods of Olympus are bathed.

One may well be astonished at the ease with which the Venetians abandoned the resources of oil-painting to which they were traditionally attached, in favour of fresco through which they were able to obtain effects of aerial transparency. While oil had allowed them to express the delicate shadings of the earth's atmosphere, fresco gave them the means to imagine that crystalline purity of absolute space which man was to discover much later when he started flying above the clouds with his own wings.

The Venetians may be said to have inaugurated a new kind of spatial invocation. The centred space of Padre Pozzo had been the symbol of eternity; the actuating forces of the Venetian ceilings seemed to thrust the spectator into a quest for the infinite.

The art of ceiling painting, elaborated in Italy, was practised extensively, later on, in the rococo palaces and churches of the German-speaking countries. The treatise written by Andrea Pozzo in 1698, *Prospettiva de' pittori e architetti . . .*, was soon translated into a number of languages, including English (*Rules and Examples of Perspective . . .*, London 1707), and served to spread the methods of *quadratura*. These methods were used as alternatives to aerial perspective, and often in combination with it, by Austrian and German painters. The finest light effects were achieved by the Austrian artist Paul Troger, whose silvery colour scheme at the Altenburg monastery has transformed the Apocalypse into a glorification of the Virgin Mary. The most proficient manipulators of space were doubtless the Asam brothers of Munich who worked in collaboration, Egid Quirin doing the stucco-work and Cosmas Damian the painting (*pl. 186*). Their most astonishing creation is perhaps the chapel of Maria de Victoria at Ingolstadt. The problem here was that they had only a very low ceiling to work with. The simulated architecture, in which the Virgin appears on the threshold of a palace, retains its vertical position only from one particular point of sight, indicated at the entry to the nave by a disc of white stone. Once this point is passed, the architecture vanishes above the spectator's head and the figures come into view in the foreground. In all these Bavarian churches, the ceiling's illusionistic space is designed to be seen by a perambulating spectator who can see figures disappear and others suddenly appear in a play of multiple perspectives; the compartments of space develop like the movements of a symphony.

By taking increasing liberties with pictorial space, German painters ended by destroying it altogether, an evolution comparable to that which saw cubism succeed impressionism. Exaggerating the obliqueness of perspectives, Matthäus Gunther dissolved space by allowing the planes to glide away from each other; Franz Josef Spiegler twisted space in the spasm of a nebula (*pl. 188*); Johann Baptist Zimmermann made it as stormy as the sea; Carlo Carlone slashed it into strips like rocaille ornament. With most of the Bavarian painters the colour becomes smoky and sulphurous; in the paintings of Anton Maulpertsch, the Magnasco of ceiling painting, the light can only pierce the thick clouds in thin shafts. As soon as it reached Germany, ceiling painting ceased being a feast for the eyes and became dramatic. Tiepolo's solar splendour, Paul Troger's delicate shades of dawn, gave way to the fires of a twilight which foreshadowed the eclipse of ceiling painting itself, about to disappear for ever after having created so many breathtaking spectacles for three centuries.

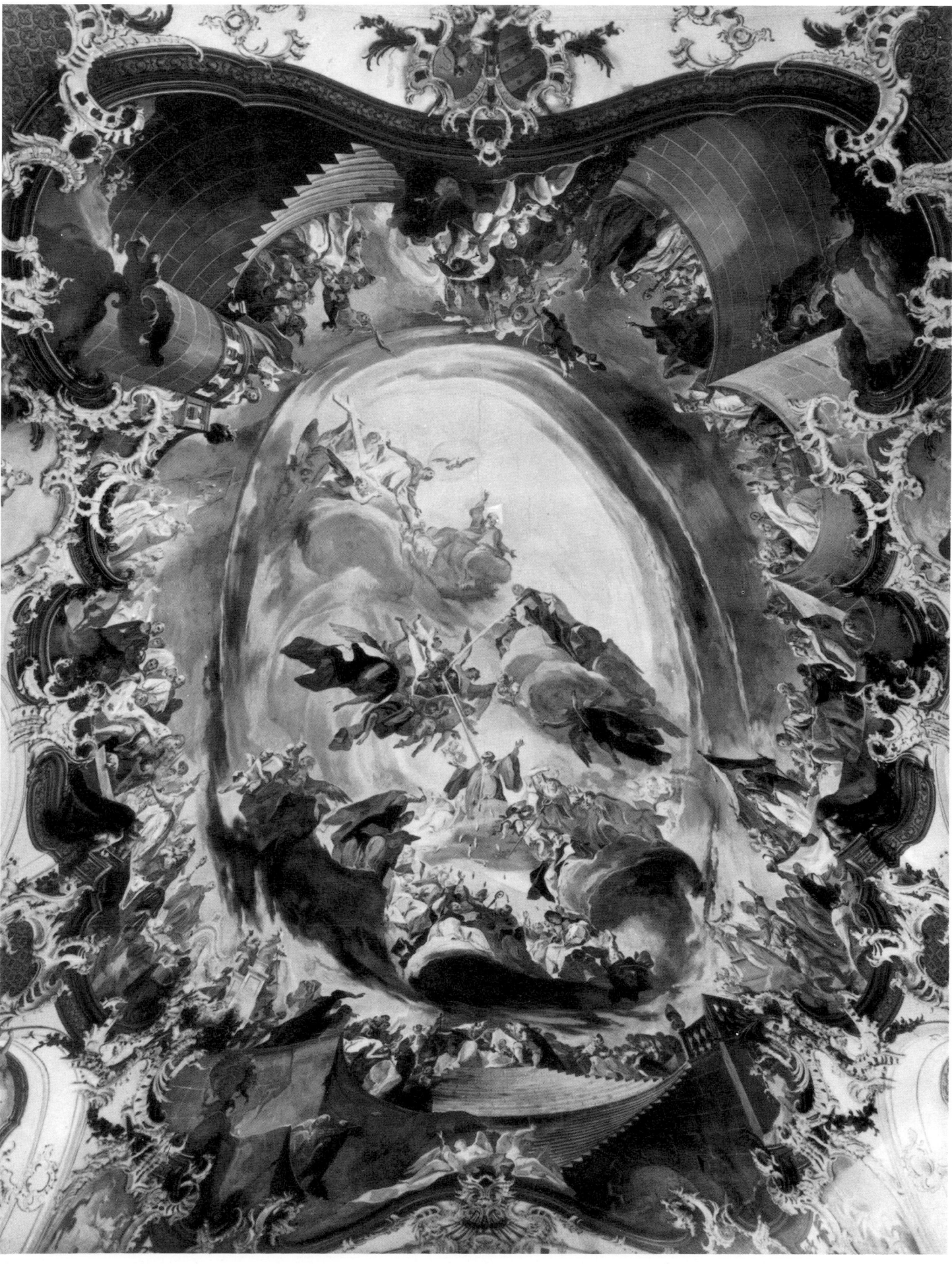

188 Franz Josef Spiegler
(1691–1757). *Vision of St Benedict*.
Fresco in the nave of the church of
Zwiefalten.

In the compositions of the German
ceiling-painters of the rococo period,
space twists and swirls like a nebula.

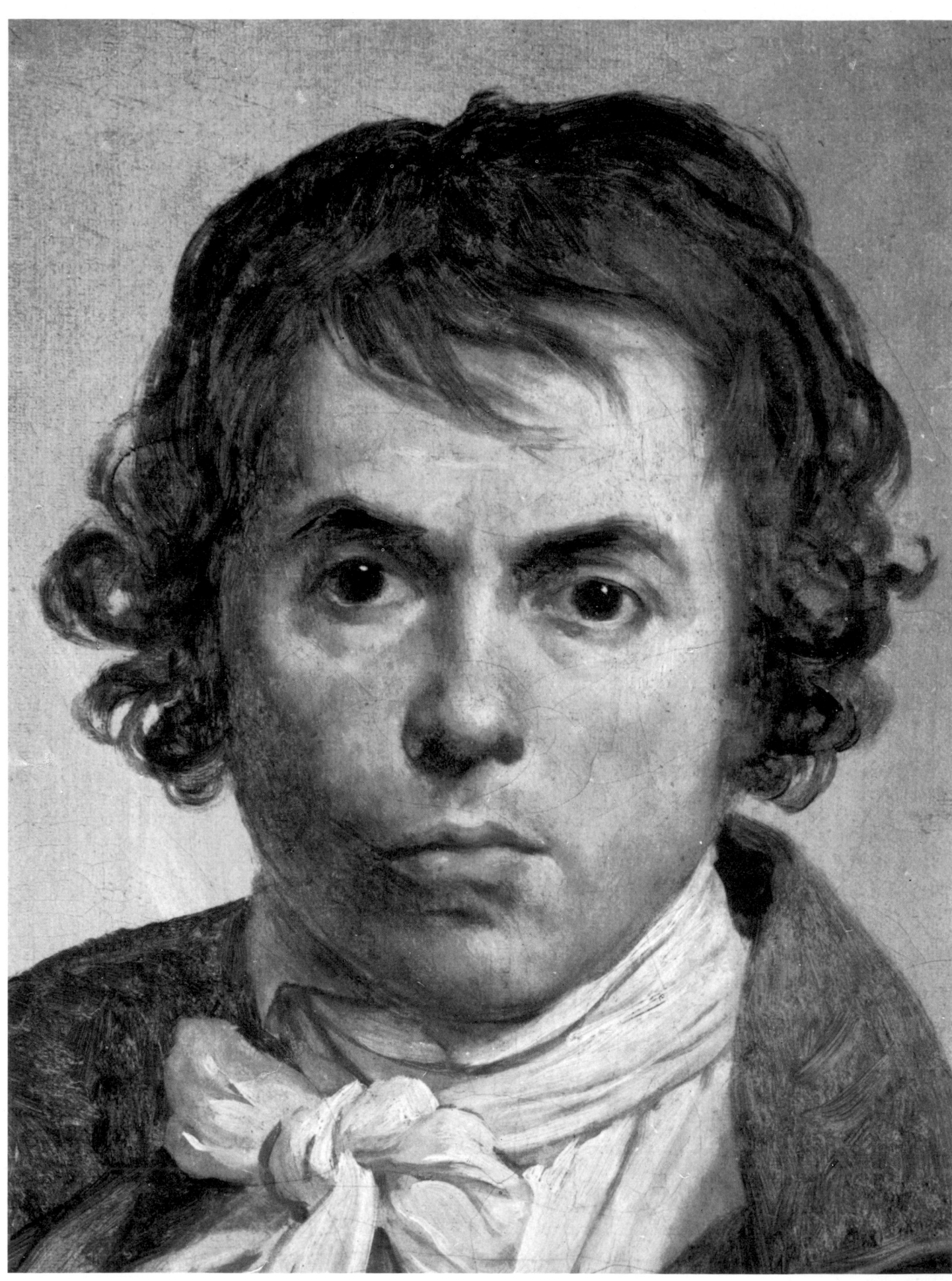

189 Jacques-Louis David (1784–1825). *Self-portrait*. Paris, Louvre.

14 Romantic conflict

In 1775, the French architect Nicolas Ledoux received a commission for an industrial building, the saltworks at Chaux; although the practical details were laid down in advance, he was given complete freedom to decide on the style, being instructed simply that it should reflect 'the simplicity of a factory'. It might have been thought that the social, humanitarian and physiocratic ideas which haunted his imagination would have inspired him to heights of inventiveness corresponding to the originality of the theme. But not at all: the design he produced was Palladian neo-Greek.

Ledoux showed rather more courage in his project for an ideal city which was to be built round the Chaux saltworks, although certain ideas, such as having the piers of the bridge look like triremes and giving a forge the shape of a pyramid, were merely eccentric. Some of his designs were so visionary that a modern German historian, Emil Kaufmann (in his *Ursprung und Entwicklung der autonomen Architektur*, Vienna 1933), has hailed him as a precursor of Le Corbusier; but these dreams of a new architecture never got beyond the theoretical stage, any more than did those of other architects of the time, such as Etienne-Louis Boullée, François-Joseph Bélanger, Louis-Jean Desprez, Pierre-Jules Delépine, studied more recently by the same author (*Architecture in the Age of Reason*, Cambridge, Mass., 1955). Ever since the fifteenth century, there has existed, alongside real architecture, a 'paper architecture' of pure speculation produced by artists and engineers; this phenomenon became particularly conspicuous towards the end of the eighteenth and beginning of the nineteenth century, but little of it was translated into fact.

After a few isolated experiments, architecture resumed the yoke of antiquity from which it did not manage to free itself again until the end of the nineteenth century. The occasional nineteenth-century attempts at liberation were designed simply to impose a different antiquarian aesthetic, that of Gothic. The German architect Karl Friedrich Schinkel, equally adaptable to Gothic and neo-Greek principles, is perfectly typical of this antiquarian horizon which limited the vision of nineteenth-century architecture.

The situation in painting was equally strange. In Rome, in 1785, the great French painter Jacques-Louis David unveiled before a stupefied public a picture that was to have a profound and lasting effect on aesthetic attitudes. This was the *Oath of the Horatii*. Inspired by a performance of Corneille's play *Horace*, and drawing admittedly upon Poussin, this picture must be considered one of the most astonishing applications of the antiquarian aesthetic of all time. More than three centuries after the dreams of Alberti, it seemed that art was still limiting its aims to the restoration of antiquity, and this on the eve of an earth-shaking revolution. But the revolution itself was undertaken in the name of antiquity; what the members of the National Convention wanted was to restore the idea of a republic based on the best possible model, that of the ancient Romans. Brutus was honoured as one of the heroes of humanity, until the establishment of the First Empire made Brutus's victim Caesar a more appropriate hero.

Humanity's capacity to project its thoughts and its conscience into the future is a contemporary phenomenon. Although the sense of spiritual adventure has always been an essential factor in Western civilization, even those most clearly driven by this sense have always masked it with curiously regressive motivations inspired by some confused dream of a golden age buried deep in our collective unconscious. Even the Christian, his whole being directed towards a future life, is in fact aspiring to rediscover primal innocence. In the fifteenth century, Italian thinkers were unwilling to admit that all their new ideas constituted more than a rebirth of Graeco-Roman civilization, a 'Renaissance', just as Luther, Calvin and Zwingli viewed their activities as simply a 'reform'. In 1793, the *sans-culottes* invoked the shades of Cato, Brutus and Scipio. Napoleon, the genius who assumed the reins of power, made Plutarch's parallel *Lives* his bible, and it remained so on St Helena. David, exiled to Brussels, advised Antoine-Jean Gros: 'Reread your Plutarch'. Indeed, the unhappy Gros, torn between his faith in antiquity and his conscience as a modernist, found the dilemma insoluble and committed suicide.

190 Jacques-Louis David. *The Death of Marat*. Brussels, Musée Royal des Beaux-Arts.

This dilemma, and the interminable quarrel that resulted between the Ancients and the Moderns, was central to the whole nineteenth century and produced its full quota of martyrs: the innovators, whether they were those first called 'Shakespearians' and then romantics, or the impressionists, were exiled from the Salons. All these pioneers were damned by the officials who had been entrusted by the establishment with the task of protecting society against any revolutionary spirit, even in the field of aesthetics.

In the romantic era, expression in the visual arts found itself completely out of joint with literary creation. The intellectual revolution had been won by the end of the eighteenth century, although it should be remembered that in order to free themselves of the shackles of classical antiquity the German and English innovators had sought for alternative precedents among the mists of northern mythology. Napoleon's favourite reading, besides his Plutarch, was provided by the poems of 'Ossian' (in fact, the contemporary Scotsman James Macpherson) which provided inspiration for another Bonapartist painter, Girodet (much to David's disgust). But the literary vogue for northern traditions at the moment of the first stirrings of romanticism still left plenty of other directions open. Jean-Jacques Rousseau, for one, was prepared to turn back as far as the 'noble savage'.

Viewed in this context, the resurgence of artistic interest in antiquity at the moment of birth of the modern world is one of the most astonishing phenomena of history. The lack of harmony between literature and the plastic arts scarcely supports Dvořák's theory of the unity of all forms of creative expression during a single era. On the contrary, such a discord would seem to lend credibility to the theories of Wölfflin and Focillon on the life of forms: if neoclassicism made a sudden appearance during the eighteenth century, it was surely because baroque in its decline called forth its opposite, despite the fact that this form was absolutely out of step with the first romantic wave which was then sweeping over minds and feelings. In addition, the neoclassical tendency was enormously encouraged by the discoveries of Pompeii and Herculaneum.

But the painters were given little chance to develop their speculations in peace and quiet. David was caught up heart and soul in the Revolution, and politics left him little time to paint. The empire offered a vast field to his imagination. When he was asked to depict the emperor distributing eagles, an exalting subject for someone so passionately attached to the idea of glory, he was not satisfied to allow the colonels bearing the standards to run

as though they were athletes: one of them even strikes a pose in imitation of Giambologna's *Mercury*. David was more at home with the *Consecration of the Emperor Napoleon I*, where he was able to give himself up entirely to his natural genius, which was bounded by his passion for antiquity on one side and his reverence for nature on the other. David's portraits, which he painted with some impatience since they distracted him from his antiquarian obsessions, display his talents at their best. With these portraits, painted with a typically French naturalness and dignity, he gave the world a final example of that beautiful traditional handling associated with the eighteenth century, and which in the nineteenth century seemed to have survived only in the crafts. He uses this traditional technique to give brilliant expression to the sense of equilibrium of man reconciled with nature and drawing from this harmony the joy of invention.

David's approach to his large, symbolic set pieces was to use the unexpected nature of the event itself to provide the impulse that would fire the spectator's imagination. Since *Le Peletier de Saint-Fargeau dying* was later destroyed by a family ashamed at having included a regicide among its ancestors, the only remaining picture in this vein is *The Death of Marat* (*pl. 190*).

Often quoted as a successful example of this revolutionary inspiration, the *Little drummer-boy Bara* does not reveal the same flair. Whatever David may have thought, the drummer-boy's nudity has nothing heroic about it, and suggests, rather, something Hellenistic, with a vague homosexual flavour which is not exactly virile; some of the pictures which Ingres was to paint later come to mind. But *The Death of Marat*, a picture of heroic simplicity, is truly the starting-point of modern painting. David undoubtedly drew all his intuitive power of expression from his republican convictions, and his later Empire compositions were false coin; *The Death of Marat* was born of harmony between man and artist, as was the *Napoleon crossing the Alps* in which he was still painting the standard-bearer of the revolution.

The painter who kept David's revolutionary spark alight was Théodore Géricault, who was not his pupil but that of another classicist, Guérin. Inspired by events, Géricault tended to consider his artistic education, which he completed by a voyage to Rome, as simply a working method rather than an end in itself. At the Restoration he had enlisted in the king's musketeers, and during the Hundred Days followed Louis XVIII on his flight. Although he soon abandoned his military career, Géricault remained in direct contact with everyday life. He

In painting *The Death of Marat* in 1797, David opened the way to modern painting.

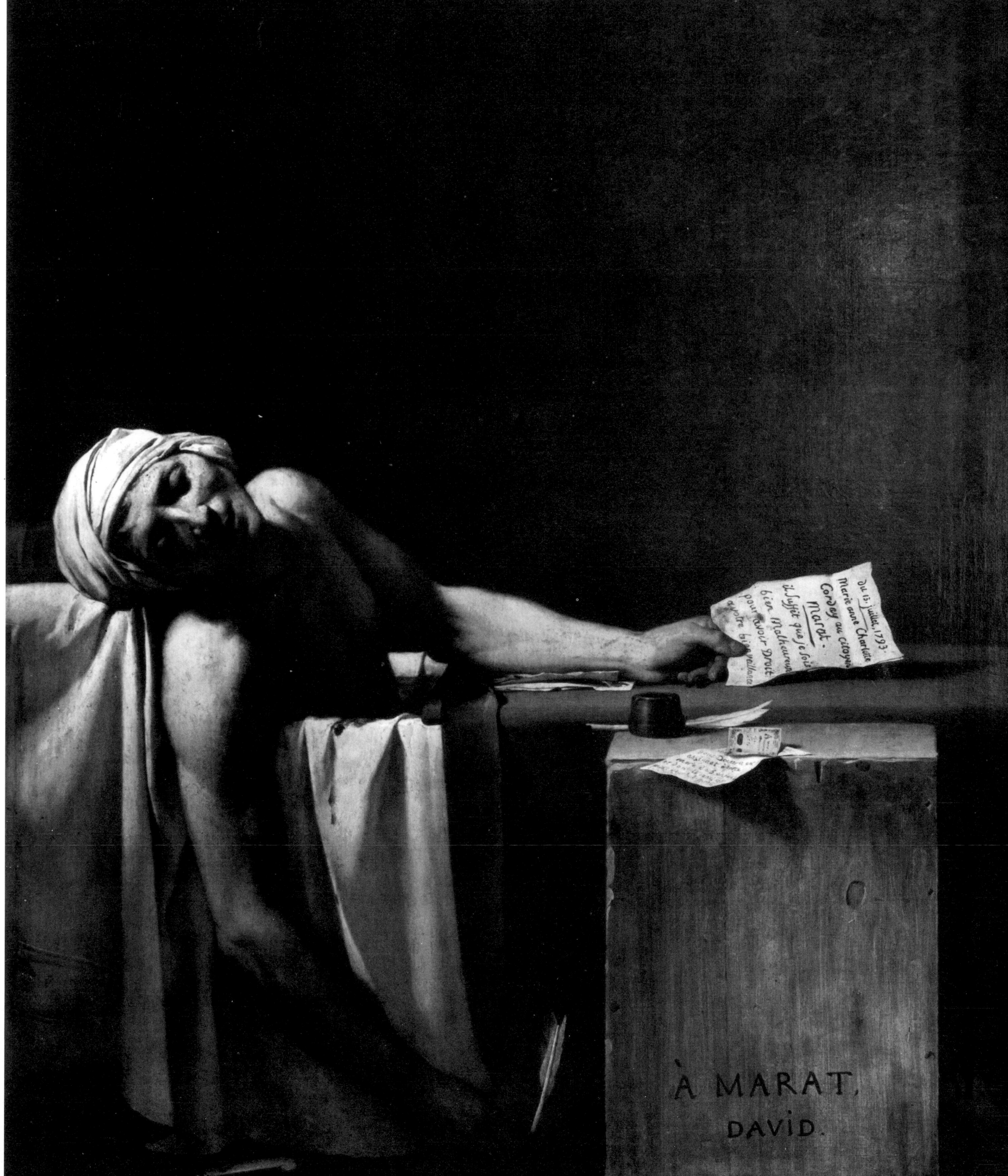

finally shook off the antiquarianism which was obsessing artists' minds and acting as a brake on their imaginations; he also managed to escape from another form of subservience to the past, the medievalism which aroused the ire of David and of the neoclassicist aesthetician Quatremère de Quincy. The example of antiquity was for Géricault a method rather than an aim. A true follower of David, he made the human body the very principle of art, the only other feature of nature which interested him at all being the horse; and that noble animal, used as a symbol of strength subdued, has always been a 'humanist' element in art.

After his return to Paris from Italy in 1817, Géricault began work on the *Raft of the 'Medusa'* (*pl. 191*), studying all the details of its composition during the course of an inquiry comparable to that of Stendhal writing *The Red and the Black*, before exhibiting the finished picture at the 1819 Salon. Although this was an entirely new kind of subject for him, he remained entirely faithful to his humanist convictions; the *Raft of the 'Medusa'* bears the same kind of relationship to David's *Horatii* as the *Laocoön* bears to the frieze of the Parthenon. Using the human body to express force, pain or death, Géricault transformed David's classicism into baroque. The conflict of rival forces provided the inspiration for his art, and he adopted subjects which would allow him to make full use of the play of muscles to demonstrate the resources of the human body. He never tired of glorifying the body, even when he painted the *Raft of the 'Medusa'*, in which, after so many preliminary studies, he still forgot that his shipwrecked mariners were supposed to be starving. His encounter in Rome with antiquity and with the work of Michelangelo had provided him with a sure knowledge of the human body. Delacroix entirely neglected this approach: for him, the body was less an anatomical organism than the clothing for a soul. Géricault also retained from classicism the feeling of those compositions constructed in bas-relief, and, in this respect again, differed from Delacroix who visualized events as occurring in a vortex.

Géricault might have provided an entirely fresh impetus to the romantic school in France had he not died tragically young. Indeed, he might well have become the greatest French painter of the first part of the century. His liberal political opinions inspired him to plan three monumental compositions, but only the *Raft of the 'Medusa'* was completed. We can only imagine how superb the *Riderless horse races, Rome* would surely have looked in the colossal dimensions he had already sketched out while in Rome. And the *Slave trade* would doubtless have

This work was conceived and painted, after much reflection, by Géricault as a veritable manifesto of modern painting.

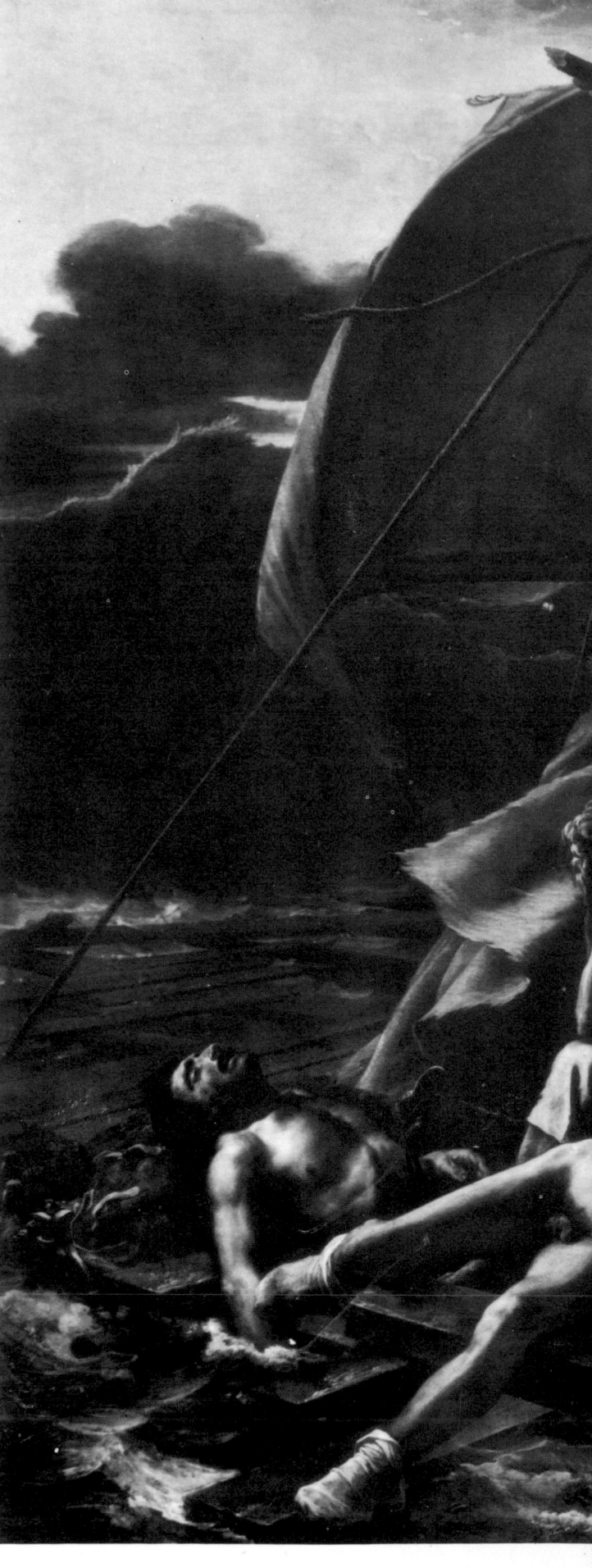

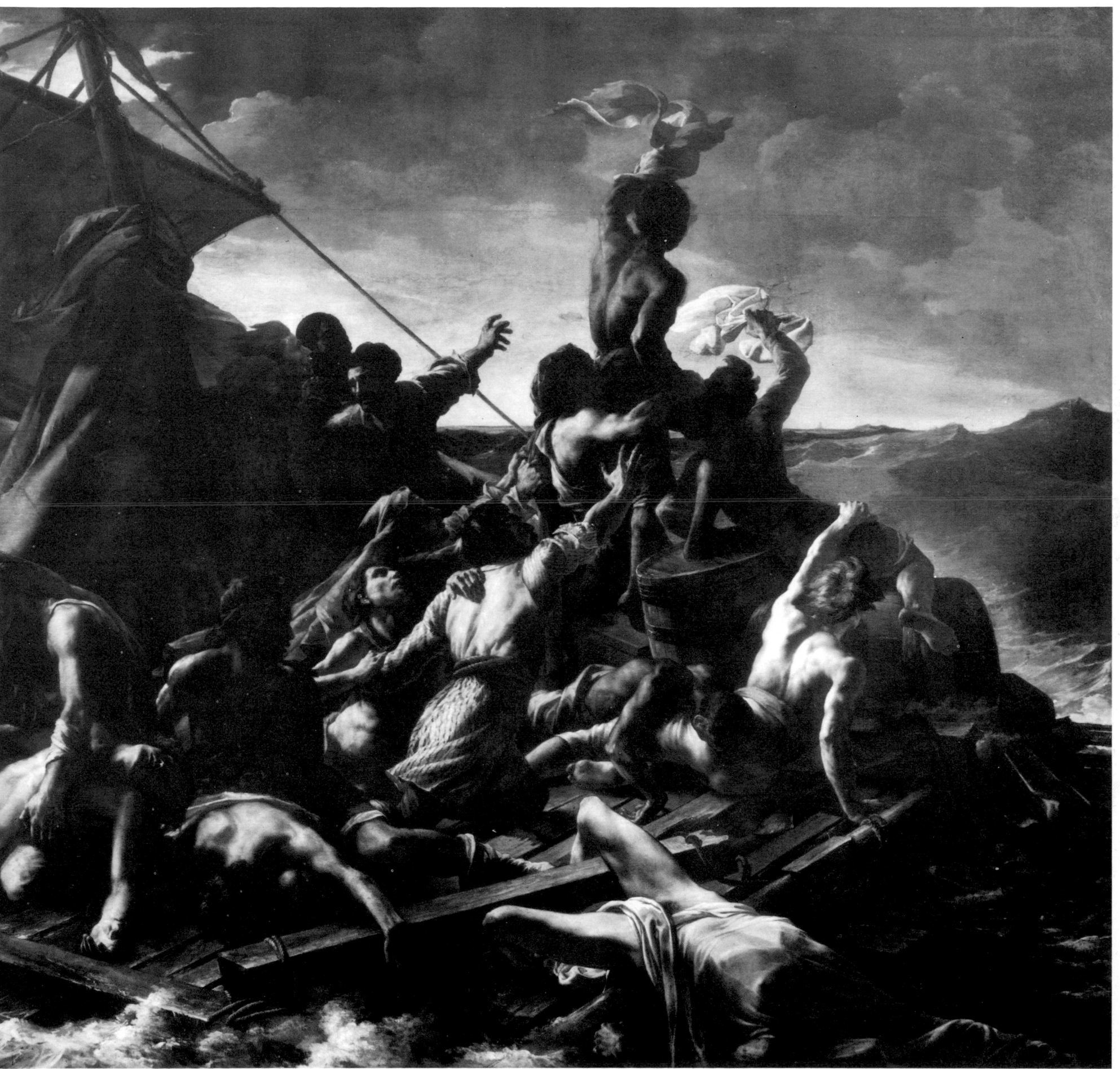

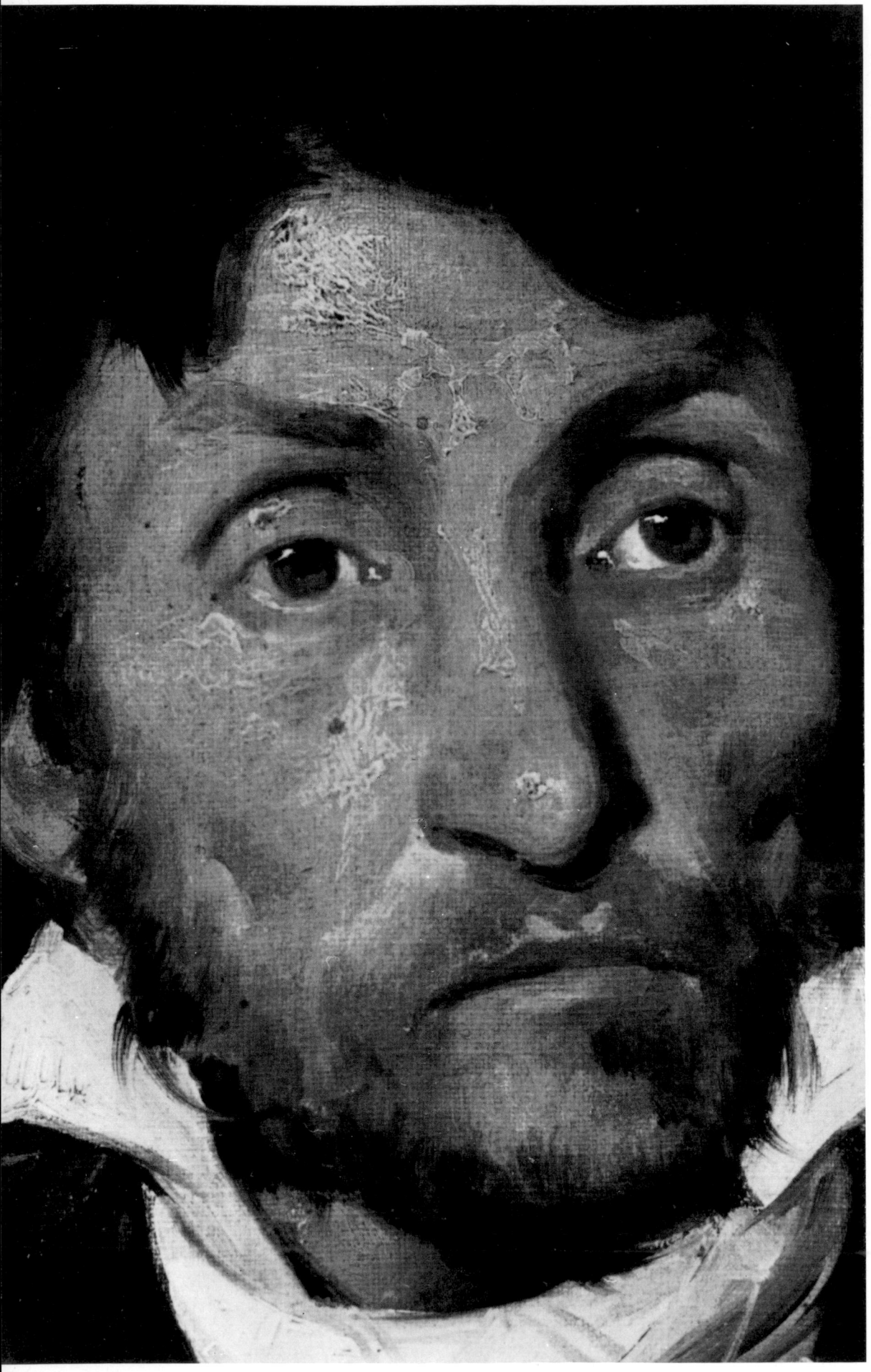

showed the world what a painter of genius might achieve when inspired by a progressive political philosophy. The *Raft of the 'Medusa'* is a grandiose composition, marred only by the lamentable consequences of painting with bitumen, a substance with which the artist was experimenting at the time. The English painting which he studied while in London, the best existing examples of technique for painters of that era, soon cured him of this eccentricity, as can be seen in the portraits of madmen he painted at the Salpêtrière for Dr Georget (*pl. 192*). These facial studies, which constitute Géricault's final group of paintings, might have opened up a new path to painting: the careful study of human psychology, paying particular attention to morbid states, leads to a better understanding of what constitutes normality. Géricault was a precursor here, too, in the interest he took in those suffering from mental illness, but this idea of seeking the individual through the byways of tortured souls, a quest demanding absolute objectivity on the part of the artist, interested no one after his death.

All the portraits emanating from this great portrait-painting century were typical compromises between the three factors traditionally present in this branch of art: the artist, the model, and the ideal human type required by the society of the time. In this direction, Géricault continued to follow David, particularly the David who had painted his own portrait and so determined, with some cruelty, to perpetuate for posterity the details of his face made hideous by a physical deformity (*pl. 189*). Working in the seclusion of a prison cell, and thus freed of all the social constraints which he respected when confronted with an unknown model, in this self-portrait David laid bare his soul. He set out to paint all that belonged to him and to him alone, and notably his disfigurement; the ardent revolutionary expressed perfectly on canvas the wild soul which, after Thermidor, caused him to be accused of having been drunk with blood. To realize his true genius, David required a model of his own stature: Marat, Napoleon or himself. The head of Bonaparte, which he painted during the three-hour sitting which was all that the emperor ever granted any artist, radiates an intensity which makes David a genuine seer, discerning in this victorious soldier the man of the coming century.

With Géricault's death there remained two artists to represent 'great French painting', Ingres and Delacroix, and they ended up loathing each other. Ingres, despite his supremely self-confident pride, was faced with an acute dilemma: he adulated David and yet at every step he betrayed his mentor, whether it was in his drawings of Greek vases, the Gothic he eyed surreptitiously without ever daring to look it in the face, his God Raphael, even his mannerism (unless the latter tendency was natural to him, as seems more likely). Ingres finally escaped from this labyrinth of feelings, as did David himself, through portraiture, and through the nude, which is, after all, the portraiture of the body. That Ingres, to make his *Reclining odalisque*'s backbone more supple, should have added a few extra vertebrae does not alter the fact that in this picture he is in the presence of the real, whereas in his theme compositions he is merely irrelevant. This great painter, perhaps the most acute example of the contradiction facing the century, was saved from disaster by his nudes and his portraits.

Was this contradiction solved by Delacroix? The sheer volume of praise at present lavished upon this artist risks obscuring the true value of one of the most original figures in the history of art. The greatness of Delacroix is in no way diminished by the spiritual torments which he suffered: indeed, this quality of suffering makes him a singularly modern figure.

When someone lauded Delacroix to his face for being a romantic he answered: 'You are mistaken, sir, I am a pure classicist.' Delacroix's greatness lies in his having been the only artist in Europe to have discovered the plastic means appropriate to the expression of romantic man in his totality; his weakness lies, precisely, in his determination to be a classicist. A painter of even disposition, Delacroix succeeded by single-minded effort in introducing the rule of reason into his art. Despite his aspirations towards classicism, he remains the brilliant incarnation of romanticism in painting. Eager to understand and interpret all the aspects of man and nature, this born painter found nothing unworthy of his brush and depicted the dark and the light sides of life with equal ease.

Delacroix has some excuse for considering himself a classicist, in view of his services to history painting, that superior genre celebrated by the academicians of ancient times and of his own age as the only one worthy to inspire a great artist. But history, as interpreted by Delacroix, derived essentially from a romantic imagination and owed nothing to classicism: his was the Shakespearian conception whereby the past is projected in an apocalyptic process of becoming, as opposed to the process envisaged by classicism, in which emotion itself is transcended in the world of ideas.

For Delacroix, history interposed itself between his art and reality, and thus his work helped postpone that moment when his own century, the century of nature, should finally recognize its natural image. On one occasion only, Delacroix trod in the footsteps of Géricault, and of the David who painted *The Death of Marat*. His enthusiastic support of the 1830 Revolution inspired him to compose his most sublime painting, in which he truly attains the grandeur of antiquity, if not in form at least in spirit, as Géricault had done before him: *Liberty leading the People (pl. 193)*, better known as *Liberty at the barricades*, may certainly be considered an avant-garde painting, as its posthumous destiny demonstrates. Exhibited at the 1831 Salon, this work outraged bourgeois opinion and provoked mainly hostile criticism. Louis Philippe, the 'king of the barricades', whose accession to power the picture celebrates, bought it to avoid offending republican opinion. Officially, the picture was intended to decorate the Throne Room at the Tuileries, but in fact it had been acquired solely so that it could be withdrawn from circulation. The new monarchist government, despite its popular mandate, was not at all pleased by this glorification of the revolutionary spirit; first it was hidden away in the Louvre's store-rooms, then it was returned to the artist under the pretext that he wished to retouch it. With the 1848 Revolution, the painting was allowed to emerge once more from its enforced obscurity, only to prove an equal source of embarrassment to the new regime; however, Napoleon III's initially liberal attitude towards artists allowed it to be hung at the Musée du Luxembourg, where it remained until transferred to the Louvre.

Delacroix's enormous output can only be described as an unexampled product of total cultural awareness: all the myths and deeds of antiquity and the Middle Ages and modern times seem to have converged in his imagination in a kind of cult of great men, a Plutarchian ethic reinforced by Shakespeare.

To appreciate Delacroix at his true value, it is as well to accept the fact that his genius is best expressed not in his large paintings but in his smaller-scale works, those marvellous drawings and sketches endowed with life by a temperament that had not yet been cooled by the false concept of the *grande machine*, the large-scale 'masterpiece' painted for the Salon. Delacroix was so determined to impose himself as a classicist that he was fatally inclined to undertake paintings solely with a triumph at the Salon in mind. It is impossible to over-emphasize the harm done, from the eighteenth century onwards, by the aesthetic of the Salon picture, imposing on the artist, as it does, the objective of pleasing a public and a jury rather than satisfying the artist himself. It might be worth while, one day, analysing the evolution of Delacroix's

192 Théodore Géricault. Detail of *The Insane Murderer*. Ghent, Musée des Beaux-Arts.

The portraits of the insane by Géricault might have given a new direction to painting, that of the psychological study of individuals.

Salon paintings in relation to the jury system. Is the fact that his earliest pictures are the finest due simply to his youth, or also because the juries of the Restoration period showed an undoubted liberalism whereas those of the July monarchy were perhaps the stupidest of the entire century?

Dante's barque, the *Massacre at Chios*, the *Death of Sardanapalus*, *Liberty leading the People*, the *Battle of Nancy*, all the pictures in which Delacroix abandons himself to the passion of his romantic temperament, are masterpieces. But his inspiration falters whenever he becomes too conscious of being a history painter, and falls into the flabbiness of the *Entry of the Crusaders into Constantinople*, the banality of the *Sultan Abd al-Rahman* or the *Battle of Taillebourg*. It is sad to compare the impoverished realism of the latter painting with the beautiful sketch of the same theme, and to consider that the clumsily executed horses are by the same hand that could create magical hippogryphs on paper or canvas prepared for sketching.

The extent to which his imagination was inhibited by this obsession with the Salon is shown by the creative inspiration which filled him when he was left to work freely on the ceiling of the Galerie d'Apollon in the Louvre or the paintings of the Library of the Chamber of Deputies in the Palais Bourbon. The Louvre panel and the decorations in the Palais Bourbon all celebrate a theme dear to Delacroix's heart: the triumph of civilization over barbarism and intelligence over instinct. As far as the two hemicycles of the Library are concerned, it must be admitted that, as a true romantic, Delacroix was more inspired by the barbaric element. However indignant he might be at such a suggestion, the fact remains that the idyllic *Orpheus coming to bring civilization to the still savage Greeks and teach them the arts of peace* is merely a well-intentioned and somewhat spectral gathering of bodies suffering from the muscular debility which afflicted all the figures painted by Delacroix after the 1830s, whereas the *Attila followed by his barbarian hordes trampling underfoot Italy and the arts* is full of febrile excitement. The terrible Hun's charger (*pl. 194*) is surely one of the most noble animals ever depicted in the history of painting, with its leonine mane recalling that of the horse in Bernini's statue of Constantine.

The whole Library of the Palais Bourbon provides an example of a decoration entirely planned and executed by a great artist, such a rare example, in fact, that one would have to go back to Michelangelo's Sistine Chapel in order to find a parallel. Usually, themes to be illustrated were dictated by scholars or patrons. A unique aspect of Delacroix's genius is that he did not illustrate history; for him,

form emanated from the idea he had conceived, a pure impulse to which his thousands of drawings bear witness, an impulse which still animates his sketches but often becomes submerged in his large compositions. He was the most literary of painters: the breadth of his culture, his intimate feeling for the spirit of his time, the vigour of his mind, the dramas of his personal life and of his artistic vocation, the absolute integrity of his genius, the moral exigencies of his thought processes, all combine to make his work as rich a hunting ground for exegetes as is that of Goethe, with whom he has so many points in common (discussed in my paper 'Delacroix et Goethe', in *Revue des Deux Mondes*, Paris 1 June 1953).

Rather than being an 'avant-garde painter', Delacroix is the last great adherent of the doctrine, summed up in Horace's tag *ut pictura poesis*, that literature and the visual arts are subject to the same laws. This theory, which has led so many artists astray, had been condemned by Lessing in his *Laocoön* (1766); but Lessing was far ahead of his time, and his demand for laws relating specifically to the plastic arts, a demand which lies at the roots of modern art, had to wait more than a century to be acted upon; then, Wölfflin and Riegl made it the cornerstone of their approach to art history and art criticism.

In confronting the modern world, which politically she had done so much to bring into being, France discovered that the way to a new pictural language was barred by a traditionalism that the Revolution had never interrupted. In other countries not subject to the same restraints, a few pioneers invented spontaneously not only a new vision but the processes best suited to express it.

In Spanish painting, there is a great hiatus between Velázquez and Goya, which, during the eighteenth century, was filled by artists summoned from France and Italy. The Bourbons were as strange to the Iberian world as were the early Hapsburgs whose artistic policy they revived, instituting a court art which ignored Spain's profound nature; this was the same policy which had been abandoned by the Hapsburg Philip IV when he gave Velázquez a free rein. Throughout most of the eighteenth century, Spanish painting represented a kind of blend of Louis-Michel van Loo, Corrado Giaquinto and Anton Raffael Mengs. It was this banal aesthetic which Goya initially practised, notably in the sixty or so tapestry cartoons which he was commissioned to produce. His portraits, however, benefited from the lessons he received from Velázquez, and he was more at ease, refashioning the master's meditative manner in a hasty, quivering treatment. In 1793 a mysterious

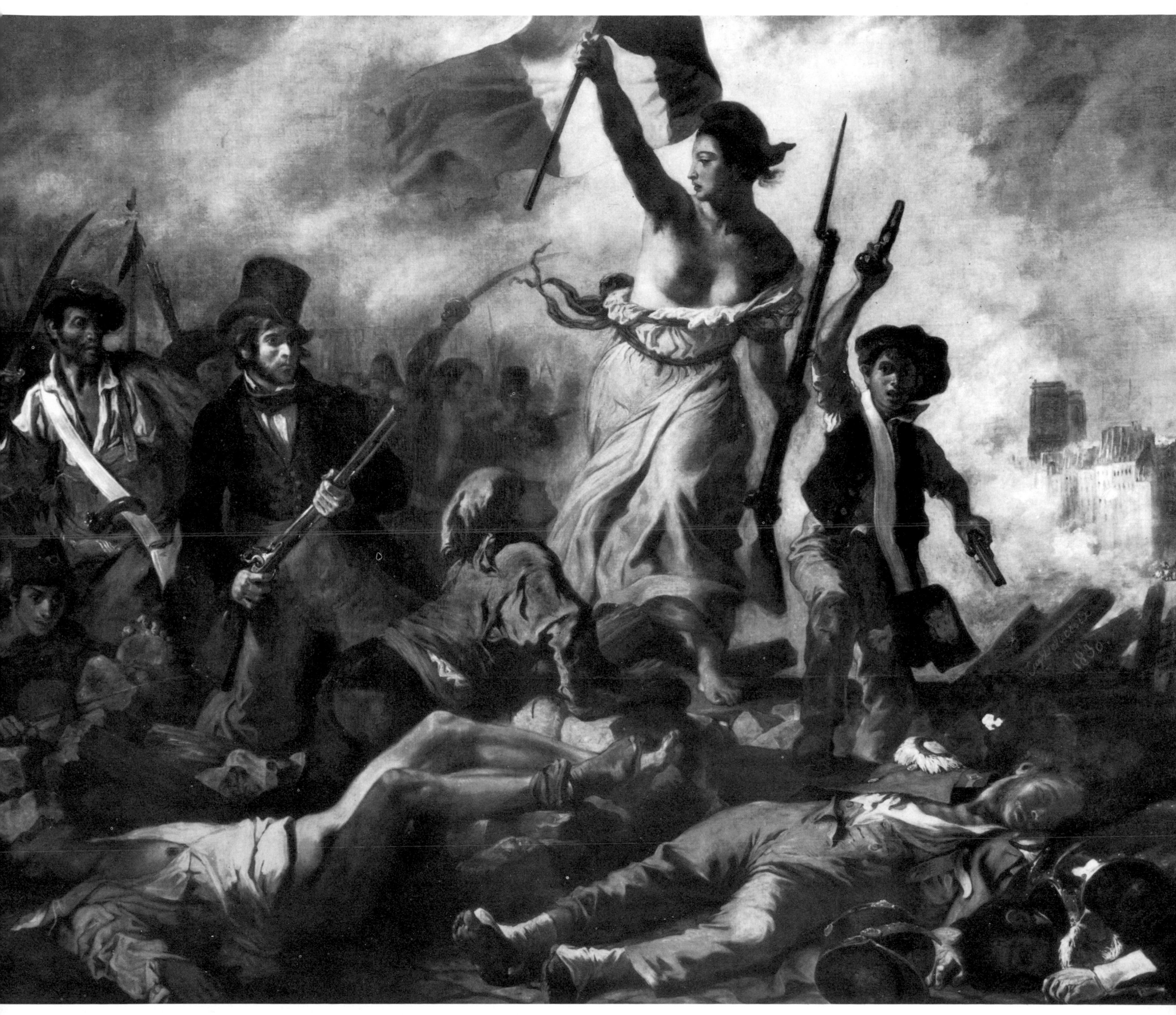

193 Eugène Delacroix (1798–1863). *Liberty leading the People*. Paris, Louvre.

Delacroix was moving towards modern painting when he painted this picture; but he later abandoned this style for a romantic approach.

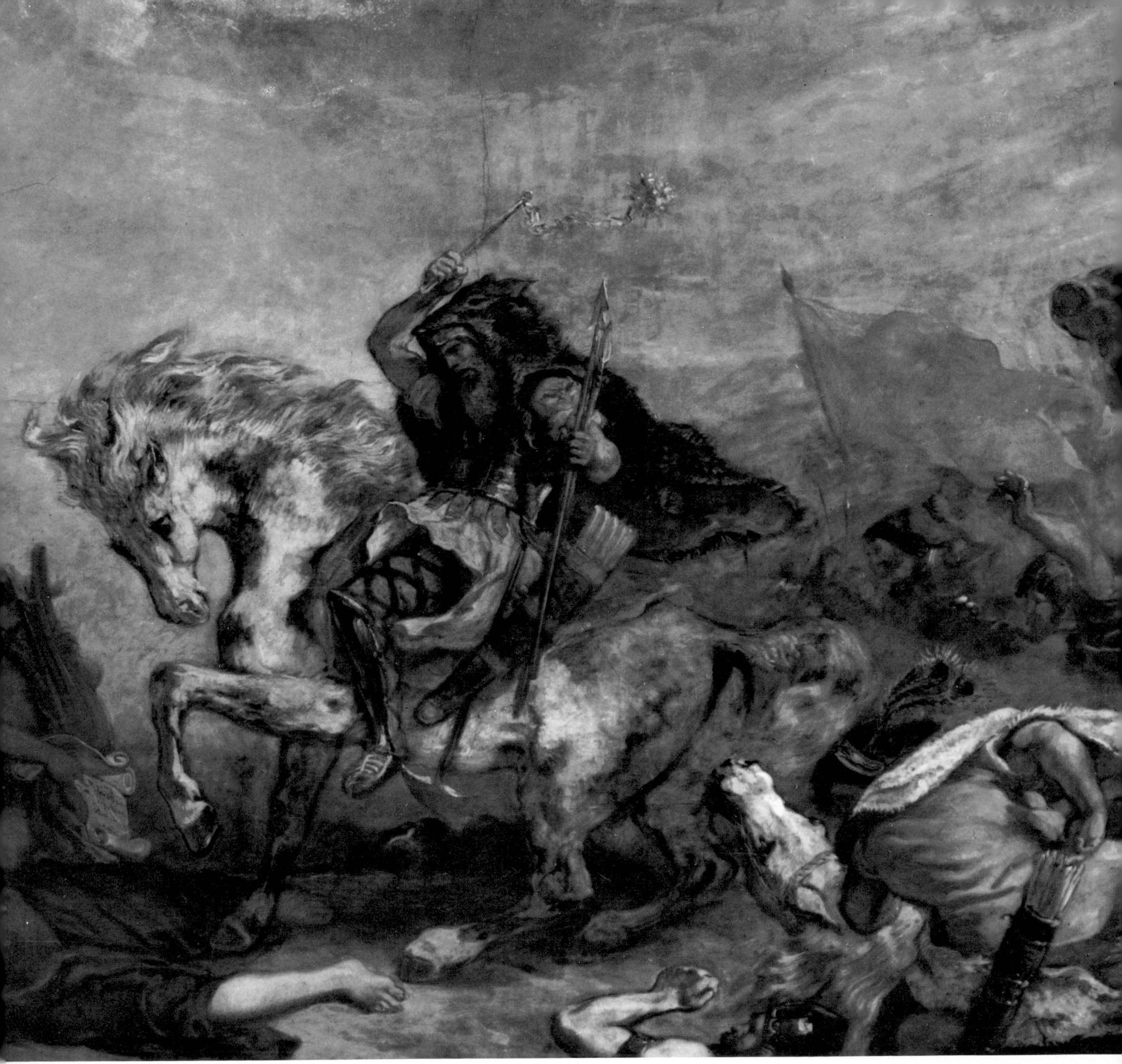

194 Eugène Delacroix. Attila on horseback, detail of *Attila followed by his barbarian hordes trampling underfoot Italy and the arts*. Paris, Library of the Chamber of Deputies.

Attila's horse proves that, despite Delacroix's misguided notion that he was a classicist, his real genius as an innovator lay in romantic expression.

ailment left him deaf, but it was at this moment that his stormy love affair with the famous Duchess of Alba commenced. Now he really assumed his true character. This court painter who had been an academician since the age of twenty-eight, this sophisticated portraitist of Madrid beaux and belles suddenly became acutely aware of the troubled times in which he lived, as a fellow Spaniard, Picasso, was to become aware just over a century later.

The two separate aspects of Goya's work provide accurate reflections of the dual character of a country about to be thrust into the drama of the modern world. This was the era when Spain was still richly endowed, thanks to its possessions in the Indies, and when the love of Queen María Luisa and the feeble-mindedness of Charles IV allowed the foppish Godoy to remain absolute master of the country's destinies for a period of thirteen years: it was truly the Spain of Goya's tapestries, warm-hearted, sensual and slightly somnolent, the Spain of fops (*petimetres*, *petimetras*), beaux and belles (*majos*, *majas*), and bohemians (*manolos*, *manolas*). But the period of Godoy's government also saw the birth of the tragic and hallucinated Spain of *Los Caprichos* and soon the *Disasters of war*, in which violent passions and the taste for blood were aroused. Originally directed towards the invader, who was welcomed at first as a liberator, this ardour was soon turned by Spain against herself; the arrival of liberal ideas in the wake of the invader served simply to reawaken religious and absolutist fanaticism as a reaction.

From a degenerate state which had nevertheless retained a tradition of resistance, there arose an anarchic state fated to be gripped by regular convulsions. Goya successfully manœuvred his way through the various regimes which succeeded each other in Spain, becoming Joseph Bonaparte's official painter, and retaining the same post under Ferdinand VII after surviving the purge instigated by the latter. An opportunity to explore the new plastic language appropriate to his new romantic inspiration was furnished Goya by the commission in 1798 to decorate with frescoes the cupola of San Antonio de la Florida in Madrid. Although this pilgrimage church was situated in the new royal domain of La Florida, he was not called upon to produce a courtly composition: on the contrary, he was specifically free to paint what and how he wanted.

The decoration of San Antonio de la Florida, begun in 1799, is one of the high points in the history of painting (*pl. 195*). The miracle of St Anthony of Padua, which Goya depicted in a continuous band around the cupola, served the artist as a pretext to

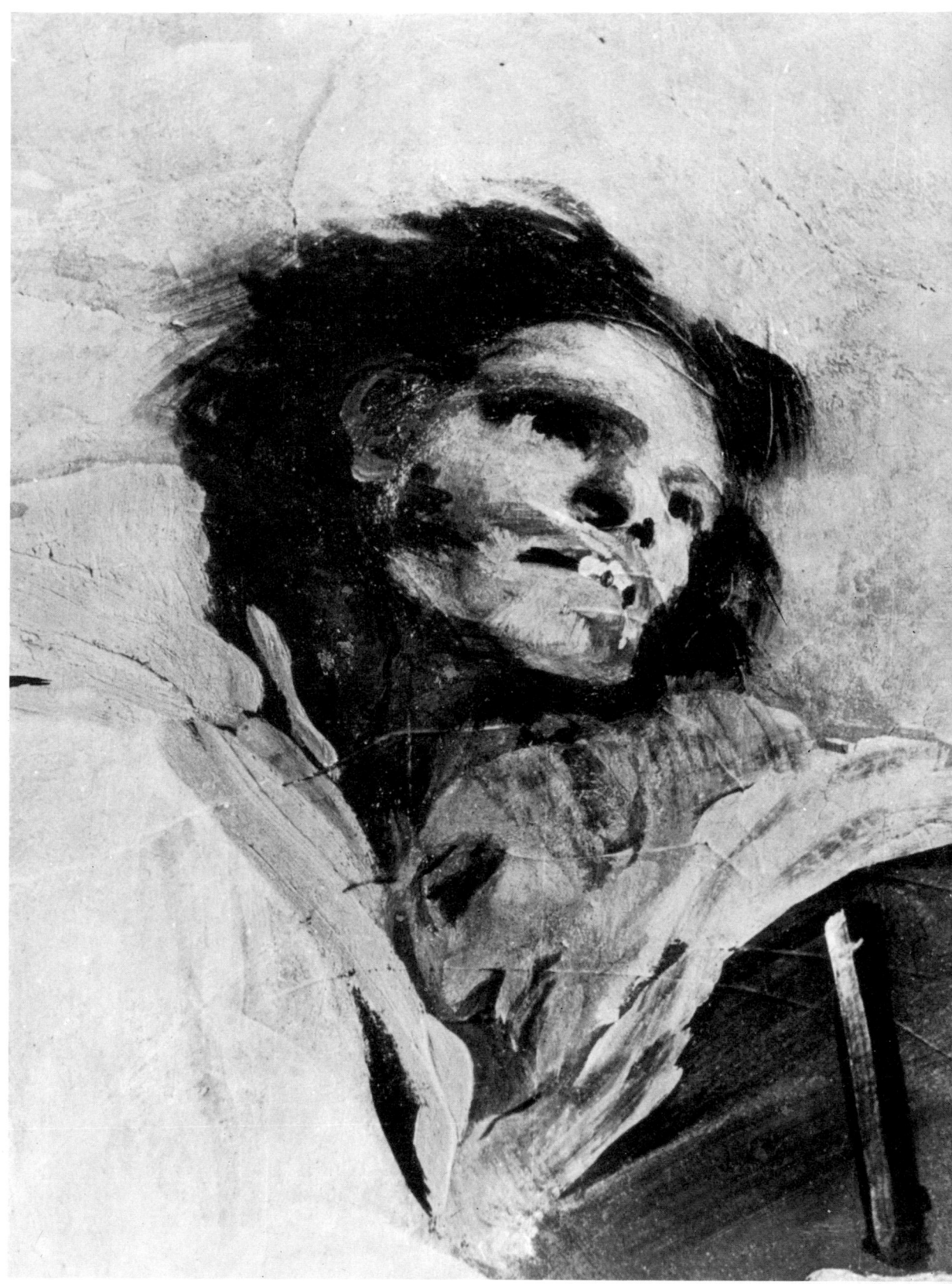

195 Francisco Goya. Detail of *The Miracle of St Anthony of Padua*. Fresco in the cupola of San Antonio de la Florida, Madrid.

With the frescoes of San Antonio de la Florida, which he painted in 1793, Goya initiated the abbreviated treatment which was to be typical of romanticism.

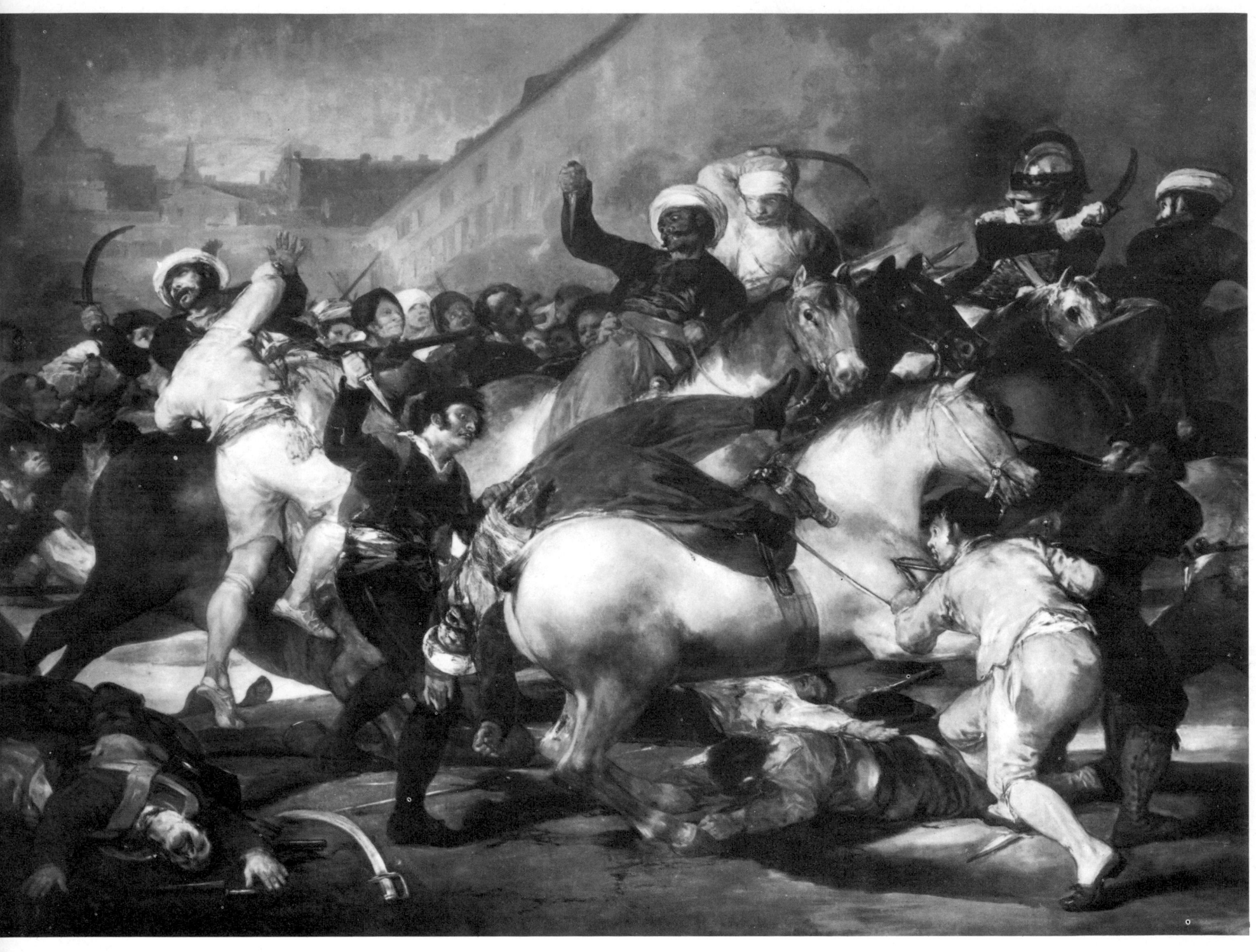

196 Francisco Goya (1746–1828). *The Second of May 1808*. Madrid, Prado.

paint a popular assembly. The emphasis on popular participation in religious scenes was an ancient tradition that had been largely abandoned during the eighteenth century: Goya revived it with these frescoes. But the true originality of his undertaking lies elsewhere. Goya's audacity lies in the fact that he painted these works in the full flush of inspiration, without any preparation or preliminary sketching (one alleged sketch is a pupil's copy), and employing a summary treatment which forms the liveliest possible contrast with the neoclassical manner of his

contemporary David. Thus, fresco, which had always been a mental operation demanding lengthy elaboration, was treated by Goya as a rough sketch to be improvised by the artist as he worked, not respecting even the original drawing incised in the plaster.

The year 1799, when the cupola of San Antonio was inaugurated, may be considered the real starting-point of modern painting. Goya deliberately put an end to the predominance of the statuary approach to painting which the neo-

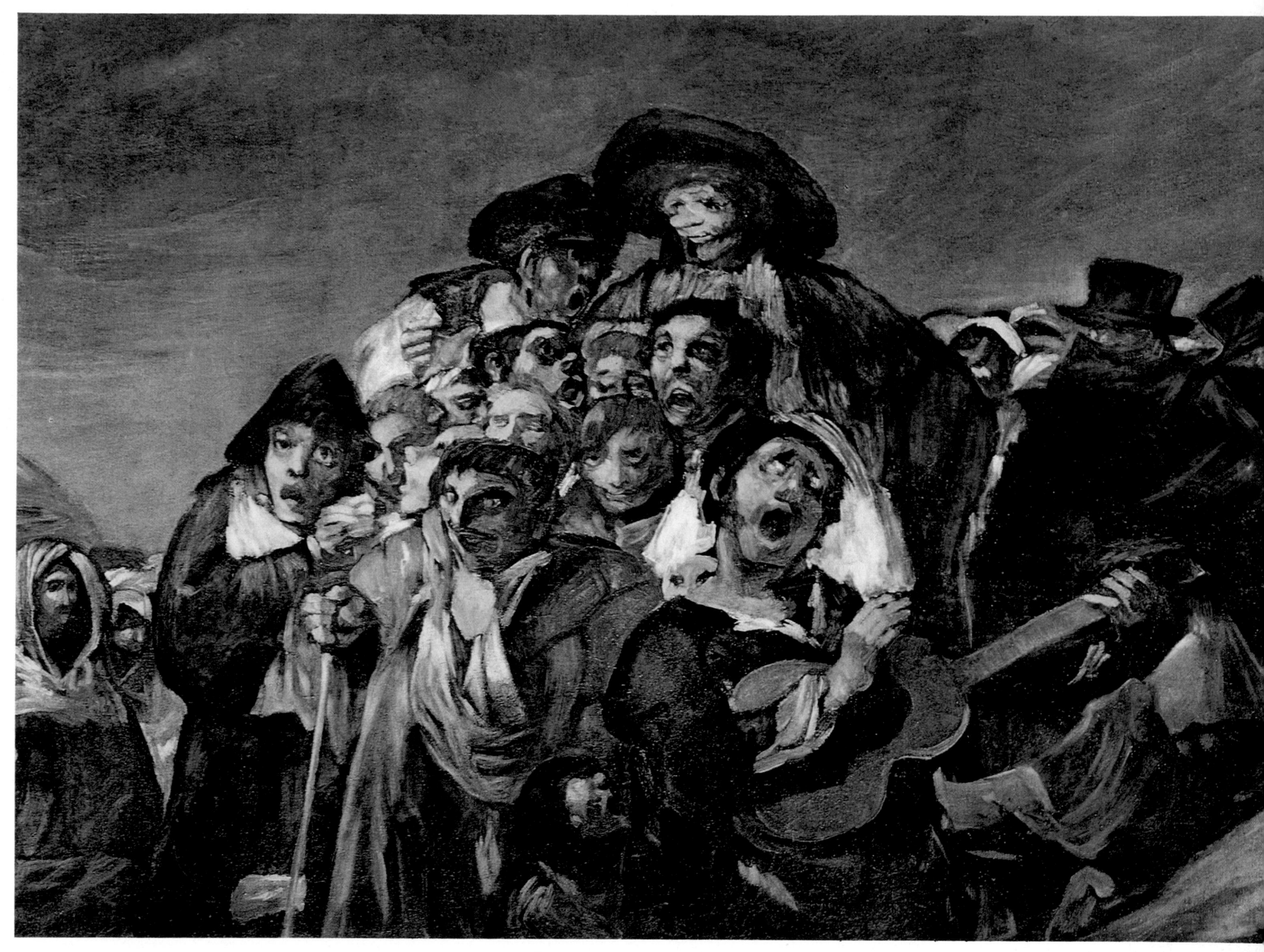

classical aesthetic had encouraged, and created the free play of forms, lending itself to all the impulses of mind and imagination, which became the very foundation of painting from then on. This kind of handling, combining the subjective and the vital, corresponded to Goya's conviction that painting was, above all, an act of delivering a specific message, and it proved ideally suited to the expressionist fervour which was to grip the romantic artists. History soon provided Goya with subject-matter for testing out the resources of his new

handling. The Madrid rebellion against the French in 1808, and the terrible repression which followed it, engendered a few years later the famous political paintings called the *Second* and *Third of May 1808*: boldly executed, the two succinct statements transform the victims of history into tragic puppets (*pl. 196*). Here, Goya is in the same heroic vein which prompted David's *The Death of Marat* (*pl. 190*), Gros's *Battle of Eylau*, Géricault's *Raft of the 'Medusa'* (*pl. 191*), Delacroix's *Liberty leading the People* (*pl. 193*), Rude's *Marseillaise*, and, much later, Picasso's

197 Francisco Goya. Detail of *The Pilgrimage to the fountain of San Isidro*. Madrid, Prado.

Goya developed an increasingly vibrant handling to express the violence and folly of the events he was forced to witness.

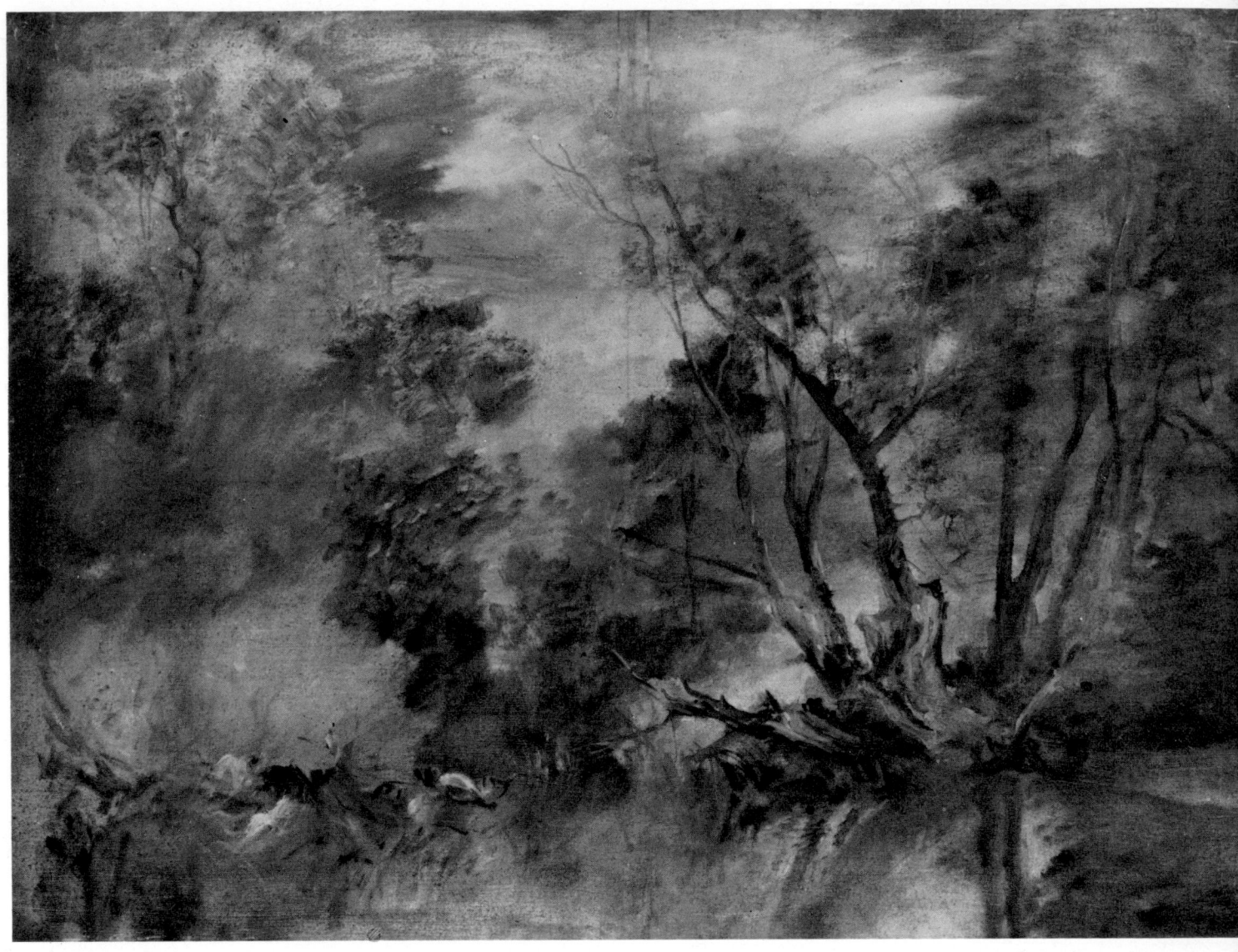

The practice of watercolour painting led Turner, very early in his career, to use an increasingly cursory handling which, in its turn, led him to create increasingly allusive forms.

Guernica (*pl. 229*). This epic vein should have provided one of the great sources of inspiration for modern painting; for various reasons, however, it was an approach which remained unfruitful, with the exception of a few isolated masterpieces.

Goya went further still. For a second time in his life, severe illness induced a change of direction in the artist's work. At the age of seventy-three, after almost dying, he painted what may be considered his testament: the fourteen paintings with which he decorated the Quinta del Sordo, a country house which he had bought near the Manzanares. These nightmarish visions are projected on to the canvas by a furious brush; Bosch's monsters, with their complex mechanisms, are children's playthings compared with the fantastic creations which Goya conjured from the powers of darkness. Like certain Renaissance philosophers, Goya seems to have derived true wisdom from the spectacle of human folly (*pl. 197*). Even the most audacious expressionists of modern times, such as Soutine, never

surpassed this stupendous wielding of a brush which might almost be the implement of an automatic handwriting. Into these explosive works (painted probably about 1820), the deaf genius, wrapped in his dreams, concentrated as much expressive violence as painting was capable of containing. His voice, the last important one in Spanish painting, delivered a supreme message which remained ignored for a long time. What is remarkable, though, is that this message already existed in essence within a deep current of Spanish painting; it can be summed up as the *vena brava* which Lafuente Ferrari invoked with regard to Herrera. Indeed, some of the figures in Herrera's pictures anticipate those to be seen in the Quinta del Sordo series.

Goya's lessons went unheeded. The romantics remained unaware of his existence, and, paradoxically, it was Manet who rescued him from obscurity. The real source of romantic handling is to be found in England rather than in Spain. It was, indeed, the influence of English painting that rescued Géricault and Delacroix from the restrictive effects of David's influence. There had been nothing to suggest that the English school was destined for such greatness. Reynolds's attempt to create a new handling had produced nothing better than the meretricious and buttery technique of Lawrence. But English painters proceeded to liberate themselve from academic conventions by establishing direct contact with nature. The source of modern landscape painting, both romantic and impressionist, is to be found in England, among those late eighteenth-century artists practising drawing and watercolour who sought inspiration from the features of the countryside, with a preference for ancient Gothic buildings.

Descriptive at first, these watercolours became increasingly frcc, and the artist tended less to copy the structure than to catch the ever-changing caprices of the light (*pl. 198*). Turner spent a large part of his life on sketching tours through Europe, completing innumerable drawings and watercolours. By maintaining contact with nature in this way, he retained a lively sensibility which might possibly have become blunted had he abandoned himself too freely to his thoughts in the privacy of his studio. Yet Turner was not, like Bonington or Constable, a man of nature; he made himself into a man of culture, learning to write with painful slowness, and teaching himself the rudiments of mythology, ancient and even modern history. Turner was tormented by the romantic spell of the past, and in his old age, when the railway was flourishing, he typically painted the visionary picture entitled *Rain, steam and speed*. Having seen his talent recognized very early – he was only twenty-seven when he was elected a R A in 1802 – he freed himself of all restraints and became, together with Géricault, the first modern artist to be no longer dependent on commissions and to be able to approach painting as a personal adventure.

A confirmed bachelor, Turner was also a hypochondriac, and when he was not travelling through Europe shut himself up in his Chelsea studio. Here he sketched out his studies for the pictures which he peopled with the phantoms of his dreams, taken from the books he read: Ulysses, Agrippina, Admiral Tromp or Nelson. He wanted to identify himself with Claude, another self-educated man. But Claude's dreams had carried him back to a golden age in which man and nature lived reconciled; Turner, on the other hand, glimpsed a world of clashing forces in the midst of which man struggled, whirlwinds of elements, mirages of light which seemed to be visions of another planet (*pl. 199*).

Turner failed to create as free a technique in oil as in watercolour: his muddy eddies derive from Reynolds's unprofitable experiments. The honour of discovering a new manner of painting in oil fell, a generation later, to another Englishman, Constable.

Before Constable, the sensory data which informed man of the nature of the universe was solely of a visual kind. The world was a kind of pageant, ordered or natural according to the outlook of the painter but always experienced as the 'external world'; these surroundings were seen as being subject to another authority, independent of that exercised by man himself, and perceived by man only when he acknowledged its relationship with him, as providing the background, the 'theatre', of his activity.

Then at one stroke Constable plunged painting into the very substance of the world. His great

199 J. M. W. Turner. *Light and Colour (Goethe's theory)*. London, Tate Gallery.

About 1835–40, Turner's art began to retreat from nature and to express, instead, the dreams of his feverish imagination. He anticipates Gustave Moreau and Odilon Redon, and his whirlpools of colour foreshadow abstract expressionism.

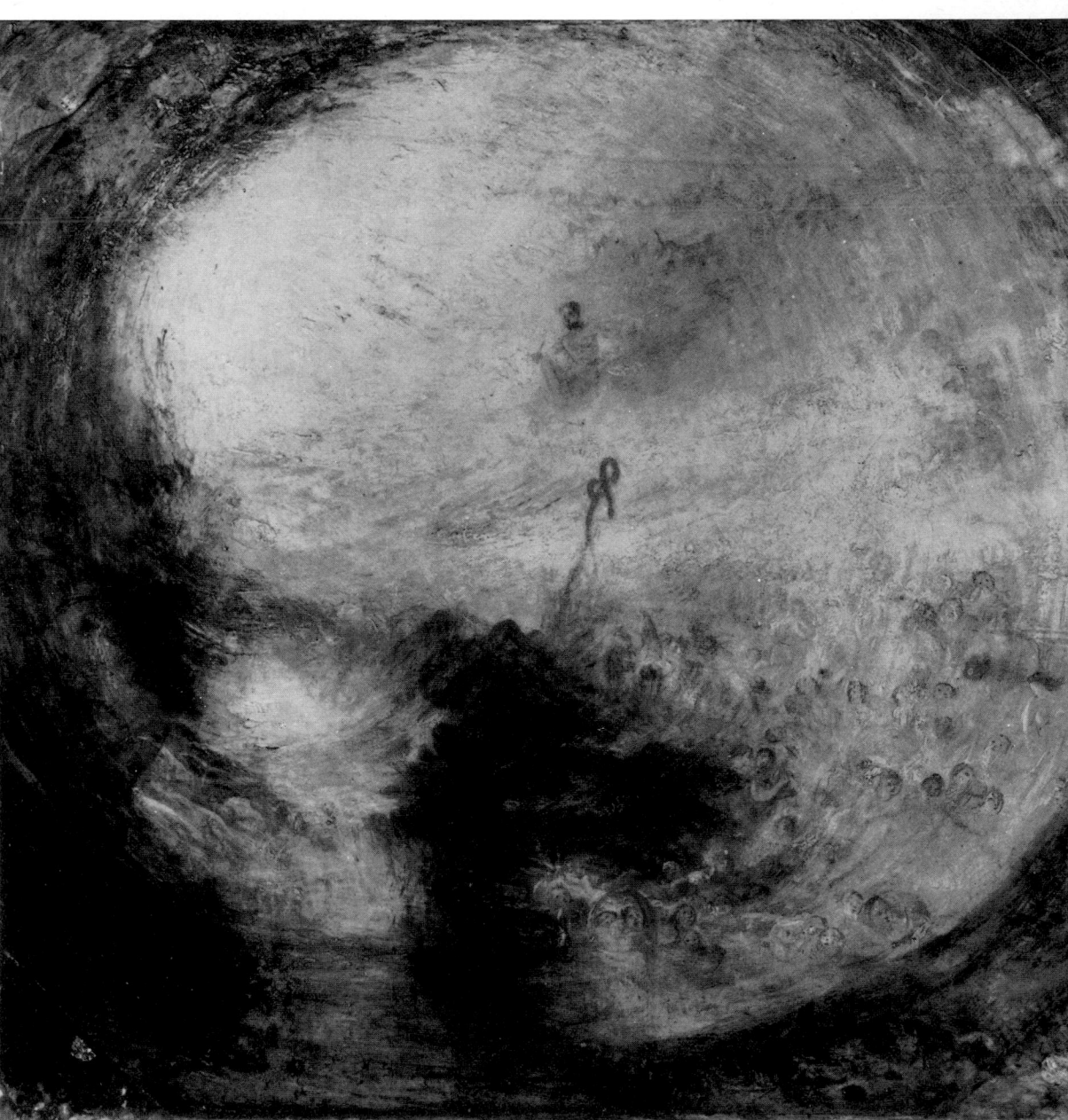

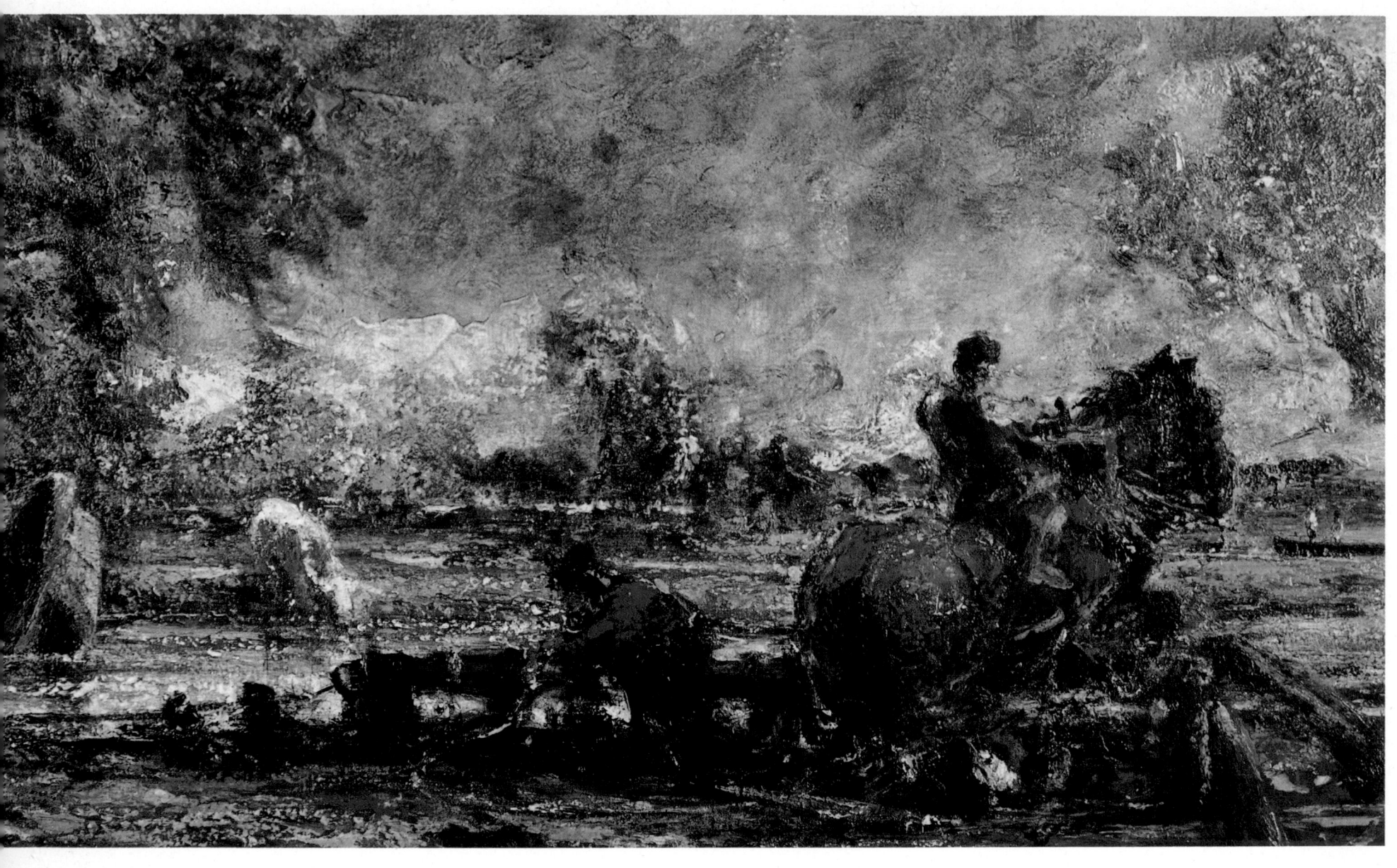

200 John Constable (1776–1837). Detail of *Horse jumping*. London, Victoria and Albert Museum.

discovery was the soil. What was the soil before Constable examined its substance? Painters had shown earth as hard as a paved surface, the base upon which man lived, either as statue or ant according to the artist's view of man's place in the world. Beneath this skin, which had been smooth and unbroken with Poussin, or hard and cracked with Ruisdael, Constable discovered the earth's warm flesh. He revealed to us the mysterious universe which autumn ploughing lays bare. This son of a Suffolk miller inhaled the heady odour of the soil which the ploughshare brings to light from beneath the dusty, anonymous crust hardened by summer.

The magnificent, glutinous, glowing red substance which constitutes the earth of Constable's pictures evokes, too, all the secret treasures which the earth harbours: the stones from which we build our houses, the coal that is our source of energy, the gems with which we adorn ourselves. This is English earth, fluid as matter on the point of melting, an aquatic earth midway between water and dry soil, a damp substance that is hardly less ductile than the muddy ocean which licks its borders, under a sky heavy with thick clouds: indeed, the three elements which compose a landscape – earth, sky and water – seem here to be fused in one inseparable substance.

Others have sought infinity in space; the eternal peasant has found it in the primordial, inexhaustible soil, fathomless as the ocean. Take Constable's sketch of a *Horse jumping*, for instance (*pl. 200*): the horseman seems scarcely able to lift his rustic steed off the ground, as though it were still heavy with the original clay from which it was moulded. Constable's heavy soil shows its love by clinging, symbolizing the affinity which unites substances and human beings.

It is this thrill of universal harmony which makes the soul of romantic man vibrate like a lyre. For centuries, man fulfilled these burning aspirations in the name of God; after renouncing God, romantic man refocused his desire for the infinite upon the universe. Ruisdael had already sensed the living nature of the world, but only as a hostile, unknown force; the 'silence of infinite spaces' frightened his Pascalian soul committed to solitude. Then Constable, in a great burst of brotherly love, acknowledged everything which bound his soul to the universe, to the eternal chain of beings and things. 'Painting is only another word for feeling', he said. He inaugurated the aesthetic of feeling. His saturated pictures reveal gorged senses, a soul bursting with impatience to unburden itself completely.

No painter has expressed romantic pantheism more profoundly than Constable. Théodore Rousseau, too conscious of himself, allowed his feelings to become congealed by the cold breath of scientific positivism. Even Courbet, the man of the soil, remained the artist of a single locality, a true Frenchman who painted a particular patch of soil rather than the soil itself. Only an English painter could have been capable of expanding his soul, in a great surge of lyricism, to the dimensions of the universal.

The glory of the French artists during this first part of the nineteenth century lay in their total involvement in conflict as fighting heroes, and their first triumph. This struggle was of extreme importance for the development of art. Apart from the stimulus given to landscape painting by the English school, European art was plunged into a sort of fatalistic acceptance of the inevitable, the majority of artists remaining blissfully unaware of the volcano on which they were living. In their desire to escape the grip of antiquity, German and English painters could see no other solution than to abandon themselves to an ever worse conformism, resulting from the inspiration they found in Italian painting of the early Renaissance. The Nazarener in Germany, the Pre-Raphaelites in England and the Ingrists in France all indulged in an absurd escapism which took them even further away from reality than from antiquity, reality being invariably associated, in the minds of the promoters of these movements, with the living model and nothing else. The Ingrists did at least make an effort to discard this yoke. Most of the others, though, as for example the artists of the 'Old Vienna' group, adapted a plastic formula based upon the imitation of statues to the expressive needs of realistic landscapes or scenes inspired by contemporary life. The results may not be works of

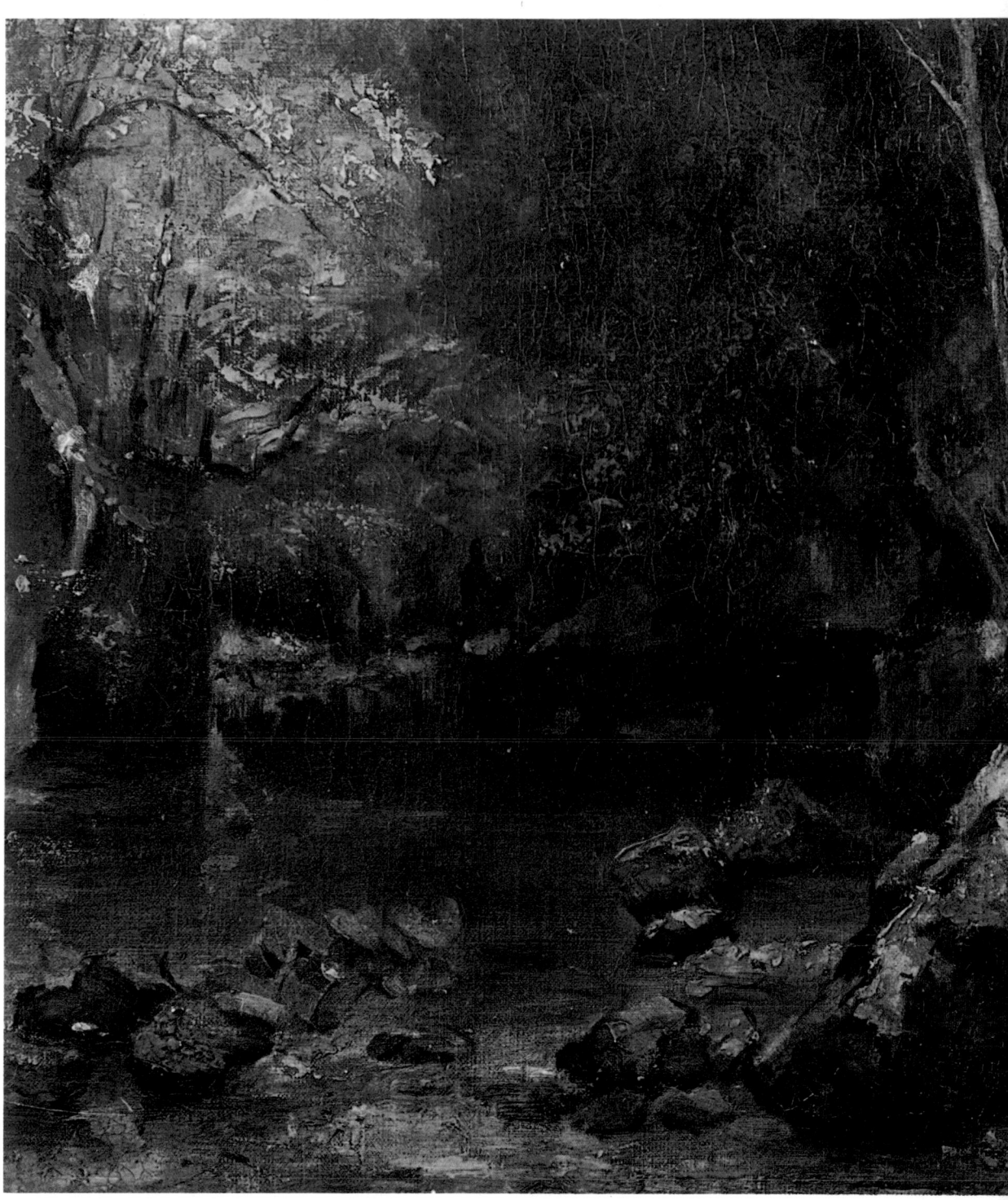

art, but they furnish a charming enough imagery tinged with a genuinely moving if superficial nostalgia.

A few men, however, dared to liberate art from history, and to give back to painting the moral and social power of expression it possessed during the Middle Ages. Millet, Daumier and Courbet, the so-called 'realists', sought inspiration in the human drama and tried to express it in terms of the harsh life which was the lot of the common people at that time. Millet exalted the tragedy of peasant life,

201 Gustave Courbet (1819–77). *The Culvert.* Besançon, Musée.

Constable and, following him, Courbet evoked the substance of the primordial earth in their paintings, and invented an appropriate technique for this purpose.

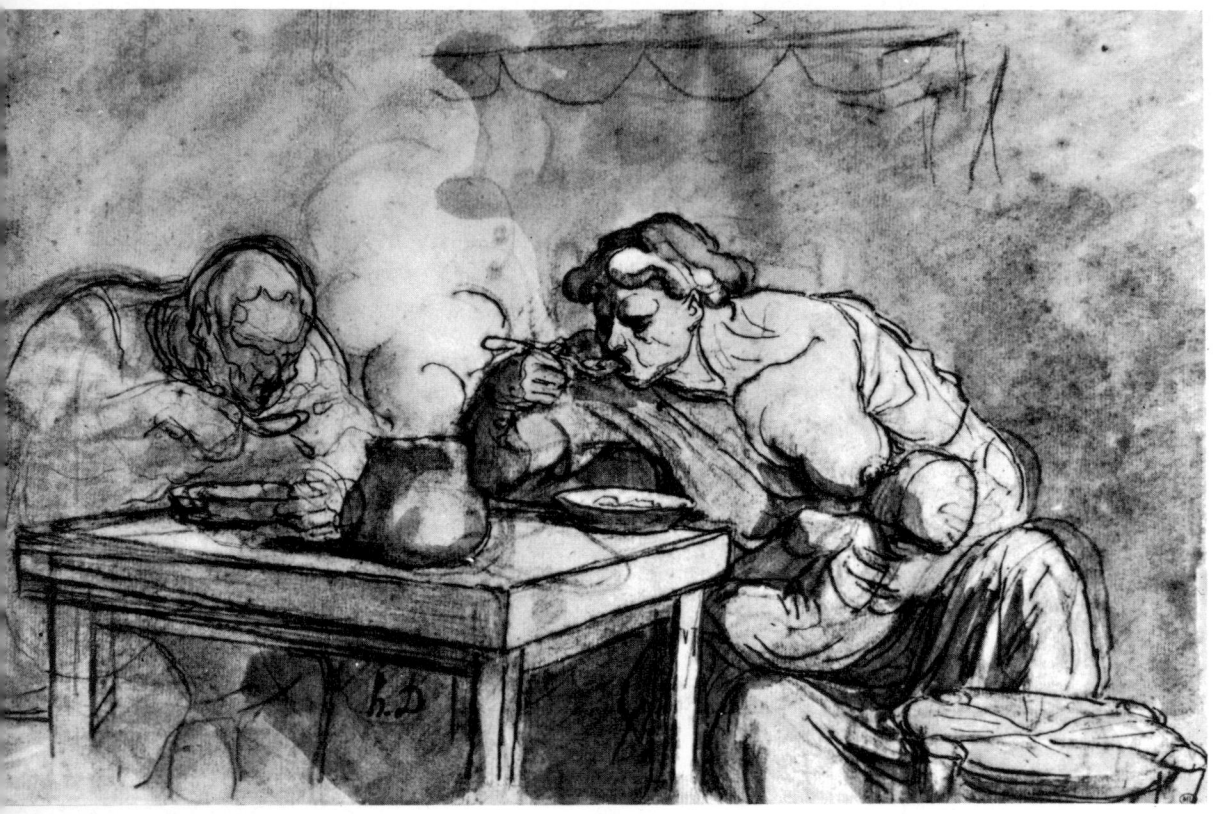

202 Honoré Daumier (1808–79). Detail of *The Soup*. Paris, Louvre.

In a few strokes, the violence of which conveys his revolutionary fervour, Daumier suggests the new emerging force: the people.

technique which he handled with great skill. In his best landscapes, the use of the brush is limited to the shadows; for the rest, the artist crushes the pigments, smearing them obliquely with his knife so that other, deeper layers can be glimpsed, thus obtaining a rich and sensual substance. As Constable had done thirty years previously, Courbet destroyed the homogeneity of the painting, opening the way to future experimentation far more effectively than Delacroix, whose influence on the impressionists has been exaggerated.

Courbet had shown that the instinctual approach of the self-taught artist provided one of the possible ways of breaking down the barriers which hindered the advance of painting. In his youth, he went through the normal process of studying the masterpieces in the Louvre attentively; it was later, when he began studying nature itself, that he elaborated his new means of plastic expression.

Honoré Daumier, on the other hand, was a self-taught painter pure and simple; he came to painting late, and learnt the craft without any assistance, his method being to start from scratch, without any preconceived notions. This non-intellectual approach makes many of his pictures formless, but in others, such as the *Republic nourishing her children and instructing them*, he immediately achieves monumental grandeur, thus proving that genius is often the prerogative of innocence.

This picture was a great success when it was entered, in 1848, for the competition which had been organized to choose an official effigy for the Republic, and in which nine other artists had participated. But its very success served to point up the loneliness of a man who was doubtless appreciated more for his revolutionary convictions than for his art. The jury, anxious to award the commission to Daumier, the glorious artist who had been persecuted by the July Monarchy, asked him to execute a larger-scale sketch and advanced him five hundred francs for this purpose. The artist was nonplussed by this impossible request. He had painted a picture in a burst of inspiration, and the jury's main interest in it appeared to be to extract a particular image; what had been for him a completed work, they considered to be merely a rough sketch. The misunderstanding on both sides was complete. Daumier had discovered the true process of romantic painting, which consists in the unselective projection of temperament on to the canvas, a process which Victor Hugo had discovered independently in his splendid drawings, and which Cézanne adopted instinctively in his first period, referring to it contemptuously later on as his *manière couillarde* ('pig-headed style').

while Courbet offered the city-dweller the vision of a towering humanity still close to brute existence.

Courbet may be considered the first genuinely scandalous painter of modern times. Before him, the scandal created by certain paintings related to their aesthetic content, but now it was the moral factor which caused concern. The bourgeois public was well aware of the socialist criticism implicit in these human figures, the like of which had never been seen before in painting. And indeed, Courbet made his intentions quite clear. When his *Burial at Ornans*, that painting filled with the gravity of a medieval Deposition, burst upon the 1851 Salon, it was denounced as disgusting. Courbet's gaze did not lift itself to the horizon, like Corot's, but concentrated, rather, on the humble clay of our origins; his instinct drew him towards wild animals, and in his landscapes he evoked the ages of the earth prior to the appearance of man (*pl. 201*).

To express his ideas plastically, Courbet needed an appropriate technique, and he promptly invented one himself, reviving unconsciously, and less subtly, the methods adopted by Constable. The superimposition of flat colours, applied with the palette-knife and then scratched so that the lower surfaces show through, provided Courbet's answer to traditional painting with its transparent technique and its magical effects of the shimmering of glazes in depth. Having established this very personal technique, Courbet incorporated it into a

At the time of the 1848 Revolution, these painters retained the epic style, the extreme audacity and the dramatic intensity of romanticism. Daumier, in particular, showed his deep concern with the urban poor, crushed by industrialism but still full of pride; there can be no more moving documents of human misery than *The Soup* (*pl. 202*), or the *Washerwoman* in the Louvre. The modern realists kept the sense of disenchantment of this 1848 romanticism, while abandoning its exalting form. Degas and Toulouse-Lautrec hounded this ancient human illusion, dissecting with pitiless objectivity the morals and foibles of their contemporaries.

Corot, on the contrary, traversed the first three-quarters of the nineteenth century without ever experiencing romantic anguish. His natural sociability prevailed over his desire for solitude, and in this era of eager hopes he achieved more as a painter through the love he showed his fellow human beings than most others did through their energy. The reflection of his landscapes, vibrating with latent humanity, can be seen trembling in the lost looks of his dreaming figures. He resolved the great dilemma which tormented other artists by dividing his painting into two categories, one for posterity, the other for his own delectation. The latter series began to receive the attention of the public only after he had been painting for twenty years; the first manner, though, he reserved for the Salons, and the success which greeted him there induced him to indulge in an increasing over-production which reached lamentable proportions during the second part of his career.

Corot's great virtue was that he developed an entirely personal technique in relation to nature itself, creating finished works from what painters would previously have considered nothing more than rough sketches. In Rome, his companions at first made fun of this painter who worked in the open air, but it was not long before they were imitating him. He painted only what he saw, as he saw it, but he was careful to look only at those scenes which satisfied his unavowed classicizing instinct: Rome, Tuscany, lakes, gentle countrysides and the villages of France. Yet, once these pictures have been visually absorbed, their contents go through a trance-like process of transformation which makes this classicist with his romantic treatment the true precursor of impressionism. Within this limited space, Corot's brush, working almost on a single spot, kneads and models the pigment over a small area, diluting it, sometimes picking out an accent of light through a more generous impasto, without ever allowing it to become an incrustation (*pl. 203*).

Romantic treatment of paint consists, precisely,

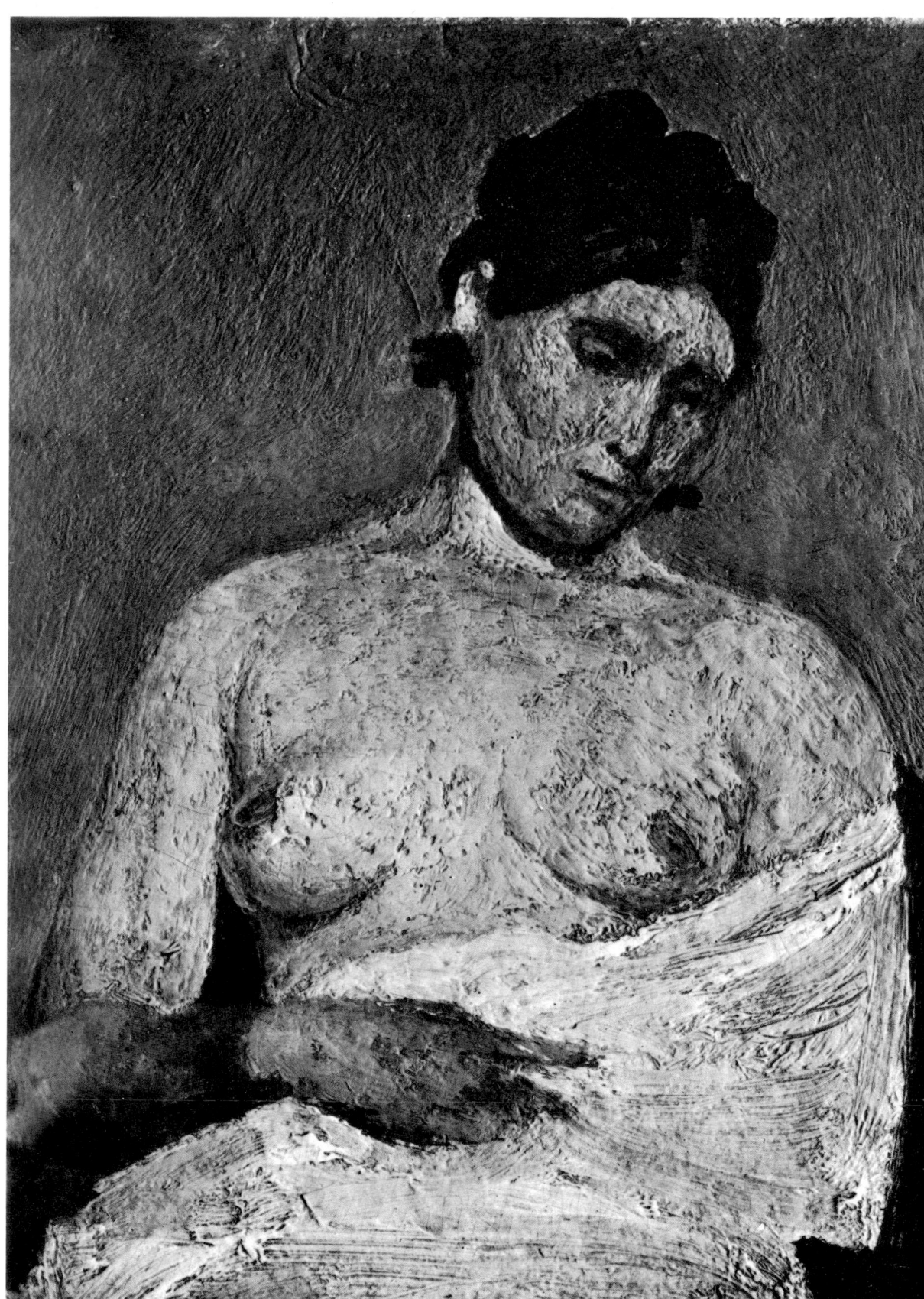

203 Camille Corot (1796–1875). *Woman with unveiled bosom*. Photograph with side lighting. Paris, collection Renan.

Corot became the master of a lively, vibrant technique, using the *demi-pâtes* traditional to French painting.

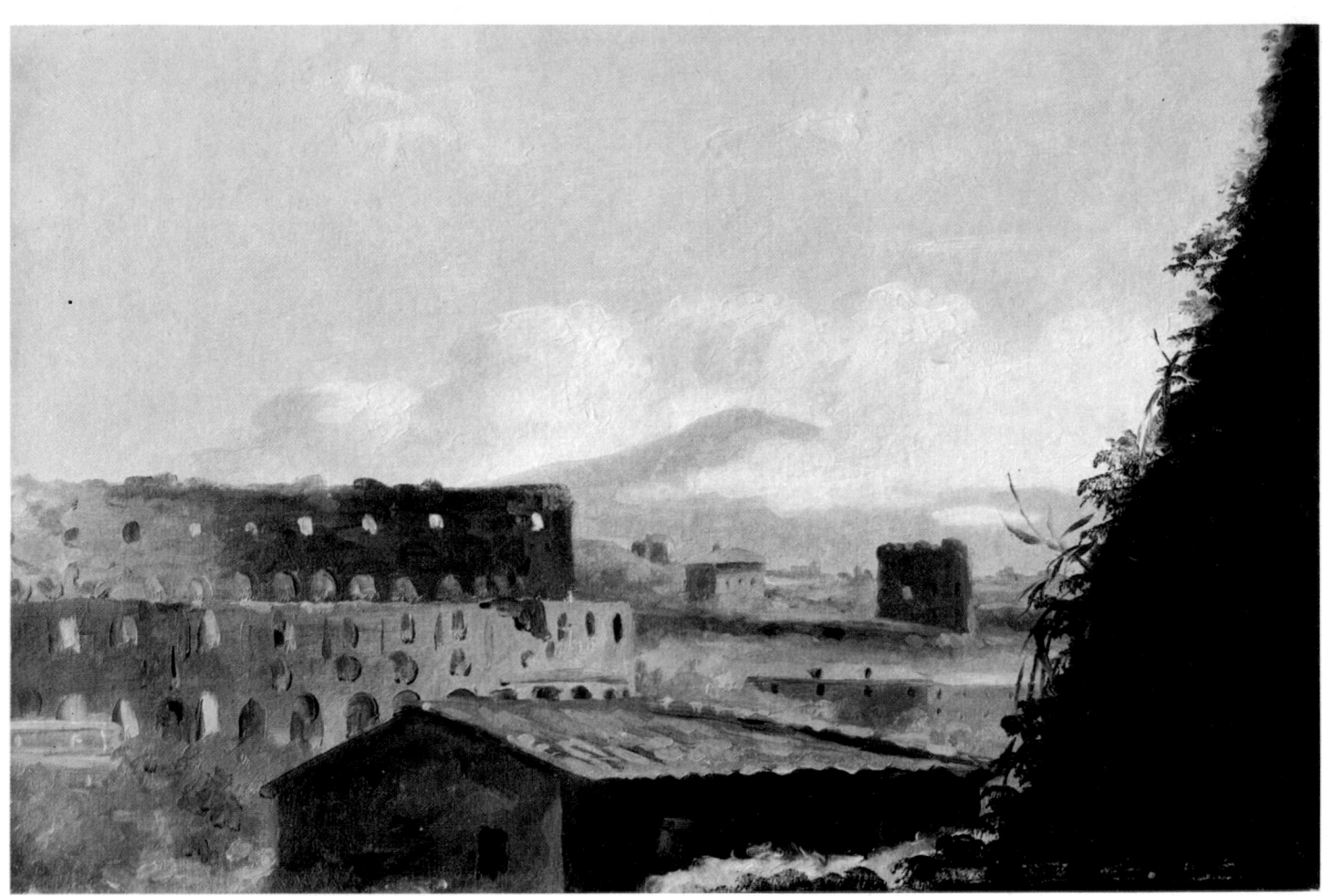

of this rapid technique responding to direct or immediate impression; the English landscape school had preceded the French in this discovery. Nevertheless, it should be remembered that the true inventor of the boldly painted impression after nature was the astonishing late eighteenth-century landscape painter Pierre-Henri de Valenciennes. Valenciennes was two painters in one: indeed he introduced into landscape painting the anomaly, to which impressionism finally put an end, which consisted in the division of an artist's output into official and private sectors. He was blessed with an exquisite sensitivity which allowed him, in his oil studies, to use a brush as light and rapid as that of a watercolourist to record the most delicate nuances of light (*pl. 204*).

These rough sketches constituted the research material of a luminarist; it is surprising to find an artist of his time and nation less interested in monuments and ancient buildings than in space, and seeking out commanding viewpoints such as the Farnese Gardens on the Palatine Hill, the Borghese Gardens, or the edge of Lake Nemi, from which to capture the effect of light passing through space. His preoccupations were a good deal more extensive

than was typical of his time, exceeded Corot's, and even anticipated those of the English romantics. He made cloud studies before Constable, painted the effects of fog, rain and storm before Turner, and, more important still, studied a single site under the effects of different lights, as Monet was to do very much later.

Everything interested Valenciennes, and his innumerable drawings reveal a universal curiosity about nature which foreshadows that of Théodore Rousseau. Valenciennes may be considered a truly modern artist: for him, to see was an operation which could be accomplished only with the active assistance of the hand – seeing and recording constituted one single process. A solitary figure, he liked to wander on foot through the Mediterranean countries, admiring his beloved nature, and savouring life in the slow rhythm of walking which suited a contemplative spirit; he was, in fact, a devotee of the kind of long walking expeditions which the 'dilettantes', the disciples of Jean-Jacques Rousseau, were in the habit of making. He left the stage-coach 'to the rich ignoramuses who travel the world like so many pieces of baggage', and advised his pupils to journey by easy stages, 'on horseback if

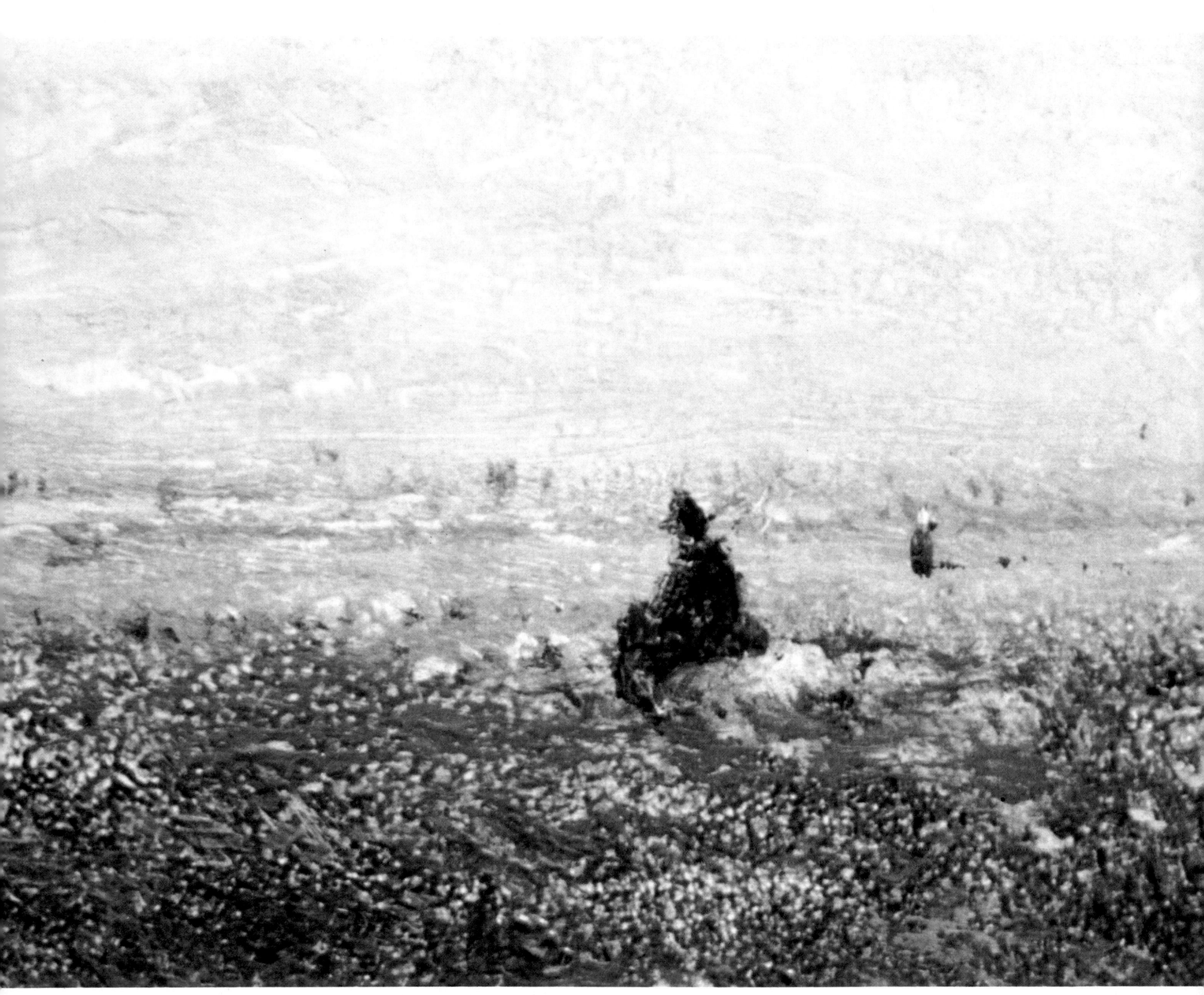

205 Théodore Rousseau (1812–67). Detail of *The Plain in front of the Pyrenees*. Paris, Louvre.

Well before Seurat, Rousseau sometimes used a divisionist technique, as Vermeer had already done, to give a vibrating quality to his paint.

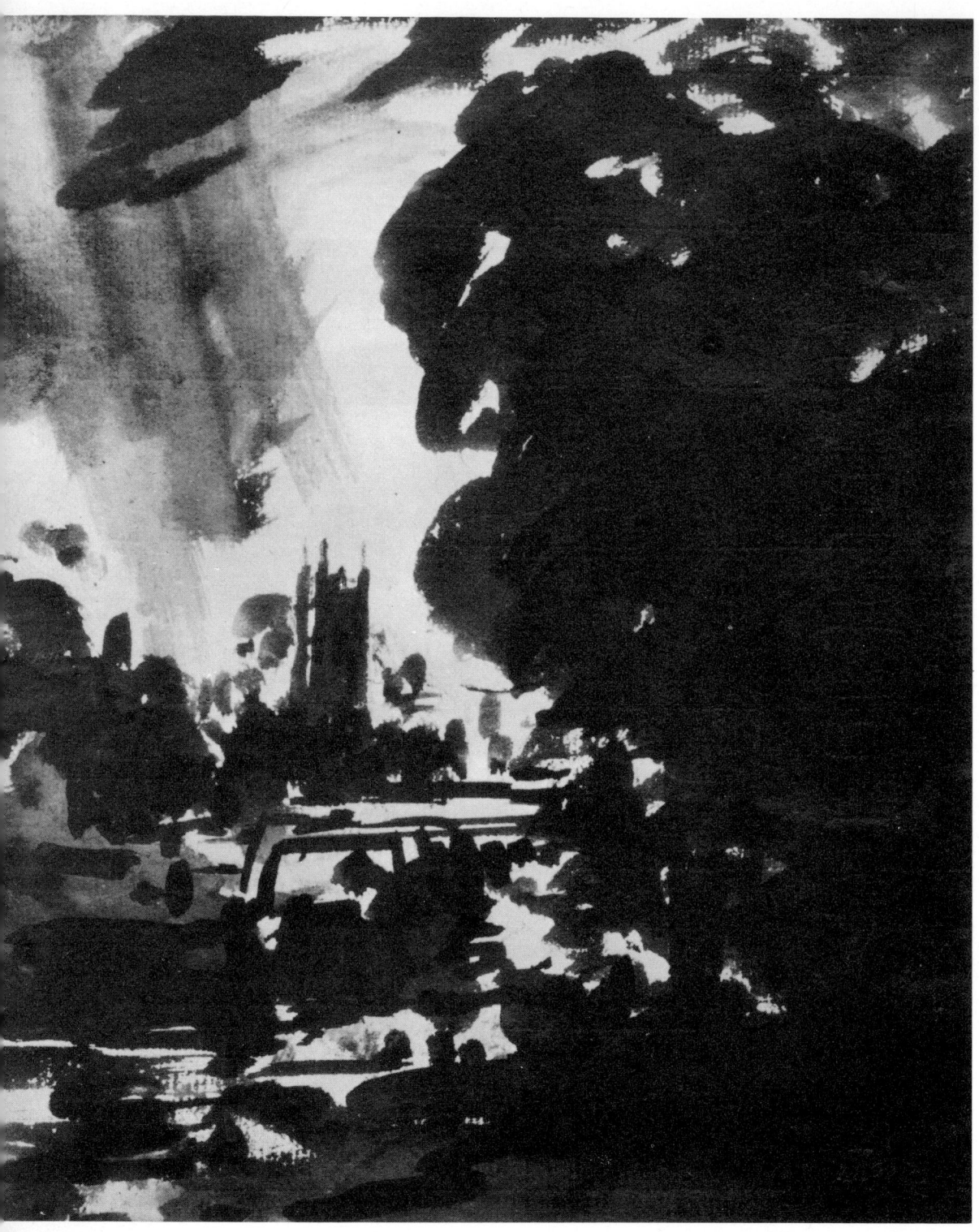

206 John Constable. *Dedham Church*. Brush and sepia. London, Victoria and Albert Museum.

possible, otherwise on foot like the Hermit'. Once back in his studio he was a different man, reinventing nature from his reading of Virgil and Homer. If he did consult his sketchbooks, none of the sensitive feeling of these studies is apparent in the composed landscapes with idyllic or bucolic themes which he painted in his studio and which made his reputation. Unlike Claude, who made good use of his nature studies, he was a true artist only in secret.

These precious sketches by Valenciennes remained so well hidden that they have only recently come to light. This kind of bold treatment reappeared in France around 1825 with Delacroix, his friend the English painter Richard Parkes Bonington and the innovating landscapist Paul Huet. The English example was one of the factors which helped these romantics to cut themselves loose from the classicists' descriptive and literary treatment of themes. Corot never assimilated this English influence, and his traditionally French technique of moulding paint differed radically from the broad, flowing impasto, derived from the English school and ultimately from watercolour painting, which was practised by Huet, Bonington and Delacroix.

Paradoxically, though, Théodore Rousseau's treatment was far less romantic than Corot's, at least during the period of his maturity, although he, too, had passed through a phase of bold treatment of direct impressions, during the 1830s, at the time of his travels in Normandy and the Auvergne. But the forest was to transform him completely. Under the spreading branches, in the deserts of stone of the forest of Fontainebleau, Rousseau felt that his profound solitude, his absolute isolation from humanity, brought him close to the secret of things. While at the artists' colony at Barbizon, he declared: 'This is how I would wish to live, surrounded by silence, watching for all that hums and glitters in a ray of sunshine.' Landscape, for this romantic, was the very opposite of a mood; his soul, open to the voices of nature, sought to rejoin 'the great chain of living beings'. He, too, forged a personal technique for himself, through close analysis.

For Corot, Delacroix, Bonington, Huet and the young Rousseau himself, the vision of the sky had inspired a fluid technique. When he turned his gaze earthward again, though, Rousseau sought to paint the permanent rather than the fugitive. During the second half of his career, his analytical approach resulted in an almost divisionist technique; he is the true inventor of divisionism, that of touch if not of colour. His stippling is so dense that the dots blend, but a keen eye can detect them, and it is this swarming of separate touches of paint that gives his ground surfaces, pools and foliages their intense and secret life (*pl. 205*). The development of impressionism, with its vogue for clear colours, and the decomposition of certain of his pictures due to his use of bituminous compounds, have combined to consign Rousseau to an unmerited oblivion.

During his lifetime, Rousseau was reduced to desperate circumstances through the implacable hostility of the Salon juries, whose power over artists was absolute in an era when the Salon represented the only outlet for an artist's work. It is to be hoped that the future will redress Rousseau's wrongs, by restoring this genuinely avant-garde painter to his rightful place of eminence.

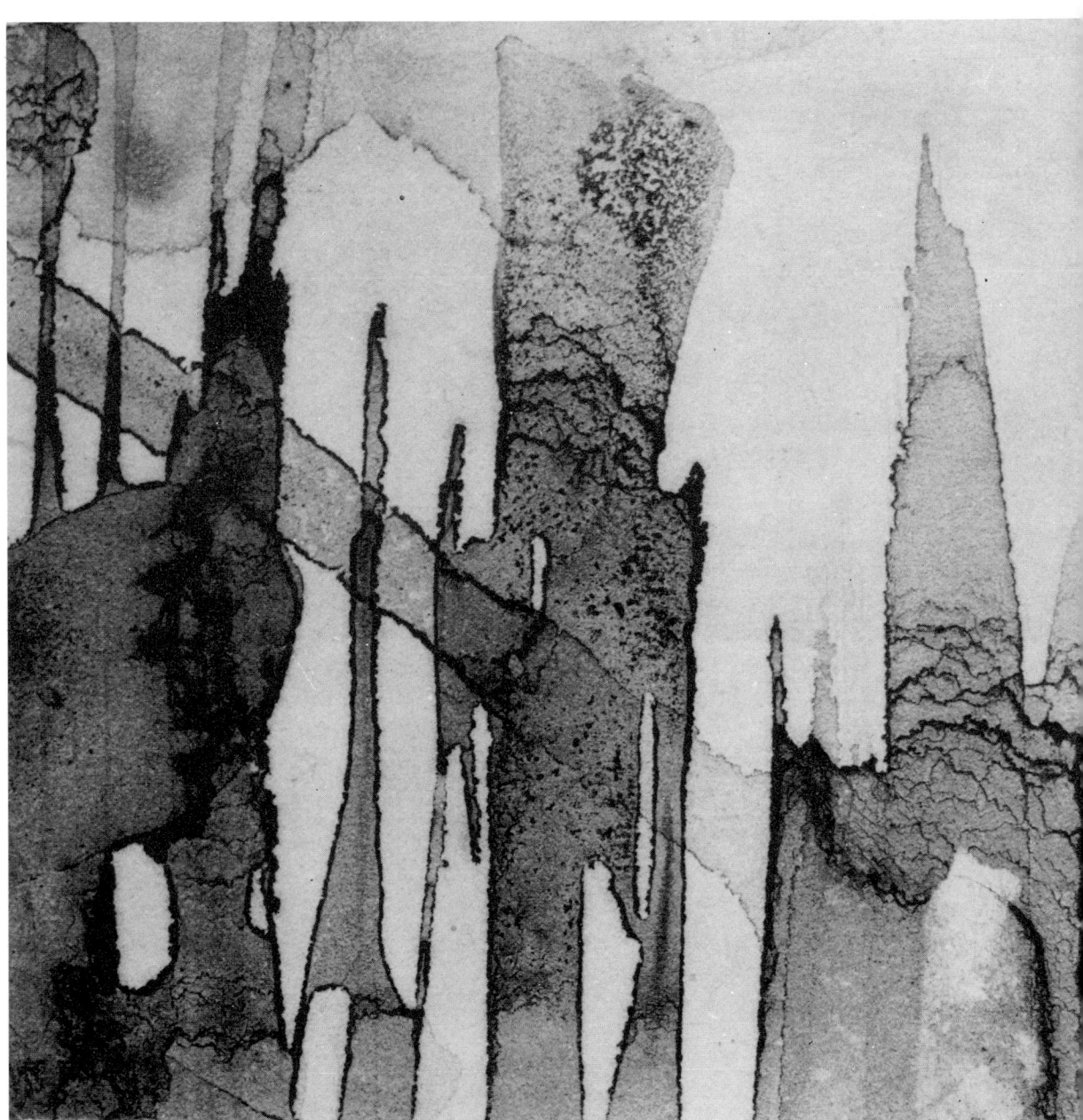

207 Victor Hugo (1802–85). *Blots*. Paris, collection Jean Hugo.

Romantic painters sometimes used a blotting technique as a means of releasing their creative impatience. In his secondary role as a Sunday painter, Victor Hugo sometimes went as far as an informal abstraction which anticipates modern art.

208 Edouard Manet (1832–83).
Detail of *Olympia*. Paris, Louvre.

15 Times of boldness

The impressionists brought with them, above all, a sense of release from all sorts of complexes. They had no illusions about being Poussins or Raphaels, and did not torment themselves with the problem of rivalling the achievements of classical antiquity or the great masters of previous centuries. They simply decided to guide painting back towards the perceived image, and went to work like good craftsmen, believing in themselves without arrogance, and displaying those virtues of simplicity and common sense which had guided Fouquet, the Le Nain brothers, Chardin and Poussin.

It is scarcely necessary to recall the huge scandal which this new approach to painting provoked. The appearance of Manet's *Luncheon on the grass* (*Déjeuner sur l'herbe*) at the Salon des Refusés in 1863 was a signal for the condemnation of the whole group in the name of morality; Manet's secret triumph was that he found himself being execrated for a composition borrowed directly from that idol of the public, Raphael. The scandal which pursued the impressionists from the date of their first group exhibition in 1874 was based overtly on aesthetic objections, but in fact after the ruthless crushing of the 1871 Commune anything that failed to conform exactly to bourgeois convention was automatically considered a menace to society.

These paintings, involving nothing more than a visual reference to nature, now seem so easy to assimilate that the original hostility towards them must appear incomprehensible to us today. But we tend to forget that the act of seeing with one's own eyes is an exceedingly rare and difficult achievement; most people, once they have grown up, no longer perceive reality as anything more than a system of references to ideas. And no public was more encumbered with ideas than that of the 1860s, burdened as it was with the twin heritages of classicism and romanticism. By daring to look at nature with an innocent eye, the impressionists showed the greatest audacity, and such an attitude was inevitably labelled subversive by their contemporaries. Worst of all, Courbet had gone so far as to claim a socialist significance for all aesthetic ideas inspired by nature.

The sun of impressionism rose from behind the dark clouds of romanticism. The impressionists have been reproached for creating a dehumanized art, but why should joy be considered a less natural feeling in the human heart than sadness? Manet celebrated the enchantment of worldly appearances. Monet, in love with light, sacrificed everything to it, going to the limit of plastic means in his desire to complete the exploration of light in space begun two centuries previously by Claude. And the exuberant Renoir, who was entirely exempt from romantic passion, fashioned an earthly paradise in which humanity could live in pagan innocence.

The year 1863 saw not only the public exhibition of Manet's *Luncheon on the grass* but also the death of Delacroix: a symbolic juxtaposition of birth and decease. Manet's purpose was to rediscover painting's true path, by clearing away all the tangled undergrowth of ideas that threatened to swallow it up. Realizing that his imagination was sluggish, and being disinclined to visualize any universe more extensive than that which could be comfortably contained within the dimensions of a canvas, Manet had the good sense to limit his ambitions to rediscovering the meaning of painting in the act of painting. It is this factor which accounts for his systematic tendency to base his work – even those compositions inspired by a contemporary event – upon some precedent borrowed from one of the old masters. Rather than claiming equality with the masters, as Delacroix did, he sought to capture their secret. The process of painting became all the easier for him because of his freedom from the necessity to invent; he created an entirely new handling, clean and precise, built up, in the French manner, with a minimum of transparency, through the interplay of heavily and lightly impasted paint, worked in calm and flowing strokes of the brush applied evenly and broadly (*pl. 208*). This technique distinguished him from the 'temperamental painting' practised at that time by Daumier, and by the young Cézanne who was sowing his wild oats of romanticism before setting out on the impressionist path.

By rescuing painting from literature and returning it to an explanation of its own resources, Manet prepared the way for Monet to create a new art starting out from art's fundamental premise, nature. To find a precedent for such an attitude, one would have to go back to the Gothic artists, who also rejected the logical outcome of entrenched forms and created new ones derived from a process of reasoning and observation. It needed the simple courage of these two men to topple the idols which had reigned in the West for four centuries, and this without any theory, manifesto or declaration of faith to bolster them – just a brush in the hand, working like those master craftsmen who built their cathedrals with trowel and chisel.

Monet was unquestionably the bolder of the two artists. While Manet prudently sought justification for his experiments in the work of the masters, Monet simply left his studio and became the first artist for centuries to dare look at the world without preconceived notions (*pl. 209*). The tragic aftermath of the 1870 War, reflected in the Salon's reactionary policy, turned Monet into a landscape painter. Previously, he had dreamed of showing modern man, life-size, in natural surroundings, thus following the path opened up by Courbet in his *Burial at Ornans*, *Stonebreakers* and *Bonjour, Monsieur Courbet*. Encouraged by the 1866 Salon, Monet undertook to paint a nature study as large in size as Courbet's *The Artist's Studio*. This composition, which he completed at Barbizon while staying at the inn there, depicted a group of men and women picnicking under the trees on a glorious summer Sunday; it was envisaged as a reply to Manet, who had arranged his art students and unclothed models in front of a theatrical setting. Dire poverty obliged Monet to leave this enormous canvas with the innkeeper, as security for unpaid bills. No doubt the huge picture would have been refused by the Salon; in any case, he subsequently cut it into sections, and today only two fragments survive (*pls 210–11*).

I have shown elsewhere (in my *Impressionist Paintings in the Louvre*, London and New York 1958) how this incident broke Monet's career, imposing upon him the more modest dimensions of easel painting, and scaling his ambition down to a delicate analysis of visual phenomena which resulted in his serial studies. Although modern art owes its whole inspiration to the stoicism of these painters, who preferred to suffer hardship rather than make concessions, officialdom succeeded nevertheless in stifling Monet's and Gauguin's first impulse towards large-scale painting. The exhibition wall space which had been given over to Delacroix in the first half of the century was reserved for Puvis de Chavannes in the second half.

The technique developed by Monet was, like that of Courbet, born of a rejection of transparent paint-ing (*pl. 212*). Instead of superimposing layers of colours in glazes, as the masters had done, Monet juxtaposed them in brief touches, the resulting 'optical mixture' being designed to produce an effect of chromatic richness analogous to that of transparent painting. Seurat was to rationalize this process, but in the hands of Monet it retained all its pristine vivacity, the freshness of the 'impression'. Renoir, on the other hand, continued to use the transparent handling he had learned in studying Rubens, Fragonard and Delacroix at the Louvre, and attained a virtuosity in this technique comparable to their own. As for Degas, his technique during his first period was influenced mainly by the judicious and precise handling of the sixteenth-century French and seventeenth-century Dutch portrait painters, as well as by Ingres. Furnished with such excellent descriptive methods, he felt able to tackle the most unusual subjects, particularly those nudes represented, so very unacademically, at various stages of their toilet. Degas's boldness as a painter encompassed all the processes which we now associate with the cinema, from close-ups to panoramic views, and so, for him too, the basic source of discovery in painting was the pure visual fact (*pl. 213*). He made use of a camera to help him in his researches, but handled it like a reporter at a time when photographers were still doing their best to produce imitations of paintings.

If Renoir owes a debt to Delacroix (a debt which he acknowledges in his 1872 *Parisian women dressed as Algerians*), Degas a debt to Ingres, and Manet to the Spanish school, it becomes evident that the boldest of them all, the one who dared measure himself against nature without any intermediary, was Monet. It was from Monet's researches, rather than from Manet's, that the future of painting flowed. His continual process of evolution, within the context of his experimentation, brought him back, towards the end of his life, to his youthful dreams of large-scale painting, only this time they were to express light, and light alone. Never satisfied with the results, frequently destroying or mutilating his canvases, Monet went on from one audacity to another, often disconcerting his friends, until his series of huge *Water-lilies* (*Nymphéas*), painted from 1916 onwards, made him the precursor of abstract expressionism (*pl. 264*).

For Seurat and Gauguin, the door was wide open. Seurat wanted to give a scientific basis to the breaking-down of the tone-scale which Monet had practised instinctively. Gauguin, on the other hand, felt a strong urge to return to the intrinsic order of classic art, where form was governed by idea; only, he chose to replace classical mythology with the

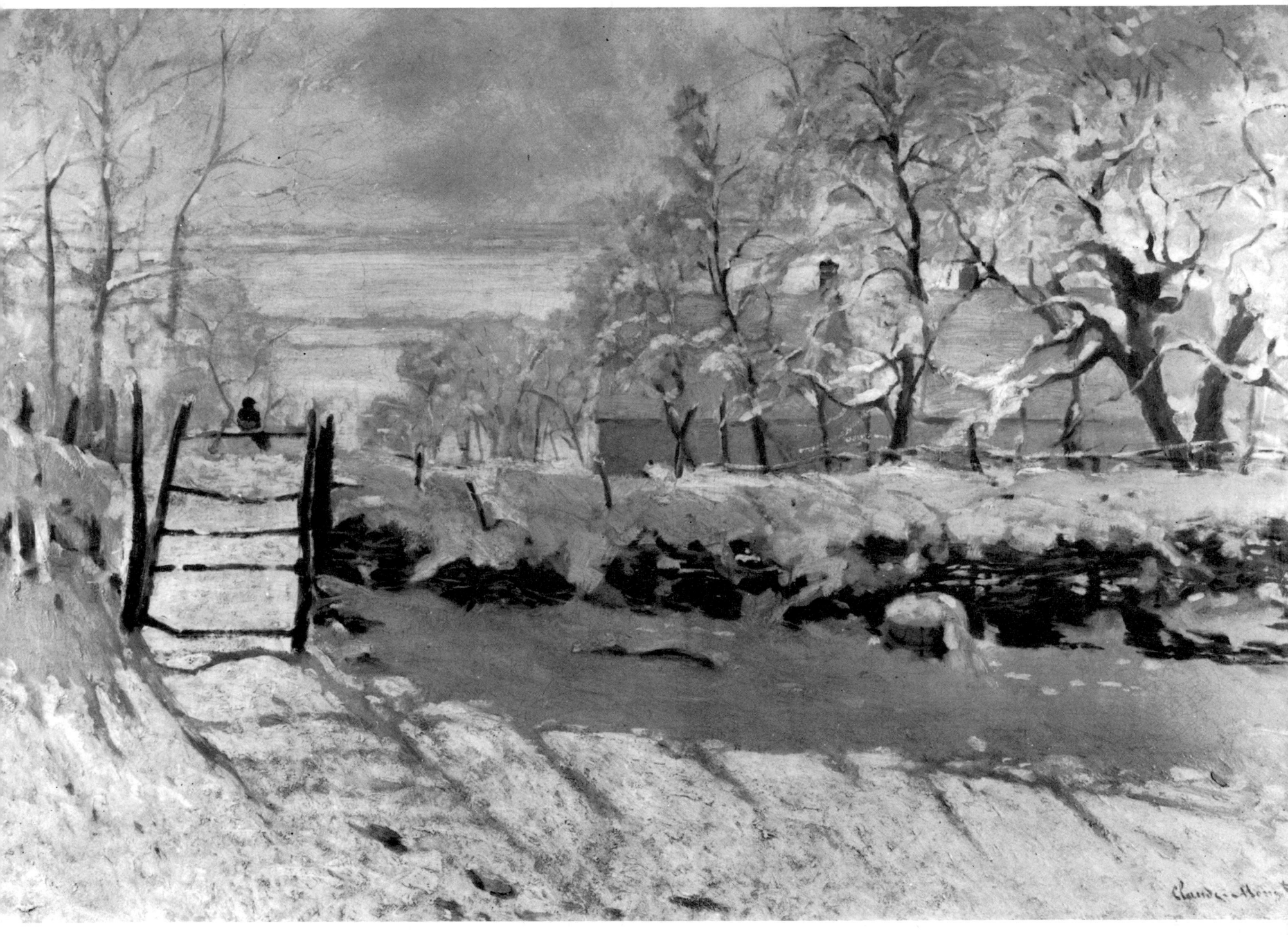

209 Claude Monet (1840–1926). *Snow effect, region of Honfleur.* Paris, collection Société Guerlain.

mythology of the Polynesian civilization. His romantic life, which has made him the very symbol of the *peintre maudit*, has masked the true nature of his art.

Van Gogh, in his turn, worshipped the idol of the sun in place of Monet's idol of light, symbolizing the fire devouring his soul by a solar furnace which turned his world into a burning mass. Van Gogh appears almost as the sworn enemy of Monet, destroying the fragile world of appearances which the latter had created. His originality lies, above all, in his handling, consisting of great sweeps of pure colour (*pls 214–15*). This handling deteriorated during his Auvers period, losing its suppleness and becoming mechanical and atomized, the strokes breaking into small licks. It may well have been because he felt his talent declining that he put an end to his life.

Van Gogh instilled new vigour into the tradition of expressionist painting and opened the way to the excesses of the fauves. In his letters to his brother Theo he continuously emphasized his romantic affiliations. In a letter to Theo dated August 1888, for example, he wrote: 'You know, whatever this sacrosanct impressionism may be, all the same I wish I could paint things that the previous generation,

Monet was the first to look at nature with an absolutely innocent eye, free of all convention or formalism.

243

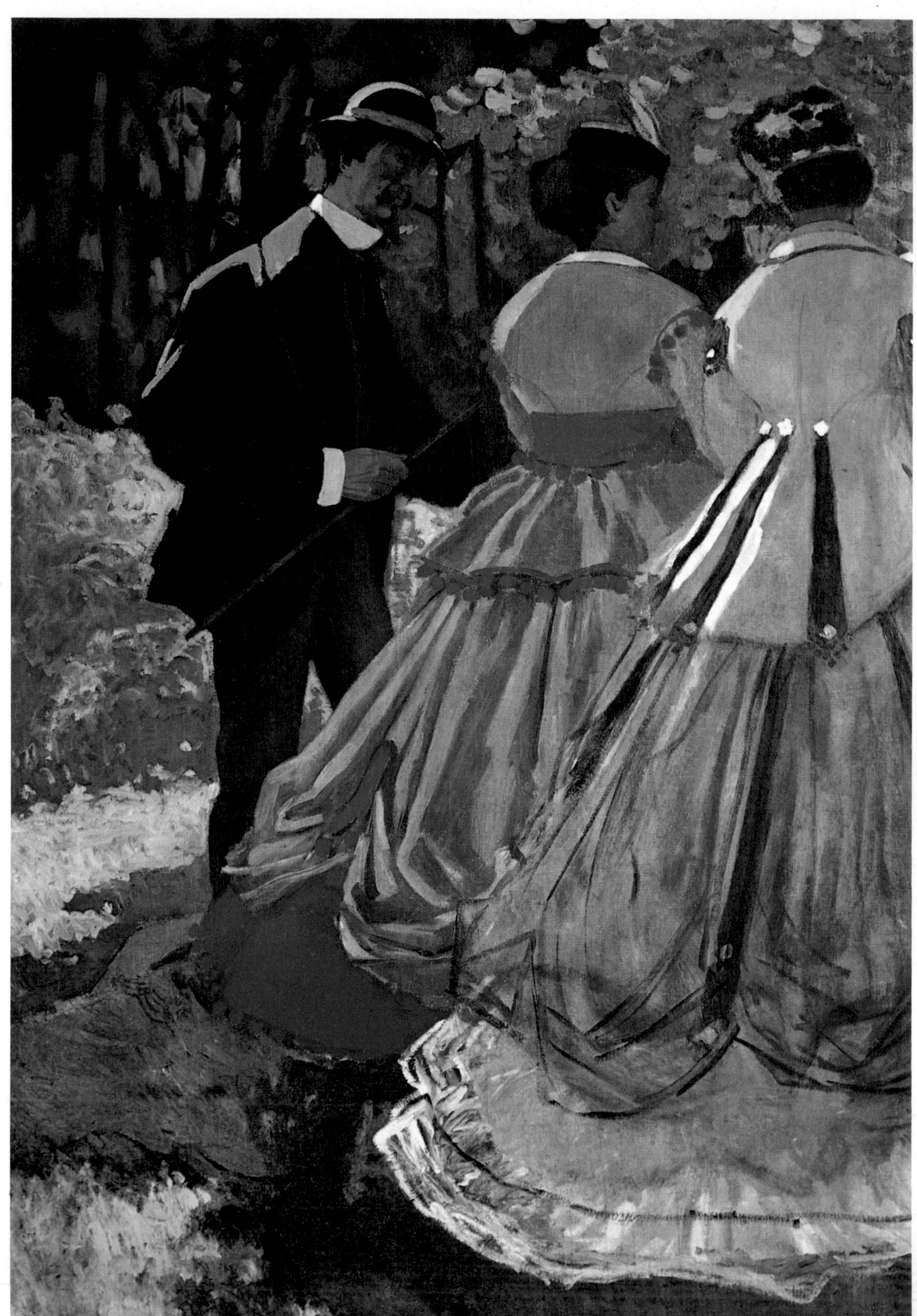

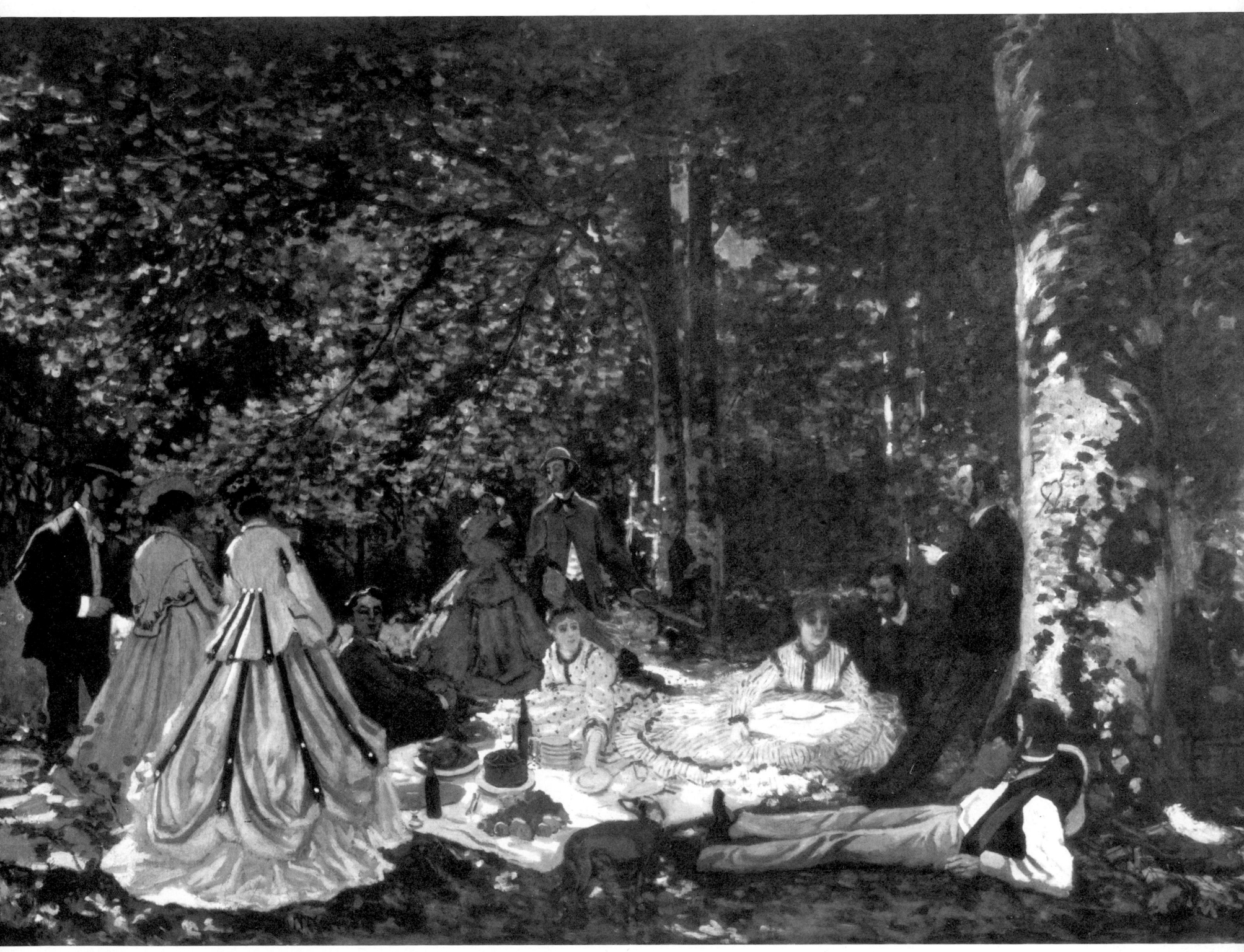

◀ 210 Claude Monet. Detail of *Luncheon on the grass* (surviving fragment). Paris, Louvre.

211 Claude Monet. Sketch for *Luncheon on the grass*. Moscow, Pushkin Museum.

In 1865, Monet was bold enough to paint a picture thirty feet square, entirely from nature. Poverty, and the incomprehension of the public, forced him to cut up this outstandingly important work, as the disappointed Rembrandt had had to do, two centuries earlier, with his *Conspiracy of Julius Civilis*.

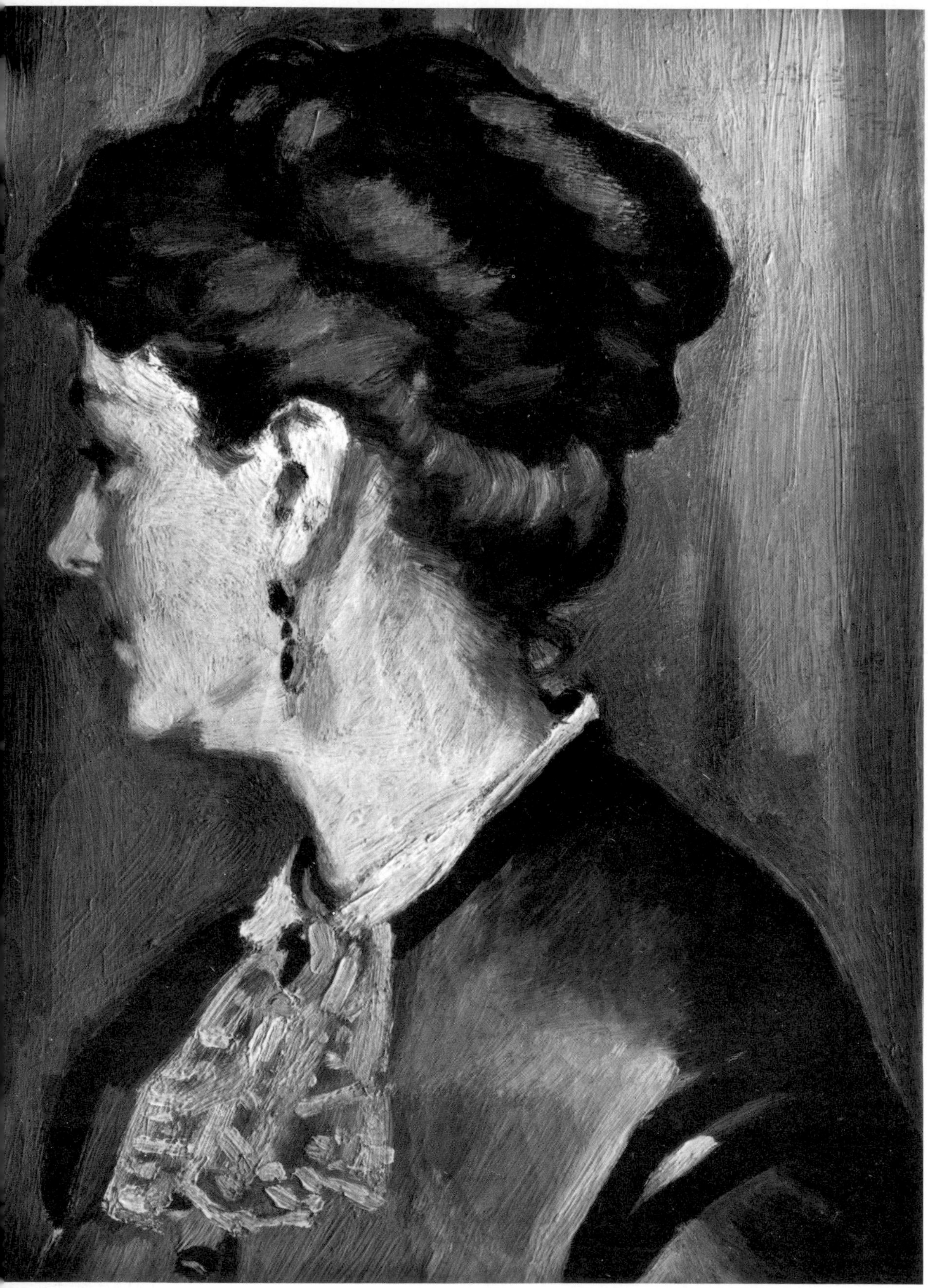

212 Claude Monet. Detail of *Madame Gaudibert*. Paris, Louvre.

Monet invented a supple handling which he improvised to suit the particular object to be painted.

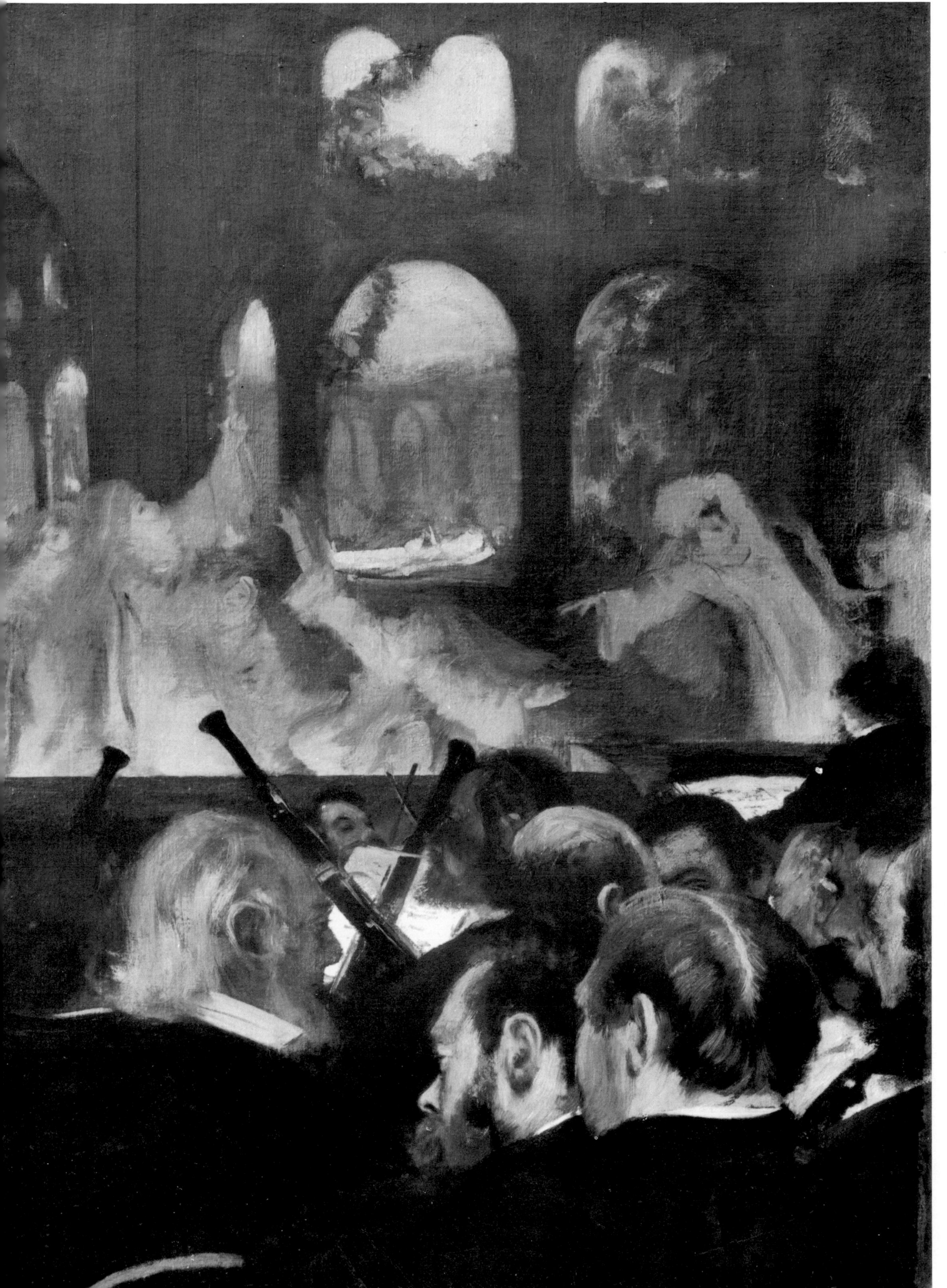

213 Edgar Degas (1834–1917).
*The Ballet Scene from Meyerbeer's
'Roberto il Diavolo'*. London,
Victoria and Albert Museum.

So intense is his curiosity that, in his
researches into previously
unrecorded aspects of reality, Degas
anticipates cinematic techniques.

247

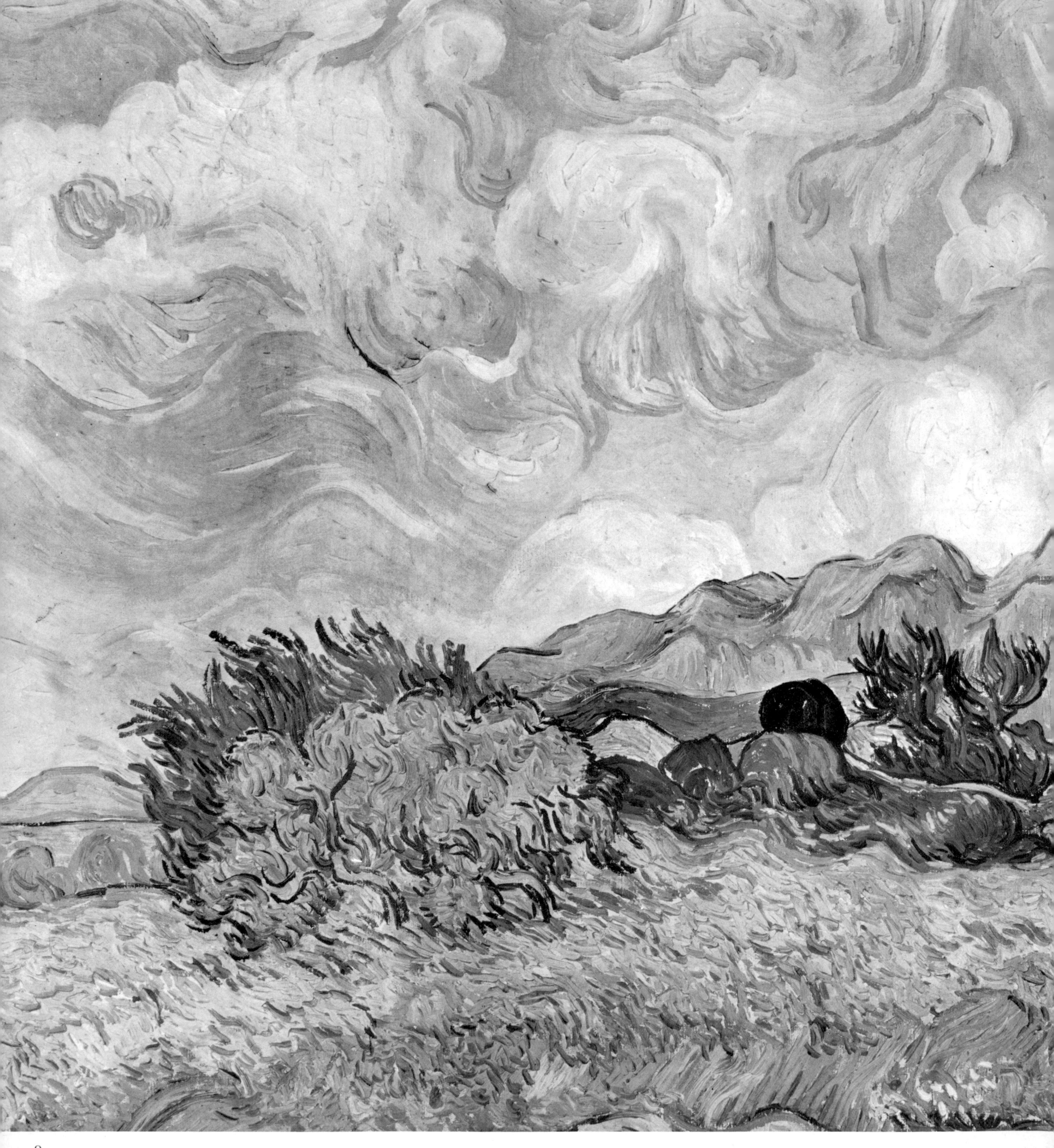

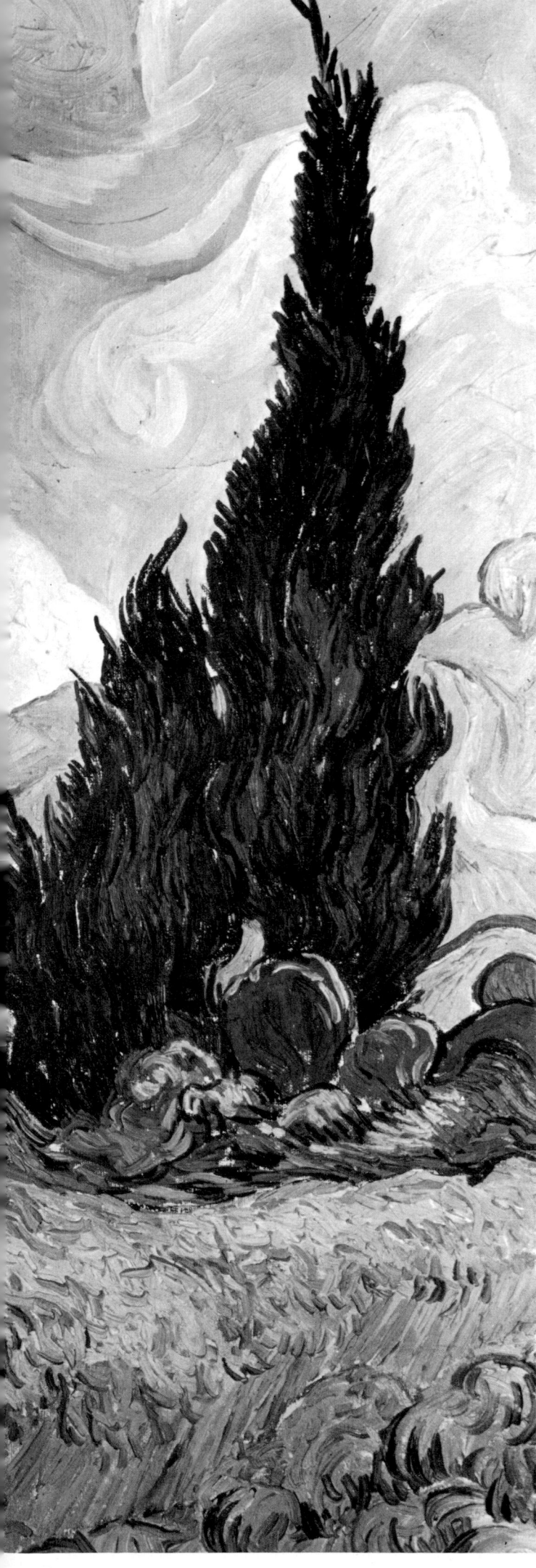

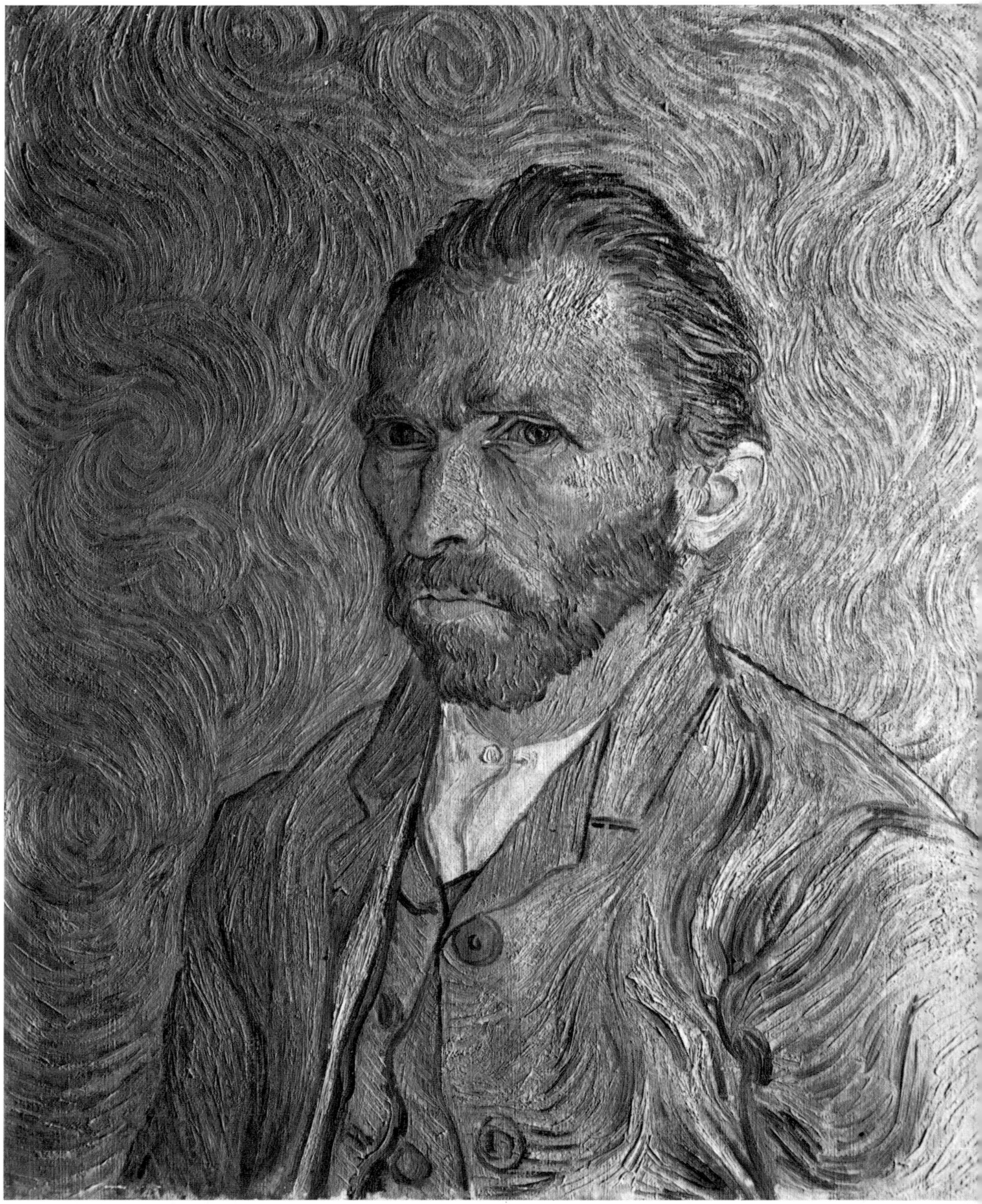

◀ 214 Vincent van Gogh (1853–90). *Cornfield and cypress trees*. London, Tate Gallery.

215 Vincent van Gogh. *Self-portrait*. Photograph with side lighting. Paris, Louvre.

Van Gogh's contact with impressionism brought to the surface his instinctive northern feeling for expressionism, and he may thus be held to have opened the way to the excesses of the fauves.

249

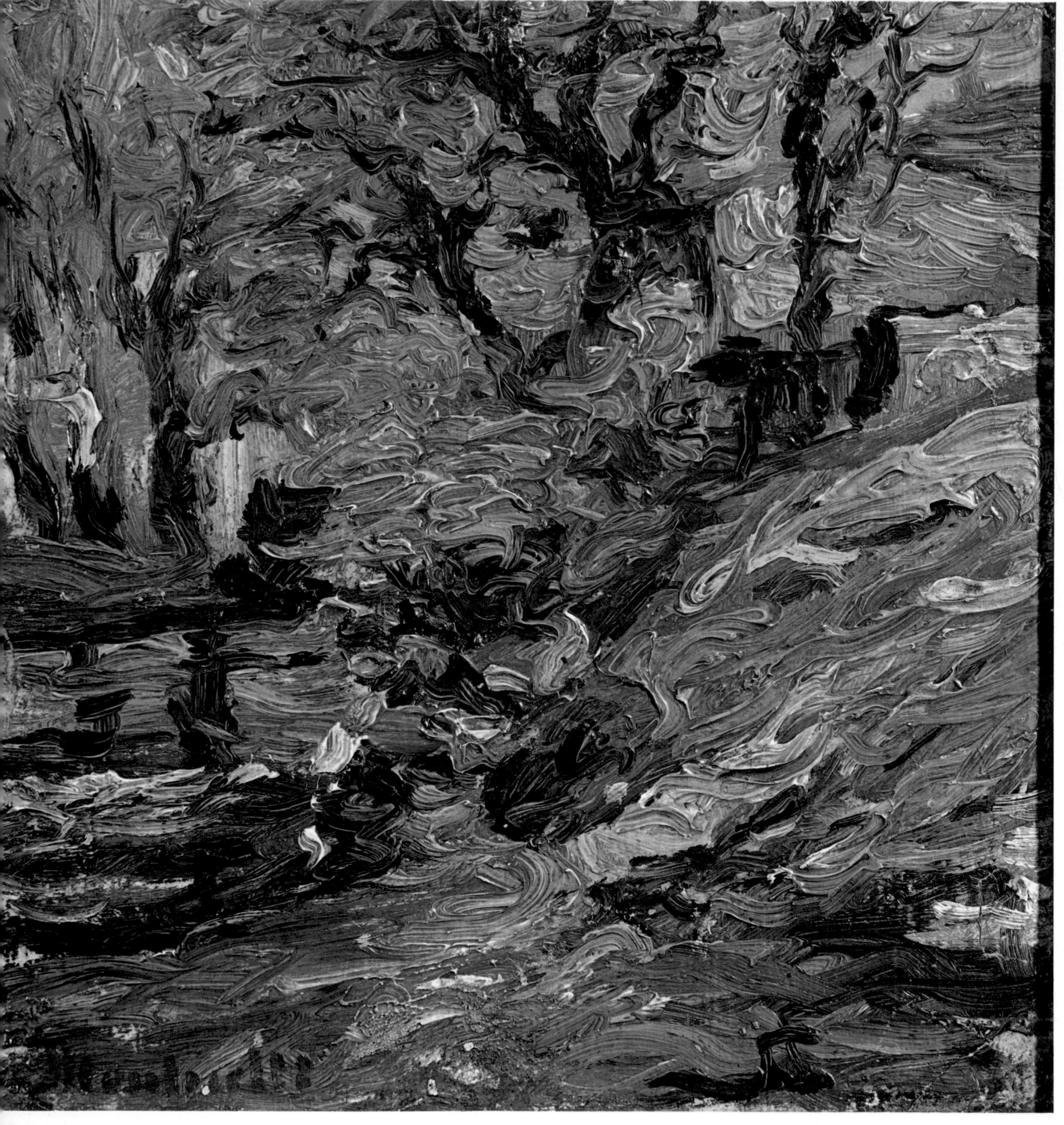

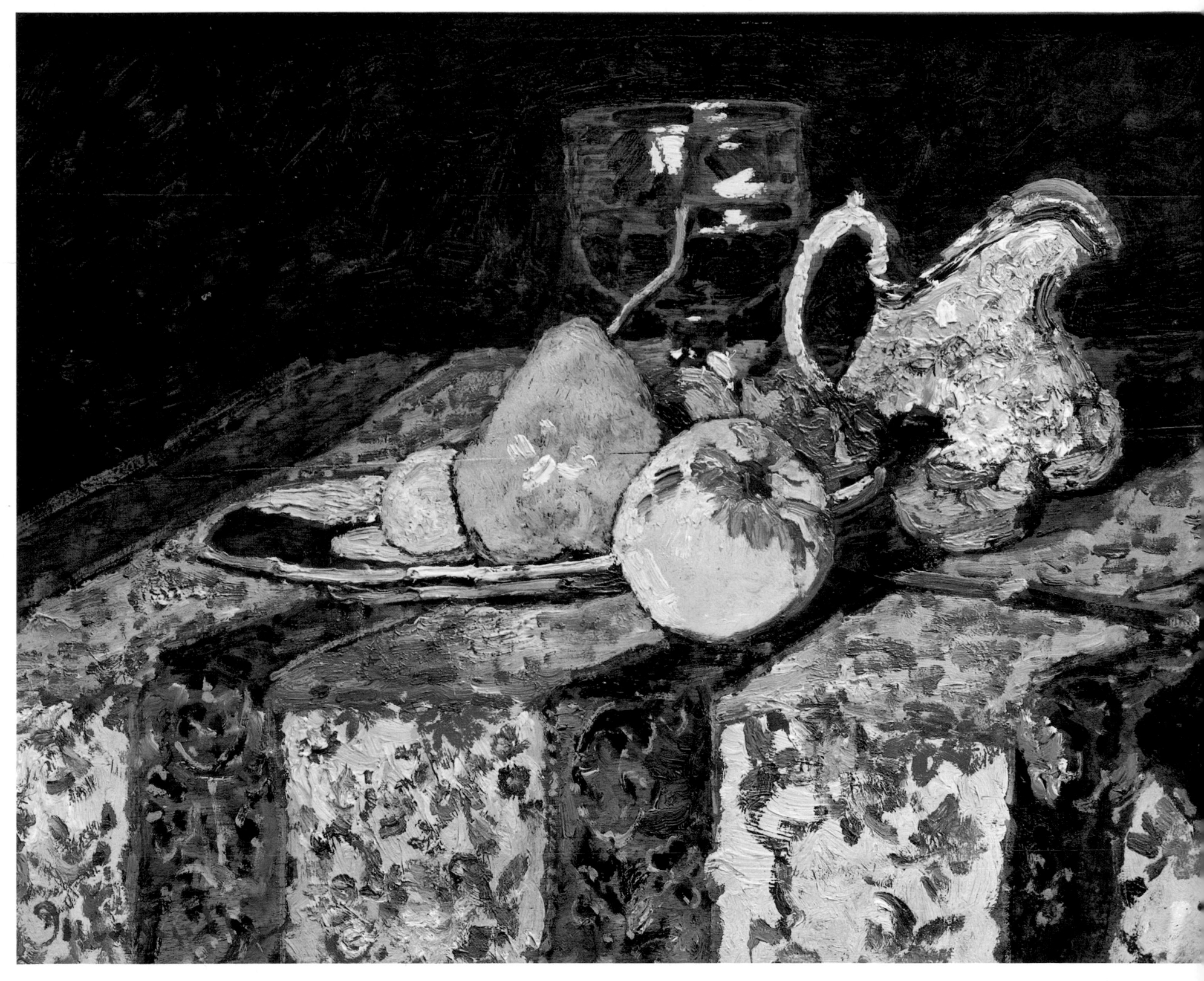

◀ 216 Adolphe Monticelli (1824–86). *Under the trees by the water's edge*. Collection Alfred Lambert.

217 Adolphe Monticelli. *The White Jug*. Paris, Louvre.

The Marseillais painter Monticelli, an astonishing precursor, invented a free technique which proved as revelatory to van Gogh as impressionism.

218 Paul Cézanne (1839–1906).
The Repentant Magdalen. Paris,
Louvre.

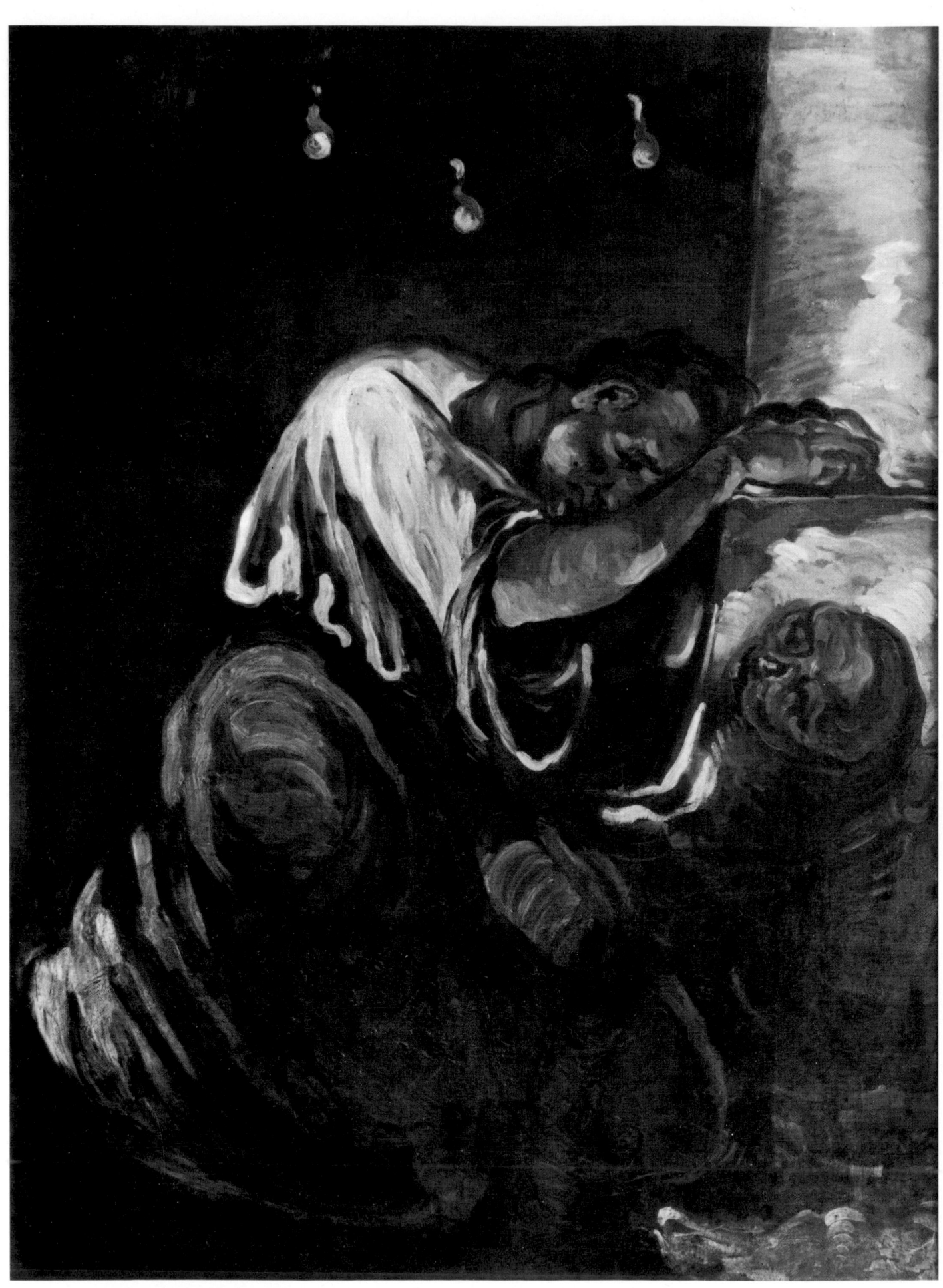

The artist who wished to base
painting on visual data started out
as a visionary, and in this early
phase Cézanne was certainly the
most passionate exponent of
'temperamental' painting.

Delacroix, Millet, Rousseau, Diaz, Monticelli, Isabey, Decamps, Dupré, Jongkind, Ziem, Israëls, Meunier, a heap of others, Corot, Jacques, etc., could understand. . . .' Van Gogh's attachment to the romantics was slightly confused, some of his preferences being literary and others artistic: the ex-missionary at Borinage admired Millet's socialism, while in the case of Delacroix he appreciated the 'suggestive' colour.

But there is a particular painter who marks the transition between the very different styles of Delacroix and van Gogh. This painter is Adolphe Monticelli, an underestimated figure who lived near Marseilles and remained aloof from all the groups and schools of the time. This obscure link between the romantic Delacroix and van Gogh was nevertheless an important one. Coming from romanticism, Monticelli transformed the style of the 1830 school into a painting of temperament, more thoughtful than was at first apparent, and based upon an intelligent exploration of the museums. Emerging from his first manner, with its earthy pigments, van Gogh's first instinct, on arriving in Paris and being introduced to impressionism, was to throw away his palette altogether. What changed his mind and made him determine to continue painting was his discovery of Monticelli, examples of whose work he had been able to see when Theo had taken him to visit a fellow art dealer, Delarebeyrette, who had been selling Monticelli's paintings for many years.

The influence exercised by Monticelli over van Gogh is attested by the frequency with which the latter mentions the Marseillais artist in his letters to Theo. Describing to his brother some spectacle of nature – a setting sun, a cypress swaying in the wind – or else discussing one of his own compositions, van Gogh often takes Monticelli as a reference point. Writing in 1888 he describes his paintings in these terms: 'The studies now are really done with a single coat of thick enamel paint. The touch is not much divided and the tones are often broken, and altogether I am involuntarily obliged to lay it on thick in Monticelli's way.' And he goes so far as to add: 'Sometimes I think I really am a continuation of that man, only I have not yet done the figures of lovers as he did.' Monticelli's genius appeared to van Gogh to be so close to his own spirit that at Saint-Rémy, at the moment when he was discussing quite lucidly his fear of losing his reason, van Gogh quoted Monticelli as an example of a painter who had died insane. Indeed, van Gogh's admiration was so great that when in 1880 Albert Aurier published a laudatory article about him in the *Mercure de France*, he reproached the critic in the following

terms: 'What I wanted to say was that all the good things you say about me should really be applied to Monticelli to whom I owe so much.'

The work van Gogh completed in Paris shows him divided between two tendencies. In some of his paintings, particularly the landscapes, he went as far as adopting divisionist technique in his desire to make use of the analytical vision of impressionism. In his flower pieces, on the other hand, he gives himself up entirely to the unrestricted joy of painting, and in these still-lifes the influence of Monticelli's flower pieces is unmistakable.

Who, then, was Monticelli, this painter who played such an important role in developing van Gogh's artistic self-awareness? Obscured during his lifetime by his independent stance and his provincial environment, his reputation suffered, after his death, from the absurd legends about him concocted by writers such as Gustave Coquiot. Although Monticelli's habits were certainly no more eccentric than those of Cézanne, he became the symbol of the dauber, the bohemian hawking his pictures around café *terrasses*, a slightly ridiculous figure always in and out of love, fond of the bottle, claiming to be a marquis descended from an imaginary dukedom of Spoleto.

Once the layers of legend have been peeled away, however, one finds an honourable painter, *déclassé*, a simple man and amiable companion, passionately devoted to his art, never exposed to the financial difficulties from which the impressionists suffered. His noble lineage becomes reduced to a family of artisans from Turin (including two gilders) whose origins can be traced back to the seventeenth century. An ancestor came to Marseilles in 1767 to get married; he was the great-grandfather of Adolphe-Joseph-Thomas Monticelli. This love-child, before being legitimized by his parents' belated marriage, passed his early childhood under conditions of secrecy, in the shadow of the ruined monastery of Ganagobie, in the harsh heat of Haute Provence, with the stars, cicadas and goats his only teachers.

Monticelli's genius was slow to mature. He took a long time to find his true path, hesitating between his admiration for various artists living and dead, Watteau, Delacroix, Diaz de la Peña, and his fellow Marseillais Gustave Ricard. He may also have been influenced by the painter Joseph Guichard, a pupil of Delacroix, whom he knew before 1863 in Lyons. Ricard's painting, a sort of glossy academicism, almost deflected him from his true vocation. Diaz de la Peña was a more wholesome influence: this Spanish adherent of the Barbizon school painted at two levels, landscapes from nature and small-scale compositions featuring nudes which he

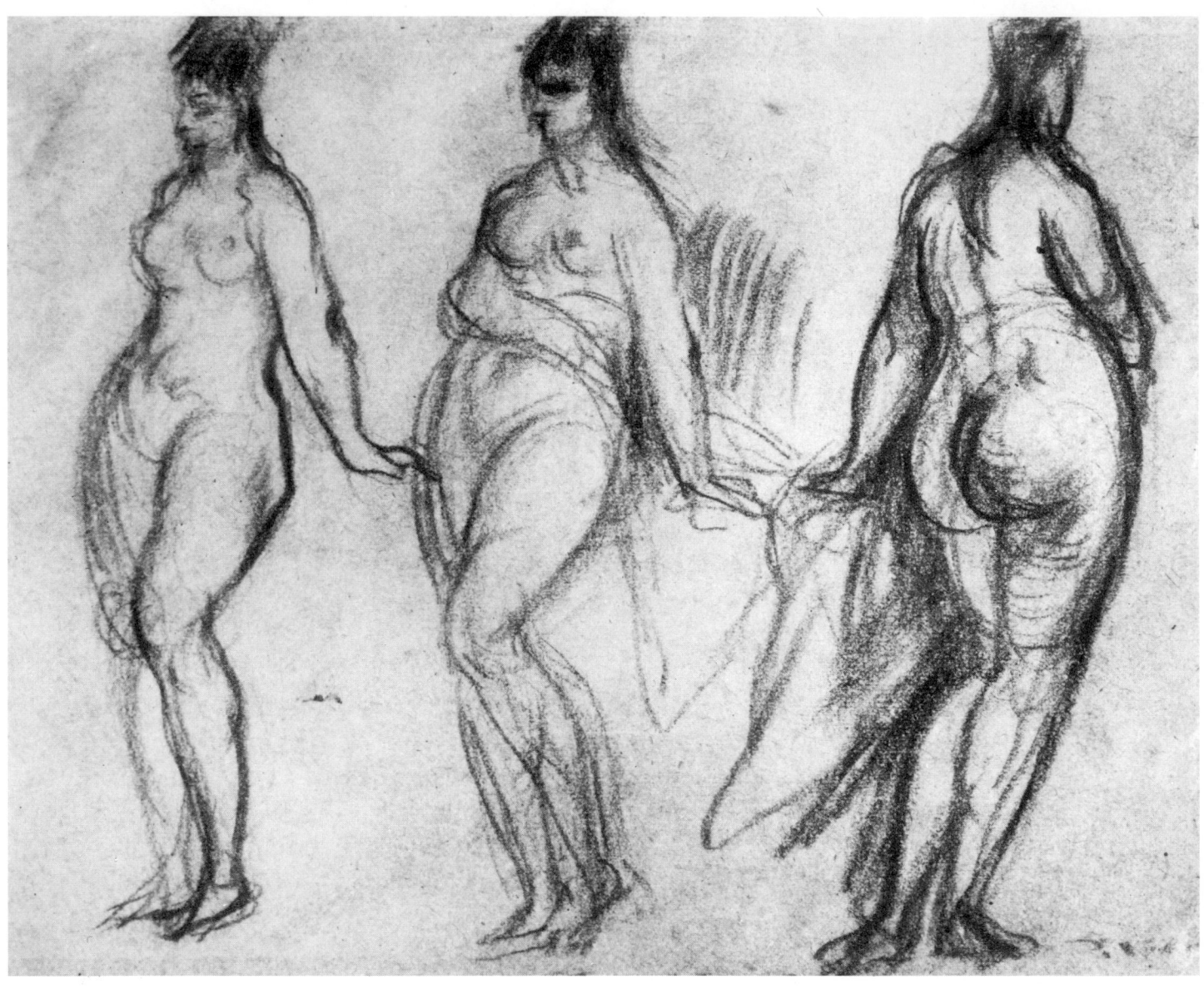

The nudes of Achille Emperaire almost certainly influenced Cézanne, who was friendly with Emperaire during his youth in Aix and was himself timid about painting from the nude female model.

dashed off in a free style and for which there was a ready market. Monticelli, who during 1856 was briefly Diaz's neighbour, imitated his painting so faithfully that a Lyons newspaper commented: 'M. Monticelli is continuing at Marseilles his sparkling pastiches of Diaz. . . .' Diaz's encouragement of Monticelli's attempts at this kind of genre painting was perhaps misplaced, since the results were comparatively weak; on the other hand, Diaz took him with him to Fontainebleau to paint from nature, encouraging him by his own example to abandon Ricard's oleaginous tones, and teaching him the marvels of colour sustained by the muted tones of the warm shadows. In Monticelli's work of the second period, during the decade from 1860 to 1870, his genius can be seen slowly emerging; the paintings are still conventional in terms of subject and arrangement, but a sense of concealed power can already be felt.

In 1871, Monticelli escaped from the horrors of war-stricken Paris and walked all the way to Marseilles. He was forty-seven, and never returned to the capital. The last fifteen years of his life were by far the most fruitful, and he spent them all in the southern port, dividing his activities, like a true romantic, between imaginative works painted in his studio and studies from nature – landscapes, flower pieces, portraits and picturesque scenes. A victim hitherto of the inferiority complex of a provincial in Paris, his imagination suddenly blossomed. Leaving the museums happily behind him, and cured of his oppressive veneration for the 'masters' of his time, he no longer sought to rival one hero or another: at last he became himself. It was none too soon; his return to Marseilles was providential.

As though determined to compensate for an overlong repression of his instincts, Monticelli, having at last discovered his true destiny, proceeded to produce a huge body of work during the next fifteen years. He worked with a passionate enthusiasm foreshadowing van Gogh's ardour, accumulating more than eight hundred pictures in less than ten years. Recording feverishly the scenes suggested to him by his own imagination or by nature, Monticelli dashed his colours on to small walnut or mahogany panels, using brushes whose bristles he had cut off half-way down to make them stiffer (contrary to general supposition, he very seldom used a palette-knife). Although he occasionally succumbed, especially in his last years, to the facility which is the hazard of all artists of 'temperament', this pictorial laxity conquered him only when his imagination became overheated in the solitude of his studio. The challenge of reality provoked magnificently inspired triumphs: still-lifes (*pl. 217*) of a rich splendour which leave those of Willem Kalf and Jan Davidsz. de Heem far behind, landscapes (*pl. 216*) depicting a golden age such as Renoir was to conceive later on when he, too, first experienced the Provençal sunshine, portraits with glowing features anticipating those of van Gogh and Soutine.

From what source did Monticelli derive his romantic instinct? What allowed him, when freed from the stifling atmosphere of Paris, to paint with a freedom never previously attempted? His art has sometimes been explained by his Provençal background, as though this region, whose imaginative and verbal fluency has been celebrated by Alphonse Daudet, should naturally produce painters of temperament. This assumption is perhaps not so far from the truth, for Monticelli is not an isolated figure. There exists in Provence a tendency towards the free artistic expression of temperament which has produced a number of painters of exceptional ability.

It is evident that the methods of painting of Daumier, and of the Cézanne of his 'black' phase, are akin to that of Monticelli. The three styles are characterized by a complete absence of aesthetic tradition, by a freedom of invention limited but also abetted by technical ignorance, and lastly by a recourse to the exaggerated impasto which is the typical approach of self-taught painters ignorant of the complex procedures involved in the expert use of transparent paint. This kind of exaggeration is the reaction of an untrained artistic temperament exasperated by the problem of expressing what masters of technique such as Frans Hals or Velázquez could say in a few diaphanous glazes. Monticelli was so prodigal with his impasto that his paintings sometimes resemble bas-reliefs: in the astonishing *Fortune-tellers*, for example, the pigment rises to craggy ridges almost an inch thick!

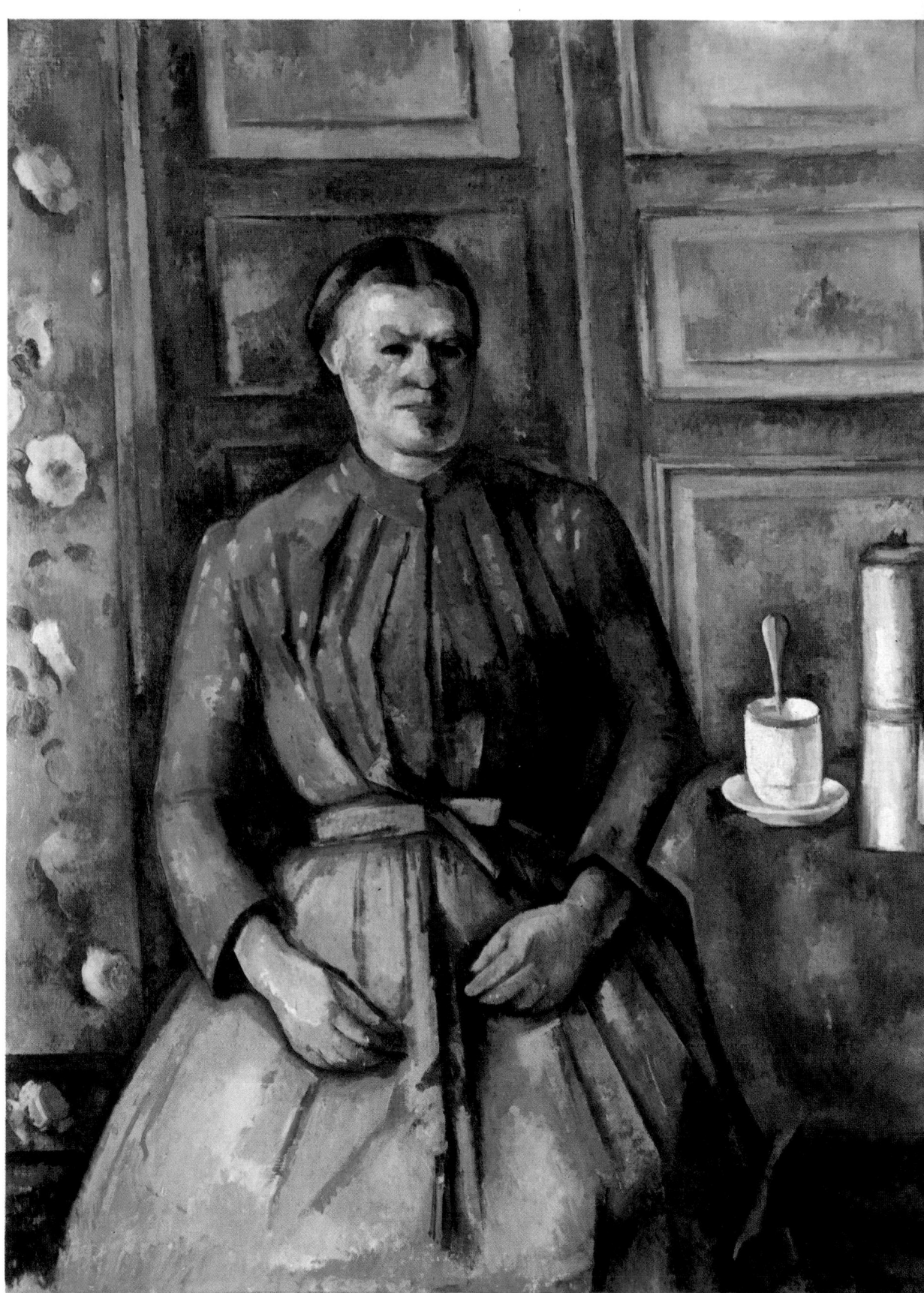

220 Paul Cézanne. *Woman with a coffee-pot*. Paris, Louvre.

After starting out as a libertarian romantic and traversing the disciplines of impressionism, Cézanne restored the grandeur of classicism in a modern form.

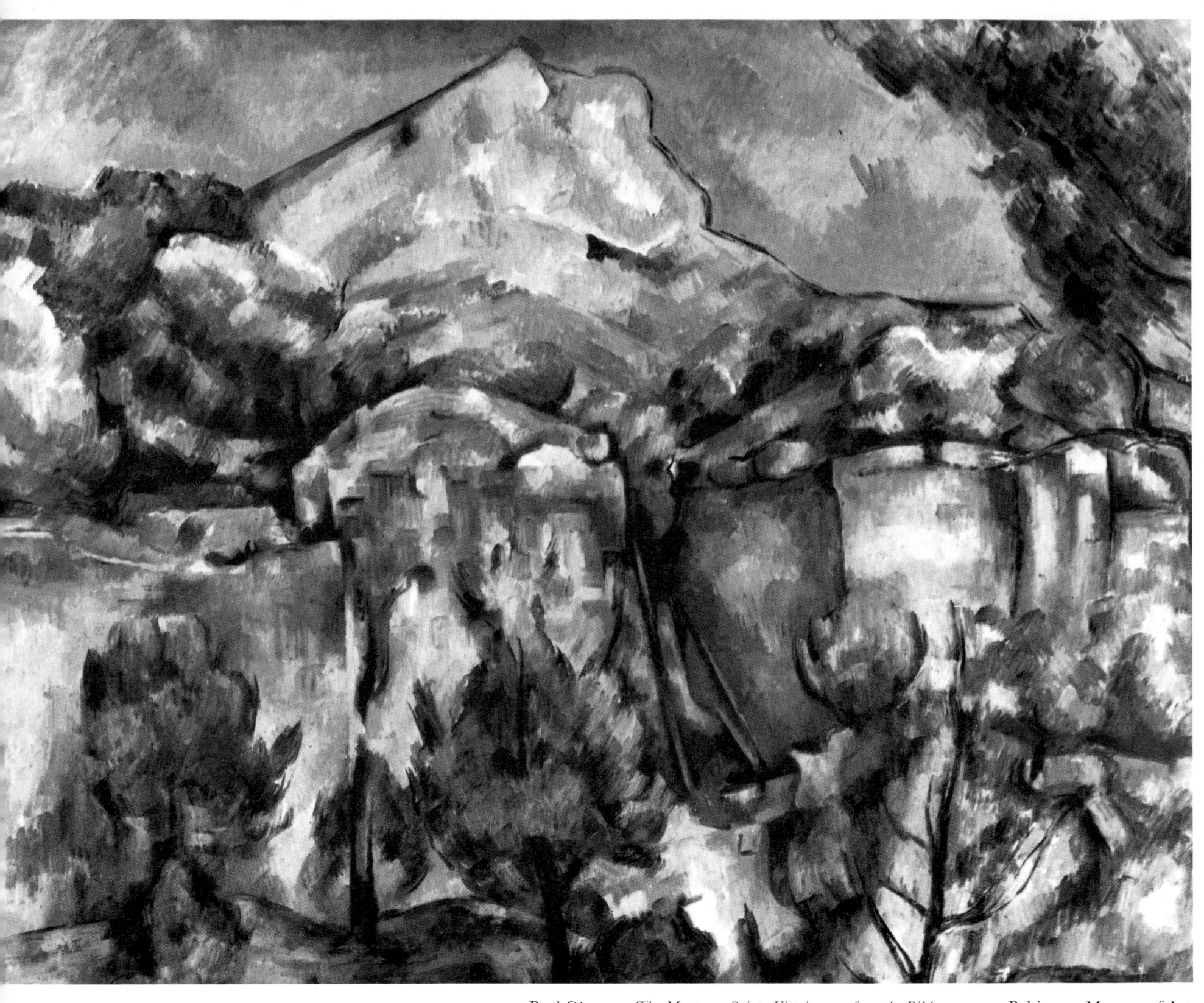

221 Paul Cézanne. *The Montagne Sainte-Victoire seen from the Bibémus quarry*. Baltimore, Museum of Art.

During the course of his long contemplation of this mountain, Cézanne passed gradually from classicism to the anxious painting of his final years.

256

During the nineteenth century, transparent painting reigned supreme in Paris, as much with the classicizing painters as with the romantics, and after a moment of hesitation (Manet, Monet) the impressionists too adopted this well-tried process (Degas, Renoir). But in Lyons and Marseilles, the only two important French centres of artistic activity outside Paris, a more or less evenly spread impasto was the technique in general use, by the most conservative of academics as well as by experimental artists such as Monticelli. In Lyons, in particular, a thick muddy technique has been practised religiously by all its artists from the romantics onwards: not only Guichard, Seignemartin, Ravier, Carrand and Vernay, but even Puvis de Chavannes himself, who retained from his Lyonnais origins this consistent, brownish treatment. In our own days, the tradition has been continued by Charmy, Couty and the extraordinary Bouche, who spent his life developing a handling with the colour and consistency of a cow-pat.

The Provençals, on the other hand, are blessed with an instinct for the baroque which has allowed them to indulge in all the freedoms of a technique in the service of the imaginary. Daumier, Monticelli and Cézanne all rejected formal texture of any kind and lashed their canvases with those great weals of colour which were already to be seen in certain paintings by Fragonard, that virtuoso who ran the gamut of feeling from Rembrandt to Rubens and from Ruisdael to Guardi.

Had Cézanne died at the age of thirty he would have belonged not to impressionism but to Provençal painting. The violence of a passionate temperament liberated itself in those first paintings, executed clumsily and brutally with a palette-knife in a sombre impasto gashed with whites and streaked with flashes of colour. The young artist visualized this dark frenzy as a demonstration of energy, and it was this phase of his painting which he referred to, coarsely, later on as his *manière couillarde*. He thought of himself then as a revolutionary, and his art made no demands on the perceived object. Obsessed by erotic dreams, he painted fantastic compositions seething with human larvae, monstrous embraces, scenes of assassination, murder and rape. On the rare occasions when he introduced nature into these compositions, it was in a twisted, tortured form corresponding to his violent instincts.

Cézanne's *Red roofs* of 1870 already contains the essential ingredients of Vlaminck, and his still-lifes of the 'black' phase have the emotional concentration of the *bodegones* of Velázquez and Zurbarán. The paintings of the youthful Cézanne are black flowers of romanticism; like those of Monticelli and Daumier they derive from the continuing tradition of southern romanticism, permeated with the idea of darkness, and leading from Tintoretto to Goya by way of Strozzi, Crespi, Francesco del Cairo, Carbone, the enigmatic Monsù Desiderio, Cavallini, Salvator Rosa, Magnasco and Jacques Gamelin. However, the Cézanne of the first manner, drawing upon the ancestral resources of baroque feeling, was also preparing himself for the future. It has been said that when this great painter, perhaps the greatest painter of the century, found his true destiny he sowed the seeds of the future of art at the same time. Certainly, if the composer of the *Bathers* (*Grandes baigneuses*) reaches out his hand to the cubists, the author of so many frenzied inventions in paint points the way to fauve expressionism. And a picture such as the *Repentant Magdalen* (*pl. 218*) embraces not only El Greco and Daumier, but premonitions of Rouault, and even the contortions of Lorjou! This inspired artist was so possessed by the demon of painting that he contained within himself its past, present and future. He himself was conscious of this future. In 1896 he wrote to Joachim Gasquet: 'Perhaps I arrived too early. I was the painter of your generation rather than my own.'

According to Cézanne's letters to Zola, and the recollections of a few of the artist's friends who were his drinking companions during that period, the circle of art students and budding poets in Aix-en-Provence was in a constant fever of anti-conformist ideas and subversive projects. As evidence of this embryonic romantic school in Aix, with Cézanne as leader, there remain the few paintings and, more important, the beautiful drawings of that strange artist Achille Emperaire, a dwarf with the face of a musketeer, of whom Cézanne has left us a touching portrait which has the harsh grandeur of Velázquez's clowns. The subject-matter and technique of Emperaire's pictures relate them to those which Monticelli was painting, with greater talent, during the same period. The drawings, on the other hand, especially the nudes with their plump outlines (*pl. 219*), evoke the graphic quality, impatient, cursive and baroque, of Cézanne's manner at that same time.

The very extent of this pictorial licence gives some idea of the degree of restraint Cézanne had to impose upon himself to conquer his 'temperament'. It is characteristic of youth to assume that the uninhibited display of instincts represents the most genuine expression of individuality. But instinct is the undifferentiated voice of the human species; personality is born from mastered passion. The discipline that Cézanne had lacked during his artistic apprenticeship he acquired, with Pissarro's help, in impressionism, to which he submitted with surprising docility considering his impetuous nature. Re-educated by Pissarro, the most theory-minded of the open-air painters, Cézanne learned to see nature and to base his imagination upon nature, investigating with the other members of the school the shared results of their researches into light and optical truth.

The Suicide's House (*La Maison du pendu*), painted at Auvers-sur-Oise in 1873, represented the point of no return for Cézanne. The pigment was still heavy, and like roughcast in texture, but the blazing colour had the brilliance of enamel. At that juncture, he was still fascinated by unctuous, granular pigment, to which the urgency of his brushstrokes communicated a living, breathing quality. Liberated from the black tones of his first period, but still retaining his sense of the baroque, Cézanne's momentary hesitation between these two aspects of himself produced a few paintings evocative of Fragonard, such as the exquisite second version of the *Modern Olympia* (Louvre).

Two or three years later, though, Cézanne deliberately entered his classic period, renouncing the eloquence of pigment and touch, and trusting to the skilful arrangement of forms and colours to reveal to him the secret of harmony. Reversing his technique, he painted from now on only in thin applications of pigment, following watercolour technique, and practised a strict economy of means (*pl. 220*). However, although Cézanne, in his still-lifes, landscapes, portraits and figure-compositions such as the *Card players*, devoted himself thenceforward to the patient elaboration of a new classicism, nevertheless certain *Bathers* and the vestiges of eroticism in a few subjects revealed that although his deep emotions had been largely repressed they were still seething under the surface.

Doubtless it is this only partially neutralized baroque urge which explains so many peculiarities and apparent *gaucheries* in Cézanne's art: those carefully constructed compositions which come tumbling down like a house of cards, those tottering vases, those fruit-dishes spilling their contents, those wobbly armchairs bringing down in their collapse the people who are sitting in them. All these defeats must be seen as reasons for the despair which constantly nagged at Cézanne, as symptoms of the ceaseless inner battle between his classical intentions and his baroque temperament.

'Contour evades me,' he once said. Contour provides the classical definition of the object, but the baroque painter deliberately breaks the object's texture in order to allow the pigment to live and breathe; Cézanne always had difficulty in imposing

upon himself a classical restraint of surface and volume. Another thing that evaded him was a sense of the vertical and horizontal; he was constantly haunted by obliqueness, the famous diagonal of baroque compositions. To exorcise this temptation, he took care to impose upon most of his pictures an imaginary graph composed of the two Cartesian co-ordinates, making a tree, the rim of a basin, a bottle or the edge of a table substitute for an axis.

In the last ten years of his life, his baroque instincts rose to the surface once more. He had no need, though, to return to the unnecessary excesses of his romantic technique, for he was now able to draw, with astonishing economy, upon the rich resources of thirty years of unremitting effort: *The Montagne Sainte-Victoire* (*pl. 221*) shaken by earth tremors, the *Château noir* devoured by flames resembling the flamboyant tracery of Gothic churches, *Bathers* (*pl. 222*) who already encompass the art of Rouault and Picasso.

The word impressionism, coined by a critic to describe Monet's picture *Impression: sunrise* which had been shown at the group's first exhibition in 1874, corresponded quite well, in fact, to the new tendency's intentions at that time. All these painters, Monet, Sisley, Pissarro and Renoir, had let themselves be carried away by lyricism and by the discovery of light; Degas had not yet revealed his 'cruel streak'; Cézanne had renounced the 'black' romanticism of his youth and was learning open-air painting under the tuition of Pissarro. But the power of the new ferment was such that impressionism not only rapidly outgrew its original objectives but through a process of natural evolution began to assume a contrary position.

Impressionism as a movement, like the Renaissance, embodied very diverse tendencies and favoured the recognition and encouragement of individual geniuses, thus providing fruitful conditions for every possible audacity. This was, indeed, the first time in the history of painting that artists had been able to create in complete freedom, having deliberately liberated themselves from all social and aesthetic restraints, at the cost, for some of them, of tragic poverty. The space of forty years witnessed the birth of experiments as different as those of Seurat and Gauguin, culminating in the searching analytical studies which Degas made, around 1880, of movement and space. The creation in 1884 of the Salon des Indépendants, the first Salon without a jury, took this liberalization a stage further by allowing self-taught artists to show in public for the first time. As the records of these Salons show, such artists were not slow to respond to this new

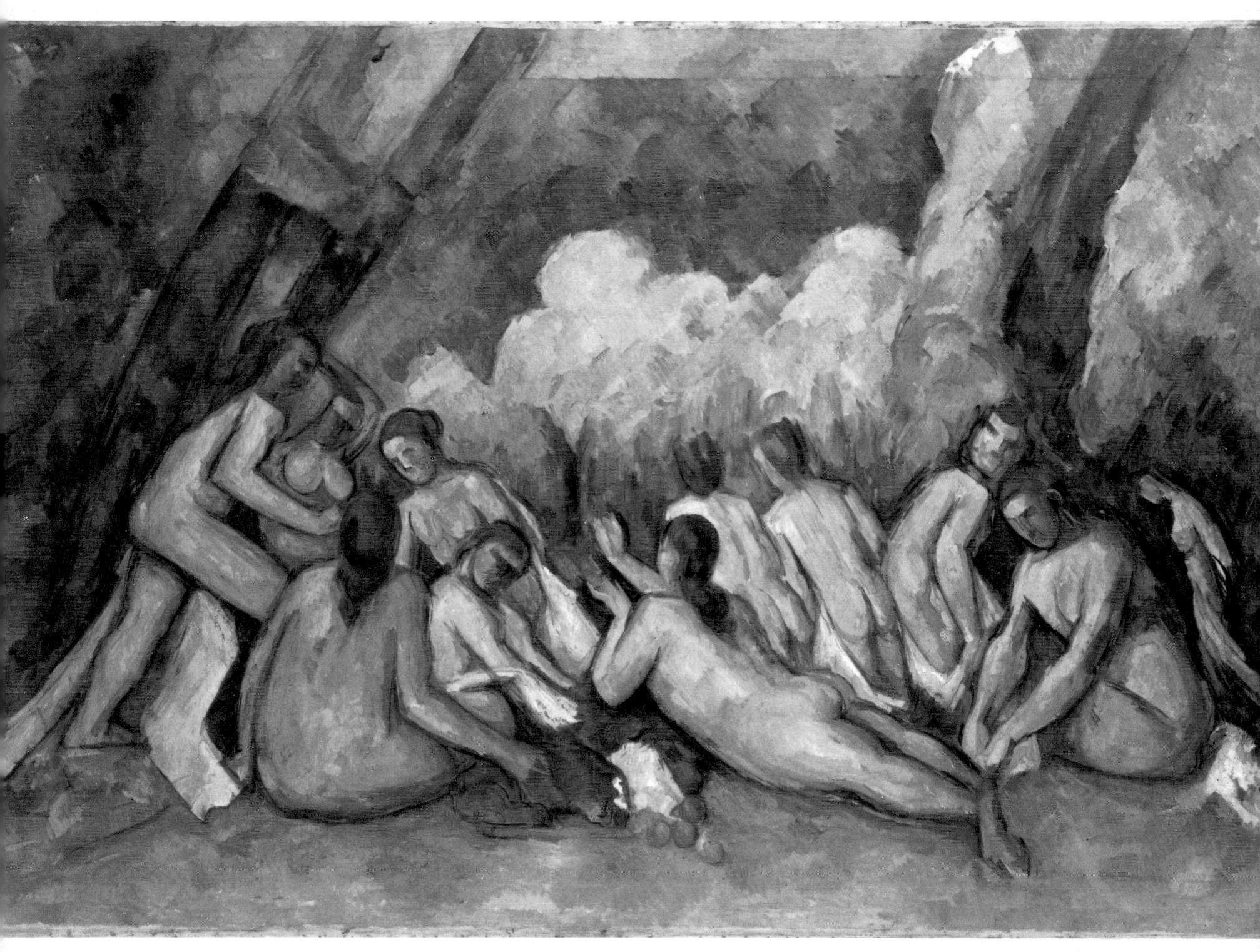

222 Paul Cézanne. *Bathers (Les Grandes Baigneuses)*. London, National Gallery.

The whole of modern art is heralded in this key picture which contains both Rouault and the Picasso of *Les Demoiselles d'Avignon*.

opportunity, although the only one with genius was Henri Rousseau, the 'Douanier', whose worth was recognized immediately by the symbolists, as it was later to be by Alfred Jarry and by the cubists. The other self-taught painters sank into oblivion, although their work serves today to reinforce the stock of fake Rousseaus in circulation. Rousseau's rehabilitation of the instinctual approach to painting gave the initial impetus to a whole branch of modern painting: the naïves (*pl. 223*).

Having run its course between two wars, the Franco-Prussian War and the First World War, during that period known rightly or wrongly as the '*Belle Epoque*', impressionism has come to seem a symbol of a joyous, carefree attitude to life. But the lyricism of Monet, Gauguin and Seurat should not blind us to the pessimistic tendency apparent in Degas's cruel analysis of human weaknesses (*pl. 224*) and in van Gogh's despair. Toulouse-Lautrec preferred to conceal his profound pessimism, derived perhaps from his Languedoc origins, beneath the frivolous mask of Paris at play; but the light-hearted air is deceptive, for these paintings are immediate precursors of the anguished compositions of Picasso's 'blue' and 'rose' periods. Lautrec is the bridge between the era that ended with the *Belle Epoque* and the era of totalitarianism (*pl. 225*).

The man of genius in the nineteenth century was a prophet who used the past as evidence in predicting the future; but the present remained deaf to his voice. That disdainful philosopher Delacroix closed his mind to the ignorant masses, preferring the spiritual company of the great men of previous ages, and his contemporaries all behaved in the same way, consciously or unconsciously. In the middle of this world of the blind and the deaf the Louvre alone stood as a sanctuary for the most revolutionary artists of the century, for Courbet, Manet and Cézanne. It is a curious paradox that a century so fertile in discoveries should have remained so solidly entrenched behind tradition. The culture amassed like treasure over the ages by the French had culminated in this great outburst of invention; and the nineteenth-century artist behaved like the profligate heir to some huge fortune, spending it with such extravagant liberality that he left nothing at all for his descendants of the following century.

One might almost say that the artists of the nineteenth-century French school decided to assume responsibility for the entire evolution of French painting in order to enrich it with new values. For example, David, the primitive of the school, re-created the sharp line, flat tints and rounded volumes of Fouquet, and shared his quality of objectivity. It was logical that the new French painting, like that of previous ages, should have rooted itself in the autochthonous tradition of sculpted form: David sought in antiquity the artistic continuity which Fouquet inherited naturally from the stone carvers of the cathedrals. There is no difficulty in detecting in Ingres, on the other hand, the effeminate mannerism and nervous arabesque of the French Renaissance. Ingres himself doubtless sensed this affinity when he transformed Jean Goujon's *Nymph* into his own *Source*.

It was left to the painters of 1830 to rediscover the gravity of the seventeenth century. Corot was, of course, a direct descendant of Poussin and Claude, but on the whole the art of the romantics, however impassioned it may have been, possessed the loftiness of ideas of the age of Louis XIV. Delacroix aspired to the universality of the great masters. In his cabin in the village of Barbizon, surrounded by sky, rock and water, Théodore Rousseau, the new Pascal, remained sunk in the anxious contemplation of the infinite and its awesome implications: the art of this romantic became so overwhelmed by intellectual considerations that it finally exhausted itself in dry stylization. In the nineteenth as in the seventeenth century, the greatness of man in the simplicity of his elemental powers was a central preoccupation of the artist's imagination, and Millet, Courbet and Daumier continued in the same path as the three Le Nain brothers.

Impressionism succeeded romanticism just as the eighteenth century rebelled against the seventeenth. The pleasures of existence were recorded for the world by artists who for the first three-quarters of their careers scarcely experienced those pleasures. The disillusioned lucidity of Degas cut through this joyous celebration, and his black hues cast a shadow over all the glowing light; but this implacable observer of human nature fulfilled the same essential role in relation to impressionism as did La Tour in relation to the century of Voltaire.

Instead of working themselves to death at their canvases like the romantics, the impressionists rediscovered the sketch as the basic inspiration of French art. Renoir inherited Fragonard's lightness of touch, but enriched it with Rubens. His paintings throb with pulsing blood and sap and the colour of flowers; his plump nymphs succeed in putting to flight the black angels of romanticism, nocturnal birds scared away by the bright daylight of impressionism.

Thus the great century of French painting drew to a close, not in a spirit of devotion to its own achievements but in a fresh burst of faith and desire. The ignorant masses were at last conditioned to

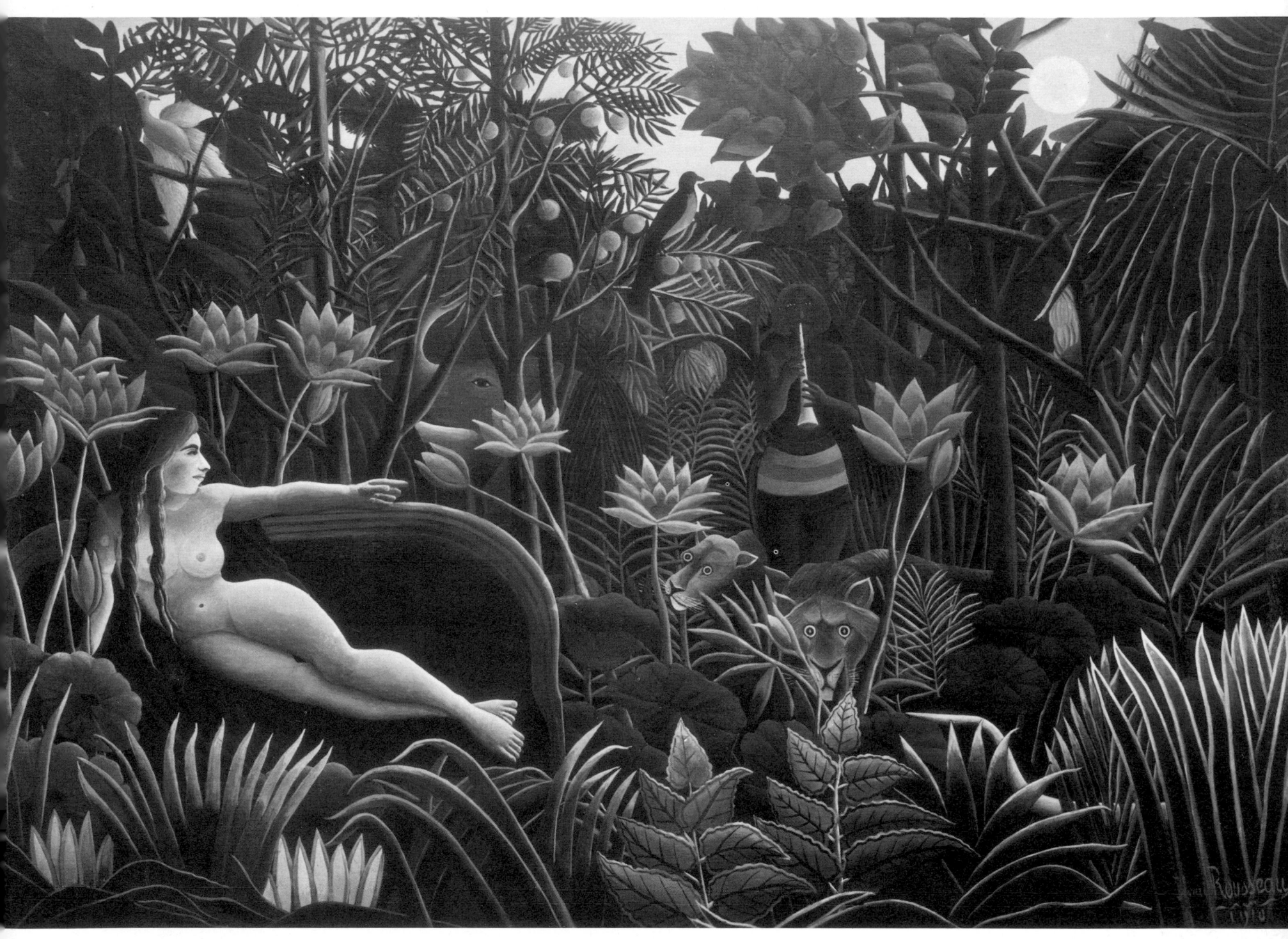

admire work that had formerly been considered audacious; but four generations had not succeeded in quenching the vital force of the French school. Young artists were to arise who would subject these men, the authors of so many masterpieces, to a ruthless criticism aimed at rediscovering in them, in its pure state, the pitiless fever of creation. These young artists, having toppled the old idol of nature that Jean-Jacques Rousseau had erected for the French to worship, launched themselves deliriously into abstract speculation, glittering fields of thought as black and icy as interstellar space.

223 Henri Rousseau (le Douanier) (1844–1910). *The Dream*. New York, Museum of Modern Art.

During the period when symbolism was flourishing in French literature, Rousseau opened the way to the dream painting and naïve painting of the twentieth century.

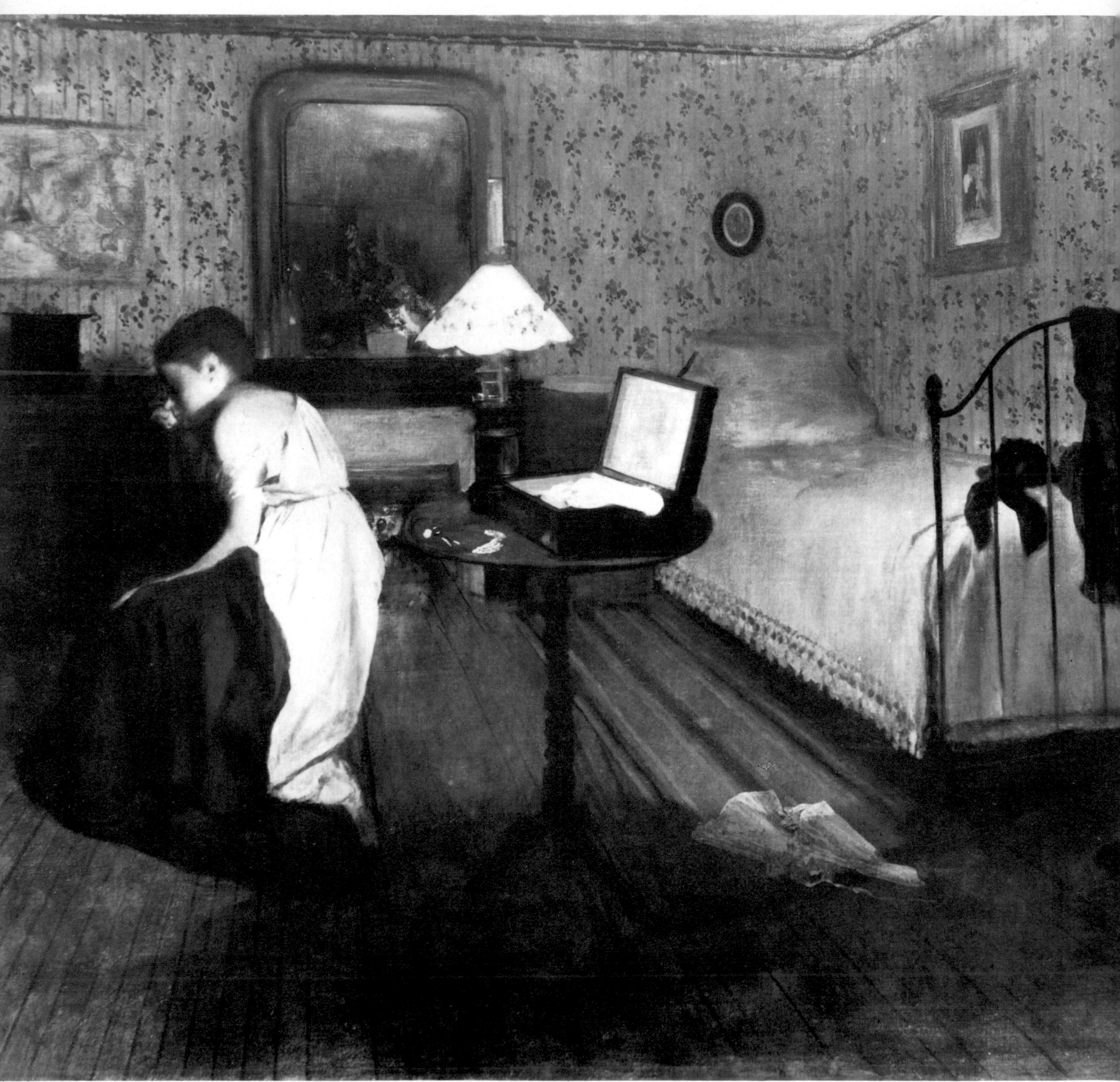

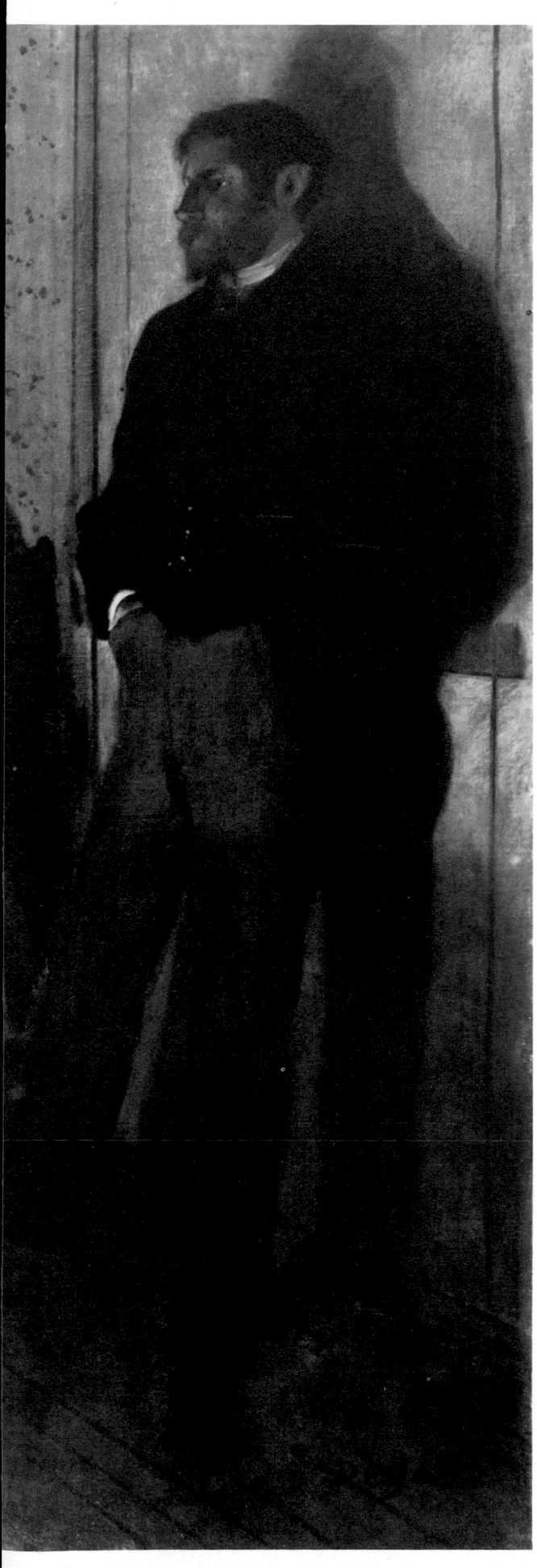

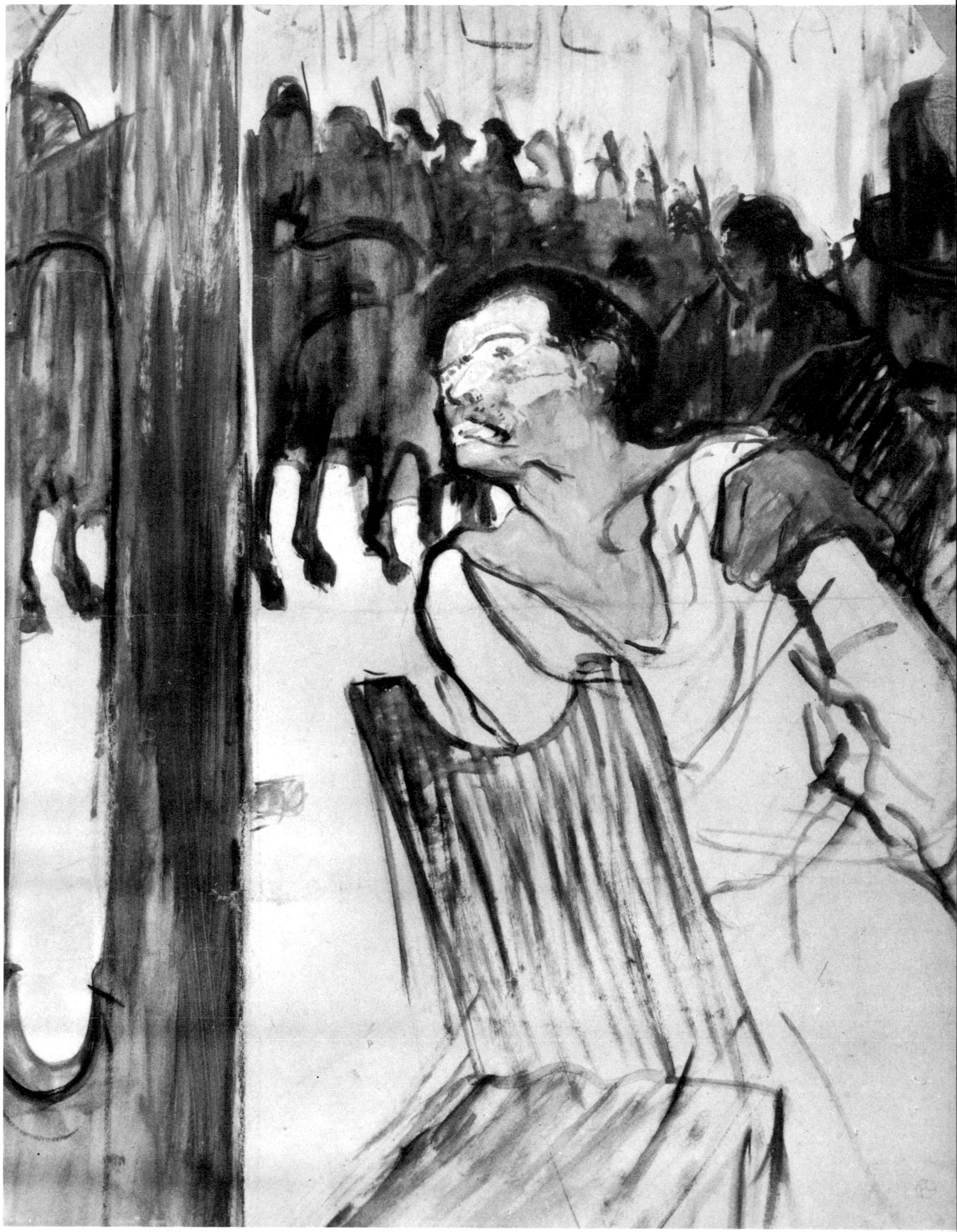

◀ 224 Edgar Degas. *The Rape*. Philadelphia, collection MacIlhenny.

225 Henri de Toulouse-Lautrec (1864–1901). *At the foot of the scaffold*. Collection Dr Doris Neuerburg.

The trenchant art of Degas and Lautrec often reflects the cruel and cynical atmosphere of the realist novels of the time.

226 Edvard Munch (1863–1944).
The Cry. Oslo, Nasjonalgalleriet.

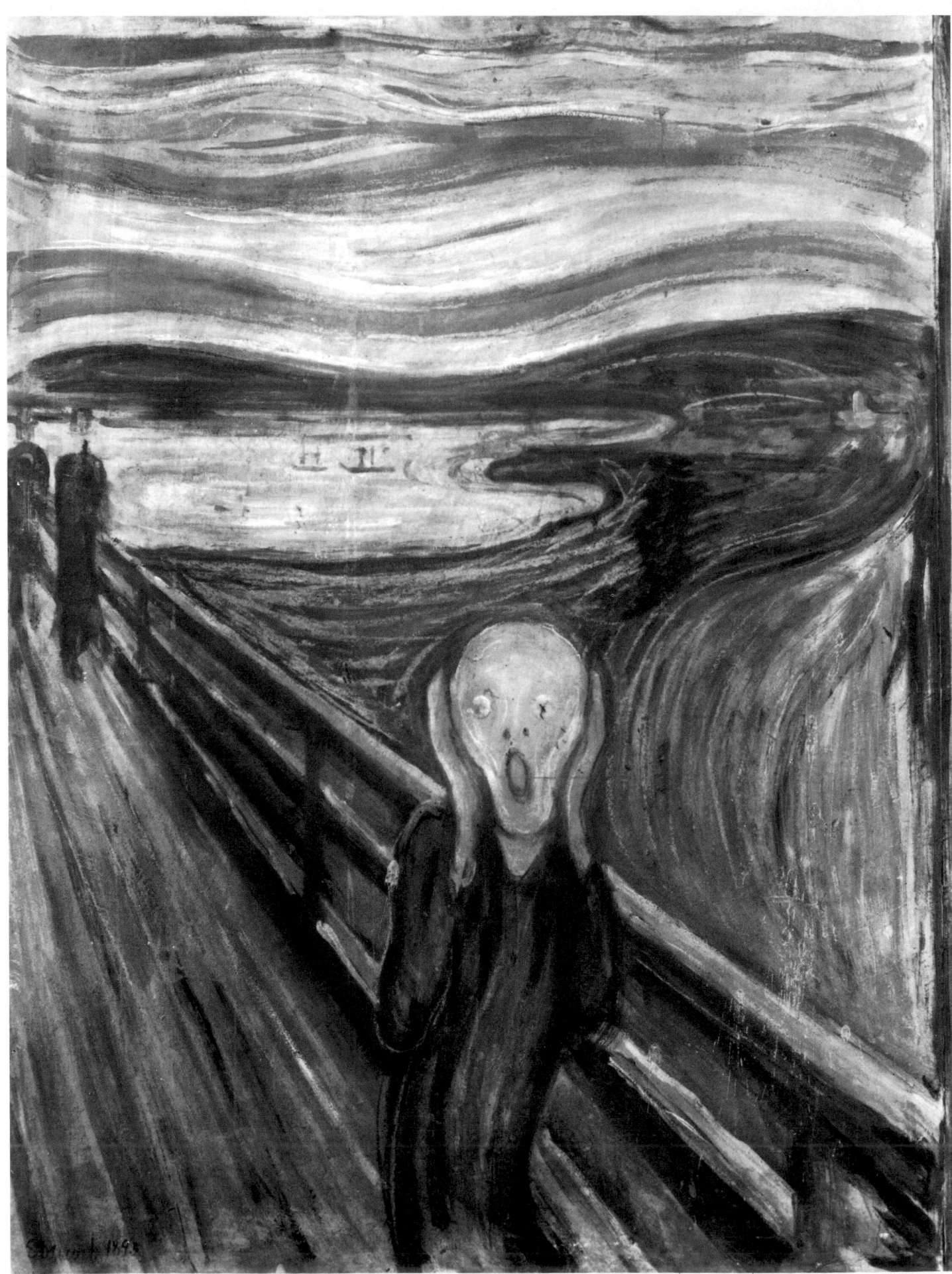

16 Revolt into conformism

'If one really thinks about it, all one really has is one's self,' said Picasso to Edouard Tériade in 1932. This individualistic declaration of faith had already been formulated twenty years previously, in a more philosophical context, by the German critic Wilhelm Worringer whose *Formprobleme der Gotik* (*Form in Gothic*, London 1927) extolled the faculty of exacerbation of the ego which he attributed to northern artists. Contemporary art springs, essentially, from a strong urge for rebellion resulting from the creative individual's acute awareness of his alienation from his environment.

The total lack of understanding shown by society towards the artist for three-quarters of a century was bound to lead to a crisis; the impressionists succeeded in postponing it only by seeking to establish with nature the communication refused them by their fellow men. In this quest for himself the artist is a discoverer who must first of all create a means of externalizing his ego, or what in Vasari's time would have been called a *maniera*. The hundreds of original painters which this libertarian attitude has helped to proliferate in every country are perfectly entitled to invoke avant-garde principles: but only a few of them can be described as precursors.

It is usual to situate the starting-point of contemporary art between the years 1905 and 1910, but even the earlier date is twenty years too late. It was in 1885, in fact, that the first open protest was made against an art of representation. This protest, in the sense of liberation of the instinct of subjectivity, expressed itself in the violence of the deformations imposed by the artist upon nature, which, after being ardently wooed for so long, now came in for rough treatment. This subversive campaign was initiated by northerners: the Dutchman van Gogh, who had learned from impressionism the eloquence of colour; the Belgian James Ensor who lived like a hermit in Ostend, in a nightmare world of phantoms wearing death's-head masks (*pl. 228*); the Norwegian Edvard Munch, whose flamboyant approach to form brings him so close to van Gogh, as well as relating him to *art nouveau* (*pl. 226*).

The work of the Swiss painter Ferdinand Hodler is typical of the state of crisis that had arisen in art.

A style might have developed out of the quest for expression apparent in a painting such as the *Student* (Zurich), inspired by Holbein and Dürer, had the artist not come up against the obstacle of Swiss Calvinism. And no doubt Hodler's attachment to his social milieu also played its part in imposing the straitjacket of academicism on his budding expressionism, which survived only in occasional landscapes. A Frenchman, Gustave Moreau, suffered from an even more marked discrepancy between the official aspect of his art and the private side represented by informal sketches; these last have been claimed as the first examples of fauvism, although that honour might more appropriately be reserved for the sculptor Jean-Baptiste Carpeaux's rare paintings, which anticipate Rouault.

Toulouse-Lautrec would figure among these pre-expressionist painters were it not for the fact that the elegance of his line brings an indefinably aristocratic aura to the street-walkers who were his models and the victims of his wit. And Gauguin's drawings have no expressionist significance, although occasionally an expressionist feeling tinges certain paintings, such as the *Devil's words* (1892).

It is possible for a mental illness to accelerate the process of liberation from aesthetic and moral constraints by contributing to the hypertrophy of a tragically alienated ego. This was the case with van Gogh, and, under totally different circumstances, with Edvard Munch. Van Gogh's art is a paroxysm of joy transformed into heartbreak, but if his soul is consumed, it is in the burning rays of the sun, like that of Mirèio, the heroine of Mistral's epic poem. Munch, on the other hand, incapacitated by his phobias, ended up a recluse on his own estates at Ekely, among his four houses and forty-three studios, painting hospital scenes, burials, and the old Germanic theme of women embracing skeletons. Like van Gogh, he was obsessed by his own face, which he painted many times; he, too, underwent clinical treatment (in 1908) for a nervous disorder; he, too, feared the contact of women.

The principal events generally considered to have opened the way to modern art are the 1905 Salon d'Automne, where the painters called *les fauves* ('the wild beasts') by Louis Vauxcelles showed as a

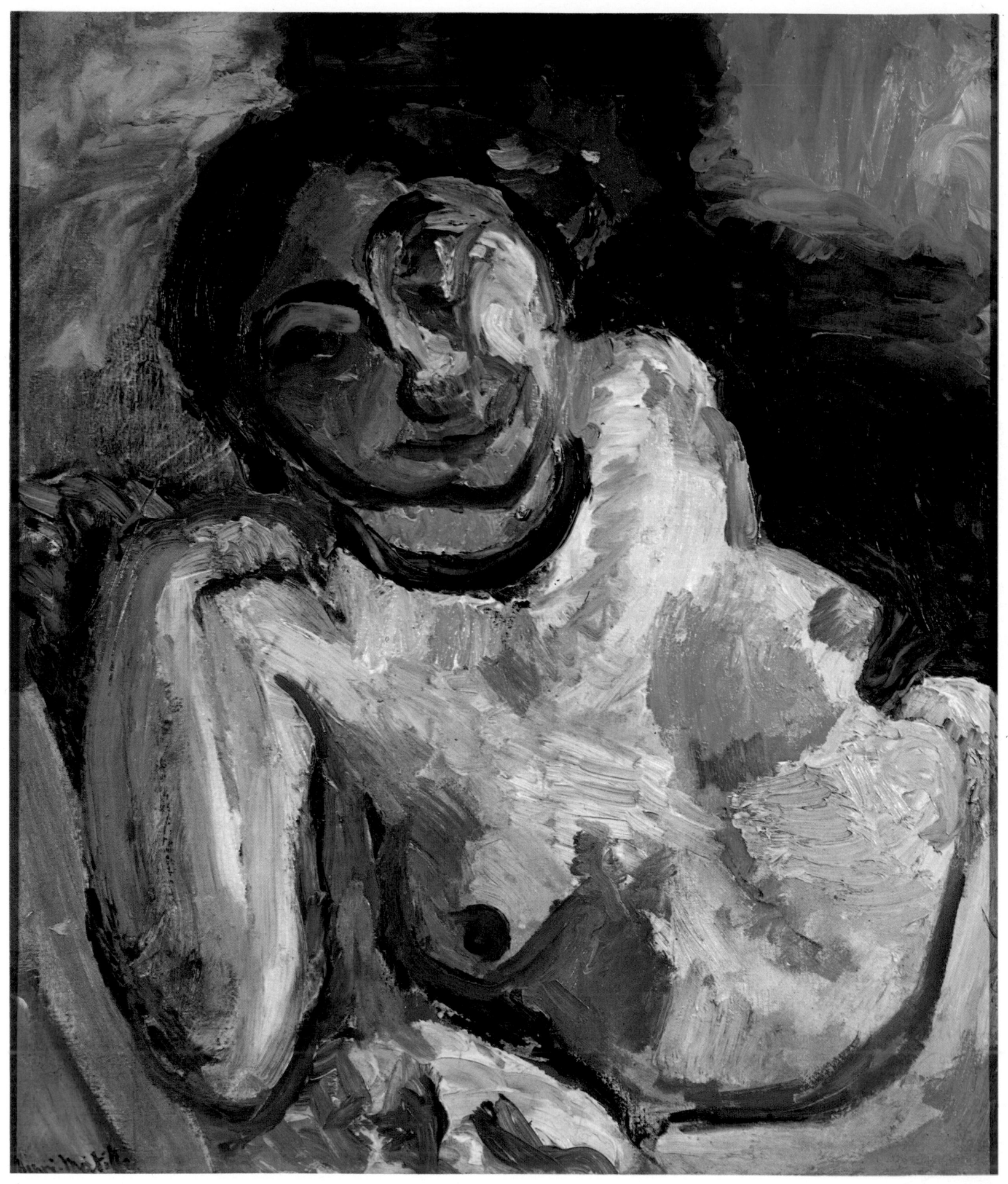

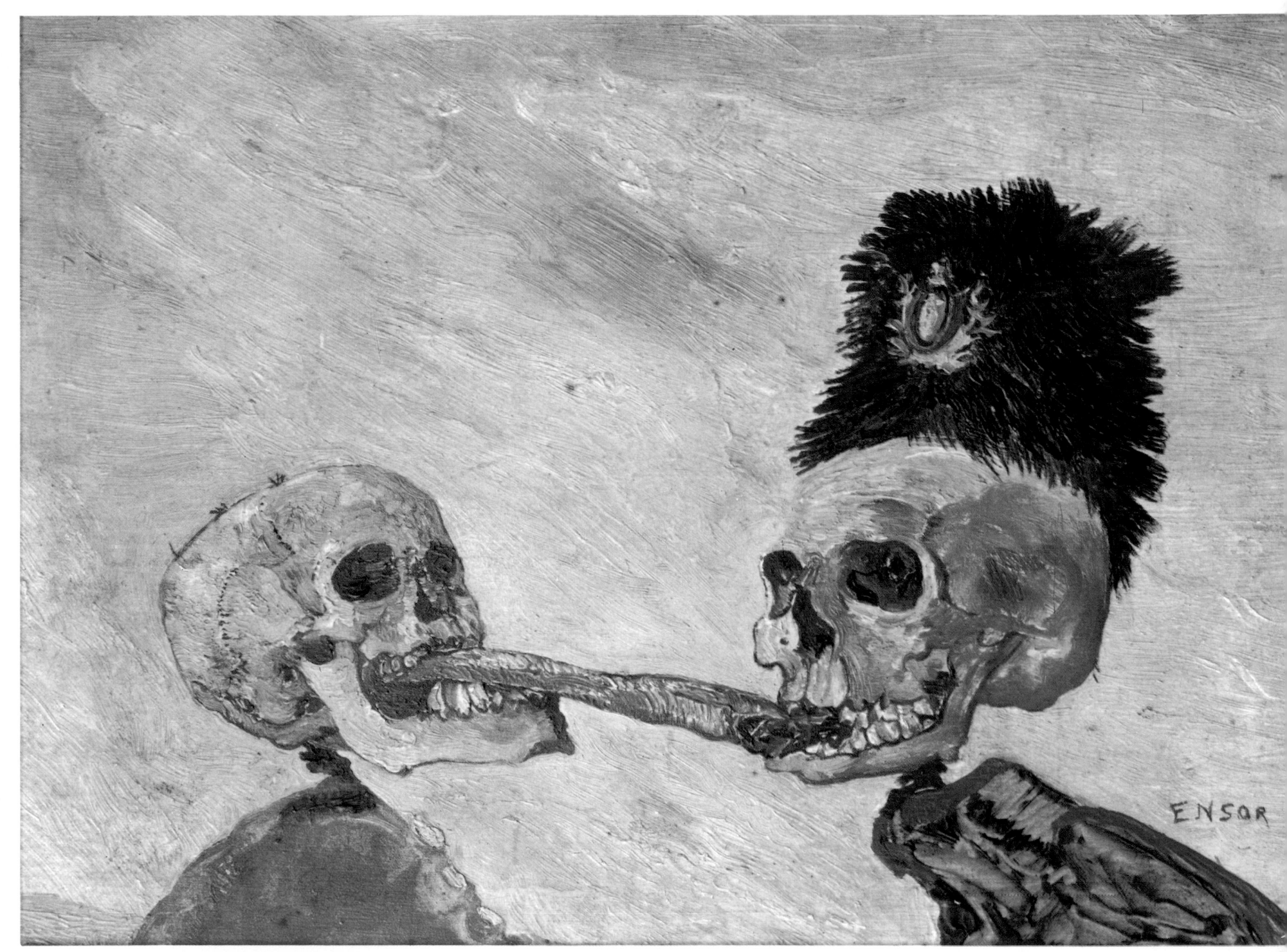

227 Henri Matisse (1869–1954). *The Gypsy (La Gitane)*. Saint-Tropez, Musée de l'Annonciade. Exhibited at the Salon d'Automne of 1905, this picture was a violent protest against all the traditions of painting, those of classicism as well as those of impressionism.

group; the 1908 Salon d'Automne which included pictures by Picasso and Braque labelled 'cubist' following a remark by Matisse; the foundation of the group called *Die Brücke* ('the bridge') in Dresden in 1905; and that of the group called *Der blaue Reiter* ('the blue horseman') in Munich in 1911. But the real point of rupture may be sought more accurately

in the 1892 exhibition by Munch of forty-five pictures at the Association of Berlin Painters, since the controversy provoked by his style resulted in the closing of the show after a few days and the break-up of the group of artists which had invited him. His supporters immediately founded in Berlin the Free Association of Artists, and the same year organized the aptly named 'Sezession' group in Munich. Resistance to modern ideas was even greater in Germany than in France, which had had half a century's experience of the polemics aroused by scandals in the world of art. In Germany, nationalistic

228 James Ensor (1860–1949). *Skeletons fighting over a herring*. Brussels, collection Benedict Goldschmidt.

Distant progeny of those of Hieronymus Bosch, the monsters of James Ensor raise a violent protest against rationalism as well as against naturalism.

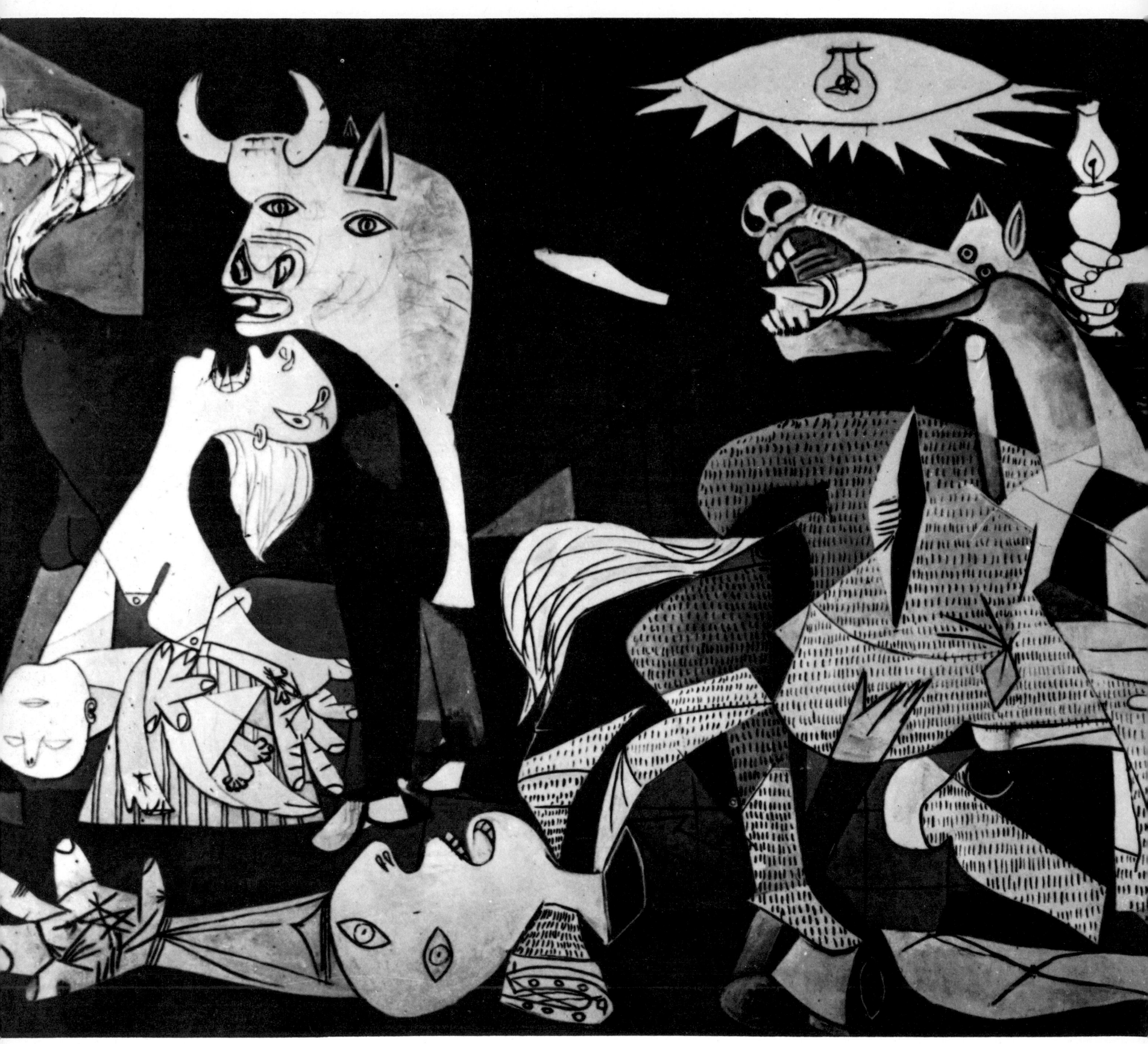

229 Pablo Picasso (b. 1881). *Guernica*. New York, Museum of Modern Art (on loan from the artist).

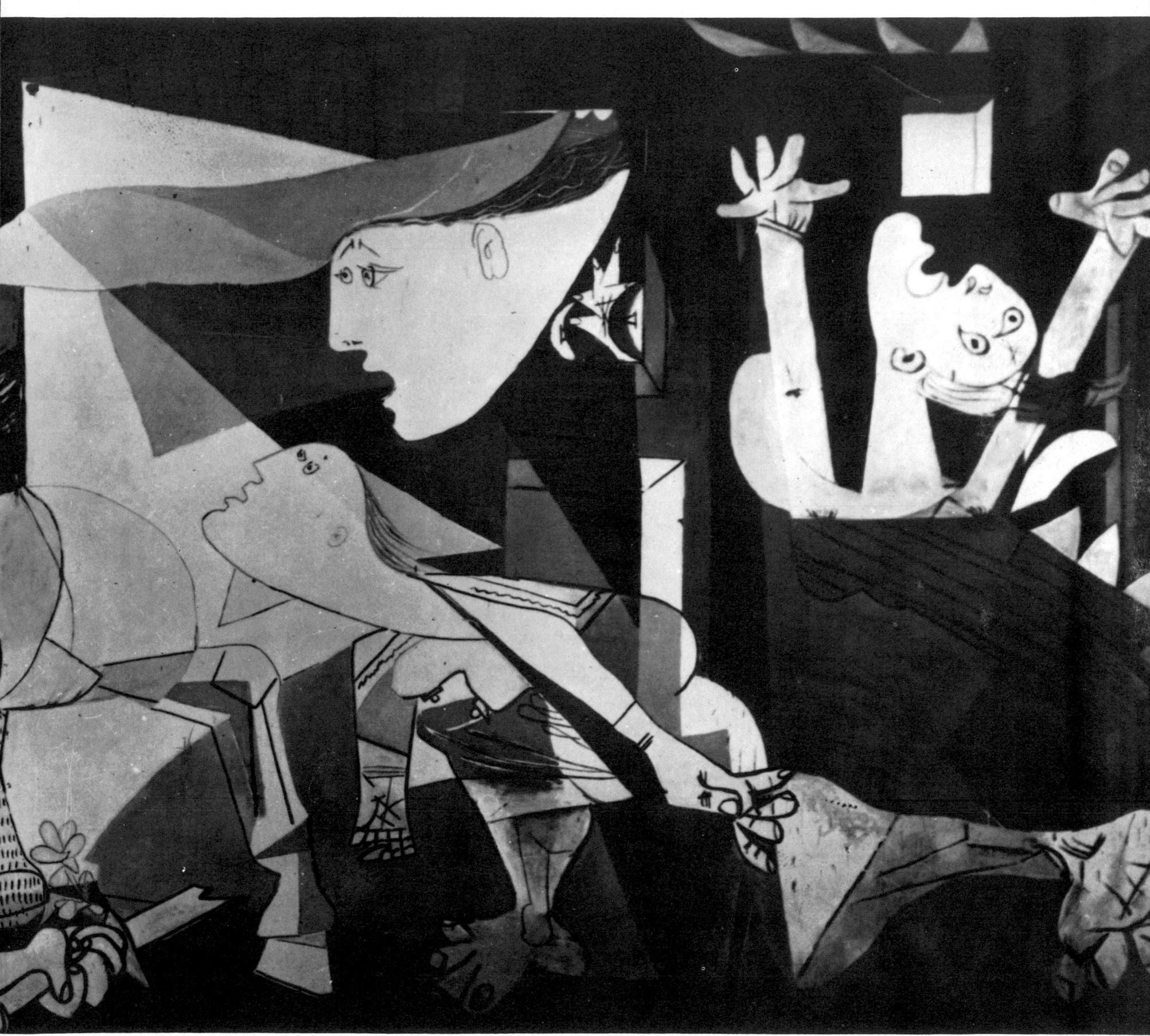

Picasso performs the mutation of plastic cubism into an
expressionist language, to execute what is surely the most
tragic work in the whole history of painting.

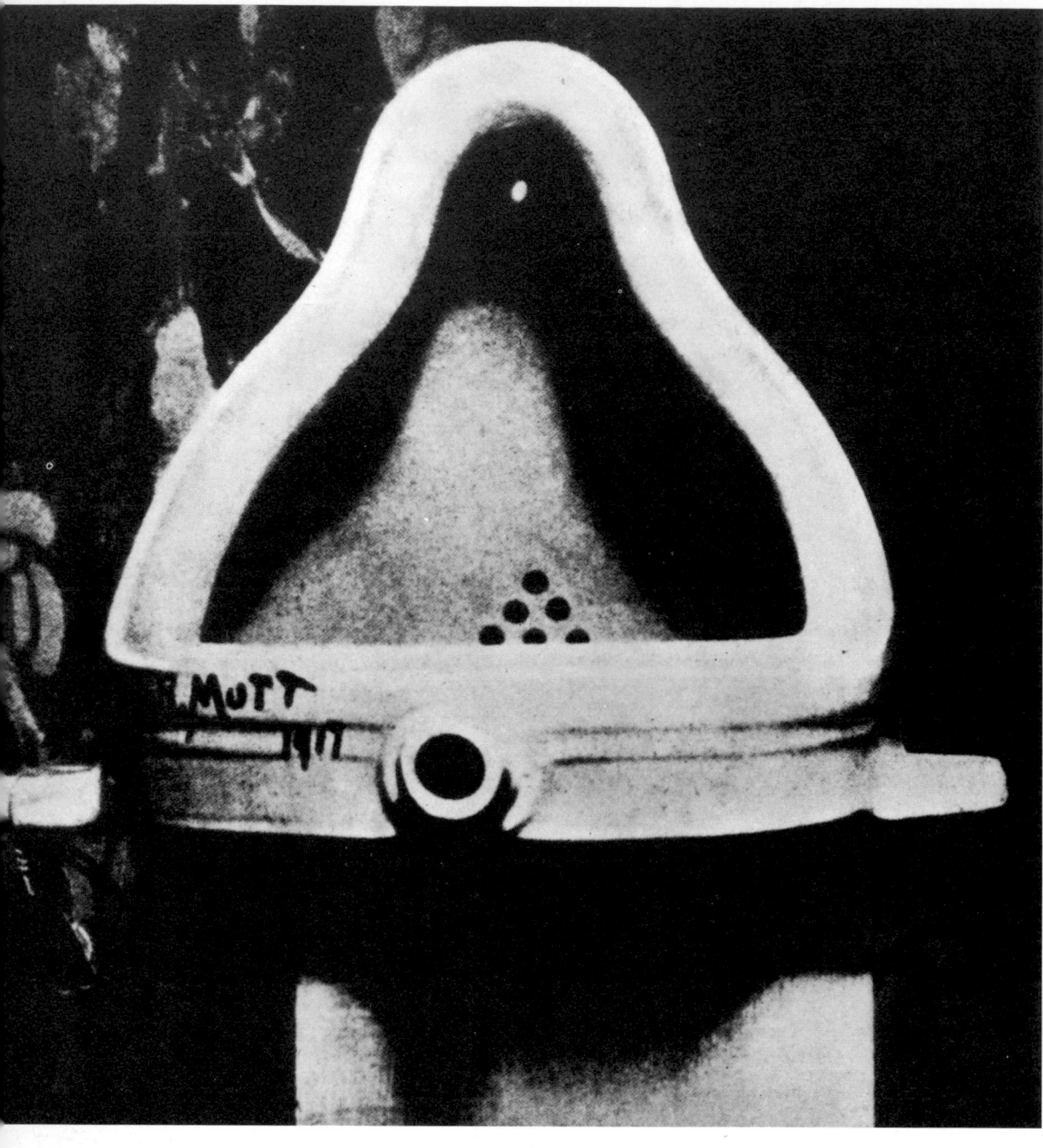

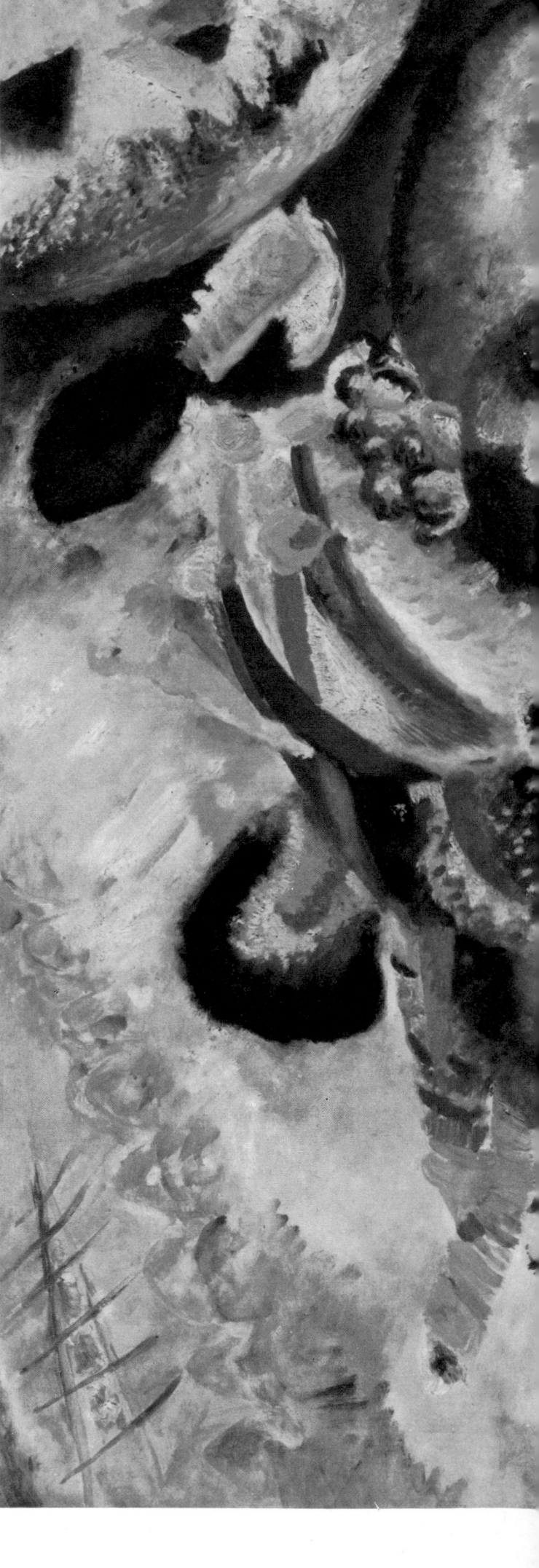

230 Marcel Duchamp (1887–1968). *Fountain*. Signed 'R. Mutt' and submitted to the 1917 exhibition of the Society of Independent Artists in New York.

Dada broke deliberately with the traditional concept of the work of art.

factors also played a part, since the Parisian artists invited to exhibit by their colleagues in Munich were widely considered to be tainted by a degeneracy from which it was necessary to preserve virtuous Germany at all costs.

Fauvism and cubism, the two great sources of contemporary art, may be said to have sprung from two separate dramas: the tragic drama of van Gogh, desperate at his inability to force a way of painting, derived from impressionism, beyond certain experimental limits; and the silent drama of Cézanne seeking, gropingly, to rediscover appearances, to re-create the texture of forms broken by Monet.

The so-called 'fauve' movement, pioneered by Matisse, Marquet, Rouault and Vlaminck, was an instinctive revolt against the fidelity to appearances

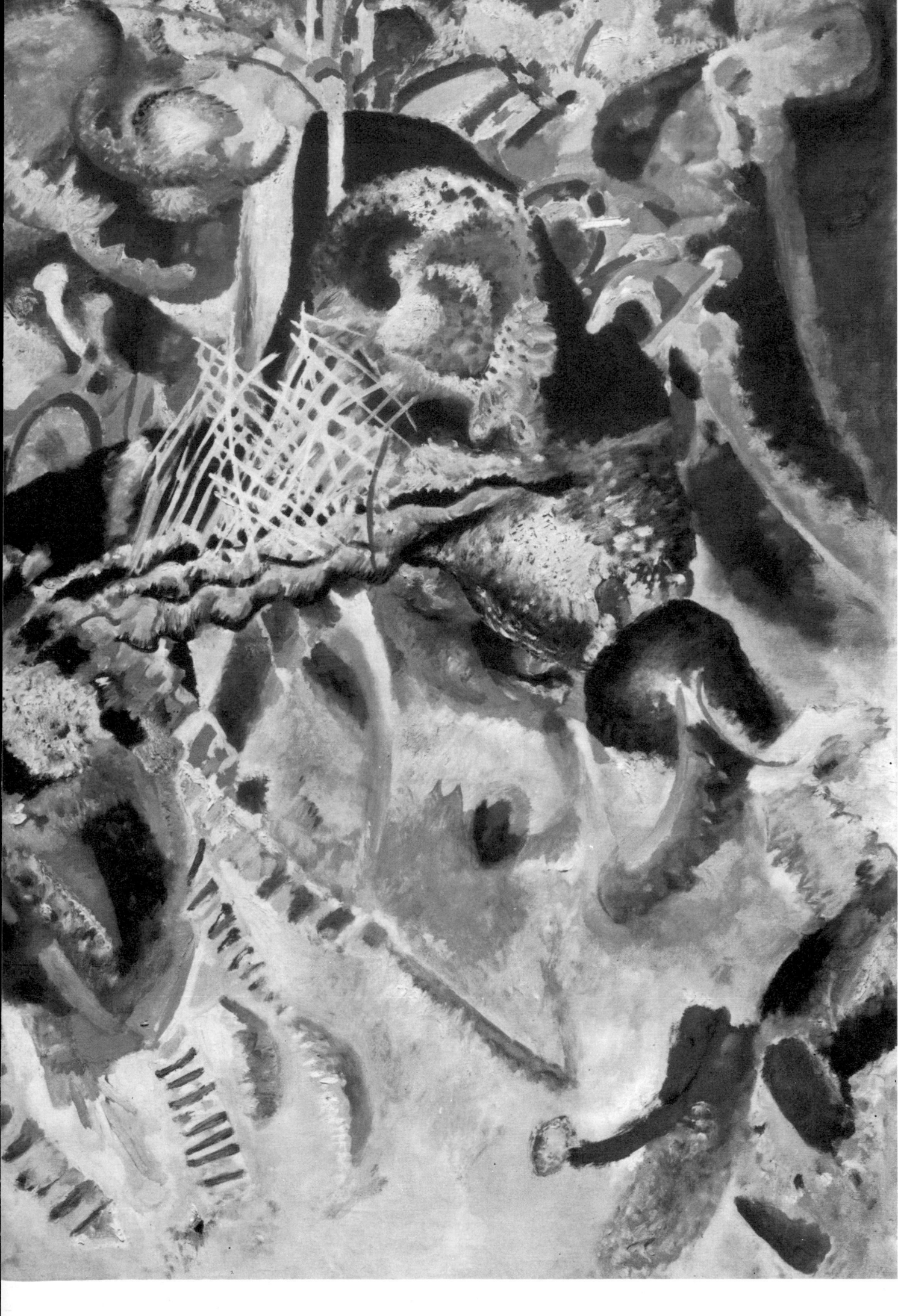

231 Wassily Kandinsky (1866–1944). *Grosse Fuge*. New York, Solomon R. Guggenheim Museum.

Kandinsky's first works are closer to the origins of abstract painting than are cubist pictures, which are the result of analysis of the object.

271

which was the principle of impressionism. This liberation, whereby colour was promoted to being a means of expression in its own right, permitted its adherents, united briefly in what has wrongly been called a 'school', to explore completely incompatible objectives and styles; it provided the means for Matisse (*pl. 227*) to develop the intellectualism of an art which was to be its own justification, for Marquet and Dufy to express their desire to revert to the representation of the external world, for Vlaminck to project his own particular temperament, for Rouault to formulate a Christian lamentation upon the miseries of the world (*pl. 237*). The fauvist liberation of colour also provided the basis for the kind of expressionism practised a few years later by the growing colony of Slav painters in Paris.

The cubism of Georges Braque and Pablo Picasso was a stricter discipline, although it drew upon sources as varied as recently discovered African carvings and the last works of Cézanne who died obsessed with cones, cylinders and cubes. Cubism was more methodical than fauvism in its attack upon appearances, breaking them up and then reconstituting them according to the principles of a geometry whose laws no longer demanded anything beyond the definition of a painted form in terms of a given surface. The resulting destruction of traditional space represented the culmination of a process already set in motion in 1895 by the movement calling itself 'Les Nabis', founded by Paul Sérusier and including among its adepts Pierre Bonnard, who spent his life attempting an impossible reconciliation between depthlessness and the impressionist mirage of appearances.

These factors all helped to create a new aesthetic climate, in which painting became a self-contained language, a willing instrument in the hands of the artist who, after having distorted appearances, ended by abolishing them.

Until 1910 the creation of modern painting in Paris remained largely the prerogative of French artists; Picasso was a major exception. However, the prestige which France gained from the glorious achievements of her nineteenth-century masters, crowned by the triumph of impressionism, brought a wealth of artistic talent flooding into Paris from all parts of the world, and especially the Slav countries. This phenomenon can be compared only to the attraction exercised by Rome in the years around 1600. It was as though artists had decided they could only express themselves in the free atmosphere of Paris. This influx of artists, escaping from their own countries' traditional attitudes in order to discover themselves in Paris, created a limitless range of expression for the new art whose language had been invented by the masters of 1910.

Invented by a Frenchman and a Spaniard, cubism soon became enriched by variations brought by the Pole Marcoussis, the Spaniard Juan Gris, the Frenchmen Albert Gleizes, Jean Metzinger, Roger de la Fresnaye, Jacques Villon, Fernand Léger; another recruit, Robert Delaunay, went beyond cubism by eventually banishing appearances of all kinds, including distortions, from his compositions, in favour of pure colour variations (*pl. 233*).

In the second decade of the century cubism, having consolidated its conquests, became a language supple enough to allow Braque to develop the aesthetic of the object-picture which he had first explored between 1905 and 1910 (*pl. 232*); and supple enough, too, to allow Picasso, in the third decade, to employ the breaking-up of forms to express in *Guernica* (*pl. 229*), and in the 'slaughtered figures' which followed, the horrors of war and genocide.

The Slav group in Paris, headed by Chagall, Soutine, Kisling and Pascin, employed the language of colour in the context of an expressionism filled with an atavistic anguish, a tendency which the Italian Modigliani transformed into the more subtle tonality of a melancholic art.

Rather than denying appearances, cubism used them selectively and freely, for plastic or expressive purposes. The movement which was to lead to the complete renunciation of all forms emanating from the external world was contained, in embryo, in Worringer's 1908 thesis *Abstraktion und Einfühlung* (*Abstraction and Empathy*, London 1953), and fully explained in Wassily Kandinsky's 1912 work *Über das Geistige in der Kunst* (*Concerning the Spiritual in Art*, New York 1947). Unlike cubism, which was entirely empirical, this new movement was therefore endowed with a theoretical basis; but, perhaps because the newly formulated ideas were too far ahead of the times, its proponents were not able at the time to emulate the cubists by setting up a group. Non-figurative painting asserted itself gradually during the first three decades of the century, represented initially by isolated artists such as Kandinsky (*pl. 231*) in Germany, Delaunay (*pl. 233*) in France, Mondrian (*pl. 234*) and van Doesburg in Holland; after the Second World War, non-figurative art blossomed in a variety of styles and theories, ranging from a formal or geometric abstraction to informal approaches characterized in general as abstract expressionism.

If these movements renounced nature as the source of inspiration for art, they did not renounce the work of art as an object in its own right; on the contrary, this objective quality was enhanced by

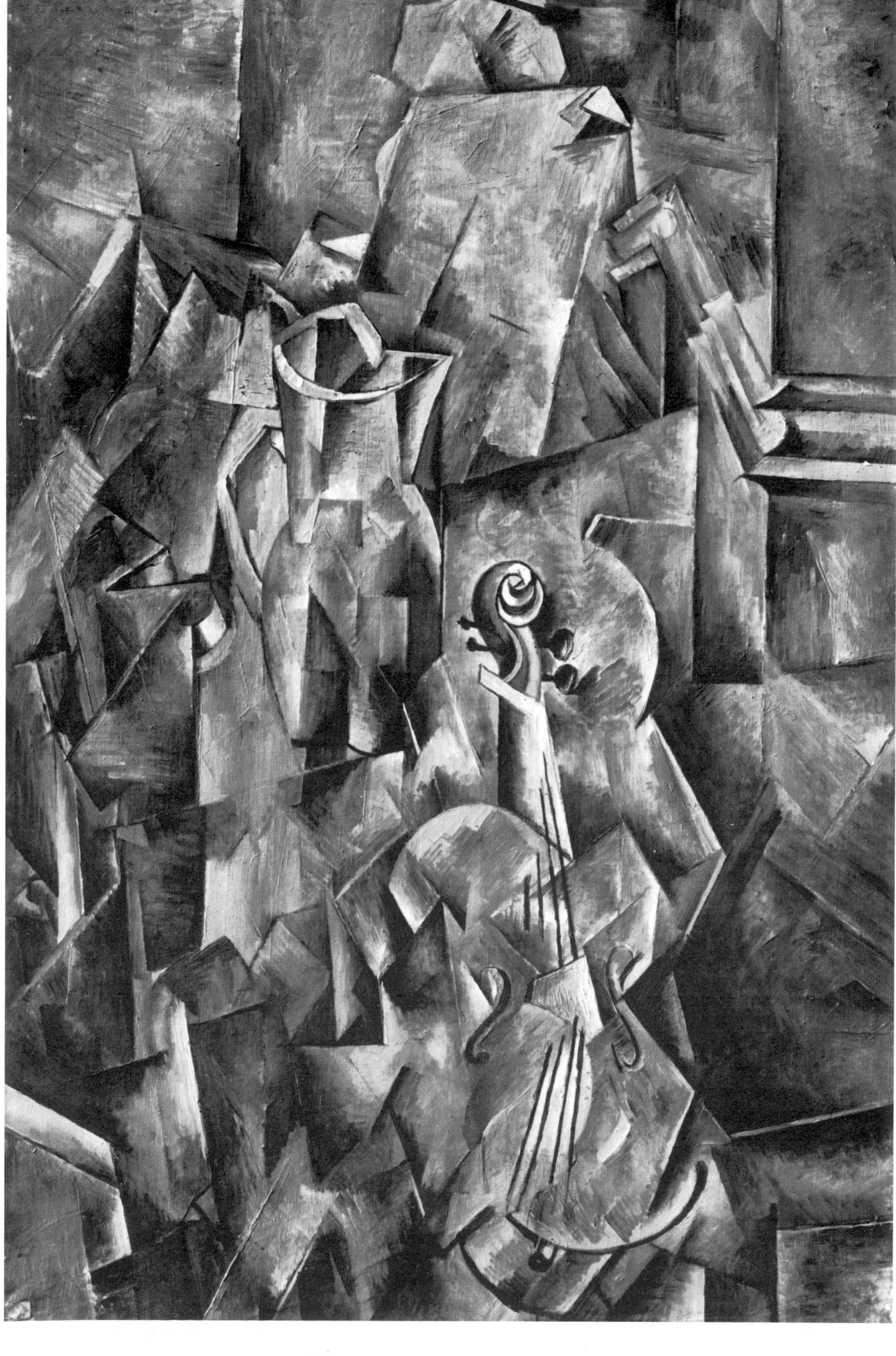

232 Georges Braque (1882–1963). *Violin and jug*. Basle, Kunstmuseum.

During their cubist period, Braque and Picasso elaborated an egocentric art in which the object is exploited as a source of formal variations on a given surface.

233 Robert Delaunay (1885–1941). ▶ *Circular forms: sun and moon*. Zurich, Kunsthaus.

273

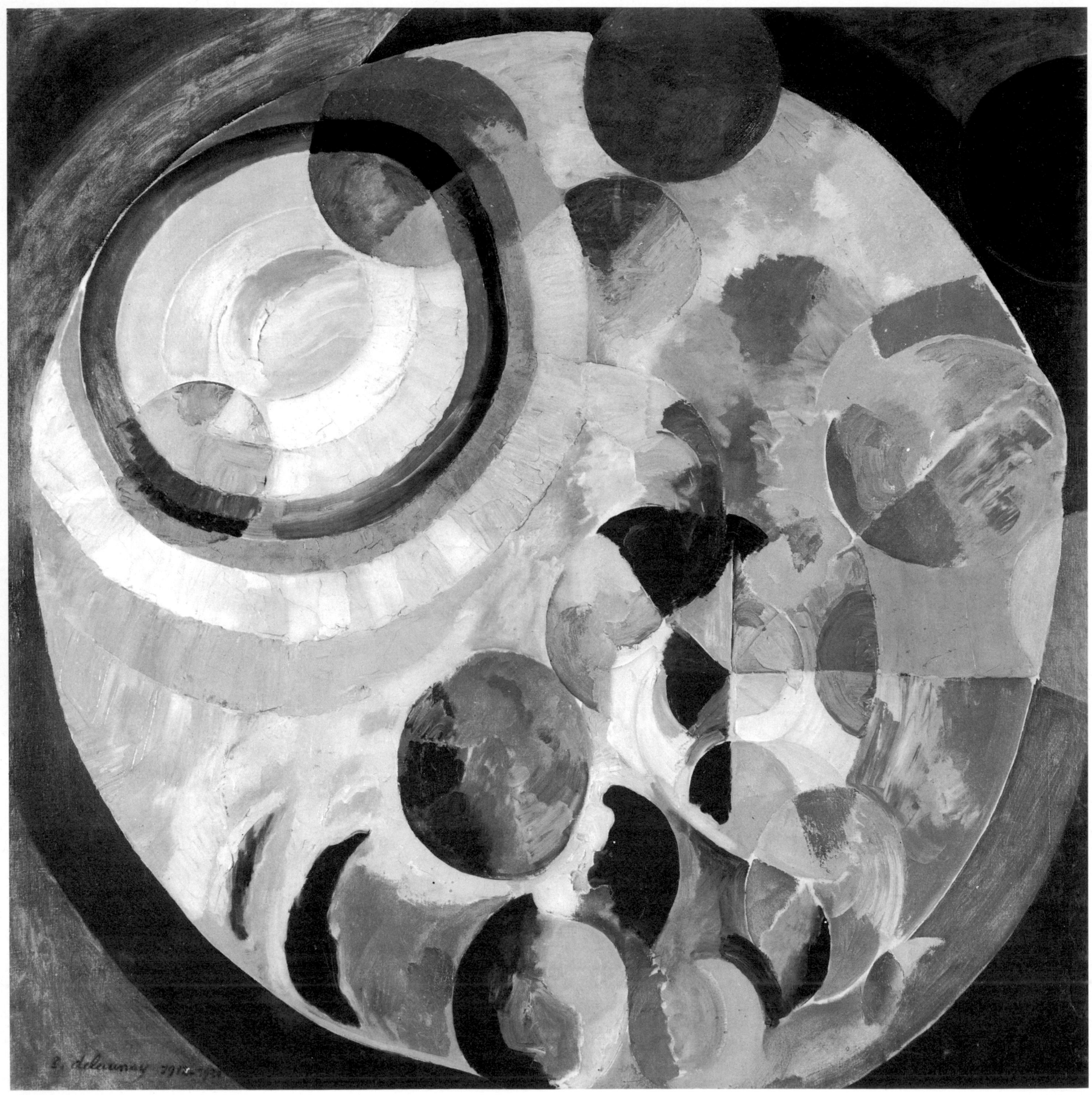

E. Delaunay 1912-1913

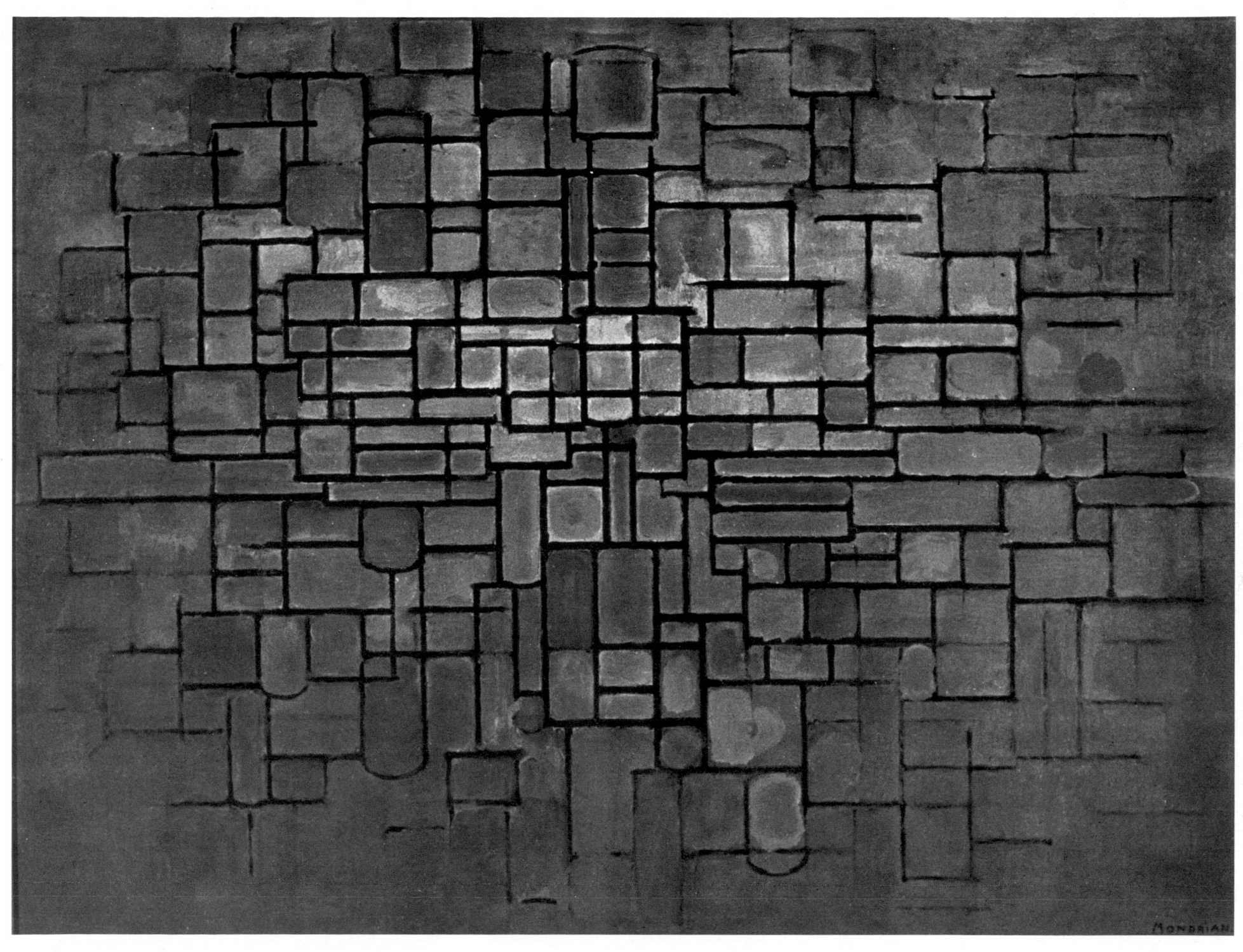

the complete break with any external reality outside the artist's own temperament. It remained to the artist to reject the work of art as an autonomous object and, by corollary, to reject art as a human activity consisting of 'fashioning' such objects.

The man to undertake this act of negation was a genuine precursor, Marcel Duchamp, one of the pioneers of dadaism and the only contemporary figure in the world of art to have remained unshakably faithful to an attitude of refusal. He had already affirmed this refusal in 1912, with his selection of 'readymades', manufactured objects of

no special significance and as far removed as possible from the idea of a work of art. The most notorious of these readymades is undoubtedly the urinal which he signed 'R. Mutt' and submitted to the 1917 exhibition of the Society of Independent Artists in New York. This initiative gave rise to innumerable variations and imitations. The 'object with a symbolic function' of surrealism may be considered a descendant, although the artificial significance attributed to such objects by their creators makes them the opposite of Duchamp's readymades whose true meaning is precisely their

234 Piet Mondrian (1872–1944). *Composition in blue, grey and red.* Otterlo, Kröller-Müller Museum.

In Germany with Kandinsky, in France with Delaunay, and in Holland with Mondrian, the year 1912 saw a simultaneous break away from all those aspects of appearances which had not already been demolished by cubism. Delaunay was already exploring the art of pure colour variations in 1912, forty years before it began to be practised on a wide scale.

275

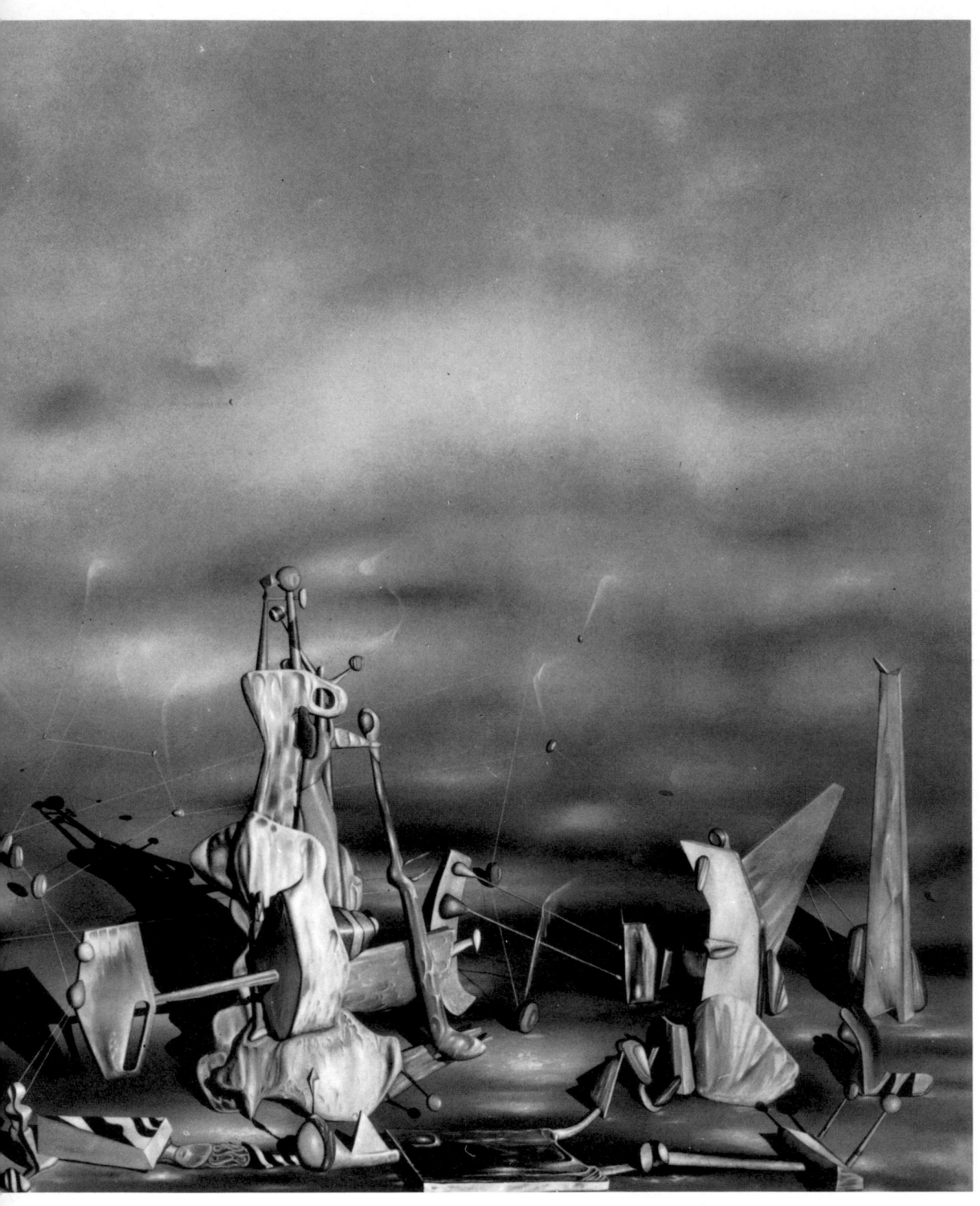

235 Yves Tanguy (1900–55). *Landscape*. Paris, Musée National d'Art Moderne.

Yves Tanguy is among those artists who have recorded most authentically the upsurge of unconscious forces liberated by surrealism.

desperate attempt to grasp at its source the power of negation of contemporary art was doomed to failure because it lacked the shock-effect of surprise and originality.

Throughout the nineteenth century the spirit of rebellion was fed by a literature of which Sade was the initiator: de Vigny, Dostoievsky, Lautréamont, Nietzsche and Rimbaud all played a part, in their different ways, in establishing a radical tradition of refusal. But the painters of the time ignored the message. Once the revolutionary fervour had subsided, the romantics became good bourgeois citizens once more, following the lead of their standard-bearer Delacroix. The first real rebel of French painting was Courbet, who refused the imperial government's offer of the Legion of Honour and desired his art to become a means of expressing social demands. The impressionists, however, never allowed this spirit of rebellion to enter into their artistic calculations. Even when, like Pissarro or Monet, they were personally sympathetic to such ideas they failed to heed Zola's appeal to join his campaign of socialist action; it may well have been this disappointment that caused the novelist to repudiate the impressionists towards the end of his life.

Nothing could have been less subversive than this most revolutionary of all movements in painting; never had such bold innovators been so entirely lacking in the will to revolt. The impressionists made no critical assessment of the achievements of their artistic predecessors. They simply worked on instinctively, in the light of their own discoveries, without realizing that the new universe they were entering was cutting them off from a social environment determined to view them solely as rebels. However keenly they felt the state of separation imposed upon them by society, they remained convinced that it was nothing more than a misunderstanding. And they avoided a feeling of isolation by remaining in close communion with nature, as well as by preserving an atmosphere of solidarity among themselves based upon the encouragement of a small group of art lovers who had faith in them. Some of the impressionists, including Degas, Cézanne and Monet, remained deeply embittered by the treatment they had received in their youth; Monet, for example, by now at the height of his glory and the friend of Clemenceau, repeated Courbet's gesture and refused the Legion of Honour. But this resentfulness was never reflected in any way in their art. It is this purity of intention which gave impressionism its unique character and allowed its influence to penetrate

meaninglessness. The origins of surrealist imagery, with its appeal to the subconscious, as manifested in dream states, should be traced back rather to the paintings which Giorgio de Chirico executed in Paris between 1911 and 1917.

By making the simple gesture of destroying the traditional subject-object relationship, Duchamp anticipated the critical nihilism of existentialism. The so-called neo-dada movement which flourished fitfully in America and Europe during the 1960s may perhaps signify a more or less conscious desire to reassert this nihilistic philosophy, but this

even an age, our own, which has witnessed the negation of all such principles.

Rebellion finally broke out with the advent of Gauguin, but it was in some ways a gratuitous rebellion affecting the man rather than the painter; Gauguin as an artist tended – apart from his imagery – to renew ties with certain classical traditions which the impressionists had set aside. Van Gogh, too, was a rebel, but in the spirit of moral dedication of a prophet such as Nietzsche's Zarathustra: no one could have been less nihilistic than this man whose heart was filled with a missionary sense of love.

It has been left to our contemporaries to raise a barrier of total opposition to all their predecessors: the art of Picasso, Matisse, Rouault, Kirchner and Nolde is based upon a spirit of contradiction, a determination to destroy the artistic capital accumulated by Western civilization. Their attitude may be compared to that of the first marxists, whose revolt against the role of capital led them to envisage the establishment of a new society not based on the accumulation of wealth: an ideal which industrial society, founded as it is on production, forced the successors of these same revolutionaries to betray in their actions.

The anarchistic position of avant-garde painters at the beginning of the century was summed up by their rallying cry: 'Burn the museums!' This impulsive attitude found expression in brutal distortions or caricatures of the human figure and of nature, thus transgressing both the sacrosanct elements of Western art which had been handed down through the centuries and which were now given an added richness by the impressionists. This rebellious instinct gradually transformed itself into a revolutionary consciousness designed to constitute a new order.

Matisse established his rigorously formal system on the basis of the wholesale destruction of values which had been achieved by fauvism. As for Picasso, it is reasonable to believe that the violence of his rebellion was tempered by the prudence of Braque who encouraged him, towards the end of his 'negro' period, to join him in setting up the experimental laboratory from which cubism was to emerge. But Picasso was incapable of remaining imprisoned in a discipline for any length of time. After a few years he reasserted his freedom, demonstrating with the monstrous figures of his 'neo-classical' period that he had abandoned the efforts of his cubist period to achieve a 'synthetic' effect deriving from a meticulously developed analysis of form.

Throughout his career, Picasso has never ceased to rebel against everything, and against himself,

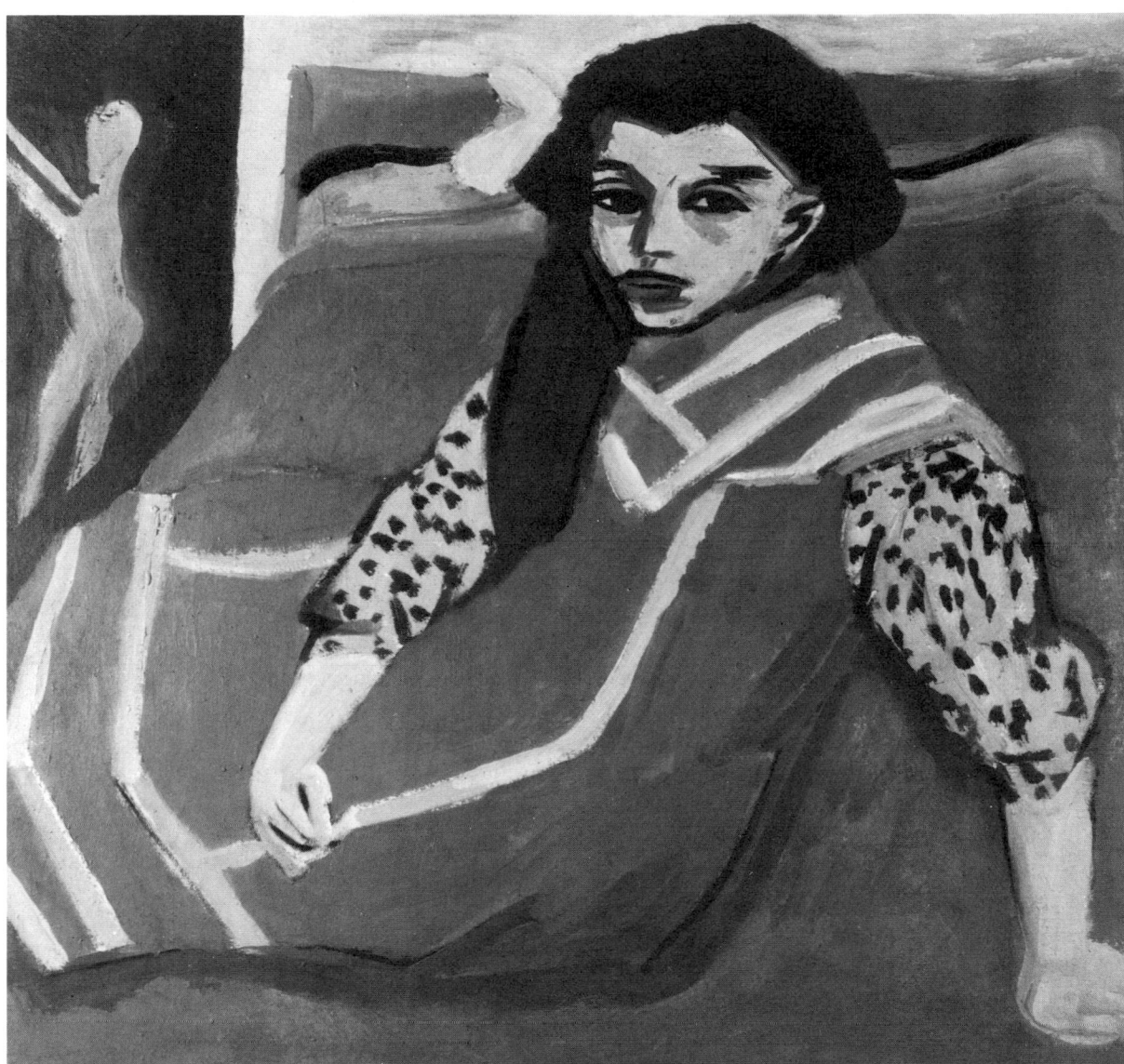

condemning himself to repeated adventures and misadventures, a few classically orientated drawings providing his sole relief. His instinct for rebellion has been strengthened by the tragic events which succeeded each other in Europe. The Spanish Civil War, and then the Second World War, seemed to justify in turn his own savage slaughter of the human form. This is not to say that he has become unmindful of the forms of the past: on the contrary, everything, from Greek vases and Chinese scrolls to the paintings of Velázquez, Cranach and Manet feeds his hunger for destruction. For Picasso, painting is an act of transgression,

236 Ernst Ludwig Kirchner (1880–1938). *Seated woman.* Minneapolis, Institute of Arts.

In the twentieth century, German painting roused itself from a long lethargy and found fresh inspiration in its deep-seated indigenous inclination towards expressionism.

a transgression of reality as much as of art. Inscrutable in his purpose, he has become the very symbol of our modern era and remains its quintessential rebel.

Braque is Picasso's antithesis. His career developed in a straight line. Towards the end of his life, rich in experience and in full mastery of his creative powers, he allowed the musician to take over from the geometrician, and indulged in the pleasures of harmony. In the pictures painted between 1938 and 1948, every possible musical approach is brought into play: counterpoint, direct or inverse mimicry, augmentation, diminution, stretto, the opposition of subject and answer, a delicate choice of timbre, a subtle knowledge of the harmonic resonance of tones. In turn austere and gracious, bold yet prudent, always discreet, a Cartesian spirit leaving nothing to chance yet possessing a sensibility as delicate as that of Corot, Braque is the most French of all the painters of this century.

With the twentieth century, the notion of an avant-garde in painting conforms more closely to the etymological and military sense of this phrase. Artistic creation remains an adventurous exploration of virgin territories, and the painter a kind of pioneer; but in contrast to the nineteenth century, this situation has become positively beneficial for him. Contemporary artists have met with far less resistance, in their campaign to destroy all the traditional values in painting, than the impressionists encountered in setting off a final firework display of that naturalism which represented the ethical basis of bourgeois society. It is an irony of fate that the nineteenth-century bourgeoisie failed to recognize this fact, and remained blinded by an academic aesthetic which it saw as one of the forces of inertia to be used as a bulwark against anything that seemed to threaten the established order.

The fauvists and cubists were more fortunate than the impressionists. Even at the beginning they could count on the support of a number of dealers, and they gradually attracted a following which seemed to grow in proportion to the subversive content of their art. Indeed, whenever passions seemed to be dying down, the artists hastily whipped up fresh antagonisms even if it meant picking a quarrel with themselves. Audacity became the stimulus of an artistic creativity which came increasingly to resemble an industrial output and which, like any industrialist, found itself forced to go on producing fresh types and models in order to attract customers and ensure a constant sales turnover. The very notion of audacity has been turned inside out, in the end, to produce a situation where-

by the 'avant-garde' has become a real conformism, and a vital necessity to the artist.

The concept of the creator is becoming increasingly confused with that of the inventor. This process, expanding as the century progressed, has now reached a point where a painter's work is launched by exactly the same publicity methods as a commercial product. It seems that our industrial civilization attaches the notion of value automatically to anything that is *new*. Indeed, there are Americans, collectors and museum curators, citizens of a country which indisputably constitutes the 'avant-garde' of technical progress, who take this relationship so much for granted that after paying enormous sums for historic works of art they have these precious objects restored, at the risk of causing irreparable damage, solely because a brand-new appearance is considered an indispensable aspect of the prestige which the works have acquired.

An artist in the public eye needs an annual exhibition in just the same way that a department store or fashion house depends upon regular displays and sales offers; the artist has become the pampered slave of a production-line, forced to produce a never-ending series of novelties for the delectation of his public. In some ways he has reverted to the days when every minor prince or great lord included a painter among his retinue, to amuse the court with fanciful inventions. In other ways he is not unlike the artist-magician in primitive cultures, whose creations are heavy with the power of mystery.

The painter of today has renounced the solitude of genius, in which the work of art took shape in a painstaking dialogue with the inner self, that lonely creative process adopted by the romantics and by some of the greatest painters in history, such as Tintoretto and Rembrandt. He is more akin to those Florentine craftsmen or Swiss watchmakers who work in their own shop-windows, in full view of the public. Exhibitionism has become a professional obligation. Profiting from the aura of heroism which has surrounded the artist since the impressionists, and from the revolutionary prestige acquired by his elders at the beginning of the century, the contemporary painter has become, whether he wants to or not, one of those products of the consumer society which are manufactured by publicity and called 'stars'. He is faced with the choice of being a 'celebrity' or being nothing at all. A 'promising young painter' has a biography before he even has a life, and the future is assured of being fully informed about the least doings of some ephemeral favourite, whereas the life story of a Théodore Rousseau or a Giorgione was allowed to sink into irredeemable oblivion.

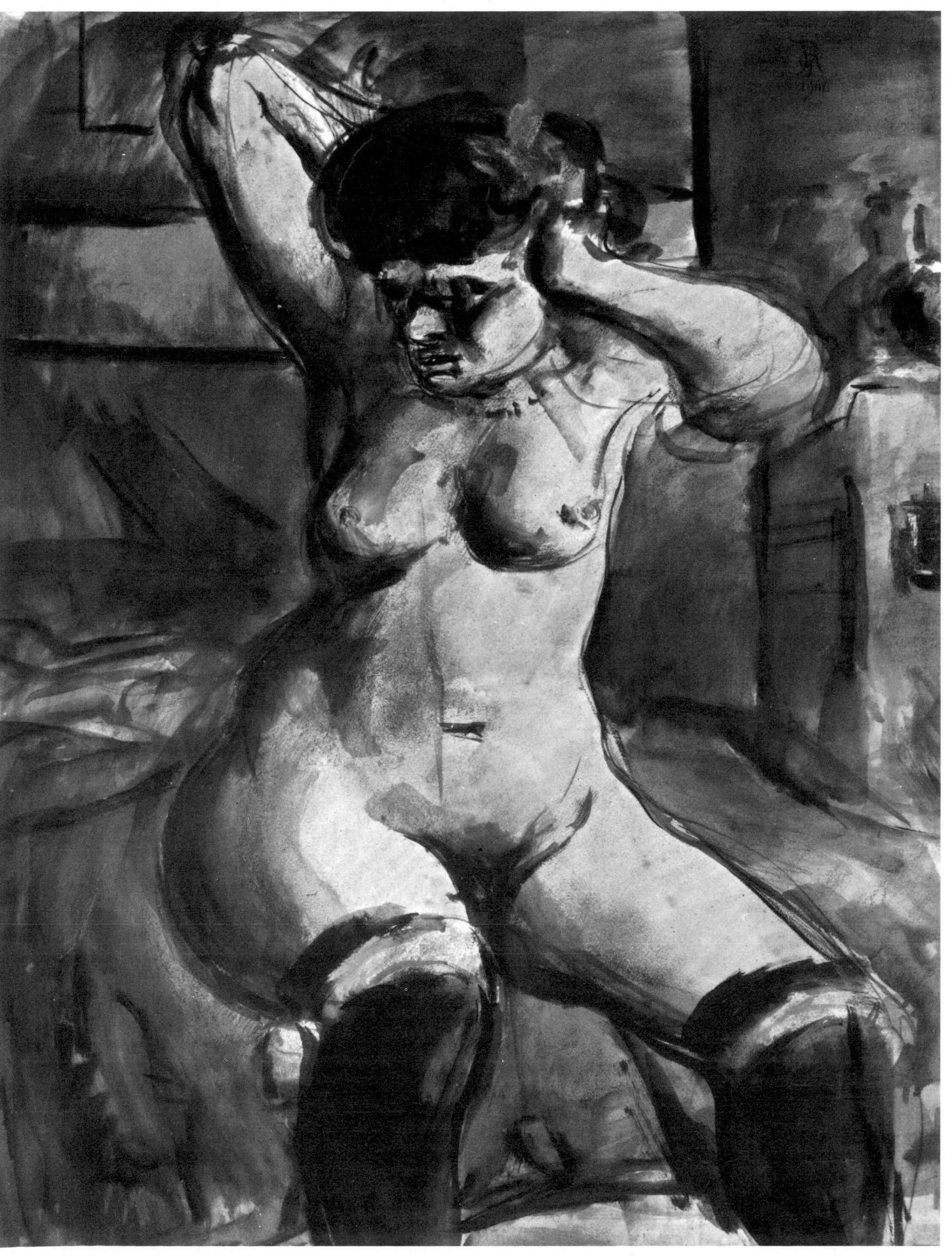

237 Georges Rouault (1871–1958). *The Prostitute*. Watercolour. Paris, Musée National d'Art Moderne.

Setting out the principles of French expressionism, and transcending Lautrec's disillusioned art, Rouault evokes the misery of prostitutes at the moment when Maillol is exalting in sculpture the beauty of the human body.

17 Beyond the avant-garde

238 Arshile Gorky (1904–48). *The Betrothal, II.* New York, Whitney Museum of American Art.

Artistic movements originating in Europe have generally taken a certain time to achieve an echo in North America. After the outbreak of the Second World War, however, the process of assimilation became accelerated with the arrival in America of a number of European artists, many of whom made their homes there, some adopting American nationality. In addition, over the last twenty-five years, America has for the first time in its history witnessed the birth of indigenous forms of art.

Abstract expression emerged in New York in 1943, more or less under the influence of the surrealists Max Ernst, Joan Miró, Yves Tanguy (*pl. 235*), André Masson and Matta. This new tendency differed radically from the abstract movement in art which received its initial impetus in France at about the same time and reached its zenith during the decade following the end of the war, in the work of Le Moal, Manessier (*pl. 241*), Bazaine, Singier, Vieira da Silva, de Staël and Piaubert. The Parisian artists, whether they proceeded from a natural impression, progressively reduced from the real until it represents little more than the translation of a perceptual stimulus, or by-passed this reductive process to confront abstraction directly, all tended to 'stylize' in the traditional manner (which was still that of cubism, inherited from Cézanne); and the end result was in either case a 'form' resulting from patient elaboration. However, the American abstract expressionists, Arshile Gorky (*pl. 238*), Franz Kline (*pl. 246*), Willem de Kooning (*pl. 245*), Clyfford Still (*pl. 247*), Jackson Pollock (*pls 239, 265*), Philip Guston, Robert Motherwell (*pl. 248*), invoking the principle of automatic handwriting extolled by the surrealists, claimed to operate under the effect of immediate inspiration, in a sort of hypnotic state.

Pollock's trance, as he squirted paint from full tubes, or even from syringes, on to canvases stretched on the ground, may be compared to the dance of a witch-doctor. The American critic Harold Rosenberg, thinking particularly of Pollock, has called this manner of painting 'action painting'. Michel Seuphor has likened de Kooning's relationship with his own paintings to an all-in wrestling match; and it is doubtless more than chance which

has led the French painter Georges Mathieu, whose work is closely related to abstract impressionism, to name a number of his paintings after battles.

Immediately after the war, an analogous movement came into being in France, existing side by side with abstract art properly so called: this movement asserted its independence of the speculative tendencies of other kinds of European abstract art, calling itself '*abstraction lyrique*'. Among its adherents were Atlan, Hartung (*pl. 249*), Wols, Soulages (*pl. 242*) and Mario Prassinos.

From 1935 onwards the American west coast painter Mark Tobey, who during his travels in Asia had studied the function of ideograms as 'abstract' elements in Japanese painting, found inspiration in Japanese calligraphy for a series of gouaches entitled 'white writings' (*pl. 243*). After the war the Frenchman Henri Michaux gave a particular expressive value to the same technique (*pl. 244*); indeed, Western non-figurative painters have found Oriental calligraphy to be a far more authentic historical precedent for their work than the frequently invoked eighth-century Anglo-Irish miniatures. Georges Mathieu, renouncing relief and shading in favour of blob and line, transposed calligraphy on to a monumental scale, completing enormous canvases in record time (*pl. 240*). Claiming to have added the dimension of speed to the artistic gesture, Mathieu explained that speed was the essential factor of improvisation. Improvisation, in its turn, was to be considered the true value of an art which rejected the composed in favour of the instantaneous and set out to be 'an exploration of the psychosensorial world active for the first time at a pure ontological level' which would thus restore to the pictural 'event' the 'primitive potentiality of the sign', freed of all the representational and illustrative irrelevances attendant on the 'spiritual ossification' of Greek art and Renaissance humanism.

The gestural aspect of the creative act now assumed such significance that it turned into a public performance. Mathieu, for example, began painting in public, as though he were a musician giving a recital of improvisations. For many artists, the act of painting began to seem more important than the painting itself. A great deal of thought was

In this late work (1947) Gorky uses the spontaneous and sensuous technique of abstract expressionism to liberate instinctual images.

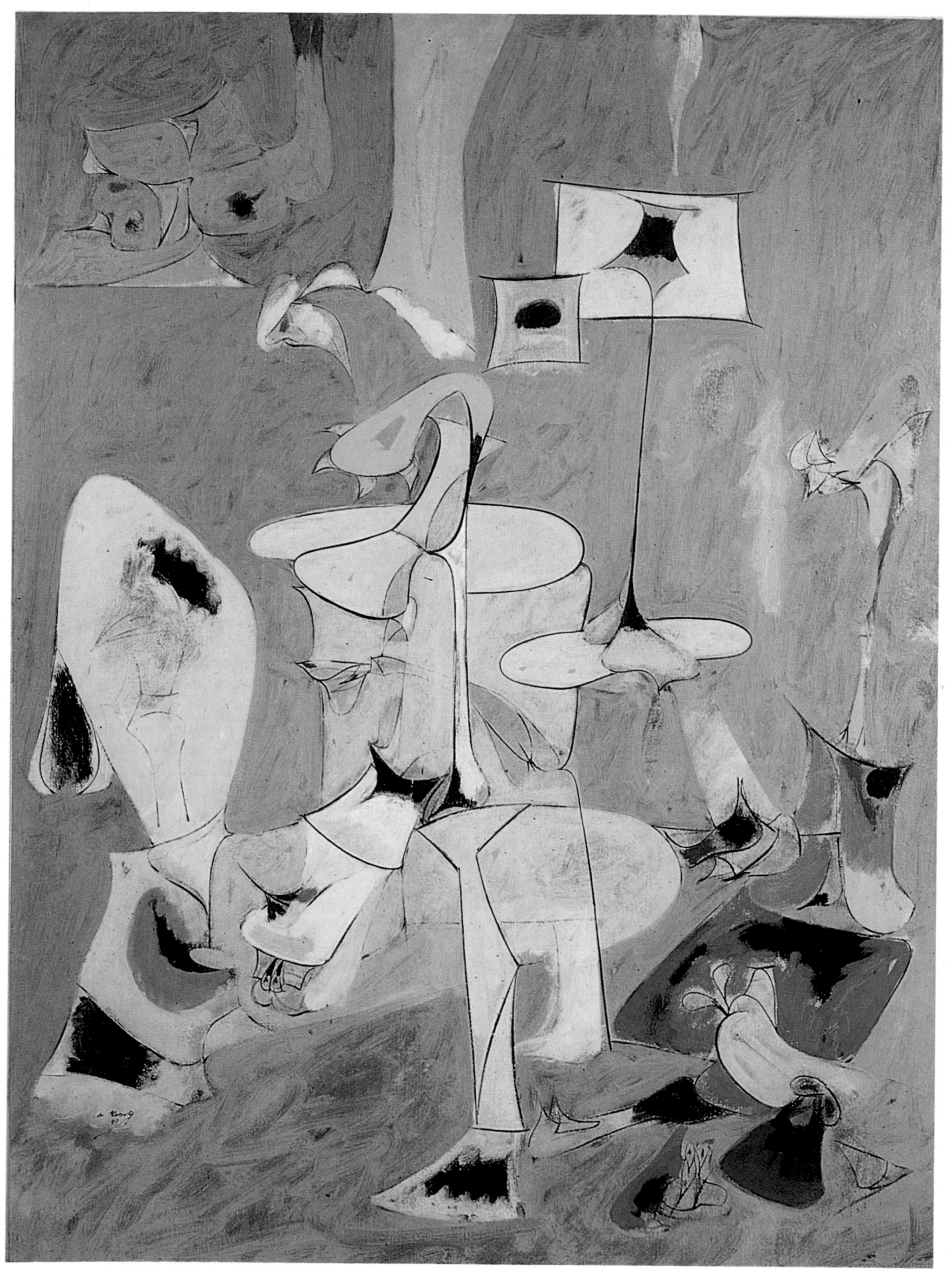

239 (overleaf) Jackson Pollock
(1912–56). *Painting*. Paris, collection
Paul Facchetti.

281

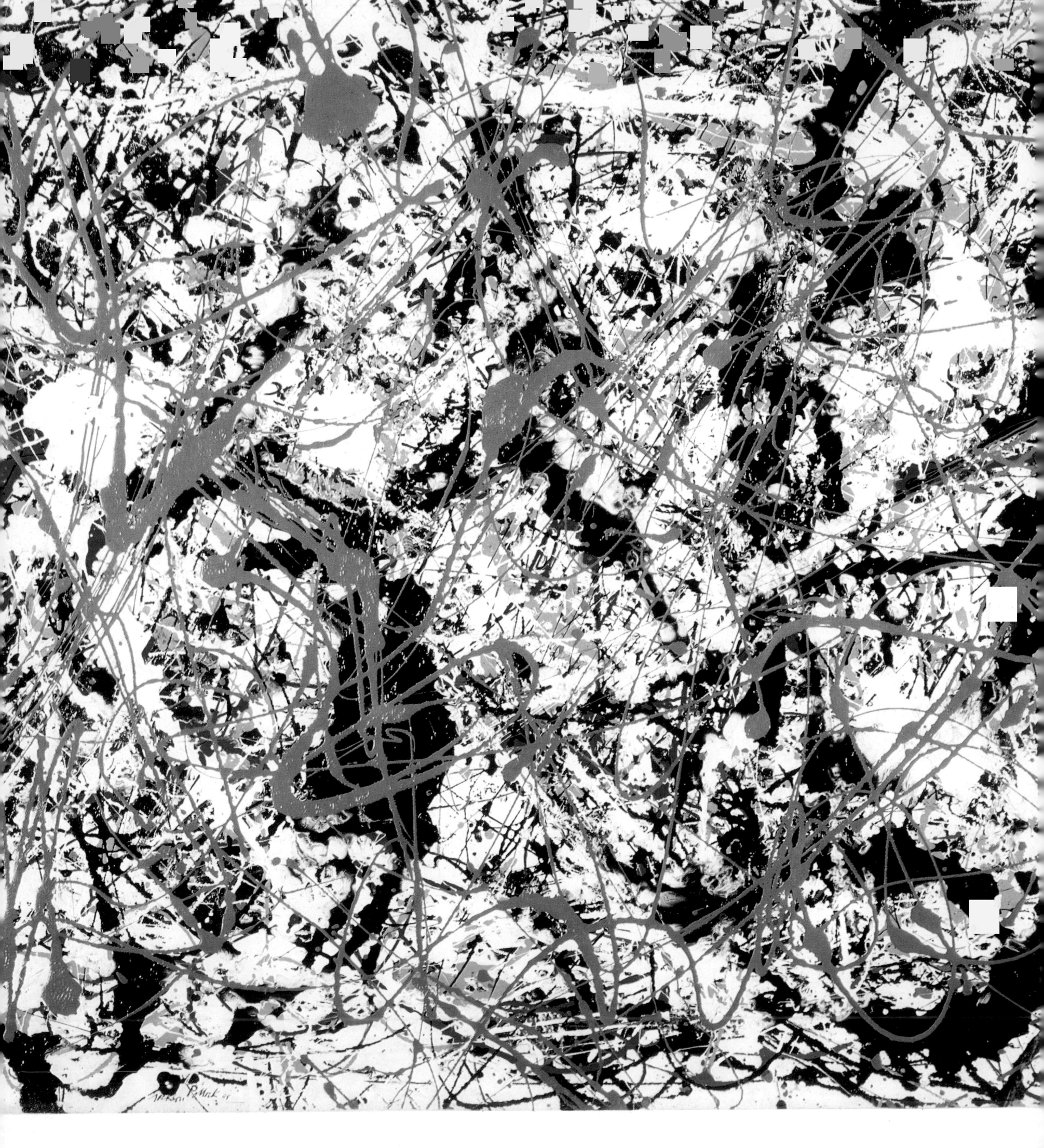

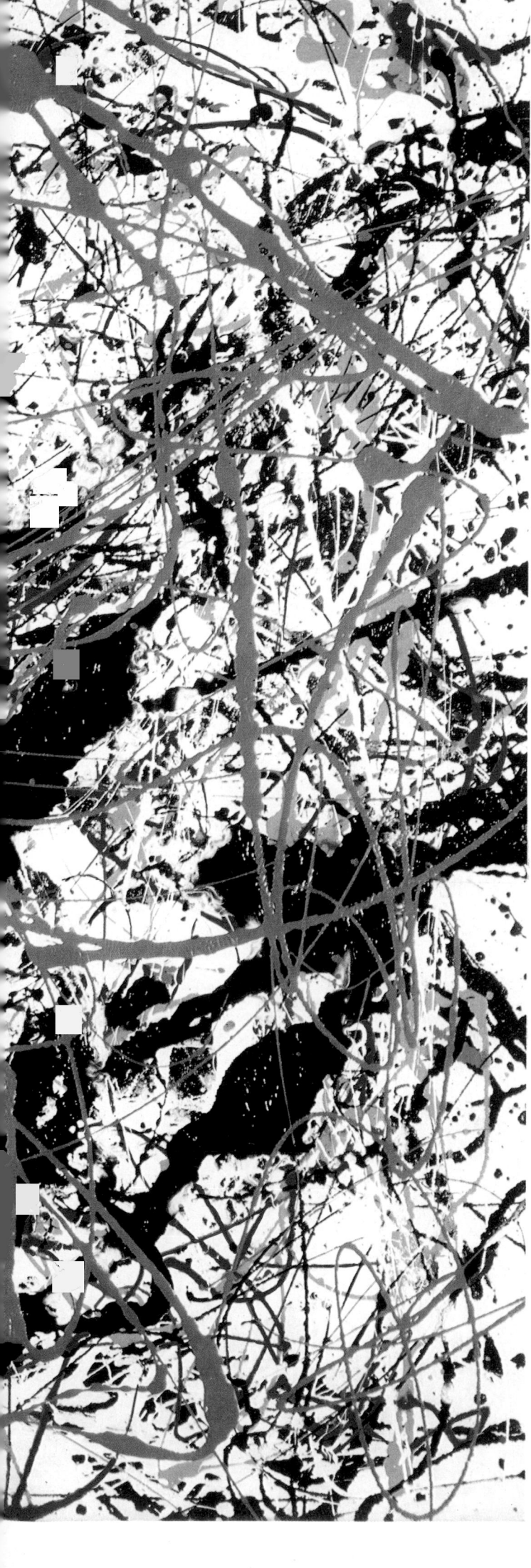

given to the ways in which colours could be projected on to the chosen bases, the criterion being the unusual nature of the method. One member of what was called the *Nouveau Réaliste* group, Yves Klein, made a naked woman press herself against a canvas after she had been smeared with paint. Another riddled his canvases with bullets from an automatic rifle. An ingenious artist had the idea of calcining the surfaces of his paintings by means of a blow-lamp. Yet another exhibited fragments of advertisements torn from billboards and hoardings. A final example of such 'inspiration' is so-called Art-Scotch, which consists in tearing off, with the aid of a length of cellophane adhesive tape, long narrow strips of the printed surface of pages of books

240 Georges Mathieu (b. 1922). *Mathieu from Alsace goes to the convent at Ramsay*. London, collection Anthony Denney.

Jackson Pollock's post-war drip paintings are, in a sense, an application to painting of the surrealist principle of automatism. The pattern produced by the 'drip' technique conveys a sense of restless movement in a number of close, parallel planes covering the entire surface of the picture. In the work of Mathieu, who arrived at his rapid, improvisatory technique independently of Pollock, single flamboyant shapes stand out against a uniform background.

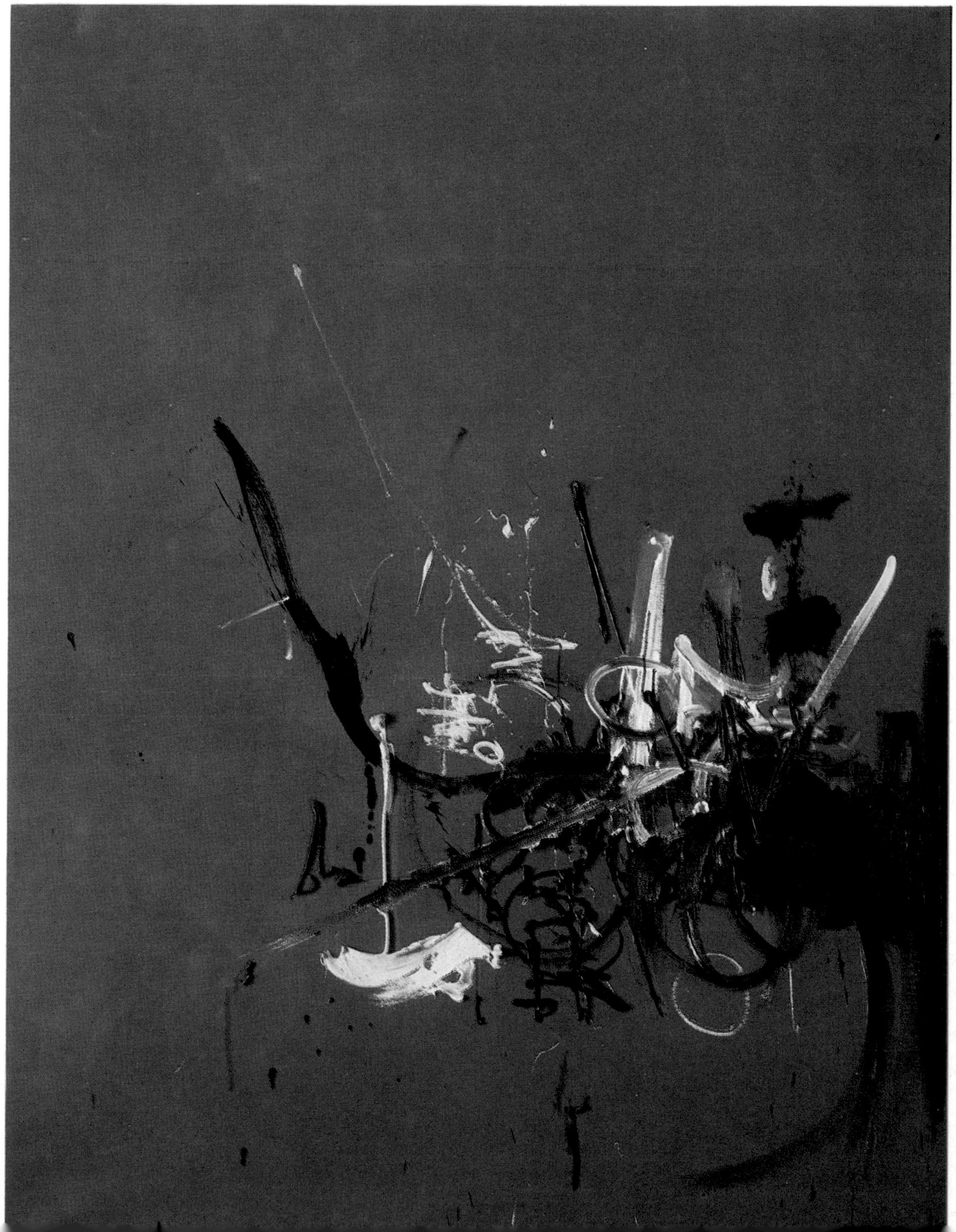

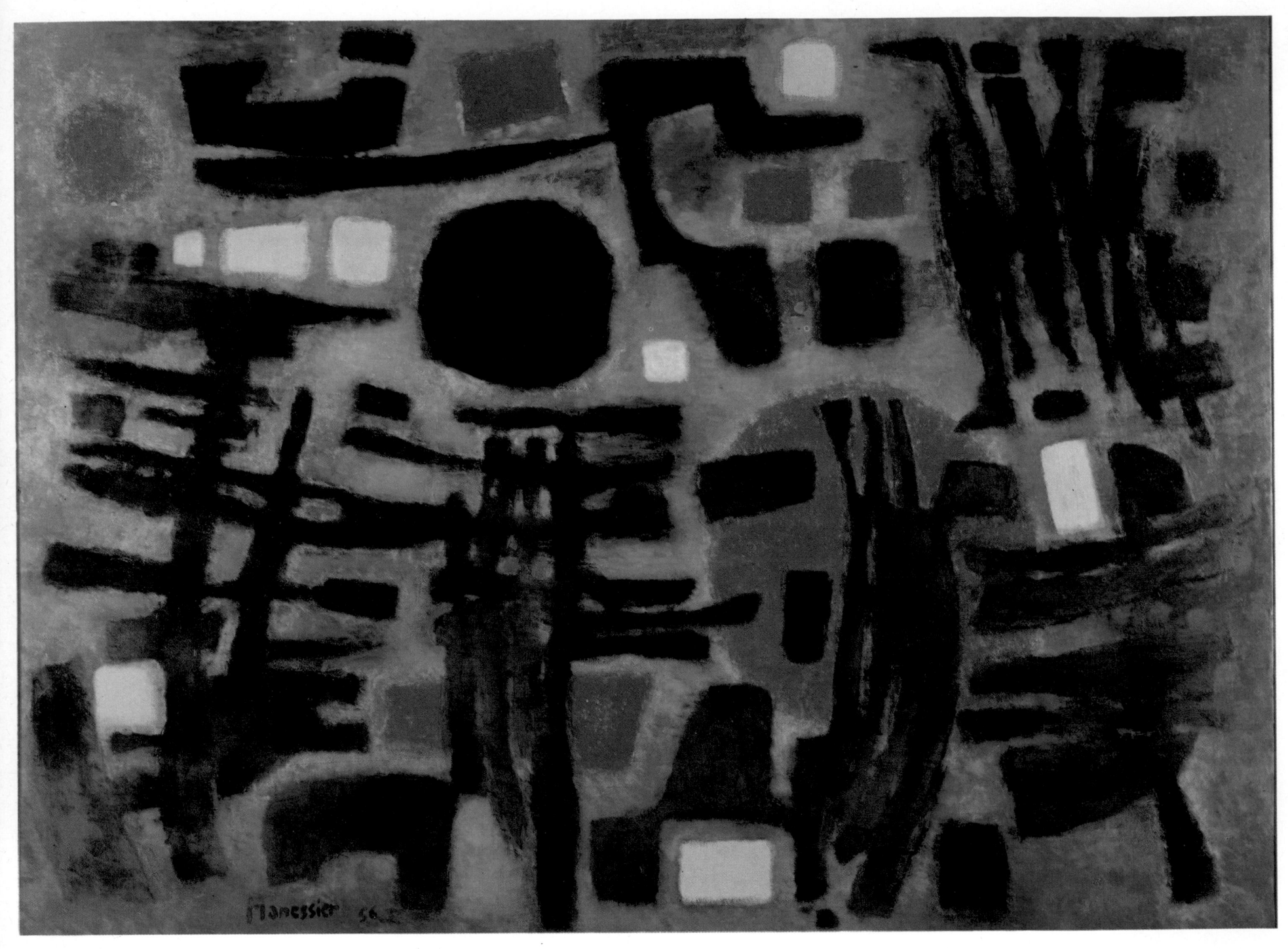

241 Alfred Manessier (b. 1911). *The Night*. New York, collection Mr and Mrs Otto Preminger.

or newspapers 'to obtain a writing which possesses a new affective dimension when arranged on a flat surface'.

This artistic production was accompanied by a chorus of literary and critical speculation. John Dewey's *Art as Experience* (1934) had as great an influence on the development of the post-war art scene in America as did Kandinsky's *Über das Geistige in der Kunst* in Europe at the same time (an English translation of Kandinsky's book appeared in 1947, and a French translation in 1949). Meanwhile, in his determination to 'deconsecrate'

Aristotle and to exorcize the 'abject' Descartes, Mathieu invoked successively the names of Heraclitus, Empedocles, Plotinus, St Augustine, Gregory of Tours, St John of the Cross, Meister Eckhart, the doctrines of Zen Buddhism, Taoism, Ch'an Buddhism and the mystical revelations of Ibn Al'Arabi.

Artists and critics began to invoke the support of science. In 1946, in my book *Crépuscule des images*, I suggested that the new forms invented by modern art might correspond secretly to the most recent conceptions in physics. This idea caught on, and artists began exploring feverishly the writings of

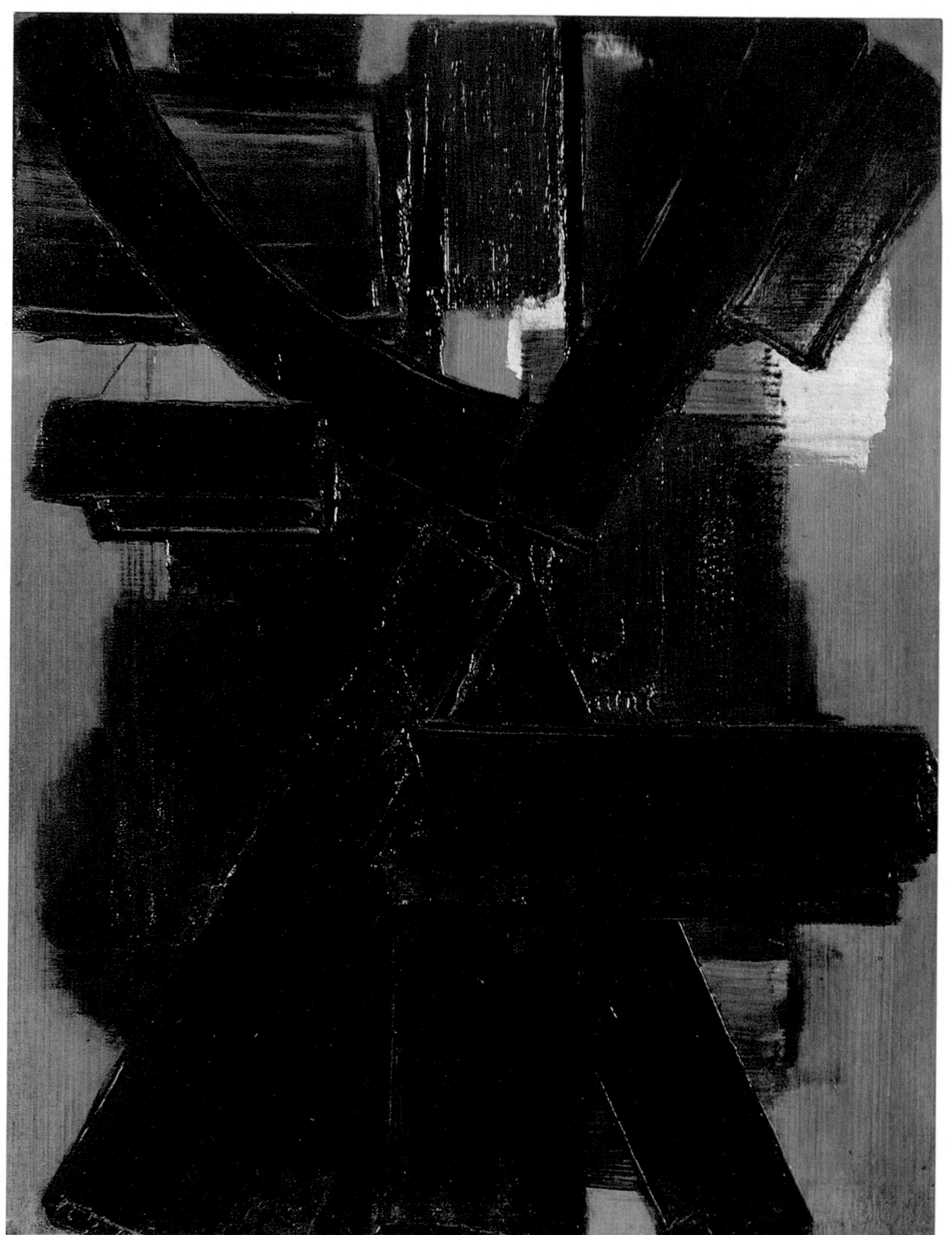

242 Pierre Soulages (b. 1919). *Painting*. Munich, Moderne Galerie Otto Stangl.

Manessier's work includes an element of stylized reality, whereas Soulages, like the other members of the *'abstraction lyrique'* movement, lays claim to the same freedom of inspiration which is inherent in abstract expressionism.

285

243 Mark Tobey (b. 1890). *Tropicalism*. Gstaad, Galerie Saqqârah.

244 Henri Michaux (b. 1899). *Gouache*. Paris, Galerie Le Point Cardinal.

Tobey and Michaux both use Oriental calligraphy as a source for their remarkably expressive forms. Tobey's all-over patterns link him clearly to abstract expressionism; Michaux, too, recalls Pollock in his deliberate exploitation of 'heightened' states of consciousness.

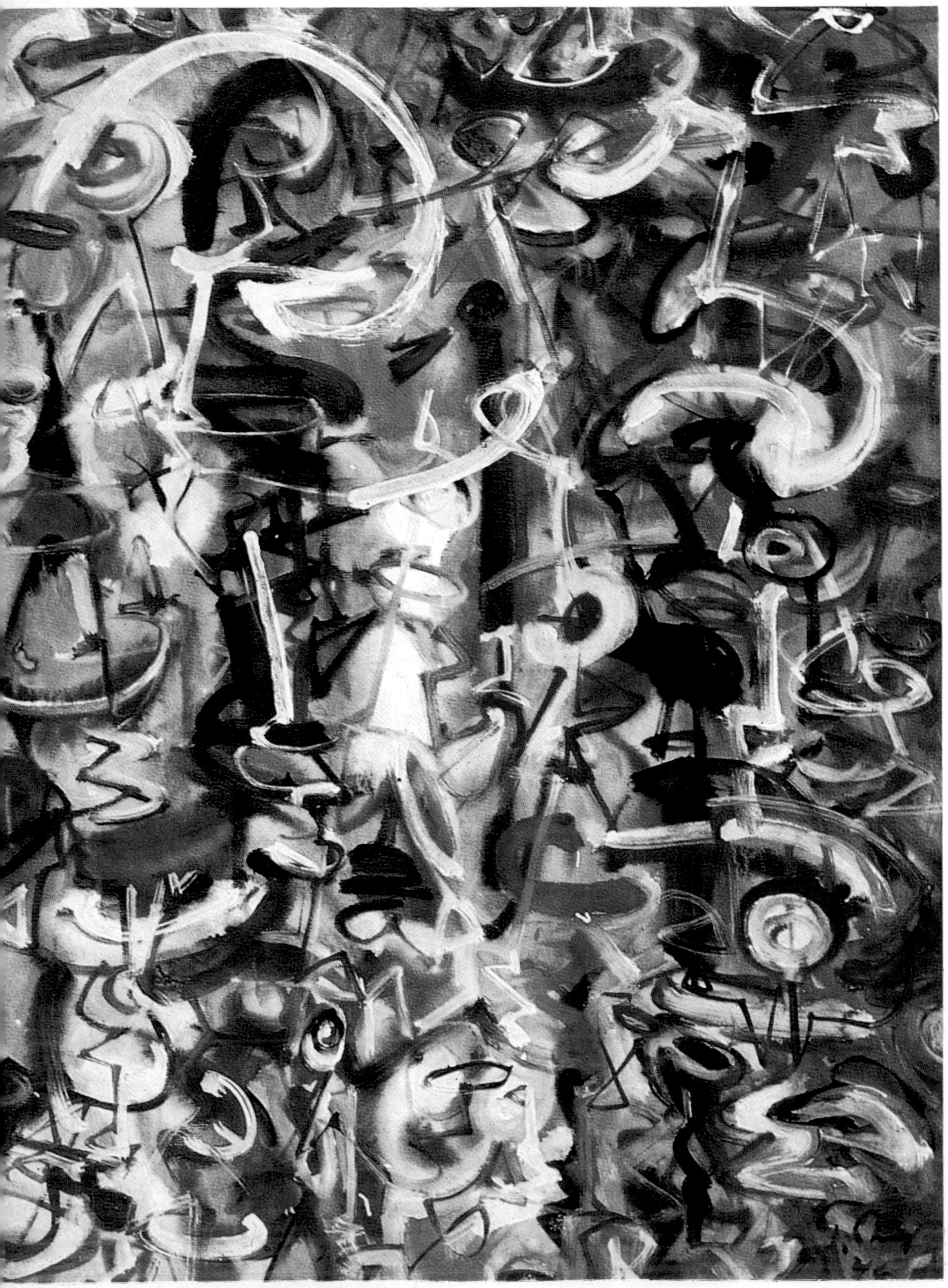

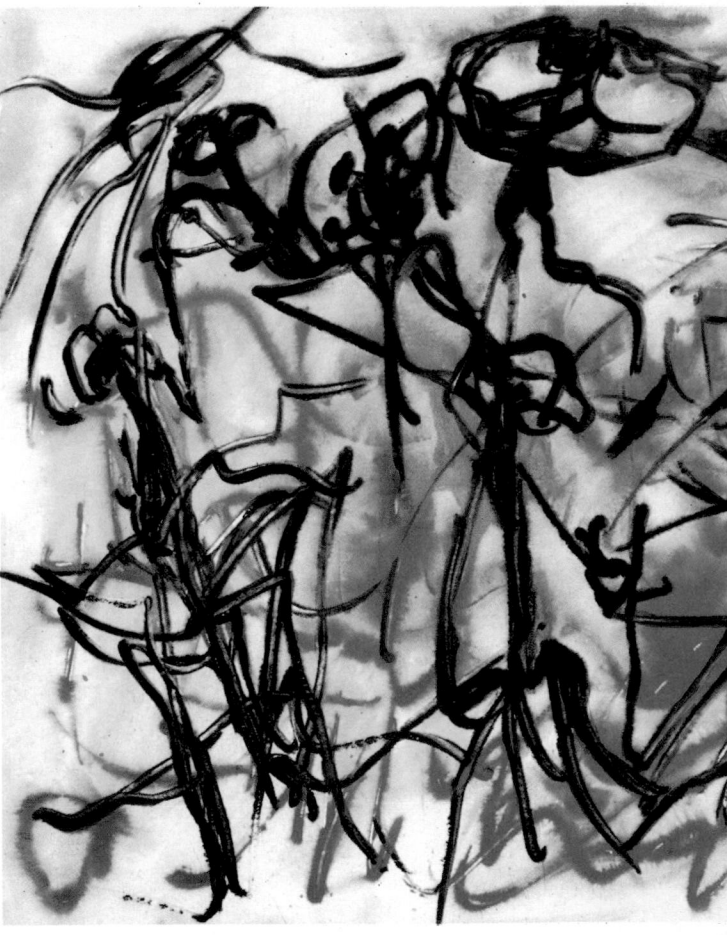

various philosophers and scholars. Heisenberg, Bohr and Planck became objects of discussion in artists' studios. Deductions from science were considered admissible, however, only in so far as they served the artists' purposes. Thus, certain theories of the physicist Louis de Broglie, the mathematician Bourbaki and even Einstein himself, were rejected as deriving from a conformist mental attitude 'still under the sway of Aristotelian superstition'. A logician, Stéphan Lupasco, the author of a theory of contradictory propositions, has exercised a certain influence on the practitioners of so-called *art informel* among the Paris-based abstract painters, and has himself written a book on the subject (*Science et art abstrait*, 1963).

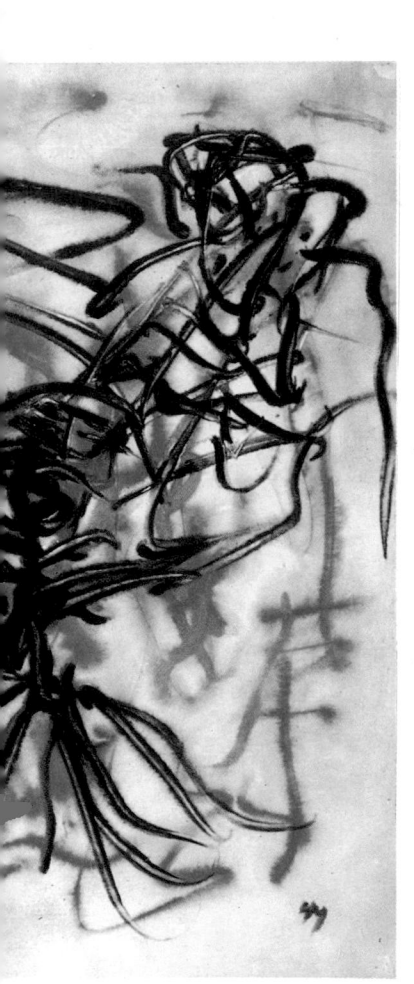

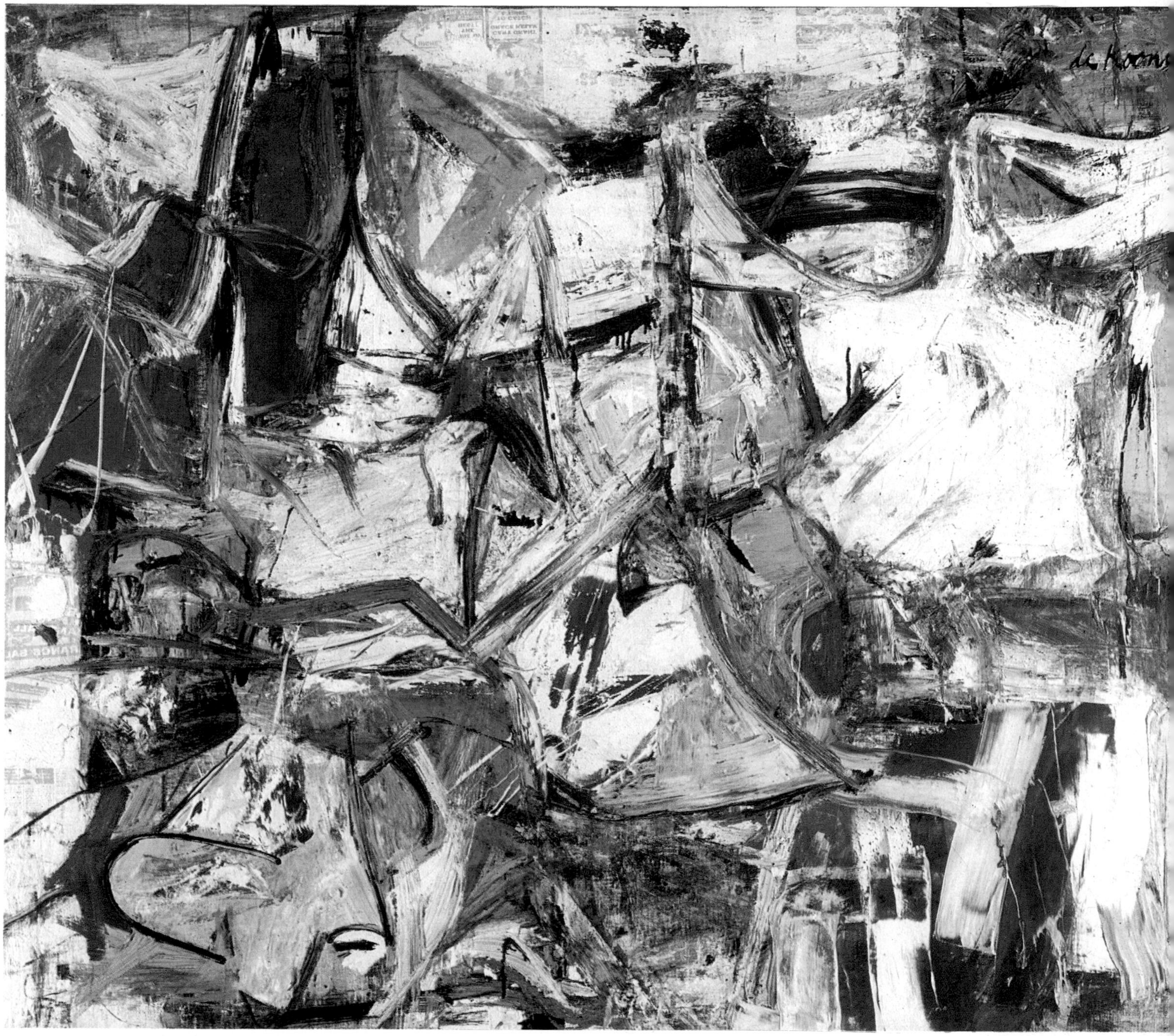

No sooner has a new fashion in painting appeared on the scene than the critics pounce anxiously on its message, as though they were Roman augurs consulting the entrails of a bird. Artists, following Kandinsky's example, have abandoned brush for pen and launched into print to explain their intentions; books by practising artists, such as Michel Seuphor's *L'Art abstrait* and Georges Mathieu's *Au-delà du tachisme*, give vivid expression to the mental climate in which large numbers of modern painters work.

I suggest that, in trying deliberately to cut painting loose both from nature as celebrated by the impressionists and from the new directions proposed by the pre-First-World-War movements, these artists who claim to have discovered an affinity with philosophers and scientists risk condemning painting to the most dreadful of all servitudes, that of being an illustrative process.

There is no disputing that an intimate relationship exists between ways of thinking and feeling and artistic creativity in any one era. What is new is that today the artists themselves emphasize connections which previously were unconscious, and which have been revealed in our times thanks only to the perspicacity of modern historians of art. Thus, the great Gothic cathedrals stood for seven centuries before Erwin Panofsky made the discovery that their structure presents profound affinities with those of scholastic philosophy; and it was not until

245 Willem de Kooning (b. 1904). *Gotham News*. Buffalo, N.Y., Albright-Knox Art Gallery.

De Kooning uses the technique of abstract expressionism in an aggressively energetic approach to figure or landscape; in his hands, action painting cuts its links with surrealism, mysticism and introspection.

three centuries after Galileo had expounded his cosmographic system that analogies were drawn, again by Panofsky, between it and certain aspects of baroque art. Similarly, it goes without saying that the Byzantine artists would have been surprised to learn from André Grabar that their vision of the world was comparable to that of Plotinus; and Picasso and Braque were doubtless unaware of the new physics which was transcending the world of appearances at the very moment that they were destroying traditional space in their paintings.

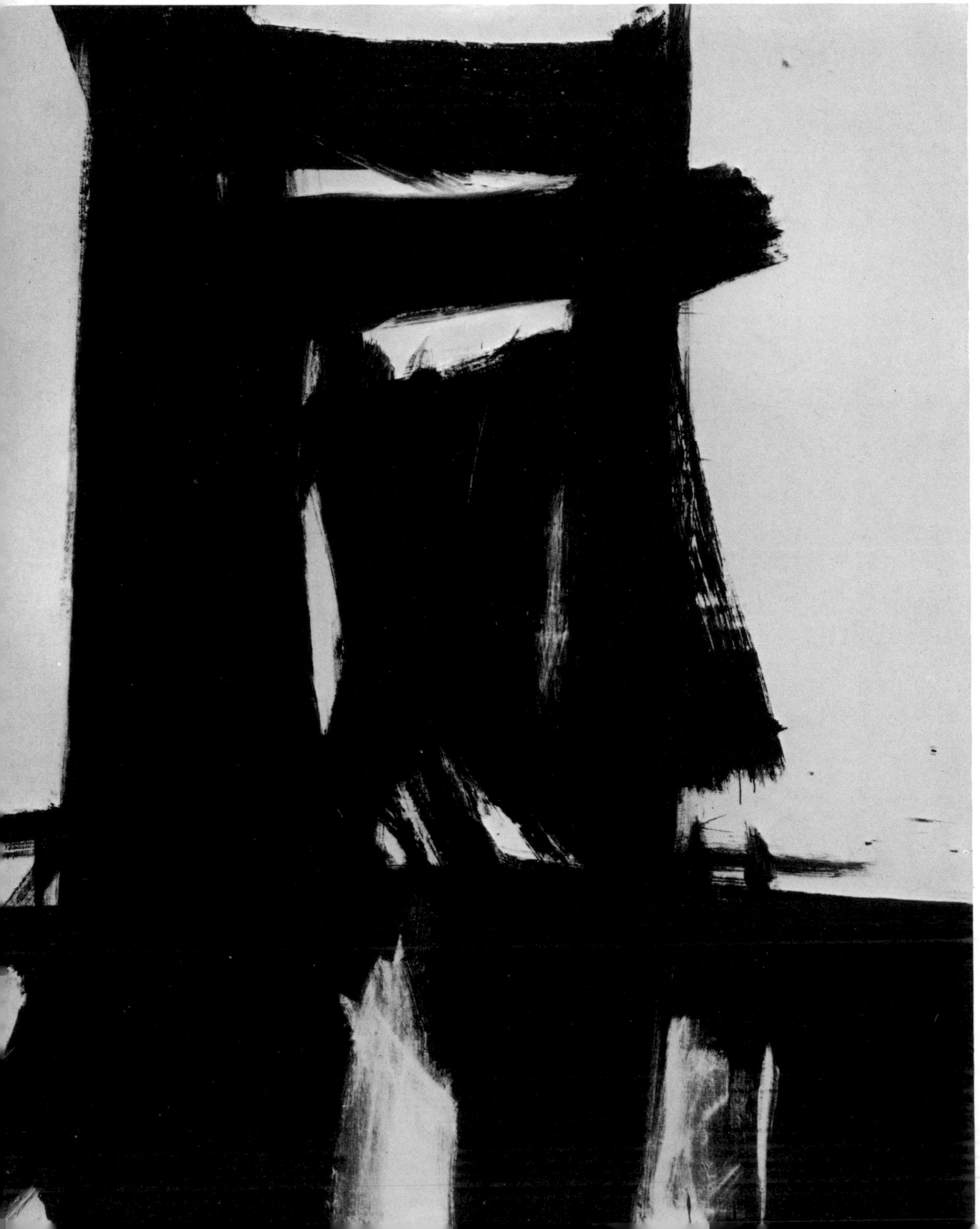

But it would seem that, for the last twenty years, artists, deprived of the authority of nature, have felt the need to appeal to an alternative system of reference, thus reimposing upon painting another

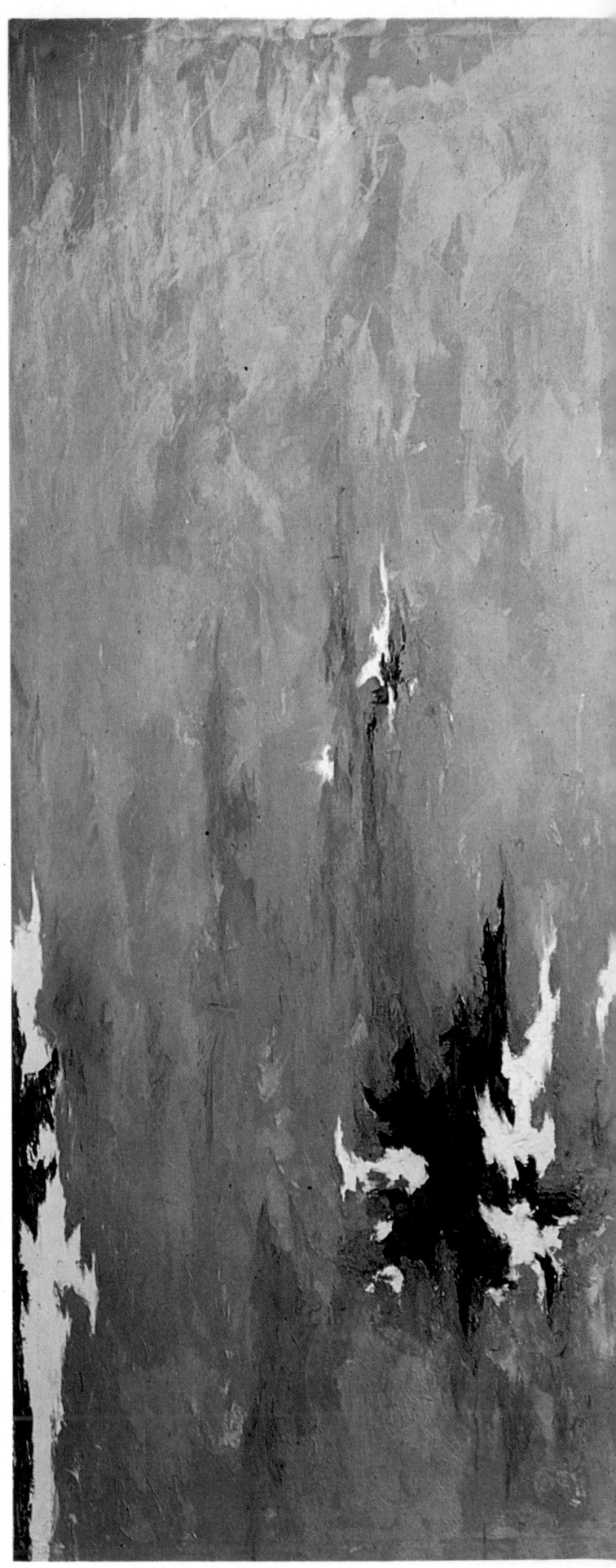

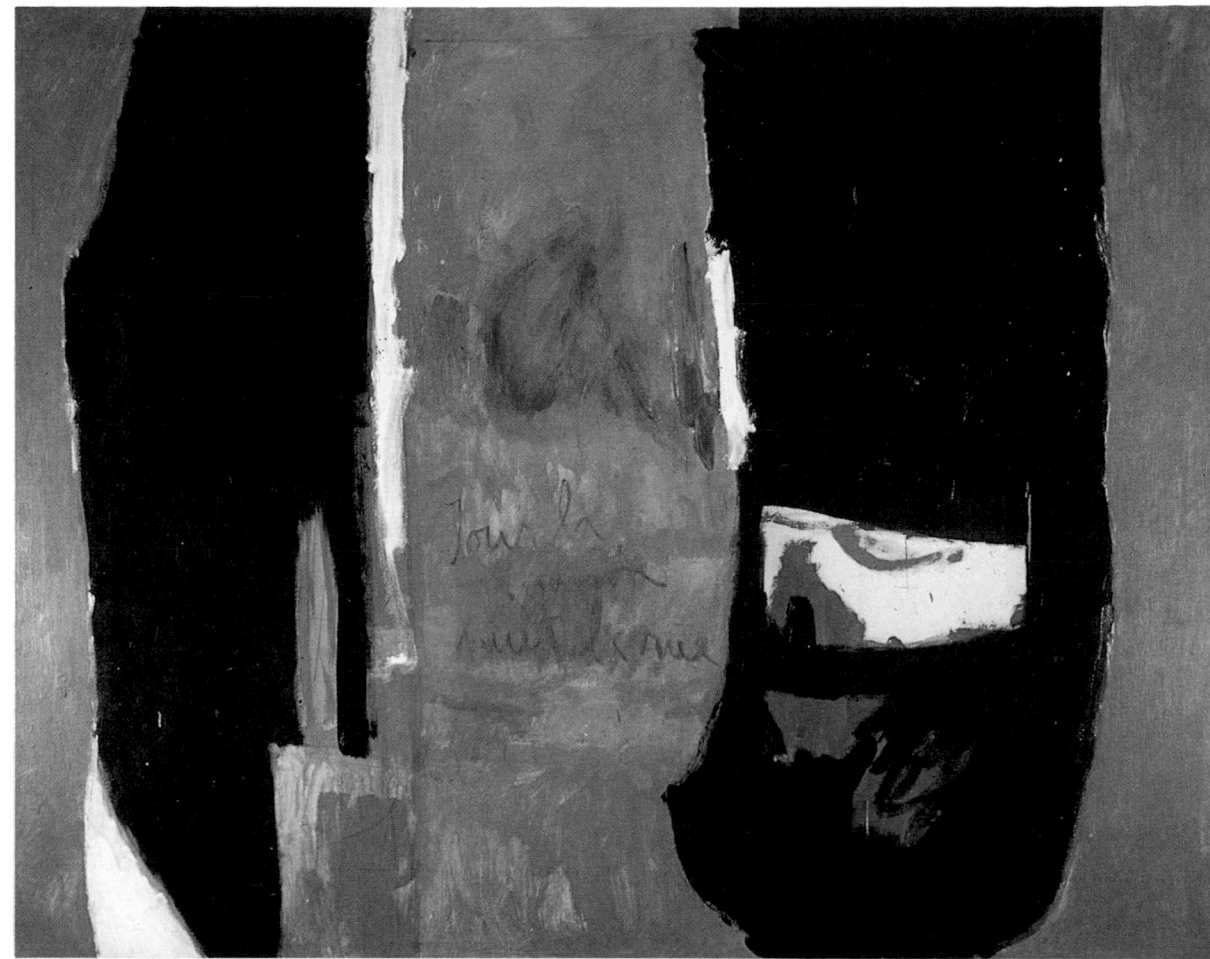

form of that literary servitude from which it had been rescued, after a heroic struggle, by Manet, and from which all the schools of painting up to fauvism and cubism had subsequently kept it free. A picture by Mathieu can arouse feelings of pleasure at its rhythmic grace, and one by Pollock may give one a voluptuous impression of opulent matter analogous to the creations of the German rococo stucco-workers (*pls 239–40*); however, wholly unjustified claims are made on their behalf. Even if one bears in mind that there exists an essential relationship between this painted non-figurative world and the world of modern science, it is fallacious to invoke the element of the 'irrational' in modern science as an analogy for so-called 'lyrical abstraction'; in science the arid path of the irrational possesses a logic of its own to which no creative frenzy can ever supply a short cut. The working methods of scientific research can be compared more accurately with the attitude of Picasso and Braque, between 1907 and 1910, as they achieved the cubist reduction of reality to abstraction through a patient programme of analysis and synthesis.

It is equally false to argue, as some have done, that abstract art in some way brings us closer to the discovery of a universe situated beyond our senses.

248 Robert Motherwell (b. 1915). *Jour la Maison, Nuit la Rue*. Idaho, collection Mr and Mrs William Janss.

Kline's massive gestures and Still's blazing expanses of colour typify 'gestural' and 'chromatic' abstraction respectively, two major and contrasting currents within abstract expressionism. The paintings of Motherwell represent a self-conscious, rhetorical use of the abstract gesture.

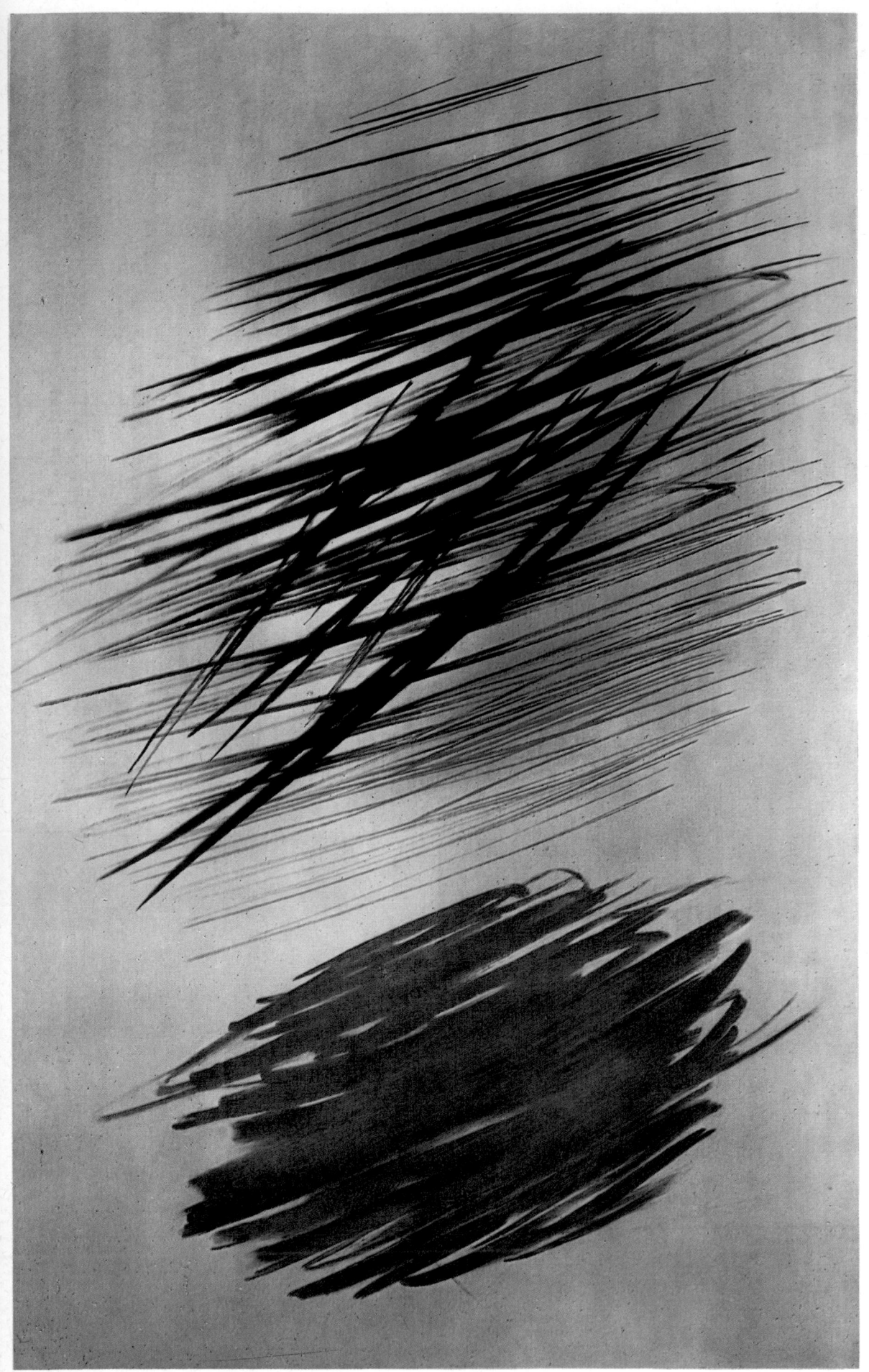

To compare the attitude of an abstract painter with that of an ecstatic mystic is sheer delusion; God is not to be found in a spasm at the tip of a paintbrush. For a painter to imagine that he can simply tear himself away in a trance from the world of representation, cross the threshold of the normal consciousness, and, like some St John of the Cross or Meister Eckhart, attain a state of pure being, is to forget the long path of asceticism that the saint needs to travel in order to detach himself from the world of appearances and attain the summit of awareness.

The notion of painting as a means of transcending the rational and the conscious so as to attain the hidden sources of human experience has inevitably led some artists to paint under the direct prompting of the unconscious. Although the surrealists had advocated this process, they had not achieved it; in the last analysis their dreams are waking dreams. In the last decade, however, a number of artists have deliberately induced in themselves mental states similar to psychosis either through the complex disciplines of Zen or yoga or by taking hallucinogenic drugs such as the peyote-derived mescalin, and LSD (lysergic acid diethylamide). Aldous Huxley, in *The Doors of Perception* (1950), had described the experiments he had conducted while under the influence of mescalin, but the artist who pioneered this kind of investigation was Henri Michaux, who, in 1957, painted the visions which resulted from his use of mescalin. Experiments with LSD, formerly carried out on a wide scale in American hospitals but subsequently banned by the government, are still frequently made in private, by artists and others.

It must be said that the artistic results of these visions are rather disappointing and are unlikely to surprise those already acquainted with the art produced by mental patients. Ever since the end of the last century, when Dr Hans Prinzhorn first argued the therapeutic effect of artistic expression on the mentally disturbed, psychiatric hospitals have made increasing use of drawing and painting materials for this purpose. The resulting works are scientifically valuable on two levels: they provide diagnostic indication of the progress of a patient undergoing specific treatment; and they furnish information about certain mechanisms of artistic creation.

It is noticeable that those artists who paint under the influence of hallucinogenic drugs employ many of the same symbols (egg, phallus, ovule, flame) and procedures as the insane, and that the paintings can often be classified in a similar way according to personality types. A practised eye can detect, by studying their work, whether such artists tend to be paranoid, manic-depressive or schizoid. Schizoid tendencies predominate, thus supporting the hypothesis that a latent schizophrenia frequently underlies the artistic psyche. The best paintings by the artificially hallucinated present the same features as the drawings executed by schizophrenics: a world closed in on itself, consisting of an endless repetition of the same patterns, and an attempt to hold fast the disintegrating personality through a rigorous

symmetry and a lapidary colour scheme which together give the painting a kaleidoscopic appearance.

The observed effects of hallucinogenic drugs on normal personalities suggest that schizophrenia is almost certainly due to a chemical disturbance of the cell-structure, since analogous effects can be produced by introducing a chemical substance into the body. Paintings so produced attain a quality rarely present in the work of the insane, except when

◀ 249 Hans Hartung (b. 1904). *T. 56–21*. Paris, private collection.

250 Ben Nicholson (b. 1894). *Still-life (off green)*. London, private collection.

Nicholson and Hartung provide examples of the two fundamental tendencies within abstract art: 'formal' or geometrical, and 'informal' or gestural.

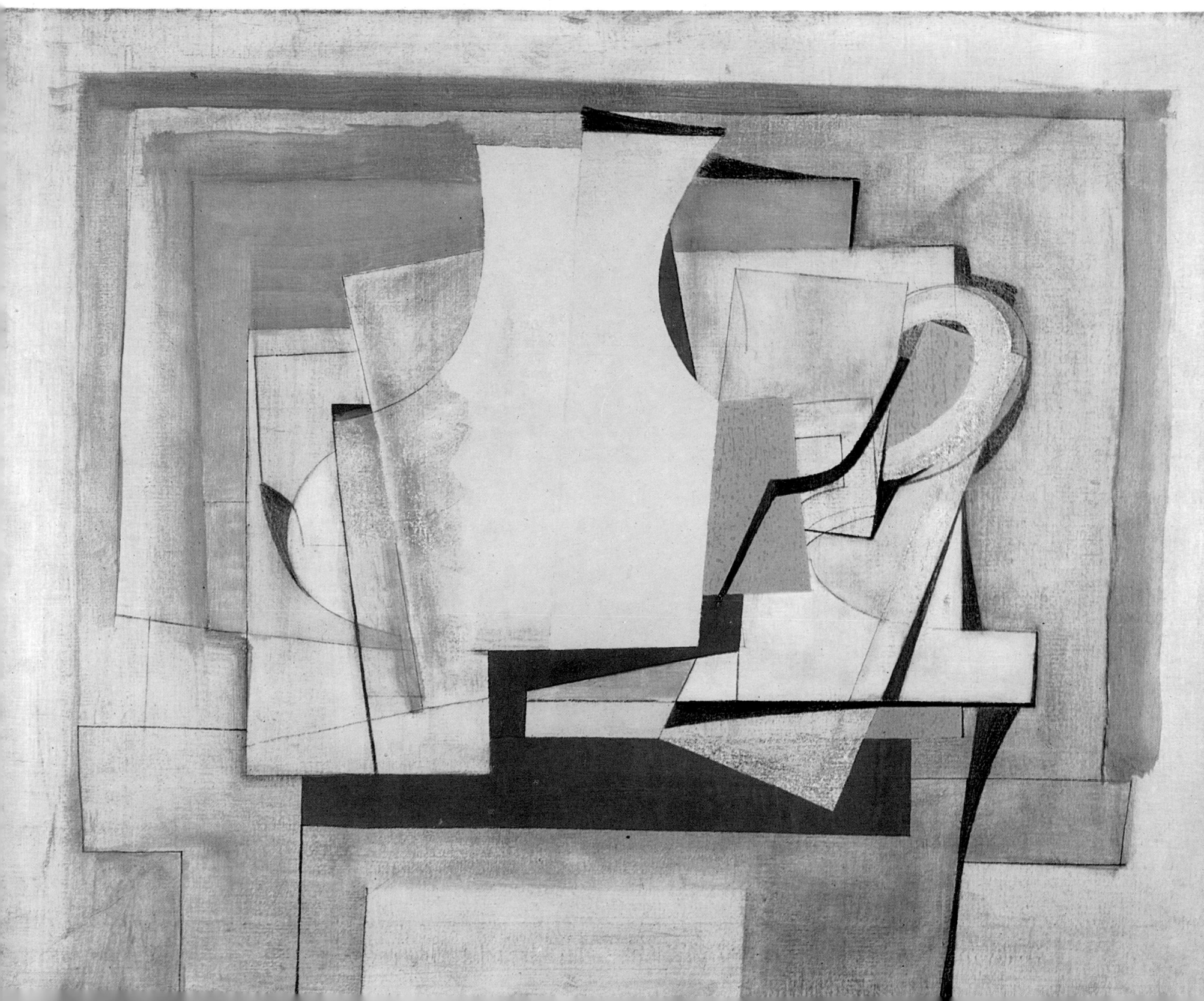

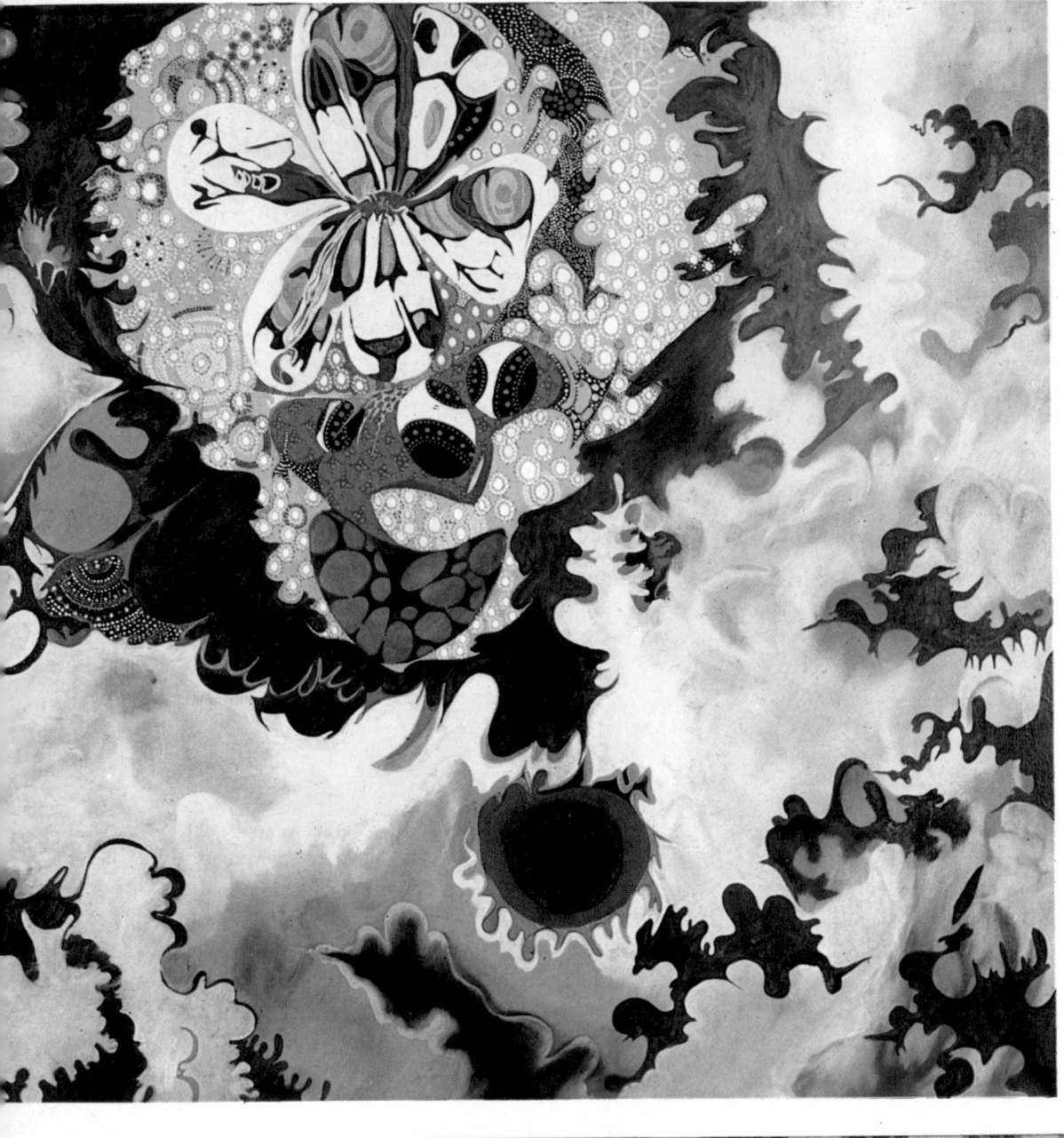

the latter are already endowed with artistic talent (a fact sometimes revealed by the shock of the illness itself), but tend to be less original than those created by artists in a normal state of health.

Paintings which are based on the sensations induced by drugs have been christened 'psychedelic art', and have exercised an important influence on fashion and the decorative arts (*pls 251–2*). Psychedelic art has in fact provided the essential ingredients of 'environmental art', which consists in placing the spectator in an atmosphere bringing together music, movement and the plastic arts in a single public manifestation.

The tendency towards large-scale painting which can be seen in the work of abstract expressionists in particular, can be traced back to Fernand Léger, and no doubt expresses the same desire to shatter the restrictive space of easel-painting and reach out towards a dynamic space. Painting, in this last decade, has gone one step further and freed itself from the flat surface, bending it, dislocating it and distributing it through the three dimensions of real space. A New York artist, Allen Atwell, for instance, has painted a 'psychedelic temple' in his studio, spreading over the walls and ceiling the coloured projections of his drug-induced visions; the spectator is no longer situated in front of the work of art, but within it, thus fulfilling an ambition which the Italian futurists had already formulated in 1910 (*pl. 253*).

In environmental art, painting itself has become no more than a single element in an interplay of light ('op art', 'lumia art'), movement (kinetic art), and music or electronic sound patterns, which confronts the spectator with a total audio-visual experience. The spectator himself is often called

251 Isaac Abrams (b. 1939). *Here it comes*. Zurich, Galerie Bischofberger.

252 Paul Ortloff (b. 1942). *Exhalation*. Halcott Center, N Y., collection the artist.

253 Allen Atwell (b. 1925). *Zurich Mandala*. Zurich, Galerie Bischofberger.

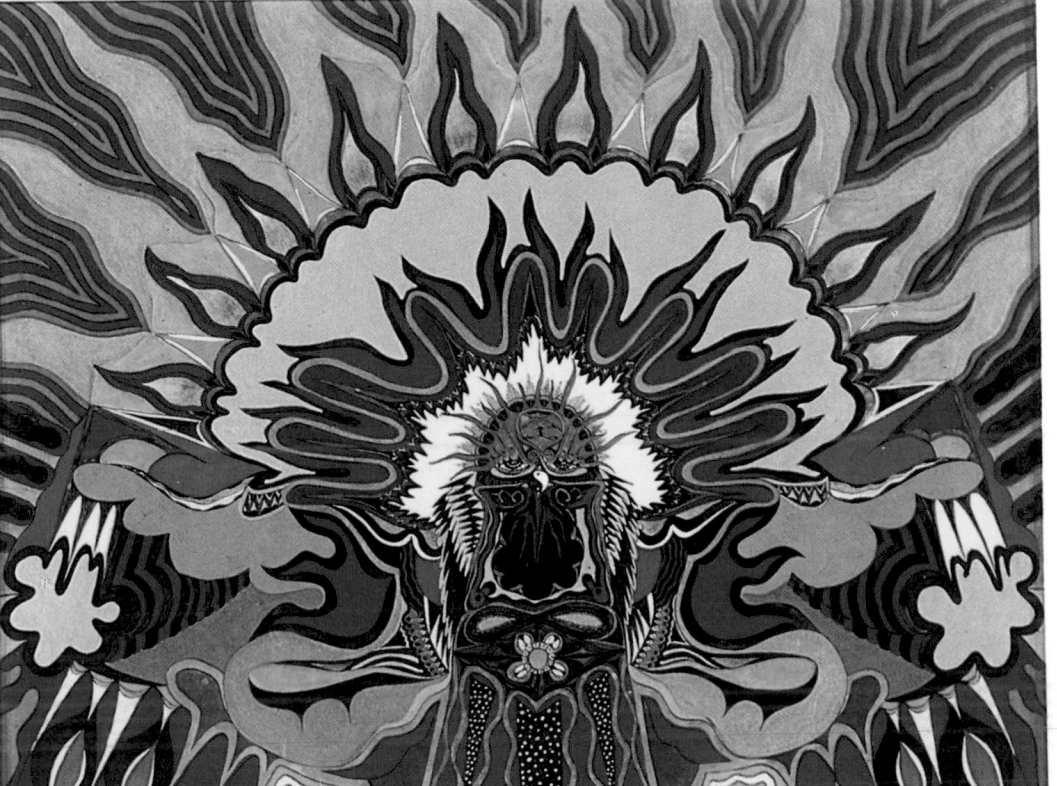

The paintings, in hard acrylic colours, of so-called psychedelic artists are an attempt to reproduce some of the perceptual distortions (and consequently, perhaps, some of the sense of heightened awareness) which result from the use of hallucinogenic drugs such as LSD. Strident and claustrophobic in effect, they bear a strong resemblance to the paintings of schizophrenic patients.

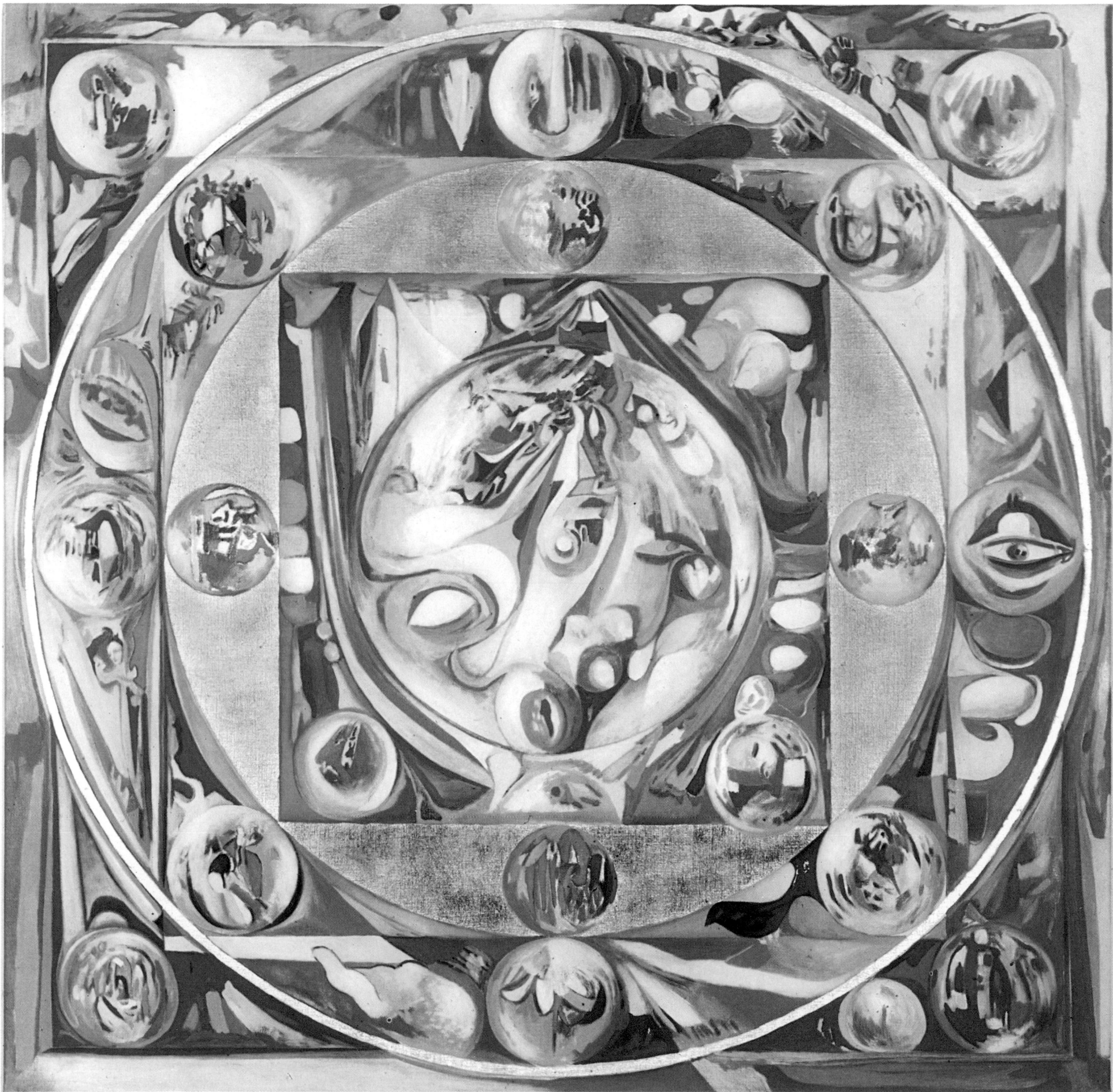

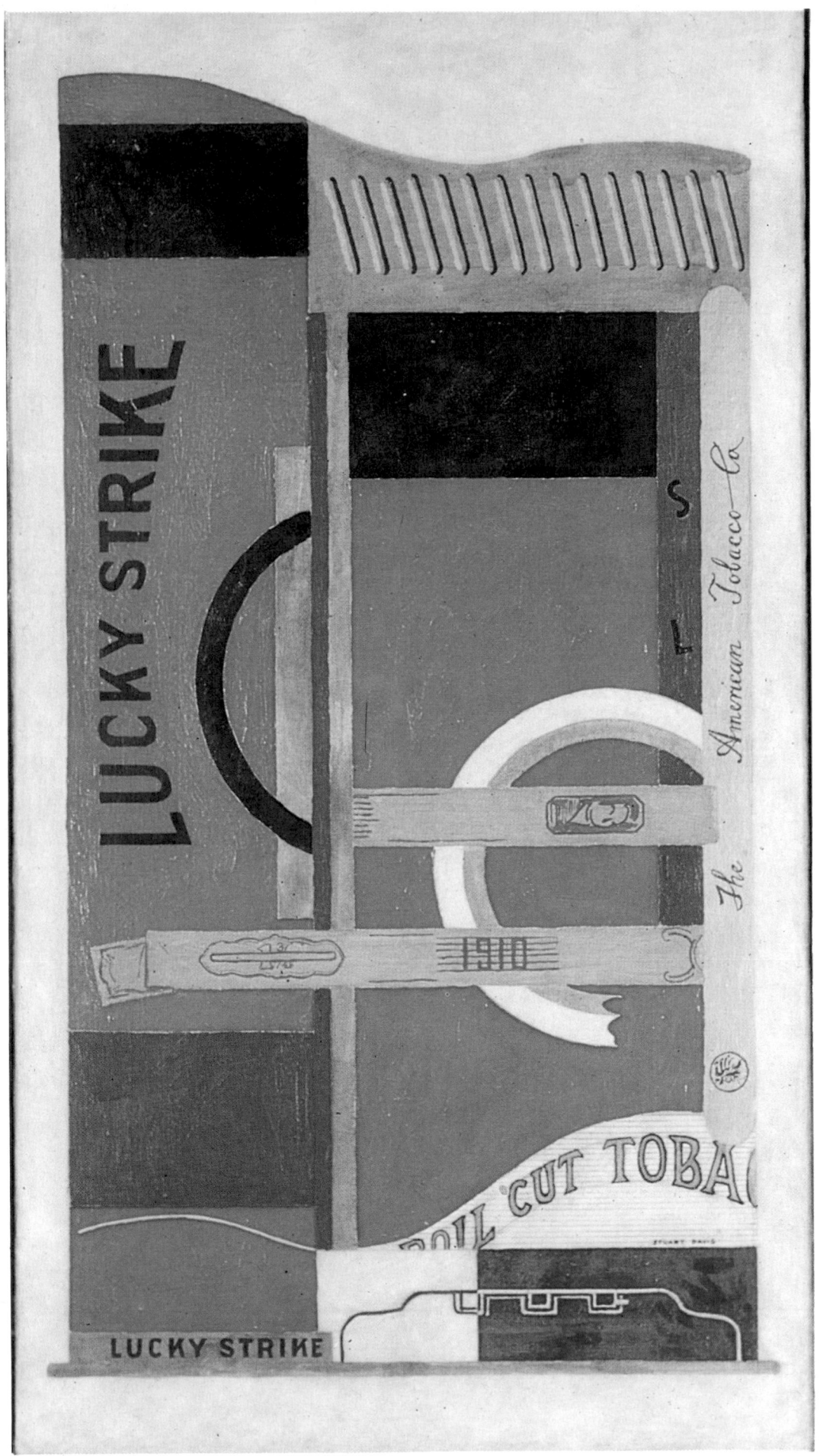

upon to participate in the development of this multi-faceted art, when the involvement of actors or dancers and the use of theatre or night club as a background convert this into an 'event'. This aspect of 'environmental art' recalls the ideal of the 'total work of art' (*Gesamtkunstwerk*) to which many German artists aspired in the rococo era.

Thus the spectator finds himself reintegrated, almost forcibly, in an art which for fifty years had seemed to be nothing more than the result of the speculations of schools, cliques and studio groups. This desire to come close to the 'public', in the widest sense of the word, was the main factor which led to a revival of figurative imagery, and, in particular, to pop art, a movement which had its origins in England. In the mid 1950s, the English critic Lawrence Alloway coined the term 'pop' which was subsequently applied to artists such as Eduardo Paolozzi (*pl. 257*), Richard Hamilton, Peter Blake, Richard Smith (*pl. 263*), R. B. Kitaj and their followers. From the early 1960s, pop art began to flourish independently in New York and California, the artists initiating this movement in New York being Andy Warhol (*pl. 256*), Roy Lichtenstein (*pl. 255*), Tom Wesselmann (*pl. 261*), James Rosenquist (*pl. 262*) and Claes Oldenburg (*pl. 259*). The principle of pop art is to present perfectly identifiable images of the external world as interpreted by the mass media (display advertising, photography, comic strips), or even to use the objects themselves, following the example set by Marcel Duchamp from 1915 onwards and repeated more recently in some of the work of the painter Jean Dubuffet (*pl. 258*), whose concept of *art brut* led him in one case to exhibit a slab of asphalt as a work of art.

The figurative simplification of pop art derives from Léger, from Herbin, from Ozenfant and Le Corbusier's purism, and from the literary imagery of certain surrealists such as René Magritte. Pop artists prefer, whenever possible, to work with industrial materials and substances. Thus, while abstract art appeals to the inner life, pop art plunges the spectator into the setting which assails him daily in the workshop and the street. The possibilities of pop are manifold. Most of the artists involved practise a literal realism, though some have adopted a geometrical formalization which brings them close to the abstract. Pop art is infinitely adaptable: it may be symbolic or dramatic, metaphysical or down-to-earth, and so becomes a natural element of environmental art.

Are the artist's avowed intentions sufficient on their own to confer aesthetic value on forms borrowed from the mass media and from *Kitsch*, both

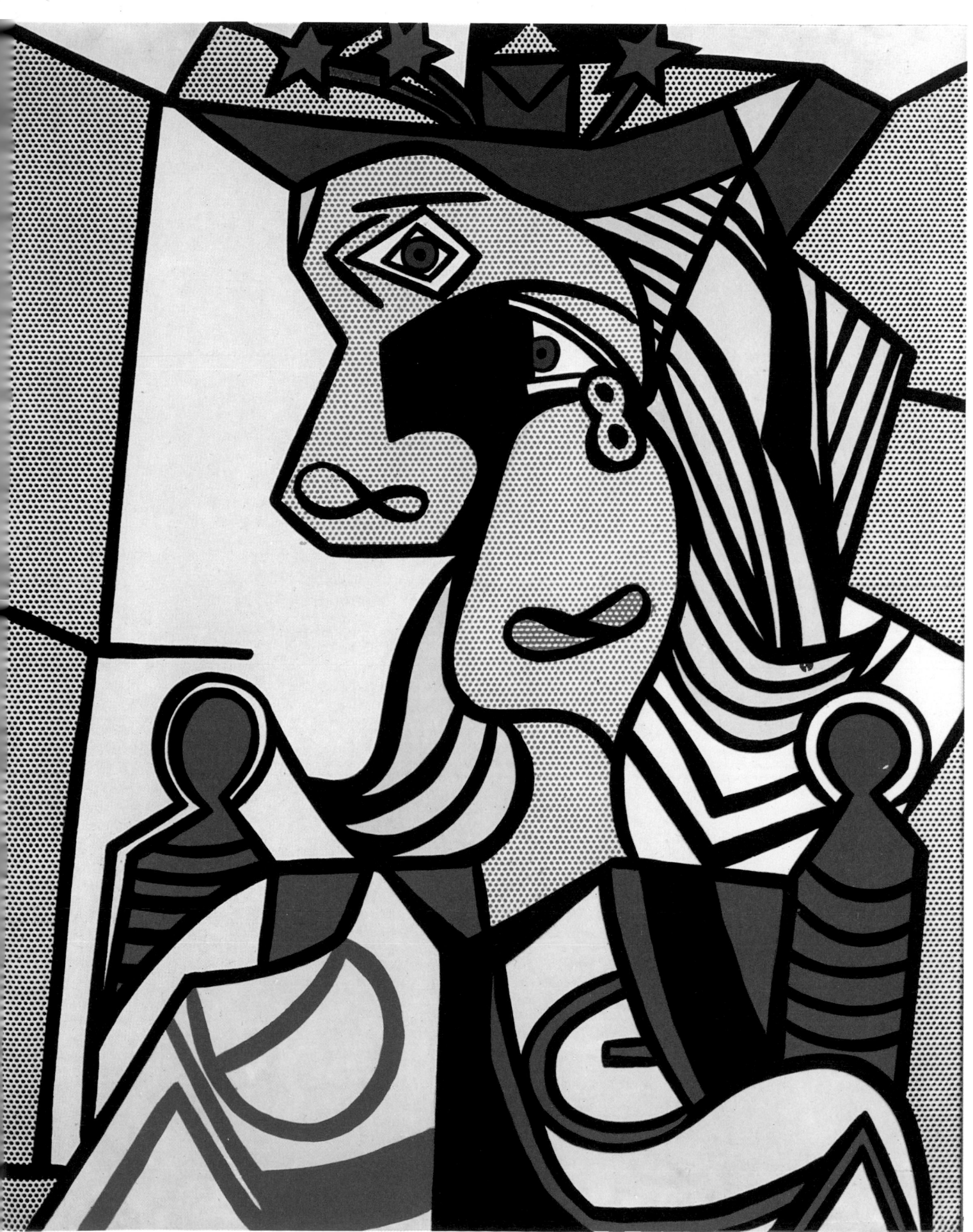

254 (opposite) Stuart Davis (1894–1964). *Lucky Strike*. New York, Museum of Modern Art, gift of the American Tobacco Co. Inc.

255 Roy Lichtenstein (b. 1923). *Woman with flowered hat*. New York, private collection.

Davis's cubist treatment of a cigarette pack (1921) and Lichtenstein's bravura marriage of comic strip and Picasso (1963) show art in direct confrontation with mass culture. This relationship is the source of pop art.

256 Andy Warhol (b. 1930). *Four Campbell's soup cans*. New York, Museum of Modern Art (upper right), collection Mr and Mrs Leo Castelli (others).

257 Eduardo Paolozzi (b. 1924). ▶ *Work sheet collage*.

of which, visually, are mere by-products of modern art? Pop art is vulnerable to criticism on the grounds that, although it may have been launched with the intention of re-establishing the 'sociability' of art, it has ended up as a renunciation of art itself.

Periodic international festivals – all modelled on the oldest of their number, the Venice Biennale – seek to persuade the public that the whole fabric of art has been refurbished during the more or less brief interval since the previous exhibition. These events are exactly comparable to those fairs at which the world's industrialists compare their wares, with the added attraction that they offer substantial prizes. At these gatherings, artists of various

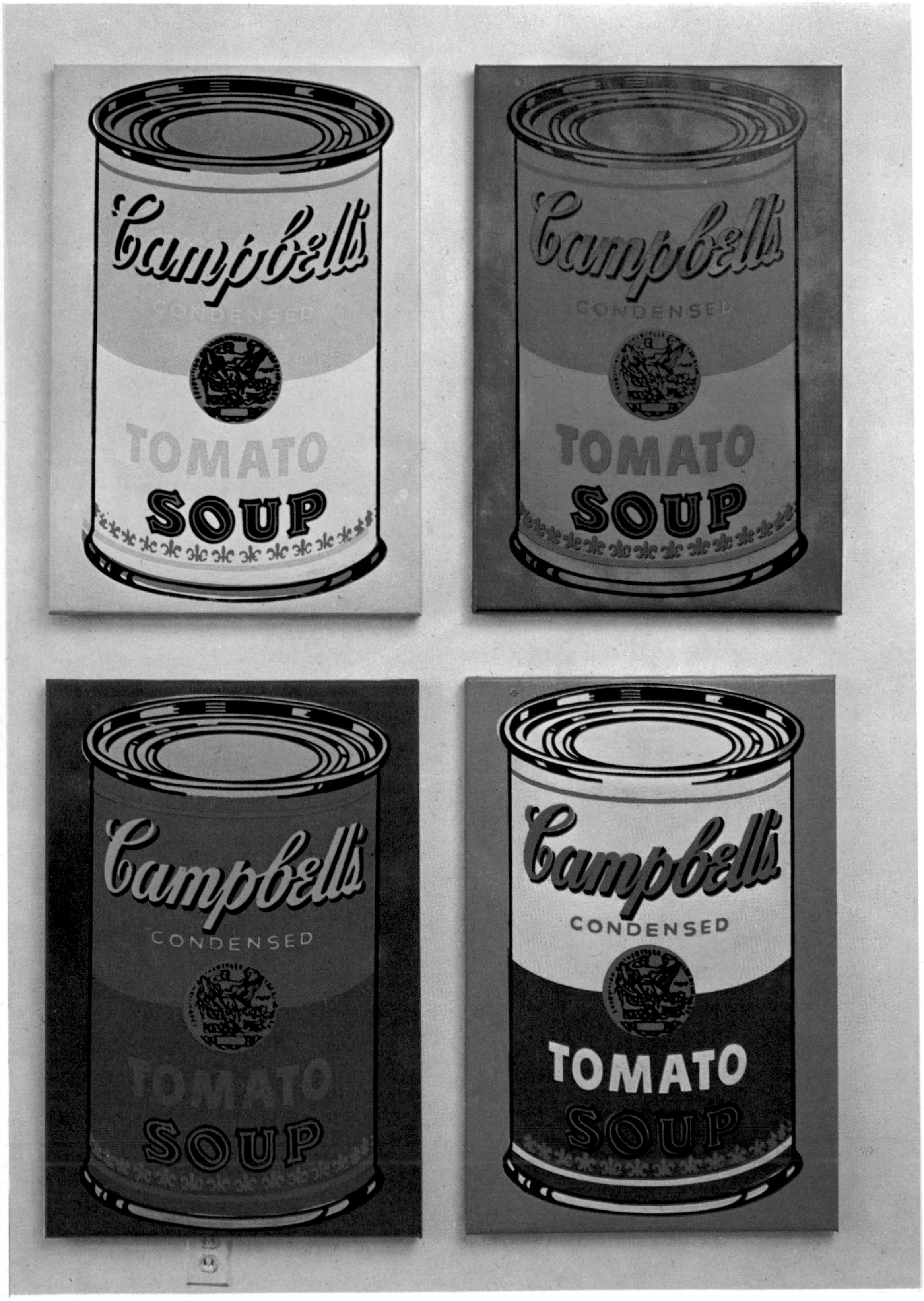

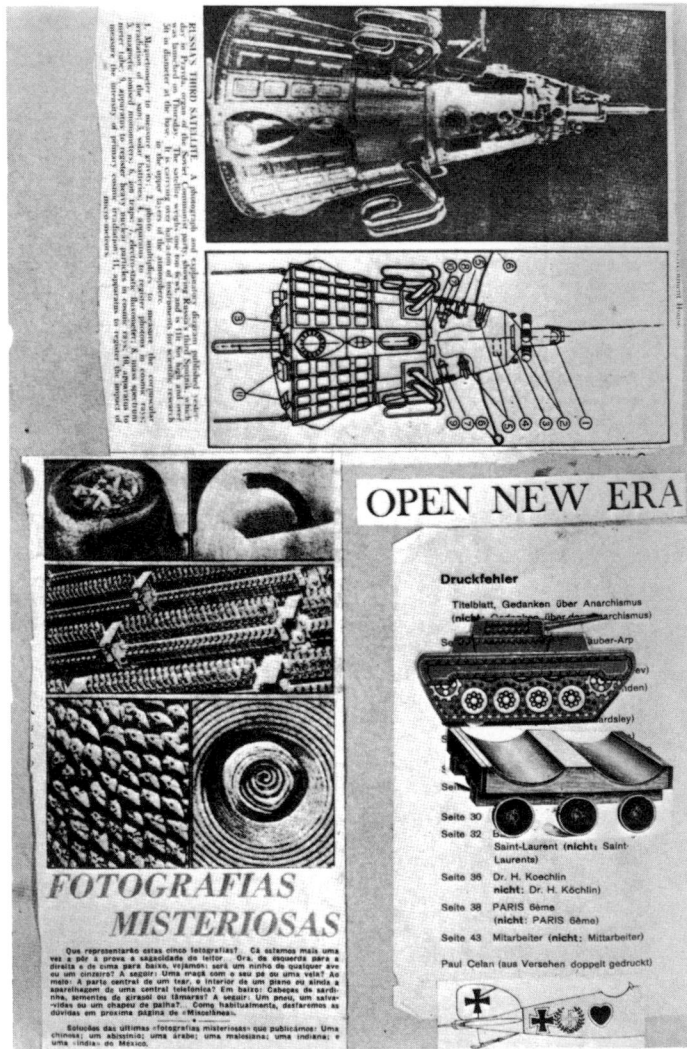

Warhol once took a leaf from Duchamp's book by signing real soup cans as works of art; in these paintings of soup cans, the artist's role extends beyond mere 'choice' to the introduction of arbitrary distortions of colour and scale. Warhol's work is characterized by a taste for mechanical repetition and for utterly banal iconography. By contrast, Paolozzi's collage of slightly esoteric printed matter is a celebration, without apparent irony, of the ramifications of 'print culture'.

258 Jean Dubuffet (b. 1901). *Danse brune*. London, collection Anthony Diamond.

Dubuffet, a painter whom the surrealists have recognized as a kindred spirit, has made a special study of what he calls *art brut*, 'crude art': graffiti, paintings by mental patients, found objects such as pieces of stone or masonry. In a sense, his own work is 'crude art', with its earthy textures and its primeval directness of expression; this example is a banana-skin collage on papier mâché.

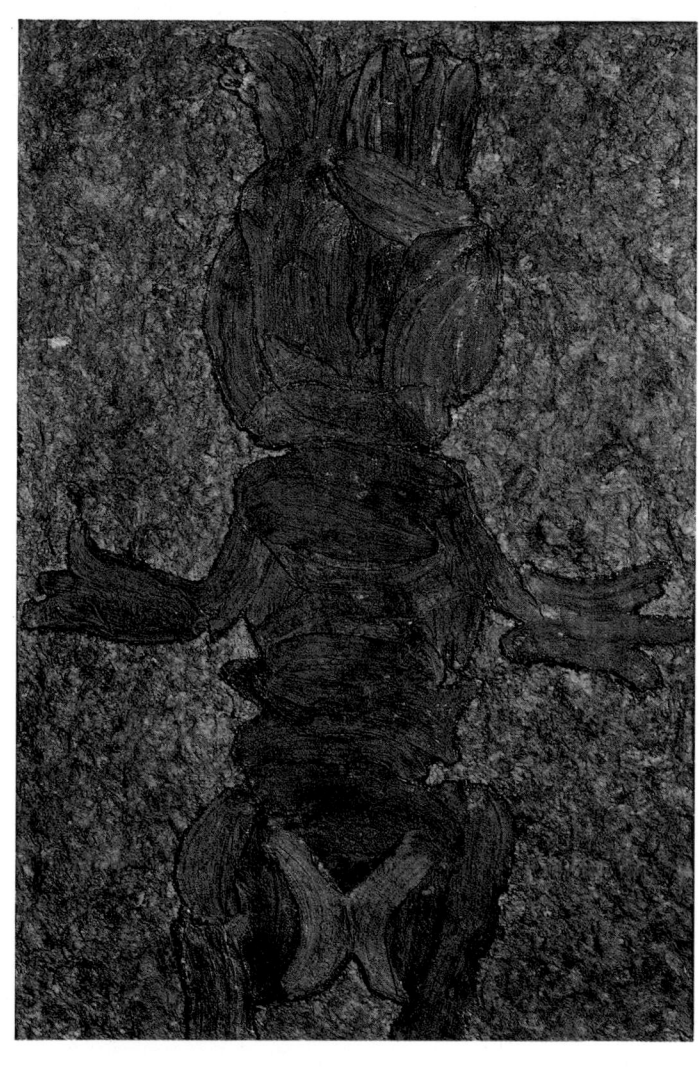

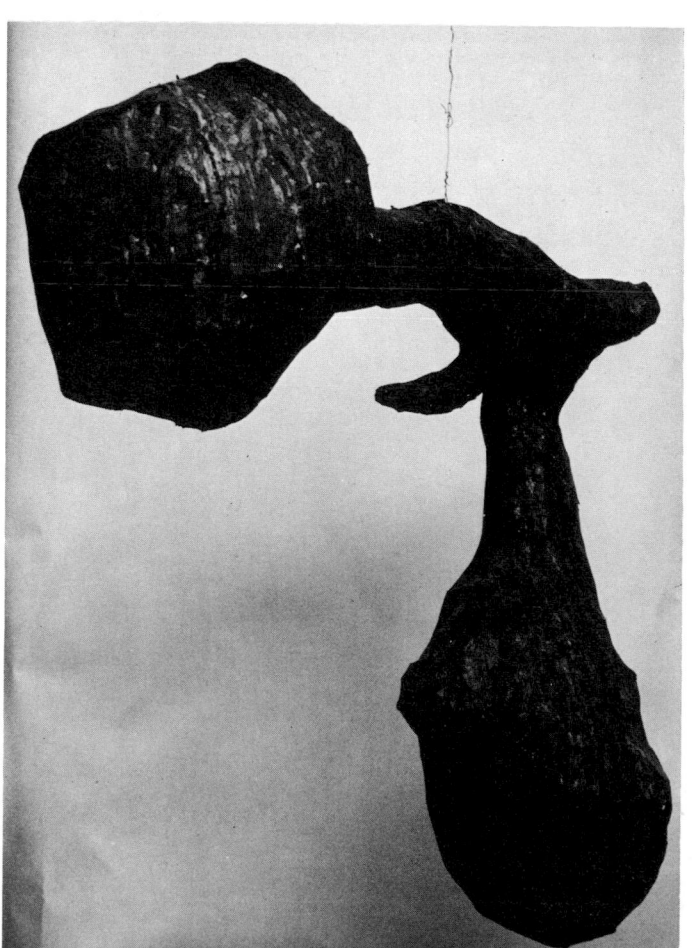

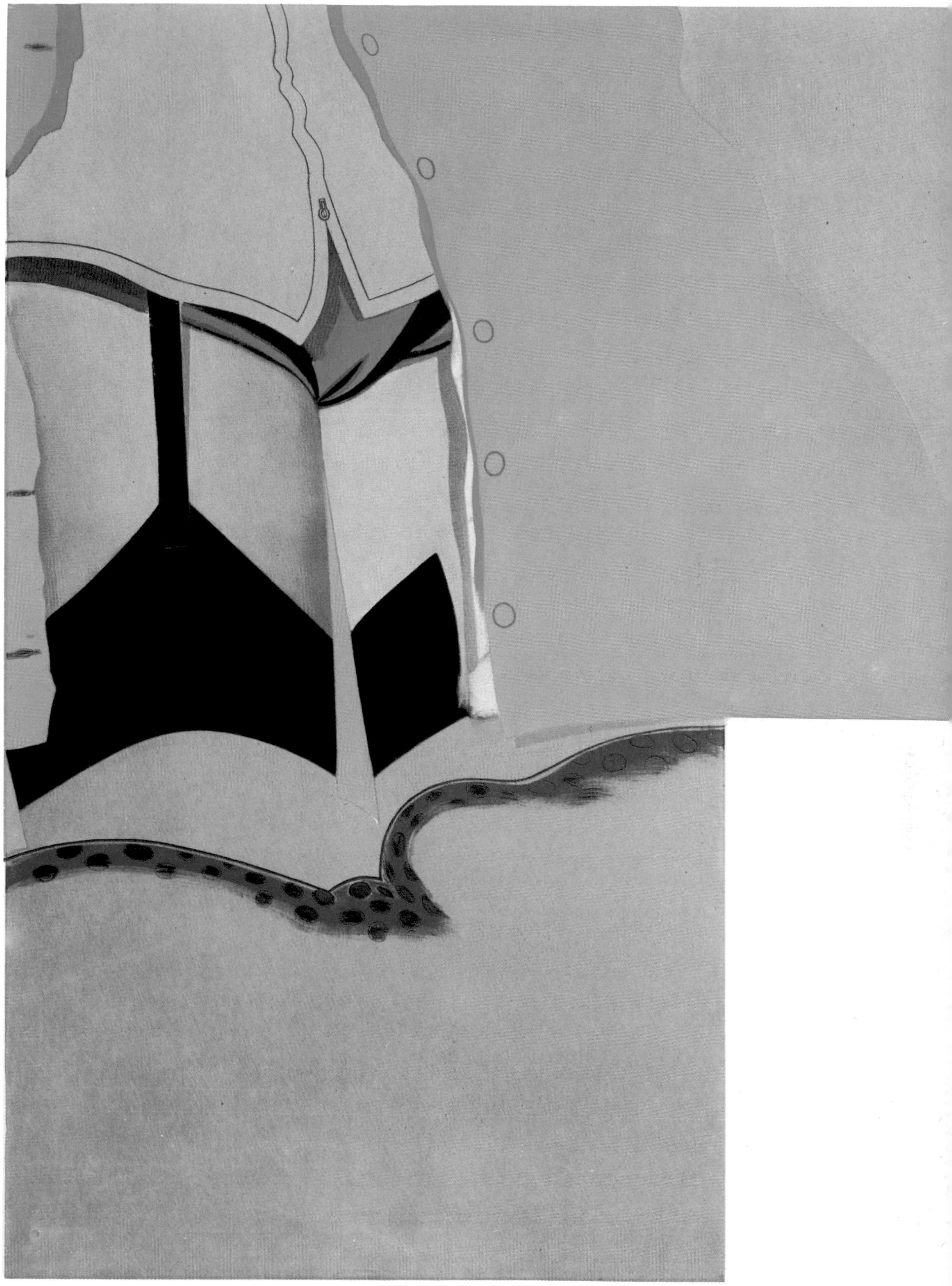

◀ 259 Claes Oldenburg (b. 1929). *Empire Papa Ray Gun*. New York, collection the artist.

260 Allen Jones (b. 1937). *Green Dress*. Zurich, collection Bruno Bischofberger.

Oldenburg, like the dadaists, is hostile to the word 'art'. In this case an object has been created by what might seem the most logically anti-artistic technique of all: fire. Jones belongs to a different pop tradition: he uses imagery from advertising art in teasingly ambiguous patterns which come close to pure abstraction.

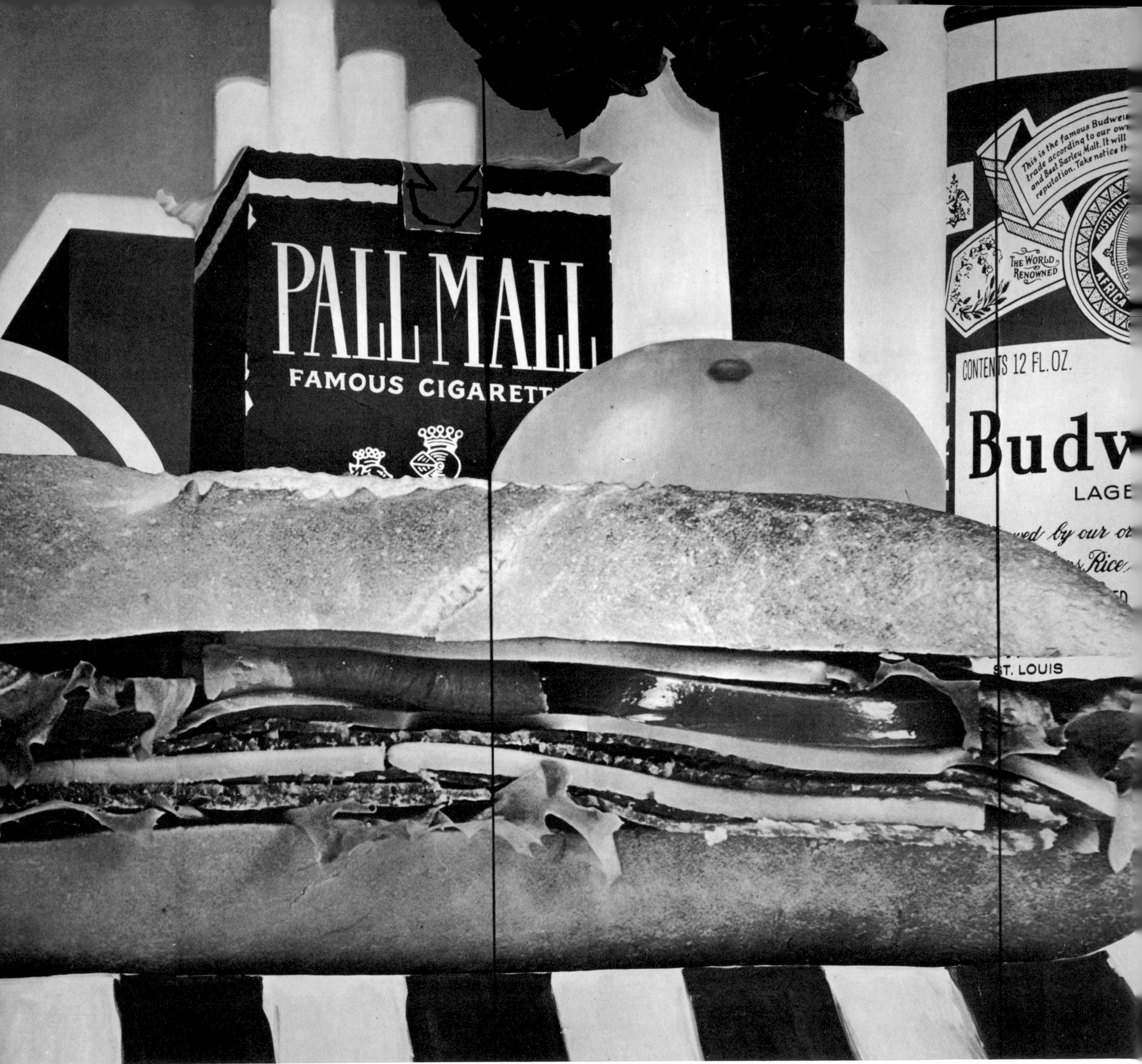

261 Tom Wesselmann (b. 1931). *Still Life No 33*. New York, courtesy Sidney Janis Gallery.

nationalities can indulge in the ecumenical pleasures of a shared pictorial language, often deriving therefrom the illusion that art has been objectified in the manner of a science.

Museums of modern art, after observing all these artistic innovations uneasily for a long time, have now transformed themselves into something like experimental laboratories, accumulating works indiscriminately as material for analysis, testing them – so to speak – as they come off the assembly line. The world of art has come to resemble a single gigantic and complex organism, and in the process

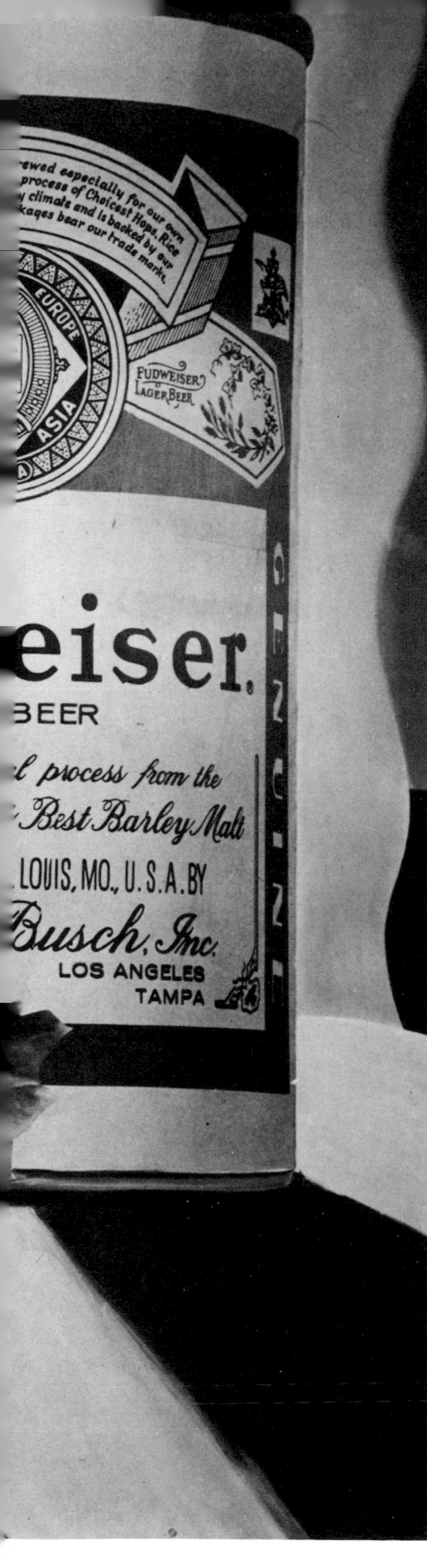

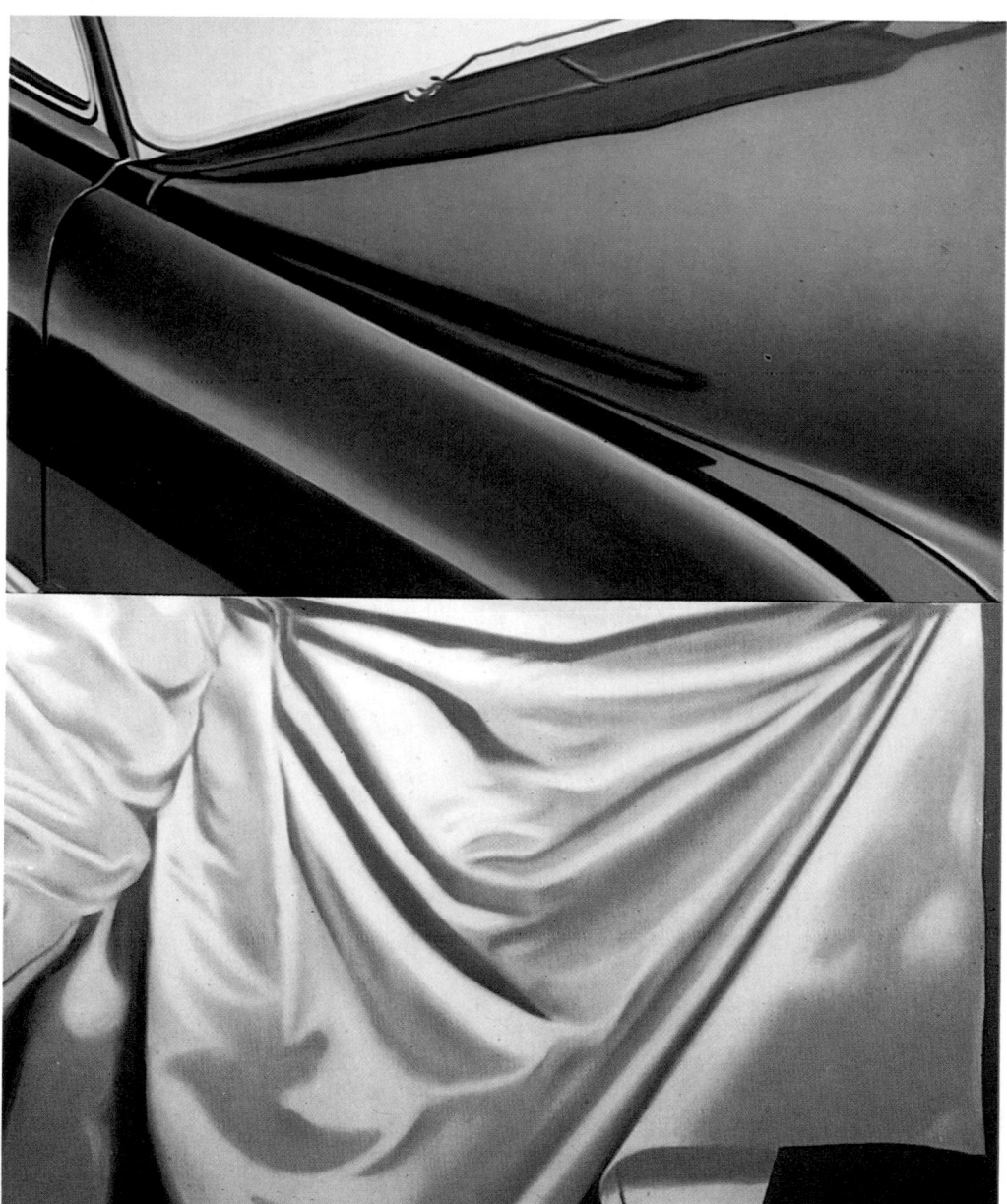

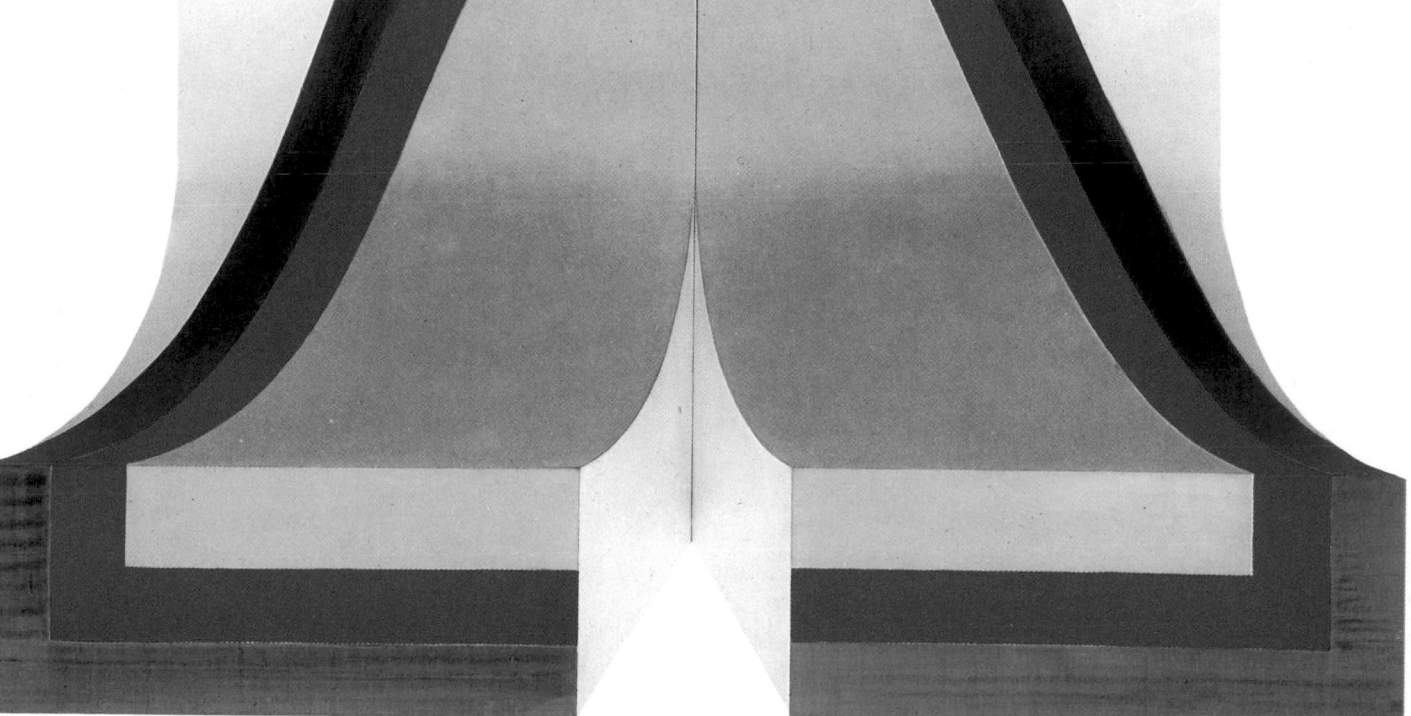

262 James Rosenquist (b. 1933). *1,2,3, and Out*. New York, private collection.

263 Richard Smith (b. 1931). *Tailspan*. London, Tate Gallery.
Wesselmann's gigantic billboards, and Rosenquist's juxtapositions of *trompe-l'œil* elements from commercial art, are obviously transpositions of reality; but there are also abstract paintings which employ a variant of the same glossy, 'post-painterly' idiom.

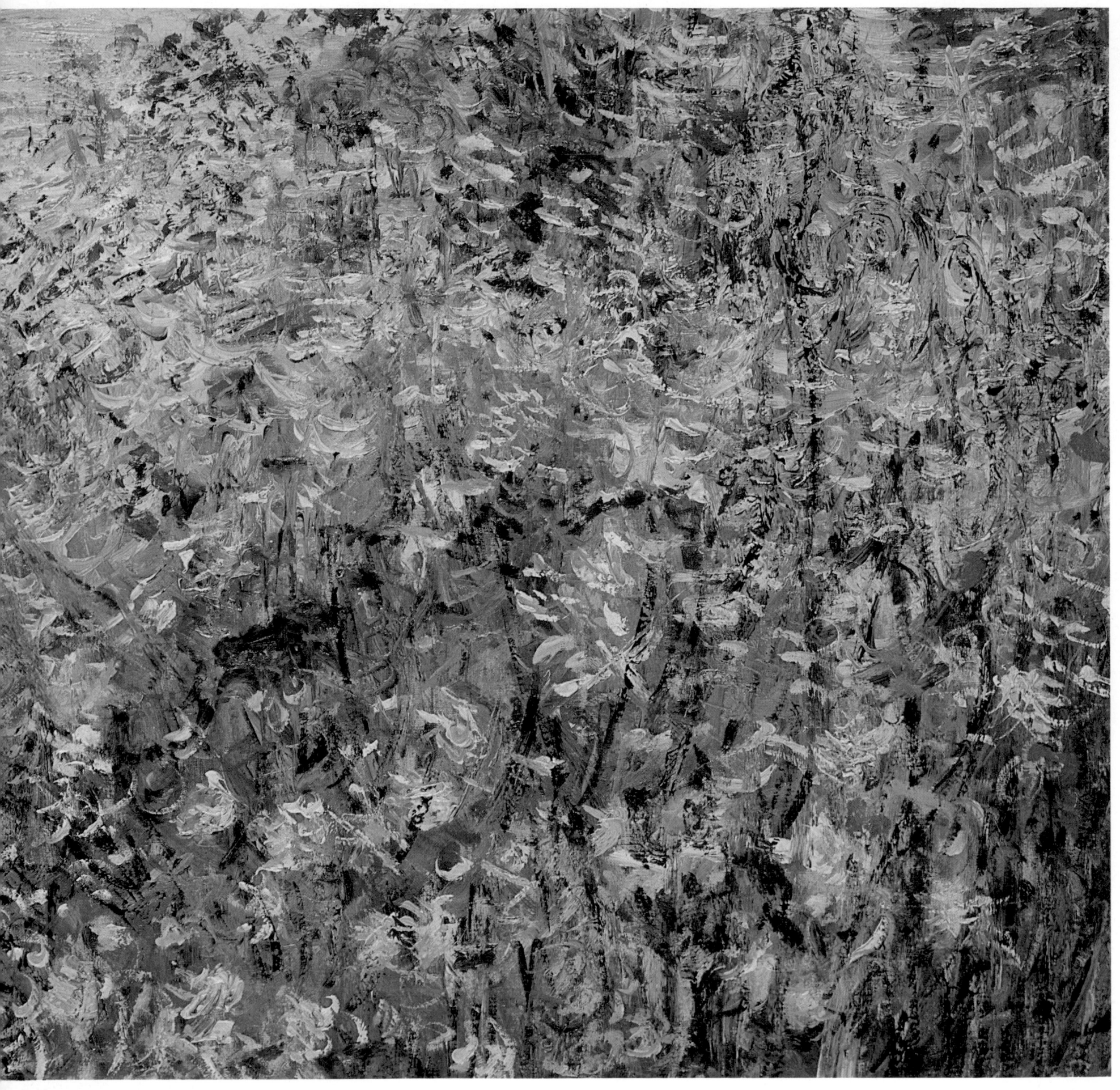

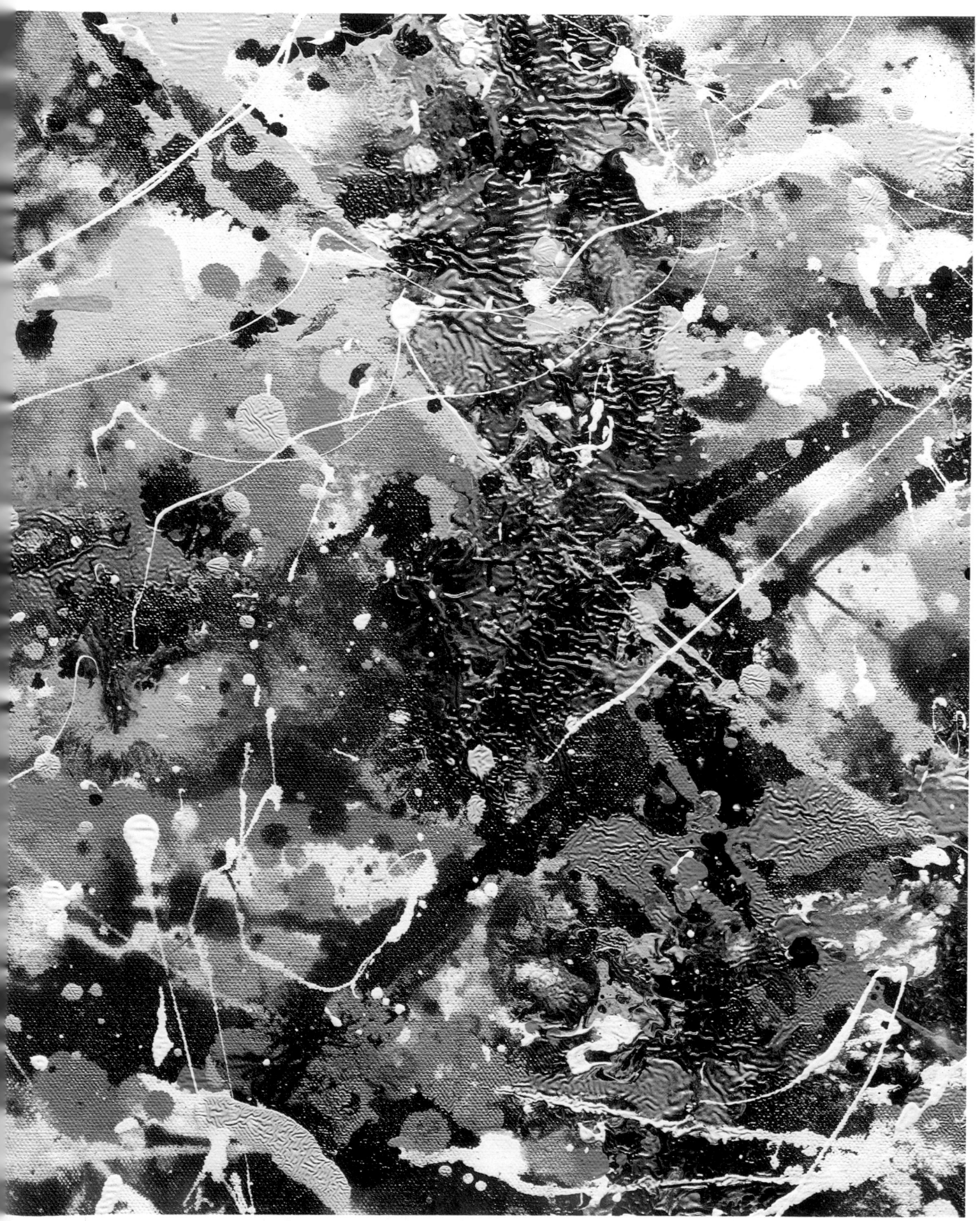

264 Claude Monet (1840–1926). Detail of *Ile aux Fleurs*. New York, Metropolitan Museum of Art, Bequest of Julia W. Emmons.

265 Jackson Pollock (1912–56). Detail of *One 1950*. New York, Museum of Modern Art.

It is not Pollock's comparatively crude 'drip' technique, nor his use of lacquer and aluminium paint, that marks him off from the tradition to which Monet belongs: in fact, the texture of his paintings is magnificently opulent. The distinction lies in the attempt made by Pollock, and other twentieth-century abstract painters, to replace the artistic representation of reality, with its indirect appeal to profound levels of the consciousness, by a direct frontal attack on the depths of the human psyche.

its creative products have become more and more remote and self-sufficient in relation to the social environment; this has happened at the very moment when, paradoxically, society is being urged to applaud their ingenuity. The pursuit of originality at all costs, which has become the basic motivating factor of contemporary art, has been interpreted by its admirers as a manifestation of individualism, bringing with it a feeling of having escaped the grip of 'mass culture'. But the opposite is perhaps the truth: in fact the dissemination of abstract expressionism, encouraging huge numbers of artists all over the world to try their hands at 'action painting', constitutes an authentic mass phenomenon.

Condemned to originality, the modern artist must retain the attention of a blasé public by constantly changing the media with which he works, and thus creating a new art form each time. The resulting proliferation of 'arts' has reached a point at which it seems that there are as many movements, groups and manifestos as there are artists, and that each artist thinks up a new theory at least once a year. Apart from the basic post-war movements such as abstract expressionism (*art informel*, *art autre*, *tachisme*), *art brut*, New Figuration, *Nouveau Réalisme* (New Realism), geometrical abstraction, post-painterly abstraction (pure colour-field abstraction), and so on, there are the various offshoots of abstract expressionism, pop art, geometrical abstraction and neo-surrealism: minimal art (primary structures), lumia art, neo-dada, assemblage, funk art, *affichage* (*décollage*), junk culture, nuclear art, *Mecanismo*, Eventstructures, etc., etc.

Sometimes the work of art itself is renounced. Certain artists create works intended to become obsolescent or to be destroyed, or amuse themselves by re-creating their gadgets at each exhibition for the delectation of the spectator, like circus jugglers or strongmen at sideshows. Painting, this realm of the eternal, has been brought forcibly 'up to date' to a point where it has become no more than a province of the ephemeral world.

An art devoid of all outside references, refusing all imagery except that provided by the most wretchedly banal themes, is deemed to offer a substitute for transcendence; nonsense is considered to be full of sense, and the insignificant is hailed as the supreme significance; non-painting is identified with the principle of non-being, but a non-being which, paradoxically, never ceases to thrust up from its depths an unmanageable proliferation of being.

Like those mutants, in some theories of evolution, fated to live only long enough to help the species accomplish a new phase, painters are chained to the invention of fashions and unusual processes in order to escape from painting itself. Creation has become synonymous with innovation, and each innovation forces the artist to take one further step along the path which separates him, ineluctably, from an external world which for thousands of years had been the source of his inspiration even when he had sought to withdraw from it.

An obsession with the absolute has gradually eliminated from the work of art everything which is not intrinsically part of it, everything outside the process of painting itself which can contribute to its realization: subject, imitation, expression, idea. This mountaineering on the high and icy peaks of the human spirit may be intoxicating, but any attempt to attain pure essence in a work of art runs the risk of depriving it of existence altogether. For pure being is inaccessible: to become manifest, it must always blend with existence. The aim of art must surely be, in Etienne Gilson's words, to 'reconcile being with what appears to be', to 'cause being and its appearance to coincide'.

Biographical notes

Fourteenth century

BARNA DA SIENA (active c. 1350/6), is said by Vasari to have died in 1381 as a result of a fall from a scaffolding in the Collegiata at San Gimignano, where he was finishing a great cycle of frescoes illustrative of the *Life of Christ*. His style shows him to have been a follower of Duccio, Simone Martini and Ambrogio Lorenzetti.

CIONE, Nardo di (active 1343; d. Florence 1365/6), was one of the three brothers of Andrea Orcagna, the Florentine painter, sculptor and architect who directed a busy workshop in which Nardo and his brothers Jacopo (also a painter) and Matteo (a sculptor) worked. Although Nardo's reputation was long eclipsed by Andrea's fame, modern criticism has tended to endorse the judgment of Vasari who considered Nardo a greater painter than his younger brother Andrea. Ghiberti's attribution to Nardo of the frescoes in the Strozzi Chapel of Santa Maria Novella in Florence (*Last Judgment*, *Paradise* and *Inferno*) have made it possible to reappraise his work and distinguish it from that of Andrea. The frescoes of the *Passion* in the Bastari Chapel of the Badia Church in Florence, long thought, on the authority of Vasari, to be by Buonamico Buffalmacco, have now finally been attributed to Nardo di Cione.

GIOTTO, real name Ambrogio di Bondone (b. Colle nr Vespignano c. 1266; d. Florence 1337): the diminutive form Giotto was doubtless derived from Angiolo. He is supposed to have worked briefly in Cimabue's workshop. About 1290 he received a commission to design a crucifix for Santa Maria Novella, Florence. In c. 1296–7 he was summoned to Assisi to paint the frescoes of the *Life of Christ* and *Allegory of St Francis* in the Upper Church of San Francesco, although his authorship is denied by some critics on stylistic grounds. About 1298, he was commissioned by Cardinal Stefaneschi to design in mosaic the *Navicella* (*Christ saving St Peter from the waves*) for the atrium in Old St Peter's, in celebration of the jubilee proclaimed in Rome in 1300, but although this still survives, frequent restoration has left little of the original. In 1304–6 he painted the frescoes of the *Life and Passion of Christ* in the Arena Chapel, Padua. From about 1311 onwards, Giotto was a wealthy man (he bought estates in Mugello) and appears to have remained from then on mostly in Florence where, after 1317, he painted the frescoes of the Bardi and Peruzzi chapels in Santa Croce. However, in 1329–33 he worked in Naples for Robert of Anjou. In 1334 he was appointed to succeed Arnolfo di Cambio as chief architect of Florence Cathedral, and designed the campanile, of which only the base was completed in his lifetime.

LORENZETTI, Ambrogio (active 1319–47), was a Sienese painter, brother of Pietro Lorenzetti and probably the younger of the two. It is possible that both died in the plague that ravaged Siena in 1348. First mentioned in 1319, he was probably his brother's pupil. He worked in Florence between 1332 and 1335.

His most important works, and those in which he shows the greatest originality, are the frescoes of the *Allegory of Good and Bad Government* in the Palazzo Pubblico of Siena, painted in 1337–9.

Fifteenth century

ANGELICO, FRA, real name Guido di Pietro (b. Vicchio di Mugello probably c. 1400; d. Rome 1455), was known in religion as Fra Giovanni da Fiesole. He is first mentioned as a painter in 1417–18, while still a layman, and must have entered the Dominican Monastery in Fiesole soon afterwards. The pictures of his first period show him working as a miniaturist, in the tradition of Dom Lorenzo Monaco and Gentile da Fabriano. On the other hand, the *Linaiuoli Madonna* (Florence, San Marco), commissioned in 1433, gives evidence of an entirely modern preoccupation with volume and perspective. Between 1439 and 1445 he supervised a workshop in decorating with frescoes the convent of San Marco which Cosimo dei Medici had ordered Michelozzi to build for the Dominican Order in Florence. In 1447 he began a series of frescoes of the *Last Judgment* for the San Brizio Chapel in Orvieto Cathedral which was later finished by Signorelli. His last work, the frescoes of *St Stephen* and *St Lawrence* in the chapel of Nicholas V in the Vatican, is permeated with Roman atmosphere. He returned to Fiesole as prior at the end of 1451. The problem of distinguishing between his own contribution and the work of his pupils in his very extensive output is often extremely difficult to resolve.

ANTONELLO DA MESSINA (b. Messina c. 1430; d. there 1479), seems to have been the pupil of the court painter Colantonio in Naples. He is known to have been living in Messina in 1456, then to have gone to Calabria, and to have returned once more to Messina where he remained until 1465; there is a gap in the records between 1465 and 1473. He paid a visit to Venice in 1475, demonstrating there his proficiency in the new method of oil-painting which he must have learnt from some Flemish painter. In 1476 Duke Galeazzo Sforza invited him to come to Milan, but it is not known whether he undertook this journey or not, since he is recorded as being in Messina in September 1476. Having become infirm, he made his will on 14 February 1479; he died before the 25th of the same month. His work consists of religious pictures and portraits, but only a small proportion of these has survived.

BALDOVINETTI, Alesso (b. Florence, c. 1426; d. there, 1499), may have worked briefly in the workshop of the engraver and goldsmith Maso Finiguerra; he also collaborated with Fra Angelico. His inquisitive mind led him to undertake technical experiments – mixing distemper, fresco and oil – which have damaged his works, a trait which he shared with Leonardo. All that remains of his fresco representing the *Nativity* in

the atrium of Santissima Annunziata in Florence (1463) is the huge-scale cartoon, showing a landscape of greater dimensions than appears in any previous known fresco.

BELLINI, Giovanni, known as Giambellino (b. Venice c. 1430; d. there 1516), was the most celebrated representative of a family of Venetian artists. He was the natural son and pupil of Jacopo Bellini; his brother Gentile was also a painter, and his half-sister Nicolosia married Mantegna in 1454. He and Gentile stayed in Padua 1458–60, at the moment when Mantegna had just completed his frescoes for the Eremitani. Between 1470 and 1480 his art developed a personal character, reaching its peak with the large altarpiece of San Giobbe (c. 1485) and the small altarpiece of the church of the Frari (1488). As the sixteenth century approached, his style broadened; in 1514 he painted a *Feast of the gods* which he left unfinished, and which his pupil Titian reworked. His reputation was great, and his workshop much frequented. The school of art he created was rich in talent and survived for a long time in and around Venice. Giorgione was his pupil, and appears to have exercised some influence on him.

BOSCH, Hieronymus (b. c. 1450; d. 's Hertogenbosch 1516), was a member of an artist family that came from Aix-la-Chapelle (Aachen), whence his alternative name of Hieronymus (or Jerome) van Aeken. He spent his whole life in 's Hertogenbosch, and may even have been born there. Between 1480 and 1512 he is mentioned several times in the records of the Confraternity of Our Lady of 's Hertogenbosch. In 1504 Philip the Fair of Burgundy commissioned a *Last Judgment* from him.

CASTAGNO, Andrea del (b. San Martino a Corella 1423; d. Florence 1457), started life as a shepherd boy. He is known to have been working in Florence about 1440, and to have arrived two years later, in July or August, in Venice where he painted a series of frescoes in the vaults of the San Tarasio Chapel in San Zaccaria. In 1444 he was enrolled in the guild of *medici e speciali*. He died of the plague at the early age of thirty-four.

EYCK, Jan van (b. probably Maaseyck c. 1390; d. Bruges 1441), probably came from the region of Maastricht. From 1422 to 1425 he was working for Count John of Holland at The Hague, and in 1425 entered the service of Philip the Good, Duke of Burgundy, as court painter and 'varlet de chambre'. He probably accompanied the duke to Aragon in 1426; in 1428 he led an embassy to Portugal to negotiate on the duke's behalf for the hand of the Infanta Isabella, and to paint her portrait. He was back in the Netherlands by the end of 1429, established in Bruges before 1431, and married in 1434. His reputation was enormous in his own lifetime, and Duke Philip, who was godfather to one of his children, held him in high esteem. A meticulous craftsman, he left few pictures. His principal work is the *Adoration of the Lamb* in Saint-Bavon, Ghent, which he completed in 1426; the question of the authorship of this polyptych is confused, in view of the problematical contribution by a brother, Hubert van Eyck, about whom little is known, but to whom some works are attributed which may in fact be by the youthful Jan.

FOUQUET, Jehan (b. Tours *c.* 1420; d. ?Tours by 1481), was the major French painter of the fifteenth century. Little is known of his early life, but his art was admired in Rome, and at some time between 1443 and the end of 1446 he painted two portraits of Pope Eugenius IV. While in Rome, Fouquet met Filarete, who speaks of him and his 'living likenesses' in his treatise on architecture. He was back in Tours probably by 1448, and in 1461 he collaborated in the preparations for the entry of the newly crowned Louis XI into Tours. In 1470, after the foundation of the Order of St Michael, he is recorded as having been paid for fashioning certain pictures for the use of this order. In 1475 he received the official title of 'King's Painter', and he died between 1477 and 1481. Fouquet was at his greatest as an illustrator of books, including the *Hours of Etienne Chevalier* (Chantilly). Apart from such miniatures, several panel portraits, some drawings and a self-portrait in enamelled copper are attributed to him.

KONRAD VON SOEST (active early fifteenth century), was the most distinguished painter of the Westphalian school, active in Dortmund from 1394, in which year he is recorded as having married. His principal work, the *Crucifixion* polyptych in the parish church at Niederwildungen, appears to be dated 1404.

MANTEGNA, Andrea (b. Isola di Carturo, between Vicenza and Padua, 1431; d. Mantua 1506), was the pupil and adoptive son of Francesco Squarcione, who is credited, perhaps over-generously, with a reform in painting comprising the imitation of the antique, the expression of relief through the study of perspective, and incisive precision of line. However, Mantegna left Squarcione at the age of seventeen, and it was no doubt through studying Donatello's sculpture in Padua that his own genius was first revealed to him. That same year, 1448, he started working with other artists on frescoes depicting the *Legends of St James and St Christopher* for the Ovetari Chapel in the Eremitani Church at Padua, which he completed alone soon after 1457; they were destroyed during the Second World War, though two sections moved to Venice remain. In 1454 he married Nicolosia, daughter of Jacopo Bellini. Between 1457 and 1459 he painted a large altarpiece for the church of San Zeno at Verona, the upper half of which has remained in this church, while the predella has been dispersed between the Louvre and the Musée des Beaux-Arts, Tours. He moved to Mantua in 1460 at the invitation of Lodovico Gonzaga, became his court painter, built a house for himself in that city and remained in the service of the Gonzagas for the rest of his life. Between 1468 and 1474 he painted the frescoes of the Camera degli Sposi in the Castello di Corte; and between 1485 and 1492 he painted a series of tempera cartoons representing the *Triumph of Caesar* (Hampton Court, Royal Collection). The frescoes he executed in 1490 for Innocent VIII's private chapel in the Belvedere at Rome have been destroyed. He completed a great number of pictures, mostly religious, during the long period

between 1468 and his death. The great *Our Lady of Victory* (*Madonna della Vittoria*), commissioned by Francesco Gonzaga to commemorate the Battle of Fornova, was completed in 1496; it is now in the Louvre. The *Parnassus* (1947) and the *Virtue triumphant over Vice* (1501–2) which he painted for the boudoir of Isabella d'Este show the belated influence of his brother-in-law Giovanni Bellini; they, too, are in the Louvre.

MASACCIO, real name Tommaso di Ser Giovanni di Guidi (b. Castello San Giovanni nr Florence 1401; d. ?Rome 1428), was the son of a lawyer. He was a pupil of Masolino, whose influence can be seen in his earliest paintings such as the *Madonna with St Anne* (between 1420 and 1424, Uffizi). His 1426 Pisa polyptych, of which the central *Madonna and Child* is now in London (National Gallery), shows a change of direction. A friend of the sculptors Ghiberti and Donatello, he sought to represent the mass and volume of objects in the round, as in the *Crucifixion* (Naples). In 1427 he worked on the cycle of frescoes in the Brancacci Chapel of Santa Maria del Carmine in Florence, which had been left unfinished by Masolino on his departure for Hungary; the *Expulsion of Adam and Eve from Paradise* and the series devoted to the Life of St Peter are definitely by his hand. His early death prevented him from completing this cycle of frescoes, which was finally terminated by Filippino Lippi half a century later.

PIERO DELLA FRANCESCA *or* DE' FRANCESCHI (b. Borgo San Sepolcro 1410/20; d. there 1492), is first recorded in 1439, when he was in Florence as assistant to Domenico Veneziano. In 1442 he was back in Borgo, serving as a town councillor; in 1445 he began work on a polyptych of the Madonna for the Compagnia della Misericordia in Borgo, in which the influence of Sassetta may be detected. Piero executed commissions for the courts of eastern Italy, and those of Ferrara, Rimini, Urbino and Bologna. Between 1452 and 1459 he painted his most important work, the fresco cycle in the choir of San Francesco at Arezzo, depicting the *Legend of the True Cross*. The frescoes which Piero painted for the Vatican in 1459 have vanished. He wrote two theoretical treatises, *De prospectiva pingendi* and *De quinque corporibus regularibus*, the last appearing after his death, its authorship ascribed incorrectly to his pupil, the geometrician Luca Paccoli. Piero was blind in his last years.

PIERO DI COSIMO (b. Florence 1462; d. there 1521), was the son of a goldsmith, Lorenzo di Chimenti, but adopted as his patronymic the name of Cosimo Rosselli, whose pupil he was and whom he assisted on his frescoes on the Sistine Chapel of the Vatican (1481–2). In his later years he became a recluse, entirely taken up by the study of nature and mythology. He blended various influences indiscriminately in his art, and was less concerned to be stylistically original than to achieve surprise through unusual imagery. Many of his pictures evoke the irrational and bizarre world of occultism.

PISANELLO, Antonio (b. Verona, 1397; d. ?Pisa, *c.* 1455), was probably the pupil of Stefano da Verona.

In 1431 he completed a series of frescoes commenced by Gentile da Fabriano for the Lateran Basilica. His gifts as a medallist and as a painter of portraits and animal studies made him much in demand by the princely courts of Italy, and he worked in Ferrara, Mantua, Rimini, Milan, Naples and Rome. There is no further mention of his activities after 1449, when he was in Naples; he seems to have been still alive in 1455, though certainly not in 1456. Only a very few of his paintings have survived, but important collections exist of his drawings (Louvre) and medals (London, Victoria and Albert Museum).

QUARTON, Enguerrand (b. Laon *c.* 1410; d. ?Avignon 1466 or later), was a native of Picardy, mentioned as working in Avignon from 1444 onwards. In 1452 he painted, in collaboration with Pierre Villatte, the *Virgin of Mercy* now in Chantilly (Musée Condé). In 1453 he signed a contract for a *Coronation of the Virgin* which was intended for the chapel of the Carthusian Monastery at Villeneuve-lès-Avignon and is now in the Hospice there. The Avignon *Pietà* derives directly from his style, although it is not possible to attribute it to him with any certainty.

TURA, Cosimo *or* Cosmè (b. Ferrara *c.* 1430; d. there 1495), was the official painter at the court of the Este in Ferrara under two successive dukes; he carried out for them numerous portraits and frescoes, designed decorative schemes and pageants, and executed large polyptychs which have now all been dispersed. He absorbed and blended northern influences (Rogier van der Weyden) and those of the school of Padua (Mantegna).

UCCELLO, real name Bolo di Dono (b. Florence 1397; d. there 1475), was called 'Uccello' perhaps because he loved birds or at some time painted them. His career as a painter seems to have started fairly late; at first he practised the minor arts, as a goldsmith, mosaic-worker and inlayer. He is first recorded, at the age of ten, as a *garzone* in the workshop where Ghiberti's First Baptistry Doors were being made. He was friendly with Donatello, and it is not surprising, therefore, that he should have sought to express volume in his paintings. In 1425 he went to Venice and worked on mosaics in St Mark's for about five years. In 1436 he gave a demonstration of his knowledge of perspective with his fresco painting, in imitation of an equestrian statue, of the English soldier of fortune Sir John Hawkwood, in Florence Cathedral. During the same period he painted scenes of the *Preachers in the Wilderness* in the cloister of San Miniato, and scenes of the *Creation* in the Chiostro Verde of Santa Maria Novella. Between 1443 and 1445 he executed two cartoons for stained-glass windows for the cathedral, painted some frescoes in Prato, and in 1445 was summoned to Padua by Donatello. On his return to Florence, probably that same year, he painted the astonishing *Deluge* in the Chiostro Verde of Santa Maria Novella. His most celebrated work is probably the *Rout of San Romano*, an episode in the war between the Florentines and the Sienese, which he depicted in three large panels for the Medici (Uffizi, Louvre and National Gallery). His last documented work is the predella for an altarpiece which he painted between 1465 and 1468 for the Confraternity of the Corpus Domini at Urbino (the *Story of the Holy Sacrament*, Galleria Nazionale delle Marche, Urbino). He appears to have given up painting in his old age. His preoccupation with perspective also found expression in a number of drawings which are exercises in the application of relief.

WEYDEN, Rogier van der (b. Tournai *c.* 1399; d. Brussels 1464), was also known as Rogier de la Pasture. He was a pupil of Robert Campin in Tournai, and became official painter to the city of Brussels in 1436. His life is well documented, and the details of a number of his commissions are known, though none of these correspond exactly to surviving works identified as being by his hand. It would seem, though, that the Escorial *Descent from the Cross* (Madrid, Prado) was commissioned by the Guild of Crossbowmen of Louvain, while the *Seven Sacraments* (Antwerp) was painted for Jean Chevrot, Bishop of Tournai between 1437 and 1460.

WITZ, Konrad (b. *c.* 1400; d. ?Basle *c.* 1447), was the son of Hans Witz, a goldsmith and itinerant painter who worked for the dukes of Brittany and Burgundy. Father and son arrived in Constance in 1412, and then settled in Tottweil, Upper Rhine, the seat of the Imperial Court of Justice. In 1431 Konrad went to Basle, attracted by the Church Council which convened there that year, and in 1434 painted there the large Altarpiece of the Redemption (*Heilsspiegelaltar*), parts of which are now missing; most of the remaining panels are now in the Kunstmuseum, Basle. He was in Geneva in 1444; the museum in that city possesses the two wings (one signed and dated) of a small polyptych which he painted for the episcopal chapel of the Bishop of Geneva.

Sixteenth century

ALTDORFER, Albrecht (b. Regensburg (Ratisbon) *c.* 1480; d. there 1538), was the son of the painter Ulrich Altdorfer who had been granted the freedom of the city of Ratisbon in 1478. His earliest known paintings are dated 1507. Drawings dated 1511, showing views of the banks of the Danube, provide evidence of a journey to Upper Austria, during which he is presumed to have met the painter Michael Pacher. In 1518 he painted a large altarpiece for Sankt Florian Monastery, near Linz. In 1529 William IV of Bavaria commissioned from him *Alexander's victory* (*Battle of Issus*), now in Munich. Towards the end of his life he became a councillor and the city architect of Ratisbon.

ARCIMBOLDO, Giuseppe (b. Milan 1527; d. there 1593), came from a noble family. In 1562 he entered the service of the Emperor Ferdinand I and spent twenty-six years in Prague as court painter to the Hapsburgs, becoming one of the favourites of Maximilian II and, more especially, of Rudolph II, for whom he was artistic adviser and organizer of princely entertainments. In the field of music, he distinguished himself by the invention of a colorimetric method of musical transcription. In 1587 he retired to Milan, and was created a Count Palatine by Rudolph II in 1591.

BASSANO, Jacopo, real name Jacopo da Ponte (b. Bassano 1510/18; d. there 1592), was the most distinguished member of a family of Venetian painters who worked in Bassano. The earliest mention of his activities is in 1530. In 1534 he became a pupil of Bonifazio de' Pitati in Venice, but his works show successive waves of influence, including that of Titian, Pordenone, Parmigianino and, later, Tintoretto. His painting evolved in the direction of naturalism and an increasingly free treatment.

BRUEGEL, Pieter I (b. *c.* 1525; d. Brussels 1569), took his name from a village which has yet to be identified precisely. The influence of Hieronymus Bosch visible in his first works has led to the theory that he may have been brought up in 's Hertogenbosch. He became pupil assistant of his future father-in-law Pieter Coeck at Antwerp, and on the death of the latter in 1550 entered the workshop of Hieronymus Coeck. He became a master in the Antwerp Guild in 1551; immediately after this he went to Italy, visiting Rome and Naples and travelling as far south as Sicily. Returning to Antwerp in 1553, he began to make drawings for a number of engravers working for Hieronymus Coeck. In 1563 he married Maria Coeck, the daughter of his first master, and moved to Brussels. His works, the best collection of which is in Vienna, all show a meticulous care and attention to detail. His earlier paintings were signed Brueghel, but in 1557 he changed his signature to Bruegel, the spelling generally adopted today.

CAMBIASO, Luca (b. Moneglia nr Genoa 1527; d. Madrid 1585), was a precocious artist who at the age of fifteen was already assisting his father, a Genoese painter, in painting frescoes for the decoration of a palace. He became acquainted with Roman art before 1557, when he was once again in Genoa, working with his father as a fresco painter and sculptor. About 1560, the influence of Correggio and Parmigianino becomes apparent in his work, following a visit to Emilia; he made further journeys to Rome and Florence which allowed him to study the mannerist art being produced in those two centres at that time. His reputation was such that in 1583 he was summoned by Philip II to finish a series of frescoes in the Escorial begun by Castello. Cambiaso never saw his native country again.

CAMPI, Antonio (b. Cremona *c.* 1514; d. there 1587 or after 1591), belonged to a Cremonese family of painters which included his father Giulio, his brother Vincenzo and his cousin Bernardino. Antonio's first known work is dated 1546. He worked in Milan and Cremona. A refined and erudite personality, he published works of history, was a cosmographer, architect and sculptor.

CONINXLOO, Gillis van (b. Antwerp 1554; d. Amsterdam 1607), was, like Pieter Bruegel, a pupil of Pieter Coeck. A landscape painter and engraver, Coninxloo travelled widely in France and Germany as well as his native Flanders before settling in Amsterdam in 1595. He was the first Flemish painter to incorporate wooded scenes into his landscapes, thus inspiring his pupil Hercules Seghers.

CORREGGIO, real name Antonio Allegri (b. Correggio *c.* 1489; d. Parma 1534), probably got his artistic education in Mantua; his first work authenticated by a document, the *Madonna of St Francis* (1514-15, Dresden), shows local influences. But the inspiration for new heights of imagination and audacity seems to have been provided by a visit to Rome, which must have taken place about 1517 and would have revealed to him the work of Raphael and Michelangelo. He worked mostly in Parma: in about 1518 he painted frescoes of mythological allegories in the Camera di San Paolo in the convent there; in 1520 he decorated the cupola of San Giovanni Evangelista with the *Vision of St John at Patmos*; in 1526–30 he decorated the cupola of the Cathedral with the *Assumption of the Virgin*. During this time he painted both religious and mythological pictures, whose sensuous charm continued to captivate other artists until the eighteenth century.

DEUTSCH, Nikolaus Manuel (b. Berne 1484; d. there 1530), became a member of the Grand Council of the city of Berne in 1510, and accompanied Albert de Stein on his military expeditions into Italy, in the capacity of *secrétaire de camp*, in 1516 and again in 1522. His artistic career was somewhat hampered by his energetic political and diplomatic activities, and his passionate advocacy of the Reformation.

DOSSI, Dosso (b. Ferrara *c.* 1479; d. there 1543), is first recorded in Mantua in 1512. His real name was Giovanni Luteri. His art was formed in the romantic atmosphere of Ferrara, but it developed after contact with Roman art and, especially, Venetian art, the influence of Giorgione and Titian being particularly strong. In fact, Dossi collaborated with Titian in painting one of the pictures intended for the decoration of the *camerini d'oro* at Ferrara. Dossi was also profoundly steeped in the romantic atmosphere of the poetry of Ariosto, and his mythological compositions were heavy with symbolism.

DÜRER, Albrecht (b. Nuremberg, 1471; d. there, 1528), was the son of a Hungarian goldsmith who had settled in Nuremberg; from 1486 to 1490 he studied painting under Michael Wolgemut, and quickly showed a precocious genius for drawing. To complete his training, he travelled between 1490 and 1494, visiting Basle, Strasbourg and then Colmar where he had intended to seek instruction in the studio of Martin Schongauer, who had just died. In 1494 he returned to Nuremberg and married, and in the autumn of that year travelled to Venice, where he became acquainted with the art of Bellini and Mantegna. On his return to Nuremberg in 1495 he opened a painting and engraving workshop which quickly became famous throughout northern Europe. His engravings met with such success that attempts were made to counterfeit them, and it was no doubt with the aim of putting a stop to this activity that he went to Venice at the end of 1505. While there he painted several works, including the *Madonna of the rose garlands* (Prague), which were strongly influenced by the art of Giovanni Bellini, whom he greatly admired, and Mantegna. He then went on to Bologna, to study the art of perspective. His success in Venice was so great that the Seigniory tried vainly to persuade him to stay there. He left Italy reluctantly at the beginning of 1517, to go home to Nuremberg. His subsequent painting was profoundly affected by this journey, which had had the effect of leading him away from the Gothic and towards an Italianate classicism (*Four Apostles*, 1526, Munich). Like Leonardo, he composed various theoretical treatises, most of which are lost. He made several copper engravings, all difficult to interpret, bearing witness to his chief preoccupations: Christian (the *Knight, Death and the Devil*, 1513), humanist (*St Jerome in his cell*, 1514), and philosophical (*Melencolia*, 1514). Fleeing the plague which was raging in Nuremberg in 1520, he made a journey to the Netherlands where he was received with great honour, and fêted by his fellow artists Quentin Massys, Joachim Patinir, Bernard van Orley and Lucas van Leyden. During this voyage he felt the first signs of the illness to which he was to succumb, probably a liver disorder.

GIORGIONE, real name Giorgio Barbarelli (b. Castelfranco 1476/8; d. Venice 1510), was not called Giorgione until after his death. The one thing really certain about his life is his death of the plague, in the autumn of 1510 at Venice, at the age of about thirty-four. In 1506 he shared a studio in Venice with Vincenzo Catena. In 1507/8 he was working in the doge's palace, and in 1508 he was painting frescoes on the outside of the Fondaco dei Tedeschi, the headquarters of the German merchants in Venice.

GIOVANNI DA UDINE (b. Udine 1497; d. Rome 1561 or 1564), was a printer, painter, stuccoworker and architect. He is mentioned as working in Rome between 1513 and 1516. In 1517 he did the stucco decoration of the Vatican Loggie, under Raphael's supervision. After a visit to Florence he returned to Udine in 1523, but was back in Rome almost immediately in response to a summons from Clement VII to execute further decorations. After the Sack of Rome in 1527 he returned to Udine once again, and thereafter worked mostly in the regions of Venice and Friuli, though paying several visits to Rome to carry out commissions there.

GRAF, Urs (b. Solothurn *c.* 1485; d. ?Basle 1527/8), was the son of a goldsmith, and was himself a goldsmith, painter, artist in stained glass, graphic artist and engraver. He led an active life, participating in the political campaigns in Basle, and became notorious for his brawls, banishment, imprisonment, and mistreatment of his wife. He fought as a mercenary in the battles of Marignan and La Bicoque.

GRECO, EL, real name Domenikos Theotokopoulos (b. Crete 1541; d. Toledo 1614), was a Spanish painter

by association, though of Greek origin. He went to Venice on leaving his native Crete, at some time between 1560 and 1570, and while there was much influenced by Titian, Jacopo Bassano and Tintoretto. He arrived in Rome in 1570 with an introduction to Cardinal Farnese, and appears to have stayed there until 1575. Some recent critics have attributed to him a whole semi-Byzantine youthful *œuvre*, but this fails to match the pictures of the Italian period which are known to be by his hand. He went to Spain in 1576, settling in Toledo the following year. He soon received major commissions, including the High Altar for Santo Domingo el Antiguo (1577–9) and the *Disrobing of Christ* (*El Espolio*) for the Cathedral. A son was born to him in 1578. In 1581 Philip II commissioned the *Martyrdom of St Maurice and the Theban Legion* for the Escorial, but the finished picture pleased neither the king nor the monastery. El Greco had to abandon the ambition of becoming court painter, and he passed the rest of his life far from court, in Toledo, where an archaic society had preserved a traditionalist outlook. In 1586 he painted the *Burial of Count Orgaz* for the church of San Tomé. His ecstatic and passionate style became heightened with time. In order to keep pace with the many religious commissions he received, he was obliged to make several replicas of some of the most popular pious images; he organized a workshop for this purpose, which raises questions of attribution.

GRÜNEWALD, Matthias, real name Mathis Nithart (b. ?Würzburg before 1480; d. Halle 1528), was wrongly called 'Matthias Grünewald' as a result of an error committed by the seventeenth-century painter-historian Joachim Sandrart, and has recently been identified as Mathis Nithart (or Neithardt) who later substituted the name Gothart and was a native of Aschaffenburg in Lower Franconia. From 1508 to 1514 he was court painter to the Archbishop-Elector of Mainz, and then to Cardinal Albrecht, Elector of Mainz. His master work, the altarpiece for the monastery of Isenheim in Alsace (it is now at Colmar), was painted between 1512 and 1513. After the Peasants' Rising of 1525 he lost his post at court and took refuge, first in Frankfurt and then in 1527 in Halle where he died. He was sympathetic to the ideas of the Reformation.

HUBER, Wolf (b. Feldkirch, Vorarlberg, *c.* 1490; d. Passau 1553), became court painter to the Prince Bishop of Passau. He is mainly noted for his drawings and woodcuts, and only a small number of his paintings survive.

LEONARDO DA VINCI (b. Vinci nr Empoli 1452; d. Château de Cloux nr Amboise 1519), learnt the art of painting in the studio of Andrea del Verrocchio in Florence. From 1482 to 1499 he lived in Milan, where he painted the fresco of the *Last Supper* in the refectory of Santa Maria delle Grazie, and worked on a project for a bronze equestrian monument to Francesco Sforza. Leonardo left Milan shortly after the entry of the French troops in 1499, returning to Florence in 1500 and remaining there until 1504. But in 1506 he went back to Milan once again, at the request of the French government. A stay in Rome between 1513 and

1516 proved unsatisfactory, since the pope made no use of his talents. He then accepted Francis I's invitation to France in 1517, spending his last years in the small château of Cloux, near the royal residence of Amboise on the Loire.

LOTTO, Lorenzo (b. Venice *c.* 1480; d. Loreto 1556), was noted both for his religious paintings and his portraits. His origins are unknown, though the suggestion that his forebears were seafaring folk has been put forward as an explanation for the restlessness which led him to spend his life moving from one town to another in Lombardy and the Marches. It is not known whether he was married and, if so, whether he had any children. He died alone and poor, although he had received lucrative commissions throughout his life. An account book which he kept from 1538 (when he was in Ancona) onwards has survived and provides us with certain details about his life; these suggest that he was a troubled and difficult character, but deeply religious. He travelled constantly between 1503 and 1512, then based himself in Bergamo from 1513 to about 1526; it was here that he produced some of his most beautiful altarpieces, though he continued, during these years, to travel through the Marches as well as paying visits to Venice and Rome. In an unsuccessful attempt to raise funds, while in Ancona in 1552, he held a lottery for his paintings. The last two years of his life were spent in the Santa Casa Monastery at Loreto, where he became a lay brother.

MICHELANGELO Buonarroti (b. Caprese nr Arezzo 1475; d. Rome 1564), was apprenticed to the painter Domenico Ghirlandaio in 1488, but remained in his workshop for only a very short time. He learnt the art of sculpture in the School set up by Lorenzo 'Il Magnifico' in the Medici gardens, where the collection of classical sculpture was under the supervision of Bertoldo, the pupil of Donatello. It was at this time that, according to tradition, his nose was broken in a fracas with a fellow pupil, Torrigiano. Between 1490 and 1492 he stayed with Lorenzo in his palace on the via Larga. He fled the revolutionary upheavals in Florence in 1492, but returned after a year to find the city sadly changed by the stern preaching of Savonarola. He was back in Rome between 1496 and 1501, when he returned to Florence yet again, remaining there this time until 1505. The only easel-painting that he is definitely known to have completed before undertaking the decoration of the Sistine Chapel is the *Holy Family* (or *Doni tondo*) executed in 1503 for his patron Angelo Doni (Uffizi), although the *Virgin and Child, St John and Angels* (London, National Gallery) may possibly have been a work of about his twentieth year. The cartoons he made for the never-completed fresco of the *Battle of Cascina* have been lost. Pope Julius II summoned him to Rome to design a fitting tomb for him, but soon diverted him from this task by commissioning him to paint the ceiling of the Sistine Chapel (1508–12). Michelangelo returned to Florence on several occasions to execute various works of architecture and sculpture (the Biblioteca Laurenziana, the Medici Chapel in San Lorenzo). In 1527, after the Sack of Rome, he placed himself at the disposal of the Florentine republic, at war against the pope and his allies, as military engineer. Paul III required him to paint the altar wall of the Sistine Chapel with the *Last Judgment* (1536–41). His last work in painting was the decoration of the Pauline Chapel with frescoes of the *Conversion of St Paul* and the *Crucifixion of St Peter*.

PONTORMO, real name Jacopo Carucci (b. Pontormo 1494; d. Florence 1556), worked under Andrea del Sarto about 1512, and was the true creator of Florentine mannerism, a tendency which can first be detected in his work in 1517. Between 1522 and 1525 he painted an important cycle of frescoes depicting scenes from the Passion in the Certosa of Galluzzo. He appears to have been highly neurotic; he lived a solitary existence and kept an obsessive Diary.

PORDENONE, real name Giovanni Antonio de' Sacchis (b. Pordenone c. 1484; d. Ferrara 1539), was named after his birthplace in the province of Friuli which was at that time under the influence of Venice. He seems to have discovered Giorgione very early (*Madonna*, 1516, Susegana), and may have gone to Rome c. 1515–16. In 1521 he painted a series of frescoes depicting scenes from the Passion in Cremona Cathedral, taking over a commission withdrawn from Romanino. He also painted frescoes in San Rocco, Venice.

RAPHAEL, real name Raffaello Sanzio (b. Urbino 1483; d. Rome 1520), was the son of a painter at the court of Urbino, Giovanni Santi. After the death of his father he was apprenticed to the painter Timoteo Viti at Perugia, and subsequently entered the workshop of Perugino there, collaborating with the latter in the Cambio. Perugino's influence on him was so great that during this first period it is sometimes difficult to distinguish between the work of the two artists. Raphael's personal style emerges fully in 1504, in the *Betrothal of the Virgin (Lo Sposalizio)*, his first signed and dated work. At the end of this year he went to Florence, where he discovered the work of Leonardo; his art now went through a transitional stage of classicism, expressed in a series of Madonnas such as the *Madonna del Granduca* (Pitti). Towards the end of 1508 Julius II summoned him to Rome and commissioned him to decorate the Stanza della Segnatura with a series of frescoes which he completed in 1511. In the last decade of his short life he was overwhelmed with work and had a large team of assistants working for him under the supervision of his favourite pupil Giulio Romano: continuing his decorative scheme in the Vatican, Raphael painted the Stanza d'Eliodoro, the Stanza dell' Incendio, the Sala di Costantino, and the Loggie. For his chief patron, the banker Agostino Chigi, he decorated the Farnesina with a fresco of *Galatea* (1514), and painted the *History of Psyche* (1518) for the garden loggia of the palace. Among innumerable other tasks he assumed the responsibility of succeeding Bramante as architect of the new St Peter's. During this period, Raphael also painted a number of easel pictures, including the *Sistine Madonna* (Dresden, Gemäldegalerie), and designed a series of cartoons for a tapestry of scenes from the lives of St Peter and St

Paul (London, Victoria and Albert Museum). He died at the age of thirty-seven, at the height of his glory.

ROMANINO, IL, real name Girolamo di Romano (b. Brescia c. 1484; d. there after 1562), formed his art under the influence of Giorgione, Titian and the German etchers. In 1519 he was commissioned to execute a series of frescoes, depicting scenes from the Passion, for Cremona Cathedral. He painted mythological scenes in the Castello del Buonconsiglio at Trent.

ROSSO, Giovanni Battista, also known as Rosso Fiorentino (b. Florence 1494; d. Paris 1540), worked under Andrea del Sarto and was one of the founders of Florentine mannerism. The most important work from his Italian period is the 1522 *Descent from the Cross* (Volterra). He went to Rome about 1524 and fled after the sack of the city in 1527, wandering around Italy until 1530 when he went to Venice. That same year he left for France at the invitation of Francis I, and took over the direction of the decoration of the palace of Fontainebleau. According to Vasari he committed suicide; he is known, in any case, to have had a neurotic temperament.

SAVOLDO, Giovanni Girolamo (b. Brescia c. 1480; d. ?Venice after 1548), was registered as a painter in Florence in 1508, but is recorded as living in Venice by a document of 1521, the same year that he married a Florentine woman. He may have worked in Milan c. 1529/35. His small output consists mainly of easel-paintings, and he seems to have had little liking for large-scale religious commissions.

TINTORETTO, real name Jacopo Robusti (b. Venice 1518; d. there 1594), acquired his familiar name from his father's occupation as a dyer (*tintore*). He may have been a pupil of Titian for a very short time, and was probably associated with Schiavone and Paris Bordone. His earliest dated work is of 1545. In that or the following year he visited Rome for the first and only time, the rest of his life being spent entirely in Venice. Here he was constantly overwhelmed with commissions, which he executed with extraordinary rapidity, with the help of a huge workshop and the use of numerous assistants. He worked for the State, the Confraternities, the churches and private patrons, and was also much in demand from outside the city. His 1548 *St Mark rescuing the slave* (Venice, Accademia) made his reputation, and he was already famous when in 1564 he won the competition for the redecoration of the Scuola di San Rocco and so assured himself permanent success. He eventually decorated the entire building, completing the scheme in 1588. He was the most prolific painter of the whole Italian school. The *Paradise* which he and his workshop were commissioned to paint for the Sala del Maggiore Consiglio in the doge's palace in 1588 is the largest work in the history of Western painting before modern times.

TITIAN, real name Tiziano Vecellio (b. Pieve di Cadore 1485/90; d. Venice 1576), learnt the art of painting in the workshop of Giovanni Bellini. With Bellini's death in 1516 Titian became the most

important Venetian master, Giorgione having died in 1510. He rapidly rose to fame, and enjoyed the esteem of the rulers of Europe. At the end of 1529 or the beginning of 1530 he was introduced to Charles V in Bologna and painted his portrait; in 1533 the Emperor rewarded him by making him a Count Palatine and a Knight of the Golden Spur. In 1546 he was created an honorary citizen of Rome. In June 1548 he went to Augsburg, where he painted several portraits, returning to Venice at the end of October; on a second visit to Augsburg in 1550 he painted Prince Philip, who was to become Philip II of Spain, and for whom he executed a number of works. In 1551 he returned to Venice, where he lived and worked for the rest of his long and glorious life.

Seventeenth century

BAROCCI, Federico (b. Urbino c. 1535; d. there 1612), went to Rome in the mid 1550s, and became acquainted with the work of the mannerists there. In 1556 he was in Urbino, but returned to Rome soon afterwards. During this second visit to Rome he claimed that an attempt had been made to poison him by colleagues jealous of his success; it is certainly true that for the rest of his life he was crippled by ill health, suffering great pain and forced, at one point, to give up painting entirely for four years. His *Deposition*, commissioned in 1576 for Perugia Cathedral, shows continued mannerist influence. He returned to Urbino, probably in 1570, and remained there for the rest of his life. Between 1575 and 1579 he painted the large altarpiece the *Madonna of the People (Madonna del Popolo)* for the parish church of Arezzo; this picture (which is now in the Uffizi) is his personal declaration of emancipation from mannerism. Although he was essentially a painter of religious themes, he completed a few portraits during his last years.

CARAVAGGIO, real name Michelangelo Merisi (b. Caravaggio 1573; d. Porto Ercole 1610), was the son of a mason in a village near Milan, and was apprenticed for four years to Simone Peterzano. At the age of about sixteen, in 1588 or 1589, he went to Rome and entered the workshop of the Cavaliere d'Arpino, painting the accessories and still-lifes in the latter's pictures. In 1590 he shared the commission for the Contarelli Chapel of San Luigi dei Francesi with his master, but finally completed the work alone, executing a *St Matthew and the Angel* (replacing an original version rejected as indecorous), together with the *Calling* and *Martyrdom* of the saint. These pictures, which appear to have been completed after 1600, embody the transformation of his art from the picturesque to the dramatic. In 1606 his *Death of the Virgin*, painted for Santa Maria del Popolo, was refused by the church's clergy, but the picture was promptly bought by Duke Vincenzo Gonzaga, on the advice of Rubens; in answer to public demand, the work was put on display for a week before being removed from Rome. Between 1605 and 1607 the police dossiers were filled with reports of his adventures: in 1606 he actually killed a man during a brawl, was wounded himself, and forced to flee from Rome, seeking refuge first of all in the Sabini Mountains and then, in 1607, in Naples. In 1608 he was summoned to Malta by the Grand Master of the Order of St John, but was soon imprisoned for assault; he escaped to Sicily, and stayed briefly first at Syracuse and then at Messina, painting pictures but still pursued by agents of the Order. Back in Naples in 1609 he was seriously wounded in a brawl and his death was generally reported. He had to flee once again, and left Naples by boat for Porto Ercole, a Spanish enclave on the Tuscan coast. Here he was imprisoned by mistake and found, on his release, that the boat had sailed without him, taking his baggage with it. He died of malaria at Porto Ercole on 31 July 1610.

CARREÑO DE MIRANDA, Juan (b. Avila 1614; d. Madrid 1685), worked under the direction of Velázquez at the Alcazar, and also formed his style by studying the Flemish and Venetian paintings in the royal collection. In 1669 he was appointed court painter to Charles II, and he later became official portrait-painter of the king's second wife, Maria Anna of Neuburg. He is chiefly known as a portraitist, but he was not happy following the style set by Velázquez, and his finest pictures are those with religious themes.

CLAUDE LORRAIN, real name Claude Gellée (b. Chamagne, Lorraine, 1600; d. Rome 1682), arrived in Rome at the age of about thirteen, and became servant-assistant to the landscape-painter Agostini Tassi. In 1625 he returned to Nancy, where he worked briefly as an assistant to Claude Dernet, but by the beginning of 1627 he was back in Rome for good. He led a tranquil life there, associating most closely with northern artists but also highly esteemed by Roman patrons of the arts. The earliest work known by him is dated 1635. He kept a reference book, which he called the *Liber veritatis* (London, British Museum), in which he made drawings of his paintings to guard against copying and forgery. He made innumerable life studies, paintings as well as drawings, but none of these have survived. All his paintings were executed in his studio.

DESIDERIO, MONSÙ (seventeenth century), is a name concealing a French origin (Monsù = Monsieur), and covers two distinct groups of works. The first group consists of some panoramic views of Naples by Didier Barra, an artist of Lorraine, who settled in Naples about 1617 and in 1647 signed a picture Desiderius Barra of Metz. The other group, which is both more extensive and more interesting, depicts fantastic architecture: the author of these *capricci* has been identified as François de Nomé, also from Lorraine, born in Metz in 1593, who went to Rome in 1602 and to Naples in 1610.

ELSHEIMER, Adam (b. Frankfurt-on-Main 1578; d. Rome 1610), left his home town about 1598 to work in Venice, then went to Rome in 1600. He remained there for ten years, producing small pictures invariably painted on copper. He introduced a Caravaggesque inspiration into landscape-painting.

GENTILESCHI, Artemisia (b. Rome 1597; d. Naples after 1651), was the daughter of Orazio Gentileschi, and the pupil of her father and of Agostino Tassi. In 1621 she left Rome with her father for Florence; she later lived in Rome and Naples, and joined her father in London during 1638–9. She was back in Naples by 1640 and continued working there for the rest of her life. Her own style, applying itself often to themes of violence and even of cruelty, gradually evolved from the Caravaggesque style of her father.

HALS, Frans (b. Antwerp *c.* 1585; d. Haarlem 1666), was the son of a draper who established himself in Haarlem soon after Frans's birth. Hals learned painting in the studio of Karel van Mander. He was in touch with Rubens, visiting him in Antwerp and possibly being visited by Rubens in return. His first important works are the group portraits, especially the *Officers of St George's Company of Archers* (1616), the *Officers of St Adrian's Company of Archers* (1622), and a 1627 version of the *St George's Company* (all at the Frans Halsmuseum, Haarlem). His late works include the great 1664 groups depicting the *Governors* and *Women Governors* of the Old People's Almshouse in Haarlem. Almost his whole life was spent in Haarlem; despite his great success as a painter he lived in constant financial difficulties.

HERRERA, Francisco, surnamed El Viejo (the Elder) (b. Seville 1576; d. Madrid after 1657), may have been the pupil of Francisco Pacheco in Seville. We have very little information about the career of this painter of frescoes and history pictures, etcher and medallist. He established himself in Madrid in 1640, and was still alive on 5 September 1657, the date on which he drew up his will before a commissioner. His first known works date from 1610 and 1617, and he achieved mastery of technique in 1629, in the pictures he was commissioned to paint for the altar of the college of San Bonaventura at Seville; for some reason he was replaced by Zurbarán when the commission was only partly completed.

LA TOUR, Georges de (b. Vic-sur-Seille, Lorraine, 1593; d. Lunéville 1652), may or may not have visited Rome, but his work suggests acquaintance with that of Terbrugghen and Honthorst, and although nothing is known of his training he was certainly influenced by Caravaggio and the Utrecht school. He was established in Lunéville by 1618, and in 1620 was certified as a master painter. He worked for Duke Charles IV of Lorraine, and he is referred to on two occasions as 'painter in ordinary' to the King of France. The pious imagery he created had a great success, and his paintings were much copied, as well as giving rise to numerous pastiches and imitations.

MAFFEI, Francesco (active Vicenza 1620; d. Padua 1660), formed as an artist by the great sixteenth-century Venetians, may be considered the true local Venetian painter of the seventeenth century, at a time when the Venetian school was composed mainly of artists from other parts of the country. He worked in Vicenza, Padua, Venice, Brescia and Rovigo. His first known work is dated 1626.

MAZZONI, Sebastiano (b. Florence *c.* 1611; d. Venice 1678), is supposed to have left Florence after composing some satirical verses which made him enemies. It is not known just when he arrived in Venice, although it was before 1648. He died as a result of a fall from a ladder.

POZZO, Andrea (b. Trent 1642; d. Vienna 1709), worked first of all in Trent, then in Como and in Milan, and in 1665 became a Jesuit lay-brother. In 1679 he created an astonishing *trompe-l'œil* decoration for the central cupola of the church of San Francesco Saverio in Mondovi (Piedmont). Brought to Rome in 1681 by Padre Oliva, the general of the Order, he designed altars for the Order's churches. Between 1691 and 1694 he painted his masterpiece, the ceiling of the nave of San Ignazio in Rome. In 1702 he was summoned to Vienna by the Emperor Leopold, to whom he dedicated his treatise on perspective, *Prospettiva de' pittori e architetti* . . . , published in Rome between 1693 and 1700. In Vienna he supervised the reconstruction of the Jesuitenkirche, and painted ceilings in the Liechtenstein Palace. A school grew up around him in central Europe, partly as a result of his direct influence and partly through the impact of his treatise on perspective, which was translated into German, French, Dutch and English.

REMBRANDT Harmenszoon van Rijn (b. Leyden 1606; d. Amsterdam 1669), was the fourth son of a prosperous miller. After about a year at Leyden University he was apprenticed for three years to a Leyden painter, Jan van Swanenburgh, then spent some six months in Amsterdam under Pieter Lastman. On returning to Leyden in 1625 he set up a workshop in company with Jan Lievens. At the end of 1631 or early in 1632 he moved to Amsterdam, and it was doubtless the success of his *Anatomy lesson of Professor Tulp* (1632, The Hague, Mauritshuis), commissioned by the Amsterdam Guild of Surgeons, that encouraged him to remain in that city. In 1634 he married Saskia van Uylenburgh, and the next few years formed the most prosperous and brilliant period of his life, during which he bought a mansion and built up a fine collection of art. But in the same year, 1642, that he painted the great group portrait, the *Company of Captain Frans Banning Cocq*, Saskia died, leaving him with a son, Titus. After 1642 Rembrandt's fortunes declined, and his bankruptcy, as a result of various unwise speculations, followed in 1656. Meanwhile he was living with Hendrickje Stoffels, but was never able to marry her because of the conditions laid down in Saskia's will, so exposing himself to persecution by the Calvinist church session. During these years his art developed in the direction of greater introspection. In 1662, his immense *Conspiracy of Julius Civilis*, commissioned for Amsterdam Town Hall, was refused by the municipal council. His work continued to become more intimate in tone and deeper in emotional content, and his many self-portraits showed an increasing power of anguished self-analysis. His death was made more lonely by the fact that he had lost Hendrickje in 1663 and his son Titus in 1668.

RUBENS, Sir Peter Paul (b. Siegen, Westphalia, 1577; d. Antwerp 1640), studied art at Antwerp under Tobias Verhaecht, Adam van Noort and Otto van Veen, and in 1598 was elected to the Painters' Guild of St Luke. Going to Italy he worked from 1600 to 1608 as court painter to Vincenzo Gonzaga, Duke of Mantua, and in 1603 went to Spain on the duke's behalf; during these years he also worked in Venice, Rome, Florence and Genoa on various commissions from churches and from the duke. He returned to Antwerp in 1608; in 1609 he was appointed court painter to the Spanish governors of the Netherlands, the Archduke Albert and the Infanta Isabella, and that same year he married Isabella Brandt. The triptych of the *Raising of the Cross*, painted for Antwerp Cathedral in 1610, assured his reputation, and he followed this with the equally important *Descent from the Cross*, painted in 1611–14, also for Antwerp Cathedral. From this point onwards he received so many commissions that he depended upon the collaboration of pupils and assistants, themselves eminent painters such as Jordaens, Snyders, Paul de Vos and Lucas van Uden. The young van Dyck joined his studio about 1617 and assisted Rubens in 1620 in the decoration of the Jesuit Carolus-Borromeuskerk in Antwerp (the ceiling paintings were all destroyed by fire in 1718). Between 1622 and 1624 he executed the twenty-one large compositions of the *Life of Marie de Médicis* for the Palais du Luxembourg (now in the Louvre). He became the confidential adviser of the Archduchess Isabella, who entrusted him with various diplomatic missions which took him to Spain, where he met Velázquez (1628–9), and to England (1629-30). At the age of fifty-three, in 1630, after the death of Isabella Brandt, he married a girl of sixteen, Helena Fourment: his passion for his young bride gave his art an emotional warmth, inspiring him to paint love scenes and to celebrate the charms of nature which he painted each year at his estate at Steen, near Antwerp. He still continued, however, to work on great decorative schemes, such as the ceiling for the Banqueting Hall in Whitehall. He spent the last five years of his life in retirement at Steen, painting for Philip IV and for his own pleasure.

SEGHERS, Hercules Pieterszoon (b. Haarlem or Amsterdam 1589/90; d. The Hague or Amsterdam before 1638), was a pupil of Gillis van Coninxloo in Amsterdam. In 1612 he became a member of the Painters' Guild of St Luke at Haarlem, but by 1614 he was living in Amsterdam. He worked at Utrecht and The Hague. He was particularly closely concerned with new methods of expression, for which he found etching the most satisfactory medium, and his paintings are comparatively few in number.

TERBRUGGHEN, Hendrik (b. Deventer 1588; d. Utrecht 1629), was a pupil of Abraham Bloemart in Utrecht before going to Italy about 1604. He remained in Italy for ten years, becoming closely associated with the aesthetic ideas of the school of Caravaggio, the *tenebrosi*. In 1614 he was working in Milan, and in the autumn of that year he returned to Utrecht, where he married in 1616. There he developed a personal style which came to owe less and less to Caravaggio as it evolved towards a lighter palette.

VELÁZQUEZ, Diego Rodríguez da Silva (b. Seville 1599; d. Madrid 1660), was of Portuguese origin, descended from a family of *hidalgos* through his father Rodríguez da Silva; he adopted the family name of his mother, who also seems to have been of noble blood. In 1613 he entered the Seville studio of Francisco Pacheco, the painter and theorist of academicism, and married his daughter in 1618, a year after he became an independent master. His early paintings show strongly the influence of Caravaggio's 'naturalism', but he detached himself from this realistic manner after contact with the court. A portrait he painted of Philip IV in 1614 was so successful that at the king's command he remained in Madrid. In 1627 he won the prize in a competition for a historical composition; he was then appointed usher of the chamber to the king and given accommodation in the palace. In 1628 he welcomed Rubens, who had arrived in Madrid on a diplomatic mission, and became friendly with him. There is no doubt that this meeting helped Velázquez to free himself of his first style, especially since Rubens painted several pictures while he was in Madrid. It was certainly Rubens, too, who advised him to go to Italy to see the works of the Renaissance painters and the moderns. While in Italy in 1629–30, Velázquez visited Venice, Bologna, Rome and Naples where he met Ribera. He was back in Madrid in January 1631, and painted the *Surrender of Breda* ('*Las Lanzas*') for a gallery of battles in the Buen Retiro Palace (now in the Prado). He returned to Italy in 1649, to buy pictures and statues for the Crown, and visited Pope Innocent X. To mark their esteem for his genius, the painters of Rome elected Velázquez to the Accademia di San Luca. Despite the king's urgent messages to him to return to Spain, he lingered in Italy until 1651. Back in Madrid, he found awaiting him the challenging task of painting the new Queen Mariana of Austria and the royal children. He benefited increasingly from the friendship of Philip IV, who in 1652 appointed him marshal of the royal household, a post involving heavy responsibilities. In 1659 the king overruled the protests of his nobles and created him a Knight of the Order of Santiago, a high honour.

VERMEER, Jan (b. Delft 1632; d. there 1675), spent his whole life in Delft. Nothing is known of his childhood upbringing. The earliest document we possess for him, after his baptism certificate, is his marriage certificate, dated 5 April 1653. The same year he was admitted to the Painters' Guild of St Luke at Delft. His first dated work is of 1656, though some other paintings are doubtless earlier. He seems to have been esteemed by his colleagues, since he was elected dean of the guild in 1662–3 and again in 1670–1. Nevertheless, he had a difficult life, selling his paintings infrequently and at low prices. He pondered his compositions deeply beforehand and was then slow in completing them: his total output is only in the region of forty paintings. Some plausible imitations of his earlier style were exposed as forgeries in 1945.

Eighteenth century

ASAM, Cosmas Damian (b. Munich 1686; d. Mannheim 1750), completed his apprenticeship in the studio of his father who was a follower of Andrea Pozzo, then studied at Rome. He worked in close association with his brother Egid Quirin, who was a sculptor, stuccoworker and architect, while he devoted himself entirely to painting. They collaborated on the decoration of a number of buildings and churches in Bavaria, the Tirol, Switzerland, Bohemia, Silesia and the Palatinate.

PIAZZETTA, Giambattista (b. Venice 1682; d. there 1754), was the son of a woodcarver, and at first followed his father's craft. The most important factor in his formation as a painter was his discovery at Bologna of the works of Crespi, whose pupil he became; Crespi's influence is apparent in his contrasted treatment of volumes in chiaroscuro, which makes him one of the last of the *tenebrosi*. Back in Venice in 1711, he specialized in easel-paintings rather than decorative schemes. In 1750 he became director of the Venice Accademia di San Luca.

RICCI, Sebastiano (b. Belluno 1659; d. Venice 1734), studied at Venice, but his stay in Emilia instilled in him a certain sense of formal strictness and, above all, allowed him to become acquainted with the work of Correggio; he was also influence by Pietro da Cortona. He worked first in Lombardy and then at Venice; his growing reputation secured him commissions in Tuscany, and in 1712 he went to London with his nephew Marco. Later he travelled in Flanders and Germany before settling in Venice.

SPIEGLER, Franz Josef (b. Wangen 1691; d. Constance 1757), commenced his career as a painter with a series of decorations for the Swabian monastery of Ottobeuren (1725). He received commissions to paint monumental frescoes throughout southern Germany, at Constance, and at the monastery of Zwiefalten (1748–51) which contains his most significant works.

TIEPOLO, Giambattista (b. Venice 1696; d. Madrid 1770), was received into the Fraglia (Guild) in 1717, and in 1719 married the sister of Guardi. Precociously talented, he was by 1729 already the most celebrated painter of his native city. The artist who exercised the greatest influence on his formation was Piazzetta, although he soon broke free from this dark tenebrist model to assume a lighter and looser style. He painted fresco decorations for various palaces and churches in Venice and throughout the Veneto, notably the Palazzo Labia in Venice (1750) and the ballroom of the Villa Pisani at Stra (1761–2). He also worked at Bergamo and Milan. In 1750 the Prince

Bishop of Würzburg invited him to decorate the ceiling of the Kaisersaal and the staircase in the Residenz. In 1762 his fame resulted in an invitation to Spain to decorate the ceilings of the new royal palace, a task he accomplished in four years with the help of his sons and a team of assistants; he died a few years after the completion of this great undertaking.

TROGER, Paul (b. Zell, Vorarlberg, 1698; d. Vienna 1762), received his training in the studio of the painter Alberti at Cavalese in the South Tirol. The grant of a bursary allowed him to spend the years between 1717 and 1722 visiting the art centres of Italy, including Venice whence he brought back a feeling for space and joyous colouring. His first work in Austria was the decoration of the cupola of the Kajetankirche Sankt Maximilian (1727–8). He completed many commissions for the monasteries and palaces of Austria and Hungary. His master work is the ceiling fresco for the monastery of Altenburg, depicting the *Apocalypse* (1733).

Nineteenth century

CÉZANNE, Paul (b. Aix-en-Provence 1839; d. there 1906), was the son of a wealthy banker who had at one time been a hatter. He was educated at Aix, with Emile Zola as a fellow pupil and close friend. In 1862 he arrived in Paris to study art, and met Pissarro, Guillaumin, Monet, Sisley, Bazille and Renoir. In the years 1846 to 1870, the initial romantic phase of his art, he divided his time between Aix and Paris. In 1871 he arrived back in Paris with his companion Hortense Fiquet who gave him a son. His so-called impressionist period then commenced, and in 1872 he and his family went to live near Pissarro at Pontoise, near Auvers-sur-Oise, where he remained until 1874, learning from Pissarro the theories of colour and light which the impressionists were then developing. That year he took part in the first impressionist exhibition, contributing *The House of the hanged man* (*La Maison du pendu*) (1873, Louvre) which marks the transition from his first to his second style. Subsequently, he painted at Pontoise, Aix, L'Estaque (near Marseilles), Auvers, Chantilly, Fontainebleau, on the banks of the Seine and the Marne, and in the studio; he completed many still-lifes. From 1881 onwards his trips away from Aix became less and less frequent. His art grew increasingly Mediterranean in feeling, and in his provincial landscapes he attempted to go beyond the atmospheric preoccupations of the impressionists. The Montagne Sainte-Victoire near Aix became his favourite theme; from about 1895 his landscapes of Sainte-Victoire, the Bibémus quarry, the Château Noir reveal a trend towards an increasingly ardent lyricism of expression. At the same time, he sought to concentrate all his artistic energies on the big compositions of *Bathers*, of which he made three versions between 1895 and 1906, preceded by numerous studies, and which herald the art of the twentieth century.

CONSTABLE, John (b. East Bergholt, Suffolk, 1776; d. London 1837), was the son of a miller. From childhood onwards, the beauty of his native East Anglia continued to stir his imagination. He was admitted to the Royal Academy Schools in 1799, but worked mostly from nature. Recognition of his talent was slow in coming, and he was not elected an academician until 1819, three years after his marriage. About this time his style began to change from a descriptive approach similar to that of the eighteenth-century watercolourists to an increasingly subjective approach. The paintings in this new manner which he exhibited at the Paris Salon of 1824, such as the *Hay-Wain* (National Gallery), had a great influence on the development of the French school. His favourite themes were Salisbury Cathedral, Weymouth Bay, Hampstead Heath and the Suffolk countryside. His daughter bequeathed a large collection of his work to the Victoria and Albert Museum, which explains the relative scarcity of his works outside England.

COROT, Jean-Baptiste-Camille (b. Paris 1796; d. there 1875), avoided academic training as a painter, and between 1825 and 1828 formed himself by painting from nature during a long stay in Italy. Back in Paris in 1829 he began a satisfying career, painting oil sketches (*pochades*) at sites in France and Italy from which he worked up the composed pictures that he sent to the Salons. He made two further journeys to Italy in 1834 and 1843. He owned a country house on the edge of the lake of Ville-d'Avray, and after 1850 his frequent stays there encouraged him to indulge rather too freely in a dreamy, rather fuzzy type of landscape; the immense popularity of the compositions led him to over-produce, sometimes with the collaboration of pupils. Happily, he retained throughout his life, and into old age, the full spontaneity of his talent when working from nature.

COURBET, Gustave (b. Ornans 1819; d. La Tour de Peilz, Switzerland, 1877), was the son of a well-to-do farmer in the Franche-Comté. He received his first drawing lessons at a private school in Besançon. He went to Paris in 1840 to study law, but soon turned to painting. His first landscapes and portraits demonstrate a rather banal romanticism of which he cured himself by means of assiduous studies at the Louvre and in the museums of the Netherlands during a visit there in 1847. He exhibited his first realist paintings at the 1850 Salon, including the *Burial at Ornans* (Louvre) which created a scandal. A stay at Montpellier, in the Midi, led him to abandon finally the dark shadings of romanticism, as is apparent in *Bonjour, Monsieur Courbet* (Montpellier). In 1855, the year of the Great Exhibition in Paris, he opened a private exhibition of forty of his paintings in a shed near the main building; this first of all 'one-man shows' included a painting refused by the French pavilion, the *Painter in his studio* (Louvre), and created a sensation. During the winter of 1858–9 he visited Frankfurt, and he returned to Germany on later occasions, attracted by the pleasures of hunting and by the welcome he received from the artists of that country. In 1870 he joined the National Guard, and took an active part in the revolutionary government of 1871. After the Commune he was declared

responsible for the destruction of the Vendôme column, imprisoned, and condemned to pay the costs of re-erecting the monument. He returned to Ornans, then fled to Switzerland in 1873 to escape arrest, going to live in La Tour de Peilz, near Geneva. In his efforts to pay off the indemnity exacted by the French government he turned out a constant stream of Swiss landscapes, helped by a team of assistants who were more or less successful in following his style.

DAUMIER, Honoré (b. Marseilles 1808; d. Valmondois 1879), was the son of a picture-framer. He went to Paris in 1816, attended several academies of painting, and in 1828 learnt the newly invented process of lithography. As a cartoonist for *La Caricature* and, later, *Le Charivari*, he became noted for his attacks on the July Monarchy, and a caricature of Louis Philippe led to his imprisonment for six months in 1831. In about 1845 he reverted to painting as a virtually self-taught artist, continuing to produce lithographs for a living. He also made a few sculptures, but not nearly as many as have been attributed to him at one time or another. He became friendly with the painters of the Barbizon school: Millet, Théodore Rousseau and Corot. His moment of official glory came when he was awarded the prize at the competition set up in 1848 for an official effigy of *The Republic* (Louvre). He gradually lost his sight, and with only a small State pension to support him he was rescued from dire poverty by Corot who bought him a house at Valmondois, where he died almost blind.

DAVID, Jacques-Louis (b. Paris 1748; d. Brussels 1825), was a kinsman of Boucher, who gave him some instruction. He then studied under Vien who gave him a grounding in the principles of neoclassicism which he consolidated during his stay in Rome between 1775 and 1780. In 1783 he became an academician, and returned to Rome to paint the *Oath of the Horatii* (Louvre) which had been commissioned by the royal administration. This picture had a tremendous success when exhibited in Rome in 1784, a success repeated the following year at the Paris Salon. Under the revolutionary government of the Convention he took an active part in politics, became a deputy in the National Assembly, and voted for the death of Louis XVI. He painted a few pictures with revolutionary themes, including *Le Peletier de Saint-Fargeau dying*, the *Death of Marat*, and the *Little drummer-boy Bara*, and was imprisoned briefly after the fall of Robespierre. Fascinated by the genius of Napoleon, he became an ardent Bonapartist and painted historical compositions such as the *Consecration of the Emperor Napoleon I* and the *Emperor distributing the eagles*. Exiled in 1815 as a regicide after the restoration of the Bourbons, he retired to Brussels. He refused Louis XVIII's offer of a pardon, and remained in Brussels, painting mainly portraits during the last years of his life.

DEGAS, Edgar (b. Paris 1834; d. there 1917), came of a wealthy family, his father being a banker. He studied at the Ecole des Beaux-Arts under a pupil of Ingres, Lamothe, and completed his classical education in 1856 by a voyage to Italy during which he made numerous studies after the masters. His first paintings showed the great influence that Ingres had had on him (the *Misfortunes of the town of Orleans*, 1865, Louvre). By the late 1860s he had begun to develop a personal style incorporating psychological analysis and realistic observation (as in the *Bellelli family*, c. 1858–9, Louvre) which he carried further, after 1870, in racecourse scenes, character portraits in offcentre compositions, and paintings of the theatre and ballet. A visit to his brother René de Gas at New Orleans (where his mother's family had settled after the Revolution) produced an interesting and typical example of his new manner in the view of the *Cotton Exchange, New Orleans* (1873, Pau, Musée des Beaux-Arts). He soon extended his interest in character studies to scenes of everyday life, in pictures such as the *Washerwomen*, *Women ironing* and *Absinthe* (1876), all in the Louvre. Nudes, dressing and bathing, and ballet dancers provided him with endless subject-matter for studies of manner and movement. From 1884 onwards, failing sight turned him to pastel and then to sculpture, and from 1898 his blindness forced him to abandon painting as a medium.

DELACROIX, Eugène (b. Saint-Maurice nr Paris 1798; d. Paris 1863), was the son of a senior Napoleonic official, who had preceded Talleyrand as foreign minister, and legend has it that his real father was in fact Talleyrand. In 1816 he entered the studio of the neoclassical painter Guérin, but also spent considerable time studying Rubens at the Louvre. His first large painting was *Dante's barque* (1822, Louvre). The *Massacre at Chios* (Louvre) was bought by the State at the 1824 Salon. A visit to England in 1825 allowed him to discover English painting, and on his return to Paris he frequented English artists, including Bonington. The *Death of Sardanapalus* (Louvre), shown at the 1827 Salon, revealed his admiration for Rubens. The 1830 Revolution inspired his *Liberty leading the People* (*Liberty at the barricades*), his masterpiece. A voyage made to Morocco in 1832, in the company of a special ambassador, made a profound impression upon him. Under the July Monarchy he received important commissions for monumental works: the library and Salon du Roi in the Palais Bourbon, the Senate library in the Palais du Luxembourg, and, later, the Salon de la Paix at the Hôtel de Ville (destroyed), a ceiling of the Galerie d'Apollon in the Louvre and, towards the end of his life, the Chapelle des Saints-Anges in the church of Saint-Sulpice. Painter, writer, moralist, art critic, man of the world, Delacroix, who kept a journal for many years, was one of the most representative personalities of his century.

EMPERAIRE, Achille (b. Aix-en-Provence 1829; d. there 1898), was a deformed dwarf who struggled to earn a living as a painter. He paid occasional visits to Paris in his efforts to get his work accepted by the Salon. A boyhood friend of Cézanne, it seems probable that he influenced the latter, especially with his drawings of nudes: Cézanne himself, as is known, was reluctant to ask models to pose for him. Emperaire's drawings are very fine; his paintings, on the other hand, of which few survive, are mediocre.

GAUGUIN, Paul (b. Paris 1848; d. Atuana, Marquesas Islands, 1903), entered the merchant service in 1865, and his sea voyages took him to Rio de Janeiro among other places. He joined a stock-broker's business in 1871, and two years later married a young Danish woman, Mette Sophie Gad. He also became a Sunday painter, and in 1883 gave up his financial career to devote himself entirely to painting. In 1885 his wife left him and returned to Denmark. His visit in 1886 to Pont-Aven, where he met Emile Bernard, marked his estrangement from impressionism, a development confirmed during his 1887 journey to Martinique. Back in Paris in 1888 he resumed contact with the Pont-Aven group, and that same year made a brief and disastrous stay with van Gogh at Arles. Back in Brittany, at Le Pouldu, he painted his first 'synthetist' pictures: *La Belle Angèle* (1889, Louvre), the *Yellow Christ* (1889, Buffalo, Albright Art Gallery), *Vision after the sermon* (*Jacob wrestling with the Angel*) (1888, Edinburgh, National Gallery of Scotland). After putting thirty of his paintings up for public sale, he left for Tahiti in 1891, and there painted pictures on Polynesian themes before returning to France in 1893. After staying once more in Pont-Aven he went back to Tahiti for good in 1895. For the remaining years of his life there he adopted the way of life of the native population. His health ruined by alcohol and syphilis, he made an unsuccessful attempt at suicide by taking poison after painting a huge picture which was intended to be his final testament, *Whence do we come? Where are we? Whither are we going?* (Boston). In 1901 he left Tahiti for Fatu-Iva in the Marquesas, where he came into conflict with the civil and ecclesiastical authorities and died in great misery.

GÉRICAULT, Théodore (b. Rouen 1791; d. Paris 1824), was born of well-to-do parents. He studied first under the painter of hunting and racing scenes Carle Vernet, 1808–10, and then under the neoclassicist Guérin, 1810–11; he completed his artistic education by studying the works of the masters at the Louvre. His first pictures were inspired by his Bonapartist enthusiasms: *Mounted officer of the Imperial Guard* (1812, Louvre), *Wounded cuirassier leaving the scene of battle* (1813, Louvre). During a voyage to Italy in 1816 he was greatly impressed by the works of Michelangelo, and on his return to Paris attempted realistic subjects in Michelangelo's grand style. He executed a colossal picture, inspired by a marine calamity of 1815, the *Raft of the 'Medusa'* (Louvre), which he exhibited at the 1819 Salon and then took to England to show in a travelling exhibition. Visiting London, he became attracted by English painting and made a close study of horses, his enthusiasm finding expression in *The Derby at Epsom* (Louvre). Back in Paris in 1822, he undertook a series of portraits of insane patients at the Salpêtrière, with the encouragement of his friend Dr Georget. His life was cut short by a riding accident which caused him severe injuries and constant pain during his last years.

GOGH, Vincent van (b. Groot-Zundert, Netherlands 1853; d. Auvers-sur-Oise 1890), was the son of a Dutch pastor. After being employed in The Hague, London and Paris by Goupil & Co., the firm of art dealers for which his brother Theo later worked in Paris, he felt the call of religion and became a missionary, but upset the evangelical authorities by his unorthodox behaviour. He began painting after he had been dismissed from his mission in 1881. Returning home to his parents in Etten he met the painter Anton Mauve, who gave him help and advice. At the same time he discovered the art of Japanese prints. During those early years he painted in a dark, heavy style, using as subject-matter the squalor of peasant life (*Potato eaters*, 1885), still-lifes and landscapes. In 1886 he joined Theo in Paris, remaining there until 1888: under the influence of Monticelli and the impressionists he entirely changed his style, evolving towards a light palette and tone division. From February 1888 to May 1889 he was in Arles, where his quarrelling with Gauguin brought on his first attack of insanity. At Arles he developed his personal style of brilliant and violently contrasting colours. From May 1889 to May 1890 he was confined in the mental hospital at Saint-Rémy; then his brother Theo arranged for him to come to Auvers-sur-Oise where he lived under the supervision of Dr Gachet. On 27 July he committed suicide.

GOYA Y LUCIENTES, Francisco José de (b. Fuendetodos nr Saragossa 1746; d. Bordeaux 1828), was apprenticed at fourteen to a local painter, José Luzán, in whose studio he remained for four years. After failing twice to secure admission to the Academia de San Fernando at Madrid, he left for Italy in 1770. The following year he was back in Saragossa, having received a commission to decorate a cupola of the Cathedral. In 1775, in Madrid, he married Josefa, sister of the painter Francisco Bayeu. In 1776 the painter Anton Raphael Mengs commissioned him to produce a series of forty tapestry designs for the royal factory at Santa Barbara, on which he was engaged until 1791. In 1798 he painted frescoes for the chapel of San Antonio de la Florida in Madrid, an important royal commission which gave him the opportunity to display his romantic manner. He remained in Madrid under the French occupation. His wife died in 1812. In 1819 he bought a country house which became known as the Quinta del Sordo (the Deaf Man's House). His position during and after the Napoleonic invasion of Spain was uneasy. When Ferdinand VII was driven out he continued to work for the usurper Joseph Bonaparte; the restoration of Ferdinand brought reaction and persecution, and although Goya was not penalized he was faced with hostility and intrigue at the court. He decided to go into voluntary exile in France, settling in Bordeaux. He visited Madrid in 1826 and again in 1827, the year before his death in Bordeaux.

MANET, Edouard (b. Paris 1832; d. there 1883), was the son of a wealthy magistrate. After a trial voyage to Rio de Janeiro as a naval cadet, he was allowed to study under Thomas Couture from 1850 to 1856, but formed himself as an artist during this period chiefly by spending much time at the Louvre copying the masters. His early work shows the influence of seventeenth-century Spanish painting (for example, *Lola de Valence*, 1861–2, Louvre). After a journey to the Netherlands in 1857 he married

Suzanne Leenhoff. His *Luncheon on the grass* (*Déjeuner sur l'herbe*) (Louvre), exhibited at the Salon des Refusés in 1863, caused a scandal. His *Olympia* (Louvre) was accepted for the 1865 Salon, and created even greater uproar, though Emile Zola came to the picture's defence in *L'Evénement* (1866). During the Franco-Prussian War he served as an officer in the National Guard. After 1870 he abandoned his 'black' painting and adopted the *peinture claire* technique discovered by Monet, while his outlook tended increasingly towards a Zolaesque realism (*Nana*, 1877, Hamburg; *Chez le Père Lathuille*, 1880, Tournai). He always longed for official recognition and refused to take part in the impressionist exhibitions, persisting in sending work to the Salon where it was nearly always accepted but usually greeted with hostile comment.

MONET, Claude (b. Paris 1840; d. Giverny 1926), was brought up in Le Havre, where his family moved when he was five. There he met Boudin who encouraged him to paint landscapes from nature. In 1859 he went to Paris to study, and met Pissarro. His art studies were interrupted by his military service in Algeria, which was cut short by illness. He returned to Paris in 1862 and entered Gleyre's studio, where he met Renoir, Sisley and Bazille: this last encounter was to prove of material importance, since Bazille came from a wealthy family and in the years to come provided regular financial help for his impoverished friend. He painted from nature at Fontainebleau, on the beaches of Normandy, on the banks of the Seine, and in the environs of Paris, but his true aim was to show figures in the reality of the open air (*Women in the garden*, 1868, Louvre). In 1870 he married his companion Camille, then, to escape the war, went to London, where he discovered Turner, and to the Netherlands. From 1872 to 1878 he worked at Argenteuil, on the banks of the Seine, and while there developed his vibrant technique for rendering the movement of light in colour. He tended to concentrate his researches into light variations on a single site *(Argenteuil; Les Débâcles)*, and soon began to paint series of pictures of a single subject (the *Haystacks*, 1891; the *Poplars*, 1892; *Rouen Cathedral*, 1892–5; the views of *London*, 1900–1, and *Venice*, 1908). Monet carried his researches beyond the sites of Normandy and the Ile-de-France to Holland, Provence and the Italian Riviera. He had already started work before 1900 on the vast luminous poem constituted by his *Water-lilies*, which he painted in the specially constructed water-garden of his house at Giverny. This vast cycle of studies was interrupted in 1922 for some time by temporary blindness caused by a cataract; the very large paintings in the series begun in 1916, which remained in his possession until his death, were bequeathed to the State and are now housed in a special museum (Orangerie, Paris). He died at Giverny at the age of eighty-six.

MONTICELLI, Adolphe (b. Marseilles 1824; d. there 1886), was of Italian descent, his family having emigrated from Piedmont in the eighteenth century. He learned to paint, between 1841 and 1844, at the local municipal art school. After a first visit to Paris in 1846, he moved constantly between the capital and his native town from 1851 to 1862, Diaz and Delacroix

being the painters who had the greatest influence on him at that time. He lived in Paris from 1862 to 1870, when he fled from the war back to Marseilles, where he remained for the rest of his life apart from landscape-painting expeditions in Provence. Unfortunately he indulged in a good deal of facile but successful studio painting, which harmed his reputation after his death, more especially since several of his pupils painted fakes of these works.

ROUSSEAU, Henri, known as 'Le Douanier' (b. Laval 1844; d. Paris 1910), spent some years in the army and claimed to have taken part, as a sergeant, in the Franco-Prussian War. After leaving the army, probably in 1871, he came to Paris and obtained a post in the municipal toll department (hence, erroneously, 'le Douanier'). He began painting, about 1880, without any training. He also opened a sort of school of music, painting and elocution, as well as writing poems and plays. He exhibited at the Indépendants (which had no jury system) from 1886 to 1898 and from 1901 to 1910; the symbolists, as well as Gauguin and Pissarro, knew and admired his work, though it was the applause of Alfred Jarry, Apollinaire and Picasso which in his later years made him known.

ROUSSEAU, Théodore (b. Paris 1812; d. Barbizon 1867), spent some time, while young, in the Jura, of which his father was a native, and his imagination was struck by the region's mountains and forests. He was a pupil of his cousin the landscapist Pau de Saint-Martin who took him to the countryside near Compiègne for painting lessons. From the age of sixteen he frequented official studios. In 1830 he made enthusiastic studies of the Auvergne mountains, then undertook an equally fruitful voyage to Normandy. In 1832 he visited Mont-Saint-Michel in company with de Laberge, a nature-loving painter. In 1834 the contemplation of Mont Blanc seen from the Col de la Faucille (Jura) inspired him to paint one of his most romantic pictures, now in Copenhagen. This same voyage also produced the *Cattle going down to the Morvan* (sketch at Amiens Museum), a picture which was refused by the Salon. The juries made such a habit of turning down his pictures that he became known as '*le grand refusé*', and he was able to show his works only when Salons without juries were introduced in 1848. From this time onwards his art evolved towards an objective devotion to nature; he worked increasingly in the forest of Fontainebleau, and finally settled down at its fringe, in the village of Barbizon. He continued travelling, though less frequently, in Vendée, the Landes, Isle-Adam, the Jura and Picardy. He lived a solitary life, often in extreme poverty.

TURNER, Joseph Mallord William (b. London 1775; d. there 1851), was the son of a barber in Maiden Lane. His general education was rudimentary, and his lifelong thirst for culture was that of a self-taught man. He was precociously talented: already selling drawings and watercolours at the age of twelve, he had started working from nature by the time he was sixteen. He studied in the Royal Academy Schools 1789–93. The Academy recognized his genius early; he became an ARA in 1799 and, at the age of twenty-seven, an RA

in 1802. He continued to travel widely and continuously in various parts of Britain as well as in Europe, particularly Italy where he was able to study the works of Claude Lorrain, whom he much admired. He lived a solitary existence and was considered something of a misogynist. He bequeathed to the nation some 280 paintings and 19,000 drawings and watercolours, which are now divided among the National and Tate Galleries and the British Museum; this is the reason for the comparative scarcity of his work in foreign collections.

VALENCIENNES, Pierre-Henri de (b. Toulouse 1750; d. Paris 1816), received his basic art training at the Toulouse Académie de Peinture, and began his peripatetic life as a painter in the Midi. He made his first journey to Italy in 1769, and later visited Touraine and the forests near Paris; at dates which it is difficult to establish precisely he also visited England, Spain and Germany. He was in Italy from the end of 1777 to 1780, visiting the Roman countryside, Campania and Sicily; he returned to Paris by way of Umbria, Tuscany, the Marches, Emilia, Lombardy, the lakes, Piedmont, Savoy and Switzerland. He returned to Italy in 1782, and there is no record of his whereabouts from then until the beginning of 1787, when the indefatigable traveller set off for Greece, Egypt, the Middle East, Turkey and the Greek archipelago. He was elected to the Académie Royale de Peinture in 1787. From then on he exhibited composed landscapes worked up from his oil studies and his drawings from nature (several hundred examples of which are now in the Louvre). Appointed a professor of perspective at the Ecole des Beaux-Arts in 1812, he wrote a treatise on landscape-painting, *Eléments de perspective pratique*, whose principles were followed throughout the first half of the nineteenth century.

Twentieth century

BRAQUE, Georges (b. Argenteuil 1882; d. Paris 1963), was the son of a painting and decorating contractor who moved to Le Havre when he was eight years old, and he learned to paint as an apprentice in his father's business. He arrived in Paris in 1900. He first painted landscapes in the fauvist manner, then his art changed radically, under the influence of Cézanne, in 1907 while he was working at L'Estaque. He exhibited at the 1908 Salon, and the conservative art critic Louis Vauxcelles described his pictures there as being made 'with little cubes'. He organized a 'one-man show' the same year. For several years he worked in close association with Picasso. Sent to the front in 1914, he was wounded in 1915, and after a long convalescence began painting again in 1917. Between 1919 and 1930 he passed through an almost 'realist' phase in which his art respected appearances to a greater degree. Subsequently his manner held a balance between the real and the abstract, with a tendency in his last years towards an increasingly summary form.

CHIRICO, Giorgio de (b. Volo, Greece, 1888), studied art at Athens and Munich. Painting in Paris between 1911 and 1915, he produced imaginative compositions incorporating incongruous elements, acknowledged by the surrealists to have provided a primary source of inspiration. Returning to Italy in 1916, he and Carlo Carrà evolved the short-lived *scuola metafisica* the following year. Since the 1920s he has devoted his time to violent attacks on modern art, and his talent to pastiches of romantic classicism and baroque.

DELAUNAY, Robert (b. Paris 1885; d. Montpellier 1941), took to painting about 1905, evolving from a naturalistic art towards cubism in 1910, a progression followed also by his wife Sonia Terk. His cubism soon developed rapidly towards pure abstraction, and in 1912 his series of *Windows* and *Circular forms* were described as 'Orphist' by Apollinaire. He was a true founder of non-figurative art.

DUBUFFET, Jean (b. Le Havre 1901), takes his inspiration from wall 'graffiti' and amateur art, especially that created by psychotics. His *pâtes* are not, strictly speaking, paintings, being composed of tar, glass, sand and pieces of junk which he colours and assembles to produce human shapes.

He studied art for a short time in Paris at the age of seventeen, gave up painting in 1924 to travel and set up a wine business, but has been devoting himself exclusively to art since the early 1940s.

DUCHAMP, Marcel (b. Blainville 1887; d. Neuilly-sur-Seine 1968), brother of the sculptor Raymond Duchamp-Villon and the painter Jacques Villon, was first influenced by Cézanne, but about 1911 changed suddenly to a kind of cubism in which the newly evolved ideas of futurism played an important part (*Nude descending a staircase*, 1912, Philadelphia). He abandoned painting in 1915, the year that he began his first preliminary studies for the 'Large Glass' ('Grand Verre') called *The Bride stripped bare by her bachelors, even*, a construction incorporating designs in oil and lead wire on glass, upon which he worked intermittently until 1923, when he left it unfinished. He was the inventor of Readymades, everyday objects promoted to the dignity of works of art by the fact of the artist's choice of them. He was one of the founders of the dada movement. From 1913, the year he exhibited the *Nude descending a staircase* and three other paintings at the Armory Show in New York, he acquired considerable fame in the United States. After 1938 he lived in New York, though returning regularly to Europe for visits to France and Spain. He became an American citizen in 1954.

ENSOR, James (b. Ostend 1860; d. there 1949), was the son of an English father and a Flemish mother. Apart from his art training at the academy in Brussels he spent his life in Ostend, working quietly in his studio, 'happily confined', in his own words, 'to the solitary realm where the mask rules'. His early works showed the influence of Turner and of certain aspects of impressionism, but about 1880 he developed a very personal manner expressing a macabre imagination.

His masterpiece is the huge *Entry of Christ into Brussels* (1888, Knocke-le-Zoute). This burst of inventive power lasted until about 1900, after which his inspiration faltered and his art became stereotyped. Together with Edvard Munch he may be considered the originator of expressionism.

GORKY, Arshile (b. Hajotz Dzore, Turkish Armenia 1904; d. Sherman, Conn. 1948), lived in the United States from the age of sixteen onwards. After being influenced successively by Cézanne, the cubists and Picasso, he came under the influence of surrealism shortly before the Second World War. His art belongs firmly to the surrealist abstract tradition of Miró, Tanguy and Matta, and he forms the link between European surrealism and American abstract impressionism.

HARTUNG, Hans (b. Leipzig 1904), left Germany in 1935 and went to Paris, where he now lives, a naturalized French citizen. He lost a leg fighting with the Foreign Legion during the Second World War. He began to paint in the abstract manner at the age of eighteen, then studied art in Leipzig, Dresden, and Munich in 1924–8. His first contact with the work of Kandinsky in 1925 encouraged him to continue in his abstract style. His paintings, usually dark on a light background and with numbers instead of titles, are represented in French, Swiss and American collections, as well as the Tate Gallery in London.

JONES, Allen (b. Southampton 1937), an English painter and graphic artist whose work is frequently based on erotic themes. He uses simple, striking colours with all the freedom of the abstract painter. He has taught at the Croydon College of Art and the Chelsea School of Art, and lives in London.

KANDINSKY, Wassily (b. Moscow 1866; d. Neuilly-sur-Seine 1944), decided to become an artist on seeing an impressionist exhibition in Moscow in 1895. In the following year he went to Munich to learn painting, and in 1901 founded the Phalanx group there, and opened a school of painting. After travelling widely inside Germany and abroad, including a visit to France in 1906, he returned to Munich in 1907. He painted his first purely abstract works in 1910, and set out the theory of his art in *Über das Geistige in der Kunst*, 1912, translated in a 1947 English version as *Concerning the Spiritual in Art*. In 1911 he was one of the founders of the *Blaue Reiter* group of expressionists. On the declaration of war he left for Switzerland, and from there went to Russia where he supported the revolutionary movement actively. He returned to Germany in 1921, and taught at the Bauhaus in Weimar from 1922, until it was closed by order of the Nazi government in 1933, when he went to Paris.

KIRCHNER, Ernst Ludwig (b. Aschaffenburg 1880; d. Davos 1938), was the principal founder, in 1905, of the *Die Brücke* group in Dresden, which moved its activities to Berlin in 1911. From 1904 the influence of African and Polynesian sculpture had led him towards a painful and gloomy expressionism. He suffered from tuberculosis, and in 1917 he left Germany

for Switzerland and settled in Davos, painting mountain landscapes. He committed suicide in 1938.

KOONING, Willem de (b. Rotterdam 1904), has lived in the USA since 1926, where he shared a studio with his friend Arshile Gorky for some years. Though his early training was influenced by *De Stijl*, he is a prominent action painter. He has taught at various American art schools and painted a mural for the New York World's Fair of 1939. His work has been exhibited at several Biennales and his pictures are in a number of American museums including the Museum of Modern Art in New York.

LICHTENSTEIN, Roy (b. New York 1923), a leading representative of American pop art, is also an experimental sculptor, using coloured plastics, brass and enamelled metal. His paintings operate with strong primary colours and with the striking effect produced by the contrast of black and white. They are mostly large, and interpret details taken from advertisements and comic strips. He uses dots of pure colour in imitation of the crude screen process used in printing comic strips.

MANESSIER, Alfred (b. Saint-Ouen, France 1911), is exceptional among abstract painters, in that he sometimes works on religious themes (a series of lithographs on the subject of Easter, 1949; stained-glass windows for churches in Bresseux, Arles and Basle, 1953). He lives in Paris and his pictures are to be found in many European galleries including the Tate, as well as in New York (Guggenheim) and Pittsburgh.

MATHIEU, Georges (b. Paris 1922), a gestural abstract painter, came to prominence after the Second World War as the leading European publicist of 'action painting', which he called *art informel*. A born showman, he once emphasized the importance of the pictorial gesture by painting a canvas in full view of an audience.

MATISSE, Henri (b. Le Cateau 1869; d. Cimiez 1954), was a pupil of Gustave Moreau from 1892 to 1897, and met Rouault, Camoin and Marquet, among others, in his studio. He did a great deal of copying in the Louvre. In 1896 he exhibited a realistic painting, the *Dinner table* (*La desserte*), at the Société Nationale des Beaux-Arts, repeating the same theme in 1908 in a fauvist version. In 1904 he was painting landscapes in the south of France. His first fauvist pictures date from 1905. From 1909 to 1910, however, his art became more refined, as in *The Dance* and *Music* (Moscow), and involved an increasing stylization of nature. In 1908–10 he ran a school which was thronged by foreigners, and began to assume the stature of the leader of a movement. After the First World War he lived for the most part on the Riviera, and during the following decade his painting became more figurative and almost sensual. The commission by the Barnes Foundation (Merion, Pa.) for a large-scale decoration on the theme of *The Dance* (1931–3) brought him back to a more abstract conception. After the Second World War he settled in Nice, and in 1947–51 he worked on a chapel for a Dominican convent at Vence which was decorated after his designs. Crippled and almost blind towards the end of his life, he came to use mostly cut-outs in coloured paper for his compositions.

MICHAUX, Henri (b. Namur 1899), moved to Paris as a young poet and began drawing only in 1926. He was preoccupied, in his writing as in his painting, with the discovery of 'new worlds' of sensation and emotion through purely spontaneous and uncontrolled creativity; calligraphic elements play a large part in his visual work. Between 1955 and 1961, Michaux experimented with mescalin, producing large numbers of pen drawings in a distinctive style in which compact and ordered abstract structures are built up with an obsessive zigzag line.

MONDRIAN, Piet (b. Amersfoort, Netherlands 1872; d. New York 1944), started as a painter of realistic landscapes. After his arrival in Paris in 1911 he came under the influence of the cubists and painted his series of *Trees*. His approach to abstraction altered gradually, and in 1914 the stylization he practised was transformed into a purely geometrical art of determined relations. Returning to Holland he joined with Theo van Doesburg and others in founding the De Stijl group; the journal of the same title, which started appearing in 1917, preached the creation of an art made of pure relations of form and colour and making no demands on appearances. He continued to paint in this manner, which he called neoplasticism, from about 1919 until his death.

MOTHERWELL, Robert (b. Aberdeen, USA 1915), studied philosophy at Harvard before taking up painting. An abstract expressionist, he was a friend of Matta and belonged to the group which also included Pollock, Gorky, De Kooning and Baziotes. Together with William Baziotes and Barnett Newman, he founded an art school in 1948. He has also taught at Hunter College in New York. His fascination with the tragic twentieth-century history of Spain and Ireland, as revealed in many of his paintings, makes him in a sense the most literary of abstract impressionists. He has edited a number of important volumes in the *Documents of Modern Art* series.

MUNCH, Edvard (b. Löten, Norway 1863; d. Ekely nr Oslo 1944), was a pupil of Christian Krogh, and in 1889 visited Paris. From 1892 to 1895 he lived in Berlin, and his exhibition of paintings in the gallery of the Association of Berlin Artists in 1892 created a scandal and led to the break-up of the group. In Paris in 1896 he frequented the symbolist group associated with the journal *Mercure de France*. For the next ten years he travelled widely, in Germany, Italy, Norway and France. In 1908 he had to undergo psychiatric treatment in a clinic, and for the rest of his life he lived in retirement on his estate at Ekely.

NICHOLSON, Ben (b. Denham, England 1894), is the leading British abstract painter and the first winner of the Guggenheim award. In the 1930s, at a time when English art was at its most insular, he was the chief link between England and the Continent. His compositions – sometimes treated plastically as

bas-reliefs – are geometrically inspired, deriving from the severer forms of cubism and from Mondrian; his art is precise, controlled, and chaste in style. His activity over the past ten years has if anything increased, and he is represented in museums all over the world.

OLDENBURG, Claes (b. Stockholm 1929), graduated from Yale University and was a newspaper reporter in Chicago before he took up art. He is chiefly known for his 'food sculptures' made of vinyl plastic, kapok, canvas, rubber and cloth and representing hamburgers, ice-cream sundaes, hot dogs and french fries. In 1960 he founded the 'Ray Gun Theatre', where he staged, in particular with Jim Dine, a series of Happenings many of which have been filmed. He has exhibited in the Judson Gallery and the Martha Jackson Gallery, New York.

PAOLOZZI, Eduardo (b. Edinburgh 1924), was a member of 'The Group', the association of artists which pioneered the term 'pop art'. Using a magic lantern to project huge images of advertisements and everyday objects, he played a major part in the early stages (in 1952) of this exploitation of mass culture. Himself an intellectual, rather literary artist, he has stood a little aloof from the mainstream of pop.

PICASSO, Pablo Ruiz y (b. Malaga 1881) began his painting career in Barcelona, and first went to Paris in 1900. Influenced by Toulouse-Lautrec he painted the disenchanted pictures of his 'blue period' (1901–4), followed by the 'rose period' (1905–6). The study of African sculpture led him to paint a large-scale picture, *Les Demoiselles d'Avignon* (1907), in which the violently broken forms anticipated the cubist formalism which he was to develop methodically, in company with Braque, until 1914. After Braque's departure for the front in that year Picasso wavered between an Ingrist classicism and the monstrously distorted female nudes of the 'antique period'. Between 1920 and 1925 a comparatively relaxed atmosphere permeated a cubism in which the forms are harmoniously and solidly disposed (*Three musicians*, 1921). From 1928 he went through a symbolist period which coincided with the development of surrealism. The horror of the Spanish Civil War inspired him to make dramatic use of cubist dislocation of forms (*Guernica*, 1937). After this he continued to paint 'butchered' figures, alternating these with purely plastic compositions inspired sometimes by the antique: this latter tendency eventually predominated (the 'Antibes period'), and it seemed that the atmosphere of the Riviera brought some relief to his dramatic tension. More recently he has involved himself enthusiastically, at Vallauris, in the design and production of pottery. He joined the Communist Party shortly after the end of the Second World War, and has produced a few more 'committed' paintings (*War and peace*, 1952).

POLLOCK, Jackson (b. Cody, Wyoming 1912; d. New York 1956), arrived in New York in 1929 to study at the Art Students' League. Influenced early in his career by the baroque dynamism of the Mexican mural painters Siqueiros and Orozco, he soon came under the spell of Picasso, and then of the surrealists. He was

subsequently to apply to painting the surrealist technique of automatism. He abandoned the use of brushes, and took to dripping paint direct on to a canvas which was stretched on the floor. Moving over his work without premeditation and without hesitation, he produced the dynamic superimposed networks and swirls of colour which are characteristic of 'action painting'. From about 1950 onwards, he was successful and famous; but there was still much incomprehension of his work, and he remained temperamentally an isolated figure. He died in a car crash at the age of forty-four.

ROSENQUIST, James (b. North Dakota 1933), started off as a billboard painter, working particularly on the vast posters in Times Square, New York. As one of the 'New Super Realists', he still works on immense canvases, enlarging certain parts of the subject and placing them as blown-up fragments across the painting, as in *Flower Garden*, where an athlete's torso is supported by an arm the size of his actual figure. Rosenquist has the same preoccupation with 'infinity' and 'totality' as the abstract expressionists, but, unlike them, he uses representational elements; he paints 'anonymous things in the hope that particular meanings will disappear. . . .'

ROUAULT, Georges (b. Paris 1871; d. there 1958), was the only one of Gustave Moreau's pupils to retain the master's influence for any length of time. In 1904 the example of Cézanne's *Bathers* inspired him to evolve a tragic distortion of form which served to evoke the harsh existence of prostitutes and clowns. He admired the vehement style of the Catholic writer Léon Bloy, and his art assumed a deeply Christian significance which is unique in our modern age. With Matisse he was one of the progenitors of fauvism.

SMITH, Richard (b. Letchworth 1931), trained at the Royal College of Art in London (1954–7) and since 1959 has divided his time between London and New York. Influenced both by American abstract painters and by pop, his paintings reflect a fascination with the forms of commercial packaging, as they appear in advertising art, and a rejection of the limitations of the two-dimensional canvas. He has summed up his work as follows: 'I set myself the task of mingling commercial atmosphere with abstract art.'

SOULAGES, Pierre (b. Rodez, France 1919), a self-taught artist and one of the leading French abstract painters, has been much influenced by the romantics and by van Gogh. He took up abstract painting in 1946, after wartime service in the army. His pictures bear no titles, being distinguished by the date of completion (as in the *23 May 1953* in the Tate Gallery). Soulages has travelled in the USA and Japan, and is well represented in American collections.

TOBEY, Mark (b. Centerville, Wis. 1890), was successively a failed technical draughtsman in Chicago, a fashion illustrator in New York, and an interior decorator, before moving in 1922 to Seattle, Wash., where he developed his own theory of art as a manifestation of inner experience. He was much influenced by

North-west Coast Indian art, and above all by the art of China and Japan. In the course of subsequent travels as a teacher of art he became an adept of Zen, and developed his technique of 'white writing'.

VLAMINCK, Maurice de (b. Paris 1876; d. Rueil-la-Gadelière 1958), was of Flemish extraction (his name means Maurice the Fleming). He professed ardently libertarian views throughout his life, even though, towards the end, both his polemics and his art began to seem slightly traditionalist. He met Derain in 1900 and shared a studio with him. Taking van Gogh as their model, the two artists painted convulsive landscapes in arbitrary colours and showed these feverish compositions at the 1905 Salon des Indépendants and Salon d'Automne. In 1906 the dealer Ambroise Vollard bought his entire output. In 1908 his colouring and treatment became inspired by Cézanne's final manner, and this period lasted until 1919. Thereafter his art became increasingly concerned with imagery.

WARHOL, Andy (b. Pittsburgh, Pa. 1927), is the most publicized member of the American pop art movement. He started as a commercial artist, working mostly on window displays. He specializes in the obsessive repetition of images from mass media (Marilyn Monroe, Jackie Kennedy), and in the theme of packaging (soup cans, Brillo boxes). He uses the silk-screen printing process, not in order to produce his works in quantity, but to achieve the effect of exact mechanical repetition. He is a prolific film-maker, setting out to shock largely through the medium of boredom (as in his six-hour film of a man sleeping), and has staged a number of Happenings. He survived an attempt on his life in 1968.

WESSELMANN, Tom (b. Cincinnati, Ohio 1931), graduated from art school and then came to New York. Like the other pop artists he makes use of images from mass culture sources such as advertisements, billboards, comic strips, films and television. He has produced a sequence of paintings called *The Great American Nude* in which a woman's body, in a series of erotic poses, is reduced to two-dimensionality and sexlessness; this is both an exercise in stylization and a commentary on the dehumanizing effect of 'glamour', as interpreted by the mass media.

Index
Acknowledgments

Index

ACKNOWLEDGMENTS

Thanks are due, in particular, to the following collectors and publishers, who have kindly authorized us to reproduce works from their collections or illustrations from their books: the Dowager Lady Aberconway (*177*); Dr Doris Neuerburg (*225*); the Earl of Pembroke (*130*); Société Guerlain (*209*); Balance House, New York (Masters and Houston, *Psychedelic Art*: *251*); Casa Editrice Ceschina (Suida, *Luca Cambiaso*: *128*); Edizioni del Milione (Ragghianti, *Pittori di Pompei*: *13*); Edizioni Le Tre Venezie (Fiocco, *Il Pordenone*: *95*); Libreria F. Valardi (Borda, *La Pittura Romana*: *5*).

PHOTOGRAPHIC SOURCES

A. C. L., Brussels *169*, *192*. Alinari *9*, *22*, *26*, *27*, *30*, *44*, *62*, *64*, *75*, *78*, *89*, *94*, *100*, *115*, *116*, *117*, *119*, *122*, *131*, *132*, *134*, *143*, *146*, *147*, *150*, *151*, *152*, *153*, *179*, *180*, *184*. Anderson *8*, *17*, *18*, *20*, *21*, *24*, *25*, *28*, *29*, *43*, *60*, *61*, *65*, *66*, *67*, *71*, *72*, *77*, *80*, *81*, *82*, *83*, *84*, *85*, *98*, *120*, *121*, *123*, *124*, *125*, *133*, *135*, *136*, *137*, *145*, *149*, *182*, *195*. Archives Photographiques, Paris *170*, *194*. Bayerische Staatsgemäldesammlungen, Munich *50*, *139*. Biblioteca Nacional, Madrid (Tomás Mayallón Antón) *172*. Bibliothèque Nationale, Paris *51*. Blauel *109*, *160*. Boudot-Lamotte *118*. British Museum, London *59*. H. Bron *207*. Bruckmann Verlag, Munich (Württ. Landesamt f. Denkmalpflege) *188*. Bulloz, Paris *42*, *54*, *55*, *58*, *86*, *87*, *99*, *111*, *165*, *221*, *225*. Canai *12*, *92*, *97*, *176*, *185*. Domínguez Ramos *53*, *164*. Editions Braun *31*. Ferruzzi *88*. Foto-Hutter *186*. Galeri Bischofberger *250*, *252*, *259*. Galerie Charpentier (J.-P. Leloir) *7*. Giraudon *36*, *38*, *41*, *52*, *57*, *79*, *113*, *114*. Brogi *3*, *19*, *91*, *126*. Graphische Sammlung der Universitäts-Bibliothek Erlangen *102*. The Solomon R. Guggenheim Museum, New York *231*. Gundermann *187*. Hachette *32*, *33*, *35*, *40*, *46*, *49*, *68*, *73*, *74*, *76*, *90*, *93*, *101*, *155*, *157*, *158*, *161*, *167*, *175*, *181*, *183*, *190*, *191*, *193*, *201*, *202*, *204*, *205*, *209*, *210*, *216*, *217*, *218*, *219*, *227*. Fleming *45*, *96*, *130*, *144*, *200*, *206*. Frans Halsmuseum, Haarlem (A. Dingjan) *163*. Graf Harrach'sche Gemäldegalerie, Vienna (Benno Key Belitz) *178*. Institut Français, Athens *15*. Johan Maurits van Nassau Foundation, The Hague (A. Dingjan) *162*. Kunsthaus, Zurich *233*. Kunsthistorisches Museum, Vienna *106*, *110*, *112*, *166*. Laboratoire du Musée du Louvre, Institut Mainini *159*, *168*, *203*, *212*, *215*. Mella (Perotti) *127*. Minneapolis Institute of Arts *236*. Musée des Beaux-Arts, Marseilles (Borel) *148*. National Museum, Stockholm *171*. Musées Nationaux de France *235*. Museo del Prado, Madrid *141*. Museu Nacional de Arte Antiga, Lisbon (A. A. de Abreu Nunes) *56*, *138*. Museum für Kunst und Kulturgeschichte, Dortmund *47*. Museum of Modern Art, New York *223*. Nasjonalgalleriet, Oslo (O. Vaering) *226*. National Gallery, London *37*, *63*, *69*, *70*, *222*. National Museum, Stockholm *171*. Öffentliche Kunstsammlung, Basle: Kunstmuseum *48*, *104*; Kupferstichkabinett *103*, *232*. Österreichische Nationalbibliothek, Vienna *39*. Österreichisches Archäologisches Institut, Vienna *11*. Pinacoteca di Brera, Milan *156*. Publifoto *2*, *6*, *10*, *11*. Pushkin Museum of Fine Art, Moscow *210*. Rijksmuseum, Amsterdam *174*. Rijksmuseum Kröller-Müller, Otterlo *234*. Roger-Viollet *105*. Scala *197*. Sidney Janis Gallery *258*. Skira *5*, *196*. Soprintendenza alle Gallerie, Naples *154*. Soviet Embassy, Paris *16*. Staatliche Graphische Sammlung, Munich *107*. Staatliche Museen, Berlin-Dahlem: Antikenabteilung (Jutta Tietz-Glagow) *14*; Gemäldegalerie (W. Steinkopf) *34*. Städelsches Kunstinstitut, Frankfurt-on-Main *129*, *173*. Szépmuvészti Muzeum, Budapest *108*. Tate Gallery, London *198*, *199*, *245*. Vernacci *140*, *142*. Victoria and Albert Museum, London *213*. Whitney Museum of American Art, New York (Geoffrey Clements) *237*.